南口茶會專車

State Legacy

RESEARCH IN THE VISUALISATION OF POLITICAL HISTORY

国家遗产：一项关于视觉政治史的研究

Contents

6

序言
Introduction
黄专　什么是我们的"国家遗产"
What is our 'State Legacy'?
by *Huang Zhuan*

26

序
Foreword
约翰·海雅特　革命的孩子们
Children of the Revolutions
by John Hyatt

38　　第一部分　帝国与国家
　　　　Part I: Empire and State

42　　赵汀阳　"天下体系"：帝国与世界制度
　　　　Rethinking Empire from a Chinese Concept 'All-under-Heaven' (*Tianxia*, 天下)
　　　　By *Zhao Tingyang*

94　　卢昊　1、项目背景简介：北京内城九门
　　　　　　2、《复制的记忆》方案
　　　　　　3、视觉档案
　　　　　　4、访谈：《复制的记忆》
　　　　Lu Hao　1. The Context of the Project: The Nine Gates of the Inner City of *Beijing*
　　　　　　2. Project: Replicated Memory
　　　　　　3. Archives
　　　　　　4. Interview: Replicated Memory

162　第二部分　一个多维的现代化模式
Part II: A Model of Multi-Dimensional Modernisation

164　汪晖　当代中国的思想状况与现代性问题
Contemporary Chinese Thought and the Question of Modernity (1997)
by *Wang Hui*

230　王广义　1、项目背景简介：中国汽车工业
　　　　2、《东风·金龙》方案
　　　　3、视觉档案
　　　　4、访谈："东风·金龙"——对皇权的最后礼赞
Wang Guangyi　1. The Context of the Project: China's Vehicle Industry
　　　　2. Project: East Wind - Golden Dragon
　　　　3. Archives
　　　　4. Interview: East Wind - Golden Dragon, A Last Tribute to the Imperial Power

288　隋建国　1、项目背景简介：中国铁路工程
　　　　2、《大提速》方案
　　　　3、视觉档案
　　　　4、访谈："大提速"——用时间和空间做影像的雕塑
Sui Jianguo　1. The Context of the Project: China's Railway Project
　　　　2. Project: Raising Speed on the Railway
　　　　3. Archives
　　　　4. Interview: Raising Speed on the Railway - A Sculpture made of Time and Space

372　曾力　1、项目背景简介：三线建设工程
　　　　2、《水城钢铁厂》方案
　　　　3、视觉档案
　　　　4、访谈："水城钢铁厂"与"国家遗产"
Zeng Li　1. The Context of the Project: The Three Line Construction Project
　　　　2. Project: The *Shuicheng* Iron & Steel Works
　　　　3. Archives
　　　　4. Interview: The *Shuicheng* Iron & Steel Works and State Legacy

442　第三部分　视觉政治神话
Part III: Visual Political Myth

444　巫鸿　权力的面容：天安门毛主席像
Face of Authority: *Mao's Portrait on Tiananmen*
by *Wu Hung*

478　汪建伟　1、项目背景简介：天安门观礼台
　　　　　2、《观礼台》方案
　　　　　3、视觉档案
　　　　　4、访谈："观礼台"作为一种"关系"
Wang Jianwei　1. The Context of the Project: The *Tiananmen* Grandstand
　　　　　2. Project: The Grandstand
　　　　　3. Archives
　　　　　4. Interview: The Grandstand as a 'Relationship'

522　附录：1、"政治学还是艺术史"座谈会纪要
　　　　　2、何香凝美术馆OCT当代艺术中心、曼彻斯特艺术设计创新研究院、后盾画廊和角屋简介
　　　　　3、参考文献
Appendix:
1. Conference Summary: Politics or Art History?
2. A Brief Introduction to OCAT, MIRIAD, The Holden Gallery and Cornerhouse
3. Bibliography

Introduction

序言

Nations rely on artists and intellectuals to create images of, and to tell stories about, the national past.

- Richard Rorty

Achieving Our Country: Leftist Thought in Twentieth-Century

每个国家都要依靠艺术家和知识分子去塑造民族历史的形象，去叙说民族过去的故事。

——理查德·罗蒂

What is our 'State Legacy'?

The text is based on an interview with *Huang Zhuan*

July 2007

什么是我们的"国家遗产"？

黄专

2007年7月

What Chinese contemporary art lacks is a foundation of political thought, an independent ability to judge political policy. In the period of modernism during the 1980s, so called 'politics' meant to rebel against traditional ideology. In the 1990s, it meant deconstruction, ironic criticism or the mocking of traditional ideology and the political system, where 'politics' was understood within a narrow and non-historical state. Actually these two attitudes or manners did not embody the quality of independent political thinking. The content of independent political thought should not simply be a negative attitude to traditional ideology or the political system, but should include a position aimed at Chinese history, culture, and reality; a position of introspection taken from within a thoughtful background. I think what Chinese contemporary art lacks is just that quality of thinking.

Contemporary art has been practised for a number of years but what is the thinking behind it? For example, what does 'state' mean? What does 'state consciousness' mean? Few people have formulated such basic or concrete questions referring to the foundations of contemporary practice. If an artist knows nothing about the configuration of his state, it is hard to say whether he is capable of adopting a real political position. But the concept of 'state' is too broad. To Chinese people, 'state' seems like a concept of the political system, a simple concept of ideology. In fact, 'state' is the basic unit within which everybody lives and the only element relative to history in everyone's lives.

The concept of a 'state/country' is very complex, including the element of independence. For instance, territorial consciousness. How was the territory of China established? How has it changed over time? What are the influences of a state's territory on our psychologies and

中国当代艺术一直缺乏一种政治思想基础，即缺乏一种独立的政治判断能力。20世纪80年代现代主义时期，所谓"政治"就是对传统意识形态的反叛，而90年代基本上是对传统意识形态和体制的解构、反讽或调侃，"政治"是在一个很狭隘、非历史化的状态中被理解的。实际上这两种态度和方式都没有体现出独立的政治思想品质。独立的政治思想包含的内容，不应是对传统意识形态或制度的一种简单的否定姿态，还应包括对中国历史、文化、生存现实的一种立场，一种有思想背景的反省立场。中国当代艺术界缺乏的就是这种反省立场。

当代艺术干了这么多年，大家在思考什么？什么叫"国家"？什么叫"国家意识"？很少有人提出这些涉及基本立场的既基础又具体的问题。如果一个艺术家连自己国家的形态都不了解，很难说他能形成一种真正意义上的政治立场。对于中国人而言，"国家"似乎就是一个政治体制概念，一个简单的意识形态的概念，其实"国家"是每个人生存的最基本的单位，也是个体生存中与历史相关联的唯一通道。

"国家"的概念特别复杂，它包括：1、自然因素，比如疆域意识。中国的疆域是怎么形成的？怎么变化的？这些疆域对于我们的心理和生活有什么影响？2、语言意识。一个国家的语言是怎么形成的？它构成一种语言心理。3、民族意识，譬如"家"、"国"意识等等。旧有"国家"与现有国家是如

lives? The second aspect is about language consciousness. How might the language of a country be formed? It encompasses a language psychology. The third aspect concerns national consciousness, home consciousness and country consciousness. Furthermore, how does a country evolve from the ancient to the contemporary? It is hard for artists to adopt a political position without an understanding of these units of discourse.

Of course, to us living in a modern society, the immediate concept of 'state' means The People's Republic of China. Our education, language, nationality, territory, life style and environment as Chinese are related to the 'state'. There was a traditional Chinese concept of 'the world', *tian xia*, and the concepts of 'nation' and 'home', but they were united as one. *Mengzi* said, 'the world roots itself in the nation, the nation takes root in the home, the home takes root in the body.' Before the late *Ming* dynasty, Chinese people believed that the centre of 'the world' was China. They called it the 'Nine States', *jiu zhou*, which served both as a concept of region and a concept of culture and psyche. According to current regional boundaries, 'the Nine States' means 'central China', *zhong yuan,* and some part of the southeast coastlands. As a concept of culture and psyche, it was a recognition of the Chinese people's spiritual territory and their understanding of the world. Therefore, we should first know our traditional concept of 'the world', *'tian xia'*.

The boundaries of ancient China moved continuously following the pre-*Qin* period, before 221 B.C. there was no fixed frontier. The *Tang* dynasty (618 – 907) was strong, but its frontier was also constantly shifting. The emperor and the people of that age did not consider the frontier to be an issue. The concept of territory was determined by the idea of

何演变的？艺术家对这些话语单位不了解，就很难形成一种政治立场。

对于生活在现代的我们来说，国家最直接的概念就是"中华人民共和国"，我们所有的教育、语言、民族、生活的疆域、生活方式和环境等等，都与这个"国家"相关。中国传统有"天下"这类概念，也有"国"和"家"这类概念，但它们的关系是一体的。孟子曰："人有恒言，皆曰：'天下、国、家'，天下之本在国，国之本在家，家之本在身"。至少在晚明以前，按照中国人的传统理解，天下 (世界) 是以中国为中心的，这个中心就是"九州"，它既是地域概念，更是文化和心理概念。"九州"从现在的地域来看，实际上就是中原和东部沿海那一块地缘空间，但作为文化——心理概念，几千年来它却一直支撑着中国人的精神疆域和世界认知，所以，中国人首先要了解"天下"的概念。

中国古代的疆域，从先秦开始都在不断地移动，它没有固定的疆界，唐代虽然强大，它的疆域也永远在变动。当时的皇帝和人民认为边界不构成问题，那时疆界的概念受"夷夏"思想支配——我是"夏"，你是"夷"，你肯臣服于我，土地归谁无所谓，只要保持这种关系就可以了。北宋到了后期变弱了，赔了很多钱给金，但是也一定要与金保持主臣关系，南宋退到南方，也绝不认为北方是夷狄的。所以中国现有的民族国家概念、疆域概念，都是从近代开始的，都是西方强加给我们，而且是在中国最弱的时段强加的，但我们又一直在用西方的各种学说和模式重构我们的国家体制。

'yi xia', 'xia' being the civilized central kingdom and 'yi' being the uncivilized barbarians or foreigners. As long as 'yi' submitted to 'xia' and maintained the relationship, who owned the land was of no consequence. The later Northern *Song* dynasty (960 – 1127) was weak and paid large sums of money to the neighbouring kingdom of *Jin* (1115 – 1234). Yet the Northern *Song* still required the *Jin* to see itself as a vassal. In the Southern *Song* dynasty (1127 – 1279), imperial control had contracted to an area of southern China, but the dynasty did not consider that the northern areas had been lost to 'foreign' control. The current concepts of state and territory were imposed on China by the West during her weakest period which was coincidentally, the beginning of China's modern era. Since then we have reconstructed our state system according to various western models and theories.

I wanted Chinese artists to have a basic understanding of the evolution of the concept of state, they could then form political thought in relation to 'state', which might bring them manners different to those of the West and make it possible for them to discover issues and methods independent from the West when making work.

Concretely speaking, the experience of our generation is the experience of The People's Republic of China (1949 -). It is a complex one. Because the People's Republic is composed of a mixture of multiple elements, it is not a place of a single ideology. For example, it feels as if the Communist Party is a one-party dictatorship, but the original plan of the Communist Party was to establish China as a democracy and a republic, *Mao* called it 'a new democracy', which was to be illustrated by the choice of name for the state. Although this 'new democracy' was mainly aimed at the Nationalist Party government's authoritarian

中国的艺术家只有对国家概念的演化有一种基本认识，才有可能形成关于国家的政治思想，在创作的时候才会真的有跟西方人不一样的方式，才有可能找到与西方人不一样的问题和思维。

我们这一代人主要是中华人民共和国的经验，这种经验特别复杂，问题在于"共和国"其实是由很多因素共同组成的，它们混杂在一起，并不是单纯的意识形态场。譬如，我们感觉中国似乎是共产党一党专政，但共产党最初的设计是要建立一个民主共和的中国（毛泽东称之为"新民主主义"），我们的国名就说明了这一点，当然这种"共和"主要是针对国民党民国政府的专制体制，这一点与西方的民主国家思想是一致的。

共和国建立之初，共产党实行的体制模式的确是多党参政制，每个民主党派都有一定的权力，这种模式很像西方，但是它的终极目标又是来自于西方的另一种"国家"学说——马克思主义的，尤其是列宁主义的"国家"学说，这种学说的逻辑是历史决定论性质的，它认定资本主义只是人类发展的一个必要阶段，最终会走到社会主义、共产主义这类以消灭阶级和国家为特征的高级阶段。《共产党宣言》就明确说："工人没祖国。决不能剥夺他们所没有的东西。"共产主义运动实际上是一种超国家的理想设计，但在新中国建立时，实现这一抽象理论的具体实践首先恰恰是要建立一个强大的现代化国家，一个西方式的工业化国家，而现代化恰恰是资本主义的产物（马克思主义同时也

system, it reflected the same view of the thoughts of the western democratic countries. At the establishment of the People's Republic, the system adopted by the Communist Party was a multi-party governmental body. Each democratic party had some power, which was similar to the West, but its ultimate aim came from another western theory of statehood, that of Marxism, especially the Leninist theory of statehood. The logic of the theory is of historical determinism, which believes that capitalism is a necessary stage in the development of human society and will progress to socialism and communism, the higher stages characterized by the elimination of classes and states. The Communist Manifesto announced articulately that: 'Workers have no motherland. You cannot deprive them of something they do not own'. The Communist movement is actually an ideal design that goes beyond an individual state. But at the beginning of new China, to accurately realize such an abstract theory, we had to establish a strong modern state, an industrialized state in the western style. Modernization is actually the product of capitalism. Marxism is a critical theory of modernization. Of course, there are some other crucial, traditional elements in the design of new China, such as the Confucian ideas of 'great unification', *'tian xia'* or 'imperial power'. New China is a compound of these thoughts.

Currently, we often simplify the Communist Party and The People's Republic of China in terms of politics, seeing it as the continuation of the Chinese feudal society or the pure model of Marxism. By now we can see that the state design and practice of the new China, especially in the period of the 1950s immediately after its foundation was very complex, including many contradictory purposes and issues: Marxism, the modernization of capitalism, nationalism,

是一种现代化的批判理论）。当然在新中国的设计中还有一些非常重要的传统元素, 包括儒家的"大一统"、"天下"观念、皇权思想等等, 所以它是所有这些思想的混杂体。

我们现在往往在政治上把中国共产党简化, 把中华人民共和国简化, 要么把它看成是中国封建社会的延续, 要么把它看成是单纯的马克思主义模式。现在看来, 新中国——尤其是50年代新中国刚刚形成的阶段, 关于国家的设计和实践实际上非常复杂, 甚至包含着很多对立的目标和因素: 马克思主义、资本主义的现代化、民族主义、意识形态理想和国家利益……, 不了解这些矛盾的复杂性就无法对我们身处的"国家"作出基本判断。

我们原来的思考没有也很少认真地面对这样的问题: 我们的国家到底是中国古代帝国的一种现代延续, 还是照搬西方民主国家的一种政治设计, 抑或仅仅是马克思主义的一种东方实践?从参照比较和感性判断上看, 新中国至少在50年代是一个非常理想化的时代, 表现在:

第一, 每个人都有了归属感, 因为我们都是中华人民共和国的公民, 都有主人感, 那是一个非常精神性的胜利。中国人原来的归属感是很混杂的, 譬如在民国时期, 特别是之前的军阀混战时期, 老百姓都不知道属于谁——既不属于满清, 也很难认同中华民国, 更不要说里面的很多地方军阀。抗日战争起到了凝聚中国的作用, 但那个时候中国刚好有两个政权: 一个合法的, 另一个非法

the ideal of ideology and national interest… Without an understanding of the complexity of these contradictions we cannot make fundamental judgments about the 'state' we own.

We rarely thought about these issues before. Indeed, is the country a modern extension of the ancient Chinese empire, a political design copying a western democratic country, or just the eastern practice of Marxism? From a comparative and perceptive perspective; new China had at least an idealistic era during the 1950s.

Firstly, everyone had the sense of belonging and of being a citizen of The People's Republic of China, a sense of ownership. It was a quite spiritual triumph. Originally the sense of belonging of the Chinese people was rather mixed. In the era of the Republic of China established in 1912, and especially during the period of the battles between the warlords, the people did not know who they belonged to. It was difficult to find sympathy with either *Qing* dynasty China or the Republic of China, not to mention the plethora of local warlords. The War of Resistance Against Japan (1938 – 1945) played a role in the cohesion of China, but there were still two regimes: one was legal and the other was illegal; the legal one was the Nationalist Party, the *Guomindang* and the illegal one was the Communist Party, the *Gongchangdang*. The people's sense of belonging to these two regimes was dependent on their region: the people in *Yan'an* and other communist-controlled areas listened to the Communist Party, in the nationalist-controlled area to the Nationalist Party, in the areas occupied by the Japanese army to the Japanese-Manchurian Government. Thus, the Chinese people only felt a real sense of belonging after the establishment of The People's Republic of China. I think this was a significant achievement for the People's Republic.

的，合法的是国民党，非法的是共产党。所以当时老百姓的归属感也不强，在延安的、边区的觉得属于共产党，在国统区的觉得属于国民党，在日军占领区的觉得属于日满。中国人从满清，即近代以后，国家归属感就很弱，所以说，中国人在中华人民共和国建立以后，才有了真正的归属感，这是中华人民共和国最大的功绩。

第二，建设民主和富强的中国为中国人构造了一个理想主义的场景，一个在现代化和工业化实践中的社会主义目标，这种集体主义的理想时代恐怕在中国历史上从未出现过，在世界范围内也可能只在前苏联有过。

第三，中国人在建立现代化这个目标下实行强制的工业化和人民公社化，这是乌托邦和现实主义的一种离奇的历史搅拌，它使上世纪50年代成为中国历史上一个非常奇特的时期，中国似乎突然真的转换成为一个具有归属感的、现代性的民族国家。到了60—70年代的文化大革命，中国历史又完成了另一次变异，以全民政治运动的方式建立一个纯正的社会主义理想代替了现代化的经济目标，极权政治代替了民主的努力，激进的世界主义代替了保守的民族主义。紧接着改革开放，国家设计的天平倒向另一个极端：政治价值上个人主义取代集体主义，经济上市场主义取代计划模式，文化上则是时尚主义、消费主义、犬儒主义完全替代理想主义。90年代以后，随着全球化时代

Secondly, the idea of building a democratic, prosperous and strong China had engendered an idealistic environment, a socialistic goal in the practice of modernization and industrialization. I would think that such an idealistic age of collectivism had never before existed in Chinese history. In a world context, it only existed in the former Soviet Union.

Thirdly, the Chinese people were subjected to mandatory industrialization and enforced people's communes within the goal of building modernity: an historical mix with Utopianism and realism as the ingredients. This mix made the 1950s a bizarre period in Chinese history in which it might seem that China suddenly became a modern nation-state with a sense of belonging. By the decade of the Cultural Revolution (1966 – 1976), Chinese history completed yet another volte face. The idea of building a pure form of socialism through a nationwide political movement, replaced the economic goal of modernization; totalitarian politics replaced democratic efforts; radical internationalism replaced conservative nationalism. Since the policy of 'Reform and Open Door' in the 1980s was applied, the designs of the state switched to other extremes: individualism replaced collectivism in the arena of political values; the market economy replaced the planned economy; fashion, consumerism and cynicism totally replaced idealism in the area of culture. After the 1990s, with the arrival of the era of globalization, China became 'strong', and the pursuit of the values of western consumerism and a fashionable life style became the norm for the Chinese people. But the basic appraisal and awareness of 'state' in the minds of the Chinese people was weakened. Radical nationalism in respect to the issues of Japan and *Taiwan* cannot be considered state consciousness. Of course, so far, I think the Chinese people's spiritual world has not

的到来, 中国变得"强大"了, 追求西方消费主义的思维价值和时尚主义的生活方式成为中国人的一种全民性共识, 但中国人对"国家"这种概念的基本判断和意识却反倒弱化了 (在对日、对台问题上那种偏激的民族主义情绪不能算国家意识)。当然, 到目前为止, 中国人的整个精神世界并不特别西方化, 也有很多学者在力图以中国传统价值抵制西方化的趋势, 但如果没有对自己国家或视觉遗产真正具有理性的判断, 这种精神建设最多只会多生产几个像易中天、于丹之类的时尚学者。

2006年开始构思策划的"国家遗产：一项关于视觉政治史的研究"计划, 正是基于这些问题的思考。这个研究计划讨论的是中国近现代"国家"概念形成的思想史和视觉史意义, 并围绕着中国由古代帝国向近代民族国家转换的思想史和视觉史逻辑, "现代化"与"反现代化"观念对中国作为民族国家形成的意识形态的影响, 国家由文化实体向政治实体、精神实体转换中的视觉形式、图像元素 (符号、产品、仪式、空间) 及其与思想史的关系等课题展开。

在这个计划中, "遗产"是中性词, 特指在中国近现代国家观念形成过程中以物质产品、政治空间、文化仪式、审美活动等方式存在的视觉性元素, 当我们将其放置于一种反思性位置时, 我们与它的关系就进入一种解放和超越的状态, 我们可以称其为"超意识形态"。这项研究的艺术史目标是：它将为中国当代艺术提供一种从史学意义和反思立场而非犬儒化、图解化把握其政治发展方向

been appreciably westernized. Many scholars are attempting to resist the trend towards westernization by advocating traditional Chinese values, but I feel that without a genuinely rational evaluation of our own state and state legacy, the task of building a national spirit can only produce more fashionable scholars such as *Yi Zhongtian* and *Yu Dan*.

The 'State Legacy: Research in the Visualisation of Political History' project which has been in the planning and design stage since 2006, is based on those thoughts I have described above. Its purpose is to discuss the formation of the concept of 'state' in modern and contemporary Chinese history and its significance in visual history. The project is designed to encourage discussion starting from the following issues: the history of thought and the logic of visual history relative to the transformation of China from an ancient empire to a modern nation-state. These include the ideological influence that the ideas of 'modernization' and 'anti-modernization' have exercised on China's forming of a nation-state; the visual forms, iconic elements of symbol, product, ceremony, space in the process of the country's transformation from a cultural entity to a political and spiritual entity and the relationship of these iconic elements to the history of thought.

In the project, the word 'legacy' in 'State Legacy' is a neutral term, referring particularly to the visual elements existing in the nature of material products, political space, cultural ceremony, and aesthetic activities during the progress of forming the concept of the modern Chinese state. When we pose it in a position of reflection, our relationship with this legacy will be advanced to a liberal and overwhelming status, which we can call 'extra-ideological'. The purpose of this project in terms of art history is to present a unique view of Chinese

的独特视野。在这种立场中，中国学术界"左派"、"右派"的争论变得没那么重要，因为了解我们这个国家历史和现状的复杂性显然比一个派别立场更为基础。

王广义、汪建伟、卢昊、曾力和隋建国五位艺术家和巫鸿、汪晖、赵汀阳三位学者分别以他们的作品和研究成果参与了这项研究计划。

王广义是一个对文化政治问题高度敏感的艺术家，他不是一个理论性的艺术家，也不是靠奇想和机灵来做作品，但他的作品都有很强的历史问题逻辑，也有很强的直觉性。他的早期艺术哲学建立在对西方现代艺术和文化的认同基础上，后来他逐步走向一种双重批判的道路，既不简单依靠西方逻辑，也不简单否定自己的文化，他总能在各种复杂的图像分析中找到某种反思的逻辑，是一个很严肃的政治批判者，同时也是一个很玩世的艺术家，他总能把高度的严肃性和高度的玩世性融合在一起，这样一种艺术家的个人气质和工作的逻辑就产生了《东风·金龙》这样的方案：他思考20世纪50年代中国人的精神价值是怎样形成的。汽车——对中国而言首先是作为一种政治象征符号（中国第一辆汽车是袁世凯送给慈禧的，现存于颐和园的德和园）而不是作为工业产品为中国人所接受，"遗产"被他具体化为一辆汽车，"东风·金龙"是新中国自己生产的第一辆汽车，实际上包含了上述所有因素：第一，它是工业现代化观念的产物，是资本主义机械时代的象征，体现的是现代

contemporary art from within its historical meaning and from a reflective position rather than one of cynicism and graphics in grasping the direction of political development. I do not consider the dispute between 'leftist' and 'rightist' important, but I feel that to know the history of our state and the complexity of its current affairs is more fundamental than to simply adopt a position.

The five artists *Wang Guangyi, Wang Jianwei, Lu Hao, Zeng Li* and *Sui Jianguo,* and the three scholars *Wu Hung, Wang Hui* and *Zhao Tingyang* have contributed their work and research outcomes to this State Legacy project.

The artist *Wang Guangyi* has a high degree of sensitivity to cultural and political issues. He is not a theoretical artist. His works are not made on a basis of whims or ingenuity, but with a strong sense of history and intuition. His early art philosophy was built on the basis of endorsing western modern art and culture, only later did he gradually turn to a road of double criticism, neither simply relying on western logic nor simply denying his own culture. He could always find a reflective logic in dissecting various kinds of complex images. He is both a serious political critic and a very cynical artist. He has always been able to integrate seriousness with cynicism at a high level. Such personal temperament and working logic was applied to his piece - 'East Wind - Golden Dragon', *'dong feng - jin long'.* This work reflects how the Chinese spiritual values of the 1950s were formed. The car, in its early appearance in China, was primarily seen by the Chinese people as a political symbol rather than an industrial product. The first car to be seen in China was the one that *Yuan Shikai* presented to the Dowager Empress *Cixi,* it is now preserved in the *De He* Park of the Summer Palace. *Wang*

化的目标：速度；但它同时又并不具备任何实用的功能，只是作为一个政治和权力象征物，这实际上包含了很多乌托邦色彩；第二，它同时也是中国传统中皇权意识的一种现代反映，只不过这种传统被赋予在一个现代政治领袖身上。王广义常说："我的作品全部来源于人民"，他的艺术也是由很多复杂的因素掺和而成。他有自由主义思想，这是他艺术的基础，但同时他对中国的民族又有很深的感情（包括对毛泽东这样的政治领袖），这样一个方案是将对民族集体主义的感情和批判性融合在一起的，特别契合这个展览主题。

汪建伟与王广义完全不同，他是一个思辩性而不是直觉性的艺术家，他的作品有一套很完整的工作方式和很严密的语言逻辑。他一直关注中国现代建筑史的一个重要个案：张开济在50年代设计的天安门观礼台。在张开济生前，汪建伟就对他进行了大量采访，并搜集了大量相关的资料。观礼台也融合了几种因素：第一，它是建国初共产党设计作为国家权力与人民之间沟通的象征空间（它附属于象征国家的天安门下），特别是它与"检阅"这种现代中国最高级别的全民政治仪式相关，这就使它具有非常强烈的政治含义。第二，它与中国传统的夷夏思想有关，譬如上观礼台的除了"人民的代表"就是各国的使节，各国的使节也有区别：与中国友好的国家领袖都站在城楼上，那些非东方集团又有外交关系的国家的使节就站在下面。所有这些格局都潜在地反映了中国传统的"夷夏"

embodies 'Legacy' as a car. 'East Wind - Golden Dragon' was the first car China produced. It embodies all the factors I have discussed above. Firstly, it is a product of concepts of industrial modernisation and a symbol of the mechanical age of capitalism. What the car embodies is the goal of modernization, speed. Yet it does not have any practical function. It is more of a symbol of politics and power and in fact includes many Utopian ideas. Secondly, it is a modern reflection of imperial power in the Chinese tradition which was later embodied in a modern political leader. *Wang Guangyi* always says: 'People are the source of all my work.' His art combines many complex elements. He has liberal thoughts, which are the foundation of his art. Meanwhile he demonstrates a deep emotional bond with the Chinese nation, even to political leaders such as *Mao Zedong*. This piece of work combined both his critical and devotional emotions towards the nation's collectivism which accurately fits the theme of the exhibition.

Wang Jianwei is a totally different artist from *Wang Guangyi*. He is a theoretical but not intuitional artist. His work displays a complete working procedure and a strict logical language. He maintains a deep concern for a unique case in the history of modern Chinese architecture: the Grandstand of *Tiananmen* designed by *Zhang Kaiji* in the 1950s. *Wang Jianwei* interviewed *Zhang Kaiji* several times and collected much relevant material. The Grandstand encompasses many factors. Firstly, its design for the Communist Party at the beginning of the People's Republic symbolized the distance in communication between state authority and the people, as the Grandstand is an accessory to *Tiananmen*, the symbol of the state. Particularly so because it is related to 'review', the highest national political ceremony in

观念 (我们在乾陵就能看出这种视觉格局)。观礼台本身的政治属性也非常能够反映50年代中国人在设计自己国家的精神环境和政治空间时的基本思路,当时整个设计的过程也非常复杂,据说周恩来把它交给张开济后提出的要求是:不能破坏天安门的整体格局,同时要满足一些功能,还分了区,哪些是工人代表的位置,哪些是农民代表的位置,等等。当然,汪建伟在这件方案中融入了更为复杂的艺术逻辑,包括材料、环境、文本、仪式的"不确定性"等等。去年张开济去世时汪建伟发给我一个短信说:"这件作品现在是真正的'国家遗产'了"。

卢昊是地道的北京人,八旗后代,我常开玩笑说他对北京有着一般人不具备的"民族感情",他的作品都与这种情感有关,当然,作为当代艺术家,他也具有对材料、空间等要素的极高的智慧和敏感。他的作品源于另一个乌托邦式的想象,他曾有过复原北京内城九座城门的想法,明建北京城内城共九座城门:北边的德胜门、安定门,西边的西直门、阜成门,东边的东直门、朝阳门,南边的宣武门、正阳门、崇文门,20世纪初这些城门已有不少自然损毁的情况,共产党1949年打进北京的时候,跟国民党谈判,希望和平解放北平,就是怕破坏古迹——毛泽东也完全是有双重性格的人,一方面他反对所有传统,一方面他对中国的文化又有很深的感情。当时谈判的结果就是国民党同意投降,共产党和平进城,实际上当时共产党准备打北平的时候,也专门联系了梁思成他们,要他们

modern China, thus it has a strong political significance. Secondly, the Grandstand is related to the traditional thoughts of *'yi xia'*. Those on the Grandstand are the envoys beside 'the representatives of the people'. The envoys are also differentiated: those national leaders friendly to China would stand on the upper level and the envoys from the countries of the non-eastern bloc having diplomatic relations would stand below. We can also see this visual pattern in *Qianling,* the tomb of the *Tang* dynasty emperor *Gaozong*. The political nature of the Grandstand reflects the basic thoughts the Chinese people held when they built the psychological environent and political space in the 1950s. The whole design process was quite complex. It is said that premier *Zhou Enlai* indicated two requirements when he assigned *Zhang Kaiji* to the project: not to undermine the overall pattern of *Tiananmen* while providing for the functions of the Grandstand with the divine sections, those which represent the workers and those represent the farmers. Based on these findings, *Wang Jianwei* applied a more complicated artistic logic to this piece of work, including the 'uncertainty' of material, environment, texture, ceremony and other factors. Last year, before *Zhang Kaiji* died, he sent me a message saying: 'This piece of work is now a true State Legacy. '

Lu Hao is a native of *Beijing*, a descendant of the *Manchu* banner men, the *ba qi,* the eight flags. I often joke that he has a greater 'national sentiment' towards *Beijing* than others. His work is entirely related to this sentiment. As a contemporary artist, he also has a heightened intelligence and sensitivity to the creative elements of his materials and space. His work comes from another kind of Utopian imagination. He had the idea to restore the nine gates of the inner city of *Beijing*. The nine gates were built in the *Ming* dynasty (1368 – 1644): the *De*

把古迹全部标识出来, 不要让炮轰到古迹, 所以共产党对当时北平的完整保存是有贡献的。但是进了北京以后, 50年代的中国反倒以"建设"的名义开始拆除古迹, 这当然也包括阻碍现代交通的城门, 现在除了正阳门 (前门) 处在北京城中轴线上没被拆除外, 其它城门都在建设中被拆除 (德胜门和崇文门还保留部分箭楼), 最近为了旅游需要又不伦不类地恢复了外城的永定门, 它们构成了一个异常吊诡的历史故事, 但历史也许正是因为包含了这么多复杂的因素才显现出它的丰富性。卢昊的《复制的记忆》也许能带来这类思考, 它也属于现代中国人的精神遗产和物质遗产的重要内容。

曾力的《水城钢铁厂》记录了另一件吊诡的历史事件。中国在50年代成立的时候, 所有的重工业布局都在东北三省, 因为当时中国跟苏联友好, 希望借助苏联的技术、能源和工业模式, 重工业对当时的中国来讲实际上是支柱。60年代末, 中苏关系恶化以后, 本来是意识形态的两个伙伴变成了最大的敌人, 中国把重工业撤到安全的地方, 于是出现了三线工程。整件事件也融合了上述的几种因素: 第一, 共产主义理想和国家利益发生了矛盾; 第二, 现代化因为这种理想的分裂造成的一系列更为复杂的人文和生态后果甚至影响到今天。三线工程这种国家性的集体搬迁也只有在一个强制性的国家体制内才能做到, 三线工程的布局, 完全是一种兵营式的管理, 体现了国家危机时的

Sheng Gate and the *An Ding* Gate in the north; the *Xi Zhi* Gate and *Fu Cheng* Gate in the west; the *Dong Zhi* Gate and the *Chao Yang* Gate in the east; the *Xuan Wu* Gate, the *Zheng Yang* Gate and the *Chong Wen* Gate in the south. Some of these gates had already been damaged in the early 20th Century. In 1949, the People's Liberation Army besieged *Beijing* and entered into negotiations with the Nationalist government for a peaceful liberation in order to protect the city's historic sites. *Mao Zedong* showed a double personality. On one hand he was radically against all tradition, on the other hand he showed a deep sense of Chinese culture. The outcome of the negotiations was that the Nationalist government agreed to surrender and the Liberation Army was able to enter *Beijing* peacefully. In fact, when the Liberation Army was preparing to do battle for *Beijing*, they contacted *Liang Sicheng*, China's first modern architect, to ask him to mark out all the historical buildings on a map to avoid them being shelled. At that time it seems the Communist Party had contributed to the preservation of the integrity of *Beijing*. But after taking power in *Beijing*, the Communist government began dismantling the historic sites in the 1950s in the name of 'construction', construction that included demolishing the city gates as they were considered to be impediments to modern traffic. Except for the *Zheng Yang* Gate which is on the north / south axis line of *Beijing*, all of the other gates were removed. Only the Arrow Towers of the *De Sheng* Gate and the *Chong Wen* Gate remain. Recently, for the needs of tourism, the *Yong Ding* Gate was restored in a nondescript manner. These are very paradoxical things, but perhaps it is because history contains so many complex factors that it enhances its own richness. *Lu Hao*'s work suggests such thinking and it also belongs to the important spiritual and material legacy of the

应急能力。《水城钢铁厂》也是一个非常典型的个案，中国人关于"国家"的精神和取向是随着历史的发展不断变异的。

　　隋建国的《大提速》是对"速度"的某种反思，所有西方的现代化都是以追求"速度"为自己的"宗教"内容，譬如蒸汽机、飞行器的发明。中国铁路史实际上是西方对中国进行强制现代化的产物，早期英美等西方国家在中缅、上海等地都曾有过修铁路的企图，因为中国政府的抵制而未遂。中国第一条自己建造的铁路是1881年洋务运动中开始建造的唐胥铁路。中国制造的第一辆机车叫"龙号"。所以它也交织着民族反抗和民族振兴两个主题。民国后铁路开始成为中国国民经济的命脉，新中国建设中铁路更是这样，迄今为止已有了6次大提速，是一个熔铸了典型的中国人追求工业化梦想的故事，所以这件作品也混杂了中国在设计自己国家时的很多因素。中国的铁路全部是国有的，反映了国家的一种控制。

　　对于"国家"或"遗产"，每个人的理解可能都不一样，也许每个艺术家在完成自己的作品方案时想法不一定与我相同，但是，他们通过这个展览提供一些有力和智慧的答案，而"遗产"这个观念在某种程度上也深化了他们的作品。

　　赵汀阳是一位哲学家，他的研究课题中有关于中国由古代帝国向近代民族国家转变历史中的

modern Chinese people.

Zeng Li's work also records yet another paradoxical historical event. In the 1950s, soon after the People's Republic was established, it was realised that all China's heavy industry was situated in the northeast, close to the border with the Soviet Union. China had befriended the Soviet Union at that time and was hoping to receive rapid assistance in the fields of technology, energy and industrial models from her neighbour to build heavy industry, the pillar of China's industries at that time. Towards the end of the 1960s, relations with the Soviet Union deteriorated, the two old ideological partners became each other's greatest enemy. China withdrew its heavy industry to safer places in the hinterland, an operation which was named the 'three-line-project'. This event also included those factors I mentioned earlier. Firstly, the communist ideal conflicted with national interests; secondly, due to the division in ideals, modernization brought a series of more complex cultural and ecological consequences which are affecting us even today; thirdly, national collective relocations such as 'the three-line-project' could only be realized within a mandatory national system. The layout of 'the three-line-project' was barracks-style management, reflecting the national capacity for crisis management, of which this is a very typical case. I think that the Chinese people's spirit and value of 'state' varies with historical development.

Sui Jianguo's work 'Raising Speed on the Railway' has the basic concept of 'speed'. 'Speed' is a very modern idea. It seems to be the 'religion' of western modernization, seen in the invention of the steam engine and the aircraft. The railway in China was a product of western policies of colonization. The early attempts to build railways in China by the English

理论模式问题。在他的著作《天下体系》中，他提出了对当代世界模式的反思问题，并提出了以中国古代"天下"理想模式替代"联合国"这种体制模式的理论猜想。汪晖的《现代中国思想的兴起》从宏观的历史场景考察中国现代化发生过程中复杂的思想变异和冲突。巫鸿的《权力的面容：天安门毛主席像》从天安门领袖图像的演变史探讨了政治、视觉空间之间复杂的互动关系。

这三项现代化研究成果的参与使"国家遗产"这一课题有了更为丰富和坚实的理论基石。

曼彻斯特既是英国工业革命的发源地，也是马克思主义的诞生地，它是现代化和反现代化两个对立历史因素共生的地方。与曼彻斯特艺术设计创新研究院的合作使这个项目有了一个多维和开放的角度，也使它具有了某种特殊的象征意味。

这个视觉研究计划重要的是体现了一种新型的立场和态度：既不是简单批判，也不是简单赞颂，更不是调侃，而是体现了一种我称之为"批判性情感"的东西。罗蒂说："一个国家和民族的形象是由艺术家和知识分子塑造的。"我想加一句："这种塑造既是一种赞美，更应是一种反思和批判。"中国当代艺术怎样真正形成一种比较独立的思想和立场？"国家遗产"也许可以作为一个问题的支点。

and the Americans had all ended in failure because of strong resistance from the Chinese government. The first Chinese built railway the *'Tang Xu'* line was completed in 1881 during the Self-Strengthening Movement (1860 – 1894). The steam locomotives that ran on the *'Tang Xu'* railway were either built in Britain or built under the guidance of British engineers. One of the locomotives was named 'Dragon' having 'Rocket of China' emblazoned on the both sides of the boiler. This shows that the twin themes of the nation's resistance and revival were tangled together in the history of the Chinese railway. When the Republic of China was established in 1912, the railway began to function as the lifeline of the national economy. It has been even more so in the People's Republic and the operating speed on the railway has been raised six times. The railway provides a typical story from the Chinese pursuit of the dreams of industrialization, *Sui's* work mixes together the various factors that emerged when the Chinese people designed their own country. The Chinese railway is state-owned, reflecting a kind of state control.

Everybody will have a different interpretation of 'State' or 'Legacy'. The thoughts of individual artists may be different from mine whilst creating his work. However, through this exhibition of 'State Legacy' I am confident that they will provide strong and intelligent answers to the project and the concept of 'Legacy' might, to some extent, make them dig deeper in their work.

Zhao Tingyang is a philosopher. One aspect of his research is the seeking of a theoretical model which will show how China transformed itself from an ancient empire to a modern nation-state. in his essay Rethinking Empire from a Chinese Concept 'All-under-Heaven',

Zhao advances reflections on the current world order, suggesting a theoretical hypothesis that would use the idealistic model of the ancient Chinese system *'tian xia'* instead of the 'United Nations' system. *Wang Hui*'s essay 'Contemporary Chinese Thought and the Question of Modernity' surveys the historical panorama of the complex changes and conflicts in thought during the modernization of China. *Wu Hung*'s essay 'Face of Authority' discusses the interactive relationships between politics and visual space using the case study of the historical background to the leaders' portraits that have hung on the front of the *Tiananmen Gate*.

Manchester in England is the birthplace of the Industrial Revolution and is also the place that influenced Marxism. It has held both the historical elements of modernity and anti-modernity at the same time. Our collaboration with the Manchester Institute for Research and Innovation in Art and Design in Manchester Metropolitan University has developed an open and multi-dimensional angle for the project, and given a kind of symbolic meaning to it.

The importance of this visual research project is to express a new type of attitude and creative stance which is not simple criticism, nor simply glorification, nor ridicule either, the project shows something that I would call 'critical sensibilities'.

Richard Rorty said, 'Nations rely on artists and intellectuals to create images of the national past.' I want to add that 'artistic creation might be a kind of praise but it also needs to be reflective and critical.' My question is how can Chinese contemporary art one day form a truly independent thinking and stance? The 'State Legacy' project may be able to provide some answers to this question.

Foreword

序

Children of the Revolutions

John Hyatt

January 2009

革命的孩子们

约翰·海雅特

2009年1月

Leaving aside genetically embedded information, we are all born blank canvases, clean pages, unburnt discs. Our infant emptiness is a field of infinite potential and possibility that is inscribed and overlaid as we change from children to adults. We begin life with vastly more neurones in the brain than we need and we discard thousands as unnecessary when we adjust our glorious and innate flexibility to the necessities of the life at hand in the context within which we grow. Our cultural circumstances, from gender, the language and artefacts of our social group, family and kinship structure, hierarchical social status and the constitution of faith groups and state play a large part in determining who we become or are made into by external stimuli. As children, we learn from adults and from their world. We are filled with tales dressed up in the clothes of knowledge, education, and officially validated histories. We learn of the world outside our bodies from experience mediated through our senses and our concepts. We order this near-chaos of being and invent stories to describe who we are, where we are from, where we are heading for or dreaming of going. We orientate ourselves with stories. In the eternal present, we get to know others by swapping these tales of our past selves and dreams of our future selves, being attracted to others where we find harmony and repelled where we find dissonance.

This is a momentous period in human history when, more than ever before, more of us can tell our stories across the globe and learn to understand the ways of the stranger: the Other. Can we grasp the opportunities for dialogue and communication that technological development grants us and engage in ideas and actions that work to harmonise our species and our planet?

如果抛开自带的基因信息不计，我们生来都是洁白的画布、干净的纸页、没有刻写过的光盘。在从儿童到成人的过程中，这种最初的空白有着无限的书写和累积的可能性。我们大脑中庞大的神经元细胞多于实际的需要，当我们根据自身环境状况的需要调整自己与生俱来的良好的适应性时，我们丢弃了那些被认为不需要的部分。我们的文化环境——从性别、语言到社会群体所有物、家庭和亲戚的结构、社会等级状况以及信仰群体的组织和国家，这些外因都在很大程度上决定了我们成为什么样的人。作为孩子，我们从大人和他们的世界中学习，被那些裹着知识、教育和官方承认的历史的外衣的故事填满。我们通过感官和思考获得的经验来学习我们身体之外的世界。我们指挥着这近乎混沌的存在，同时发明故事来描述我们是谁，从什么地方来，要到什么地方去或者说梦想去哪里。我们用这些故事给自己定位。在无止境的当下，我们通过和别人交流我们过去自我的故事和我们未来自我的梦想来认识对方，找到和谐时我们彼此吸引；发现不一致时相互排斥。

这是一个人类历史上重要的时期，我们之中的大多数可以享有比以往任何时候都要多的机会，在全球范围内讲述我们自己的故事，并且学习懂得作为陌生人的另一方的方式。我们能不能抓住这个技术发展给我们提供的机遇进行对话和交流、进而把让我们的物种与星球和谐相处的理想和行动付诸实践？

'State Legacy' represents the results of one of those opportunities for dialogue that led to a two-year research and curatorial collaboration with my Chinese colleague and now good friend, *Huang Zhuan*. 'State Legacy' is a transport of stories across the world communicated in visual forms and, therefore, arguably more immediately accessible than the written or spoken word, especially when the languages of the two cultures look and feel as different as English and Chinese. This exhibition, with its inaugural showing in the self-described 'original modern city' of Manchester, overlays the rich narratives of the Industrial Revolution upon those of more recent Chinese industrialisation. 'State Legacy' thematically explores the consequences of the Chinese industrial revolution through original artworks made especially for this research project and as yet unseen in the United Kingdom.

During the nineteenth century, North West England was the epicentre of the waves of technological change which led to unprecedented transformations in culture that continue to the present day. Important social ideas and ideals of the twentieth century sprang from those inventive times resulting in the global challenges we now face in the twenty-first century. In countries, such as China, industrialisation has been and is being re-enacted and re-interpreted. Chinese society continues to strive to balance the forces of change and disruption.

The artists who were chosen for this exhibition are all critically reflective. To reflect upon who we happen to be, our circumstances and why things are the way they are is a necessary condition for understanding how to act in the world. To behave purposefully and according to our will, rather than be merely automata reacting to external pressures requires critical

"国家遗产"项目在曼彻斯特的展览代表着这样一个对话的机会，是我和我的中国同事、现在的好朋友黄专两年以来研究策划合作的成果。展览从世界的另一端带来故事，用视觉形式和观众交流。有证据表明视觉语言比说和写的语言更能被直接感受，特别是面对两种文化的语言的时候——中文和英文这样看着、觉着差距都很大。"国家遗产"展在曼彻斯特这个自定义为"最初的现代城市"的地方揭开序幕，给新近的中国工业化故事叠加了丰厚的最原始的工业革命的背景。展览中原创的艺术作品集中探讨了中国工业革命的后果。这些作品是特别为这个研究项目制作的，都是第一次和英国的观众见面。

19世纪的英国西北部是技术革新浪潮的中心，其引领的空前的文化变革一直持续到今天。重要的社会思想和20世纪的理想从这个富于创造的时代喷涌而出，孕育了我们现在21世纪所面临的全球性的挑战。在像中国这样的国家中，工业化的故事也已经正在被再次上演和再次演绎。中国社会至今仍然在努力维持变化和分裂这两种力量的平衡。

入选这个展览的艺术家都具有批判性的反思精神。反思我们怎样成为现在的我们、我们的生存现状、为什么事情按照它们的方向去发展——这是理解怎样应对世界的必要的条件。有目的地、按我们的意愿去表现而不是仅仅机械地对外部的压力做出反应这需要批判性的反思精神。艺术是

reflection. Art is inquiry as much as science is inquiry and, amongst other things, art tests the received world. Art is the science of shining a subjective light onto the constructs we have inherited.

'State Legacy' explores the aftermath of the industrial revolution in China through the visual languages of five contemporary Chinese artists acting as perceptive observers, representing a critical reflection upon recent historical experience translated into visual art.

For an artist to exhibit in a foreign country is to look back on one's home in a fresh light. The world of the new land can be a mirror to see not only yourself but also your construction made by your circumstance and social history. In an illumination of imagination, it allows a magic opportunity to momentarily step out of your self and your social context: it shakes the structure. It is a persistency in human history that big ideas often happen in the heads of émigrés and refugees – it is a common enough cultural feature to warrant a book on that subject alone.

For our purposes one pertinent example, of the many available, might be that in Manchester, one hundred and fifty years ago, Karl Marx and Frederick Engels developed their story of the world's economic and political evolution that was to compete with the capitalist worldview. Communism was an ideology of capitalism turned upside down – as French theorist, Jean Baudrillard[1], pointed out, it was a 'mirror' world of production. The

---

[1] Jean Baudrillard (1929 – 2007), French cultural theorist, sociologist, philosopher, he wrote the book, The Mirror of Production, in 1973.

一种探索，就像科学是一种探索一样。在事物中，艺术尤其检验被普遍接受的世界，艺术是科学的一束主观的光，照亮了我们所继承的结构。

"国家遗产"展通过五位当代中国艺术家的视觉语言探索中国工业革命的后果，他们扮演了敏锐的观察家的角色，在视觉艺术中阐释对当前历史经验的批评性反思。

一位艺术家到外国做展览，回首自己的家园时会有新的见解。新大陆的世界可以作为一面镜子，不仅仅用来对照着看你自己，而且看被你的环境和社会历史造就的你的构成。给这个想象的场景画一个插图，允许一个短暂的魔法时刻出现——你从你自身和你的社会关系中走出来：于是那个固有的结构被动摇了。这正是为什么在人类历史上伟大的思想常常从移居者和流亡者的头脑中诞生——这是一个太平常不过的文化特点，可以确保单独就这个话题写一本书。

如果要举些例子来说明我们的观点，有一个很贴切的：可能就是在150年前的曼彻斯特，卡尔·马克斯和弗里德里希·恩格斯发展了他们和资本主义的世界观相匹敌的、关于世界经济和政治进化的学说。共产主义是一种把资本主义颠倒了的意识形态——像法国理论家让·波迪亚[1]指出的，

---

[1] 让·波迪亚（1929–2007），法国文化理论家、社会学家和哲学家。著有《生产之镜》，1973年。

two ideologies were powerful competing stories: a *yin to a yang*, they were opposing forces tied together, intertwined, and each interdependently creating the other in turn for much of the twentieth century. Through the mediating agency of Soviet Russia, pursuit of the Communist mirror model of production by the forces led by *Mao* changed the face of Chinese society's power elite. Since the end of Maoism, over the past thirty years, China has encouraged the emergence within its system of the old mirror twin of *laissez-faire* capitalism without appearing to ditch communism.

A current question is how big will the communist bird allow the capitalist cuckoo chick to grow?

One purpose of this exhibition, with its accompanying publication and related programmes of discussions and events, is to develop a deeper and richer understanding of his historical complexity, or at the very least to provide an introduction to a wide panorama of debate.

Between Britain and China, and consequently between their artists, there was little open exchange of each other's stories for many years during the Cold War. We could only vaguely see our eastern neighbours through the dark glass of global politics. However, it has been revealed that the lives of these artists have since been heavily influenced by the technologies and ideas of the West, especially the influence of the Industrial Revolution.

Images of China, in the western media, continue to be simultaneously anachronistic or futuristic. Strange mixtures of Orientalism, Confucianism, Maoism and communist totalitarianism swirl confusedly with images of cheap plastic goods and burgeoning

它是一个"镜像"的生产世界。这两种意识形态是强有力的竞争者——像阴和阳的较量：两种相反的力量绑在一起、缠绕在一起，在20世纪大部分时间里一方独立地轮换地来创造另一方。通过借鉴前苏联、俄国这个中间媒介，中国共产党在毛泽东领导下武力夺取政权，追求共产主义那一边镜像的生产模式，改变了中国社会领导精英的面貌。在毛主义结束后，过去的30年间中国鼓励在它的制度中出现自由放任的资本主义，而且是在不抛弃共产主义的状态下，就如同那面老"镜子"里的孪生子。

当前的问题是共产主义的鸟会允许资本主义的疯狂的小鸡长多大？

我们这个展览以及相关的讨论和活动的一个目的，是达到对历史的复杂性的一个更深和更有收获的理解，或者至少是要给讨论提供一个广阔的全景介绍。

在冷战时期的岁月里，中英之间进而在两国艺术家之间开放式的交流和了解非常少。我们只能从全球政治的有色眼镜里很模糊地看到我们东方的邻居。但是冷战结束后，展览中的艺术家揭示了他们的生活被西方的技术和思想——特别是工业革命深深地影响着。

中国的形象，不是过时的就是超前的，继续同时存在于西方媒体对中国的描述中。东方主义、儒家哲学、毛泽东思想和共产主义集权的奇怪组合使人困惑地与便宜塑料制品的形象和急速成长

vigorous capitalism. China is chop suey stir-fried in a media satellite dish – a crazy mix of representations. The Chinese state is conscious of trying to manage that image to ensure that the rise of China's modernism is seen as a non-threatening 'development' rather than an economic, military and cultural threat. It pursues a foreign policy of strategic development of influence in terms of 'soft power'. Amongst other strategies, this pursuit of 'soft power' involves letting other friendly states and trading partners, which it sees as not being a part of China, self-determine. In this, China sets its internationalist image against that of the interventionist United States yet its own record continues to attract and encourage international criticism.

However, China is a complex country with a degree of sanctioned inner debate. It is involved in contested balancing acts between centralised power and regional variations, exploring a variety of interesting and often adventurous social models that test different blends of capitalism, socialism, democracy, totalitarianism, openness, censorship, liberalism, environmentalism, public and private wealth.

China continues to rise as an economic power, a military power and a cultural power whilst, within its borders, cities and regions resembling autonomous states vie for status: if one has a giant art gallery or opera house designed by an international architect then so must its neighbours. As in the West, competing city-states vie for international attention. One only has to look at the magnificent town halls of the Manchester region to see a similar architectural competitiveness, scale and pride evident in the British Industrial Revolution.

The artworks chosen for the exhibition speak about many aspects of social,

的强有力的资本主义盘绕在一起。中国是在媒体卫星接收天线盘上翻炒的什锦杂碎菜——各种表现的疯狂混合。中国有意识地试图控制这个形象，来确保中国现代化的崛起看起来不是一个经济、军事和文化的威胁，而是没有任何威胁的"发展"。它追求的外交政策是策略化地发展自己影响的"软实力"。在别的策略之间这个追求"软实力"的策略包括让那些不被视为中国的一部分的——中国的友邦和生意伙伴自己决定自己国家的事物。在这里，中国让自己的国际主义者的形象和美国的干预主义者的形象相对照，但是它自己的纪录也继续吸引和招致国际批评。

但是，中国是一个复杂的国家，在一定程度上支持内部的讨论。这包括辩论在中央集权和地方自治之间保持平衡的举措，探讨多样化的和有意思的、又经常是冒险性的社会模式——尝试把资本主义、社会主义、民主、集权主义、开放、审查、自由主义、环境主义、公共和私人健康体系做不同的混合。

中国继续崛起为一个经济、军事和文化大国，同时在它的疆界内，和自治州有些相似的城市和地方之间相互为地位而竞争：如果一处拥有了一个国际建筑师设计的巨大的美术馆或者歌剧院，那么它的邻居也一定要有。这就像在西方，城邦之间竞争国际的注意力。在曼彻斯特地区，只要看看壮丽的市政府大楼就可以想象在建筑物方面的类似的竞争，在英国进行工业革命时显示出的规

psychological, and political change. To bring them to Manchester, the birthplace of the Industrial Revolution and a relatively successfully regenerated post-industrial city, is to construct a critical examination of the legacy of the Industrial Revolution in China within a larger global background.

Recently, contemporary Chinese art has received much attention and it has been criticised for being too westernised and not 'Chinese' enough and looking like western Modernism and Post-modernism. These are the views of critics and are not of interest to this curator. If the works look western, this is a point of interest for inquiry and examination. This is one reason why it is appropriate that 'State Legacy' is subtitled 'Research in the Visualisation of Political History'. These artists make art whilst involved in processes of change. When we look at the works in this show we witness artists honestly struggling along their own life-paths in time and space together with the problem of understanding and representing. The issues and the artworks are full of contradictions, open-ended and are complex to navigate: it is not simple to represent when you are in the middle of the turbulent seas of change.

Change continues in the East and West and also in the North and the South too. The only constancy is change. Understood realities crumble and are seen to have been built on sand or, indeed, are almost revealed to be the fictions and illusions that they truly are. Such are the recent revelations about the state of the western economy and banking system. All that is solid melts into air[2], and not least the ice caps are melting, which graphically illustrate

---

[2] Karl Marx and Friedrich Engels, Communist Manifesto, 1848

模和自豪。

参展的入选作品讲述了社会、心理和政治变迁的诸多方面。把这些作品带到曼彻斯特——这个工业革命的诞生地、同时也是一个复兴成功的后工业化城市来展出，是给这个对中国工业革命的遗产所做的批评性审查提供一个全球化的大背景。

近来中国当代艺术引起了很多的注意，也有被批评为太西方化、不够"中国"，看起来像西方的现代主义和后现代主义。这是批评家而不是策划人感兴趣的东西。如果作品看上去像西方，那是调查和审视的兴趣点。这是为什么"国家遗产"展的副标题叫做"一项关于视觉政治史的研究"的一个原因。这些艺术家做作品的同时也经历着社会的变化过程。看这个展览中的作品，我们见证了艺术家们在他们自己的生命轨道上诚实地奋斗——在时间和空间里、也在理解和表现的问题上。现实问题和艺术作品充满了对立、开放式结局而且描述起来非常复杂：当你身处的变化像海一样动荡不息时，不可能简单地去表现。

变化在东方和西方继续着，同时也发生在北方和南方。只有变化是永恒的。理解现实如何被粉碎，看清它们是建筑在沙子上的，或者说，甚至几乎揭示了它们真的是被虚构的或者就是幻觉。这

the point that the present reverberations are global. We no longer live isolated in our own states. It is not possible to achieve a total news blackout to hide contentious events. With the complicity of the internet companies, the Chinese state attempts to censor content and does quite well at it but it must know that this is an attempt to build sand walls against the tide and wisdom would suggest careful management towards openness should be effected to avoid social upheaval in the future. Global communications and an interconnected economy call for a political 'Declaration of Interdependence': we are citizens of a world community where we are all facing the same severe consequences of our past revolutions and the ecology of our planet is dramatically endangered and requires urgent care, love and attention.

There is a new challenge of representation for all artists of the East and the West, the North and the South – for all children of the revolutions. New worlds demand new forms. There is a need for optimistic and creative futurists, born into whatever nationality, gender, form, class or creed, to converse and engage positively in dialogues of resolution. This explains the will on *Huang Zhuan*'s part and mine to bring this conversation to the public so that they might join in. There is a planetary need for artists, scientists and people of all interest groups to take the lead in dialogue and forge friendships, trust and networks in order to mandate the politicians and corporate servants to be open explorers of selfless new models of world order. Communism, as manifest to date, has led to repression and stagnation; Capitalism has led to the unequal distribution of wealth. Both are socially disharmonious. To create a harmony of human inventiveness within ourselves, our fellow species and our planet's ecological systems seems to be an achievable social design task that can be undertaken

是近期西方经济衰退和银行系统危机带来的启示。一切固有的东西都烟消云散了[2]，消失的不仅仅是冰壳，消失的冰壳只给我们提供了一个形象的插图来显示当前的危机的范围是世界性的。我们不再是孤立地生活在自己的国家里。用完全的信息封锁来隐藏引起争论的事件是不可能做到的。和网络公司共谋，中国试图审查互联网络的内容而且还做得比较成功，但它一定知道这种企图就像用沙子建墙来阻挡潮水，明智的建议是小心地管理、逐渐开放就能有效避免未来的社会动乱。全球交流和相互联系的经济呼唤一个政治的"互相依赖的宣言"：我们是世界社区的公民，在这里，我们都面对同样的我们过去革命的严峻后果和我们地球生态戏剧性恶化的危险，这需要我们紧急的关注、关心和倾注我们的爱。

　　新的表现是对所有东方和西方的艺术家、北方和南方的艺术家——所有革命的孩子们的挑战。新的世界要求新的形式。需要乐观和创造性的未来主义者——无论他们的国籍、性别、外形、阶级和信条，都来对话，积极地讨论决议。这解释了黄专与我决定把这个对话带给公众的意愿，这样他们可以加入讨论。这是一个全球的需要，艺术家、科学家、和所有利益群体的人们都来领导对

[2] 出自《共产党宣言》，马克思和恩格斯著，1848年。

together in the realisation that monetary wealth is but a shadow of true wealth and that true power is the state of not needing to exert it.

I make a call to optimistic futurists to creatively research our existing models and apply human imagination and creativity to the job of seeking new and conscious designs for living. This is deliberately not a call for a new revolution but for a controlled and sensible resolution: a new harmony between people and planet that might well involve a cyclic resurrection of older wisdom, as *Lao Zi* wrote:

'Only those that value themselves for the world can undertake its important tasks. Only those who love the world above themselves can be entrusted with the rule of it.'[3]

It is my hope that this exhibition will engender an environment and a moment for the exchange of stories of our past and present in order that we might more clearly understand ourselves, our neighbours and the appropriate action in a global present upon which hinges the very future, not just of the planet, but of the human project. Continuation of humanity relies upon a diversity of models of society from which evolution can choose the most appropriate to its context. Diversity is a pre-requisite of evolution and evolution equals survival.

In a world context of radical interconnectedness the benefits to the individual rely upon benefiting the whole. Co-operation and selflessness become the sensible selfish choice. Therefore, let us embrace diversity and be selfishly selfless.

[3] Chapter 13 of *Lao Zi*

话，缔结友谊、信任、建立网络，为了授权政治家和企业家去做开放的、无私的世界秩序新模式的探索者。共产主义到目前被证实导致压制和停滞；资本主义导致财富分配不均。两者都是不协调的社会制度。当理解了金钱的财富只是真正的财富的影子、真正的权力是不需要一个国家去行使的权力时，在我们、我们的物种和我们地球的生态系统之间用人类的聪明才智创建和谐看起来是一项可以达到的、共同完成的社会设计任务。

我呼吁乐观的未来主义者来创造性地研究现存的模式，运用人类的想象力和创造力来追求——那些新的有意识的为生活而做的设计。这不是去呼吁一个新的革命，而是呼吁一个有控制的和明智的解决：人们和星球之间的新的和谐很可能再次实践一个古老的哲学，像老子所写的：

故贵以身为天下，若可寄天下；爱以身为天下，若可托天下。[3]

我希望这个展览将为我们交换过去和现在的故事创造一个环境和契机，由此可以更加清楚地理解我们自己、我们的邻居和当下在全球的恰当的行动，这关系到的不仅是星球而且是人类计划的

[3] 出自《老子》第13章，"以贵身的态度去为天下，才可以把天下寄付给他；以爱身的态度去为天下，才可以把天下托交给他。"《老子注译及评介》，陈鼓应著，中华书局，1984年5月版，第110页。

未来。人性的继续依赖于社会模式的多样性，从中为进化提供最适合的生存模式。多样性是进化中必须的，而进化等同于生存。

在一个根本上相互联系的世界语境中，个体的利益依赖于整体的利益。合作和无私成为明智的自私的选择。因此让我们拥抱多样性，并且自私地成为无私的人。

Part I

第一部分

Empire is materializing before our very eyes.

- Michael Hardt and Antonio Negri

Empire

我们眼睁睁地看着帝国正在成为事实。　　　　　——哈特和尼格瑞

Rethinking Empire from a Chinese Concept 'All-under-Heaven (*Tianxia*, 天下)' *

Zhao Tingyang

* This is an edited version of the article originally published in Social Identities, Vol.12, No. 1, January 2006, pp 29-41

"天下体系"：帝国与世界制度 *

赵汀阳

* 本文为"普遍知识和互动知识"国际会议主题发言论文 (India, Goa, 2002/11/25-29)；"帝国与和平"
国际会议研讨对象主题论文 (France, Paris, 2003/2/15-18)。原文为英文，在翻译成中文时有所增
删。2002年应法国Le Robert出版社和Transcultural研究所之邀写成此文。

'Empire' is not only a geographical but also a cultural institutional concept. There have been great empires in the past, always reminding us of their splendid victories and their fatal collapse. The modern age has been mainly an age of nations/states, in which the concept of empire has been distorted in terms of the imperialism that should assume responsibility for the most terrible wars recorded in history. As is now realized, because of penetrating globalization and astonishing technological developments, the modernity of the nations/states system has been weakened, while a still-vague new age emerges,[1] an age of globality, the consequence of globalisation. But what is the most likely form of global governance? Personally I feel as if the steps toward a new empire can be now be heard and indeed have already been discussed (see Hardt & Negri, 2001). What ideal of empire could we expect for a new empire? It seems an important and serious question. Here I would like to introduce the Chinese traditional concept of world governance, which is quite different from the usual understanding of empire, and which might give a more constructive and positive way to rethink the best idea of an acceptable empire.

1 The Concept of 'All-under-Heaven'

In contrast to the western concept of empire, China has a three thousand year-old traditional concept, 'All-under-Heaven', very closely relevant to the idea of empire. We are

---

[1] But not all think so. Smith (1996, Chapter 6), for instance, insisted the system of nation/states would not be broken up as many think, because no new system could be stronger than nationalism in the coming future.

就理论可能性而言, 帝国可以只是个文化/政治制度而不一定是个强权国家实体。古代伟大帝国的兴衰留下了神话般的历史故事, 是耽于梦想的人的永远梦想。现代的"民族/国家"体系终结了古代模式的"伟大帝国", 使之成为并仅仅成为社会记忆, 以至于人们现在已经非常习惯于用民族/国家作为分析单位去理解现实、过去乃至未来。其实, 帝国体系曾经长时间地作为自然生成的社会制度而存在, 民族/国家却只不过是现代的产物。现代不仅结束了传奇的帝国古代传统, 而且挫败了各种理想和乌托邦, 除了技术和经济, 几乎没有别的什么事业能够在现代获得神话般的成功。

"帝国"这个概念在现代演变成为一个失去了自然朴实品质的改版概念"帝国主义"。"帝国主义"是到了19世纪后期才被创造出来的一个反思性概念[1]。在很长的时间里, 帝国主义被认为主要是马克思主义关心的论题, 其中一个重要原因是马克思主义是对资本主义的批判, 而帝国主义被认为是最大化资本主义的方式, 从列宁主义到依附理论都假定控制海外资源和市场对于资本主义的自身

---

[1] 据霍布斯鲍姆的说法, "帝国主义"一词在19世纪70年代才出现, 直到19世纪90年代才"突然变成一般的用语", 并且"挂在每个人的嘴上"。这个概念如此晚近才出现, 以至于马克思都没有使用过这个如此重要的概念。《帝国的时代》, 第64-65页, 南京, 江苏人民出版社, 1999。

led to think that a thing always has, in Platonic philosophy, its idea that essentially makes it as it is. An idea also implies, if further interpreted, the perfect concept for a thing to be as it is expected. That means a perfect idea turns out to be an ideal of a thing. Here the concept of All-under-Heaven could be considered as a supposed ideal of a perfect empire.

The term 'All-under-Heaven' (*Tianxia*, 天下), found in almost the oldest Chinese texts, means firstly the earth, or the whole world under heaven.[2] It is almost equivalent to 'the universe' or 'the world' in western languages. Its second meaning is the 'hearts of all peoples' (*Minxin*, 民心), or the 'general will of the people'. The world is always the home-for-people, that is, the earth as it is ours more than the earth as it is. All-under-Heaven therefore consists of both the earth and the people. Consequently, an emperor does not really enjoy his empire of All-under-Heaven, even if he conquers an extraordinary vast area of land, unless he receives the sincere and true support from the people on that land. Just as Philosopher *Xunzi* (313BC - 238BC) said in his essay 'On kingship and supremacy':

Enjoying All-under-Heaven does not mean to receive the lands from people who are forced to give, but to satisfy all people with a good way of governance.

---

[2] Two thousand years ago, the popular Chinese imagination of the so called 'All-under-Heaven' was interesting in its square division of the world into 'nine regions' (九州) spreading from the central region to the rest in eight directions. And the land consisting of the nine regions was the area of ancient China while the oldest capital city in China is rightly in the central region. But *Zou Yan* (邹衍), one of China's earliest geographers, exceptionally had a much wider sight of the land that was thought to comprise 81 'nine regions - reckoned by multiplying by nine - and he said that ancient China was 'just the one of the eighty-ones' in the world. See *Shima Qian*, 91BC, p. 2344.

最大化是必不可少的，因此，现代化、资本主义、殖民主义和帝国主义是密不可分的系列概念。可以说，帝国主义是基于民族/国家制度的超级军事/经济力量而建立的一个政治控制和经济剥削的世界体系。欧洲传统帝国和帝国主义的共同理念都是"以一国而统治世界"——背后的哲学精神是"以部分支配整体"这样的欲望——而民族/国家的概念使得帝国主义以民族主义为原则来重塑帝国眼光从而精神变得更加狭隘，不仅失去了传统帝国兼收并蓄的胸怀，而又把帝国的强权好战方面发展到了极致（历史上最大规模的战争都是现代帝国主义的作品）。

今天有迹象表明世界似乎正在走向一个新的时代和新的世界体系，许多人相信民族/国家体系正在受到全球化的挑战（但并非所有人都相信民族/国家体系会被破坏[2]）。那么，未来将是一个新帝国时代吗？哈特和尼格瑞富有挑战性的热门著作《帝国》甚至认为现在就已经开始了新帝国时代，他们指出："我们眼睁睁地看着帝国正在成为事实"，"民族/国家的统治权力的衰落并不意味着统治权力这一权力事实本身（sovereignty as such）的衰落……新的全球统治形式就是所谓帝

---

[2] 例如A. D. Smith就坚信许多人过于心急地认为民族/国家体系将被打破，他认为事实上在可见的未来里我们还很难发展出一种比民族主义更强大的精神，因此也就难以发展出新的体系。参见*Nations and Nationalism in a Global Era*, Chapter 6, Polity Pr., 1996。

Its third meaning, the ethical and/or political meaning, is a world institution, or a universal system for the world, a Utopia of the world-as-one-family. This political/ethical ideal of the world boasts of its very distinctness in its philosophical and practical pursuit of world governance ensured by a world institution. The ideal of All-under-Heaven as the philosophical concept of a world institution essentially distinguishes itself from the pattern of the traditional military empire, for instance the Roman Empire, or that of an imperialist nation/state, for example the British Empire. The conceptually defined Empire of All-under-Heaven does not mean a country[3] at all but an institutional world instead. And it expects a world/society instead of nation/states. All-under-Heaven is a deep concept of the world, defined by the trinity of the geographical, psychological, and political worlds. From the viewpoint of this political ontology, our supposed world is now still a non-world, for the world has not yet been completed in its full sense. World institution and full popular support are still missing. We are talking nonsense about the world, for the world has not yet been fulfilled within its world-ness.

The concept of All-under-Heaven shows its uniqueness in its political and philosophical world-view that creates the world-wide measure, or the world-wide viewpoint, of seeing the affairs and problems of the world within the measure of worldness. It defines the world as a categorical rethinking unit of viewing and interpreting political life, constitution and

[3] A Chinese philosopher, *Liang Shuming* thought that ancient China had been developing itself as a 'world' rather than a 'country'. See Collections of *Liang Shuming*, 1992, p. 332.

国"[3]。这不是想象，而是非常值得深思的问题。正如人类所能够发明的社会制度种类并不多，所能够想象的世界体系形式也不多，事实上帝国是最典型的世界体系。帝国问题属于那种复杂的大规模问题 (comprehensive problem)，它几乎涉及生活和社会的所有方面，应该说是个"问题组"。大规模问题的凸现往往是面向新时代的思维特征，因为在面向新时代的时候人们就试图重新思考关于整个世界、社会和生活的理念。帝国正是这样一个理念 (eidos, idea)。在这里不可能全面讨论帝国的问题，我准备讨论的是，在哲学的意义上，中国传统的"帝国"理念对于任何一种可能的世界体系会有什么样的理论意义。

进一步说，不管未来是什么样的时代，至少我们知道全球化已经把所有地方的问题世界化了，几乎任何一个地方性问题都不得不在世界问题体系中被思考和解决。现代性的一个一直隐藏着的困难突然明显起来：现代制度只是国内社会制度，而不是世界制度，或者说，现代制度的有效范围或约束条件是民族/国家的内部社会，而不是世界或国际社会。于是，即使每一个国家都成为民族/国家并且建立了标准的现代制度 (民主政治和自由市场) 以保证每一个国家内部社会秩序，在国家

[3] Michael Hardt and Antonio Negri: *Empire*, Harvard Univ. Pr., 2001, Preface.

institution. This methodology is essentially different from that in the west. In western political theory, the biggest political unit to be found is a country or nation/state, while in Chinese theory it is the framework of the 'world/society'. States have always been seen as subordinate units inside the framework of the world/society that are regarded as a necessary and the highest political unit. Chinese political philosophy defines a political order in which the world is primary, whereas the nation/state is primary in western philosophy. Certainly, westerners do think about the world, but the western image of the world is nothing higher nor greater than international alliances or unions of nation/states, not going beyond the framework of nation/states. Such projects have essential difficulties in reaching the real integrity of the world for they are limited by their perspectives of nation/states, due to the lack of a vision of world-ness. To see the world from its world-ness is different from seeing it from part of it.

All-under-Heaven should be understood together with another closely related concept the 'Son of Heaven' (*Tian-zi,* 天子), that is, structurally pertaining to All-under-Heaven. The concepts of All-under-Heaven and the Son of Heaven make a philosophical foundation for the system of empire. The Son of Heaven, analogous to an emperor,[4] is entitled to 'enjoy his reign of the world under the heaven' (see The Poems). He is born to have 'All-under-Heaven as his home', just as naturally as a man has a home of his own according to his natural rights,

---

[4] In Chinese history, before the King of *Qin* the Great self-nominated as 'the first emperor' in 221BC, the King in general was called the Son of heaven and kept as the interpretive name for emperor.

之间也仍然是无制度的。因此是无约束、无秩序或无法则的失控空间 (尽管有一些国际组织在假装建立国际制度)。这种国际无政府状态完全满足"霍布斯状态",即"所有人反对所有人的状态"。从形而上学角度看,现代世界体系在本质上是"无序状态" (chaos)。希腊哲学认为,只有当"无序状态"变成"有序状态" (kosmos) 才形成自然和世界 (kosmos正是宇宙的词源[4]),而chaos要变成kosmos又首先需要发现世界的理念 (eidos)。从这个角度看来,今天的世界仍然没有成为"世界",仍然停留在chaos状态,它只不过是个无序的存在,是个"非世界" (non-world)。希腊哲学的kosmos (有序存在) 所表达的也只是关于自然世界的充分意义,还不是关于人文世界的概念。与kosmos相应的、同样具有充分意义的"人文世界"概念可以在中国哲学里找到一个表达模式,这就是"天下"。"天下"不仅是地理概念,而且同时意味着世界社会、世界制度以及关于世界制度的文化理念,因此它是个全方位的完整的世界概念。这一概念的重要性正在于它与世界制度问题的密切关系。

---

[4] Kosmos原义为军队纪律,被用来表达有秩序的宇宙,就是说,自然必须有其"形式"才成为宇宙。参见J. Burnet: *Early Greek Philosophy*, p. 9, Adam & Charles Black, 1930。

and 'nothing left there out of his world of home'. Whilst not even the strongest empires have controlled the entire world, it is not difficult to conceive of the world controlled by a conceptual empire. Of most importance is that a Son of Heaven does rather than is . In other words, one could self-claim one's destiny as the mandate of heaven, but one has to be reconfirmed as the Son of Heaven if and only if there is evidence to justify this qualification. That is, as a Confucian master Mencius argued, one's being supported by the people.[5] The people's choice is conceived as the final evidence or examination of the legitimacy/justification of the governance. The Chinese theory of political legitimism allows two ways to prove the rightness of the reign, one of them is the legitimacy of establishment of an empire - that is to save people from a terrible situation when, and only when, welcomed by most of the people - and the other is the justification of enjoyment of the reign, which is to keep the world in the order that most of the people want.

According to Confucius' theory of justification, 'p is p if p does as p is conceptually meant to do', we do not say that a king, an institution or a political system is better but rather does better as evidenced.[6] However, what is considered evidence in the Chinese way is not always

[5] Mencius argued that people were of greater weight than the government and the support from people was the final confirmation of the reign. And he insisted that the king would lose his reign if he lost his people's support, and he lost his people's support because he was against the people's hearts. And Interpretation of Rites also said:'enjoying the reign when receiving the support from the people, and losing the reign when losing the support of the people.' (see Mencius, c. 220BC, as well as Interpretation of rites)

[6] Confucius had claimed his famous theory of justification as 'p is p if p does as p is meant to do', for instance, a king should do as the concept of king requires. See Confucius, The Analects, c. 500BC.

当今天的所有问题都变成世界性问题时，就不得不思考"世界制度"的问题。弗朗西斯•福山曾经通过分析现代社会制度而得出结论认为，现代制度虽然有缺点，但已经是足够好的制度，因此不再有制度革命的可能性，历史也就完成了（通常翻译为"历史的终结"，但不够准确[5]），或者说，历史最后实现了历史的最高目的。这一"历史的完成"的断言显然过于匆忙，即使不去讨论社会制度的革命可能性而仅就任意给定的某个社会制度而言，我们也必须要求一个社会制度具有逻辑完备性，即它不仅能够处理国内社会，而且能够处理国际社会。这一逻辑其实很简单：一个社会制度不能止步于"国家"这一单位，而必须考虑到"世界"这一最大的政治/社会单位，不能对世界视而不见[6]。显然，一种社会制度仅仅在国家层次上获得成功仍然还没有完成其最大和最终目的，如果它在世界场合中不再有效，那么就不是一个充分有效的制度。作为比较，我们可以考虑马克思的制度理

[5] 参见Fukuyama: The End of History and the Last Man, Free, Pr., 1992。其中的关键词"end"的表面意思是"终结"，深层意思是"历史目的之最后实现"。这是来自德国古典哲学的观念。作为参考，马克思也是在德国古典哲学的习惯意义上想象共产主义社会的，共产主义社会也被理解为既是历史的终结又是历史目的之最后实现。

[6] 在"北京对话"（2003年3月17日）会议上，我与福山教授讨论到这个问题，但是福山教授坚持认为，政治自由主义的社会制度尤其是民主制度用于国际社会，是不合适的而且也没有实践的可能性。

based on statistics, a democratic election, but rather that collected by means of observation of social trends or preferences, and especially by the obvious fact that people autonomously choose to follow and pledge their allegiance, instead of voting for one of several dubious politicians. In fact, careful and sincere observation can better detect truth and come to a better reflection of public choice than do democratic elections, which become spoilt by money, misled by media and distorted by strategic votes. The autonomy of people to follow or not to follow is regarded as a fundamental question in Chinese political philosophy as the matter of 'people's heart' (*Minxin,* 民心), is considered closer to the truth of political reality than democracy. The problem of the people's heart, the term might better be translated as 'demo-allegiance', must, theoretically, be a better form of representation than democracy with the problem of public choice. If we follow the facts, it seems to be the case that the masses always make the wrong choices for themselves by the misleading of democracy.

The knowledge of public preference has never been an epistemological problem to Chinese minds, for evidence of public preference is thought to be apparent. Instead, the Chinese have taken the ethical problem of the 'sincerity' of concern for the people most seriously. The unspoken theory is that most people do not really know what is best for them, but that the elite do, so the elite ought genuinely to decide for the people. In the late nineteenth century, many Chinese influenced by western discourse, began to think that the best way of carrying out the Chinese principle of 'people's hearts' was democracy. But the problem of public choice remains unsolved today and has become an ever greater difficulty, for democracy represents the misled much more than the independent mind, the

论,马克思和福山都拥有黑格尔哲学背景,但马克思所思考的共产主义社会才是一个世界规模的社会。共产主义可能不是个最合适的社会制度,但马克思至少考虑到了世界制度问题。毫无疑问,世界必须被理解为一个思考和分析的最大单位,否则所有国际问题或者世界性问题都不可能被有效地分析和解决,甚至,如果不能有效地分析和解决世界性的问题,那么也不可能充分有效地分析国内社会制度问题,因为世界问题是任何一个国家问题的必要约束条件。我们不能想象,每一个子集都是有序的,但是总集却是无序的,在这样的条件下能够有效地理解、分析和解决问题。

在这里要讨论的主要是中国的"天下理论",我试图论证,天下理论是任何可能的世界制度的形而上学。所以在这里使用哲学来分析世界政治问题,是因为哲学是分析任何理念的方法。"天下"也是个乌托邦,不管什么样的乌托邦都不同程度地有它不现实的方面。讨论乌托邦的意义并不在于能够实现乌托邦,而在于有可能获得一种比较明确的理念,从而使世界制度获得理论根据,或者说,我们至少能够因此知道离理想有多远。

false want much more than true needs and illusive advantages much more than real goods and virtues.

In Chinese philosophy, the legitimacy of All-under-Heaven is asserted as absolute whereas a Son of Heaven is not, which indicates three implicative principles: 1) the political legitimacy of reign of All-under-Heaven is independent of and prior to any ideology or religion; 2) the reign of All-under-Heaven is open to any qualified candidates who best know the Way (*Dao*, 道) to improve the happiness of people universally; and 3) this will not be a dictator or a superpower, but one who has the right and power to justify the governance of All-under-Heaven. *Laozi*, the founder of Daoism, pointed out:

a king could rule a state by his orders, win a war by strategies, but enjoy All-under- Heaven only by doing nothing to decrease the freedom and to deny the interests of people. (see *Laozi, Tao Te Ching*, c.500BC)

The appeal to the evidence of the people's support had become the justified reason for another political group to launch a revolution, a 'rewriting of the mandate of heaven' in Chinese terms. In fact the justification of revolution has become a 4000-year-old tradition. And the theory of All-under-Heaven has no discriminating rule to deny the opportunity for any nation to be in charge of the governance of All-under-Heaven. Historically, the Mongolians and the *Manchu* governed China for 400 years and their governance had been considered as legitimate dynasties of China. More interestingly, both the Mongolian and the *Manchu* emperors adopted the theory of All-under-Heaven in establishing their legitimate

一、"天下"理念

1. 饱满的或完备的世界概念

与西方语境中的"帝国"(empire)概念不同,"天下"这一中国传统概念表达的与其说是帝国的概念, 还不如说是关于帝国的理念。概念和理念虽然大体一致, 但有一点区别: 理念不仅表达了某种东西所以是这种东西的性质 (希腊人认为是一种决定性的"形式"), 而且表达了这种东西所可能达到的最好状态。在柏拉图的意义上, 理念总是在本质上使得某个东西成为这个东西。于是这就逻辑地蕴涵着, 理念又是为某个东西所可能设想的完美化概念。因此理念 (idea) 就必定意味着理想 (ideal)。概念和理念的这一区别对于自然事物或许是没有意义的, 因为在自然事物身上, 概念和理念几乎完全重合, 我们不能要求石头长得更"理想"。但这一区别对于人为事物来说则有着不可忽视的意义, 因为人为事物要承担着比自然事物更多的意义, 我们对我们要做的事情总可以有理想, 而在事实上, 概念未必总能够赶上理想。这就是为什么我们不但能够知道一个东西是什么样的, 而且还能够指望它成为什么样的。理想的意义就在此。

"天下"要表达的正是关于帝国的一种理想或者说完美概念 (尽管具体制度和实践永远是个难题)。每种文化和思想体系中的关键词往往都有着多层复合的意义, 而且很难完全被说明, 永远有

reigns.[7]

In the Chinese system of ideas, family-ship is very powerful in interpreting ethical/political legitimacy, for family-ship is thought to be the naturally given ground and resource for love, harmony and obligations and thus a full argument that 'exhausts the essence of humanity'.[8] Chinese philosophy has developed the very consciousness of the virtue of family-ship.[9] The essence of humanity, fundamentally constituted as family-ship, is claimed as the 'first thing with which a Lord is concerned most' and the only thing 'impossible to be altered forever', while all other rules and knowledge are alterable.[10] Family-ship is the minimal and irreducible location of harmony, cooperation, common interests and happiness, so that it is arguably the universal framework through which to interpret all possible cases of harmony,

---

[7] In 1271, the Mongolian emperor changed the empire name Mongolia into a Chinese name 'Da-yuan' (大元), meaning 'as vast as the vastest', for he thought the name Mongolia was rather local thus not good for his empire of All-under-Heaven (see *Song Liang*). And the *Manchu* nation had ruled China successfully for nearly 300 hundreds years with the support from people. The *Manchu* king had written an interesting letter to the Chinese emperor of the *Ming* dynasty before its declaration of a war on *Ming*, in which the *Menchu* king took advantage of the theory of All-under-Heaven to speak for his justice. He wrote: 'all kinds of things from insects to humankind in the world are created and nurtured by the nature itself, not by your empire, so that nothing is your private property. And Heaven is always so fair that your empire will be blamed and punished for your abusing the governance . . . All under-Heaven will be given to one who has greater virtues' (see *Pang, Sun & Li*, 1984, pp. 289/96).

[8] Interpretations of rites (c. 500BC), chapter on *Da-zhuan*.

[9] Only a few Chinese philosophers had the opposite opinion to the principle of family-ship. For instance, *Shang-yang* said that the ethics of family-ship encouraged selfishness and evils rather than kindness and goodness, and he thought laws were the most important things. See *Shang-yang* (c. 300BC).

[10] Interpretations of rites (c.500BC), chapter on *Da-zhuan*.

着解释和争论的余地。"天下"也是这样一个概念。一般地说，它的基本意义大概是：

1) 地理学意义上的"天底下所有土地"，相当于中国式三元结构"天、地、人"中的"地"，或者相当于人类可以居住的整个世界[7]；

2) 进而它还指所有土地上生活的所有人的心思，即"民心"，比如当说到"得天下"，主要意思并不是获得了所有土地（这一点从来也没有实现过），而是说获得大多数的民心。[8]这一点很重要，它表明"天下"概念既是地理性的又是心理性的；

3) 最重要的是它的伦理学/政治学意义，它指向一种世界一家的理想或乌托邦（所谓四海一家）。这一关于世界的伦理/政治理想的突出意义在于它想象着并且试图追求某种"世界制度"以及

---

[7] 古代中国的天下概念虽然在理论上的所指是整个世界，但由于实际知识的有限，因此实际上理解到的世界并不太大，最早时的理解是"九州"，只相当于今天的数省面积，而且按照想象，是几何上很整齐的土地，以都城为核心而向四面八方展开。不过也有眼界更大的学者，如邹衍想象的世界由多达81个"九州"组成，而中国只是其中之一。这个想象又似乎过大。参见《史记》卷七十四。

[8]《荀子·王霸篇》："取天下者，非负其土地而从之之谓也，道足以壹人而已矣……用国者，得百姓之力者富，得百姓之死者强，得百姓之誉者荣。三得者具而天下归之，三得者亡而天下去之。"

cooperation, common interests and happiness.

The virtue of the-world-as-All-under-Heaven is always understood and interpreted in terms of family-ship. It analytically implies the claim for the wholeness and harmony of the world to be a world, for the necessary conditions of family happiness are always the world's wholeness and harmony. As also implied logically, anything against the wholeness and harmony of the world is defined as politically unacceptable (the interference in the liberty of an individual might be an unacceptable political mistake, whilst the damage to harmony, the first political mistake). Thus the principle of harmony, originating in the ideal of family-ship, is made a paradigm applied further to the explanations of the possibility of any kind of harmony in the world. All-under-Heaven is nothing but the greatest family, a world-family; that said, all political levels, defined as 'All-under-Heaven, states and families', should be essentially homogenous or homological so as to create a harmonious system. This is the key to understanding Chinese political theory. The world's effective political order must progress from All-under-Heaven, to state, to families, so as to ensure universal consistency and transitivity in political life, or the uniformity of society (just like the uniformity of nature), while an ethical order progresses from families, to states, to All-under-Heaven, so as to ensure ethical consistency and transitivity. It implies that a world is of order if and only if it is ordered with the highest world institution, while the world institution must reflect the virtue of family-ship. Under this principle, Chinese political and ethical theories are made one. We all have reason to highlight the importance of political/ethical consistency and transitivity, because any inconsistency or contradiction in the system would be a disaster. For instance,

由世界制度所保证的"世界政府"。显然,"天下"虽然是关于世界的概念,但比西方思想中的"世界"概念似乎有着更多的含义,它至少是地理、心理和社会制度三者合一的"世界",而且这三者有着不可分的结构,如果分析为分别的意义则破坏了天下的存在形式。"天下"意味着一种哲学、一种世界观,它是理解世界、事物、人民和文化的基础。"天下"所指的世界是个"有制度的世界",是个已经完成了从chaos到kosmos的转变的世界,是个兼备了人文和物理含义的世界。与"天下"相比,西方的"世界"概念就其通常意义而言只是个限于科学视野中的世界(尽管可以在比喻的意义上指任意什么世界[9]),而"天下"则是个哲学视野中的世界,它涉及世界的各种可能意义,是个满载所有关于世界的可能意义的饱满世界概念(the full concept of the world)。不过,在西方的世界概念里也有一个概念是涉及人文和生活传统的,或者说也是纯粹哲学性的,即胡塞尔提出的"生活世界",它是个历史的世界或者说是关于世界的历史视界(horizon)[10]。生活世界是个主观性的世界,但它

---

[9] 波普尔曾经把"世界"理解为三个:物质的、心理的和图书馆式的,仍然还是科学视野中的世界。而且这一区分意义不大,似乎画蛇添足(参见Popper:*Objective Knowledge*,1972)。

[10] Husserl: *The Crisis of European Sciences and Transcendental Phenomenology*, Northwestern Univ. Pr.,1970.

democracy, equality and liberty have been developed in western domestic society, but never extended to the international society. This case of political inconsistency and intransitivity could greatly damage the reputation of democracy, equality and liberty.

The Chinese system of families, states and All-under-Heaven, which differs fundamentally from the western system of individuals, nations and internationals, is often criticised for its neglect of the individual as well as individual rights, but this is a misunderstanding of Chinese philosophy and a poor understanding of political society. There is no Chinese denial of the value of the individual, but rather a denial of the individual to be a political foundation or starting point, because the political makes sense only when it deals with 'relations' rather than 'individuals', and the political is meant to speak for co-existence rather than a single existence. In a very Chinese way, politics aims at a good society of peaceful 'order' (*Zhi*, 治), which is the first condition for any possible happiness of each and all, and at keeping a society from the'disorder' (*Luan,* 乱) that destroys all possibilities of individual happiness. This political conception could find a strong argument in Chinese ontology, the ontology of relations, instead of the western ontology of things .

According to the grammar of Chinese philosophy, the political philosophy focusing on the absoluteness of the individual or nation misleads political questions and logic, for it encourages conflicts and consciousness of the enemy, which creates more problems than solutions. Carl Schmitt's wonderful theory of recognition of enemy/friend could be an example. Schmitt's theory rightly reflects the typical wrong in western political consciousness, or sub-consciousness, in which political impulse divides and breaks up the

被认为是客观知识的原始基础, 是被科学世界所掩盖和遗忘的本原性经验世界, 它被胡塞尔用来批评科学的"忘本"。在"天下"和"生活世界"这两个关于世界的非常不同的概念之间, 其实可以发现有着一些遥远但重要的相关性, 也许可以说, 相对于"生活世界"来说, 天下是个"制度世界"。

"天下"构成了中国哲学的真正基础, 它直接规定了这样一种哲学视界: 思想所能够思考的对象——世界——必须表达为一个饱满的或意义完备的概念。既然我们总是负担着制度而生活在世界上, 所以, 世界必须被理解为一个有制度的世界, 否则就不可能说明生活。同时"天下"概念还意味着一种哲学方法论: 如果任意一个生活事物都必须在它作为解释条件的"情景"(context) 中才能被有效地理解和分析, 那么, 必定存在着一个最大的情景使得所有生活事物都必须在它之中被理解和分析。这个能够作为任何生活事物的解释条件的最大情景就是"天下"。只有当解释条件是个饱满的或意义完备的概念, 才能够说拥有充分的世界观。我们将看到, 缺乏充分意义的世界观的哲学 (例如西方哲学) 在解释世界性问题时存在着根本性的困难。

2. 天下体系: 世界尺度和永恒尺度

既然"天下"是个"有制度的世界", 那么, 天下理想就可以理解为关于世界制度的哲学理论。它

world. In contrast, one of the principles of Chinese political philosophy is said 'to turn the enemy into a friend', and it would lose its meaning if it were not to remove conflicts and pacify social problems - in a word, to 'transform'(*Hua,* 化) the bad into the good. Today, some investigations in game theory seem to support Chinese philosophy in that in a game, maximizers will find a limit to improving their own interests, because Pareto efficiency for common happiness would be impossible without trusted cooperation.

The concept of All-under-Heaven is meant to be an empire of world-ness responsible for the common happiness of all peoples. It refers to a theoretical or conceptual empire that has never really existed. I do not say that Chinese dynasties, for instance the *Qin* (秦) dynasty, were not empires. Quite the opposite, China had been an empire in its usual sense for a long time. Every dynasty of the Chinese empire had tried to apply the concept of All-under-Heaven, but had never been able to realize it because of practical limitations. All-under-Heaven means a very different empire, that is not necessarily a world superpower, but a world under a commonly agreed institution, a plan to make the world a place of world-ness. The ancient Chinese empires had no power to accomplish the plan of world-ness, but had tried to be an exemplar empire of family-ship. The comprehensive view of the world as All-under-Heaven surely takes the whole world as a single political system that is much greater and higher than a single country or nation/state. Consequently, the empire of All-under-Heaven highlights the problem of time rather than of space, that is, the problem of its duration rather than of its territory; and it has been apparent in the Chinese concern for the legitimacy of its dynasties rather than actual territorial conquest.

所想象的天下/帝国从本质上区别于西方的各种帝国模式，包括传统军事帝国如罗马帝国模式和现代帝国主义的民族/国家如大英帝国模式以及当代新帝国主义即美国模式。最突出的一点是，按照纯粹理论上的定位，天下/帝国根本上就不是个"国家"尤其不是个民族/国家，而是一种政治/文化制度，或者说一个世界社会。正如梁漱溟所指出的，"天下"是个关于"世界"而不是"国家"的概念[11]。天下理论的重要性在于它把"世界"看作是一个政治单位，一个最大并且最高的政治单位，同时也就成为一个思考所有社会/生活问题的思想分析单位，也就是最大的情景或解释条件。中国关于政治/社会各种单位的层次结构，即"家—国—天下"的结构[12]，意味着一种比西方分析单位结构更广阔因此更有潜力的解释框架。在西方概念里，"国家"就已经是最大的政治单位了，"世界"就只是个地理性空间。不管是城邦国家，还是帝国，或者民族/国家，都只包含"国"的理念，没有"世界"的理念。从概念体系的逻辑上看，西方政治哲学的分析单位系列是不完全的，从个人、共同体到国家，都是包含着物理、心理和制度的意义饱满概念，可是到了"世界"这个最大的概念，却缺乏必须配备的制

---

[11] 《梁漱溟学术论著自选集》，第332页，北京：北京师范大学出版社，1992。

[12] 比较早的表述更多是天下在先，如《孟子·离娄上》曰："人有恒言皆曰天下国家。"

The ancient Chinese practical project of the empire of All-under-Heaven had many sub-states (*Guo*, 国) that were institutionally loyal to the empire, which were institutional centres, but independent in their governance. These sub-states were not nation/states at all but ruled by kings or noble families and politically recognized by the emperor. Before the centralized government of the vast Chinese Empire was set up in 221BC, China had been an 'ideal' empire, close to the concept of All-under-Heaven, consisting of many 'sub-states',[11] independent in their economies, military powers and cultures, but politically and ethically dependent on the empire's institutional centre. There was a tributary system between the suzerain centre and the sub-states. The suzerain centre enjoyed its authority in recognizing the legitimacy of the substates, but never interfered unless a sub-state declared war on another sub-state member of the family of All-under-Heaven.

The Chinese institution of empire experienced revolutionary reform in 221BC when the First *Qin* Emperor conquered China and created a country with centralized governance over many provinces, instead of sub-states. But this institutional reform did not change the ideal of All-under-Heaven. On the contrary, it seemed to lead the Chinese to the idea of an even wider understanding of the world, a nearly 'global' picture of the world in which all foreign countries, near and far, were seen as the theoretically acquired sub-states. So the former

[11] A Chinese sub-state in the ancient times appeared similar to a Greek city-state in many but not all aspects. The oldest word for state in Chinese is '或', meaning 'a militarily guarded city' while the land outside is called the 'field' (野), and later added a wall or border around the city to make a new word '国'. A sub-state was considered a member in a family-like empire.

度文化意义而只是个自然世界概念，就是说，"世界"只是个知识论单位，而没有进一步成为政治/文化单位。政治/文化单位到"国家"而止步，这就是西方哲学的一个重要的局限性，它缺少了一个必要的视界。

西方一直到现代才开始有似乎比"国家"更大的关于政治单位的想象。例如康德关于"人类所有民族的国家"（civitas gentium）或者所谓"世界共和国"的想象，但这种想象并不认真，事实上在康德的论文中只是被草草提及而已，只有空洞的概念，并无论述。康德认为比较现实的想象应该是弱一些的"自由国家的联盟制度"[13]，其潜台词是不能超越民族/国家体系（这个理由在当代自由主义政治理论中终于变得直截了当了）。不过后来马克思的共产主义社会概念则是个关于世界政治制度的认真想象，但马克思主义并没有成为西方思想主流，相反几乎是个异端。从实践上说，现在的联合国看上去几乎是康德想象的实践，但只是个准世界性的单位，即使这种准世界性也是非常象征性的，因为联合国这样的政治概念至多意味着目前规模最大的政治单位，却不是理论上最大而且地位最高的政治单位，因为它不拥有在国家制度之上的世界制度和权力，而只不过是民族/国家之间

[13] 康德：《历史理性批判文集·永久和平论》，商务印书馆，1997。

smaller picture of All-under-Heaven had been just mapped onto the enlarged one. And the legal tributary system had also been redefined and transformed into the voluntary tributary system, in which foreign countries volunteered to decide whether or not to join.

The voluntary tributary system expresses much of the diplomatic strategy of the ancient Chinese empire. It had developed stipulated reciprocity into the voluntary in a tributary system and always ran it in a pattern of much greater returns for any tributary gifts. Reciprocity has been a leading idea in Chinese thinking. And it has been performed within the norms of practical life to express mutual respect. The Interpretation of Rites says: 'the reciprocal repay is mostly preferred in the rites. And no pay or no repay no respect'. [12] Reciprocity is a truer echo of the other's heart-felt respect than an economically equal exchange. And it has been argued that the ideal of social relations is rooted in the essence of reciprocity as heart-for-heart, much more than the reciprocity of interests-for-interests. The primary concept or principle in Confucian theory is *Ren* (仁), literally meaning the best relationship 'of-twopersons'.[13] And even more interesting, the oldest literal meaning of *Ren* was the best relationship of a 'thousands hearts' (*Ren*, 忎). *Ren* had been considered the only fundamental principle by which the harmony of peoples could be developed. Reciprocity understood in the Chinese way has less to do with the reciprocal utilitarianism or balance in commercial exchange and much more to do with the reciprocity of hearts.

---

[12] Interpretations of rites (c. 500BC), chapter on *Qu-li*.

[13] *Ren* has often been translated as 'humanity' or 'kindness'. These are not good translations.

的协商性机构，所以从实质上说就只是个从属于民族/国家体系的服务性机构。

"天下"概念的重要性表现为这一哲学概念创造了思考问题的一个"世界尺度"，它使得度量一些用民族/国家尺度无法度量的大规模问题成为可能。这一尺度的意义在古代并不十分明显，而在今天却极其突出。至于为什么古代中国在3000年前就思考到这样一个世界尺度，这或许已经很难解释清楚，但大概可以肯定，古人不可能预料到这个理念在今天世界的意义，古人在表达这个概念时就好像它是个理所当然的理想，因此，"天下"概念在古代应该是个信仰或者是纯粹的哲学而不是经验知识，事实上当时也没有相应的经验知识可以支持它。

"天下"把"世界"定义为一个范畴性的 (categorical，康德意义上) 框架和不可还原的反思单位，用于思考和解释政治/文化生活和制度。它意味着一种完全不同于西方的方法论。西方思考政治问题的基本单位是各种意义上的"国家" (country/state/nation)，"国家"被当作是思考和衡量各种问题的绝对根据、准绳或尺度。而按照中国的天下理论，"世界"才是思考各种问题的最后尺度，"国家"只是从属于世界社会这一解释框架的次一级别的单位，这意味着：

1) 超出国家尺度的问题就需要在天下尺度中去理解；

2) 国家不能以国家尺度对自身的合法性进行充分的辩护，而必须在天下尺度中获得合法性。

The principle of voluntariness is key to the Chinese understanding of 'relations' from the viewpoint of other-ness. Some scholars have argued that the general Chinese ethical principle appears the same as the western Golden Rule (see Kung & Kuschel, 1993), but it differs essentially in the philosophical presuppositions wherein western philosophy sees in terms of subjectivity, but the Chinese in terms of other-ness. The Bible's golden rule, 'do unto others as you would have them do to you' sounds promising, but it would encounter challenges and difficulties when other hearts are taken into account. The other-ness of the other heart is something absolute and transcendent, so the other heart might reasonably want a different life. In terms of other-ness, the Chinese ethical principle thus runs: 'let others reach their goals if you reach yours'. It is easy to see the subtle difference between the western and Chinese rules. I have rewritten the Bible's rule in a negative representation to be a better representation of the absoluteness of other-ness: 'never do to others what the others would not want you to do to them'. When facing the problem of the irreducible diversity of the hearts of others, Chinese philosophy found a solution in the highlighting of voluntariness. The 2000-year-old Interpretation of Rites says that harmony can be developed under two conditions:

To be heart to heart closed when congenial to each other; to respect reciprocally when different from each other ... rites differ in forms but equal in essence as the expression of respect, just as in the same way, music differs in styles but is equal in essence as the expression of heart.[14]

---

[14] Interpretations of rites (c. 500BC), chapter on *Yue-ji*.

因此，天下理论是典型的世界理念，以至于可以成为判断一个理论是否具有世界理念的结构性标准，就是说，具有不同的价值观的其它世界理念也许是可能的，但任何一种可能的世界理念在逻辑结构上应该与天下理念是同构的。根据这一结构性标准就很容易判断一个世界体系是否表现了一种世界理念，例如很容易看出帝国主义不是一种世界理念而是国家理念，因为帝国主义仅仅考虑国家自身的利益，它把自己国家利益当成了世界利益以及判断世界所有事情的价值标准，甚至以自己国家的利益作为判断其它国家合法性的标准[14]。于是有理由认为，如果一个全球体系具有世界理念，那么就是一个"天下体系"，否则就只是一个世界体系。

由于思考的基本单位和解释标准的不同，在严格意义上说，西方思想传统里只有国家理论而几乎没有世界理论（马克思主义是例外）。这当然不是说，西方没有关于世界的思考，而是说，由于立足点不同，尺度不同，对世界的思考方式就不同——按照希腊人的说法就是"logos"不同，而按照胡塞尔的说法则是不同的生活世界给定了不同的"视界"。如果说西方对世界的思考是"以国家衡

---

[14] 最典型的例子是美国帝国主义，它现在宣称它拥有"先发制人"的权利，假如任何其他国家构成对美国安全的潜在威胁的话。而且它还按照自己的国家利益，把阿富汗的塔利班政权、伊拉克的萨达姆政权等定义为非法的，并以武力摧毁之。

That means that to love that whch is is the same as ourselves is not a problem at all, and thus it proves nothing of the essence of humanity. And our brilliant virtue of humanity could show its excellence only in respecting the dissimilar forms of life. And to respect others in their otherness is at least to respect his voluntariness or rights in developing his culture.

It is proper to learn values from others whereas unjust to impose one's values onto the others. Or to say, the values are to be learnt by rather than to be taught to the others.[15]

Accordingly, an empire of All-under-Heaven could only be an exemplar passively in situ, rather than positively become missionary. Here we see the difference between the western and Chinese ethics: western philosophy sees humanity through the eyes of subjectivity, while the Chinese sees it through the eyes of other-ness. This is a clue in distinguishing cultural empire from cultural imperialism.

2. The Relevance to Contemporary Problems

The All-under-Heaven pattern of all-states-in-a-family reminds us of the similarities with the United Nations pattern, one of which is that they are both world organizations dedicated to solve international problems and to ensure peace and order in the world. But their differences might be more important, taking into account the successes of the All-under-Heaven pattern in Chinese history to have brought long periods of peace and stable

[15] Interpretations of rites (c. 500BC), chapter on *Qu-li*.

量世界", 那么, 中国的天下理论则是"以世界衡量世界"——这是老子"以天下观天下"这一原理的现代版[15]。西方关于世界统一性的想象基于国际主义原则, 基于"之间关系 (inter-ness)"观念而发展出来的世界性方案无非是联合国或其他类似的各种"国际组织", 都没有也不可能超越民族/国家框架, 因此就很难通过联合国等方案来真正达到世界的完整性。民族/国家的视界注定了在思考世界问题时总是以国家利益为准而无视世界性利益——世界性利益并不是指其他国家利益 (如果要求首先考虑其他国家的利益, 未免要求太高, 也不合理, 但互相尊重各方利益是必须的), 尽管世界性利益的具体内容还需要讨论和分析, 但至少可以抽象地说, 它是指与各国都有关的人类公共利益, 既包括物质方面也包括精神方面, 它是保证人类总体生活质量的必要条件。尽管人类公共利益的最大化在某个时段里未必与某个国家的利益最大化能够达到一致 (更可能的情况是不一致), 但从"长时段" (布罗代尔) 的尺度去看, 或者从几乎永恒的时间性去看, 那么, 人类公共利益的最大化必定与每个国家或地方利益的最大化是一致的。

在这里可以发现, 天下理念不仅是空间性的而且是时间性的, 当它要求一个世界性尺度时, 就

[15] 《道德经·五十四章》。

to society over many dynasties, in contrast with the inability of the United Nations pattern to deal with international conflicts. Furthermore, we might be encouraged to find in the All-under-Heaven pattern the theoretical potential to resolve international and inter-cultural problems.

The comparison of the All-under-Heaven pattern with the United Nations might still sound a little far fetched for the United Nations is not an empire system, but it would also be a mistake to neglect the flexibility and inclusiveness of the concept of All-under-Heaven. One factor that could reduce the unreasonableness of this comparison is that the utopia of All-under-Heaven is not a narrowly defined empire but an extendedly-defined world society with harmony, communication and cooperation of all nations, guaranteed by a commonly-agreed institution.

In spite of history's uncontrollable causes and conditions, the successes and failures of these two patterns, All-under-Heaven and the United Nations, are due to the different philosophical presuppositions upon which their world system concepts are built. All-under-Heaven presupposes the Oneness of the world, and the oneness shows itself in all its diversities.[16] Oneness of the world is also reflected in the political principle of 'inclusion of all' in All-under-Heaven in terms of family-ship. Oneness means the denial of the existence of any pagan, so that nothing in the world can be defined unacceptable, no matter how strange it

_____

[16] *Laozi* said: 'the Way of the world produces the Oneness of its own. And the Oneness has its two-ness. Then the two-ness self-develops into the three-ness. And the three-ness is the minimal base for the diversities in the world.' See *Laozi* (c. 500BC) *Tao Te Ching*.

逻辑必然地进一步要求一个永恒性尺度，因为世界性利益需要通过永恒性的时间概念来彻底表达。只有当"世界"被看作是个先验的 (apriori) 政治单位，才能够考虑到属于世界而不仅仅属于国家的利益和价值。"以天下观天下"的眼界显然比"以国观天下"的眼界更加广阔和悠远。天下理念可以说是一个考虑到最大尺度空间和最大时间尺度利益的概念。只有把"世界"理解为一个不可分的先验单位，才有可能看到并定义属于世界的长久利益、价值和责任。而对于民族/国家的眼睛，所看到的是"属于国家利益的世界"而没有看到"属于世界的利益"。

为什么在中国哲学中有着"天下"这个高于国家的利益、价值和责任单位，而在西方哲学中却没有？这很可能与基督教改造了西方思想有关。希腊哲学虽然没有等价于"天下"的概念，希腊的世界概念虽然是单薄的而非全方位意义的世界，但它考虑到了chaos必须成为kosmos才能成为世界这样的普遍形而上学问题，因此它有可能在逻辑的路上进一步发现意义饱满的世界概念。但是基督教的胜利把分裂的世界概念带进西方思想，它剥夺了关于人间世界的完美的和永恒理想的想象权利，并且都归给了天堂世界，于是，世界就仅仅是个科学问题，而生活变成信仰问题，所谓世界观就停留在自然的世界观上而不再发展为人文的世界观。宗教的真正危害并不在于无神论所批判的虚妄性上 (幻想是无所谓的)，而在于它理解世界的分裂性方式，它把世界划分为神圣的和异端的，而

might seem. But, slightly differently, the pattern of the United Nations relies on two divergent presuppositions: pluralism and universalism. Pluralism is of reluctant 'political correctness' to please the developing countries, and the universalism to satisfy the developed, especially the major western powers. In order to reconcile this divergence, the United Nations has made great efforts to validate rational dialogue to replace conflicts. There is no doubt that rational dialogue has had an impact in reducing wars and fighting, but not in conflict reduction, and instead has encouraged the strategic game of non-cooperation, thus universally enhancing the personality of the selfish maximizer. And, worse, the United Nations has no power to stop a superpower from universalizing itself alone in name of globalisation. The UN is more of a political market for nations and less of an institution for the world itself.

The consequential difference between these two patterns is rooted in their different understandings of the Oneness of the world. The concept of All-under-Heaven commits us to the Oneness of the world as the intact wholeness that implies the acceptance of the diversities as they are and are meant to be in the world. The concept of the United Nations has taken Oneness as a mission of western modernity to be accomplished. It is apparent and not surprising that Oneness as a mission has been developed from universalism. Unfortunately, universalism is a type of fundamentalism. The reason is quite simple: universalism means to universalize something rather than everything and to universalize the self instead of others, thus a sort of fundamentalism that insists on the ideology of making others the pagan. Political modernity has inherited from and never gone beyond the format of Christian ideology that had invented, among others, unacceptable others, cultural clashes and wars,

这种分裂性的理解是几乎所有无法调和或解决的冲突和战争、迫害和征服的思想根源。

3. "无外"原则

要进一步理解天下/帝国就还需要讨论"天子"。"天子"大概相当于西方的"皇帝"（emperor）概念（在中国，秦始皇以后才有"皇帝"之名[16]），但就像"天下"不完全等于"empire"，"天子"也不完全等于"emperor"。"天子"是"天下"的配套概念，天下和天子共同构成了天下/帝国的理论基础，"天下"主要是个世界制度概念，而"天子"则主要是世界政府概念。应该说，天下比天子在理论意义上要重要得多，而且更为基本，因为制度是政府合法性的保证，而反过来政府并不能保证制度的合法性。显然政府本身有可能是坏的。事实上中国历史上的皇帝好的不多——如果不说是根本没有的话[17]。好皇帝所以少见，就是因为制度理念没有得到很好的实现和贯彻。在中国历史上，"天下/天

---

[16] 在中国古代早期，天子、皇、帝、王等称号的所指大致相同，但各自所强调的含义略有不同。商周时代，天子为王，诸侯国君称公、侯、伯等，春秋时南方的楚、吴、越诸国不合礼仪地称王，战国时各国纷纷称王。秦始皇并六国而自觉功盖三皇五帝，遂自创"皇帝"号，后世沿用，而"王"自汉以来成为最高爵位。

[17] 甚至如明末清初唐甄所说："自秦以来，凡为帝王者皆贼也。"（《潜书·屋语》）

ideological dogmas and propaganda. The worst is the universalism that tries to universalize the others in a way they do not want.

The theoretical problems of understanding Oneness as a mission to be accomplished has already been shown. The United Nations is an international organization mapping onto an individualist society. It inherits and enlarges the problems of an individualist society, for instance, international conflicts copy social conflicts. Worse, it does not enhance international democracy over social democracy. As has been observed, a superpower has every opportunity to invalidate an international organization such as the United Nations. Furthermore, it would be the All-under-Heaven system, instead of an international organization, that would be a more effective channel to the ideal of the world-as-one, because of the logical impossibility of an always-justified international choice through democracy, according to Arrow's theorem. I am not criticizing the United Nations; it has tried its best. What I am discussing is the given limitations in the potentiality of the United Nations pattern. The United Nations is supposed to be an international organization, conditioned by the interests of every nation/state, dealing with international problems in an age of nation/state rather than in an age of globality. And it seems to enhance rather than weaken, as Giddens pointed out, the system of nations/states as the modern political form (see Giddens, 1985). To be fair to the United Nations, it is not designed to take care of the world but of nations, it is of, not beyond, modernity. In short, internationality is not and cannot be world-ness. The question of world institution has now become more urgent since the world plunged into globalisation.

It is interesting to consider the pattern of the European Union, maybe the European

子"理论在实践中被贯彻的更多的是天子观念。这一片面的或残缺的实践损害了天下理论的形象，也引来许多深刻的反思，如黄宗羲曰："三代之法，藏天下于天下者也；后世之法，藏天下于筐箧者也。"[18]显然，如果天下社会制度没有被实践，而仅仅单方面地实行天子政府，则天子徒有其名而无实。孔子对春秋礼崩乐坏的痛心疾首现在看来是非常深刻的，因为那不仅是个乱世，而且是天下制度的破坏，事实上从春秋以后就不再有比较接近天下制度的努力了。

在天下/帝国的纯粹理论上，天子享有天下，所谓"君天下"或天下"莫非王土"[19]，尽管实际上从来没有一个帝国拥有过整个世界，但"天下/帝国"是个理论，在理论上则完全可以设想天下一家的帝国。天子以天下为家，因此产生"无外"原则[20]。天下为家而无外，这是个意味深长的观念，它非常可能是使得中国思想里不会产生类似西方的"异端"观念的原因，同样，它也不会产生西方那样界限清晰、斩钉截铁的民族主义。既然世界无外，它就只有内部而没有不可兼容的外部，也就只有内在结

---

[18]　《明夷待访录·原法》。

[19]　《礼记·曲礼下》曰："君天下曰天子。"《诗经·小雅·北山》曰："溥天之下，莫非王土，率土之滨，莫非王臣。"

[20]　蔡邕《独断·卷上》曰："天子无外，以天下为家"；司马迁《史记·高祖本纪》亦曰："天子以四海为家。"

United States in the future. The EU is an excellent invention of a real and institutionally organized region. But it is still not a system that could be extended to the world, for it is just a company of nations/states, and it is difficult to form and give priority to a European common interest over the interests of each of its member nations/states, let alone a world interest. Theoretically speaking, the EU has gone not as far as Kant's idea. A well-organized region such as the EU is essentially an enlarged nation/state meant to compete with other world regions or powers, rather than an ideal for the world in its lack of its world-view of world-ness. The EU pattern enhances the integration of a region but also deepens separation from the world.

Globalisation is breaking the world system of nations/states. It is not new. It is a composition of universalism and fundamentalism, in which fundamentalism, whether though capitalism, modern industry, post-modern technologies, self-claimed world religion or ideology, tries to universalize itself. And within the process of globalisation itself,[17] it is likely for one or more nations/states to transform themselves into new empires, different from the imperialism of nations/states. Is there an age of new empires to come? Will there be a new form of empire, or just a post-modern return to the old way? We should consider

---

[17] The Manifesto of the Communist Party was one of the earliest texts discussing something of globalization. It said: 'The bourgeoisie has, through its exploitation of the world market, given a cosmopolitan character to production and consumption in every country.' And 'as in material, so also in intellectual production, the intellectual creations of individual nations become common property. National one-sidedness and narrow-mindedness become more and more impossible, and from the numerous national and local literatures, there arises a world literature.'

构上的远近亲疏关系。尽管和所有地域一样，中国也自然而然地会有以自己为中心的"地方主义"，但仅仅是地方主义，却缺乏清楚界定的和划一不二的"他者"（the others）以及不共戴天的异端意识和与他者划清界线的民族主义（中国的民族主义是引进西方观念的现代产物，是建立了现代民族/国家以来形成的"新传统"）。于是，与本土不同的他乡只是陌生的、遥远的或疏远的，但并非对立的、不可容忍的和需要征服的。对于天下，所有地方都是内部，所有地方之间的关系都以远近亲疏来界定，这样一种关系界定模式保证了世界的先验完整性，同时又保证了历史性的多样性，这可能是唯一能够满足世界文化生态标准的世界制度。假如把世界看作是给定的分裂模式，那么世界的完整性就只能通过征服他者或者"普遍化"自己来获得，而这样做的代价是取消了作为生态活力必要条件的多样性。

无论如何，至少在理论上，"无外"的原则已经排除了把世界作分裂性理解的异端模式和民族主义模式。至于在实践上，"无外"原则虽然不能完全克服作为人之常情的地方主义，但也很大程度上减弱了天下/帝国与其他地方的矛盾。清朝许多学者都自觉地利用"无外"原则来解释规模空前的帝国内部的复杂民族关系，可以看作是这个原则的一个典型应用[21]。也许会有疑问说，清朝以少数民族入主中原，所以对"无外"这一原则特别感兴趣。这可能的确是个原因，但更值得思考的是，"

whether there a more reasonable and commendable concept of empire. Comparative study would help to clarify the concept of empire, though this is beyond the scope of this paper. The differences among the ideas of empires can be detailed as follows:

1. The pattern of the Roman Empire. This is the typical ancient empire, not referring only to the Roman Empire but also to others. It is considered a military superpower with territorial expansion. It would encompass the whole world if it were possible in its claimed or hidden ideal. Consequently it always has temporary frontiers instead of clearly-settled boundaries. We know this pattern has not worked since the age of nations/states.

2. The pattern of the British Empire. This is the typical modern empire based on a nation/state under the mixed ideals of nationalism, imperialism and colonialism. It has definitely divided boundaries except in disputed areas. The definite boundaries do not indicate the self-restraint of imperialism, but the safeguard of their national interests against the free entry of others. Instead of territorial expansion, imperialism has created colonies to develop and maintain its control of the world and the division of the world into the developed and the undeveloped. This pattern has become impossible since the Second World War because of the universalizing of the system of nations/states, together with nationalism and the consciousness of independence.

3. The new pattern is of the American 'empire'.[18] It is a new imperialism, inheriting many characteristics of modern imperialism, but transforming direct control into the hidden, yet totally dominating world control by means of hegemony or the 'American leadership' as Americans prefer to call it. This hegemonic imperialism is occurring not only in political

无外"原则确实有着良好的实践效果。而且，中原主体民族对清朝的效忠更加能够证明"无外"原则所蕴涵的宏大意识。清朝学者龚自珍甚至为"无外"原则给出了形而上学的论证："圣无外，天亦无外者也"[22]。就是说，既然"天无外"是个毋庸疑的、被给予的存在论事实，那么，天下当然也应该"无外"才能够与无外的天相配。而假如天与天下在形而上学原理上是分裂的，没有共通之"道"，那么就意味着"存在"是分裂的、不和谐的，各种危险的冲突就会产生。显然，如果不在哲学上先验地承诺和谐完整的存在和世界，那么就不会有和谐的思想，就更加不会有和谐的行动。只有以"同一片天"为准，才不会产生不共戴天的分裂世界意识。

在这里，关于"内外"的问题还需要略加分析：中国自古也有内外意识，可以说"无外"意识和"内外"意识并存，但特别需要注意的是，在"无外"原则和"内外"原则中关于"外"的概念并不在同一个问题层次上，所以并没有构成矛盾。"无外"原则是世界制度原则，所说明的是"没有任何他者作为异端"的四海一家观念，而"内外"原则是国际关系原则，说明的是亲疏有别的远近关系。自商朝开

---

[21] 汪晖在其新著《现代中国思想的兴起》中，详细地讨论了清朝学者在这方面的作为。

[22] 龚自珍：《龚定庵全集类编·五经大义终始答问七》。

and economical spheres but also in knowledge, especially through globalisation, in which it has the greatest power to universalize its own.[19] This new imperialism differs from the traditional empire in that it is much more than a game winner as it also defines the rules. The world would become disordered if a player in the game also became the rule-maker.

4. The pattern of All-under-Heaven. All-under-Heaven appears much like globalisation, but is essentially different as it contains no such sense of the '-isation'. All-under-Heaven indicates globalism instead. It means an institutionally ordered world or a world institution responsible to confirm the political legitimacy of world governance as well as local governance, and to allow the justification of systems. Its political goal is to create 'All-under-Heaven', the trinity of the geographical world (the earth), the psychological world (the hearts of all people) and the political world (the world institution). It is a grand narrative, maybe the grandest narrative in political philosophies. The very virtue of the All-under-Heaven pattern is its world view of world-ness, which could let us understand correctly and discover solutions to world problems. World-ness is a principle higher than internationality.

My conclusion is that the most important political problem today is not the socalled 'failed states' but the failed world, a disordered world of chaos. This is why I maintain that

[18] Hardt and Negri (2001) had argued in their Empire that the new empire of today is different from the European imperialism and mainly produced in American constitutionalism that is more akin to Roman empire than to European imperialism.

[19] But the American empire seems still not satisfied with its 'leadership'. Nye calls upon the USA to enhance its 'soft power' as complement to its 'hard power', for the USA is still not powerful enough to 'go it alone' even though it is the strongest power since Rome. See Nye, 2002.

创"王畿"制度，至周朝而完善，就规定了"外服"和"内服"的亲疏关系，内服即王畿，乃天子所直辖的"千里之地"，外服即诸侯领地，围绕着王畿按五百里一圈的比例向外排开（这是理想化的规划，事实上并非如此整齐。）内外服共"五服"之多（又有时认为有"九服"）[23]。这种内外意识可能在后来发展成为所谓"华夷之辨"的意识，但由于毕竟有无外原则的制约（蛮夷戎狄仍然在五服之中），它表达的是文化差异而不是设立作为不可共存的对立面或者异端的他者，这一点不可不察。在中国意识里，蛮地番邦或许会成为利益竞争者，但并没有被定义为意识形态和种族上受歧视者，甚至不同文化的长短得失是可以客观讨论的（"由余使秦"关于文化政治的讨论则是实例[24]）。这说明天下

[23] 《国语·周语上》曰："夫先王之制，邦内甸服，邦外侯服，侯卫宾服，夷蛮要服，戎狄荒服。"《周礼·夏官·大司马》曰："方千里曰国畿，其外方五百里曰侯畿，又其外方五百里曰甸畿，又其外方五百里曰男畿，又其外方五百里曰采畿，又其外方五百里曰卫畿，又其外方五百里曰蛮畿，又其外方五百里曰夷畿，又其外方五百里曰镇畿，又其外方五百里曰番畿。"又可参见《尚书·禹贡》及《尚书·酒诰》。

[24] 《史记·秦本纪》记载：戎王使由余于秦，秦缪公问曰："中国以诗书礼乐法度为政，然尚时乱，今戎夷无此，何以为治，不亦难乎？"由余对曰："此乃中国所以乱也。夫自上圣黄帝作为礼乐法度，身以先之，仅以小治。及其后世，日以骄淫……夫戎夷不然。上含淳德以遇其下，下怀忠信以事其上，一国之政犹一身之治，不知所以治，此真圣人之治也。"于是缪公退而问内史廖曰："孤闻邻国有圣人……"

our world is not yet a world, but still a non-world. And there are so many world problems too major to be resolved by a nation, a region or by any international contract. International theory in the framework of internationality finds its limitation in dealing with world problems, the common or shared problems of the world. World-ness cannot be reduced to internationality, for it is of the wholeness or totality rather than the between-ness. Our globe needs a world theory, rather than an international theory, to speak for the world. And the theory of All-under-Heaven as a world theory could provide a better view for political philosophy and political science.

References

Burnet, J. (1930). *Early Greek philosophy*. 4th ed. London: Adam & Charles Black.

Confucius (c. 500BC). *The Analects*.

Folsom, K. (1968). *Friends, guests and colleagues*. University of California Press.

Giddens, A. (1985). *The nation-state and violence*. Cambridge: Polity Press.

Hardt M. & Negri, A. (2001). *Empire*. Harvard: Harvard University Press.

Interpretation of rites (c.500BC).

Kung, H. & Kuschel, K.-J. (Eds.). (1993) *A global ethic: The declaration of the parliament of the world's religions*. New York: The Continuum Pub. Co.

Laozi (c. 500BC) *Tao Te Ching*.

Mencius (c. 220BC). *The Book of Mencius*.

Nye, J. (2002). *The paradox of American power: Why the world's only superpower can't go it

理念能够克服文化原教旨主义。

根据天下理论的"无外"原则，"天子"也相应地具有非专属性。中国关于身份（identity）的观念归根到底是一种责任制观念，可以看作是"名实论"的一个重要组成部分。先秦的名实论包含许多复杂论点，在此不能详细讨论，但其中特别重要的一个原则是"名有待于实"或者通常所谓的"名副其实"原则，其中"名"远远不仅是名称，而是一个关于事物或人的伦理意义结构，至少包括两个原理：

1）任何事物都必须理解并定义为"在生活中的某物"而不仅是"在自然中的某物"，任何事物都按照它的社会位置以及该位置的社会关系来定义，于是，"名"定义的是某个社会位置的价值以及它在关系网络中的意义，而不是知识论上的一组摹状词（descriptions）；

2）"名"所定义的那个社会位置意味着一组责任/诺言，承担这些责任和诺言是占有这个社会位置的充分必要条件，于是有：p是p，当且仅当，p做了p规定要做的事情。可以看出其中暗含着这样一个思想结构："做"优先于"是"。这个思想结构虽然没有在古典文献中被表达，但我曾经论证它是中国哲学语法的必然理论要求，并且表述为"存在即做事"（to be is to do）[25]或者"做什么因而

[25] 参见赵汀阳《一个或所有问题》，南昌：江西教育出版社，1997。

alone. Oxford: Oxford University Press.

Pang, Sun, & Li (Eds.) (1984). *The early history of Qian Dynasty.* Beijing: Press of the People's University of China.

Poems (c. 1000BC).

Shang-yang (c. 300BC). *The Book of Shang-yang.*

Shima Qian (91BC). *The history.* 74: 2344.

Shuming, L. (1992). *The collections of Shuming Liang.* Beijing: Beijing Normal University Press.

Smith, A. D. (1996). *Nations and nationalism in a global era.* Cambridge: Polity Press.

Song, L. (c. 1370). *The history of Yuan Dynasty.* Section 4 of *Yuan-shi-zu,* Vol. 7.

Xun-zi (c. 200BC). On kingship and supremacy. In *The book of Xun-zi.*

是什么" (to do thus to be)。

　　一个人 (包括天子在内) 到底有什么资格当什么人, 并不取决于他的出身, 最终要取决于他的德行和作为, 所谓"君君, 臣臣"之类[26]。于是, 即使对于帝王, 也有渎职的问题。而如果渎职, 那么就失去任职的资格。因此, 天子可以宣称他受天命而为天子, 但天命并非无条件的, 还需要得到经验上的重新确认, 即必需有无可怀疑的称职证据 (evidence) 来完成其资格论证。这种称职证据, 按照儒家理论尤其是孟子的理解, 就是获得民心[27]。这个论证似乎可以大概解释为: 天子虽然是天命的而不是民选的, 但这只意味着天子的位置是先验的, 却并不意味着具体某个天子是天定的。而先验的天子位置规定了天子以民为贵的先验义务, 假如没有尽到这个义务, 那么, 即使他暂时利用权力窃据天子的位置, 他也已经在理论上失去了这个位置, 即失去了合法性——而这正是中国革命理论的基础。革命的合法性是以获得天意民心为根据的 (以汤武革命为经典模式), 中国

---

[26]　《论语·颜渊》曰："君君, 臣臣, 父父, 子子。"

[27]　《孟子·尽心下》："民为贵, 社稷次之, 君为轻。是故得乎丘民而为天子";《孟子·离娄上》："桀纣之失天下也, 失其民也；失其民者, 失其心也";《礼记·大学》："得众则得国, 失众则失国。"

历史上针对暴君、昏君的革命总是很成功，而没有明显合法性的夺权即使获得成功也被认为是篡位，即不算"正统"。当一个朝代之立国能够顺天命得民心从而得天下，就算正统。成功夺取政权和土地并不等于得天下，因为"天下"远远不仅是个地理事实，而更是个社会事实（按照这个标准，传统欧洲帝国以及现在的美国新帝国主义所推崇的征服和统治就只不过是夺取"世界"而不是获得"天下"）。得天下意味着拥有社会承认，意味着代表了社会公共选择，所以得天下和得民心是一致的。老子早就意识到统治世界和得天下的根本区别，老子曰："以正治国，以奇用兵，以无事取天下"[28]。

按照中国民本主义的信念，民众的选择总与天意吻合，所谓"民之所欲，天必从之"。又曰："汤武革命，顺乎天而应乎人"[29]。这其中并非巧合，而是被认为存在着必然的吻合。这种必然的吻合需要论证。根据天人合一假设，似乎可以这样分析：存在必定是整体和谐和自身一致的，否则，被破坏的存在就变成不存在；既然存在是整体和谐的，那么天、地、人就必定是和谐呼应的；而天命不可见，它是隐藏着的，但是天命这种隐性的事实必定有其显性的表现途径，否则我们就会根本不知道存在着天命（希腊人也论证说我们不可能知道本来不知道的东西）。天道虽然遥远而不显[30]，但是与之呼应的人道却近在眼前，人道的表现是民心，因为天是所有人的天，所以天先验地代表所有人的选择，于是，民心就是天命的显形。以天意和民心的一致性来证明统治的合法性的理论优势在于取证的方便。天意本身虽然并非直接可见，但民心却是明摆着的确证（evidence），因此，即使声称知道了天命，也必须通过民心这一确证而得到验证，否则就是没有得到证明。所谓"天畏棐忱，民情大可见"（疏谓：天威之明，惟诚是辅，验之民情，大可见矣）[31]，又有"天亦哀于四方民，其眷命用懋，王其疾敬德"[32]。

至于"验之民情"，古代中国显然没有数字化的验证方式，比如现代的民主选举方式[33]。但实际上知道民情并不需要数字化的"准确"统计，因为民情总是表现为能够直观的或者直接感受到的社

---

[28] 《老子·五十七章》曰："以正治国，以奇用兵，以无事取天下。"

[29] 《尚书·泰誓》："民之所欲，天必从之。"《易传》："汤武革命，顺乎天而应乎人。"

[30] 这一原则自古有之，如《左传·昭公十七～十八年》子产曰："天道远，人道迩，非所及也，何以知之？"天人原则正是在天道和人道之间建立了呼应关系。

[31] 《尚书·康诰》；孙星衍：《尚书今古文注疏》。

[32] 《尚书·召诰》。

[33] 严格意义上的现代民主选举制度一直没有被中国采用，这是个非常复杂的问题，似乎西方民主制度一直没有能够获得中国人的充分支持。尽管从清朝末年就有人相信民主制度是表达民心的最好方式，尤其有趣的是有人相信以民为贵的原则本为中国之思想发明，但是实现这一原则的方式却是西方的发明，"其惟泰西之议院"（郑观应：《盛世危言·议院》，1990）。

会气氛，而且，人们关于民情的直观、对社会气氛的感受似乎从来不会出错。原因可能是，民情的表现或流露是自然真诚的反应，直接表达了真实的社会选择。而现代的民主投票反而往往是民情的错误反映，数字虽然显得精确，但产生如此这般的数字的程序却往往导致失真，因为人们被告知进入了投票选举这个博弈，于是就有了斤斤计较的理性选择，就会出现所谓策略选举或不真诚选举和违心选举等情况（可以参考阿罗的"不可能性定理"所证明的完全公正选举的不可能性），而且还会受到偏心的不真诚的宣传误导。既然天命的最后证明只能落实在民心这一直观的确证上，天子保有天命唯一方法就是"敬德"，即以民为重，体察民情。总之，天命落实在天子的位置上，而不是具体人上。可以看出，在中国的帝国理论中，"天下"是个具有先验合法性的政治/文化单位，是关于世界社会的绝对必然的思想范畴，但是任何具体的政权或宗教统治却不具有先验合法性；"天子"这一位置也具有先验合法性，但是任何具体的皇帝却不具有先验合法性。因此，"天下/天子"意味着一种先验的世界社会和世界制度，是一种世界理论或世界理念。

既然天下/帝国的"无外"原则是个世界尺度的原则，"天下/帝国"的理念，就其理论本身而言，就意味着在整个世界范围内都不包含任何歧视性或拒绝性原则来否定某些人参与天下公共事务的权利，就是说，天下的执政权利是对世界上任何民族开放着的。天下作为一个先验概念，它在关于世界和人民的经验事实之前就已经在概念上包括了地理上的整个世界又包括了世界的所有人民。把经验事实当成先验概念来肯定，这在哲学上并不多见。在古代中国，人们所感觉到的或实际上知道的"世界"非常有限，但天下概念本身却事先就意味着至大无边的世界，并不依赖着关于实际世界的经验知识。这一对世界的普遍认同在结构上有些类似罗尔斯的"无知之幕"。不同的是，罗尔斯以无知之幕为条件所导出的是人人确保自己不吃亏的自私自利原则，而中国以类似无知之幕的条件导出的却是天下为公的原则。这表明了自由主义对生活的理解是不全面的，非常可能忽视了在个人利益和权利之外还存在着公共利益，尤其是那些与个人利益并非总是吻合的公共利益[34]。

天下概念这个世界观的基本性质是兼容万事，其"无外"原则是先验的，所以在中国的理解中没有异教徒[35]。这样就不难理解为什么中国帝国不仅像其他帝国一样没有明确的地理边界，而且没

---

[34] 比如说，交通规则属于与个人利益非常吻合的公共利益，没有人愿意取消交通规则。但是，自然资源（能源、水和矿物等）以及世界和平、世界公正和社会正义等公共利益就不一定与个人或个别国家的私利总能吻合，因此就往往被破坏。美国是典型，它过度地消费了世界的25%的资源而不愿意节制，还经常为自己的利益而发动战争，破坏世界公正。

[35] 盛洪曾经论证说中国文明在文化上是最宽容的，而基督教是最不宽容的，尽管基督教有"爱你的敌人"这样的伦理原则，但又绝不容忍别的宗教和意识形态，这是自相矛盾的。他论证说，宽容异教徒是证明宽容的必要条件。参见《为万世开太平》，第113~122页，北京大学出版社，1999。

有文化边界。"天下"概念所具有的兼容并蓄的灵活性和解释力在历史实践中明显地表现出来，例如，历史上大元帝国和大清帝国统治中原数百年而它们的统治在后世（甚至在当时）能够被承认并解释为合法的天下王朝；另一方面，蒙古和清朝统治者也都采用了天下理论来建立和解释其统治的合法性，都自认所建立的帝国属于天下/帝国这一模式和传统，如蒙古帝国的国号更改为"大元"所显示的天下意识[36]，而大清帝国则甚至对作为天下/帝国的正统传承有着更加明确和提前的意识和理论论证[37]。历史上还有其它许多民族曾经不同程度地入主中原，如北朝五胡以及辽、金、西、夏，虽然只是割据一方，但大多都接受天下/帝国的想象[38]。在宋、辽、金时代，由于各国实力大致相当，因此只是逐鹿天下的竞争者，而在媾和时则成为暂时分有天下的"兄弟之邦"，甚至更为"正统"的宋往往还要向辽金进贡。无论中原对外族的承认还是外族对中原思想的接受，都显示了天下/帝国概念的开放性。现代中国在西化的运动中更显示出极端的开放性，百年来世界的现代化运动与西化运动是基本同一的，东方国家以及几乎所有第三世界国家基本上都接受了西方的现代社会/政治制度、经济制度和物质文明，但只有中国进一步发生了文化最深层的、釜底抽薪式的文化革命（这里远不是指毛泽东那种特定的"文化大革命"，而是广义的文化革命。毛泽东的"文化大革命"其实只是广义的文化革命中的一次并不具有历史决定性的革命）。中国现代文化革命表现为在整个文化理念、基本价值观和语言的革命——这里"革命"主要是在中国传统概念上使用，即不仅指社会制度和社会结构的根本改变，而且指这些改变合乎新的天命。既然西方文化被认定代表着新的天命，所以在中国可以顺理成章地获得权威地位。可能没有别的国家像中国这样推翻了自己传统的意识

---

[36] 1271年，忽必烈把蒙古帝国改名为"大元"，"盖取《易经》乾元之义"（《元史·世祖纪四·建国号诏》），"元者也，大也，大不足以尽之，而谓之元者，大之至也"（《国朝文类·经世大典序录·帝号》）。忽必烈认为蒙古概念显得是地方性的，而不足以表达他那个"大之至"的天下帝国。

[37] 甚至远在清兵入关之前，满族统治者就对未来的天下帝国有了意识准备。在努尔哈赤给明万历帝的一封信中，他说："天地之间，上自人类下至昆虫，天生天养之也，是你南朝之养之乎？……普养万物之天至公无私，不以南朝为大国容情……自古以来，岂有一姓之中尝为帝王，一君之身寿延千万……天命归之，遂有天下……或天命有归，即国之寡小勿论，天自扶而成之也"。《清入关前史料选辑1》，第289~296页，北京：中国人民大学出版社，1984。

[38] 后晋皇帝石敬瑭称臣于辽太宗或许是中原皇帝由外族皇帝册封的最早事例。而辽太宗进一步决定成为中原模式的皇帝，公元947年采用中原礼仪宣告成为中国式皇帝，并改国号为"大辽"，改元为"大同"，其含义与"大元"相似，都源于"天下/帝国"理论。金太祖采纳杨朴建议："大王创兴师旅，当变家为国，图霸天下……愿大王册帝号，封诸番，传檄响应，千里而定"（《三朝北盟会编·政宣上帙三》），金太祖听到天下概念大感兴趣。而金海陵帝试图迁都至开封，也基于天下帝国的理由，他自认已经"君临万国"，而都城仍然偏居一隅，不能"光宅于中土"，实在不合道理（《大金国志·海陵炀王》）。

形态和价值观, 而代之以"他者"的意识形态和价值观[39]。接受一种新的物质文明并不会也并不必然要求根本改变一种传统文化, 中国现代文化革命如此剧烈, 其背后必有宏大思想根据。正是天下概念决定了中国没有文化边界。

4. 分析的单位及其后果

正是天下/帝国的这种开放性使得它具有完全不同于民族/国家的价值标准。天下作为最高的政治/文化单位意味着存在着比"国"更大的事情和相应更大的价值标准, 因此, 并非所有事情和所有价值都可以在"国"这个政治单位中得到绝对辩护, 就是说, 有些事情是属于天下的, 有些事情是属于国的, 有些则属于家, 如此等等, 各种层次的事情必须不同地理解。如老子所说: "以身观身, 以家观家, 以乡观乡, 以邦观邦, 以天下观天下。"[40]老子这一原则可能是"天下体系"的最好的知识论和政治哲学, 它意味着每个存在单位或政治单位都有着属于自己的、不可还原的利益和主权, 于是就意味着: 既不能随便以一个层次单位的要求来牺牲另一个层次单位的利益, 同时又意味着一个规模更大的层次单位必定存在着比小规模层次单位多出来的公共利益。按照老子原则, 既然世界存在, 那么就存在着属于世界的而不是属于国家的世界利益, 只有承认和尊重世界利益才能够形成对世界中任何一种存在都有利的天下体系。天下体系与"世界体系"(world-system)有所不同, 尽管天下体系也可以看作是世界体系的一个最佳模式或乌托邦, 但它至少与历史上存在过的世界体系有本质不同。按照沃勒斯坦的概念, 世界体系是"一个社会体系, 它具有范围、结构、成员集团、合理规则和凝聚力。世界体系的生命力由冲突的各种力量构成, 这些冲突的力量由于压力的作用把世界体系结合在一起, 而当每个集团不断地试图把它改造得有利于自己时, 又使这个世界体系分裂了"[41]。显然, 世界体系是由国家之间的冲突和互相合作形成的, 其中起决定性作用的是国家利益。而天下体系强调的是, 存在着某些世界公共利益, 这些公共利益的力量达到"一荣俱荣, 一损俱损"的程度, 以至于没有一个国家愿意破坏这些利益。如果与纳什均衡比较的话, 似乎可以说天下体系

---

[39] "五四"运动打倒了孔家店之后, 经过选择, 中国接受了马克思主义作为基本意识形态和价值观, 现在个人主义和自由主义又作为相当一部分人的意识形态和价值观。当年陈独秀在《吾人最后之觉悟》文中论证说: "吾人果欲于政治上采用共和立宪制, 复欲于伦理上保守纲常阶级制……自家冲撞, 此绝对不可能之事……存其一必废其一——伦理的觉悟, 为吾人最后之最后觉悟"。这多少说明了文化革命的理由。

[40] 《道德经·五十四章》。

[41] 沃勒斯坦:《现代世界体系·卷1》, 第460页, 北京:高等教育出版社, 1998。

能够创造一种"天下均衡"，它是这样一种最佳均衡：不但满足帕累托最优，而且满足"一荣俱荣，一损俱损"的互蕴均衡 (p iff q)。

　　与老子所表达的思考单位系列略有不同，作为中国思想主流的儒家的思考单位系列通常表达得更为简练[42]，称作"家"、"国"、"天下"。一般而言，"家"和"天下"这两个概念在中国思维中最具支配性地位，并且以此形成基本的解释框架，就是说，"家"和"天下"这两个概念被赋予比其他所有可能设想的思考单位以更大的解释能力或解释权力（作为比较，西方思想则以"个人"和"国家"作为解释框架）。赋予某些概念或思考单位以更大的解释权力是思考社会/生活问题的一个必要的思维经济学策略：人没有无穷多的时间可以做所有的事情，所以必定需要选择，做事情需要选择，解释事情也同样需要选择，优先被选择或被考虑的东西就具有更大的支配性权力或话语权。不同的价值排序会产生不同的社会生活，于是，选择什么样的价值排序，又成为关于价值选择的元问题（这个问题非常复杂，在此不多讨论）。比较简单地说，现代西方的价值重心落在"个人"和"民族/国家"上，其中的极端重心是"个人"，当一个事情被追问到最后解释时，问题就还原到个人价值上；而传统中国的价值重心则落在"家"和"天下"上，其中极端重心是"家"，同样，当需要最后解释时，问题就还原到"家"。因此，对于中国思想来说，"国"就被解释为只不过是比较大的家，"天下"则是最大的家，所谓"四海一家"。在这个思维模式中，天下各国以及各民族之间的冲突实质上只是各个"地方"之间的矛盾，而不是现代理论所认为的国家和民族之间的矛盾。

　　"家、国、天下"这个政治/文化单位体系从整体上说是"家"的隐喻，所以，家庭性 (family-ship) 就成为大多数中国人理解和解释政治/文化制度的原则[43]。"家、国、天下"由于贯穿着家庭性原则而形成大概相当于三位一体的结构。按照家的隐喻，天子虽然有着父母般的管理权力，但对子民也必须有着父母般的关怀义务[44]。按照这种设想，除了远古的面目含糊的圣君尧舜禹汤之外，实际上的皇帝对义务的实践总是非常可疑的。天下/帝国始终是个乌托邦，是尚未实现的理想，但确实是作为理念和标准而存在。

[42] 道家比较关心个人生命，所以老子的分析单位中有"身"（个人），对于道家来说，个人不仅是个利益单位也是个道德单位。儒家并不否认个人利益，但似乎倾向于以家庭作为伦理基本单位。当然儒家并不忽视"身"，只不过儒家是在修养的意义上重视"身"。如孟子曰："天下之本在国，国之本在家，家之本在身"（《孟子·离娄上》）。
[43] 历史上只有很少的中国思想家相对轻视家庭以及以家庭关系为基础的伦理体系，例如商鞅认为儒家所鼓吹的家庭性伦理实际上鼓励了人们不关心社会公共利益，因此社会性的法律是更重要的。参见《商君书·开塞》。
[44] 《尚书·洪范》曰："天子作民父母以为天下王。"

　　在选择政治/经济理解的出发点上, 个人和家庭都是同样显眼的自然事实, 中国思想选择"家"作为制度的最后根据, 这一点往往归因于, 如果从人类学和社会学的角度看, 古代中国的农业社会 (或费孝通著名的说法"乡土社会") 的结构——据说由于农业社会的基本经济单位是家庭, 所以强化了家庭的重要性并且赋予了伦理意义。这是个重要原因, 但恐怕不充分。问题是, 不同的选择会导致不同的理念或哲学效果。在中国传统语境里, 家庭是一个具有自身绝对性的、不可还原的最小生活形式, 而且任一个体都必须通过他在家庭中的存在而获得作为这个特定个体的意义 (这一点和马克思主义所认为的人的本质是社会关系的总和的观点相当接近)。如果不在家庭中存在, 那么一个人就无法被定义为某人, 就是说, 当我们说到"存在着某个体a", 必定是在说"存在着某个体a, 当且仅当, (a∧b) ∧ (a∧c) ∧ (a∧d) ……", 个体a的意义必须表现在他与家庭的其他成员的关系中。这直接否定了个体具有自足的价值 (所以中国传统主流与个人主义格格不入)。也许可以说, 假定选择了"家庭"作为政治理解的出发点, 由于家庭的逻辑性是"并且" (∧), 那么要维护这一"并且性"就必然重视和追求"关系"、"和谐"、"责任"以及"和平"等系列概念; 而假定选择了"个人"为政治理解的出发点, 由于其逻辑性是"或者" (∨), 于是就必然更关心和追求"权利"、"主权"、"利益"和"征服"等系列概念。

　　传统中国意义上的家庭不能简单地理解为西方意义上的那种由个体组成的"共同体" (community), 共同体是两个以上的自足个体的协议组合, 而在中国理解里的家庭则是一种先在的人际制度和给定的生活场所, 它具有纯粹属于家庭概念的先验生活形式和道德意义, 简单地说, 家庭是个先验形式, 个体形成家庭只不过是"进入"了家庭这一先验形式而不是"组成"了家庭。个体自身不足以使他成为具有完整或成熟人性的人, 而家庭正是个体将其自然本性 (所谓"性") 实现为社会人性 (所谓"德"或"人道") 的必要条件或前提[45]。像"天下"概念一样, "家庭"也成为一个理想化的先验概念, 它的所指是理想化的家庭 (显然实际上大多数家庭并不能达到理想指标)。按照这个理想概念, 家庭应该是生活中利益计较趋于最小化的一种生态环境, 应该最有利于发展人之间无条件的互相关心、和谐和互相责任。于是, "人性"和"家庭性"便在理想条件下被认为是一致的。就儒家思想传统而言, 家庭性几乎构成了对人性的完全充分论证, 所谓"上治祖祢尊尊也, 下治子孙亲亲也, 旁治昆弟, 合族以食, 序以昭穆, 别之以礼义, 人道竭矣。"[46]

---

[45] 关于人的自然本性和社会人性, 中国哲学家有大量的讨论。简略地说, 自然本性是告子所最早定义的"生之谓性" (《孟子·告子上》) 或荀子定义的"性者天之就也……不可学不可事而在人者谓之性" (《荀子·性恶》); 社会人性则是孟子定义的"人之所以异于禽兽者" (《孟子·离娄下》) 或朱熹定义的"德性犹言义理之性" (《朱子语类·卷六十四》)。

[46] 《礼记·大传》。

如果还需要关于家庭性作为人性原则的直观确证（evidence），那么可以注意到中国哲学基本上都使用了"情感证明"。孔子所以把"亲亲"看作是万事之本，就是因为"亲亲"是无可置疑的直接事实和所有情感的开端。显然，亲情是无条件的感情，人类所有其它有条件的情感都基于与亲情的距离而确定。在儒家看来，感情亲疏的距离正是伦理规范的绝对基础，甚至所谓文化也无非是人类各种情感关系的恰如其分的制度表现[47]。"亲亲"的绝对性表现在它的直接性上。这一确证在结构上的完美性可以与笛卡儿"不能怀疑我在怀疑"的论证或者胡塞尔"我思其所思"（ego cogito cogitatum）命题相比。孔子关于"亲亲"的论证甚至有着更强大的力量感，因为它非常可能是我们在情感事实方面所能够想象的唯一绝对的论证。而这一情感证明的文化后果是巨大的：既然在实际生活中能够找到人类情感的绝对支持，那么就不需要超越人类情感的信仰（这或多或少能够解释为什么中国人不需要宗教）。情感证明是直证，是可以实现的普遍事实，而超越的宗教世界是不可证明的[48]，不可证明就等于人人都可以给出对自己有利的解释，而且没有理由接受任何别人的解释，所以宗教是形成所有不可调和的冲突的根源。

既然家庭性被假定能够充分表现人性，那么，家庭性原则就是处理一切社会问题、国家问题乃至天下问题的普遍原则。儒家声称只要人道/家庭性原则万世不移，那么在其他事情上都可以根据实际需要而进行移风易俗，于是"圣人南面而治天下必自人道始矣"。[49]如果理解了家庭性是处理天下万事的基础原则，就不难理解"天下"概念所蕴涵的世界先验完整性和先验和谐——天下和家庭性之间构成一种循环论证。一般来说，当试图论证任何一种基本观念时，几乎无法避免地会遇到"循环论证"或者"无穷倒退"这样的情况，我们很难想象还有第三条道路，因此很难完全消除怀疑论[50]。但是至少可以肯定循环论证比无穷倒退要好得多，而且还存在着一种特殊的良性循环论证，它不仅不构成知识论困难，相反还构成知识的严格的绝对基础，即所谓的超验论证

[47] 《礼记·三年问》曰："称情而立文。"

[48] 在中国思想里，相信某些东西是必要的，但是信仰某些东西则没有必要。《论语·雍也》曰："务民之义，敬鬼神而远之，可谓知矣。"中国式的智慧就是在力所能及的实践范围内找到思想和行动的绝对根据。当然，人们可以信仰某种实践之外的东西，但不可以真的相信它。如果利用维特根斯坦的"不可说"的概念，很显然，我们可以信仰某种不可说的东西，但却不能相信它，因为我们不能相信某种我们不知道的东西。假如我们盲目地相信某种所不知道的东西，那么，在逻辑上说，我们被正确地引导或者被误导的机会相等。关于这一点可以参考柏拉图"美诺篇"的"美诺悖论"：即使我们遇到了我们在寻找但不知道的东西，既然不知道，那么我们不可能知道那就是我们所寻找的东西。

[49] 《礼记·大传》曰："圣人南面而治天下，必自人道始矣。立权度量，考文章，改正朔，易服色，殊徽号，异器械，别衣服，此其所得与民变革者也。其不可得变革者则有矣，亲亲也，尊尊也，长长也，男女有别，此其不可得与民变革者也。"

(transcendental argument)。天下和家庭性之间非常可能存在着超验论证的结构。

家庭性所意味的幸福必定基于它的完整性与和谐，这一真理是分析性的，因此是绝对的——显然，父母与子女、夫妇之间的幸福是互为条件和互相促进的，所以家庭的完整性与和谐是每个成员各自幸福的共同条件——那么，任何不利于完整性与和谐的事情也就被先验地定义为不可接受的事情。于是有这样一个一般性模式：关于幸福、和谐或和平的唯一有效原理就是，给定一个共同体或人际制度，它必须能够满足：

1) 这个共同体的完整性是任何一个成员各自幸福或利益的共同条件。

2) 这个共同体的总体利益与任何一个成员各自的利益成正比，或者说集体利益和个人利益总是挂钩一致，因此任何一个成员都没有反对另一个成员的积极性。

按照这一完美共同体标准，家庭性模式是最合格的。于是，当我们幻想世界的幸福、和谐或和平，至少在理论上，就有理由把家庭性原则推广地应用到整个世界。当然这一推论并非逻辑推论，即并不能由家庭的和谐模式"推理"出天下的和谐模式，这种推论是数学的"映射式"(mapping-into) 的，即既然家庭模式在形成和谐关系方面具有优越性，那么，如果把天下建设成家庭模式就也能够形成和谐关系。这种映射式的推论是中国思维惯用模式。

但是，对由家而国至天下这一推广并不是没有任何疑问。至少有一点是相当可疑的。家庭是人的情感中心，其它情感关系则围绕着这一中心按照其亲疏程度层层向外远去 (按照费孝通的比喻，它是个波纹同心圆的结构[51])，这就很容易想象，当情感关系走到非常疏远的层次时，淡化了的情感就恐怕无力再来维持家庭性模式的互相爱护了，就是说，家庭性原则会在情感的淡化过程中消于无形。看来，由家庭性而世界性的推广还缺乏某些实践条件。不过家庭模式仍然是世界模式的理想，这一点不成问题。费孝通对家庭性模式的著名批评恐怕是对经典理论的误读，费孝通认为，《大学》里的"古之欲明明德于天下者，先治其国，欲治其国者，先齐其家，欲齐其家者，先修其身……身修而后家齐，家齐而后国治，国治而后天下平"，这段经典论述意味着一个自私的制度："一个人为了自己可以牺牲家，为了家可以牺牲党，为了党可以牺牲国，为了国可以牺牲天下。"[52]这样的

---

[50] 宗教的解决也许算是第三条道路，即给定一种信仰，不许怀疑，不许争论。但这不是知识论的解决而是政治性的解决。如果从知识论角度看，信仰的解决是完全不成立的，因为如果能够任意相信某种东西，那么在逻辑上就可以随便相信另一种东西，并且任何人都可以任意的理由来拒绝其他人的思想。所以，宗教的解决是知识的堕落和意识形态冲突的根源。

[51] 费孝通：《乡土中国》，第25页，北京三联书店，1985。

[52] 费孝通：《乡土中国》，第27页，北京三联书店，1985。

结论在逻辑上是推不出来的 (不过有趣的是, 商鞅倒是早就有类似解读: "其道亲亲而爱私, 亲亲则别, 爱私则险"[53]) 。费孝通把"自我中心"的思维归于中国主流文化难免让人迷惑 (自我中心的思维倒是西方现代个人主义价值观的典型表现, 而且表现在一些典型的西方哲学概念如"个体"、"主体"和"个人权利"之中。中国固然也有自我中心的理论, 如杨朱的利己主义和道家个人生命价值理论, 但这些都不是中国的制度主张) 。真实情况可能是个理论与实践的差距问题: 儒家的家国天下理论是一个事实上总也做不到的乌托邦, 却不能说成是一个自我中心的制度主张, 由于它有着实践上的局限性, 理想难以实现, 所以人们观察到的社会学事实并非理想的社会主张。如何改进家庭/天下理论使得社会以至世界的和平和谐在实践上也成为可能, 这才是重要的问题。

5. 制度最大化问题以及作为完成式的和作为使命的世界

就历史的情景 (context) 或历史发生学而言, 天下理论所直接设想的是一个天下/帝国, 但就其理论的深层意义来说, 它蕴涵着关于"世界"的饱满概念和世界制度的先验理念, 即作为天下体系的世界制度。天下理论最重要的创意就在于它的世界概念以及世界制度的先验理念, 尽管历史上实际存在的帝国从来没有很好地表现这一理念, 但这个关于世界制度的先验概念始终是天下/帝国的深层结构, 而天下/帝国则是它的某个表现模式。我们无法断言天下/帝国是不是天下体系的唯一可能的表现模式, 但很可能是天下体系的一个有效模式。正如前面说到的, 以人类本性和生活欲望作为约束条件, 我们所能够设想的社会制度的花样并不多。许多思想家都希望能够在理论上 (也就是提前于充分的实践经验) 分析出哪一种社会制度对于人类生活是最适宜的。通过理论分析而发现最佳选择其实可以看作是人类心智的精明之处, 也最合乎经济学, 因为通过实践经验来选择很可能是不能承受的代价, 历史不仅是不可逆的, 而且有时候还很可能是不可逆转的, 即一旦错了就永远错下去, 即使知道错了也没有条件改正错误 (潘多拉盒子模式) 。自马克思以来的批判理论就是在不断提醒人们说, 现代性所带来的社会发展是以扭曲人性为代价的, 而且这种错误很可能难以逆转。不过, 自由主义思想家们则致力于论证, 在给定自私和贪婪人性的约束条件下, 自由主义社会制度已经足够好了 (所以才会有历史的终结的说法) , 如果有更好的, 那就是不现实的。自由主义论证相当有力, 但是有一个无法回避的困难: 自由主义社会制度总是仅仅在"国内社会"的约束条件下有效, 它不能超越国家这个约束条件, 因此它不能满足制度最大化和普遍化要求, 不能成为

---

[53] 《商君书·开塞》。

一种对所有规模的社会都有效的社会制度。这是一个致命的问题，也是经常被忽视的问题。

所谓制度最大化和普遍化是指如果一个社会制度是最好的，那么它必须能够成为一个普遍有效的社会制度，以至于能够尽可能地扩展成为在任何一个政治/社会单位上有效的社会制度，否则它就是个不彻底的社会制度。一个社会制度所以需要成为普遍有效的，至少有这样一个基本理由：各种政治/社会单位并非各自独立互相无关，而是互相影响、互相制约着的，尤其是这些政治/社会单位之间的关系是包含关系，即按规模层次一个包含另一个，于是，规模比较大的单位就形成了比较小的单位的外部环境和存在条件（这一点在全球化时代变得更加突出），如果忽视一个社会的外部环境（尤其在今天的世界），或者说各个层次的单位之间没有一致性，就几乎必然要产生无法控制的混乱、失序、矛盾和冲突。因此有理由认为，假如一个社会制度不能成为世界性制度，那么它就不是一个完善的制度，它就还没有能力建立人类生活所必需的完整秩序。社会制度的最大化和普遍化必须被看作是一个社会制度的必要指标。

缺乏世界性制度的原因除了历史和现实所给定的实践困难之外，在思想上或理论上的原因是人们在理解世界时缺乏理论准备，没有给予世界一个世界观。只有当能够从世界的整体性上去理解世界才能够有"世界观"，否则就只是关于世界的某种地方观，只不过是"管窥"（the view of the world from somewhere），就不会关心世界性利益。在这个意义上，"天下"作为一种世界观的重要性就明显起来。"天下"所认定的世界是个在概念上已经完成的世界（conceptually completed world），是个已经完成了它的完整性结构的世界，它承诺了世界的先验完整性。既然世界具有先验的完整性，那么世界的存在论意义就在于保护其内在和谐。基于这种完成式的世界概念，世界的历史就不可能有一个进化论的终点，即一个要等到最后才实现其目的性（finality）的目的地[54]。对于天下理论，历史是维持世界先验理念及和谐状态的无穷过程。可以看出，天下的世界观深刻地影响着中国的历史观，这种历史观以理解生命和生态的方式去理解存在，即存在（being）的目的在于维持良好的存在的状态（state of being），而不是为了存在之外的某种目的。所以中国总是以存在状态的情况去分析历史，特别是以"治/乱"模式去判断一种存在状态是否良好[55]。

西方对世界的理解可以看作是与此不同的典型例子。西方对世界的理解，无论是帝国的还是

---

[54] 黑格尔、马克思和福山式的历史终结论对于中国哲学来说是不可理喻的，如果不假定一种finality，就无所谓the end of history。

[55] 关于"治/乱"模式，我在另一篇论文中有更多的讨论。参见《历史知识是否能够从地方的变成普遍的？》，见《没有世界观的世界》，第113页。

帝国主义的, 都把世界看作是分裂的, 把世界的完整性看作是尚未完成的历史使命 (往往同时又是宗教使命)。一旦把世界的完整性看作是"使命"而不是给定的概念, 就不可避免地为了克服所想象的分裂而发动战争, 进行殖民, 从事政治、经济和文化的征服。西方对征服的迷恋不是出于恶意, 而是出于作为意识或潜意识的"使命感"。可以看到, 天下/帝国理论与帝国主义理论在对世界的理解上有着顺序颠倒的结构: 天下/帝国的理论是个由大至小的结构, 先肯定世界的先验完整性, 然后在给定的完整世界观念下再分析各个地方或国家的关系。这是世界观先行的世界理论; 而帝国主义是由小至大的结构, 先肯定自己的民族和国家的绝对性, 然后以自己国家的价值观把"其他地方"看作是对立的、分裂的和未征服的。这是没有世界观的世界理论。也许我们无法比较哪种理论本身是更正确的 (因为在社会和历史方面没有绝对真理可言), 但假如我们需要世界正义、世界制度和世界和平这样一些事情, 那么天下理论更有助于达到这些目标。

与天下这一先验概念相配, 天下的完整性是依靠内在的多样性的和谐来维持的, 因此又有一个关于世界和谐的先验原理, 所谓"和"。一个东西本身无所谓"和", 因为没有什么可以与之构成"和", 至少必须有两种以上的东西才能够形成"和"。然而, 假如只有一种东西存在, 不是更具典型的完整性吗? 对于完整性而言, "和"似乎是多余的。关于这个问题, 中国哲学在至少2000年前就进行了不同寻常的深入反思, 其中关键的论证是这样的:

1) 至少两种以上东西之间的和谐是任何一种东西能够生存的必要条件, 就是说, 单独一种东西靠它自身不可能生存, 任何一种东西都不得不与另一种东西共存, 于是, 共存 (co-existence) 成了存在 (existence) 的先决条件。

2) 足够多样的东西才能够使得任何一种东西具有魅力或者说价值和意义, 因此, 足够多样的存在方式是生活意义的基础。经典的表述有: "道始于一, 一而不成, 故分为阴阳, 阴阳合和而万物生"[56]; "和乃生, 不和不生"[57]; 以及"夫和实生物, 同则不继。以他平他谓之和, 故能丰长而物生之, 若以同裨同, 尽乃弃矣"[58]。基于这样的考虑, 只有多样的和谐这一模式才能够同时满足世界的完整性和生命力双重要求。不过应该指出, 这样两个论点都是出于直观的, 这样的直观虽然神奇而且实践经验也几乎总能够给予验证, 但却不能被绝对地证明。不过, 假如再加上

[56] 《淮南子·天文训》。

[57] 《管子》。

[58] 《国语·郑语》。

一个约束条件"对于人类生活而言"，这两个论点可能就能够在某个超越论证 (transcendental argument) 中被证明。

6. 不完美的帝国实践

天下理论显然过于完美，往往被认为只属于古老的圣贤时代 (其实即使圣贤时代的完美性也是想象的，未必真的完美)。不过重要的不在于理想不能实现，而在于理想是必要的标准。没有理想就等于没有尺子。尽管事实上的古代中国帝国的确与天下/帝国理想有相当的距离，以至于在许多方面只不过是个寻常模式的帝国，但古代中国帝国毕竟在文化追求上一直试图按照天下/帝国的文化标准去行事。至少有这样几个方面是明显的：

1) 在天下一家的理想影响下，在中国的意识里不存在"异端意识"，于是，中国所设定的与"他者" (the others) 的关系在本质上不是敌对关系，其它民族或宗教共同体都不是需要征服的对象。这不是说古代中国与其它民族和宗教共同体没有冲突，关键是，那些冲突在本质上只是地方利益的功利冲突，而不是在精神上或知识上否定他者的绝对冲突，因此所有冲突都不具有不共戴天的性质。这显然要归因于"天下"与"天"一样都是不可分的公共空间和公有资源这样一个理念。

2) 天下公有而为一家的意识还抑制了天下/帝国作为军事化帝国的发展趋势。按照"天下"概念所理解的帝国不是一个超级力量的存在。事实如此，中国古代帝国在人口和经济方面都非常突出，但按照比例，其军事实力并不十分强大，以至于西北人口很少的少数民族军事集团永远成为中原帝国之大患。[59]天下/帝国的理想追求不是征服性的军事帝国，而是文化帝国，而且这个文化帝国也不是致力于普遍化自身的统治性文化帝国，原因在于中国式的文化帝国以"礼"为基本原则而形成自我限制。

3) 天下/帝国所设想的根本不是一个国家。如果说全世界变成一个国家，这个说法在逻辑上显然没有意义，所以天下/帝国设想的是一个世界制度。它把世界理解为一个完整的政治单位，这种理解在民族/国家思维模式中是不可能的。天下/帝国虽然是一个完整的政治制度性存在，但它允许按照各个地方分成许多"国"，就是说，天下制度是共享的，但是各个地方在经济、统治和文化上是独立的。

---

[59] 即使在似乎很强大的王朝如汉、唐、明、清，西北威胁仍然严重，更不用说像宋这样比较弱的王朝。但是元帝国除外，元帝国仍然是军事帝国的模式。历史上个别"穷兵黩武"的皇帝也除外，他们对军事征服的兴趣应该归于个性而与帝国理论无关。

4) 在天下/帝国的理想指导下，既然空间问题（土地的征服和空间占有）不是根本问题，于是时间问题就被突出。古代中国王朝帝国确实重视"时间性"问题超过"空间性"问题，即它总是优先思考帝国的持久性而不是领土的开拓。这样，帝国的主要问题就是制度的可持续性，即所谓"千秋万代"的问题。中国帝国制度设想者们的思考重心显然不在经济发展速度和管理效率的最大化上，而是在生活方式的稳定性和社会和谐的最大化上，因此总是以最大程度减少社会冲突和规避冒险性发展作为基本原则。这大概是为什么几乎所有的王朝都选择了儒家制度的一个原因，因为儒家制度具有无与其匹的稳定性。但是我们决不能认为儒家制度是一个足够好的制度，就儒家制度所能够提供的可能生活而言，它有着非常严重甚至不可接受的局限性（鲁迅对表面温厚的儒家制度处处都在"吃人"的深刻批判不能被遗忘），何况这个制度在今天已经失效（回归儒家社会是个不切实际又毫无想象力的主张）。当然，我们所熟悉的儒家社会其实是以宋明儒学为原则的退化了的或歪曲了的儒家社会，并非原本意义上的（fundamental）儒家社会[60]。

5) 由于天下/帝国不是个国家，而是世界性政治单位，于是在天下/帝国这个概念下的"国际关系"就不同于通常意义上的国际关系。天下单位之下的"国"不是民族/国家，而应该说是"地方性统治"。中文的"国"最开始时本来就指的是王都以及地方都城。商周时代人们对天下范围有着纯概念的想象：在天子的直辖地之外一圈一圈地围绕着各个伯侯之国，这些属国与天子有着法律上的朝贡关系。秦始皇一统六合，虽然不能说天下尽属王土，但也几乎海内尽属王土，于是整个中原都变成了王朝直辖地，在王朝辖地之外的地方就在理论上变成了环绕着的各国。原来规模比较小的天下视野就在结构上映射到规模比较大的天下视野中。而由于那些遥远的地方并不属于同一文化体系，而且也较少往来，于是原来的"法定朝贡体系"就转化为"自愿朝贡体系"，即中原正统王朝虽然认为其他国家应该尊崇天下王朝而发展朝贡关系，但并不强迫这样做。朝贡的自愿性从表面上看似乎是由于在控制世界方面实力有限，但更重要的原因应该是中国关于礼的理解，而礼被认为是处理人际和国际等一切"际间"（inter-ness）关系的普遍原则。

---

[60] 中国早期古代生活显然存在着很大的自由生活空间，但宋明以后的儒家原则发生了无节制的自身膨胀以至于取消了生活的所有方面和所有细节上的自由，所以变成了严重压抑的社会。

7. "礼不往教" 原则

特别需要讨论的是"礼"这一充分表达了中国心灵 (heart) 的实践原则。礼的精神实质是互惠性 (往来)，所谓"礼尚往来，往而不来，非礼也；来而不往，亦非礼也"[61]。这种中国式的互惠性虽然也包括经济意义上的互惠，但似乎更强调心之间的互惠，即心灵的互相尊重和应答。如果说经济上的互惠能够带来利益，那么心灵的互惠则产生幸福，所以心灵互惠是更加深刻的互惠。由礼所规定的社会关系被认为是最优的，因为据说它表达了人性基本原理"仁"。仁的直接意义是"二人"，这一语义结构意味深长。仁的更古写法为"忎"，似乎表达的是千心所共有的人性或共同认可的人性原则，可以理解为对人性的普遍意识，即仁是人的普遍要求[62]。因此可以想象，二人关系的人性要求就是众人关系的人性要求的最基本模式，因为二人关系是最基本的人际关系。

不过"二人模式"是可以争论的。至少从现代社会的结构来看，把众人关系还原为二人关系似乎有些过分，更合适的基本模式可能应该是三人关系。一个重要的理由是，一个社会，不仅是现代社会，总是包括陌生人的。尽管古代中国社会据说是个熟人社会，但陌生人仍然存在并且同样构成问题。三人模式可以解释为"至少存在着一个陌生人的人际关系"。但如果进一步看，孔子的二人模式则另有道理，他试图说明的是人类所能够指望的最好人际关系的伦理条件，而不是关于社会的科学描述的经济学或社会学条件，所以在这个意义上，二人模式仍然是最优的。道理很简单，在二人关系中，另一个人必定是自己的存在条件以及生活意义的条件，失去另一个人只剩下自己的生活不仅没有意义而且几乎不能生存。因此二人模式是发展和谐关系的最优模式。列维纳斯也有类似的见识，在二人面对面的关系中，另一个人就不再是形同路人的"他"而变成了与我息息相关的"你"，因此二人模式是个"我与你"的亲密关系模式，在其中人之间的互相尊重和关心成为无条件的。不管是孔子还是列维纳斯都无非是想论证道德的先验条件。正是基于二人模式的条件，孔子才能够说出"己所不欲勿施于人"和"己欲立而立人，己欲达而达人"这样的道德完美主义原则[63]。

仁这个"二人模式"的幸福境界就成为分析社会和生活的伦理学原则和好生活/好社会的乌托邦。正如前面论证的，二人模式是发展和谐、幸福以及和平的最优条件，因为在二人模式中，要最

---

[61] 《礼记·曲礼上》。

[62] 从千心变化而为仁，关于其中的理由似乎并无确切记载，但从孔子的学生不断问仁，至少可以说明孔子对仁的用法包含有新的含义，所以需要不断解释。

[63] 《论语·颜渊》；《论语·雍也》。

大化自己的利益的唯一可能途径就是同时去最大化他者的利益, 否则必定损害自己。这就是孔子名言"己欲立而立人, 己欲达而达人"的深层含义。当然, 这个"二人模式"不是指仅仅有两个人的社会, 而是指众人之间的人际关系达到相当于二人关系的良好水平。不过, 由于存在着利益冲突, 所以在实际上并不能真的在所有人的关系中实现互惠, 于是, 仁就不得不限制在具体情景中, 人们只能在某些特定关系中才能发展超越利益互惠的心灵互惠 (reciprocity of hearts)。所谓"义"和"礼"就被发展为实现仁的具体规则。

有一个非常典型的义气规则是"豫让原则"[64], 即给定特殊的人际关系, 别人给我什么样的价值待遇 (不等于物质待遇), 我就以配得上这种价值待遇的行为给予回报。豫让原则是伦理原则和策略原则的结合, 就其行为策略方面而言, 它非常接近于现代博弈论中据说被证明为在长期博弈中最成功的"回应性"模式, 即首先采取与他人合作的策略, 但以后的每个行为步骤都模仿他人的上一个步骤以回应他人。其中充分体现了以他者而不是自己为思考核心的"他者性原则"。

在礼方面的一个重要原则是自愿原则。这个原则一直没有被充分表述, 但它是明显存在的。中国伦理强调的是"以身作则"而不是把自己的价值观加之于人 (后者是西方的"传教"模式)。中国伦理的基本原则 (例如孔子原则) 表面上看起来有些类似于西方的金规则, 有些西方学者就这样认为[65], 但这是典型的貌合神离, 其本质区别在于西方的哲学假设是主体性原则而中国的哲学假设是他者性原则。因此西方的金规则的眼界就比较狭隘, 它只能按照自己的价值观去定义什么是不应该对他人做的事情, 而没有考虑他人对生活的不同想象。这一缺陷使得西方伦理原则只能满足形式或程序上的公正而不能满足实质上的公正。中国哲学显然考虑到了他者心灵, 即他人的价值观、生活想象和情感方式, 是不可还原的, 于是在与他者的关系中引入了自愿性原则。如《礼记》所说:"同则相亲, 异则相敬……礼者殊事, 合敬者也, 乐者异文, 合爱者也。"[66]又曰:"礼, 闻取于人, 不闻取人, 礼, 闻来学, 不闻往教。"[67]等待别人来学, 与强加于人显然是完全不同的原则。于是, 不管自己认为自己的文化多么优越 (似乎绝大多数的民族都有这样的自我感觉), 也不能因此认为自己的文化有更大的权力去获得普遍化。其中显示的正是他者性原则。

---

[64] 《史记·卷八十六》。

[65] *See A Global Ethic: the Declaration of the Parliament of the World's Religions*, ed. by Hans Kung and Karl-Josef Kuschel. The Continuum Pub. Co., 1993.

[66] 《礼记·乐记》。

[67] 《礼记·曲礼上》。

历史事实显示，中国古代帝国在扩大其文化影响方面的确实践了"不取人、不往教"的原则，尽管中国古代帝国连续3000年保持着优势的帝国文化，但是其文化影响的扩大速度非常缓慢，基本上只影响了近邻地区，甚至几乎只限于其属国范围（日本除外）。相反，中国一向引进"西方"文化，大规模的引进至少有胡服骑射、佛教和现代欧洲科学文化。可以说，以"礼"和"仁"为表里而定义的天下/帝国想象的是一种能够把文化冲突最小化的世界文化制度，而且这种文化制度又定义了一种以和为本的世界政治制度。文化制度总是政治制度的深层语法结构，亨廷顿也意识到了这一点，所以在文明关系上重新理解了国际关系，可是他只看到了冲突，这毫不意外，因为这只不过是主体性思维和异端模式的通常想法。

二、天下理论与当代问题的相关性

1. 联合国模式

按照家庭性关系而想象四海一家的天下/帝国模式有时候会让人联想到今天的联合国模式，它们或多或少有些相似性，比如它们都被假定是某种世界组织，而且有义务解决国际冲突、保证世界和平和秩序。然而它们的差异则是本质性的。就事实而言，天下/帝国模式尽管在实践中远远没有达到所预期的标准，但已经在中国古代许多朝代的实践中被证明比较成功地维护了和平、社会稳定秩序和传统的延续。而联合国的实践却不能说是很成功的，它在保证世界和平和世界秩序方面显然有非常大的局限，而且联合国几乎没有能力创造世界性的公正体系，何况它的有些成就在今天还被超级大国毁于一旦。从根本上说，联合国的概念并不是一个清楚的理念，它没有提供一种世界性的社会/生活理想。在缺乏相应的世界性理想的情况下，一种世界性的制度是可疑的和没有确定性的，它不能为自身辩护从而没有能力去解释和解决世界性问题，所以与其假定的身份不匹配。而就世界的理念而言，天下理念却是基本清楚的，它是个世界乌托邦，从而它不是一般意义上的帝国，而是世界社会制度，它指望的是有着共同的世界理念却不存在着霸权的天下体系，在其中，和谐、沟通和合作通过一个共同认可的世界制度而得到保证。当然，联合国所以虚弱自有"各方面的"实际原因。在这里我们只分析其理论假设方面的缺陷。

为了更单纯地在理念层面上进行分析，我们回避掉天下模式和联合国模式在历史语境中的具体得失成败，而只考虑它们的理念和假设。天下模式预设了世界的先验一体性（Oneness a priori）。如前面所论证，既然天下是个先验理想，那么，世界中的所有可能生活就被认定为天然合法的，因为生活方式的任何可能性都是世界一体性的可接纳部分，甚至是构成生活意义的必要条件。当然，这一逻辑包含着一定的危险性，因为的确存在着某些可能生活是危险的或有害的。这一点可以这样解释：天下理想在可能生活上并非完全没有限制，凡是与天下理想得以成立的条件（至少是"世界完整性"原则以及"和谐"原则）互相冲突的生活方式就被认为是不可接受的。那些危险的生活既需要获得天下模式的支持又准备破坏天下模式本身，而按照"超验论证"的标准——任何一个东西p不可以构成对p所依赖的某个条件q的否定，既然反对自身的存在条件是不成立的，那么就证明q是必要的约束条件——那些危险生活就被排除了。由此我们可以更准确地理解天下模式的有限性：所有可能生活，如果与天下模式的存在条件没有冲突，那么都是天然合法的。

从理论立意上说，天下的概念默许了世界的多样性。不同的生活就仅仅是不同的生活而已，而不是某些必要修改或必须消灭的异端，因为任何一种所谓不同的可能生活都分有着世界的先验一体性。按照老子理论，多样性是一体性必然需要生长出来的，否则世界就什么也没有[68]。把"多"看作是"一"的存在需要甚至存在的条件，这一哲学原则几乎是所有中国哲学所共同强调的，如前面讨论到的所谓"道始于一，一而不成，故分为阴阳，阴阳合和而万物生"，以及"夫和实生物，同则不继。以他平他谓之和，故能丰长而物生之，若以同裨同，尽乃弃矣……声一无听，物一无文，味一无果，物一不讲"[69]，等等。既然世界的一体性是先验的，世界就是一个完成式的概念，既然世界多样性成分是一体性的必要生存条件，那么就不可能把其中某种东西理解为不可兼容的、不可接受的异端，无论它是如何陌生和异己。因此，天下模式不包含"普遍化"（universalization）的要求。这里需要分辨的是，普遍化并不等于标准化。标准化的确建立了各种普遍统一的标准，但是那些普遍化的标准基本上都是生产、社会管理和政治制度所必需的实用性标准，正因为实用性标准是生活所必需的，所以任何文化都包含大量的普遍性标准，即使是特别强调灵活和变通精神的中国文化也不例外[70]。所以"普遍化"不包括物质层面的普遍标准，而是指统一精神和心灵的企图，即试图把属于自己的价值观和意识形态、观念体系和知识体系给予单方面的推广，从而剥夺其他观念和知识体系的生存空间。由此来理解，秦始皇的"书同文、车同轨"应该属于标准化而不是普遍化（不过，秦始皇"焚书坑儒"以及汉朝的"独尊儒术"则属于意识形态方面的普遍化，可以说是天下模式的反例）。

---

[68] 《道德经·四十二章》曰："道生一，一生二，二生三，三生万物。"

[69] 《国语·郑语》。

[70] 参见翟光珠《中国古代标准化》，太原，山西人民出版社，1996。中国古代的标准化涉及文字、纺织、农业、道路、车辆、度量、货币、建筑、航运、桥梁、工程等等方面，标准化的范围和项目与其他文化大同小异，可见标准化出于生活需要而并非文化风格。

什么事情都会有反例, 这倒不奇怪）。

与天下理论的单纯性不同, 联合国模式表面上是众多国家的联合机构, 但实质是第二次世界大战后对世界权力关系的重新规划。联合国在发展其多种功能的过程中也发展了许多混杂的思想观念, 其中特别包括了多元论和普遍主义这样两个有严重分歧甚至互相矛盾的原则。当然, 联合国模式本来就是以众口难调和"什么都要照顾到"的复杂情况为背景的, 一方面它要以各国所"共同认可"的原则为基础来把各国联合起来追求某些"普遍的"价值和目标, 另一方面, 既然联合国并非一个"世界国"或严格意义上的世界性单位, 各国就必定仅仅考虑或至少优先考虑自身的利益, 这样的"联合性"或"合同性"的制度显然不可能形成甚至不可能去发现属于世界整体的价值观、世界性利益和世界性理念。那些所谓的"普遍"价值和目标一方面是伪装成普遍价值的超级大国的利益, 另一方面又被各国多元地解释, 显然只不过都是各自利益的表述而已。多元论和普遍主义本来应该是"或者"的关系, 但是在联合国那里似乎被伪装成"并且"的关系。

也许可以更准确地说, 联合国根本不是个世界性制度 (institution), 而只是个世界性组织 (organization), 是个关于各国利益的一个谈判场所或机构, 而且还是个不健全的谈判机构。原因是明显的 : 当不存在一个世界性制度时, 就不存在超越国家利益和力量而做出解释/决定的可能性, 也就不存在超越民族/国家的游戏规则, 而且也没有能力去控制一个超级力量滥用实力, 比如说超级大国单方面地普遍化其自身的利益、价值和知识而剥夺他者的发展机会甚至发动战争。这里并非在批评联合国, 事实上联合国已经尽了很大的努力试图通过理性对话来减少可能发生的战争或严重冲突, 但由于这一模式在理论上的局限, 它不可能减少世界中的利益冲突和世界性的不公正, 相反, 它维持着世界上各种不合作博弈和自私的最大化者思维。无论从理论准备上说还是从实践上看, 联合国模式不但没有超越民族/国家思维, 而且是附属于民族/国家体系的一个服务性组织。由于联合国模式关于世界的概念以及对世界中政治/文化关系的理解从属于民族/国家体系, 因此, 联合国必定为各个民族/国家的国家利益所约束, 它要照顾的并非世界这个整体的利益, 而是各国的利益, 它也就在事实上很容易被某些甚至某个特别强大的民族/国家的帝国主义所利用。即使它不愿意被帝国主义所利用, 帝国主义也有能力超越它。所以, 就联合国的概念而言, 它不可能把世界引向一个新的体系、新的国际社会和新生活, 相反, 如吉登斯所指出的, 联合国似乎没有削弱而是加强了作为现代政治形式的民族/国家体系。[71]可面前的问题是, 今天的全球化运动

[71] cf. Anthony Giddens: *The Nation-state and Violence*, Chapter 10, Polity Pr. 1985.

已经使得世界制度问题成为一个迫切问题。世界从来没有像今天这样需要一个世界制度，也没有像今天这样难以创造一个世界制度。这可能就是前面讨论到的那种不可逆转的历史性堕落。

2. 现代游戏

作为现代性的最重要特征之一的民族/国家体系在基本价值观上与西方思想中"个体"或"主体"这样的基本概念或者基本思考单位是一致的，并且存在着映射关系，只不过民族/国家单位更大。我们可以看到从个人主义到民族主义或国家主义、从个人权利到民族或国家主权之间的一致逻辑，即有意义的存在形式总是某种自身独立的单位（个人或国家），而且，任何一个独立单位的思维模式必定是并且仅仅是对自身利益的最大化。按照这一逻辑，各个独立单位之间的冲突是不可避免的，因为其他独立单位，不管是他人还是它国，都被先验地假定为"负面的外在性"；而且利益的最大化是个永远的过程，无休止的过程，所以冲突永远不可能消解。就民族/国家体系而言，如果一个民族/国家足够强大，那么它就会发展成为帝国主义（列宁早就分析了现代世界如何必然要产生帝国主义，尽管他的论证不是很充分）[72]。

不过我们没有必要对哪一种游戏进行价值批判，不能认为哪一种游戏本身是错误的，而只能说由于不具备适合该游戏的充分条件而导致游戏不成功——意识到这一点是重要的，否则就会陷入无助于解决实际问题的意识形态批评。真正的问题是：给定某种游戏，这种游戏在它的制度设计或规则体系上是否有能力去避免这个世界所不能承受的各种困难、危险甚至毁灭？如果这样去思考，我们就能够把价值或意识形态的立场之争转换为能够无立场分析的问题。当意识到帝国主义与民族/国家以及民族主义的关系，当意识到"利益最大化"思维与无止境竞争的关系，当意识到对他者的否定与异端思维的关系，我们就会发现今天世界的危险根源，就会意识到以主体性原则、经济人原则和异端原则作为元定理而设计的现代社会游戏根本没有能力来维护游戏的合理性。应该说，人们对"现代游戏"（任何单位意义上的利益最大化运动）的危险性已经有了明确的意识，因此，不管在社会制度问题上还是在世界体系问题上，人们都希望能够有一个足以避免危险和毁灭的制度设计。由此可以看到公正、规则、法律、权利、权力、秩序、对话和合作等事情所以成为今天

---

[72] 列宁努力论证帝国主义是资本主义的必然产物。不过，尽管资本主义和帝国主义之间存在着历史事实上的密切关系，但是否存在着绝对必然关系则仍然需要充分的论证。或许资本主义只是其中一个因素，而观念和文化传统，包括宗教意识，可能需要考虑在内，甚至有可能是更深层的因素。参见列宁：《帝国主义是资本主义的最高阶段》。

世界的关键"问题"的理由。

那么，现代游戏是否能够通过自身完善而发展出一个足以保证游戏正常运作和合理性的制度？一般地说，现代的制度想象是这样的：如果有一个由合格的法律和政治制度所保证的个人或任何独立实体的政治权利、社会秩序和自由市场，那么，个人的利益最大化行为不但不会导致互相的损害，反而会在"看不见的手"的指引下促进共同利益，或者说，只要制度在技术上（程序上）是公正的，那么就可以规避危险的直接冲突而形成公平的市场交易，于是互相获利。这个亚当·斯密式的推论其实非常可疑，因为没有理由能够证明利益冲突形式由直接的暴力争夺变成和平竞争就必然能够导致互利。这一论证的缺陷居然长期不被觉察，一直到纳什均衡被证明才被普遍意识到[73]。甚至现代民主政治制度本身也被发现存在着理论上的严重缺陷，阿罗的"不可能性定理"说明了，不存在完全公正的民主选举方式[74]，尽管据说实际的选举并没有那么不可救药。现代民主政治和自由市场制度尽管存在着许多缺陷，但仍然被大多数人认为是个比较好的制度，而且要寻找一种明显更好的制度似乎并不容易，这正是福山宣称"历史的终结"的重要理由。

我们在这里不打算卷入关于现代制度作为一种国内社会制度是否合理的讨论（当然这是非常需要讨论的，尤其是现代制度绝不像通常想象的那么乐观），因为这里所讨论的是世界制度的问题。只要面对世界性问题或者国际问题，就很容易发现，到目前为止还没有一个实际存在的世界制度，所以不可能有效地解决世界性和国际问题。联合国的概念并不是一个世界制度（the world institution），而只是一个试图解决世界性和国际问题的"国家间机构"（an international organization），正如前面论述的，它的思考方式和利益分析单位仍然以民族/国家为标准，它至多只能照顾国家而不是世界。人们虽然"被抛入"世界，但是人们不看护世界。迄今为止，"世界"只是作为一个地理事实而存在，仍然不是作为一个制度事实和文化事实而存在，这意味着世界还没有完全充实"世界"这个概念。"世界"在西方一直是个很单薄的哲学概念，一直没有充分地、全方位地、多层次地被思考。而中国的"天下"则是个丰厚得多的哲学概念，在其中，地理和人文、制度与情感是浑然一体的。当思考世界制度时，天下概念显然是个重要资源。

正因为世界还没有一个以世界为单位的制度，所以国际问题最后在实质上只能是通过国与国

---

[73] 纳什均衡证明了由于自私的个体互相不信任从而形成不合作的博弈，结果不可能形成共同利益的最大化，或者说，由互相受害向互相得益的帕累托改进总是不可能。

[74] 许多政治学家和经济学家试图通过一些有限的条件修改来克服阿罗定理所证明的困难，但是困难并没有得到真正的解决。

之间的对话、协议或者冲突来解决, 联合国的"决议"的实质上仍然是国与国的协议, 因为它最终可以还原为国与国的协议, 或者说和与国与国的协议等价, 而在这种协议的背后只不过是国与国的利益博弈, 并不存在高于民族/国家概念的世界制度依据。许多人以为, 人权可以成为世界普遍的法律基础, 所以有了"人权高于主权"这样貌似世界性原则的口号。但人权是个非常空洞的概念, 它的具体内容的解释权就成了问题。显然, 人权概念并没有获得一个世界性的解释, 而是由各个国家各自解释, 于是就出现了"解释的解释"这样的知识论的元解释问题, 还出现了福柯式的"知识/权力"知识政治学问题, 简单地说, 关于人权的解释本身就是一件缺乏世界性依据和世界性公正的事情。即使仅就西方主流认可的人权概念来说, "天赋人权"的基本假设也存在着严重的逻辑错误[75]。

现代制度的局限性在世界性和国际问题上就特别明显地暴露出来。现代制度是以民族/国家为思考单位的产物, 它所设计的是一个国家内部社会的制度, 所考虑的人民也是国家内部的人民, 它本来就没有或几乎没有考虑到世界整体的利益。既然现代制度只是国家制度而不是世界制度, 它就没有能力处理世界问题。尽管现代制度所推崇的种种主要观念如"民主"、"自由"、"平等"和"公正"等就其理论概念而言看上去似乎应该是普遍有效的, 但是这种"普遍性"实际上只在国家内部社会中有效, 而不是在世界上普遍有效。诸如"民主"和"公正"这些原则从来都不被应用于国际关系中, 那些现代的"普遍"原则只要一进入世界性和国际问题就立刻化为乌有。当考虑到现代制度不是一个世界制度时, 现代制度就更加不让人乐观了。现代制度不具备处理世界性问题的能力配置、义务或责任界定以及道德与德性理想, 而在这个全球化时代, 几乎所有国家内部社会的问题都已经无法避免地与国际问题联系在一起, 在这个世界上, 现在已经不可能有与世界无关的"自己的"问题, 这一点决定了现代制度不是一个充分的社会制度, 也说明了世界社会需要有一个世界制度。

3. 遗弃世界

由于文化上的偶然, 中国最早思考了世界制度的问题, 即"天下理念"。中国的"天下"概念是严格具有世界眼光的世界理念, 即能够达到老子标准"以天下观天下"。有一些西方现代思想家, 例如从康德、马克思到罗尔斯, 也都思考过这个问题, 但是除了马克思, 西方思想家并没有能够发现一个超越了国家眼光的世界眼光。马克思的思想在西方传统中多少显得独辟蹊径。马克思超越了国家

---

[75] 参见我的"预付人权"理论, 《赵汀阳自选集》, 桂林: 广西师范大学出版社, 第191～203页, 2000。

概念, 发现了普遍存在于各个社会中的"阶级"以及全球化的阶级剥削[76], 于是马克思想象总有一天"全世界的无产阶级联合起来"建立一个没有国家的共产主义世界性社会, 而这种超越了国家的世界人民的联合之所以是必要的, 马克思主义论证说是因为只有解放全人类才能真正解放自己。马克思主义在西方之外特别是在"东方"被接受并不偶然, 因为尽管关于世界的理解不同, 但马克思主义显示出一种世界尺度的思维, 这一点至少与中国思想在"形式上"有所沟通。不过, 马克思主义在西方并不太成功, 就西方主流思想而言, 民族/国家是人们更喜欢的概念, 人们在思考到世界问题时仍然是以国家为最大的独立单位去计算的, 因此, 所谓世界问题就只不过是"国际问题"而不是以世界为单位的世界整体问题。西方的这种主流思维在实践上表现为联合国等国际组织或国际契约, 在理论上则典型地表现为康德—罗尔斯观点。

罗尔斯主要是继续了康德的工作, 如果说多少有些新意的话, 他主要是突出了美国式的政治自由主义和人权高于主权的观点。康德的思想则的确是开创性的, 康德关于"世界公民"、"各民族的联盟" (foedus amphictionum) 或"和平联盟" (foedus pacificum) 的理论基本上涉及了以个人权利和民族/国家权利为准则所能够想象的国际关系最优模式[77]。罗尔斯在细节上发展了康德的观点, 并且进一步提出了部分类似于一种世界制度的"万民法" (law of peoples) [78], 但他在康德没有考虑的两个问题上提出了非常阴险和危险的两个观点。

1) 适合于国内社会的公正原则不适用于国际社会, 特别是涉及分配公正的那一条有利于弱者的"差异原则"是万万不能在国际上使用的。在一个自由社会里, 差异原则用来限制不公正的社会关系, 即使不从伦理学上去论证, 而从经济学的角度去看, 差异原则也是维持社会秩序的必要条件, 因为维护弱者的生存条件是一个社会必需付出的代价和投资, 否则活不下去的弱者就会成为破坏者。当罗尔斯在国际社会中取消了差异原则, 就等于取消了国际公正, 也就鼓励了弱肉强食的国际社会。而差异原则是保证一个社会免于退化成为弱肉强食社会的唯一条件, 取消差异原则的危险结果是绝对无法辩护的。

---

[76] 《共产党宣言》是最早讨论全球化的文献之一, 它宣称: "资产阶级, 由于开拓了世界市场, 使一切国家的生产和消费都成为世界性的了……物质生产是如此, 精神的生产也是如此。各民族的精神产品成了公共的财产。民族的片面性和局限性日益成为不可能, 于是由许多种民族的和地方的文献形成了一种世界的文献。"参见《马克思恩格斯选集》, 第1卷。原文中"literature"一词, 往往译成"文学", 不是非常准确, 在此译成"文献"。

[77] 参见康德: 《历史理性批判文集·世界公民观点下的普遍历史观念·永久和平论》, 北京: 商务印书馆, 1997。

[78] 罗尔斯: 《万民法》, 长春: 吉林人民出版社, 2001。

2) 假如给定的只有弱肉强食的世界, 别无选择, 那么按照弱肉强食的逻辑, 弱者就没有义务与强者合作去维护强者的压迫和剥削, 而一定会奋不顾身、不择手段地反抗, 这是强者不愿意为秩序而投资的必然结果。这样危险的世界从对等性上说也算是正常的和公正的。可是罗尔斯还是决心彻底取消国际公正, 他另外想到了解决方法, 他认为应该剥夺弱者的不合作或反对的权利和力量, 不是让弱者不想反抗, 而是使弱者没有能力反抗。在这一点上所依据的是"人权高于主权"的干涉主义。他说: 如果必要的话, 法外国家将被"强行制裁甚至干涉", 理由是"在万民法之下, 自由和合宜的人民有权利不去宽容法外国家"[79]。罗尔斯的理论等于主张了一种新帝国主义。这种新帝国主义就是美国现在所推行的, 美国不愿意为国际社会的秩序而投资, 却愿意为战争投资。其实康德关于世界契约的理论本来是相当谨慎的 (尽管存在着民族/国家思维的局限), 康德的头脑异常清楚, 他已经提前反对了罗尔斯式的国际理论: "双方中的任何一方都不能被宣布为不义的敌人 (因为这就得预先假定有一种法庭判决。)"[80]

要保证一种契约的有效性就必须有制度的支持, 而一种制度是有效的就必须是一个权力体系而不仅仅是一个权利契约。现在世界上的国际组织, 比如说联合国, 所以不像国家那样有效, 就是因为没有相匹配的有效的世界制度作为支持, 进一步说就是没有一个仅仅属于世界而不是属于任何国家的权力体系的支持。因此, 一个有足够实力的强国只要愿意就可以超越联合国之类的国际契约性组织。这就是关键问题之所在。在"个人"、"民族"、"国家"、"宗教"、"异端"等计算单位所构成的概念体系中不可能理解和解决世界性的问题。这些概念不是为世界而准备的。只有新的概念体系才能够产生新的知识体系。马克思曾经以"阶级"这一概念作为旧概念体系的突破口而发现了世界性问题, 类似地, 今天的哈特和尼格瑞以新马克思主义的姿态通过"帝国"和"普众" (multitude) 这些概念再次试图突破旧概念体系的框架来重述世界性问题。他们论证说, 全球化会产生出"普众"来消解新帝国, 从而最后建立起全球的民主社会 (这听起来有些类似于马克思说的资产阶级自己生产出了作为资本主义掘墓人的无产阶级[81]) 。不过, 即使是当年马克思主义那样狂风骤雨般的观念革命, 也并没有完全超越西方思维模式。"阶级"定义了另一种意识形态和另一种异端, 阶级虽然是任何国家都存在的, 它以一种横切面方式解构了民族主义而制造了国际主义, 但是仍然假设了世界

---

[79] 罗尔斯:《万民法》, 第86页, 长春:吉林人民出版社, 2001。

[80] 康德:《历史理性批判文集》, 第102页。

[81] 参见Hardt & Negri: *Empire*, Harvard Univ. Pr. , 2001。

的分裂性和斗争性 (阶级斗争)。自从基督教征服了希腊文明之后, 西方就形成了固定的异端模式思维, 它以各种方式把世界看作是分裂的和战争性的。可以说, 基督教在西方哲学中毁灭了"世界"这一概念, 使"世界"在精神上和理论上失去了先验给予的统一性和完整性, "世界"变成了一个永远没有完成的使命—— 甚至在逻辑上也永远不可能完成, 因为按照异端模式思维习惯, 即使某个异端被消灭了, 那么就必须把另一种东西定义为异端, 否则就不知道该与谁进行斗争了。冷战的结束也是"共产主义异端"的结束, 亨廷顿马上就发现了新的异端和文明的冲突。

正如前面讨论到的, 天下这一概念所承诺的世界一体性是先验给予的整体性, 而世界的先验一体性又构成了对世界内部多样性的承认, 因为多样性不但是既定事实, 而且是任何东西的存在条件, 必须有某些东西可以"和"才有各种东西的"生"。世界的先验一体性所以重要, 就在于它在理论上拒绝了"异端"、"战争"、"冲突"这样的危险思维。从哲学上说, 天下是关于"世界"的全方位概念, 不仅是个地理概念而且是文化和制度概念;从政治学和经济学上说, 天下是危险性最低的世界制度理念, 它拒绝了把物质上的统一世界在观念上又理解为分裂的至少两个世界 (或许多个世界)。假如未来需要一个世界制度, 或许天下理论就是一个适宜的理论基础。

三、 结论或者开始:世界还不存在

今天的全球化是否正在解构还是在加强民族/国家体系, 这是个非常暧昧的问题。但几乎所有人都承认, 在今天, 任何一个地方的本地问题都联系着世界上的所有问题, 任何一个地方的生活都联系着其他地方的生活:跨国公司、全球市场、网络、知识推广、文化交流、跨国迁徙[82]和新帝国主义政治等。但是在"一个问题和所有问题"或者"一个事情和所有事情"的知识、利益和权力互动结构中, "世界"还不存在, 我们看不到"世界", 看不到一个具有属于世界整体的世界利益、世界制度和世界秩序的"世界", 就是说, 在作为地理事实和财富资源的物质世界之外, 还不存在一个精神、制度和价值意义上的世界。一个没有世界制度和世界利益的世界仍然不是世界。今天世界的各种问题已经形成了对世界制度和价值的迫切需求, 而且这一需要正在变得越来越强烈, 于是我们需要一个全方位意义的"世界"概念, 同时需要一个相应的世界事实。西方哲学没有完整意义上的世界观, 在西方概念体系里, 国家已经是个具有完整意义的最大概念, 西方的世界概念虽然比国家更大, 但却不是全方位的世界概念。天下概念作为全方位的"世界", 显然是重新思考今天世界问题的一条重

---

[82] 不必是传统意义上的移民, 更大量的情况是, 许多人持有其本国护照, 却在世界各地工作。

要思路。

帝国以及帝国主义就其理念来说总是世界性的，但是除了天下/帝国模式，其他的帝国模式都没有世界观，都只有国家观，只是以国家为主体单位而试图扩展至整个世界，无论扩展到什么程度，其利益、价值观以及制度设想都是基于国家尺度的视界。这里不妨对几种典型的帝国模式进行简单的比较：

1. 罗马帝国模式

这是具有普遍性的典型古代帝国模式。帝国（imperium）原义指罗马执政官代表国民利益的行政统治权力，分成内政统治和对外征服两方面责任。一般来说，这种帝国是个领土扩张型的军事大国，往往包括多民族。就其公开声称的或者隐蔽的目的而言，假如条件允许，它将扩张至全世界。于是，这种帝国只有临时性的"边陲"（frontiers）而没有法律明确认定的"边界"（boundaries）。这种古代帝国不管在实践上还是在理念上，在现代民族/国家时代以来就已经不可能了。

2. 大英帝国模式

这是基于民族/国家体系的典型的现代帝国主义。它总是一个帝国主义的民族/国家，以民族主义、资本主义和殖民主义为帝国理念和行动原则。帝国主义就是以现代化的方式来实现民族/国家利益的最大化。现代化本身可以理解为一种"最纯正的帝国主义"，现代化推行普遍主义来"生产一种全球规模的形式或结构上的同质性"，但是，"资本的全球扩张却决不产生真正实质上的同质性，而是产生了不均匀和断层的全球体系，因为不平等的发展就是资本主义的一个最基本的要求"。[83]这种帝国有着明确划定的边界，不过明确的边界并不意味着帝国主义准备自我克制，边界的意义在于用来禁止其他人随便进入而危害帝国或分享帝国的利益。与古代的领土扩张主义有所不同，帝国主义在控制世界方面主要表现为：首先，在条件允许的地方开拓境外殖民地；其次，在不容易通过征服而变成殖民地的地方，则强行发展不平等贸易（"大英帝国的性格是商业性"，它是个国际贸易体系[84]）；最后，通过现代性话语重新生产关于事物、社会、历史、生活和价值的知识或叙事，以此把世界划分成中心的、发达的、有神圣法律地位的一些主权"国家"和边缘的、不发达的、没有自主性的"地区"；划分成"有历史的和进化的"世界和"没有历史的或停滞的"世界，通过这种不平等的知识生产来造成其他地方的知识退化。"二战"之后殖民地纷纷独立并加入民族/国家体

[83] S.Makdisi: *Romantic Imperialism: Universal Empire and the Culture of Modernity*, Cambridge Univ. Pr. , 1998, 第177~182页.
[84] D.Armitage: *The Ideological Origins of the British Empire*. P.8, Cambridge Univ.Pr. , 2000.

系，同时世界各国都强化了民族主义意识和主权要求，于是现代帝国主义也就与时俱进地转变为全球化帝国主义。

3. 全球化帝国主义就是美帝国主义模式[85]

首先，全球化帝国主义尽量继承了现代帝国主义能够被继承的特性，主要表现为对其他国家的政治霸权、经济支配和知识霸权从而形成"依附"格局[86]。依附的政治和经济格局虽然是现代帝国主义的特性，但只有在全球化时代才可能被强化到极致，以至于全球化帝国主义能够形成对世界的全方位控制和霸权，按照美国自己喜欢的说法则是"美国领导"（American leadership）。这种"美国领导"被J.奈生动地解释为"硬力量"和"软力量"的双重领导[87]，即由美国领导和操纵的全球政治权力体系、世界市场体系和世界文化知识市场体系，而且这些"世界体系"都达到仅仅最大化美国利益和仅仅普遍化美国文化和价值观。也许奈是对的：建立文化知识的统治比政治和经济的统治更是一劳永逸的解决。因为只有文化知识的统治才能够通过使其他文化知识传统作废而达到使其他心智（the other minds）作废。要达到这样宏大的目标，如果仅仅是发展了现代帝国主义的手段，显然是不够的。于是，全球化帝国主义创造了一种超越了现代帝国主义的新游戏。如果说在现代帝国主义游戏中，帝国主义依靠强大实力而永远成为赢家（比如说总能够签订不平等条约），那么，在这个全球化帝国主义新游戏中，帝国主义不仅由于强大实力而永远是赢家，而且还是唯一有权选择游戏种类的主体以及游戏规则的唯一制定者。于是，美国就成功地成为世界游戏中唯一的法外国家。很显然，当集参赛选手、游戏规则制定者和游戏类型指定者这三个身份于一身，就必定是个法外选手。不过美国的无法无天并非完全归因于美国的野心，更重要的原因应该是世界缺乏世界理念、世界制度和足以支持世界制度的力量，而这正是这个时代提出来的严重问题。

4. 天下模式

在思考或许可能的世界制度的问题上，天下模式至少在世界理念和世界制度的基本原则上具

---

[85] M. Hardt and A. Negri 论证说，新帝国与欧洲老帝国非常不同，它产生于美国的宪政主义（American constitutionalism），它更像罗马帝国而不是欧洲帝国主义。参见 *Empire*, Harvard Univ. Pr., 2001。

[86] 所谓"依附"，就是指"一些国家的经济受制于它所依附的另一国经济的发展和扩张……依附状态导致依附国处于落后和受统治国剥削这样一种局面"。多斯桑托斯：《帝国主义与依附》，第302页，北京：社会科学文献出版社，1999。

[87] J. Nye 呼吁美国加强它的软力量以补充其硬力量，尽管美国已经是"自罗马帝国以来最强大的力量"，但单靠硬力量还不足以"在世界上为所欲为"。参见 J. Nye: *The Paradox of American Power: Why the World's Only Superpower Can't Go It Alone.* Oxford Univ. Pr., 2002。

有哲学和伦理学优势 (virtue)，它具有世界尺度，所以能够反思世界性利益，它又是一个冲突最小化的模式，最有利于保证世界文化知识的生态。由于天下概念意味着先验的、完成式的世界整体性，因此它是个全球观点 (globalism) 而不是全球化要求。必须强调的是，虽然天下理念是中国提出来的理论，但天下体系的理想不等于中国古代帝国的实践。由于中国古代帝国仅仅部分地而且非常有限地实践了天下理想，所以这一不完美的实践主要是形成了专制帝国，而并没有形成一个今天世界所需要的榜样。显然，天下理念只是一个理论准备，它仅仅是个值得研究的问题和值得利用的思想资源，特别是天下理念所包含的世界先验一体性观念、他者哲学以及和谐理论。

世界制度在现实性上尽管遥远，可是它又是世界的迫切需要，这一点有些悖论性。美国对伊拉克的战争本身就是这个世界作为"问题世界"的集中表现。为了不卷入烦琐论证，在这里我们不讨论哪一方比较正义或不正义，重要的是，这一事件说明了这个世界没有能力解决世界性问题。世界的无能在各种冲突还没有极端化的时候并不明显，因为人们似乎可以指望"对话"，尤其是哈贝马斯想象的满足了理想商谈条件的长期理性对话。但是哈贝马斯忽视了两个致命的问题：其一，有一些事情无论经过什么样的理性对话都仍然是不可互相接受的，即"理解不能保证接受"的问题；其二，还有一些事情涉及当下利益，假如不马上行动就会错过机会而失去利益，即"时不我待"问题，它说明了在对话上的时间投资会导致利益上的损失。于是，当问题以话语的方式提出来总是不太严重的，而当问题以行动的方式提出来，世界就茫然失措，因为没有什么样的话语能够回应行动的问题。这就是"对话哲学"的破产。

传统哲学曾经试图独断地给出关于事物的真理，但是各种文化和不同的知识体系的存在使得单方面的真理成为不可能，于是当代哲学的一个努力是把真理的证明转化为观念的对话，"同意" (agreement) 优先于"真理"。但是现在我们又看到了对话哲学的破产，当行动提出话语无能力回应的问题时就破产了。哲学在追求真理与知识然后又是利益和对话的路上走到了头，现在有理由认为，我们通常用来表述和分析各种问题的"概念体系"非常可能有着严重缺陷，以至于不能正确地理解事物。概念体系构成了思想的"计算单位"，假如计算单位不合理，即使思想的计算在逻辑上都是正确的，仍然可能错过重要的问题。前面的分析正是试图分析西方概念体系中的一种偏好，它总是选择诸如"个体"和"民族/国家"这样的实体作为决定性的计算单位，这种计算单位隐藏着一个内在的秘密：它的利益是独立的，不必与他者的利益挂钩。于是，对自身的利益最大化就可以：第一，不把他者的利益考虑在内；第二，如果涉及对他者利益的计算，那么就只想损人利己。这种行为不是伦理上的无耻或缺陷，而是一个利益能够单独成立的存在单位的存在论逻辑 (ontological necessity)。假如给定生活目的是利益，那么这种个体存在论 (the ontology of individuals) 是合适的，但是假如生活的目的是幸福，那么那种个体存在论是不成功的，因为，幸福的存在论条件是"关系"，幸福只能在成功的关系中产生，幸福只能是他者给的，自己不可能给自己幸福。中国哲学概念体系所偏好的"计算单位"往往强调一种存在论单位的关系结构，典型的如家庭和天下。中国哲学更为关心的是关系存在论 (the ontology of relations) 具有关系结构的存在论单位所提供的是关于幸福的逻辑，即它假定他者是自己的幸福条件甚至存在条件。基于"关系"而不是"个体"的哲学便形成了"无立场的眼界" (the view from everywhere) 而不是"特定角度的眼界" (the view from somewhere)。这样的概念体系对于分析和解决世界性问题是必需的，否则甚至不可能发现世界性问题的症结所在。

不过，传统天下理论还只是关于世界制度的初步理论准备，仍然有大量疑难问题存在，尤其是目前缺乏足够的实际条件来实现一种世界共同认可的世界制度。其中尤其缺乏的是能够形成世界性利益的社会结构，就是说，现在世界上的社会运动和人们的行为基本上都趋向个人利益和国家利益，而很少去发现和发展世界共同利益，所以很难形成人们之间或国家之间的"正面外在性"，即各方的行为碰巧在客观上形成互惠结构配置，也就是各方之间存在着利益的互相依附关系。许多人追求世界各国或各地在政治社会制度的同质性，这种做法很可能无助于解决任何冲突，因为政治制度的同质并不逻辑地蕴涵实际利益的对等和公正。因此，对全球政治社会制度同质化的追求 (不管是自由主义还是共产主义) 也许不是错误的，但非常可能是无效率的。各地人们所能够普遍满意的真实条件其实是物质利益和权力、知识和话语的发展水平的等量化，这样才能消解世界上的冲突、矛盾和战争。简单地说，凡是仅仅能够兑换成权利 (rights) 的东西都是虚的，凡是能够兑换成权力 (power) 的东西才是实的。

世界性利益不能仅仅是观念，而必须是实际存在的利益，否则没有人有追求它的积极性。如果在将来也不能慢慢地形成客观利益上的互惠结构，那么世界制度就遥遥无期而仅仅作为理想而存在。即使如此，理想仍然是重要的，它至少能够让我们知道错在什么地方。

The Context of the Project:
The Nine Gates of the Inner City of _Beijing_

项目背景简介

The Nine Gates of the Inner City of *Beijing*

The history of the city of *Beijing* extends back for over 2200 years. The city can be traced back to the slave societies of *Yan* and *Ji* during the *Shang* dynasty (1600BC – 1046BC). It was within the territory of these two small states. *Beijing* was known as *Nanjing* in the *Liao* dynasty (916 – 1125) also being known as *Yanjing*. In the *Jin* dynasty (1115 – 1234) *Beijing* formally became the capital. The *Yuan* (1279 – 1368), *Ming* (1368 - 1644), and *Qing* (1644 – 1911) dynasties all adopted *Beijing* as their political and cultural centres on the basis of the previous dynasties.

The construction of *Dadu*, the capital of the *Yuan* dynasty was a crucial turning point in the urban development and planning of *Beijing*. The city wall of the *Ming* dynasty was built on the foundations of *Dadu*'s city walls. The reconstruction of the inner city of *Beijing* was begun in the tenth year of the *Zhengtong* reign period (1445) during the *Ming* dynasty. The names of the nine gates were changed except for the *Desheng* and *Anding* Gates in the north wall. The *Lizheng*, *Wenming*, and *Shuncheng* Gates in the south wall were renamed respectively the *Zhengyang*, *Chongwen*, and *Xuanwu* Gates; the *Chongren* and *Qihua* Gates in the east wall were renamed the *Dongzhi* and *Chaoyang* Gates; the *Heyi* and *Pingze* Gates in the west wall were renamed the *Xizhi* and *Fucheng* Gates. The construction of the outer city was undertaken in the years of the *Jiajing* reign period (1522-1567) during the *Ming* dynasty.

The overall length of the inner city walls of *Beijing* are 6650 metres on the east-west axis and 5350 metres on the north-south axis. The overall length of the outer city walls are 7950 metres on the east-west axis and 3100 metres on the north-south axis. The city gates are the

北京内城九门

北京城市存在的历史至今长达两千二百多年, 可追溯至奴隶社会时代——商代的"燕"和"蓟", 当时作为这两个小国的领土; 辽代称北京为"南京", 又称"燕京"; 金朝时, 北京正式成为首都都城; 元、明、清三代王朝在之前朝代的基础上, 将北京作为政治、文化中心。

元大都的兴建在北京城市发展与规划上是一个重要转折点。明城墙是在元大都城土城垣基础上改造而成, 北京内城的改造是在明朝正统十年 (1445年)。九门的名称除北城墙的德胜、安定两门而外, 南面的丽正、文明、顺承改称正阳、崇文、宣武; 东面的崇仁、齐化改称东直、朝阳; 西面的和义、平则改称西直、阜成。外城的修筑是在明朝嘉靖年间。

北京城墙的内城墙东西长6650米, 南北长5350米; 外城墙东西长7950米, 南北长3100米。城门是城墙的重要组成部分。内城九门虽然在用途上没有明确分工, 但其名称不同, 含义也不同。

正阳门, 也称前门, 功能主要是政治上的, 有"国门"之称; 崇文门和宣武门, 其名称相对应, 按五行学说, 东为木、主生, 西为金, 主死, 进京赶考的举人要进崇文门, 死人出殡要走宣武门; 安定门和德胜门对称, 军队出征走安定门, 凯旋时从德胜门进城, 安定门也叫"生门", 有丰裕之意, 德胜门也叫"修门", 有品德高尚之意; 朝阳门对应于阜成门, 朝阳门有"粮门"之称, 阜成门多走煤车; 东

crucial components of the city walls. Although the nine gates of the inner city had no specific function, they had different names with different significances.

The *Zhengyang* Gate is also referred to as the Front Gate, *Qianmen*, the function of which was and is political. It is also known as the State Gate, *Guomen*. The names of the *Chongwen* Gate and *Xuanwu* Gate complimented each other. According to the theory of the Five Elements, East is associated with wood and governs life; West is associated with metal and governs death. The candidates attending the imperial examinations had to pass through the *Chongwen* Gate and funerals were obliged to leave the city through the *Xuanwu* Gate. The *Anding* Gate was symmetrical with the *Desheng* Gate. Armies set off from the city through the *Anding* Gate and returned through the *Desheng* Gate when they were victorious. The *Anding* Gate was also called the *Sheng* (to live) Gate and implies 'being in plenty'. The *Desheng* Gate was also called the *Xiu* (to cultivate) Gate and signified moral superiority. The *Chaoyang* Gate corresponded to the *Fucheng* Gate. The *Chaoyang* Gate was also known as the *Liang* (food/grain) Gate, and the coal vehicles always passed through the *Fucheng* Gate. The *Dongzhi* Gate corresponded to the *Xizhi* Gate. The *Dongzhi* Gate was also known as the *Shang* (business) Gate and was the focus of daily transactions; the *Xizhi* Gate was also called the *Kai* (open) Gate, meaning the gate from which the Government issued explicit instructions or directions to the people. The component structures of the city gates included a gate tower *chenglou*, an arrow tower *jianlou*, a barbican *wengcheng*, and a portcullis tower *zhalou*. Among the nine gates of the *Ming* and *Qing* dynasties, only the Gate Tower and the Arrow Tower of the *Zhengyang* Gate have survived together with the Arrow Tower of the *Desheng* Gate. The

直门和西直门遥相呼应，东直门有"商门"之称，多集中于从事日常买卖；西直门，又称"开门"，开放之门，意即晓喻之门。

城门的组成建筑包括城楼、箭楼、瓮城、闸楼。明清北京内城的九门中，现今只有正阳门的城楼、箭楼，和德胜门的箭楼得以保存。内城九门的拆除情况记录如下：

1、正阳门：1915年拆除掉瓮城和闸楼，城楼和箭楼保存至今。

2、崇文门：1920年拆除掉残存的箭楼废墟，1950年拆除掉瓮城，1965年拆除掉城楼。

3、宣武门：1927年拆除掉城楼，1930年拆除掉箭楼和瓮城。

4、阜成门：1935年拆除掉箭楼和闸楼，1953年拆除掉瓮城和箭楼台基，1965年拆除掉城楼。

5、西直门：1969年一并拆除掉城楼，箭楼，闸楼及瓮城。

6、德胜门：1915年拆除掉瓮城和闸楼，1921年拆除掉城楼，箭楼保存至今。

7、安定门：1915年拆除掉瓮城和闸楼，1969年拆除掉城楼和箭楼。

8、东直门：1915年拆除掉瓮城和闸楼，1927年拆除掉箭楼，1958年拆除掉城台，1965年拆除掉城楼。

9、朝阳门：1915年拆除掉瓮城和闸楼，1953年拆除掉城楼和城台，1957年拆除掉箭楼。

records of the demolition of the nine gates of the inner city are as follows:

The *Zhengyang* Gate: the Barbican and the Portcullis Tower were demolished in 1915; the Gate Tower and the Arrow Tower survive.

The *Chongwen* Gate: the ruins of the Arrow Tower were demolished in 1920; the Barbican was demolished in 1950; the Gate Tower was demolished in 1965.

The *Xuanwu* Gate: the Gate Tower was demolished in 1927; the Arrow Tower and the Barbican were demolished in 1930.

The *Fucheng* Gate: the Arrow Tower and the Portcullis Tower were demolished in 1935; the Barbican and the earthworks of the Arrow Tower were demolished in 1953; the Gate Tower was demolished in 1965.

The *Xizhi* Gate: the Gate Tower, Arrow Tower, Barbican and the Portcullis Tower were all demolished in 1969.

The *Desheng* Gate: the Barbican and Portcullis Tower were demolished in 1915; the Gate Tower was demolished in 1921; the Arrow Tower survives.

The *Anding* Gate: the Barbican and Portcullis Tower were demolished in 1915; the Gate Tower and Arrow Tower were demolished in 1969.

The *Dongzhi* Gate: the Barbican and Portcullis Tower were demolished in 1915; the Arrow Tower was demolished in 1927; the foundation platform was demolished in 1958; the Gate Tower was demolished in 1965.

The *Chaoyang* Gate; the Barbican and Portcullis Tower were demolished in 1915; the Gate Tower and the foundation platform were demolished in 1953; the Arrow Tower was

至于拆除的原因，在历史上复杂多样。比如正阳门、德胜门、安定门、东直门和朝阳门这五个城门都在1915年被拆除掉部分建筑，是由于当时北京城在修建环城铁路，为了改造交通所导致的；又比如崇文门的箭楼是在八国联军入侵时被炸损的，因为没有得到及时修复，于1920年拆除掉其箭楼废墟。

北京城的内城九门，虽然大部分实体建筑已不复存在，但它们确是北京城市发展及规划史上——乃至国家文化史上无法忽略不计的组成因素。

demolished in 1957.

The reasons for the demolition of the structural elements of the gates are complicated and various. For example, some parts of the *Zhengyang* Gate, *Desheng* Gate, *Anding* Gate, *Dongzhi* Gate and the *Chaoyang* Gate, were demolished in 1915 due to the construction of the railway around *Beijing*, intended to ease the flow of traffic through the city. The Arrow Tower of the *Chongwen* Gate was destroyed by the Eight-Nations Allied Forces when it entered *Beijing* during the so-called Boxer Uprising. The ruins of the Arrow Tower were demolished in 1920 due to their not having been repaired.

Although most of the structures of the nine gates of the inner city of *Beijing* no longer exist, they are indeed elements that cannot be ignored in the history of the urban development and planning of *Beijing* and even more so in the context of the country's cultural history.

Lu Hao
Project: Replicated Memory

卢昊 《复制的记忆》方案

Archives

视觉档案

　　城墙，是人类文明发展到一个重要阶段的产物和象征，也是冷兵器时代规模最大、最有效的防御体系。而在中国，城市的出现是以城墙的建造为标志的，它经历了数千年的演进。高耸而壮美的明清北京城墙、城门，既是古都北京历史上最高大雄伟、最坚固完美的军事防御体系，也是其最鲜明生动而又独具特色的形象标志。

　　在中国古代建筑城池的观念中，城墙既是统治者护卫自己政权主要的军事防御设施，也是统治者中心形象的扩大。在城市设计中，建城又等于计划一座庞大的建筑物。因此，作为国都的围墙，始终是都邑规划和建筑形制不可或缺的组成部分。换言之，北京城从它的产生、演变，乃至其平面构成出现"品"字形的格局，都具有历史意义。北京城墙，以及宏丽嶙峋的城门楼、箭楼、角楼等，也构成了整个北京城整体环境中不可分割的艺术构成部分。而对北京城的认识也往往是从城墙、城门伊始的。

A diagram of the changes to and
movement of *Dadu* during the
Yuan dynasty and *Ming* dynasty
Beijing.
元大都城与明北京城变迁示意图

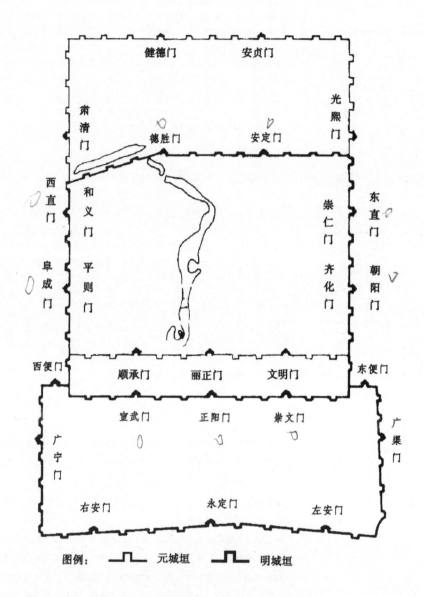

健德门　　安贞门

光熙门

肃清门

西直门

和义门

平则门

阜成门

德胜门　　安定门

崇仁门

齐化门

东直门

朝阳门

西便门　　顺承门　　丽正门　　文明门　　东便门

宣武门　　正阳门　　崇文门

广宁门

广渠门

右安门　　永定门　　左安门

图例：⎍⎎ 元城垣　⎍⎎ 明城垣

　　城门实际是一组防御设施建筑的总称，一般包括：城楼，筑在略高略宽于城墙且与城墙连为一体的城台上，其下城台正中辟城楼门，是城门防御的最后一道防线；瓮城，是建在城楼前的一座小城堡，其墙体高、宽略同于城墙且与城楼左右城墙连为一体，平面呈方形、长方形或半圆形，起到防御线外移保护城楼的作用；箭楼，筑在瓮城上对着城楼之处，对外的三面每层辟有对外攻击或防御的箭窗数孔至十数孔，其下城台略高略宽于瓮城墙体且与瓮城连为一整体，城台不辟或辟箭楼门，视其位置和需要而定；闸楼，形似"小箭楼"，亦三面辟有箭窗，筑在瓮城之上或左、或右、或左右皆有，其下辟门，但不设门扇，而设有闸楼控制的可吊起或放下的"千斤闸"，内城的闸楼门一般是与邻近瓮城闸楼门两两相对。

The changes in position of
Beijing's walls
北京城址变迁图

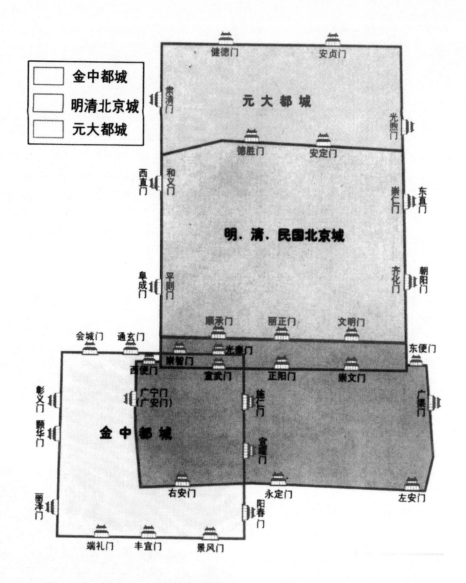

1995 年 10 月，中科院院士、历史地理学家、北京大学教授侯仁之先生，为矗立在今广安门立交桥北侧滨河公园内的"蓟城纪念柱"题写了"北京建城记"：

北京建城之始，其名曰蓟。《礼记·乐记》载，孔子授徒曰："武王克殷反商，未及下车而封黄帝之后于蓟。"《史记·燕召公世家》称："周武王之灭纣，封召公于北燕。"燕在蓟之西约百里。春秋时期，燕并蓟，移治蓟城。蓟城核心部位在今宣武区，地近华北平原北墙，系中原与塞上来往交通之枢纽。

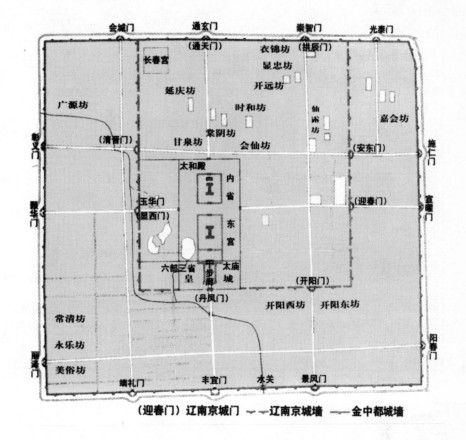

Diagram of the walls of *Nanjing* during the *Liao* dynasty, and of *Zhongdu*, the central capital of the *Jin* dynasty.
辽南京城与金中都城示意图

蓟之得名源于蓟丘。北魏郦道元《水经注》有记曰："今城内西北隅有蓟丘，因丘以名邑也，犹鲁之曲阜、齐之营丘矣。"正以同书所记蓟城之河湖水系，其中心位置在今宣武区广安门外。

蓟城四界，初见于《太平寰宇记》所引《郡国记》其书不晚欲唐代。所记蓟城"南北九里，东西七里"，呈长方形。有可资考证者，即其西南两墙外，为今莲花河故道所经；其东西墙内有唐代悯忠寺，即今法源寺。

西唐至辽，初设五京，以蓟城为南京，实系陪都。今之天宁寺塔，即当时城中巨构。金朝继起，扩建其东西南三面，改称中都，是为北京正式建都之始。惜其宫阙苑囿湮废已久，残留至今者惟鱼藻池一处，即今宣武区之青年湖。

金元易代之际，与中都东北郊外更建大都。明初缩减大都北部，改称北平；其后展筑南墙，始称北京；及至中叶，加筑外城，乃将古代蓟城东部纳入城中。历明及清，相沿至今，逐为成人民首都之规划建设奠定基础。

综上所述，今日北京城起源于蓟，蓟城之中心在宣武区。其地承前启后，源远流长。立石为记，永志不忘。

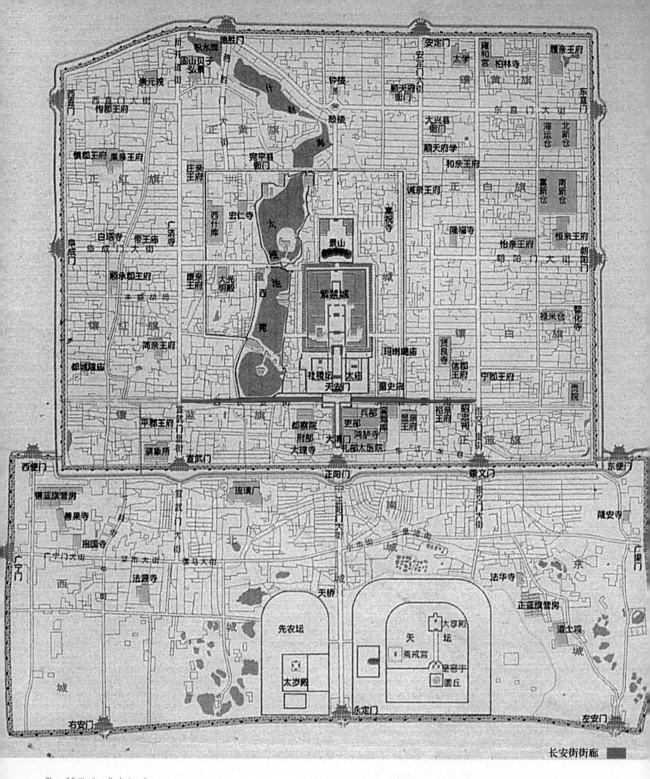

Plan of *Beijing's* walls during the
Qing dynasty (1750)
清代北京城平面图（1750年）

城市规划属于上层建筑范畴。其理念、方法无不受到政治制度、社会经济、科学技术水平、传统文化的强烈影响。明清北京城的规划建设，首先秉承了"天人合一，象天设都"的规划理念，同时也受到了《周易》《尚书》《周礼》《礼记》《史记》《管子》《诗经》《孙子》《山海经》《葬经》等古代著名典籍的深刻影响。而这条被称之为"基本定式"的中轴线，便是自周秦以来，尤其是隋唐以来，都城建设"天人合一，象天设都"高度抽象化的表达方式。

老北京城建筑布局中的中轴线是很出名的，像这样恢宏，这样壮观的中轴线在世界城市中不敢说绝无仅有，至少也是极罕见的。在这条中轴线上，有闻名世界的紫禁城，有太庙和社稷坛，有如盆景一样的景山，有风格独特的钟楼和鼓楼……还有新中国成立后修建的天安门广场、人民英雄纪念碑、人民大会堂、历史博物馆和革命博物馆，还有毛主席纪念堂。在中轴线的两侧，有天坛、北海、皇史成等等。总之，体现北京作为政治和文化中心、历史文化名城，以及千年古都的标志性建筑，似乎在这条中轴线上都得以展示。甚至代表共和国的五星红旗，每天清晨和傍晚、都是由国旗班的战士，踏着正步、走在广场的中轴线上去升降。

相比之下，贯穿世界上很多有名的城市中心的往往是一条河。考古界通常认为，人类最初的城市大都建立在河流两岸，那体现得更多的是人与自然的关系，是人类生存的需要和文明发展的选择。

而北京的中轴线却是人造的，因此它能有严格的左右对称和层次递进，设计精确和起伏有序，有实用性和意识形态的高度统一，它的构成是我们祖宗两千年封建伦理、皇权至高无上的观念在城市建设中的体现。当然，任何一种建筑形式，都不中避免地要反映时代的思想和审美取向。今天，中轴线所包容的建筑形式和理念作为宝贵的文化遗产被研究和发扬。

比较而言，北京的中轴线或许缺乏一点人与自然的协调，但它毕竟是屹立在世界东方的大国首都的一条龙脉，有它特有的庄严之美、堂堂正正的气派和丰富的人文内涵。它是老北京城永远不倒的品牌，老话说：是招牌。

The Arrow Tower, *Desheng* Gate
德胜门箭楼

　　明嘉靖三十二年修建了外城，于是出现了"内城"。明清的北京内城是在元代大都城的基础改建而成。明洪武元年（1368）太祖朱元璋定都南京；派徐达攻克大都城后，改大都为北平，将其北垣向南缩五里新筑。大都城原北二、东西南各三、共十一座城门。徐达废原光熙、肃清、健德、安贞四门，其余门名仍依元旧，于新北垣辟德胜、安定二门，则北平城共九门。洪武二年（1369）改北平崇仁门为东直门，和义门为西直门，并在各门外筑瓮城，将城墙外侧以砖包砌。永乐元年（1403）改北平为北京，并定都。永乐四年，诏建北京宫殿、修城垣城门。永乐十七年（1419）将原大都城南垣南拓二里，是为北京城南垣。永乐十八年（1420）北京宫殿城垣成，明都城自应天（南京）迁至北京。明正统元年（1436）诏修北京九门城楼、瓮城及角楼，二年兴工，四年修讫；改丽正门为正阳门，文明门为崇文门，顺承为宣武门，齐化门为朝阳门，平则门为阜成门。清依明旧，相沿至今。内城九门的瓮城内均设庙宇，除正阳门为两座庙外，其余八门各一座；除德胜门、安定门为真武庙外，余皆为关帝庙；正阳门除一座关帝庙外，尚有一座观音庙；除德胜门、安定门的庙是在箭楼下正中面对城门洞处外，余皆在城门洞或左或右，多偏于闸楼门处。城门瓮城内设庙始于明代。目前在明清北京内城的九门中，仅正阳门城楼、箭楼、德胜门箭楼得以保存，其余都消失在历史的尘埃中。正阳门城楼、箭楼于 1988 年 1 月被国务院公布为全国重点文物保护单位；德胜门箭楼于 1979 年 8 月 21 日被北京政府公布为北京市文物保护单位。

The southern aspect of the
late *Qing* period *Desheng* Gate
Tower, demolished in 1921
清末德胜门城楼南侧，1921年
拆除

The *Zhengyang* Gate Tower and
Arrow Tower
正阳门城楼及箭楼

Zhengyang Gate

The demolition of the barbican
of the *Zhengyang* Gate in 1915
1915年拆除正阳门瓮城时的情形

The north face of the
Zhengyang Gate before building
modifications, photograph
taken before1915.
未改建之前的正阳门北侧，摄于
1915年之前。

The *Zhengyang* Gate after the
demolition of the barbican and
the construction of the two
walkways through the wall
1915年被拆除瓮城并在两侧增
建券洞后的正阳门

　　正阳门城楼南面的全貌，是 1916 年之后不久从箭楼向北拍摄的。左右城墙上各辟两个门洞，是城门改造的工程项目之一。东门洞直通户部街，西门洞直通刑部街。工程于 1916 年完工。当时有人写道："人马纷纷不可论，插车每易见前门。而今出入东西畔，鱼贯行来妙莫言。"其注曰："出入车马，前门最多。往日一经插车，动致时许；今则东出西入，井井有条，往来行人，无不称便。"（《京华百二竹枝词》）

Panoramic photograph of the
south side of the *Zhengyang*
Gate Tower
正阳门城楼南面全景

The present day *Zhengyang* Gate
现在的正阳门

South-east aspect of the
Desheng Gate, late *Qing* dynasty
清末德胜门城楼东南侧

The *Desheng* Gate in 1915
德胜门（1915年）

The *Desheng* Gate
德胜门

***Chongwen* Gate**

The *Chongwen* (*Wenming*)
Gate during the period of the
Republic of China
崇文门（文明门，民国时期）

The Tower of the *Chongwen*
Gate before demolition
即将拆掉的崇文门城楼

The *Chongwen* Gate in 1909,
The Eight Nations Allied Army
demolished the Barbican and
the Portcullis Tower and the
Guandi Shrine, allowing railway
lines to pass across the gateway,
the track may be seen in the
photograph.
1909年的崇文门，八国联军拆
掉崇文门瓮城闸楼及关帝庙，
使火车穿瓮城而过。图中可见
到铁轨。

Xuanwu Gate

The *Xuanwu* (*Shuncheng*)
Gate during the period of the
Republic of China
宣武门（顺承门，民国时期）

The Noon cannons of the *Xuanwu* Gate
宣武午炮

　　这幅是 20 年代拍摄的著名的"宣武午炮"现场照,地点是宣武门东侧的城墙顶上。宣武门有很多史迹、典故、功能、作用值得述说,但最值得一提的是"宣武午炮"。炮有五尊,铁铸,但不是用于战争,而是鸣放报时。民国时的《最新北平指南》载:"午炮有两处,一在宣武门以东的城墙上,一在德胜门以东的城墙上。每日午时燃火药炮一声,声震遐迩,用于城中人们对时之用。人称'宣武午炮'"。

Fucheng Gate

The East aspect of the Gate
Tower of the *Fucheng* Gate in
the 1930s, demolished in 1965.
20世纪30个代的阜成门城楼东
侧，1965年拆除。

The *Fucheng* (*Pingce*) Gate during the
period of the Republic of China
阜成门（平侧门，民国时期）

Xizhi Gate

The Eastern aspect of the *Xizhi* Gate Tower
西直门城楼东侧

A panoramic view of the *Xizhi*
Gate after rebuilding in 1950
1950年修整后的西直门全景

The *Xizhi* Gate during demolition
拆除中尚余立柱的西直门

The *Anding* Gate during the
period of the Republic of China
安定门（民国时期）

Anding Gate

An exterior view of the *Anding*
Gate in 1860
1960年的安定门外景

The *Anding* Gate with scaffolding,
in preparation for its demolition
正在搭架准备拆除的安定门城楼

The *Dongzhi* Gate during the
late *Qing* dynasty
清末的东直门

Dongzhi Gate

The *Dongzhi* Gate during the 1920s
20年代的东直门

The western aspect of the Arrow
Tower of the *Dongzhi* gate in 1951
1951年的东直门箭楼西侧

Chaoyang Gate

The *Chaoyang* Gate at the end
of the *Qing* dynasty
清末的朝阳门

The *Chaoyang (Qihua)* Gate
during the period of the
Republic of China
朝阳门（齐化门，民国时期）

Other gates from the Inner City
其他外城门

The *Yongding* Gate
永定门

The *Yongding* Gate at the time
of the Republic of China
明国时期的永定门

The Gate Tower of the *Yongding* Gate
永定门城楼

The Arrow Tower of the
Guangan Gate, at the time of
the Republic of China
民国时期的广安门箭楼

Replicated Memory

Based on an interview with *Lu Hao* in *Beijing*
on 7th July 2007

《复制的记忆》

时间: 2007年7月5日
地点: 北京
采访对象: 卢昊

I advised the curator *Huang Zhuan* of my plan to build a light-box, about 10 square-metres in size, then place an old city map of *Beijing* on top of it. Although my original idea was to reproduce the nine city gates on a large scale, it was not realistic when one considered the budget available. I used transparent acrylic sheet to build the models of the nine city gates, so this work has a sense of 'State Legacy'.

In expressing the subject of *Beijing*, I think it was interesting to use transparent acrylic sheet. It's there and yet it's not there. It's illusory. Moreover transparent acrylic material feels modern in itself.

I tried to find the plans of the nine city gates. Later I found out that they are the same in structure. I used to think they were different. I also found a lot of information about the gates, finishing my investigation at the end of last year. Nowadays, it is easier to get the information one needs. My information was obtained from traditional Chinese landscape architectural engineering companies and construction teams, also from the Internet.

My creative work is all about the buildings of *Beijing*. I regard myself as a native *Beijing* artist and have a right to have my say on the affairs of *Beijing*. Somebody has called me 'an aboriginal artist'; I feel that is a great honour. I do not want to be referred to as 'an international artist', that is ridiculous. I am an aboriginal artist, or a folk artist. My interests are always with my city – *Beijing*, the small street of *Beijing* known as *Hutong*, my neighbours and what happens around me.

The words that artists want to express are all said through their works. What I have to do is to present this piece of work to people, so they will understand the message in my work.

问：能具体讲讲您构思《复制的记忆》这件作品的过程吗？

卢：复制九城门起初是按照北京城市规划委员会重新复制永定门的想法做的。我觉得很不可思议，在考古学这么发达的时候，居然能够把这么重要的人类文明都毁掉了！我觉得所有这些正在被复制的古城门都应该用有机玻璃来复制才有意思。我原来跟策展人黄专谈过，我的作品要做一个灯箱，按比例大概是10平方米左右，放有老北京的地图，原来构想大规模复制九城门，但是已经不可能，投资太大。后来我的方案就是用有机玻璃来实现这个作品，下面是一个灯箱，做一个北京地区的老地图，在这个基础上放置九个城门。这件作品也有"国家遗产"的意味。

问：您是按照什么样的比例来复制九城门？

卢：应该是1：300或1：500，太大了做不了。

问：为什么选择有机玻璃？

卢：对于北京的主题，我觉得选择有机玻璃挺有意思。它介于存在与不存在之间，用透明的有机玻璃来做一种虚拟的概念。而且这种透明的有机玻璃化学材料，本身有现代感，它不同于青铜、

If you ask me to express my concept, I have to admit that I feel saddened by these years of large-scale urban reconstruction and modernization in *Beijing* which uprooted the city in this way. It is not just that the buildings have disappeared, the living habits of the people, the stories that were formed in those old buildings; some of the characteristics of the city of *Beijing* have disappeared.

The city gates and walls of *Beijing* have nearly all been demolished. Many of the gates were demolished after 1949, when the city was being re-planed. At the time experts in architecture and city planning proposed to build a new city to the west of *Beijing*, leaving the old city untouched. Of course this plan could not have been easy to approve. The newly established state lacked investment and *Tiananmen* Square is a popular space for people to gather together. In such a conflict, it is a certainty that culture will always give way to politics. Thus the demolition of all the city gates together with sections of city walls went ahead, also demolished was part of inner *Tiananmen* Gate. I heard that *Liang Sicheng*, the first modern architect in China, cried and bent his knees to plead for the demolition to be stopped. I think the Chinese should build statues to commemorate people like *Liang*, who dare to do what they think is right despite being under political pressure. I felt that the damage done to the city compared with the bombing of Berlin during the Second World War. I am speechless at what the Chinese have done. If we had preserved *Beijing*'s old city, it might have compared favourably with Rome?

I feel that the concept of restoring antiques and making fake antiques are different. If the nine city gates still existed we might have made some repairs to their beams or pillars. This

铁，不同于雕塑手法的其它材质，我对这种化学材质的现代感很感兴趣。

问：重新复制永定门是已经下了文件的吗？您是如何看待这种"复原的"？
卢：没有下文件，是象征性的。永定门的城楼在原有的遗址上复原了，就是说在永定门的遗址上重新建了一个新的楼，我觉得这挺荒唐的，有点像琉璃厂，它实际上是一个假文物，已经跟"文物"没有什么关系了。北京内城九门比较有代表性，这也是我复制它们的一个理由，多了我也复制不了，条件有限。

其实这个事情我也不是很了解，当时开车经过那看到一个复原了的永定门，很惊讶。但我觉得其它几个城门的复原就不太可能。这种复原就是造假古董，有什么意义呢？它无法给我们传递原有的信息和符号，就像我们去挖一个古墓，一开始我们为了保存它，就很小心翼翼地去找，因为这些东西是无法再生的，而且这些东西被破坏了以后，它传达的信息就不准确了。但是如果我们把这整个东西都填平了炸塌了以后，再按照以前的设想重新盖一个古墓，这就没有任何意义。它除了变新了，变成一个好看的景观之外就没有什么了。

我去过梵蒂冈，当时去的时候我不是去那些旅游的景点，我有一朋友在意大利工作，他的工作

is quite different from demolishing the whole thing and then building a brand new one. We know that the *Tiananmen* Gate is a newly renovated building. Although it is slightly bigger that the old gate, it was restored based on the original earthworks and structure. That seems acceptable.

Today, the *Yongding* Gate, one of the outer city gates and demolished in the 1950s has been rebuilt on its old site. The whole thing is absurd. I drove past it and felt astonished - it is a fake antique. What is the point of it? It has none of the original symbolism and message. It is brand-new, just part of the view, a folly - nothing else.

I have been to the Vatican, one of my friends works there restoring the old frescoes. He draws grids on the frescoes first and then repairs one grid square at a time. The repair of one fresco took three to four years to complete. Many ancient Roman buildings have been restored during recent centuries. Neither granite nor calcareous buildings last long. I came to know that in Italy, France…or indeed in the whole of Southern Europe, the rain is acidic and strongly corrosive. Does that mean that people are unable to preserve buildings? Later I found that, as long as people have no intention of dismantling them, these buildings would last anyway.

The will of the people is the decisive factor in the preservation of ancient buildings. If we want our buildings to be long lasting, we will find a way to protect them. Are there other ways to protect the Imperial Garden of the Summer Palace or the *Ming* Dynasty Tombs? Many tourists tread these sites everyday, I don't know if that is a good thing or a bad thing. If we want to preserve those historical relics, we may have to consider not opening them to the

就是每天在梵蒂冈里面修复这些古壁画, 在这些壁画上面打上网格来进行修复, 修复一幅壁画有可能需要三、四年的时间。

我觉得修复跟造假还是不一样的, 就好像一个人生病了, 他需要板蓝根, 但没找到板蓝根, 找到感冒冲剂, 也可以。区别取决于一开始的态度。比如现在如果九个城门都还保存着, 但房梁塌了, 我们找一些梁、柱子对它进行修复, 跟我们把这些东西全部推倒了重新再盖, 不是一个概念。其实现在的天安门也是新的, 老的天安门比现在这个小, 它已经扩大了, 但原来的地基之类的都没动, 就只是修复了一下, 这就还是不一样。所以如果我们喜欢老爷车, 我们不断地在修理它, 这车还在, 就传递了一个符号给别人, 但如果我们把这车整个儿往河里面扔, 找一个类似的零件安装在现在的车上, 那就不叫老爷车了, 那没有任何意义, 现在很多婚纱车也使用这种车, 但那也不是老爷车, 从出厂的时候, 这个车上面的配件所经历的年代跟这个车就没有关系了。

问：据您所知, 目前北京内城九门的状况怎样？
卢：城门和城墙几乎都拆了。北京内城九门 (德盛门、安定门、西直门、阜城门、东直门、朝阳门、宣武门、正阳门、崇文门) 只有正阳门 (前门) 保留, 崇文门、德盛门保留的只是箭楼而非城门。我觉

public. They are more like art galleries, not all the people appreciate them. Why give people who have no sense of understanding access to these sites they only throw rubbish and spit mucus around? There is no support in the work of protecting these buildings. It is only for the benefit of the management team – although the workers can earn a bit more selling tickets.

Aside from the Summer Palace, the Forbidden City has not been properly protected - some of its ancient buildings have been demolished; new buildings have been added without any historical consideration, many of the remaining buildings are in need of renovation. Parks in other countries we visited are places of quiet and comfort. I cannot believe that parks have been turned into supermarkets in our country. As soon as you enter them you feel clamour and noise. I remember the Long Corridor of the Summer Palace when I visited it as a little boy, except for those who were viewing or interpreting the paintings on the Corridor, few people were around. Parks should be a place for people to relax. But you can't find such a place in *Beijing*.

We add new buildings beside ancient ones. The Historical Museum, now the National Museum and the Great Hall of the People are European style buildings and have nothing to do with Chinese tradition. Although we have to accept such things now, there were huge arguments as to whether we should build these kinds of buildings at the time. However, because our leaders visited the Soviet Union and saw what they had built, they must have decided that we must have bigger buildings than the USSR. The Grandstands of *Tiananmen* Gate are ridiculous building, from which to review army parades, a facility just for that purpose. Was that not cynical? In my opinion, only *Liang Sicheng* can be called an architect, he

得只有在二战德国被炸毁的时候才会有这种情况，我挺"佩服"中国人的……其实按我的想法，我想在北京九个城门的地方用有机玻璃装起城门城墙——当然这是不可能的。

问：您知道具体是什么时候拆这九个城门的吗？

卢：据我所知，是1949年以后拆的，1949年以后北京要改变城市格局，当时在50年代有一些建筑专家和规划专家讨论过这样的问题，他们提议在北京的西边再建一个新城，而保持老城的原有不动，在那基础上再盖一个新城，当然，这个东西肯定会受限制，因为当时刚刚建国没有钱，而且天安门广场是一个天然形成的广场。碰到这样的矛盾，通常是文化给政治让步，所以就拆掉了这些老城门，拆掉了天安门里面的一部分，保存了天安门的另一部分，然后把北京的很多城墙都给拆了。听说当时拆这些城墙的时候，梁思成哭了，还上去给人下跪了，说千万别拆这些东西……我觉得中国应该为梁思成和马寅初这样的人立铜像，他们是多了不起的人，他们面对政治压力的时候，仍然在做良心让他们做的事情，这种人现在太少了。如果保留这些东西，就很难说北京跟罗马比怎样。

问：能具体讲讲您掌握九城门相关资料的情况吗？

protected structures of cultural importance. What were the other intellectuals doing? Some of them sang high praises for the Grandstands and said that it did not affect the outlook of the *Tiananmen* Gate Tower. The cart was put before the horse. Black was sworn to be white.

The only fortunate thing for *Beijing* is that it has thousands of years of history; all the things accumulated over those thousands of years cannot be destroyed in a couple of decades.

I cannot say that I am optimistic, because we are forced to accept changes. I know an old man who used to live in central *Beijing*. He was offered some ten thousand *yuan* to move to a suburb of *Beijing*. Such a move presented all manner of problems for him. Firstly, how would his grandson continue his education? Secondly, how would his family members get to work everyday? The money he was offered was not enough to buy another house, how could he solve those problems? Did he even have any choice over whether he moved to the suburb or not? He had no choice. This is what I mean when I say that people are forced to accept being pushed out of their homes, they have no way to resist.

Artists should always be concerned about social issues, they should care about the most common problems; not overlook them. For me, the most common problem in *Beijing* today is the scale of the city, people are being pushed out; old buildings are being demolished to build new, this is our social reality. We can see these things happening every day and we must do something about it.

My earliest consciousness of the state basically came in the form of confrontation. At that time I believed the only state bold enough to confront the two strongest countries in

卢：我找过九城门的设计图纸，我原来以为九个城楼的结构有差别，后来发现它们的外形结构都一样，当然功能是不一样的。

我找了很多资料，从去年就搜集完了。先把建筑的大概结构、比例了解了。现在获取资料比较容易，城门的古建队、古建公司都会提供的，网上也可以查到很多资料。

问：《复制九城门》这件作品是否延续了您一直以来创作的关注点？

卢：我基本上是以北京的建筑为创作题材。我觉得我是一个北京籍的艺术家，对于北京城市的成长变化，我觉得我有发言权，如果去了别的地方，我就觉得起码我不比当地人有发言权，所以到现在，除了北京，我对中国的其它城市都不感兴趣。我所有的作品都是围绕着北京的胡同、我的邻居、我周围发生的事情，我对周围和我生活有关的东西感兴趣。有人说我是一个北京的"土著艺术家"，我觉得这是对我特大的赞扬，我特怕别人说我是一个"国际艺术家"，这挺可笑的，我觉得我就是一土著艺术家，或者是一个民间艺术家。

问：能否讲讲您创作这件作品的想法？

the world was China. In my mind, leaders like *Mao Zedong* and *Zhou Enlai* appeared the icons of the state. Now the impression I have of the concept of 'state' has been turned into one of 'chief steward' that manages billions of people, a bit like some of the biggest tycoons and corporations. The state is no longer a concept that embraces democracy and confronts others with ideology, now the state embraces global economic unification – we demolished the old buildings of the *Hutong* and built so called new architecture, what do those new buildings mean to us? We are working hard to demolish our culture and turn our state into the offices and warehouses of other developed countries, this appears to be our main effort at this moment, I feel the state is more like a 'chief steward'.

卢：我觉得艺术家要说的话，全都在他的作品里面说了，我要做的就是把这个作品呈现出来，至于这个作品呈现的方式是什么，我觉得是在它展出之后大家就明白了，但是让我来叙述自己的观念，只能说北京这些年来，大规模的城市改造，现代化建设的这种连根拔起的状况让我很惋惜，因为这里面，不光是一个建筑消失了，人的生活习惯，老的建筑里面发生过的故事，北京的一些城市特点，也全随着消失了。

　　除了颐和园，故宫——故宫还是拆了一部分，现在里面盖了很多乱七八糟的东西，很多梁柱也都残破了。我们通常看国外的公园，会觉得那是一个特别安静和舒适的环境，但我惊奇的是我们的国家把公园变成一个超级市场了，你一进去会有特别喧哗的感觉。我小时候看过的颐和园的长廊，没有几个人，只有一些在看长廊的画和讲解画的人。公园应该是一个让人休息的地方，但在北京现在基本上找不到这样的地方。

　　我觉得可能也只有艺术家能做这个工作，因为艺术家跟民工差不多，都是弱势群体，艺术家的作品除非有参加展览被人关注以外，已经没有任何人管，除了个别靠新闻做作品的艺术家以外，大部分人都还是弱势群体，所以，我觉得我情绪的流露，只能在我的作品里面体现出来。

问：对于古迹来说，可能还面临着老化之类的问题，所以需要修复改造，这与我们想永久保存它们也存在一个矛盾。

卢：古罗马的很多建筑也是近几百年经过修复的，实际上花岗岩和石灰岩的建筑也不能保持很久，我后来了解到，整个南欧的雨水含酸性很大，腐蚀性也很强——难道人就没有办法保存它了吗？后来发现，人只要不是有意识地去拆，这些东西保存的时间还是会很长的，比如敦煌的莫高窟。

其实我不觉得这是个问题，难道古罗马那些建筑矗立在那里就肯定不会塌吗？千百年之后肯定塌，但是还有人的主观愿望在那儿，我们希望它塌还是希望它矗立在那儿？如果我们希望它矗立，我们会找到一个办法来保存它，现在的颐和园和十三陵，不是都找到了更好的办法来保存了吗？我就觉得颐和园比以前新了，但是每天去那么多人在上面踩来踩去的，我也真不知道是好事还是坏事。我觉得这些建筑，包括这些历史遗存，不一定要对外开放，每天有人耷拉着脑袋进去颐和园看了，就说是好事了？他看不懂他能干嘛呢？他除了破坏——在里面扔点垃圾，吐点痰，他干不了什么，我觉得这其实跟美术馆是一样的，不是所有的人都能进去看，好比一个歌剧不是所有的人都能欣赏。这样的对外开放，除了有一个个别的单位的利益存在以外，实际上对文化保护并没有特别好的作用，颐和园的那些员工不都是为了多卖一些门票，赚钱改善自己的生活吗？就这么简单。

问：这种情况跟大众的心态和审美是否有关系？

卢：大众的审美是需要引导的，不是说他爱听"二人传"，我们就每天给他唱"二人传"；他喜欢《还珠格格》，就46个台都放《还珠格格》，天天循环播放。这也有问题。这些文艺节目的东西在我看来都是精神毒品，麻醉和软化了神经，老百姓们几个人，下班了，一打开电视机一看就是这些，再吃着饭，就high了，所以我觉得电视里面的这些垃圾有问题。没办法，一打开电视就全是这些，就只能在这些当中挑一个，自己觉得还行就行了，比如说我还可以看看凤凰卫视，看看新闻节目，尽管新闻节目也不一定是真的，但起码还能看看。

问：您觉得对"文物"的糟踏是每个朝代更替时所重蹈的悲剧吗？

卢：清朝除外，清朝除了把宫殿修复了一遍，和增加了一些新的设施之外，其它基本上没动，而明朝和其它朝代都是在拆的基础上来进行改造。我们也一样，比如人民大会堂、历史博物馆，还有观礼台——我觉得这个建筑挺荒诞的，我觉得在我眼里，只有梁思成配叫做建筑师，为什么？因为他在保护这些东西，而有的知识分子是在做什么事情呢？为了在天安门城楼检阅部队，为了完善设施，就做了像观礼台这样的东西，这不是犬儒吗？但是还有人因为做了这个东西而大书特书，说做这个东西没有影响原来的风貌——这是本末倒置，黑白颠倒。

我打一个比喻，比如说像历史博物馆和人民大会堂，它们完全是欧式建筑，实际上跟中国的传统建筑并没有关系，尽管现在我们能接受这个事了，但当时为了这个方案肯定也有很大的争议，是否真的要盖这样的东西？但当时我们的领导人出国就去了苏联，那心理就跟现在朝鲜人的领导是一样的：一定要盖比它还大的！

问：北京现在留存下来的东西很少？

卢：还有很多，北京好就好在，这么几千年，沉淀下来这么多东西，拆个几十年也拆不干净，并不是有意识地在保留，实在是因为没法全拆了，能拆的都拆。我听说最早的时候，连天安门都计划要拆掉，广场的面积，就是玄武门和端午们的位置计划要比现在的大，后来被拦住了，说应该保留这些，天安门城楼就没被拆。

问：您对中国目前的状况持悲观的态度。

卢：你觉得我应该乐观吗？因为我们所做的所有事情都是被迫接受的，就像我所知的北京有一个老头，本来住在市区，现在给了他几万块拆迁费，让他搬到郊区去，他一系列生活的问题就出现了，他孙子上小学的问题怎么解决？家里人上班的事情怎么解决？到了郊区，给他的那拆迁费也不够另买一房子，怎么解决这一系列的问题？但是他有什么权力决定不搬这个家？他没有什么权力，这种排挤对老百姓来说是被迫的，是没有办法的。

问：这也是艺术家的一种社会关怀了。

卢：艺术家总要去关心问题，关心一个显著的问题，而不是视而不见。在我看来，这种大规模的拆迁改造就是显著的事实，这种排挤现象，这种拆老的建新的，就是咱北京特别显著的社会现实，每天都能看得到的：建筑工地上那么大的塔标，那么多机器的轰隆声……把旧的的拆掉盖新的，这是你不能视而不见的。

问：您是如何理解"国家"这个概念的？

卢：我最早有国家意识的时候——基本上那时候是以对抗的形式存在的，那时候觉得敢于跟世界上两个最强的国家对抗的就是中国。在我脑子里，毛泽东、周恩来这样的领导人即作为一个国家的形象出现。现在我觉得国家的概念成了"管家"的概念了，就像是世界上几个最大的资本家、资本集团来管理十几亿人口的国家，它不再像以前，是个有民主意识的并形成对抗的国家，现在全球经济一体化——我们拆掉了所有的胡同、老房子，然后在上面盖了很多所谓的新楼房，但这些新楼房的实质是什么呢？我们在做的工作就是努力消除自己的文化，然后努力把自己的国家变成发达国家的办公室和厂房，这就是现在我们最大的工作，所以我觉得现在"国家"给我的感觉更像是"管家"。

Part II

第二部分

A Model of
Multi-Dimensional
Modernisation

一个多维的现代化模式

Contemporary Chinese Thought
and the Question of Modernity (1997)*

Wang Hui

* This is an edited version of the article originally published in China's New Order: Society, Politics, and Economy in Transition (pp. 139-187) by Harvard University Press, paperback edition 2006. It was first published in the journal *Tianya* (Frontiers) in 1997; the article was translated by Rebecca E. Karl and republished in Social Text in the United States.

当代中国的思想状况与现代性问题

汪 晖

The year 1989 was a historical watershed; nearly a century of socialist practice came to an end. Two worlds became one: a global-capitalist world. Although China's socialism did not collapse as did the Soviet Union's or Eastern Europe's, this was hardly a barrier to China's economy from quickly joining the globalizing process in the arenas of production and trade. Indeed, the Chinese government's persevering support for socialism does not pose an obstacle to the following conclusion: in all of its behaviors, including economic, political, and cultural - even in governmental behavior - China has completely conformed to the dictates of capital and the activities of the market. If we aspire to understand Chinese intellectual and cultural life in the last decade of the twentieth century, we must understand the above transformations and their corresponding social manifestations.[1]

Before moving into an analysis of contemporary Chinese thought, we must first explore several premises that bear an intimate relationship to thinking within intellectual circles in the 1990s.

Firstly, the 1989 *Tiananmen* incident did not change the fundamental reform path China has followed since the end of the 1970s; on the contrary, under state promotion, the pace of

---

[1] It would be better to call this essay a set of notes on my thought process rather than an academic article. I wrote a first draft in 1994 and have revised it several times since, but because of the limitations of the original version, and the fact that most of my efforts of late have been devoted to research on the intellectual history of the late *Qing* to the modern period, I have not been able to inclued any analysis of any of the discussions that have taken place since 1994. I am well aware that the essay's framework and content need further revision and augmentation. But my friends have urged me repeatedly to publish it, and I do so now mainly in the hope of eliciting further discussion.

1、历史已经终结?

1989, 一个历史性的界标。将近一个世纪的社会主义实践告一段落。两个世界变成了一个世界：一个全球化的资本主义世界。中国没有如同苏联、东欧社会主义国家那样瓦解, 但这并没有妨碍中国社会在经济领域迅速地进入全球化的生产和贸易过程。中国政府对社会主义的坚持并未妨碍下述结论：中国社会的各种行为, 包括经济、政治、文化行为甚至政府行为, 都深刻地受制于资本和市场的活动。如果我们试图理解20世纪最后十年的中国思想和文化状况, 就必须理解上述变迁及其伴随的社会变化。[1]

在进入对当代中国知识界的思想分析之前, 有必要提及几个与20世纪90年代中国知识界的思考密切相关的前提：

---

[1] 本文与其说是一篇学术论文, 不如说是一篇个人的思想札记。此文初稿写于1994年, 此后做过若干修订, 但限于原稿的状况, 以及我自己的精力主要在晚清至现代时期的思想史研究, 1994年以后发生的一些讨论没有能够成为讨论的对象。当时写作的动机主要是清理我自己的思想。我非常清楚这篇文章的框架以及所涉及的材料都有待进一步的修改、论证和补充。在朋友的一再鼓励下, 现将此文发表出来, 主要是为了引起讨论。

the reforms has been faster than even during the most open period of the 1980s (by reforms, I refer primarily to the adaptation to marketization and to the process of economic and legislative structural reforms). Through the stepped-up reforms in the systems of production, trade, and finance, China has increasingly entered into the competition of the world market, with the result that the restructuring of the domestic social and production mechanisms has been undertaken under restrictions imposed by the contemporary market system. Moreover, commercialization and its attendant consumer culture have thoroughly penetrated every aspect of social life, thereby demonstrating that the painstaking creation of markets by the state and by enterprises is not merely an economic phenomenon. Rather, this social process ultimately seeks to use market rules to regulate all social life. In this context, not only have the original social and professional roles of the intellectuals profoundly changed, but so has the state, particularly the social and economic roles the government plays at every level - by daily becoming more intimately related to capital.

Secondly, in the 1990s, Chinese intellectual voices did not all emanate from China; rather, they also came from abroad. The 1989 *Tiananmen* incident precipitated a large westward outflow of prominent intellectuals; in addition, many scholars and others went abroad for different reasons and then either stayed or chose to live in exile. At the same time, a number of those who went to study in Europe, the United States, and Japan under the state policies on study abroad of the late-1970s have now received their degrees. Of those, there are some who are employed abroad and some who have returned to China. From the perspective of intellectual subjectivity, these two generations of Chinese intellectuals have

首先，1989年的事件没有改变中国自20世纪70年代末期以来的改革路线，相反，在国家的推动下，改革（主要是为适应市场化而进行的经济体制和立法方面的改革）的步伐较之20世纪80年代最为开放的时期更为激进：通过生产、贸易和金融体制的进一步改革，中国日益深入地加入到世界市场的竞争之中，从而内部的生产和社会机制的改造是在当代市场制度的规约之下进行的；另一方面，商业化及其与之相伴的消费主义文化渗透到社会生活的各个方面，从而表明国家和企业对市场的精心创制并不仅仅是一个经济事件，相反，这一社会过程最终要求用市场法则规划整个的社会生活。在这一历史情境中，不仅知识分子原有的社会角色和职业方式经历了深刻变化，而且国家、特别是各级政府在社会生活和经济生活中的角色相应地发生了变化，它们与经济资本的关系变得日益密切了。

其次，20世纪90年代中国知识界的声音并不都来自国内，而且也来自国外。一方面，1989年的事件造成了当代中国历史上大规模的主流知识分子的西迁，许多学者、知识分子基于不同的原因出国访问、滞留海外或选择流亡生涯；另一方面，20世纪70年代末期国家执行的留学生政策在20世纪90年代产生了影响，因为自那时起赴欧美和日本留学的许多学生陆续获得学位，其中相当一部分在这些国家获得职位，另一部分回到中国。从知识主体方面来说，这两代中国知识分子基于不同的经

undergone different experiences, but both have had the opportunity to fundamentally understand Western society and intellectual trends. They have brought their observations on Western society to bear on their analyses of Chinese questions, thus opening up a different perspective on China from that of those who stayed at home. From the perspective of the institutionalization of knowledge, contemporary education and research in China have gradually become structurally transnational, that is, the production of knowledge and research activities have been incorporated into the globalization process.

Thirdly, after 1989, intellectuals in China could not help but rethink their historical experiences.

Under pressure from the harsh environment and through their own choices, a large majority of intellectuals engaged in the humanities and social sciences gave up their 1980s New Enlightenment mode. After discussing the problem of intellectual norms and taking up increasingly specialized research, they clearly turned to a more professional mode of work. Owing to the dissolution of intellectual groups such as those devoted primarily to the introduction of Western scholarship under rubrics like 'Culture: China and the World', and the appearance of such periodicals as The Scholar that had research on Chinese history and thought at their cores, some people saw the intellectual activity in the 1990s as moving toward a revival of 'Chinese studies' (guoxue). This characterization is, however, inaccurate, no matter from what perspective one approaches it. To begin with, the 1989 incident obliged the scholarly world to review the implications of the intellectual movement of the 1980s and to reflect on the relationship between Chinese history and the cultural movement in which

验，得到了深入了解西方社会和西方学术的机会，并把他们对西方社会的观察带入对中国问题的思考之中，从而也形成了与国内知识分子看待问题的差异。从知识制度方面来说，中国教育和学术制度正在逐渐地与西方、尤其是美国体制接轨，成为跨越国界的学术体制的一个独特方面。在这一条件下，中国的知识生产和学术活动已经成为全球化过程的一个部分。

第三，1989年以后，国内的知识分子不得不重新思考他们所经历的历史事变，出于环境的压力和自愿的选择，大部分人文和社会科学领域的知识分子放弃了20世纪80年代启蒙知识分子的方式，通过讨论知识规范问题和从事更为专业化的学术研究，明显地转向了职业化的知识运作方式，而这个学术转向正好与中国大学体制和学术基金制度的转变相一致。由于"文化：中国与世界"等以介绍西方学术为主的知识群体的解体，以及《学人》等以研究中国历史和思想为中心的刊物的出现，有人把20世纪90年代的知识转向看成是"国学"的复兴。但这一概括在任何意义上都是不确切的。首先，1989年学生运动的失败促使知识界重新思考20世纪80年代的思想运动的含义，反思自身从事的文化运动与中国历史的关系，因此，把研究的目光转向中国历史包含了内在的现实需要，而不是某种单纯的学术复兴；其次，尽管学术史研究一度成为知识圈内的话题，但新一代人的学术研究难以被放在"国学"的范畴内加以概括。值得注意的是，这一知识转向虽然直接地表现在知识

they had participated. Because of these, the scholarly gaze turned toward the practical demands implicit in Chinese history rather than to the revival of any sort of pure scholarship. Second, even though research on the work of this new generation of scholars as simply being 'Chinese studies'. It is worth pointing out that although this epistemic shift was most directly registered as a move of intellectual interest from the 'West' to 'China', these efforts at self-adjustment were at the time based on Weberian theories of 'academic professionalization'. After 1992, the process of marketization accelerated the tendency toward social stratification, a tendency seemingly in accord with the internal professionalization of scholarship; the progress of professionalization and institutionalization of intellectual life gradually effected a fundamental change in the social role of the intellectual. Basically, the intellectuals of the 1980s were gradually transformed into experts, scholars, and professionals.

Of course, there are many other circumstances that could be listed here; in general, however, it is possible to say that the above three conditions produced a vastly different cultural space from that inhabited by intellectuals of the 1980s. Not only has this profoundly altered the relationship of intellectuals to the state, but the unity of the intellectuals as a group no longer exists. Chinese intellectuals have responded to these transformations in various ways: some, to appeals to the spirit of humanism; some, to a self-conscious sense of professional responsibility; and some have called for a renewal of the sense of the intellectuals' mission. On the one hand, these different and contradictory efforts have allowed Chinese intellectuals to maintain their critical and moral condemnation of contemporary society; on the other hand, these very attitudes have become the basis for

兴趣从"西方"向"中国"的某种转变，但这种自我调整的努力在当时是以韦伯有关"作为职业的学术"的理论为依据的。在各种知识取向的变化之中，学术的职业化似乎是更为明显的趋势。在1992年以后，市场化进程加速了社会科层化的趋势，这一趋势似乎与学术职业化的内在要求不谋而合。职业化的进程和学院化的取向逐渐地改变了知识分子的社会角色，从基本的方面看，20世纪80年代的那个知识分子阶层逐渐地蜕变为专家、学者和职业工作者。

我们当然还能举出一些重要的现象。但概括地说，上述三个方面共同创造了一种不同于20世纪80年代中国知识界的文化空间，不仅深刻改变了原有的知识分子与国家的关系，而且知识界自身的同一性也不复存在。从寻求传统的价值，到人文精神的呼吁，从职业责任的自觉承担，到重新呼唤社会使命感，当代中国知识分子的这些各不相同又相互交叉的努力一方面是对当代社会变迁所做的一种批判性的和道德化的姿态，另一方面又是以这些姿态来进行自我重新确认的社会行为。20世纪80年代的知识界把自己看作是文化英雄和先知，20世纪90年代的知识界则在努力地寻求新的适应方式，面对无孔不入的商业文化，他们痛苦地意识到自己已经不再是当代的文化英雄和价值的塑造者。

当代中国的社会进程进入了一个极为复杂的历史时期，而知识群体对社会问题的看法也变得

their own social reorientation. Intellectuals during the 1980s saw themselves as cultural heroes and trendsetters; 1990s intellectuals are urgently seeking new ways of adapting. Facing a pervasive commercial culture, they have become painfully conscious of the fact that they are no longer contemporary cultural heroes or arbiters of value.

Contemporary Chinese society has entered a complex era and the views of social issues held by intellectuals as a group have become ambiguous. Throughout the modern period the reflections of China's intellectuals have centered on how China can modernize and the reasons for its failure to do so. During the 1980s, intellectual critiques focused on a reevaluation of Chinese socialism, which was generally denounced as antimodern in its very methods. In reality, though, the clarification of thinking came from the elucidation of social questions. For intellectuals, modernization was on the one hand a search for wealth and power along the path to the establishment of a modern nation-state; on the other hand, it was the process of reevaluating their society and tradition against the yardstick of Western society and its cultures and values. Therefore, the most conspicuous feature of the Chinese discourse on modernity is its location within the 'China/West' and 'tradition/modernity' binaries.

Those young intellectuals who reside in the West (particularly the United States) and have come under the influence of Western critical theory, however, have become dubious about the so-called Western path as a model of China. For intellectuals residing in 'the market with Chinese Characteristics', the goal of reform has become similarly ambiguous. The 'good society' promised by the Chinese enlightenment thought of the 1980s has not only failed to

含混起来。自近代以来，中国知识界的历史反思集中于中国如何实现现代化和为什么中国未能成功地实现现代化。在整个20世纪80年代，问题则集中在对中国社会主义的反思，社会主义的方式也经常被视为反现代化的方式。思想状态的明朗化实际上来自社会问题的明确化。现代化对于中国知识分子来说一方面是寻求富强以建立现代民族国家的方式，另一方面则是以西方现代社会及其文化和价值为规范批判自己的社会和传统的过程。因此，中国现代性话语的最为主要的特征之一，就是诉诸"中国/西方"、"传统/现代"的二元对立的语式来对中国问题进行分析。

然而，对于那些身处西方（特别是美国）、又受到西方批判思想影响的年轻知识分子而言，所谓"西方道路"能否作为中国的楷模变得可疑了；对于那些身处中国特色的市场经济之中的知识分子而言，改革的目标到底是什么也同样变得含混起来。20世纪80年代中国的启蒙思想所许诺的"好社会"不仅没有伴随经济市场化而到来，市场社会本身呈现了新的、在某种意义上说是更加难以克服的矛盾。[2]资本主义的全球化不仅意味着在经济、文化甚至政治领域打破民族国家的界限，而且也

[2] 所谓"市场社会"不等同于市场，也不等同于市场经济，而是指社会的基本构造和运作方式是一种市场运作方式。根据卡尔·博兰尼的解释，市场社会就是现代资本主义社会。see Karl Polanyi: *The Great Transformation: the political and economic origins of our time*, Boston: Beacon Press, 1957.

accompany the market economy in coming into existence, but the market society has given rise to new and in some ways even more intractable contradictions.[2] The globalization of capitalism signifies not only the breakdown of the borders of the nation-state in the realms of the economy, culture, and even politics, but also the clarification of the benefits to the people in both global and domestic economic relations. It is worth noting that the advance of economic globalization is still guaranteed politically by the system of nation-states, so that even though the function of the nation-state has changed, its significance as a unit that benefits from the advance of economic globalization is even more important. To a very real extent, the clarification of the relations of interest in the international economic system has assisted the internal integration of the nation-state. In China's case, the tension between state and society engendered by the 1989 incident have to a certain extent actually been alleviated.

From the ideological perspective, the problems facing Chinese intellectuals in the 1990s have become much more complex. Firstly, the cultural and ethical crises of contemporary society can no longer be attributed to manifestations of an outmoded Chinese tradition (even as there are those who maintain to the contrary that these crises are the result of the decline

---

[2] So-called market society if equivalent neither to the market itself nor to market economics, but refers instead to a situation in which the basic structures and functions of society are market structures and functions. As Karl Polanyi explains, market society means modern capitalist society. See Polanyi, The Great Transformation: the Political and Economic Origins of Our Time (Boston: Beacon Press, 1957).

同时意味着人们对自己在全球经济关系和内部经济关系中的利益所在更为清楚了。值得注意的是，全球化的经济进程仍然是以民族国家体系为其政治保障的，因此，尽管民族国家的功能发生了变化，但它作为一个全球经济进程中的利益单位的含义反而更加凸现出来。在一定意义上，国际经济体系中的利益关系的清晰化反而有助于民族国家内部的整合。对于中国而言，1989年事件所产生的那种国家与社会的紧张关系在一定程度上反而获得了缓解。

从思想层面来看，20世纪90年代中国知识分子所面对的问题也已经大大复杂化了。首先是当代社会的文化危机和道德危机已经不能简单地视为中国传统的腐败的结果（因而有人反过来说这些问题是传统的失落的结果），因为许多问题恰恰产生于现代化的过程之中；其次是在中国经济改革已经导致市场社会的基本形成和国有企业仅占国民生产总值30%左右的时候，我们也不能简单地将中国社会的问题说成是社会主义的问题；再次是在苏联、东欧社会主义体系瓦解之后，资本主义的全球化过程已经成为当代世界的最为重要的世界性现象，中国的社会主义改革已经将中国的经济和文化生产过程纳入全球市场之中。在这样的历史条件下，中国的社会文化问题，包括政府行为本身，都已经不能在单一的中国语境中加以分析。换句话说，在反思中国社会的问题时，那些通常被作为批判对象的方面已经难以解释当代社会的困境：在亚洲资本主义兴起的历史语境中，传

of Chinese tradition); many of the problems are produced by the process of modernization itself. Secondly, China's problems cannot be simply blamed on China's socialism, as economic reforms have already brought into being an essentially market society. Thirdly, since the disintegration of the Soviet and Eastern European socialist systems, global capitalism has advanced to a new historical stage and China's socialist reforms have already led to the complete incorporation of the country's economic and cultural processes into this global market. Under these conditions, China's sociocultural problems-including the very behavior of the government - can no longer be analyzed from the position of a single context. In other words, in rethinking Chinese society, the usual targets of criticism can no longer explain contemporary difficulties. In the historical context of the rise of Asian capitalism, tradition can no longer be used as a self-evidently derogatory term; in the context of the globalization of production and trade, the nation-state is also no longer a self-evident unit of analysis. (This does not imply that the contemporary world has succeeded in establishing a supranational political system. On the contrary, the transnationalization of production and trade has been guaranteed by the original form of the nation-state. The problem is that the nation-state system is less and less able to adapt itself to the process of globalized production and culture. It is in this sense that the nation-state system and the capacity of nation-states to control sociopolitics are facing profound transformation.) With the complete interpenetration of the activities of capital and social life, the government and the behavior of all other organs of the state, as well as the workings of state power, have also been tightly linked to the market and to capital; it is thus insufficient to apply a simple political perspective to the problem. (This

统不可能再是自明的贬义词；在生产过程和贸易过程跨国化或全球化的历史语境中，民族国家也已经不是自明的分析单位；（这决不意味着当代世界已经成功地建立了超越民族国家的政治体系，相反，生产和贸易的跨国化是由旧有的民族国家体系作为它的政治保障的。问题是民族国家体系越来越不能适应全球化的生产和文化过程。正是在这个意义上，民族国家体系和民族国家的社会政治功能面临深刻的变化。）在资本活动渗透到社会生活各个领域的历史语境中，政府和其他国家机器的行为和权力运作也已经与市场和资本活动密切相关，从而也不能简单地从政治角度来分析（这也不是说政治分析是没有意义和价值的）。那么，中国的问题是怎样的问题，或者，用什么样的方式以至语言来分析中国的问题呢？在多元主义文化、相对主义理念和现代虚无主义的各种理论姿态瓦解了任何重建统一的价值和规范的时候，以批判性为其特征的各种理论开始意识到在它们所进行的激烈的批判过程中，批判性本身正在悄悄地丧失活力。因此，需要重新确认批判的前提。然而，迄今为止，改革/保守、西方/中国、资本主义/社会主义、市场/计划的二元论仍然是具有支配性的思想方式，在这种思想方式中，上述问题几乎是无法得到揭示的。

当代中国思想界放弃对资本活动过程（包括政治资本、经济资本和文化资本的复杂关系）的分析，放弃对市场、社会和国家的相互渗透又相互冲突的关系的研究，而仅仅将自己的视野束缚在

does not imply that political analyses are not significant or valuable.)

So, just what are China's problems? Or, what methods or even language should be used to analyze them? In a time when the various theoretical stances of pluralism, relativism, and nihilism have eliminated the possibility of the resurrection of any unitary parameter of value, the proponents of various alternative theories, the major characteristic of which is their critical edge, have begun to recognize in the course of their heated debates that the very idea of critique is gradually losing its vitality. It is thus necessary to first confirm the premises of critique. At present, however, the binaries of reform/conservatism, the West/China, capitalism/socialism, and market/planning are still hegemonic concepts, and in such a discursive situation the problems described above can hardly even be brought to light.

Contemporary Chinese intellectuals have abandoned their analysis of the workings of capital (including the complex relationship between political, economic, and cultural capital); they have also abandoned research into the interpenetrating and mutually conflicting relations between the market, society, and the state. Instead, they have confined their gaze to the level of morality or to the ideological frameworks of modernization, something especially important to note.

Contemporary Chinese social and cultural problems are linked to the question of Chinese modernity in a number of complex ways, but my question is simply this: if China's historical practice of socialism is the major characteristic of Chinese modernity, why have the New Enlightenment intellectuals who have borrowed from Weber and other theorists to critique socialism not been logically led to a critical reflection on the question of modernity itself?

道德的层面或者现代化意识形态的框架内，是一个特别值得注意的现象。当代中国社会的文化问题涉及中国现代性问题的许多复杂方面，我的问题仅仅是：如果说中国的社会主义历史实践正是中国现代性的特殊形态，那么中国启蒙知识分子借助于韦伯或其他理论对中国社会主义的批判为什么没有同时成为对于中国的现代性问题的反思？在当代世界性的变化之中，中国社会的改革实践一方面深刻地重组了中国社会的基本结构（知识分子被迫进行的自我确认的行为本身表明，社会文化的主体已经从中心地位向边缘转化。社会特定阶层的社会地位变动无疑是中国社会结构重组的表征之一），另一方面对于世界资本主义的发展方向提供了至今不能确定的因素。（关于中国道路的独特性的讨论最终回答的是如下问题：有没有偏离资本主义的历史形式而产生的现代社会，或者对现代化具有反思意义的现代过程？）我认为，所有上述问题是隐藏在当代知识分子的道德姿态背后的更为深刻的问题，这些问题本身揭示了当代思想的暧昧状态的历史原因。

2、三种作为现代化的意识形态的马克思主义

讨论当代中国思想的批判性的丧失，需要首先了解中国的马克思主义与现代化的历史联系。那些依据现代化理论对中国问题进行研究的西方学者，简单地把中国的现代化理解为科学和技术的

In the context of contemporary global change, Chinese reforms have on the one hand profoundly reorganized the basic structures of Chinese society. (That the intellectuals have been forced to affirm themselves is itself a demonstration that they have moved from being central subjects of society and culture to being marginal. This alteration in the fixed positions of social classes is clear evidence that the social structure is being reorganized.) On the other hand, the Chinese reforms have also contributed in unknowable and unspecifiable ways to the direction in which global capitalism itself is developing. (Debates on the uniqueness of the Chinese path have in the end only managed to address the questions of whether there can be a modern society that deviates from the historical model of capitalism or whether there can be a process of modernization that causes a rethinking of the concept of modernization itself.) I think that the above questions are implicit in the moral stance of contemporary intellectuals and are more profound then the stance itself. The questions themselves reveal the ambiguous historical reasons for the current state of contemporary thought.

Three Versions of Marxism

Prior to any discussion of decline of critical discourse in contemporary Chinese thought, it is necessary first to understand the historical relationship between Chinese Marxism and modernization. Those Western scholars who rely on modernization theory to analyze Chinese history reduce the problem of Chinese modernization to a problem of scientific and technological development, that is, to the transformation of an agrarian economy

发展、传统的农业社会向都市化和工业化的巨大转变。[3]由于现代化理论从欧洲资本主义的发展中理解现代化的基本规范，因此，现代化的过程也经常被理解为资本主义化的过程。对于马克思来说，现代化意味着资本主义的生产方式。但是，中国的情况稍有不同，因为当代中国的现代化问题不仅是由中国马克思主义者提出的，而且中国的马克思主义本身就是一种现代化的意识形态；不仅中国的社会主义运动以实现现代化为基本目标，而且它本身就是中国现代性的主要特征。当代中国流行的现代化概念主要指称政治、经济、军事和科技的从落后状态向先进状态的过渡和发展，但这一概念并不仅仅是技术性的指标，也并不仅仅是指中国民族国家及现代官僚体制的形成，而且还意味着一种目的论的历史观和世界观，一种把自己的社会实践理解为通达这一终极目标的途径的思维方式，一种将自己存在的意义与自己所属的特定时代相关联的态度。正因为这样，社会主义现代化概念不仅指明了中国现代化的制度形式与资本主义现代化的差别，而且也提供了一整套的价值观。

中国语境中的现代化概念与现代化理论中的现代化概念有所区别，这是因为中国的现代化概

[3] 请参见由Gilbert Rozman主编的《中国的现代化》，国家社会科学基金"比较现代化"课题组译，江苏人民出版社，1988。

into an urban industrial one. [3]Because modernization theory derives from the historical development of European capitalism, modernization has often been understood as the process of becoming capitalist. Marxism, too, sees modernization as the mode of capitalist production. However, China's situation is different not only because the question of its modernization was posed by Marxists, but because Chinese Marxism itself is an ideology of modernization; not only was the goal of the Chinese socialist movement modernization but the movement itself constitutes the main characteristic of Chinese modernity. Although the popular understanding of modernization in China focuses primarily on the process of transforming the state, the economy, the military, and science from backwardness to an advanced condition, this concept does not merely set technological goals, and it does not point only to the formation of the nation-state and a modern bureaucracy. Rather, it also includes a teleological historical perspective and worldview. It is a type of thinking through which China's social praxis is understood as a path toward an ontological historical goal, which in turn fosters an attitude that links existential meaning to the historical period in which one finds oneself. As a result, socialist modernization is a concept that not only points out the difference between the institutions of Chinese modernization and capitalist modernization, but that also provides a whole set of its own values.

Thus, the 'modernization' in Chinese discourse and the 'modernization' in modernization

[3] For example, see Gilbert Rozman, Ed., The Modernization of China (in Chinese) (*Nanjing: Jiangsu renmin chubanshe,* 1988).

念包含了以社会主义意识形态为内容的价值取向。像毛泽东这样的马克思主义者相信历史的不可逆转的进步，并力图用革命的或"大跃进"的方式促成中国社会向现代化的目标迈进。他所实行的社会主义所有制一方面是为了建立富强的现代民族国家，另一方面又是以消灭工人和农民、城市和乡村、脑力劳动与体力劳动之间的"三大差别"这一平等目标为主要目的。通过公有化运动，特别是"人民公社"的建立，毛泽东使自己的以农业为主的国家实现了社会动员，把整个社会组织到国家的主要目标之中。对内，这是要解决晚清和民国政府都未能解决的国家税收的问题，通过对农村的生产和消费的剥削为城市工业化积累资源，并按照社会主义的原理组织农村社会；在这个意义上，农村公有制是以更为深刻的城乡不平等为前提的。[4]对外，通过有效地将社会组织到国家目标中，使落后的中国社会凝聚成为一个统一的力量来完成民族主义任务。毛泽东本人多次谈到他所领导的社会主义革命是对孙中山的民主主义革命的继承和发展，实际上是将这个革命理解为对上个世纪以

[4] 有关20世纪50年代中国在推进现代化过程中的城乡关系问题，也涉及中国共产党放弃新民主主义而直接进入社会主义的原因问题。金观涛、刘青峰所著《开放中的变迁——再论中国社会超稳定结构》(香港：香港中文大学，1993) 一书第九章《从新民主主义到社会主义》对此有深入清晰的研究，第411–460页。此处不缀。

theory are different. This is because inherent within the Chinese concept of modernization is a tendency toward values based on a content of socialist ideology. *Mao Zedong* believed in irreversible historical progress and used revolution and the methods of the Great Leap Forward to push Chinese society along the modernization path. He used the socialist system of public ownership to establish a prosperous and powerful modern nation-state while at the same time working toward his principal goal of equality by striving to eliminate the 'three differences'- between workers and peasants, between town and country, and between mental and manual labor. Through the movement to nationalize the economy and particularly through the establishment of People's Communes, *Mao* led his primarily agricultural nation to social mobilization; he thus successfully subsumed society under state goals. Internally, this resolved the tax-collection problems that were a legacy of the late *Qing* and Republican periods; resources for urban industrialization were now to be secured by exploiting production and consumption in the countryside, which was organized according to socialist principles. In this sense, public ownership in the countryside was premise on even more inequality between the urban and the rural sectors.[4]Externally the effective subsumption of society under the state enabled China's backward society to coalesce into

[4] The problem of the urban-rural relationship and its position in China's modernization process through the 1950s is also related to the decision by the Chinese Communist Party(CCP) to abandon New Democracy and move directly into socialism. On this Question, see *Jin Guantao* and *LiuQingfeng, Kaifangzhong de bianqian*: *Zailun Zhongguo shehui chaowending jiegou*(Changes in the course of opening: a further discussion of the superstable structure of Chinese History) (Hong Kong: Chinese University of Hong Kong Press, 1993), 441-460.

来的整个中国现代化运动的基本问题的解决，并为这个现代化运动制定未来的方向。[5]毛泽东的社会主义一方面是一种现代化的意识形态，另一方面是对欧洲和美国的资本主义现代化的批判；但是，这个批判不是对现代化本身的批判，恰恰相反，它是基于革命的意识形态和民族主义的立场而产生的对于现代化的资本主义形式或阶段的批判。因此，从价值观和历史观的层面来说，毛泽东的社会主义思想是一种反资本主义现代性的现代性理论。从政治后果方面来看，毛泽东消灭三大差别的社会实践消灭了独立于国家的社会范畴存在的可能性，不仅造成了一个前所未有、笼罩一切的庞大的国家体制，而且把社会生活的各个方面组织到先锋政党的周围。

　　"反现代性的现代性理论"并不仅仅是毛泽东思想的特征，而且也是晚清以降中国思想的主要特征之一。"反现代"的取向不仅导因于人们所说的传统因素，更重要的是，帝国主义扩张和资本主义现代社会危机的历史展现，构成了中国寻求现代性的历史语境。推动中国现代化运动的知识分子和国家机器中的有识之士，都不能不思考中国的现代化运动如何才能避免西方资本主义现代性的种种弊端。康有为的大同空想、章太炎的平等观念、孙中山的民生主义，以及中国各种各样的社会

[5] 请参见毛泽东《中国革命与中国共产党》等文章，《毛泽东选集》，第610－650页。北京：人民出版社，1966。

a united force to finish the unfinished task of nationalism, *Mao* often said that his socialist revolution was the heir to and the development of *Sun Zhongshan's [Sun Yat-sen's]* democratic revolution; in reality, he saw his revolution as the final resolution to the modernization movement that had been ongoing since the nineteenth century and as having set its future direction.[5]

Mao's socialism is both an ideology of modernization and a critique of Euro-American capitalist modernization. But this critique was not a critique of modernization itself. Quite the contrary: it was a critique of the capitalist form or stage of modernization based on a revolutionary ideology and a nationalist standpoint. For this reason on the perspective of history and values, *Mao's* socialism is a modernization theory opposed to capitalist modernization. From the perspective of its political impact, *Mao's* elimination of the 'three differences' in actual practice eliminated the possibility of the existence of a public sphere autonomous from the state. This not only produced a huge structure of unprecedented size and overarching scope, but brought all social activity under the organization of the vanguard party.

This 'antimodern theory of modernization' is a characteristic not just of *Mao Zedong* thought, however; it is one of the major characteristics of Chinese thought from the late *Qing* onward. The tendency towards 'anti-modernism' was not only a function of what

---

[5] See *Mao Zedong*,'The Chinese Revolution and the Chinese Communist Party', in *Mao Zedong's* Selected Works(*Beijing: renmin chubanshe*, 1996), 610-650.

主义者对资本主义的批判, 是和他们在政治、经济、军事和文化等各个领域构筑的各种现代性方案 (包括现代性的国家政治制度、经济形态和文化价值) 相伴随的。甚至可以说, 对现代性的置疑和批判本身构成了中国现代性思想的最基本的特征。因此, 中国现代思想及其最为重要的思想家是以悖论式的方式展开他们寻求中国现代性的思想努力和社会实践的。中国现代思想包含了对现代性的批判性反思。

然而, 在寻求现代化的过程中, 这种特定语境中产生的深刻思想却在另一方面产生出反现代的社会实践和乌托邦主义:对于官僚制国家的恐惧、对于形式化的法律的轻视、对于绝对平等的推重, 等等。在中国的历史情境中, 现代化的努力与对"理性化"过程的拒绝相并行, 构成了深刻的历史矛盾。对于毛泽东来说, 他一方面以集权的方式建立了现代国家制度, 另一方面又对这个制度本身进行"文化大革命"式的破坏;他一方面用公社制和集体经济的方式推动中国经济的发展, 另一方面他在分配制度方面试图避免资本主义现代化所导致的严重的社会不平等;他一方面以公有方式将整个社会组织到国家的现代化目标之中, 从而剥夺了个人的政治自主权, 另一方面他对国家机器对人民主权的压抑深恶痛绝。总之, 中国社会主义的现代化实践包含着反现代性的历史内容。这种悖论式的方式有其文化根源, 但更需要在中国现代化运动的双重历史语境 (寻求现代化与对西方现代

people refer to as traditional factors, but was even more importantly a result of the fact that the discourse on China's search for modernity was of shaped in the historical context of imperialist expansion and a crisis in capitalism. Thus, those intellectuals and state officials who promoted modernization in China could not help but consider how China's modernization could avoid the multiple abuses of Western capitalist modernity. *Kang Youwei*'s one-world utopia (*Datong*), *Zhang Binglin*'s egalitarianism, *Sun Zhongshan*'s principle of the people's livelihood (*minsheng zhuyi*), and the various socialist critiques of capitalism all went hand in hand with programs and plans for the construction of political, economic, military, and cultural programs and plans. (Including those for a modern national political system, economic forms, and cultural values). It is even possible to say that the basic characteristics of Chinese thought on modernity are doubt and critique. As a result, at the heart of the search for Chinese thought on modernity are doubt and critique. As a result, at the heart of the search for Chinese modernity in Chinese thinking and in some of China's most important intellectuals stands a huge paradox.

Modern Chinese thought includes critical reflection on modernity. Yet in the search for modernization, among the profound ideas that this particular discourse has produced are both antimodern social practice and utopianism: fear of a bureaucratic state, contempt for the formalization of legal structures, an emphasis on absolute egalitarianism, and so forth. Indeed, in China's historical context, the struggle for modernization and the rejection of rationalization have proceeded together, something that has produced profound historical contradictions. For example, on the one hand, *Mao* centralized power to establish a modern

化的种种历史后果的反思）中解释。

以"文化大革命"的结束为界标，以不断革命和批判资本主义为特征的社会主义宣告终结。1978年开始了延续至今的社会主义改革运动。从思想方面说，对先前的社会主义的批判主要集中在：（1）理想主义的公有制及其平均分配制度导致了效率的低下；（2）专制作风导致了全国范围内的政治迫害。因此，在对历史进行清算和总结的同时，以寻求效率为轴心，中国的社会主义改革从农村公社制的解体和土地承包制的实行开始，逐步地发展为城市工业的承包制和股份制的实行，并在开放的改革实践中把中国逐渐纳入世界资本主义的市场之中。[6]改革的进程明显地推进了经济的发展，改造了原有的社会结构。但是，它放弃的仅仅是毛的理想主义的现代化方式，继承的则是

[6] 对于1979年以后农村改革的意义需要在20世纪50年代以后的历史中加以理解。从动机上看，集体化模式似乎一方面可以避免资本主义弊病，又可以通过对小农经济的改造走向现代化。然而，由于缺乏激励机制，集体化在一定程度上导致了效率的低下。（参见林毅夫：《制度、技术与中国农业发展》，上海三联书店，1992，第16－43页）更重要的是，"阻碍了农业外就业机会的扩展。政府虽然把工业化作为目标，但在农村，却极力限制农业以外的就业机会。由于政府……对乡村控制空前严密，这种限制非常有效。这样与以前相比，集体化时期个人选择的自由度不仅未增加，反而缩减，严重束缚了农村经济发展。"1979年以后的农村改革，"提供了一个较自由的'机会结构'，给地方共同体和个体农民提供了自主性和实验自由，这样他们便可以灵活地

state system; on the other hand, he launched the Cultural Revolution to destroy that system. On the one hand, he used People's Communes and collectives to promote China's economic development; on the other hand, he designed the social distribution system to avoid the severe social inequalities of capitalist modernization. On the one hand, he used the nationalization of the economy to subsume society under the state goal of modernization, in the process stripping individuals of their political autonomy; on the other hand, he abhorred the use of state mechanisms to suppress the autonomy of 'the people'. In sum, inherent in the practice of China's socialist modernization is a historical antimodernity. This paradox has cultural roots, yet it is even more important to search for an explanation in the double-edged historical context of Chinese modernization (namely, the search for modernization and reflections on the various historical consequences of Western modernization).

The end of the Cultural Revolution marked the end of a socialism characterized by perpetual revolution and the critique of capitalism. In 1978, the socialist reform movement that has lasted to this day began. On the level of ideology, the criticism of the prior socialism focused first on its idealistic system of public ownership and egalitarianism, both of which led to a decrease in efficiency, and second on the dictatorial methods that caused political damage to the whole country. At the same time as the evaluation and the historical summing-up were proceeding, China's socialist reforms, with improved efficiency as their central focus, were launched. They began with the disbanding of the agricultural communes and their replacement by the responsibility system in the countryside. Gradually, these were extended to responsibility and shareholding systems in the urban industrial sector.

现代化的目标本身；当代改革的社会主义同样是一种作为现代化的意识形态的马克思主义，也是一种实用主义的马克思主义。与改革前的现代化不同，中国现在正在进行的社会主义改革的主要特征就是经济领域的市场化，它通过中国经济以及社会文化与当代资本主义经济体系的接轨，把中国社会纳入全球性的市场社会。与改革前的社会主义相比，当代社会主义虽然是一种作为现代化的意识形态的马克思主义，但是，它已经基本不具有前者的那种反现代性倾向。

当代中国社会的改革所创造的惊人成就并不仅仅是经济性的，而且也蕴含了深刻的政治内

寻找多种多样的经济发展途径和就业机会。"（参见高寿仙：《制度创新与明清以来的农村经济发展》，《读书》1996年5期，第123–129页。）黄宗智则指出：改革以来的变化"不是由于一些人想象的自由市场化的家庭农业的高度刺激力导致农业生产的戏剧性突破，而是由于农村经济的多种经营，以及农业剩余劳动力向农村外就业的转移。"他进一步指出："在中国80年代的改革中，具有长期的最大意义的农村变化是随着农村经济多样化而来的农业生产的反过密化，而不是广泛设想的市场化农业生产。……随着80年代家庭生产承包责任制的引进，农业产量停止了增长，而极少有农民沿着静电模式和官方宣传机器预言的道路致富。直率地说，80年代的市场化农业在作物生产上并不比在1350至1950年的600年间或集体化农业的30年间干得好。""长江三角洲乡村的真正重要的问题过去不是、现在也不是在于市场化家庭农业或计划下的集体农业，不是在于资本主义或社会主义，而是在于过密化还是发展。"（《长江三角洲小农家庭与乡村发展》，第16–17页，北京：中华书局，1992）

In addition, in the course of reform and opening up, China was gradually absorbed into the global capitalist market. [6]These reforms have plainly advanced economic development

---

[6] The significance of the post-1979 rural reforms must be understood in the post-1950s historical context, when it seemed that the collective model could avoid the motivational problems of capitalism at the same time as it transformed a small-scale peasant economy into a modern one. Yet, without the encouragement of incentives, once collectivization reached a certain point, it led to a decrease in efficiency. See *Lin Yifu, Zhidu, jishu yu Zhongguo nongye fazhan* (Systems and technology in China's rural development)(*Shanghai: Sanlian Shudian*, 1992), pp.16-43. More important still, according to *Gao Shouxian*, '[this situation] obstructed the expansion of employment opportunities outside the agricultural sector. Although the government made industrialization a primary goal, in the culture. Because the government…exerted unprecedented control over the gone on previously, during collectivization the degree of individual freedom of choice not only did not increase, it contracted severely. This radically restricted the development of the rural economy.' In *Gao*'s opinion, the post-1979 rural reforms 'offered a relatively free'structure of opportunity' and gave local collectivities and individual peasants both autonomy and the freedom to experiment. In this way, they could more flexibly search for and find different paths to economic development and other employment opportunities.' *Gao Shouxian*, '*Zhidu chuanxin yu Ming Qing yilai de nongcun jingji fazhan*'(Institutional innovation and rural development since the *Ming* and *Qing* dynasties), *Dushu* 194(May 1995):123-129.Philip Huang points out that the changes since the reforms came not from the 'private crop production and petty commerce that were given so much press, but rather from rural industry and new sidelines.'He adds that 'in the reformist China of the 1980s…the rural change of the greatest long-term import was the de-involution in crop production that cam with the diversification of the rural economy, and not the turn to marketized farming in crop production as is commonly assumed…[C]rop yields failed to advance with the introduction of the household responsibility system in farming in the 1980s, and few peasants grew rich along the lines predicted by the classical model and official propaganda. To put it bluntly, marketized farming in the 1980s did no better in crop production than it did in the six centuries between 1935 and 1950, or than collective agriculture did in the preceding three decades.' Huang continues: 'The really important issue for the Yangzi delta countryside, in other words, was not - and is not - between marketized family farming and planned collectivist agriculture, or capitalism and socialism, but rather between involution and development.' (Philip Huang, The peasant Family and Rural Development in the Yangzi Delta, 1350 -1988(Stanford: Stanford University Press, 1990), pp.17, 18.

含。中国社会主义改革通过经济的发展进一步完成了中国近代民族主义所要完成的历史任务,同时深信科学技术的发展、经济形态向资本主义市场的过渡是历史的巨大进步。"让一部分人先富起来"的口号表明,中国的社会主义改革者认为"一部分人先富起来"是一种权宜性的策略,而不涉及生产关系的变化和社会资源的公平分配。人们通常用"竞争机制"的形成或"效率的提高"解释"家庭联产承包责任制"在农村改革中取得的巨大成功,却忽略了土地再分配过程所蕴含的平等原则,以及在此过程中逐渐形成的相对平等的城乡关系。事实证明,公正和平等正是促使生产效率提高的基本因素。根据农业经济专家的研究,1978-1985年城乡收入的差距是缩小的,从1985年起扩大。1989年到1991年农民收入增长基本停滞,城乡收入差距又恢复到1978年以前的情况。1993年以后,由于国家提高粮食价格、乡镇企业增长快、外出务工人口收入增长等原因,农村收入增长较快,但在城市劳动力大量剩余的情况下,这一势头正在改变。[7]农村经济发展的状况与相应的社会平等(特别是城乡经济关系的平等)直接相关。与农村改革相比,在城市进行的市场改革和私有化

---

[7] 罗峪平:《始终不能忘记农村的发展——访国务院研究中心农业问题专家卢迈》,《三联生活周刊》,1998年7月31日,1998年第14期,总第68期,第26页。

and reshaped the preexisting social structure, but what they have abandoned is *Mao's* idealistic modernization methods while continuing the goal of modernization; the socialism of the contemporary reforms is at the same time an ideology of Marxist modernization and pragmatism. Different from prereform modernization, the most important characteristics of the socialist reforms that China is now implementing are marketization in the economic arena and the convergence of the Chinese economy, society, and culture with the contemporary capitalist system. In contrast to prereform socialism, while contemporary socialism is a type of Marxism as an ideology of modernization, it has already in effect been stripped of the antimodern character of the prior socialism.

The astonishing achievements brought about in China by the contemporary socialist reforms are not limited to the economic arena, but also entail profound political implications. The socialist reform has, through economic development, moved the country one more step toward completing the unfinished nationalist project of the modern period; at the same time there is deep belief that, along with the development of science and technology, the transition to a capitalist commodity economy represents great historical progress. The slogan 'allow some people to get rich first' clearly demonstrates that China's socialist reformers consider that the policy is an expedient measure that bears neither on fundamental changes in the relations of production nor on the equal distribution of social resources. People generally use the formation of 'mechanisms of competition' or 'increased efficiency' to explain the great success of 'the household responsibility system' in agricultural reform. This overlooks the principles of equality embedded in the redistribution of land,

的过程中，社会财富（特别是国有资产）的再分配甚至没有遵循在起点平等状态下找到"最初所有者"，在规则平等的状态下找到"最终所有者"的市场规则。[8]人们常常忽略的是，这种将效率置于一切之首的实用主义，为新的社会不平等创造了条件，也为政治民主化制造了障碍。如果社会财富的再分配是在充分公开化或者民主监督的程序下进行，以瓜分国有资产为特点的社会再分配就不可能如此严重地进行。现在人们寄希望于用私有产权的合法化来解决当前的社会矛盾，然而，如果私有化过程不是在民主和公正的条件下进行，这个合法化过程保护的就只能是不合法的分配过程。

自1978年以来，围绕改革问题发生过一系列的论争，这些论争的核心问题并不是要不要现代化，而是用什么方式现代化。我把它们概括为这样的冲突：反现代性的现代化的马克思主义意识形态与现代化的马克思主义意识形态的斗争。在今天，这样的争论已经不能说明当代经济和政治斗争的基本特点。

第三种作为现代化的意识形态的马克思主义具有深刻的空想社会主义特点，我指的是1978年

---

[8] 参见苏文：《山重水复应有路——前苏东国家转轨进程再评述》，《东方》1996年1期，第37–41页。该文讨论前苏联、东欧经济改革问题，这里提到的基本原则是指捷克的经验。

and the gradual equalization of urban-rural relations that was part of this process. The facts demonstrate that justice and equality were the basic factors that furthered the efficiency of Chinese agriculture. According to the research of agricultural economists, the income difference between city and country decreased between 1978 and 1985, only to increase again after 1985. Between 1989 and 1991 agricultural income essentially was stagnant, and the inequality between urban and rural income returned to the levels that had existed prior to 1978. After 1993, because the state raised the price of grain, the rapid advance of rural enterprises, and the increase of income of rural migrants to urban areas, rural income grew relatively quickly, but in circumstances of a great surplus of urban labor, this situation began to change.[7] The status of rural economic development is directly of urban-rural economic relations in particular. In contrast to the reform in rural areas, in urban areas the process of market reform and privatization that has redistributed social wealth (particularly state-owned assets) has not been carried out on the principle of a level playing field, where ownership is assigned to the original owner, but rather on a de facto basis that grants it to the last owner.[8] What is often neglected is that the pragmatism that focuses solely on

---

[7] luo Yuping.'Shizhong buneng wangji nongcun de fazhan - fang guowuyuan yuanjiu zhongxin nongye wenti zhuanjia Lu Mai' (Never forget rural development - an interview with the agricultural expert Lu Mai of the Research Institute of the State Council), in *Sanlian shenghuo zhoukan* (Sanlian life weekly)14(1998):26.

[8] See *Su Wen*, '*Shangchongshuifu ying you lu: Qian Su Dong guojia zhuangui guocheng zai pinglun*' (There should be a way out: a further discussion of perestroika in the former Soviet Union and Eastern Euiope), *Dongfang* 1(January 1996): 37-41. This article discusses economic reform in the former Soviet Union and Eastern Europe. It focuses on the experience of the Czech Republic.

以后在中国共产党内以及一些马克思主义知识分子中出现的"真正的社会主义"思潮，其主要的特征是用人道主义来改造马克思主义，并以这种改造了的马克思主义批判改革前的主导意识形态，从而为当代社会主义改革运动提供理论上的依据。这个思潮是当时中国的"思想解放运动"的一部分。人道主义的马克思主义一方面批判国家社会主义忘记了马克思学说中有关人的自由和解放的思想，从而在"人民民主专政的名义"下产生了残酷的社会专制；另一方面也与社会主义改革思想发生了矛盾，我把这种矛盾理解为空想社会主义与实用主义的社会主义的冲突。中国人道主义的马克思主义关注的主要理论问题是马克思《1844年经济学——哲学手稿》中所讨论的"异化"问题。早期马克思继承了费尔巴哈等西方人本主义哲学中的异化概念，并把它用于对资本主义生产关系的分析，特别是用于对资本主义生产过程中的劳动的分析，他所指的异化首先是指资本主义生产关系中的劳动的异化。中国人道主义的马克思主义把马克思的异化概念抽离开批判资本主义现代性的历史语境，转而把这一概念用于传统社会主义的批判。就主要的方面来说，这一思潮把毛的社会主义、特别是其专制主义当作传统的和封建主义的历史遗存来批判，也涉及社会主义社会本身的异化问题，但对社会主义的反思并没有引向对现代性问题的反思。正像文艺复兴以后西方人文主义对宗教的批判一样，中国人道主义的马克思主义对传统社会主义的批判催生了中国社会的"世俗化"运

efficiency has created the conditions for social inequality, and it also poses obstacles to political democratization. Had the redistribution of social wealth been implemented openly or with some degree of popular supervision, the partitioning of national assets that is its characteristic could not have proceeded so unequally. People currently place their hopes for solving our contemporary social contradictions on the legitimization of private property rights, but if this privatization if carried out under undemocratic and unjust circumstances, this 'legitimization' will guarantee only an illegitimate process of distribution. Since 1987, there have been many debates about reform. The heart of these debates has not been the question whether to modernize; rather, it has been the question of modernization methods. In general we can characterize this as a struggle between Marxism as antimodern ideology of modernization and Marxism as an ideology of modernization. As things stand now, however, this debate has been unable to encompass the essentials of the contemporary economic and political struggle.

A third kind of Marxist modernization ideology is utopian socialism. By this, I mean what has since 1978 been called 'authentic socialism' by some Marxist intellectuals in the CCP. Its major characteristic is the use of humanism to reform Marxism. Such a 'humanistic Marxism' was mobilized as a critique of the ideological mainstream of the prereform period and could have become the theoretical foundation for the contemporary socialist reform movement. This trend was part of the 'thought liberation movement' in China at the time. On the one hand, humanistic Marxism criticized state socialism's disregard for the Marxian ideals of individual freedom and liberation, which was responsible for the cruelties of the social

动——资本主义的市场化的发展。在特定的语境中，马克思对西方资本主义现代性的批判被转换为一种作为现代化的意识形态，并成为当代中国"新启蒙主义"思想的重要组成部分。中国人道主义的马克思主义的主要任务是分析和批判毛的反现代性的现代化的意识形态及其历史实践，在中国向资本主义开放的社会主义改革中，它的抽象的人的自由和解放的理念最终转化为一系列现代性

[9] 有关马克思主义人道主义的讨论并不是周扬首创，但他在纪念马克思逝世一百周年的大会上的报告引发了对马克思主义人道主义的批判。他的报告的删改稿发表于1983年3月16日《人民日报》，原文在发给与会代表后，很快收回。他的报告题为《关于马克思主义的几个理论问题的探讨》。对马克思主义人道主义的最为有力的批判来自当时的党内理论家胡乔木，他于1984年1月3日在中共中央党校发表讲话，不指名地对周扬和其他理论家的观点进行理论批判。他的讲话先发表在中共中央党校的《理论月刊》，而后由人民出版社出版了单行本，题为《关于人道主义和异化问题》（北京：人民出版社，1984年1月版）。实际上，关于这一问题的讨论早在1978年后就引起了一些理论工作者的注意，人民出版社于1981年1月出版了题为《人是马克思主义的出发点——人性、人道主义问题论集》（北京：人民出版社，1981）的论文集，内中收录了王若水、李鹏程、高尔太等人的文章。值得注意的是，在讨论中，人道主义的抽象的人和人性概念是论证的基础。而作为人道主义的对立面的是神道主义和兽道主义，前者指的是宗教专制，在中国的语境中隐喻文革中的"现代迷信"；后者指的是封建专制和法西斯主义，在中国的语境中隐喻"文革"中的"全面专政"。也许是受到苏联、东欧国家相关讨论的影响，中国的马克思主义人道主义者认为马克思主义是重视人的问题的，但斯大林的《辩证唯物主义和历史唯物主义》对此问题没有给予充分的注意。此外，他们还指出，列宁根本不知道马克思

dictatorship. On the other hand, it was in direct contradiction to socialist reform thinking, a contradiction I regard as a conflict between utopian socialism and the pragmatism of socialist reformism. The core of China's humanistic Marxism is Marx's theory of alienation, as outlined in his Economic and Philosophical Manuscripts of 1844. The early Marx took this concept of alienation from Feuerbach and other Western humanist philosophers and used it to analyze the problem of labor in capitalist production. He pointed very specifically to the problem of the alienation of laborers in capitalist relations of production. Chinese humanist Marxists wrested this concept from production. Chinese humanist Marxists wrested this concept from the historical context in which Marx used it to critique capitalism and turned it into a tool for the critique of traditional socialism. This trend of thought specifically critique of traditional socialism. This trend of thought specifically critiqued *Mao*'s theories of dictatorship as the historical legacies of tradition and feudalism; it also engaged the problem of alienation in socialism itself. However, these Chinese humanist Marxists offered no critical reflection on the question of modernity.

Just as with the Western humanist attack on religion after the Enlightenment, China's humanistic Marxist critique of traditional socialism has accelerated the 'secularization' of society - the development of capitalist commodification. In certain contexts, Marx's critique of Western capitalist modernization has been transformed into an ideology of modernization, and has become an important part of contemporary Chinese New Enlightenment thinking. Thus, the major task of China's humanistic Marxism has been to analyze and critique the historical experience of *Mao*'s antimodern modernization. Yet in the context of the capitalist

的价值观；换句话说，它本身就是作为现代化的意识形态的马克思主义，因此几乎不可能对现代化和资本主义市场本身所产生的社会危机作出相应的分析和批判。在市场社会及其规则日益成为主导形态的中国语境中，以批判传统社会主义历史实践为主要目标的批判的社会主义已经衰亡。[9]中国人道主义的马克思主义如果要重新焕发它的批判活力，就必须从它的人本主义取向中走出来，把它对人的关注重新置于一种具有时代特点的政治经济学的基础之上。

3、作为现代化的意识形态的启蒙主义及其当代形态

在整个80年代，中国思想界最富活力的是中国的"新启蒙主义"思潮；最初，"新启蒙主义"思潮

的《1844年经济学——哲学手稿》（1932年发表）。王若水在题为《人是马克思主义的出发点》的文章中还提到，1964年毛泽东曾经表示赞同"异化"概念，认为异化是普遍现象。所有这些都表明，中国的人道主义马克思主义为了对中国社会主义的历史实践进行批判，一方面采用了一种隐喻式的方式，即把中国的社会主义实践问题解释为封建主义的问题，另一方面又利用了人道主义和异化概念的普遍主义特征。这两个方面都暗示了对现代价值观、特别是启蒙运动的价值观的肯定。在这种解释模式中，社会主义从未作为一种非资本主义的现代性形式进行检讨。相反，对社会主义历史实践的批判是对欧洲现代性的价值观的充分肯定。

opening in China's socialist reforms, abstract theories of human freedom and individual liberation in the end have become the very definition of the values of modernity. In other words, humanistic Marxism itself has become a Marxist ideology of modernization. For this reason, it cannot possibly launch either an appropriate analysis or a critique of the multiple social crises that have resulted from modernization and the capitalist market. In a context in which the market society and its norms are increasingly dominating discourse, the type of critical socialism that primarily targets the traditional historical experience is already obsolete.[9] If Chinese humanistic Marxism wants to revivify its critical power, it must take leave of its humanistic tendency and refocus its attention on people to concentrate on a

---

[9] Although the debates on Marxist humanism were not started by *Zhou Yang*, the report he gave at the conference in commemoration of the centennial of Marx's death attracted much criticism. The revised and edited version of his report was published in People's Daily.(16 March 1983) but the original text, distributed to the conference delegates, was confiscated. The report's original title was 'An Exploration of Several Theoretical Problems in Marxism'. The most trenchant criticism came from then party theorist *Hu Qiaomu*, who, in a speech to the Central Party School on January 3, 1984, took *Zhou Yang*'s and others' perspectives on Marxism to task without naming them. His speech was first published in the Central Party School's *Lilun yuekan* (Theory monthly), and it was followed by a pamphlet published under the title *Guangyu rendao zhuyi he yihua wenti* (On humanism and alienation)(*Beijing: Renmin chubanshe*, 1984). Actually, this issue had already attracted the attention of several theorists after 1978, and the People's Publishing House had already put out an anthology in 1981 title *Ren shi makesizhuyi da chufadian: renxin, rendaozhuyi wenti lunji* (Man is the starting point of Marxism: a collection of articles on human nature and humanism), which included essays by *Wang Ruoshui*, *Li Pengcheng*, and *Gao Ertai*, among others. It is worth nothing that in those discussions, an abstract conception of man and human nature were the bases of the debates on humanism. 'Theism' and 'bestialism (*shoudao zhuyi*) ' are the two terms most often used as opposites of 'humanism'. The former indicates the tyranny of religion, and in Chinese discourse it is a metaphor for the Cultural Revolution's 'contemporary superstition'; the latter indicates feudal dictatorship or fascism, and in Chinese discourse it is a metaphor for the 'complete

---

是在马克思主义人道主义的旗帜下活动的，但是，在80年代初期发生的针对马克思主义人道主义的"清除精神污染"运动之后，"新启蒙主义"思想运动逐步地转变为一种知识分子要求激进的社会改革的运动，也越来越具有民间的、反正统的和西方化的倾向。"新启蒙主义"思潮并不是统一的运动，这个思潮中的文学和哲学方面与当时的政治问题没有直接关系。我想特别指出的是，如果简单地认为中国当代"启蒙思想"是一种与国家目标相对立的思潮，中国当代"启蒙知识分子"是一种与国家对抗的政治力量，那就无法理解新时期以来中国思想的基本脉络。尽管"新启蒙"思潮本身错综复杂，并在20世纪80年代后期发生了严重的分化，但历史地看，中国"新启蒙"思想的基本立场和历史意义，就在于它是为整个国家的改革实践提供意识形态的基础的。中国"新启蒙知识分子"与国家目标的分歧是在两者之间的紧密联系中逐渐展现出来。当代启蒙思想从西方的（主要是自由主义的）经济学、政治学、法学和其他知识领域获得思想的灵感，并以之与正统的马克思主义意识形态相对抗，是因为由国家推动的社会变革正在经由市场化过程向全球化的历史迈进。在这个意义上，"新启蒙知识分子"与正统派的对抗不能简单地解释为民间知识分子与国家的对抗，恰恰相反，从总的方面看，他们的思想努力与国家目标大体一致。20世纪80年代中国思想界和文化界的活跃知识分子（其中一部分在1989年之后流亡国外），大多是深受重用的国家研究机构或大学的领导者，

political economy that takes account of the current situation.

Enlightenment as an Ideology of Modernization and Its Contemporary Form

The most dynamic intellectual current of the entire 1980s was the New Enlightenment movement. Initially, it proceeded under the banner of humanistic Marxism, but after the Spiritual Pollution Campaign of the early 1980s that was aimed at humanistic Marxism, the New Enlightenment movement gradually was transformed into an intellectual movement with radical demands for social reform that increasingly took on a popular and anti-orthodox pro-Western tendency. The New Enlightenment movement is by no means unitary; its literary, philosophical, and political aspects have no direct relationship to one another. However, I wish to particularly point out that to regard China's New Enlightenment thought as simply an intellectual trend in opposition to the goals of the state and China's

---

dictatorship' of the Cultural Revolution. Perhaps because of the influence of related discussion in the Soviet Union and Eastern Europe, Chinese Marxist humanism considers the rethinking of man to be the primary problem of Marxism; it points out that Stalin's Dialectical Materialism and Historical Materialism paid insufficient attention to this problem. In addition, Chinese Marxist humanists point out that Lenin was not familiar with Marx's Economic and Philosophical manuscripts of 1844(which was published only in 1932). *Wang Ruoshui*'s essay 'Man Is the Starting Point of Marxism' mentions that *Mao* in 1964 supported the concept of alienation and thought it an omnipresent phenomenon. This all makes it clear that Chinas Marxist humanism was launched as a critique of China's socialist historical experience, using, on the one hand, an allegorical strategy to subsume China's socialism under feudalism and, on the other hand, taking advantage of the universality of the concepts of humanism and alienation. Both these features of the argument suggest an affirmation of the values of the New Enlightenment movement. In this explanatory model, socialism was never a noncapitalist critique of modernization; on the contrary, the critique of the socialist historical experience was a complete affirmation of the values of European modernity.

其中的一部分在20世纪90年代成为中国国家立法机构的重要的高级官员。[10]问题的复杂性更在于，变革的过程不仅改造了社会，也改造了国家，并在国家内部形成了结构性的裂痕，进而形成了不

---

[10] 20世纪80年代思想启蒙运动的构成是极为复杂的。大约是在1979年曾经召开过一个理论工作务虚会，与会者多为党内理论家。由南京大学哲学系教师胡福明初稿，王强华、马沛文、孙长江等人修订的文章《实践是检验真理的唯一标准》于1978年5月11日在《光明日报》刊出，实际上为思想解放运动提供了理论的依据。尽管参与者关于文章的产生过程的回忆有所出入和差别（胡复明认为该文是在他的文章基础上修订而成，孙长江则说这篇文章是两篇文章捏合而成），但他们都承认文章的修订和刊出是当时特定的政治情境的产物，也是国家意志的表现。孙长江明确地说："这场讨论绝不是由于某个'秀才'，或某几个'秀才'的灵机一动或苦思冥想而引发起来的。这场讨论是历史的产物，《实践是检验真理的唯一标准》这篇文章也是历史的产物。""直接参加讨论的，不仅是理论家，而且有政治家。"值得注意的是，所谓"国家意志"不能被理解为统一的国家意志，因为当时的国家或党内部存在着重要的分歧，这篇文章正是这一分歧的表达。在这个意义上，"国家"或"党"都不能被看作是铁板一块的存在。（关于这篇文章刊出前后的情况，请参见胡福明的回忆文章《真理标准大讨论的序曲——谈实践标准一文的写作、修改和发表过程》，载广州《开放时代》杂志1996年1、2月号，以及孙长江的文章《我与真理标准讨论的开篇文章》，载《百年潮》1998年第3期，第25–29页）。从后来刊出的李春光等人的回忆来看，那时的思想解放运动与上层官员的关系非常密切。以《走向未来》这样较为年轻的知识分子群体为例，虽然其中部分人在1989年后因各种原因滞留海外或一度身陷囹圄，但另一部分却是高级官员。《走向未来》丛书的情形是有代表性的。在1989年以后，"新启蒙"知识分子中的许多人流亡国外，但他们的一些当年的

New Enlightenment intellectuals as simply political dissidents makes it impossible to explain the basic sequence and logic of Chinese thought in the new era. Despite the fact that the history of the New Enlightenment movement is confusing and complex and that serious divisions had emerged by the end of the decade, nevertheless, in historical perspective, it is clear that the movement has served as the foundational ideology of the reforms. Indeed, the split between the New Enlightenment intellectuals and state establishment emerged gradually from their intimate relationship to one another.

The intellectual fountainhead of New Enlightenment thought derives from Western (especially Western liberal and modernization) economics, political science, and legal theory. This was all posed in opposition to orthodox Marxist ideology and is directly attributable attributable to the fact that the Chinese reforms were striding toward globalism via a process of commodification. In this respect, it is impossible to explain the split between New Enlightenment intellectuals and the state establishment simply as an opposition of civil society and the state. Quite the contrary, from an overall perspective, the efforts of the intellectuals and the goals of the state were completely compatible with one another. The active intellectuals in both the intellectual and cultural spheres in China in the 1980s, some of them have become leading officials in the state's legislative bodies.[10] A more

[10] The history of the formation of the 1980s New Enlightenment movement is exceedingly complex. One can probably point to a 1979 conference on theory attended mostly by CCP theorists, as an origin. Previously, *Nanjing* University professor *Hu Fuming* had circulated a draft of the article 'Practice Is the Sole Criterion of Truth', which was revised by *Sun Changjiang*, *Wang Qianghua*, and *Ma Peiwen* and published in the *Guangming* Daily (11 May 1978). This article provided the theoretical

同的政治集团。某些知识分子集团与国家的对抗实际上反应了国家意志内部的冲突。所有这些复杂的状况，都为1989年后中国的政治状况以及流亡知识分子的身份转化所遮盖。事实上，对于国家的内部分歧与"新启蒙"知识分子思想活动的复杂关系的自觉和不自觉的遮盖，已经造成了认识20世纪80年代中国思想状况的重要障碍。

中国的"新启蒙主义"不再诉诸社会主义的基本原理，而是直接地从早期的法国启蒙主义和英美自由主义中汲取思想的灵感，它把对现实的中国社会主义的批判理解为对于传统和封建主义的批判。不管"新启蒙思想者"自觉与否，"新启蒙"思想所吁求的恰恰是西方的资本主义的现代性。换句话说，"新启蒙主义"的政治批判（国家批判）采用了一种隐喻的方式，即把改革前的中国社会主义

同道者仍在国内，并身任要职。例如，在20世纪80年代因为介绍西方经济学思想名噪一时的北京大学经济学教授厉以宁现在是全国人民代表大会法制委员会副主任。与这些群体不同的是一些文学群体和人文知识分子群体，例如早期的《今天》派群体和20世纪80年代中期成立的"文化：中国与世界"编委会。这些群体基本上不是政治性的群体，而是文学或知识的社团或群体。值得注意的是，《今天》派的代表人物北岛虽然在当时以政治性的朦胧诗著名，但却是文学的独立价值的热情赞颂者。"文化：中国与世界"也是以"文化"为标帜，不直接地卷入政治问题。这种一定程度的非政治主张当然有其政治性的后果，即为知识分子的独立地位和价值创造了空间。

complicated aspect of the problem is that the process of reform has transformed not only society, it has transformed the state. It has created cracks in the internal structure of the state and deepened factionalism among the ruling elites, which has led to the formation of different political cliques. The apparent opposition of some intellectuals to the state in

justification for the Thought Liberalization movement. Even though there are different accounts of the creation of this article from those who wrote it (*Hu Fuming* considers it to be a revision based on his earlier essay, while *Sun Changjiang* believes it be a hybrid of *Hu*'s work and the revisions), they all allow that it was the product of the particular political circumstances of the time and an expression of the national will. *Sun Changjiang* said quite clearly: ' This discussion was not the product the brainstorming or deep thoughts of any particular whiz kid or group of whiz kids. The discussion was a product of history, and Practice is the Sole Criterion of Truth was the product of history.' 'The direct participants in the discussion included politicians as well as theorists.' It is worth pointing out that what we refer to as 'the national will' cannot be understood as a united national will, because there were significant fractures at both the state level and in the party, and this essay was precisely the expression of those fractures. The 'state' or the 'party' thus cannot be seen as monoliths. For an account, see *Hu Fuming*'s reminiscence, '*Zhenli biaozhun da taolun de xuqu: Tan shijian biaozhun yiwen de xiezuo, xiugai he fabiao guocheng*' (Prelude to the great debate on the criterion of truth: a discussion of the writing, revising, and publication of the practice criterion essay), *Kaifang shidai* (*Guangzhou*) 1-2(1996):1-25. From the memoirs of *Li Chunguang* and other protagonists in the event, it is clear that the Thought Liberalization movement was closely tied to top-level leaders. The *Zouxiang weilai* (Toward the Future) Group of young intellectuals is representative of this: although a good number of them have gone abroad since 1989, there are still some in China who are in important posts. *Beijing* University professor *Li yuning*, who, in the 1980s, was for a time quite famous for introducing Western economic thought, is now a vice director on the legal committee of the Chinese People's Consultative Congress. In contrast to that group, there are also the literary and humanist groups, such as the early 1980s *Jintian* (Today) faction and the mid-1980s Culture: China and the World editorial board. These groups were basically apolitical, committed as they were to literature and knowledge. It is worth noting that even though *Jintian*'s representative voice, *Bei Dao*, was implicated in the then political Misty Poetry movement, he is a strong supporter of literary autonomy. The Culture: China and the World group took 'culture' as its mission and also did not get directly involved in political questions. Both groups' relatively apolitical stances of course had political consequences, yet they also helped forge social space for autonomous intellectual activity and values.

的现代化实践比喻为封建主义传统，从而回避了这个历史实践的现代内容。这种隐喻方式的结果就是：把对中国现代性（其特征是社会主义方式）的反思置于传统/现代的二分法中，再一次完成了对现代性的价值重申。在20世纪80年代的思想解放运动中，中国知识分子对社会主义的反思是在"反封建"的口号下进行的，从而回避了中国社会主义的困境也是整个"现代性危机"的一部分。"新启蒙"在传统/现代的二分法中进行自我理解，从而忽略了现代国家体制、政党政治、工业化过程，以及由此产生的社会专制和不平等主要是一种"现代"现象。从许多方面看，在寻求把中国纳入世界资本主义的经济体系的现实目标方面，中国的"新启蒙主义"与改革的社会主义有许多共同的东西。把传统社会主义理解成封建主义的历史传统，这不仅是中国"新启蒙主义"的斗争策略，而且也使它获得一种自我的认同，即把自己理解成与反对宗教专制和封建贵族的欧洲资产阶级相似的社会运动。在这种自我理解中被遮盖了的，是作为现代化的意识形态的"新启蒙主义"与作为现代化的意识形态的马克思主义的共同的价值目标和历史理解方式：对进步的信念，对现代化的承诺，民族主义的历史使命，以及自由平等的大同远景，特别是将自身的奋斗和存在的意义与向未来远景过渡的这一当代时刻相联系的现代性的态度，等等。指出这种联系并不是为了抹杀二者逐渐呈现的历史矛盾，也不是否认新启蒙知识分子作为一个特定的社会群体与"国家"的区别，更不是否定作为一种

essence reflects these internal structural divisions. This complexity was concealed by the post-1989 political situation and the transformed position of exiled intellectuals. Actually, it is precisely this conscious or subconscious concealment of the internal divisions within the state and their complex relationship to the activities of New Enlightenment intellectuals that has already become a huge obstacle to the analysis of the 1980s Chinese intellectual situation overall.

The theoretical fountainhead of the Chinese New Enlightenment movement was not socialism but early French Enlightenment thinking and Anglo-American liberalism. Its critical stance toward Chinese socialism was understood as a critique of tradition and feudalism. Consciously or unconsciously, New Enlightenment thinking pursued Western capitalist modernity. In other words, the New Enlightenment critique of politics (and of the state) was couched in an allegorical critique of Chinese socialism as feudal tradition; it thus avoided discussing the modern content of this historical experience. The result of this allegorical strategy is that reflections on China's modernity (whose major characteristic is socialism) are subsumed under the tradition/modernity dichotomy, where modernity is completely reaffirmed. In the movement for the liberalization of thought of the 1980s, intellectual reflections on socialism were undertaken under the slogan of antifeudalism, thereby avoiding any discussion of how the difficulties of socialism were part of a 'crisis of modernity'.

In its self-understanding as part of the tradition/modernity dichotomy, the New Enlightenment overlooked the fact that the state system, party politics, industrialization, and

价值的知识分子独立精神。我在此所谈论的是实际的历史关系。如果知识分子把自己的认同建立在一种虚幻的关系之上，那么，无论他（她）如何强调自己的独立性，这种独立性都将是可疑的。因为我们不能相信：一个不能确切地认识自己的人，能够确切地把握现实。

中国"新启蒙主义"思想不是一个统一的整体，就思想的体系性而言，它远不如中国马克思主义那样完整。事实上，中国"新启蒙主义"是一种广泛而庞杂的社会思潮，是由众多的各不相同的思想因素构成的。这些各不相同的思想因素只是在批判传统的社会主义和寻求作为目标的"改革"过程中才结为同盟。不过我们仍然可以冒险对这一社会思潮的基本方面作出不完整的归纳，这是因为这些相互歧异又相互关联的思想实践以寻求和建立中国的现代性方案为基本的要务。这个现代性方案的主要标志就是在经济、政治、法律、文化等各个领域建立"自主性"或主体的自由。在经济学方面，通过对传统的社会主义计划经济的批判，重新确认市场经济的正当地位以及商品流通过程中的价值规律，进而把市场和私有制理解为现代经济的普遍形态，并最终实现将中国经济纳入世界市场的目标（它被理解为经济自由）；[11]经济改革的思想最初是从价值规律等古典经济学（特别是马克思主义经济学）的理论中汲取灵感的，但是，隐藏在古典马克思主义的价值规律学说中的对于资本主义的批判却逐渐地消失了，价值规律在意识形态的层面日渐地等同于现实的资本主义市场，

the social despotism and inequality that resulted are in themselves products of 'modernity'. In many respects, particularly in its desire to incorporate China into the global capitalist economic system, China's New Enlightenment has many points in common with the socialist reforms. Painting traditional socialism as a relic of feudal tradition was not merely a tactic on the part of the New Enlightenment intellectuals, it was also a means of self-identification. It allowed them to identify themselves with the antichurch and anti-aristocratic European bourgeois social movement. However, such a self-understanding obscures the fact that both the New Enlightenment movement and Marxism, as ideologies of modernization, have many common values and common modes of historical understanding: belief in progress, acceptance of modernization, belief in the historical mission of nationalism, and particularly, belief in the ideals of freedom, equality, and universal harmony. These latter ideals are linked to individual struggle and the existential significance of the individual - both hallmarks of the modern attitude that understands the present moment as the temporal transition to a better future. To point out this link is not an attempt to erase the gradually emerging contradiction between the two, nor is it to deny the status of the New Enlightenment intellectuals as a group distinct from the state at this particular time. Still less is it an attempt to deny an independent value orientation on the part of the intellectuals. What I am talking about here is an actual historical relationship. If the intellectuals build their self-identity on an imaginary relationship, then no matter how much they stress their independence, it will be in doubt. This is because we have a hard time believing that those who cannot accurately know themselves can accurately grasp reality.

从而丧失了这一概念可能具有的对于一切垄断形式的深刻揭露。在政治方面，要求重建形式化的法律和现代文官制度，通过扩大新闻和言论的自由，逐步建立保障人权、限制统治者权力的议会制度（它被理解为政治自由）；[12]但是，由于对毛泽东时代的群众运动的恐惧，许多人对于政治民主的理解主要集中于"形式民主"、特别是法制建设方面，从而把"民主"这一广泛的社会问题局限于上层社会改革方案的设置和专家对于法律的修订和建议方面，不仅忽略了广泛的政治参与乃是民主的必要内容，而且完全无视这种政治参与与立法过程的积极的互动关系正是现代民主变革的基本特征。令人惊异的是，有些学者无视现代宪政民主中包含的直接民主与间接民主的内含（无论它采取什么形式），完全排斥直接民主在民主实践中的意义，甚至把民众的普遍参与看成是专制主义的温床。这种"民主观"在任何意义上都是和民主的精神背道而驰的。在文化方面，一些学者用科学的精

---

[11] 关于价值规律和商品经济的讨论是在马克思的政治经济学范畴中提出的，其中影响最大的是孙冶芳。但根据最近披露的材料，在孙之前，顾准已经思考过同一问题，并曾经与孙讨论过。有关价值规律的讨论典型地揭示了20世纪80年代中国思想的特征，即通过重新探讨马克思主义的基本理论范畴，为现实的市场化改革提供理论的依据。

[12] 法制问题的提出与重新审理"文革"中的错案相关，曾任全国人民代表大会常务委员会委员长彭真提出的"法制面前人人平等"是"文革"结束后流行的口号。但在理论上提出建设性意见的还是于浩成、严家其等学者。

China's New Enlightenment movement, unlike Marxism, is by no means a coherent or unitary intellectual system. In reality, it is a far-flung and jumbled social trend that is constituted by various and sometimes incompatible elements. These elements were initially united by their shared critique of traditional socialism, a unity forged in the process of their common support for the goals of "reform." Nevertheless, we can risk some generalizations about the basic features of this social trend because the mutually exclusive yet mutually linked trends of thought that constitute it take as their basic task the advocacy and establishment of a Chinese modernity. The core of their modernization project lies in their support for the establishment of 'autonomy' or subjective freedom in the economic, political, legal, and cultural spheres. In the economic sphere, through its condemnation of traditional socialist economic planning, the New Enlightenment movement reaffirmed the rightful position of the market economy and its associated law of value in commodity exchange; it upheld the market (understood as the free market) and private ownership of property as elements of a universal, modern economic mode; and it sought thereby finally to integrate the Chinese economy with the world capitalist market (which it takes as economic freedom). The ideas behind the economic reforms gained their initial impetus from the notions of value in classical economic theory (particularly Marxist economic theory). The critique of capitalism embedded in the theory of value in classical Marxist economics, however, gradually disappeared and the theory of value on the ideological level eventually became identical to that of the market in capitalism. As a result, this idea lost its profound capacity to reveal structures of monopoly.[11]

神或科学主义的价值观，重建世界历史和中国历史的新图景，从而将对传统社会主义实践的批判建立在对整个中国封建历史的社会结构的系统研究和批判之上；[13]而另一些学者则通过在哲学和文学等领域中的主体性概念的讨论，一方面吁求人的自由和解放，另一方面则试图建立个人主义的社会伦理和价值标准（它被理解为个人的自由）。主体性概念包含了对现代过程及其意识形态的某种程度的疑虑，但在当时的语境中主要是指个人主体性和人类主体性，前者的对立面是专制国家及其意识形态，后者的对立面是整个自然界，它的积极意义在于为后社会主义时代的人的基本政治权利提供了哲学的基础。这样的主体性概念建立在主体—客体的二元论之上，洋溢着18－19世纪欧洲启蒙主义的乐观主义气息。[14]值得注意的是，在寻求个人的自主性的过程中，启蒙思想既从西方的宗教改革和古典哲学（特别是康德学说）中汲取思想资源，也从尼采、萨特等思想家那里得到灵感。但是，在中国的语境中，尼采、萨特等人对西方现代性的批判却被省略了，他们仅仅是个人主义的和反权威的象征。[15]中国启蒙主义思想内部的冲突经常表现为古典的自由主义伦理与激进的极端个人主义伦理的二元对立。主体性概念即使在今天也是包含着内在的可能性的，但是，如果我们不能把这一概念从上述二元对立中解放出来，置于新的历史条件之中，这一概念就可能僵化为一种没有批判潜能的概念。总的说来，新启蒙思想蕴含的批判潜能在20世纪80年代曾经焕发过青春活

In the political sphere, it demanded the reestablishment of formal legal frameworks and a modern civilian bureaucracy; it also demanded the gradual establishment of human rights and a parliamentary system to limit the power of the rulers through the expansion of freedom of press and speech (this was understood as political freedom). [12] Because of a fear of the mass movements of the Maoist period, however, the understanding of political democracy on the part of many people was limited to 'formal democracy', and the establishment of the rule of law in particular. They thus took the broad social question of 'democracy' as applying only to plans for reform coming from the higher reaches of society and to suggestions for revisions to the law from experts. They thereby not only overlooked the fact that widespread participation is a necessary constituent of democracy, but also failed to realize that a positive interaction between widespread participation and the legislative process is the very hallmark of modern democratic change. What was particularly surprising was that some scholars ignored the mutual implication between direct and indirect democracy in modern

[11] Initial discussions of the law of value and of a commodity economy were conducted within the framework of a Marxist political economy. The most influential contributions were those of *Sun Yefang*. But recent scholarship has revealed that *Gu Zhun* first raised the issue and discussed it with *Sun*. These discussions of the law of value are representative of the major developments in Chinese thought in the 1980s. It was these rethinkings of basic categories of Marxism that served as the theoretical foundation for the implementation of the market reforms.

[12] The calls for legal reform were connected to the reevaluations of wrongly adjudicated cases of the Cultural Revolution and were initially undertaken under the aegis of the popular post-Cultural Revolution proposition that 'everyone is equal before the law', put forward by *Peng Zhen*, the former chairman of the Standing Committee of the National People's Congress. But the theoretical foundations for these ideas derived from scholars like *Yu Haocheng* and *Yan jiaqi*.

力, 但在被组织到现代化意识形态的框架内的过程中, 这些批判潜能正在逐渐地丧失了活力, 以至我们可以说:无论中国的启蒙主义思想内部存在多大的冲突, 也无论中国启蒙主义者对启蒙主义的社会功能的自觉程度如何, 中国启蒙主义是中国当代最有影响力的现代化的意识形态, 它在一个短暂的历史时期内由一种富于激情的批判思想转化为当代中国资本主义的文化先声。

在80年代后期, 由于社会控制的事实上的削弱, 中国"新启蒙主义"的内部分化逐渐表面化。在1989年的世界性变化之后, 中国"新启蒙"运动的内在同一性不复存在。由于中国"新启

[13] 金观涛、刘青峰于1984年在一家地方出版社发表的《兴盛与危机》(长沙:湖南人民出版社, 1984) 一书, 用系统论方法研究中国历史, 提出中国封建社会是一种"超稳定结构"。关于"超稳定结构"的基本观点一直延伸到他们于1993年在香港写作发表的有关中国近代历史的著作《开放中的变迁——再论中国社会的超稳定结构》中。

[14] 主体性问题首先源自李泽厚对康德哲学的解说, 而后他先后发表了几篇关于主体性问题的论纲。(参见:李泽厚:《批判哲学的批判》增订本, 北京:人民出版社, 1984) 但是, 将李泽厚有关主体性的讨论推向整个思想界的是深受其影响的刘再复。他在《论文学的主体性》等文章中将一个形而上学问题变成了一个文学和思想运动的旗帜。(《文学评论》1985年第6期, 第11-26页, 1986年第1期, 第3-15页)

[15] 当代中国知识界对尼采学说的理解甚至还不及大半个世纪前的鲁迅。当代知识分子眼中的尼采、萨特不过是西方个人主义的代表, 而鲁迅早在1907年就已经注意到尼采等人的反现代内容。

constitutional democracies - no matter what forms this entailed. In thus completely excluding the significance of direct democracy to democratic practice, these scholars even came to regard the widespread participation of the populace as the hotbed of authoritarianism. This sort of 'idea of democracy' runs in complete opposition to any actual understanding of the spirit of democracy.

In the cultural sphere, some scholars have used the scientific spirit or scientism to adopt Western modernization as the yardstick for the reconstruction of world and Chinese history, thereby basing their critique of traditional socialism on a total critique of Chinese feudal history and social structure. [13] Other scholars, by contrast, have used philosophy and literary criticism to raise the question of subjectivity to call for personal freedom and liberation while trying to establish social norms and values based upon individualism, something understood as individual freedom. The notion of subjectivity includes certain misgivings about the procedures and ideologies of modernity. In this context, however, subjectivity means both individual subjectivity and the subjectivity of the human species, where the former is counterposed to the dictatorial state and its ideology and the latter is counterposed to the natural world. Its positive significance lies in its provision of a philosophical foundation for the notion of postsocialist political rights. This theory is suffused with the optimism of the eighteenth - and nineteenth- century European Enlightenment and is couched in the binary framework of subjectivity/objectivity. [14] It is worth noting that in the quest for individual autonomy and subjectivity, New Enlightenment thinkers have derived inspiration not only from Western Reformation thinking and classical philosophers (particularly Kant) but also

蒙运动"与社会主义改革存在着目标上的部分一致性, 这个运动的保守的方面成为体制内的改革派、技术官僚或者作为现代化的意识形态的新保守主义的官方理论家; 这个运动的激进方面逐步的形成了政治上的反对派, 其主要的特点是按照自由主义的价值推进中国的人权运动, 促使中国在进行经济改革的同时在政治领域实行西方式的民主化改革。在文化上, "新启蒙主义"的激进方面(激进在这里指的是文化上的对传统的态度) 开始意识到作为社会目标的"现代化"有可能导致 (也可能已经导致价值的危机, 其中一些敏感的年轻学人以基督教伦理为依据, 提出中国现代社会思想中的价值问题和信仰问题。[16]这一问题的提出也明显地配合着韦伯的《新教伦理与资本主义精神》在中国知识界的传播, 其中最为简明的逻辑是: 如果资本主义的发生与新教伦理相关, 那么中国的现代化实践就必须在文化上作出更彻底的变革。一般来说, 20世纪80年代中国的启蒙知识分子普遍地信仰西方式的现代化道路, 而其预设就是建立在抽象的个人或主体性概念和普遍主义的立场之上的。

---

[16] 刘小枫出版于1988年的《拯救与逍遥》(上海:上海人民出版社, 1988) 是首先提出这一问题并引起知识界的重要反响的著作。他本人也逐渐从德国哲学的研究转向基督教神学的研究。

from Nietzsche and Sartre. Yet in the Chinese appropriation of Nietzsche and Sartre, the latters' critique of Western modernity has been conspicuously ignored, and they are seen simply as symbols of individual autonomy opposed to a powerful state. [15] The internal conflict in Chinese New Enlightenment thinking is thus often reflected in a split between classical liberalism and radical individualism. While the notion of subjectivity holds real potential for the present, if we cannot liberate it from the dichotomy described above and situate it in our new historical circumstances, then the idea might calcify into one without critical potential. In general, in the 1980s the critical potential implicit in New Enlightenment thought brought forth a flourish of ideas, but in the process of being deployed and reduced to the ideology of modernization, this critical potential has gradually lost its force. We

---

[13] In its systematic study of Chinese history, *Jin Guantao* and *Liu Qingfeng*'s *Xingsheng yu weiji* (Booms and crises) (*Changsha: Hunan renmin chubanshe*, 1984) was the first book to argue that the structure of China's feudal society was 'superstable'. Underlying this thesis is the question of why China did not succeed in achieving Western-style modernization. This thesis continues to inform their most recent book, *Kaifangzhong de bianqian* (Change in the course of opening up) (Hong Kong: Chinese University of Hong Kong Press, 1993).

[14] The problem of subjectivity was first put forward by *Li Zehou* in his work on Kantian philosophy; he later published several essays on the question. *See Li Zehou, Pipan zhexue de pipan* (A critique of critical philosophy), This theory was made known to a wider audience through its substantial influence on *Liu Zaifu*. In '*Lun wenxue de zhutixing*' (On subjectivity in literature) and other essays, *Liu* turned a metaphysical problem into the banner for a literary and thought movement. See *Liu Zaifu, 'Lun wenxue de zhutixing'*, part 1,*Wenxue pinglun* 6 (1985):11-26; part 2, *Wenxue pinglun* 1 (1986):3-15.

[15] Contemporary Chinese intellectuals' understanding of Nietzsche is not nearly so profound as that of the early-twentieth-century *Lu Xun*. While today's intellectuals take both Nietzsche and Sartre as representatives of the Western notion of individual autonomy, *Lu Xun* as early as 1907 noted the antimodern strain in Nietzsche and other thinkers of his time.

　　只是在启蒙主义发生分化的过程中，对这种普遍主义的质疑才成为可能。其最初的表征是相对主义的文化理念的出现。我指的是在20世纪90年代初期，一些早先的启蒙主义者转而吁求传统的价值，特别是儒教的价值，他们开始怀疑西方社会的各种发展模式是否适合于中国的社会和文化。这一思想倾向特别地受到日本以及韩国、新加坡、台湾和香港等所谓"亚洲四小龙"的鼓励，这些国家和地区的现代化的成功被视为"儒教资本主义"的胜利。"儒教资本主义"这一概念掩盖了三个基本问题：第一，它掩盖了东亚各国的完全不同的发展道路和儒教文化圈内部的社会差异和历史差异，例如日本、韩国、越南和中国都属于儒教文化圈，但为什么所走的道路却如此不同？第二，它实际上把资本主义看作是唯一的现代性模式，通过把儒教与资本主义挂钩，它暗示儒教传统不再是阻碍现代化的历史负担，而是实现现代化的历史动力。换句话说，对儒教价值的怀念并不是传统主义，也不是拒制资本主义的文化力量；在这些学者的眼里，儒教在中国现代化过程中的作用就如同韦伯所说的新教伦理对于欧洲现代资本主义的作用一样。第三，它掩盖了整个现代过程与殖民主义历史的无法分割的联系。如果把儒教资本主义上升到某种规范的高度，就掩盖了现代历史形成的基本动力：全球市场及其规则对民族国家内部的经济关系的制约和规范较之任何其他力量都更为基本。"儒教资本主义"仍然是一种现代化的意识形态；通过对西方价值的拒斥，"儒教资本主义"

can thus say that, however large the internal conflicts and contradictions within the New Enlightenment movement, and regardless of the degree of consciousness the proponents of the New Enlightenment movement have about its social effects, Chinese New Enlightenment thinking is without a doubt the most influential of all ideologies of modernization, and in a short historical period it has been transformed from a mode of ardent critical thinking into the pioneering voice of contemporary Chinese capitalism.

In the latter half of the 1980s, because of the real decrease in social controls, divisions within the New Enlightenment movement gradually came to the surface. After the earthshaking changes of 1989, the essential unity of that movement could not be restored. Because the Chinese New Enlightenment Movement and the socialist reforms had many points in common, the conservative wing of the movement was absorbed by the reform faction of the state to serve as technocrats or theorists of neoconservatism, the official itself into a political opposition, focusing on promoting the liberal idea of human rights and pushing for political reform in the direction of Western democracy. Culturally, the radical faction of the New Enlightenment movement (here, 'radical' indicates a cultural attitude toward tradition) began to become conscious of the possibility that the social goal of modernization could become (or could already be) a crisis in values. Within this group a number of insightful young scholars used Christian ethics to highlight crises in morality and belief in modern Chinese society.[16] The derivation of this question clearly came from the transmission into Chinese intellectual circles of Max Weber's Protestant Ethic and the Spirit of Capitalism. The book's most important message (in this context) was: if the spirit of capitalism

所达到的则是对资本主义生产方式和世界资本主义市场这一导源于西方的历史形态的彻底肯定, 只是多了一层文化民族主义的标记。在中国的语境中, "儒教资本主义"与当代中国改革的社会主义只是同一问题的两种表述罢了。

与这种"儒教资本主义"相似, 另一些学者则致力于论证中国原有的宗族和地缘力量在中国当代经济生活中的意义, 他们相信以"社群"或"集体"为特征的中国的乡镇企业将引导中国走一条既非资本主义、又非社会主义的现代化道路。[17]"乡镇企业的现代化论"有重要的现实依据, 这种以地缘和血缘为核心的集体所有制形式在许多地区创造了经济的奇迹。中国的修正的启蒙主义者试图将乡镇企业当作一种独特的现代化模式, 为的是在理论上回避资本主义与社会主义的冲突, 并在全球资本主义的语境中找到一种区别于西方现代化的道路。在1993–1995年间, 中国一些从事社会研

[17] 甘阳:《乡土中国重建与中国文化前景》,《二十一世纪》(香港), 1993年4月号, 第4–7页。对于甘阳论点的批评, 参见秦晖:《"离土不离乡":中国现代化的独特模式?——也谈乡土中国重建问题》,《东方》(北京), 1994年第1期, 第6–10页。关于乡镇企业的讨论请参见杨沐:《中国乡镇企业的奇迹——三十个乡镇企业调查的综合分析》、王汉生:《改革以来中国农村的工业化与农村精英构成的变化》、孙炳耀:《乡镇社团与中国基层社会》(均见《中国社会科学季刊》总第9期, 第5–17页, 18–24页, 25–36页)。

arises from the Protestant ethic, then the process of modernization in China must undertake some fundamental cultural transformations. In general, while the 1980s New Enlightenment intellectuals wholeheartedly believed in a Western-style path to modernization, their hopes were built on an idealistic individualism or subjectivity and based on universalism.

It was only in the course of the split in the movement that doubts about universalism cropped up. Its first manifestation was in the emergence of relativism. By this, I mean that in the early 1990s some of the early New Enlightenment scholars resorted to traditional values, particularly to Confucianism, to question whether the Western model of development was appropriate to Chinese society and culture. This trend of thought was strongly encouraged and inspired by the experiences of Japan and the so-called Four Small Asian Dragons - Korea, Singapore, Taiwan, and Hong Kong - whose successful modernization had been called a victory for 'Confucian capitalism'. This concept of Confucian capitalism conceals three basic matters: first, the completely divergent paths of development and the cultural and historical differences within the Confucian cultural sphere; for example, if Japan, Korea, Vietnam, and China all belong to this sphere, why have their historical paths diverged so widely? Two, this idea takes capitalism as the sole form of modernity, and in this articulation of Confucianism to capitalism, Confucianism is no longer regarded as an obstacle to modernization but rather

---

[16] *Liu Xiaofeng, Chengjiu yu xiaoyao* (Salvation and leisure1) (*Shanghai: Shanghai renmin chubanshe*, 1988), was the first book to raise this issue, around which there was much subsequent debate in the intellectual world. *Liu* himself has gradually moved from the study of German philosophy to the study of Christianity theology.

究的学者通过深入的调查，终于获得了显著的成果。这些学者的基本问题是：人民公社解体以后，农民是否已成为无组织的完全自由的社会个体？依靠集体致富，是不是等同于再度集体化？个体私营经济的发展是否意味着私有化的开始？随着市场经济的发展，人民公社三级合作组织是否依然存在？它们发生了哪些变化？乡村社会各类组织要素之间，是处于无序的发展状态，还是处于有序的整合状态？乡村社会的组织整合具有什么特点？根据深入的调查，研究者详细分析描述了公社解体以后，集体与个体关系的演变，个体农民与社会化农业生产的关系，乡村组织与乡村组织网络的变革，勾勒了乡村社会发展的社区化趋势，提出了"新集体主义"的概念。根据作者的看法，新集体主义组织方式，既体现了现代市场经济的竞争原则，又符合现行的社会制度，以及共同富裕的奋斗目标，而且承继了传统家族文化的精髓，体现了中国"群社会"的本质，是真正体现中国特色的社会发展之路。[18]乡镇企业的现代化理论和新集体主义观念都没有忘记公社制时代的历史教训，它们

---

[18] 王颖的《新集体主义：乡村社会的再组织》（北京：经济管理出版社，1996）以及她和折晓叶、孙炳耀合著的《社会中间层：改革与中国的社团组织》（北京：中国发展出版社，1993）对改革以后中国社会、特别是乡村的组织和工业化进行了细致的研究，是研究当代中国发展问题的文献。文中所涉及的内容引自《新集体主义》一书的内容提要。

as a key motivating factor for its realization. In other words, this nostalgia for Confucianism has nothing to do with traditionalism, nor is it a cultural barrier to capitalism. Indeed, in the eyes of these scholars, Confucianism plays the same role as that assigned by Weber to Protestantism in the development of Western capitalist modernity. Three, this idea obscures the unbreakable connection between the entire process of modernization and the history of colonialism. If one takes Confucian capitalism as an outstanding example of a norm, one obscures the basic motive power of the formation of modern history: the regulation and standardization imposed by the global market on the economic relationships of nation-states has been a much more important historical factor than anything else. Clearly, 'Confucian capitalism' is an ideology of modernization. In its rejection of Western values, Confucian capitalism enables exponents to embrace the capitalist mode of production and the global capitalist system - phenomena born of Western historical specificity - while adding a layer of cultural nationalism on top. In this context, 'Confucian capitalism' and the contemporary Chinese socialist reforms are simply two sides of the same coin.

A derivative of 'Confucian capitalism' is the theory put forth by some scholars that emphasizes the role played by lineage organizations and localism in Chinese economic life. These theorists argue that rural enterprises based on various types of social collectives are leading China along a unique path of modernization that is neither capitalist nor socialist. [17]

---

[17] *Gan Yang, 'Xiangtu Zhongguo Chongjian yu Zhongguo wenhua qianjing'* (The reconstruction of rural China and the prospects for Chinese culture), *Ershiyi shiji* 16 (April 1993): 4-7.For a critical view of *Gan Yang,* see *Qin Hui,' Litu bu lixiang:*

对"集体"所有制的研究也严格地区别于中国社会主义历史实践中的集体主义，其中最为重要的区别显然是对"个人利益"的强调，即"新集体"的基础是以个人利益为基础的自愿合作的产物。集体与个体以共同利益与地缘乡情为纽带，"合作"本身的目的是"为适应市场经济形势"、更有效地获取经济利益。

乡镇企业的现代化理论和新集体主义理论的提出都意味着在全球资本主义的历史情境中进行理论创新和制度创新的努力。"集体"、"合作"、"地缘"、"乡情"等概念的重新使用，明显地强调了社会生产和分配过程中的"公平"或"平等"问题。在"新集体主义"的理论视野中，中国农民在貌似对传统的复归中，走出了农村多少世纪以来封闭的领地和领域，第一次以乡村工业的高速发展、现代企业制度的迅速推开为主要方式，发展市场，促进都市化（非国家投入的就地造城），成为中国经济改革持续深入进行的重要推动力和开展城市国有企业改革的稳固的后方基地。这是中国农民第一次以经济改革领先，推动中国走向现代化。[19]然而，乡镇企业的现代化论和"新集体主义"的案例研究都带有明显的把个别案例普遍化和理想化的倾向。由于这种理论努力过于急切地试图提出"非西方

---

[19] 同上，第204页。

To be sure, this theory of rural enterprise led modernization has an important empirical base, and these types of local and collective formations have indeed wrought economic miracles in many places. Yet revisionist Chinese New Enlightenment thinkers want to render rural industry as a unique model of modernization to avoid a theoretical confrontation between capitalism and socialism and to find within the discourse of global capitalism a non-Western path to modernization. From 1993 to 1995, some Chinese social scientists undertook full-scale research programs and came up with striking results. The basic questions these scholars asked were: After the dismantling of the People's Communes, did the peasants become autonomous and unorganized social actors? Is relying on the collective to reach prosperity the same as recollectivization? Is an economy of individual enterprise tantamount to the beginning of privatization? In the wake of the development of a market economy, do there still exist organizational forms akin to the People's Communes' "three in-one" structure? What changes have there been in these? Is there essential order or disorder in the articulation of various rural social organizations? What is the general characteristic of village social organization?

Zhongguo xiandaihua de dute moshi?' (Leaving the land without leaving the village: is this a unique Chinese model of modernization?),*Dongfang* 1 (1994): 6-10. On rural industries, see *Yang Mu, 'Zhongguo xiangzhen qiye de qiji: Sanshige xiangzhen qiye diaocha de zonghe fenxi'* (The miracle of China's rural industries: a general analysis of investigations into thirty rural industries); *Wang Hansheng, 'Gaige yilai Zhongguo nongcun de gongyehua yu nongcun jingying goucheng de bianhua'* (Transformations enabled by rural industrialization and village elites since the reforms in China); and *Sun Bingyao, Xiangzhen shetuan yu Zhongguo jiceng shehui'* (Village-level collectives and Chinese grassroots society), *Zhongguo shehui kexue jikan* 9 (Fall 1996): 5-17,18-24,25-36.

的现代化道路",最终却像现代化理论一样把现代化理解为一种中性的技术化的指标;它真正回避掉的恰好是乡镇企业的生产方式与整个资本主义的国内市场和国际市场的关系,是乡镇企业与致力于市场化的国家目标的关系。从技术上看,"乡镇企业的现代化论"和"新集体主义"理论试图把乡镇企业描述成一种独特的现代性的生产和社会组织模式,对乡镇企业和村社组织在中国大陆的不同地区的极为不同的发展方式注意不够, [20]并严重忽略了以追求"效率"为主要目的的乡镇企业在破坏资源和环境、忽略劳动保护等方面的"现代性后果"。

　　"乡镇企业的现代化论"通过对乡镇企业的理想化描述和对其生产关系中的内在矛盾的忽略,

---

[20] 乡镇企业在江苏、浙江、广东等地区的发展可以说是极为成功的,但是,根据中国社会科学院社会学研究所黄平等人的调查,1992年以后,这些地区的乡镇企业的形态也正在发生重要的变化。其中一个突出的变化就是,许多乡镇企业,包括很多成功的乡镇企业纷纷开始与外资合资,转化为新的合资企业。另一方面,由于中国地区间的差异,乡镇企业在各地的情况也有极大的差异。即使在乡镇企业获得巨大成功的许多地区,也没有采取相应的采取保护环境的措施,结果是对环境和自然资源造成了严重的破坏。我曾有机会到河北大丘庄考查,该地是全国闻名的乡镇企业和集体化发展的典型。但是,在巨大的产值和富裕的生活掩盖之下的,是严重的环境污染,生产环境的恶化和严重的不法行为。所有这些都表明,对乡镇企业的状况需要具体地进行分析。关于当代中国乡村的变化,请参见《读书》1996年第10期上的一组笔谈,总题是"乡土中国的当代图景"。

The researchers analyzed and described in detail the changing relations between the collective and the individual after the dismantling of the People's Communes, the relationship between individual peasant activities and socialized rural production, and the transformation of rural organizations and rural organizational networks. They mapped out the trends in rural social organization and localization, from which they derived the concept of 'new collectivism'. In their view, the organizational methods of new collectivism reflect the principles of competition in the modern market economy and are entirely compatible with the current social system and its efforts toward shared prosperity. Moreover, as a continuation of the quintessence of traditional lineage culture, they reflect the essence of China's 'collective society' and the unique characteristics of China's current path of social development. [18]

Neither the theory of modernization via rural and township enterprise nor the concept of new collectivism has neglected the historical lessons of the era of People's Communes, and their delineation of 'collective' is rigorously differentiated from the collectivism of China's socialist period. The most important difference is in the emphasis given to 'individual interests'; indeed, the new collectives are founded on the premise that they are the product

---

[18] See *Wang Ying, Xin jitizhuyi: Xiangcun shehui de zaizuzhi* (New collectivism: the reorganization of rural society) (*Beijing: Jingji guanli chubanshe*, 1996); and *Wang Ying, She Xiaoye*, and *Sun Bingyao, Shehui zhongjianceng: Gaige yu Zhongguo de shetuan zuzhi* (The middle stratas of society: reform and China's social organization) (*Beijing: Zhongguo fazhan chubanshe*, 1993). These books analyze Chinese society in detail after the reforms, particularly with reference to rural organization and industrialization. They are both extremely valuable for the study of contemporary Chinese development.

扬弃了启蒙主义对传统社会关系的批判，又不把私有化的资本主义视为替代社会主义公有制的唯一方式，似乎开掘了一条现代化的第三条道路。从乡镇企业的实践出发理解中国现代性问题是有重要的依据的。但由于它完全不考虑中国经济已经成为世界资本主义市场的一个活跃的部分，同时又把现代性作为中性的技术指标，因此，它不能对现代性或现代化本身的问题作出相应的诊断。我们不妨问一句：作为一种独特社会模式的乡镇企业在进入市场之后的活动也是独特的吗？用乡镇企业的内部特征来抵抗全球资本主义的社会预言是一种可以理解的智力活动，这种智力活动用文化的和数据的方式揭示了中国的现代化道路的独特性。但它的创造者忘记了它所说的独特性（我并不否认这种独特性的存在，正如我不否认中国和日本或者美国和英国之间存在差别一样）如今只能建立在全球资本主义的市场关系之上。这只能是一种"中国特色的现代化理论"，它的整个论证建立在现代化的目的论框架内。在最近几年的社会发展中，许多地区，包括江苏、浙江和广东等地，乡镇企业的结构正在发生重要的变化，一方面表现为集体企业的私有化，另一方面则表现为合资化，即与跨国资本结成新的经济体制。因此，乡镇企业究竟是一种现代化的途径，还是一种现代化的模式，仍然需要深入持续地观察。进一步地说，我的看法是，乡镇企业的形式的确构成了中国的现代化、特别是工业化道路与西方及其他国家的重要的区别，以此为根据而提出的"乡镇企业的现代化

of a voluntary cooperation among individuals based on their individual interests. The collective and the individual are linked by mutual benefit base on localism and local feeling; the goal of cooperation is to adapt to the conditions of the market economy, through which the new collectives attain the most effective economic results.

The emergence of the theory of modernization via rural and township enterprises and the theory of new collectivism has implications for theoretical and systemic innovations amid the historical conditions of global capitalism. The revived use of such concepts as 'collective', 'cooperation', 'localism', 'local feeling', and so forth clearly emphasizes the problems of 'fairness' and 'equality' in social production ad distribution. Under new collectivism, Chinese peasants, seemingly through the revival of traditional forms, are for the first time moving out of their centuries-old isolation and rapidly developing rural industries. They have developed market and promoted urbanization (not goaded by the state but created by the locality) and have become in the process an important motivator of and stable basis for the expansion of China's economic reforms to the urban industrial sector. This is the first time that the Chinese countryside has led in economic reform and has been the primary motive force for the nation's modernization. [19] Yet the study of individual cases of 'new collectivism' and the theory of modernization via rural and township enterprises both have clear tendencies to generalize and idealize particular situations.

Because these theories rather too urgently wish to promote 'non-Western paths of

---

[19] *Wang, Xin jitizhuyi*, p.204.

理论"在批判的意义上主要针对的是将西方资本主义当作唯一模式的看法, 这一看法的提出具有重要的理论和实践意义。但是, 这一理论仍然是以效率为标准的, 它没有涉及的是这种乡镇企业的生产与分配制度是否能够扩大经济民主, 乡镇企业的文化能否有利于建立保障经济民主的政治民主及其制度形式, 乡镇企业的生产方式对自然生态是否具有保护作用, 乡镇企业的组织方式是否有利于社会的政治参与能力, 乡镇企业在全球资本主义的情境中能否为经济平等 (国内的和国际的) 创造制度的和伦理的基础。因而, 这一理论的批判性受到了很大的限制。换言之, 乡镇企业的现代化理论并没有从乡镇企业的经济结构和运行规则中发掘对于现代社会经济和政治活动过程的批判源泉。

20世纪80年代的启蒙思潮曾经为中国社会的改革提供过巨大的解放力量, 它曾经是、而且仍然是支配中国知识界的主要思想倾向。但在迅速变迁的历史语境中, 曾经是中国最具活力的思想资源的启蒙主义日益处于一种暧昧不明的状态, 也逐渐丧失批判和诊断当代中国社会问题的能力。这并不是说中国新启蒙主义的那些思想命题已经完全没有意义, 我也不是说20世纪80年代的思想运动已经达到了目的。我的意思仅仅是, 中国的启蒙主义面对的已经是一个资本化的社会: 市场经济已经日益成为主要的经济形态, 中国的社会主义经济改革已经把中国带入全球资本主义的生产

modernization', they both suffer from the same problem as modernization theory itself, that is, they treat modernization as a neutral technical indicator. They thereby evade a central problem, namely, the relationship between the modes of production of rural enterprises and the international and domestic capitalist market, as well as their relationship to the state goal of marketization. From a technical perspective, both theories want to see in village enterprises a unique modernity in their mode of production and social organization, and they ignore the different modes of development such enterprises have taken in different regions of China [20] and seriously overlook 'the after-effects of modernization', the environmental degradation, and the neglect of labor protection that have come in the wake of their pursuit of efficiency first.

---

[20] In regions like *Jiangsu, Zhejiang*, and *Guangdong*, village and township enterprises have developed extremely successfully; however according to research done by *Huang Ping* and others under the aegis of the Institute of Sociology of the Chinese Academy of Social Sciences, the form of these enterprises has been undergoing great transformation since 1992. One particularly telling change is that many rural industries, including many successful ones, are beginning to link up with foreign investors and are being transformed into jointly owned enterprises. On the other hand, because of regional differences within China, village and township industries differ widely by region. More important, those regions where rural industries are the most successful have not put in place any measures for the protection of the environment. The result has been severe environmental degradation. In 1992, I had the opportunity to to on a research trip to *Daqiuzhuang, Hebei* Province, where rural industries and collectivized development are nationally famous. But obscured by the productivity and the prosperous lifestyle were serious instances of environmental pollution, the degradation of the environment around production sites, and serious illegalities. This all makes it clear that concrete analysis needs to be done regarding rural industries. On changes in contemporary Chinese villages, see *Guo Yuhua, Shi Ran, Wang Ying*, and *Huang Ping 'Xiangtu Zhongguo de dangdai tujing'* (Perspectives on the contemporary Chinese countryside), *Dushu* 10 (October 1996): 48-70.

关系之中，在资本主义化的过程中，国家及其功能也相应地发生了虽然不是彻底的、但却是极为重要的变化。资本主义的生产关系已经造就了它自己的代言人，启蒙知识分子作为价值创造者的角色正面对深刻的挑战。更为重要的是，启蒙知识分子一方面既愤慨于商业化社会的金钱至上、道德腐败和社会无序，另一方面却不能不承认自己已经处于曾经作为目标的现代化进程之中。中国的现代化或资本主义的市场化是以启蒙主义作为它的意识形态基础和文化先锋的。正由于此，启蒙主义的抽象的主体性概念和人的自由解放的命题在批判毛的社会主义尝试时曾经显示出巨大的历史能动性，但是面对资本主义市场和现代化过程本身的社会危机却显得如此苍白无力。一些坚持启蒙主义姿态的人文学者把现实的资本主义化过程所产生的社会问题归结为抽象的"人文精神的失落"。[21]他们重新回向西方和中国的古典哲学，寻找终极关怀和伦理规范，最终把问题落实于以安身立命为目的的个人的道德实践。在这样的历史语境中，启蒙主义似乎只是一种神圣的道德姿

---

[21] 有关"人文精神"的讨论首先是在《读书》杂志（北京）上展开的，而后波及到许多其他刊物。问题的首先出现，请参见张汝伦、王晓明、朱学勤、陈思和：《人文精神寻思录之一，人文精神：是否可能和如何可能》，《读书》杂志1994年3期，第3－13页。自那以后，《读书》杂志在1994年3－7期陆续发表了来自上海的年轻学者的多次谈话录。

Through its idealized description of and disregard for the serious internal contradictions in the production relations of rural industries, the theory of modernization via rural and township enterprises has effectively discarded the New Enlightenment critique of traditional social relations as well as allowed for the idea that capitalist privatization is not necessarily the only alternative to socialist public ownership. It has seemingly opened the possibility for a third road to modernization. There are solid grounds for setting out to understand the question of Chinese modernity through the experience of China's rural and township enterprises. Yet because this theory does not take into account the fact that China's economy is already a very active part of the global capitalist market and because it takes modernity as a neutral technical indicator, it has been unable to make appropriate diagnoses about either modernity or modernization. We cannot help but ask whether rural industries, for all their uniqueness as a social model, have behaved in unique ways after joining the marketplace. Positing the internal uniqueness of rural industries does have the understandable intellectual attraction of rejecting global capitalism's social predictions; this can then be mobilized along with cultural data to explain China's unique path to modernization. But the inventors of this theory have forgotten that the very uniqueness of which they speak (I am not denying the existence of uniqueness, just as I would never deny that China, Japan, the United State, and England are all different) is today made possible only because of its relation to global capitalism. There can be a 'theory of modernization with Chinese characteristics' only where the notion of modernization is teleologically assumed.

Over the past several years of social development, the rural industries in many regions-

态（而它曾经是以反道德为特征的），它的那些抽象而含混的范畴无力对无处不在的资本活动和极为真实的经济关系作出分析，从而丧失了诊断和批判已经成为全球资本主义一部分的中国现代性问题的能力。更为重要的是，什么是所谓的"人文精神"。如果它真的失落了，那么是什么力量导致它的失落？启蒙主义的思想家们曾经奢望"理性化"的过程不仅导致对自然的控制，而且也能促成人的主体的自由、道德和公义的进步以及人类的幸福。但是，这样的信念正在遭到深刻的质疑。因此，如果我们要讨论"人文精神的失落"，就必须先澄清这一失落与中国"新启蒙主义"所致力的现代化运动的历史联系。这场关于"人文精神"的讨论从1994年初开始，持续了一年多的时间，参与者众多，但却没有触及这样的问题：如果所谓"人文精神"是和20世纪80年代的知识分子的思想运动直接相关的话，那么，1989年以后的急剧社会变迁如何瓦解了作为一个独特群体的"知识分子"？这些改变中国"知识分子"社会身份的社会变迁包括：现代社会日趋分工严密的职业化过程，现代企业和公司内部的科层制的发展，国家体制内部的技术官僚化，以及与之相伴随的社会价值取向的转移。原有的知识分子阶层正在分化为专家、学者、经理人员、技术官僚，并被组织到中国社会日益发展的科层制度之中。把当代"知识分子"的变化归结为某种"精神"的失落，而回避导致"知识分子"阶层发生变化的社会条件，其根源之一就是"启蒙主义"知识分子对这个社会过程本身持有极为暧昧的矛盾

including *Jiangsu* and *Guangdong* – have undergone profound transformations; one of these is the privatization of collective enterprises, another is their transformation into [Sino-foreign] joint ventures, in which a new economic system is being forged in collaboration with multinational capital. It remains to be seen whether rural industries are a transitional avenue to modernization or whether they constitute a new model of modernization. Moreover, I think that the rural industries that have led Chinese modernization have trodden a path that is quite different from the industrialization paths of Western and other countries. To use this, as does the theory of modernization via rural and township enterprises, as the basis for a critique of the Eurocentrist notion that there is only one model of modernization has great theoretical value and significance. But this theory still uses efficiency as its yardstick; it is silent on the questions of whether the system of production and distribution in the rural enterprises promotes the expansion of economic democracy, whether their culture is conductive to a political democratization that will guarantee economic democracy, whether their mode of production can protect the environment, whether their organizational methods are conducive to political participation, and whether, in the context of global capitalism, they are capable of setting the systemic and ethical foundations of economic equality, both domestic and international. The critical quality of this theory has, however, been sharply limited. In short, this theory has failed to identify targets of criticism in the economic and political processes of modern society.

The New Enlightenment thinking of the 1980s provided an enormous source of liberation for the reform of Chinese society and it dominated and still dominates intellectual

.

态度。

　　中国的所谓"后现代主义者"正是利用了这种含混，把西方的后现代主义直接作为批判中国"新启蒙主义"的武器，尽管中国的"后现代主义"比中国的"启蒙主义"更加含混。我在这里不能对中国的"后学"作全面的分析，因为其中也包含了各种因素和复杂性。我在此所作的分析，主要针对的是"后学"的一些代表性人物的代表性文章。"中国的后现代主义"是在西方、特别是美国后现代主义影响之下形成的，但它们的理论内涵和历史内涵都极为不同。我仍然把这种"中国的后现代主义"作为现代化的意识形态的补充形式来看待。"中国的后现代主义"的主要理论来源是解构主义、第三世界理论和后殖民主义。然而，"中国的后现代主义"从未对中国的现代性问题作出历史分析，也从未见到一位中国的"后现代主义"的信徒对中国的现代文化与西方的现代文化的关系作细致的历史分析。在文学的领域里，他们所解构的历史对象与启蒙主义曾经作过的历史批判是一样的，都是中国现代的革命及其历史理由；稍有不同的是，他们对启蒙主义的主体性概念加以嘲笑，却从未将中国启蒙主义的主体性概念置于特定的历史语境中加以分析。当"中国的后现代主义者"嘲笑"启蒙主义"历史姿态的时候，他们不过是在说作为一个历史过程和社会运动的"启蒙主义"是如何地不合时宜，因为他们已经置身于受商业化的大众传媒支配的、消费主义的"后现代"社会。后殖民主义可以被视

discourse in China. But in the rapidly changing historical context, what used to be China's most vigorous source of ideas has increasingly descended into equivocation; it has gradually lost not only its ability to critique but also its ability to diagnose problems in contemporary Chinese society. This is not to say that the issues raised by New Enlightenment thought have lost their significance, nor is it to say that the intellectual movement of the 1980s has already attained its goals. My point is simply that China's New Enlightenment movement now faces a fully capitalized society: the market economy is increasingly the dominant economic formation, and China's socialist economic reforms have already brought China completely into the global capitalist mode and relations of production. As part of this process, the state and its capacities have witnessed corresponding and extremely important changes, even if they have not been complete. Capitalist relations of production have already created their own spokespeople. New Enlightenment intellectuals, as the definers of values, face a profound challenge. More important, New Enlightenment intellectuals, while deploring commodification, moral bankruptcy, and social disorder, cannot help admitting that they are in the middle of the very process of modernization that they have longed for.

China's modernization (or the process by which capitalist markets were created) has enlightenment as its underlying ideology and cultural harbinger. Because of this, the abstract concept of human subjectivity and the concept of human freedom and liberation, which played significant roles in the critique of *Mao*'s socialist experiment, lack vigor in the face of the social crises encountered in the process of capitalist marketization and modernization. Some humanists committed to the notion of enlightenment have attributed the crisis to

为西方（主要是美国）文化制度内部的自我批判，它从边缘文化立场对西方中心主义文化所作的批判（对后殖民主义理论本身的讨论不是本文的任务），揭示了殖民主义在文化和知识领域的表现形式，其中也包括西方民族国家理论被殖民地人民用以抵抗殖民者的复杂过程。在"中国后现代主义"的文化批评中，后殖民主义理论却经常被等同于一种民族主义的话语，并加强了中国现代性话语中的那种特有的"中国/西方"的二元对立的话语模式。例如没有一位中国的后殖民主义批评家采取边缘立场对中国的汉族中心主义进行分析，而按照后殖民主义的理论逻辑这倒是题中应有之义。具有讽刺意味的是，有些中国后现代主义者利用后现代理论对西方中心主义进行批判，论证的却是中国重返中心的可能性和他们所谓"中华性"的建立。在这种典型的现代性宏伟叙事中（虽然打着后现代的旗号），中国的所谓后现代主义者对中华性的未来性预见不仅没有触及作为资本主义中心的新中国与自己的文化、与西方现代历史的关系，而且与传统主义者有关21世纪的预言和期待完全一致。[22]这倒并不使人惊讶。

中国后现代主义的另一特点是以大众文化的名义将欲望的生产和再生产虚构为人民的需要，

---

[22] 请参见张法、张颐武、王一川：《从"现代性"到"中华性"》，《文艺争鸣》1994年2期。第10–20页。

an abstract 'decline of the spirit of humanism'.[21] They have gone back to Western and Chinese classical philosophy to seek moral norms and final answers; in the end, they reduce the problem to one of the moral foundation of selfhood. At this historical juncture, New Enlightenment thought has seemingly become a spiritual moral stance (whereas formerly its hallmark was to condemn moralism). Its abstract and indistinct categories are incapable of critically examining the activities of a ubiquitous capital and actual economic relations; it has thus lost its ability to diagnose and criticize the problems of a Chinese modernity that is already part and parcel of a global capitalist system.

An even more important question is what is this spirit of humanism, and how has it been lost, if it has? The wild hopes that Chinese New Enlightenment intellectuals harbored about this process of 'reason' – that it would lead to the control of nature, to the formation of subjective freedom, to the progress of morality and justice, and to the happiness of human beings – are now subject to large doubts. As a result, if we wish to explore the 'lose of the humanistic spirit', we must first understand the historical relationship between this loss and the efforts of the New Enlightenment intellectuals during the modernization movement.

The recent discussions on the humanistic spirit began in 1994 and lasted for more than a year. There were many participants, but they did not even touch on the following problem: if

---

[21] Discussions on 'the spirit of humanism' began in the magazine *Dushu* and later spread to many other journals. For the first mention of the subject, see *Zhang Rulun, Wang Xiaoming, Zhu Xueqin*, and *Chen sihe, 'Renwen Jingshen Xunsilu Zhiyi'* (Meditations on the spirit of humanism, part 1), *Dushu* 3 (March 1994): 3-13. In later issues that same year, (nos.4-7), *Dushu* published a series of responses sent by young scholars in *Shanghai*.

将市场化过程中受资本制约的社会形态解释为中性的、不受意识形态支配的"新状态"。[23]在这种理论分析中，既缺少对大众文化内部的不同层次、不同方面的调查和分析，又没有对商业化的或消费主义的意识形态作出相应的阐释和批判。当他们以中性化的欲望、状态、人民、大众文化的名义对他们所属的知识分子群体进行攻击的时候，以消费主义为其主要内容的市场意识形态却经由他们的后现代主义理论而合法化了。"中国的后现代主义"否定掉的是"新启蒙主义"的严肃的社会政治批判，他们对一切价值进行解构的同时，却没有对构成现代生活主要特征的资本的活动作出分析，也没有对这种资本的活动与中国社会主义改革运动的关系作出评价。在他们经常指称的"官方或主流与大众文化"的二元对立之中，看不到这两者通过资本的活动而形成的复杂关系，而这恰恰是当代中国社会文化的主要特点之一。事实上，中国的后现代主义者正是把希望寄托于"市场化"："'市场化'意味着'他者化'焦虑的弱化和民族文化自我定位的新可能"，"市场化的结果，必然使旧的'伟大叙事'产生的失衡状态被超越，而这种失衡所造成的社会震撼和文化失落也有了被整合的可能"，"并

---

[23] "新状态"这个概念被一些当代文学评论家用于描述当代中国文学的主要特征。其意思是当代中国文学中的"新状态"是一种不受意识形态支配的原生态。

this so-called humanistic spirit is directly linked to the intellectual activity of the 1980s, how have the dramatic social changes since 1989 collapsed the category of the "intellectual"? Changes in the social position of the intellectual in China include a higher degree of division of labor and a concomitant professionalism, increased stratification within corporations and enterprises, the technocratization of the state machinery, and consequent changes in many of society's values. The original intellectual stratum is now dividing into experts, scholars, managers, and technocrats and is subjected to the same relentless process of stratification as everyone else in Chinese society. The ascribing of the changes among intellectuals to a loss of 'spirit' and their silence on the social conditions that lead to stratification can be attributed to the fact that New Enlightenment intellectuals have an extremely contradictory and equivocal attitude toward these social processes.

China's 'postmodernists' have exploited this ambiguity in their deployment of Western postmodernism as a tool for the critique of New Enlightenment thinking, even though China's postmodernism is even more ambiguous than the latter. I cannot undertake a full-scale analysis of Chinese 'post-ism' (houxue) here, because it contains so many factors and complexities. What I analyze here are some of the principal essays of 'post-ism' by some of the representative players. Postmodernism in China emerged under the influence of Western, and particularly U.S., postmodernism, but Chinese postmodernism's theoretical intentions and historical contents are very different from the West's. I consider Chinese postmodernism to be a supplement to the ideology of modernization. Its major sources are deconstruction, third-world theory, and postcolonialism. Yet Chinese postmodernism has never carried

提供了一种新的可能的选择、一条民族的自我认证和自我发现的新道路。"[24]所谓"市场化"不是一般地对市场的赞同，而是要把整个社会的运行法则纳入到市场的轨道，"市场化"不是一个经济学范畴，而是一个政治、社会、文化和经济的范畴。在20世纪90年代的历史情境中，中国的消费主义文化的兴起并不仅仅是一个经济事件，而且是一个政治性的事件，因为这种消费主义的文化对公众日常生活的渗透实际上完成了一个统治意识形态的再造过程；在这个过程中，大众文化与官方意识形态相互渗透并占据了中国当代意识形态的主导地位，而被排斥和喜剧化的则是知识分子的批判性的意识形态。在有些后现代主义者所采用的学院政治式的批评方式中，隐含的是他们的文化政治策略：用拥抱大众文化（虚构的人民欲望和文化的市场化形态）、拒斥精英文化的姿态重返中心——中国特色的社会主义市场。中国后现代主义文化批评的一部分已经成为中国大陆的独特的市场意识形态建构的有效部分。

在当代中国的情境中，思想界和知识界对上述问题的回应是极为无力的。一些来自大陆中国、留学欧美的年轻中国学者与他们在中国的合作者们试图借助于分析的马克思主义等西方理论提出

---

[24]张法、张颐武、王一川：《从"现代性"到"中华性"》，《文艺争鸣》1994年2期，第15页。

out a full-fledged historical analysis of Chinese modernity, nor have I ever seen any adept of Chinese postmodernism subject the relationship between Chinese modernization and Western modernization to serious historical analysis. In the field of literature, the historical target of postmodern deconstruction and that of the New Enlightenment thinkers is the same – namely, China's modern revolution and its historical roots. The one difference is that postmodernists sneer at the New Enlightenment concept of subjectivity without taking into account the historical context of this concept's emergence. When Chinese postmodernists mock the historical position of enlightenment, they are merely saying how as a historical process and social movement enlightenment is outmoded in a postmodern society dominated by the mass media and consumerism.

For its part, postcolonialism can be seen as the cultural self-criticism of the West (principally in the United States), a critique launched from the perspective of peripheral cultures against the culture of Eurocentrism. It reveals the extent to which colonialism is implicated in culture and thought, and it also indicates the complicated process through which colonized peoples used Western theories to resist their colonizers. In Chinese postmodernism, postcolonial theory is often synonymous with a discourse on nationalism, which reinforces the China/West paradigm. For example, there has not been a single Chinese postcolonial critique of *Han* centrism from the standpoint of peripheral culture. What is particularly amusing is that Chinese postmodernists turn the postmodernist critique of Eurocentrism on its head to argue for Chineseness and to search for the prospects for China repositioning itself at the center of the world. In this typical metanarrative of modernism

问题。尽管他们对现代中国历史的把握让许多学者感到不满，但我仍然认为，他们的问题意识具有现实尖锐性。在思想的方式上，这些年轻学者也一定程度地超越了那种在中国/西方的二元论述中讨论中国问题的启蒙主义的思想方式。他们考虑的问题与冷战的结束有密切的关系，其主要出发点是：冷战时代的旧的概念范畴已经不能满足中国和世界的需要，时代呼唤制度创新和理论创新。他们中的代表者认为可以从"新进化论"、"分析的马克思主义"和"批判法学"中汲取一些有益的启发；然后以中国深厚的土壤为基础，将中国已经出现的一些制度创新和理论创新的萌芽培育、壮大起来。所谓"新进化论"倡导的是超越传统的"社会主义/资本主义"的二分法，对中国社会主义经济制度中的一些遗传因素如乡镇企业及某些农村组织形式进行制度创新，从而获得发展。将John Roemer、Adam Przeworski等美国学者提出的"分析的马克思主义"引入中国，目的在于对马克思的学说严格解说，以在当代条件下推动人类全面解放、个人全面发展的理想的实现。其中最核心的思想是，社会主义的理想历来是以广大人民的"经济民主"来取代少数经济、政治精英对社会资源的操纵。实际上，这一理论的提出直接针对的是俄国已经实行、中国正在实行的国有资产的股份化或私有化运动。因此，他们的观点恰好是：政治民主是保证公有资产不被少数人"自发私有化"的必要条件，如果说"资本主义民主"是"资本主义"和"民主"的妥协，而社会主义则是经济、政治民主的

(even though it proceeds under the banner of postmodernism), the vision of the future of Chineseness not only says nothing about the change in China's position within a process of globalization but is also silent regarding any predictions and hopes for the twenty-first century. The Chinese postmodernists' vision not surprisingly replicates those of the traditionalists. [22]

Another of the most salient features of Chinese postmodernism is that in its treatment of popular culture, it misrepresents the production and reproduction of desire as people' 'needs', and it interprets the marketized social mode as a neutral and ideology-free 'new mode' (*xin zhuangtai*).[23] In this type of analysis, there is neither differentiation between levels and aspects of popular culture, nor any attempt to undertake a hermeneutic and critical appraisal of the ideology of consumerism and commercialism. Rather, postmodernism appears as the champion of the people and popular culture and as the defender of their neutral desires and their 'unmediated state'. It is used to attack other intellectuals and as a legitimation of market ideology and consumerism. At the same time as it deconstructs all values, postmodernism jeers at the serious sociopolitical critical intent of the New Enlightenment intellectuals while ignoring the formative role of capitalist activity in modern life and neglecting consideration of the relationship between this capitalist activity and China's socialist reforms.

---

[22] See *Zhang Fa, Zhang Guwu, Wang Yiquan, 'Cong xiandaixing dao Zhonghuaxing'* (From 'modernism' to 'Chineseness'), *Wenyi Zhengming* 2 (1994):10-20.

[23] The new mode is seen by some contemporary literary critics as a major feature of contemporary Chinese literature. It indicates an ideology free, 'pristine' condition.

同义词。"批判法学"的一项重要理论成果是揭示出西方18世纪以来民法的最核心内容———绝对财产权,即财产"最终所有者"对财产的排它性处置权——已经解体。这一理论在中国的语境中的意义仍是与如何扩大经济民主、扼制大规模私有化运动相关的。用他们自己的观点来说就是,在概念层次上,超越"私有制/国有制"的两分法,从而把注意力转移到如何通过"财产权力束的分离与重组"来扩大经济民主,并将生命与自由的权利置于比财产权更重要的宪法地位。总之,以"新进化论"、"分析的马克思主义"和"批判法学"为理论基础的中国学者试图以经济民主和政治民主为指导思想,超越非此即彼的两分法,寻求各种制度创新的机会。[25]

是否继续使用社会主义或者资本主义的概念并不重要。当代中国社会面对的问题也显然无法用资本主义或社会主义这样的概念来简单地加以解释。问题仅仅在于能否真正触及当代中国社会面对的社会问题,能否在具体的情境中作出审慎有度的分析。中国新马克思主义的出现与美国大学里的经济学、社会学以及法学中的马克思主义思潮有深刻联系,这也可以看作是所谓全球化条件

---

[25] 崔之元:《制度创新与第二次思想解放》,《二十一世纪》(香港),1994年8月号,第5-16页。对于这篇文章的批评,请参见季卫东:《第二次思想解放还是乌托邦?》,《二十一世纪》(香港),1994年10月号,第4-10页。

In constantly pitting popular culture against official culture, the postmodernists fail to see that the complex relationship the two have developed through the mediation of capital is one of the main features of contemporary Chinese society and culture. Actually, the hopes of the postmodernists ride on commercialism: 'Marketization' means the weakening of anxieties over Othering and the possibility for the confirmation of the self through national culture... The result of Marketization is the inevitable transcendence of the imbalance produced by the old metanarrative and the possibility that the shocks produced by these imbalances and by cultural decline can be realigned... It also offers the possibility of new choices a new path towards self-confirmation through nationality and self discovery.'[24] Their so-called marketization is not simply an affirmation of the market, but represents an effort to subsume all the rules of social activity to the functions of the market. As a result, the scope of this marketization is not limited to just the economic sphere, but includes politics, society, and culture as well. In the 1990s Chinese context, the rise of consumerist culture is no longer merely an economic event, it is also a political event because the penetration of such culture into people's daily lives is carrying out the task of the reproduction of hegemonic ideology. In this process, it is the interaction between popular and official culture that is the main feature of contemporary Chinese ideological hegemony, and what is being excluded and ridiculed is the critical consciousness of elites. The academicism of some of these postmodern critiques conceals their cultural strategy of embracing popular culture (as

---

[24] *Zhang Fa, Zhang Yiwu*, and *Wang Yichuan, 'Cong xiandaixing dao Zhonghuaxing'*, p.15.

下的"理论旅行"。除了由于忽略历史的具体过程而产生的对西方理论的简单搬用外，这些研究的一个欠缺是，作者的注意力完全集中于经济领域，[26]而很少涉及文化领域。如果说中国新马克思主义已经提出了经济民主的问题，但却没有提出和讨论文化民主的问题。在市场条件下，文化资本的运作是整个社会活动的重要方面。对文化资本的控制和媒体的掌握，决定着社会的基本文化倾向和主流意识形态的取向。例如当代最重要的媒体是电视系统，除了国家对媒体的控制之外，中国的电视剧生产正在市场化，那么在大众文化与国家之间建立的这种联系能否提供文化民主的内在机制呢？许多中国知识分子乐观地认为"市场化"能够自然地解决中国社会的民主问题，实在是天真的幻想。在媒体和大众文化已经相当发达的中国当代情境中，特别是中国的文化生产与国际的和国内的经济资本的活动密切联系的时代，放弃对文化生产、文化资本的分析，也同样不能真正理解中

---

[26] 崔之元对当代中国经济改革中的问题的诊断也是引起争论的问题。苏文发表于《东方》1996年第1期上的论文《山重水复应有路》虽然是讨论前苏联和东欧国家的改革问题的文章，但基本的思想却是针对崔之元关于中国私有化进程的观点的。这是因为崔之元对中国改革道路的分析是在与前苏联和东欧改革的比较关系中进行的。由此可见，关于中国当代改革道路的讨论不只受到中国改革本身状况的影响，还受到前苏联和东欧地区改革状况的影响。在可以预见的将来，前苏联和东欧的改革的成败对中国学者思考中国问题将会产生重大的影响。

the defender of neutral desire and the commercialization of culture) to adopt a posture of negating elite culture in order to effect a conquest of the cultural center stage. This is none other than the socialist market with Chinese characteristics. Some postmodernist critics have effectively participated in the establishment on the Chinese mainland of a unique market ideology.

In contemporary China, the responses to the above problems in intellectual circles is quite without vigor. Some Western-trained mainland Chinese scholars in conjunction with their mainland collaborators have been exploring new theoretical approaches (such as Marxism) to these problems. The understanding of these young scholars of modern Chinese conditions leaves something to be desired. Nevertheless, I think that their consciousness of these problems has poignant relevance and their mode of thinking has transcended to some extent the West/China binary that remains the focal point of New Enlightenment thought. Intimately linked to the end of the Cold War, their point of departure is that old concepts and categories born of the Cold War era are no longer sufficient to accommodate the realities of post-Cold War China or the world. A new world situation demands new theories. A number of them want to apply insights gained from 'neo-evolutionism', analytical Marxism, and critical legal studies to China's situation by building on the foundation of new systems and structures within China that then nourish their theoretical innovations.

So-called neo-evolutionism seeks to transcend the traditional dichotomy of capitalism/socialism to introduce theories that can explain the institutional innovations, such as rural enterprises, in the legacy of the socialist economic system. Analytical Marxism, a theory

国当代社会和文化的复杂性。新马克思主义特别注重经济民主的分析，但文化民主问题似乎基本上没有涉及，这也多少显示了中国现代化的目标和现代化理论对他们的潜在的影响。在中国的语境中，国家机器与市场的关系错综复杂，而文化的生产一方面受制于国家机器的运作，另一方面则受制于经济资本和市场的活动。但是，经济和市场本身从来就不是脱离国家的领域。在当代的条件下，文化生产就是整个社会再生产的一个部分。因此，对文化问题的分析需要超越马克思有关"经济基础"与"上层建筑"的二分法，而将文化理解为整个社会生产和消费过程的有机的部分。换句话说，对于中国学者来说，文化批判一方面需要与对社会政治经济过程的分析相联系，另一方面也要在方法论的意义上寻找文化分析与政治经济分析的结合点。在这方面还很少有学者提出系统的理论和观点，因为真正的理论创造需要大量的经验分析和历史研究，而后一方面的工作仍然是相当不够的。但是，这并没有妨碍一个最为基本的结论，即争取经济民主、争取政治民主和争取文化民主事实上只能是同一场斗争。

对于中国社会来说，对经济民主的讨论涉及的是整个社会分配制度和生产方式，因此必不可免地涉及政治民主问题。在这个意义上，讨论经济民主和文化民主问题为讨论政治民主提供了实质内容。20世纪90年代以来，有关政治民主的讨论明显减少，这显然是因为这一话题仍然充满禁

promoted by U.S. scholars such as John Roemer and Adam Przeworski, has been imported to China with the goal of rigorously explicating Marxist positions on the possibilities for the realization of the all-round liberation of human beings and the development of individual potential. Its core theory is that the historical emphasis of socialist ideals has promoted the expansion of mass economic democracy in opposition to economic benefit for the few and as a way to prevent the monopolization of social resources by an economic and political elite. Clearly, this theory stems from opposition to the largescale privatization of state property that has already been completed in Russia and is well under way in China. Analytical Marxists believe that political democracy is necessary so that the few can be prevented from becoming the exclusive beneficiaries of privatization; if 'capitalist democracy' is a compromise between capitalism and democracy, then socialism is synonymous with political and economic democracy. As for critical legal studies, its major theoretical contribution lies in its discovery that the basis of Western civil law since the end of the eighteenth century – that is, the concept of absolute property rights, or the exclusive right of disposal by the 'final owner' of a property – has collapsed. In the Chinese context, the significance of this theory is once again connected to the expansion of economic democracy and restraint of the privatization movement. It seeks to transcend the private/public ownership dichotomy and to focus on 'the separation and reconstitution of the cluster of powers over property', to expand economic democracy, and to give priority to the right to life and freedom over the right to property in the constitution. In sum, Chinese scholars subscribing to neo-evolutionism, analytical Marxism, and critical legal studies strive to transcend the either/or

忌。除此之外，如何在冷战结束以后的情境中界定民主和规划切合实际的历史目标的确成为需要思考的问题。政治民主不仅是社会实践的目标，而且也是文化反思和历史反思的课题。对政治民主的诠释一方面受制于不同的文化价值观，另一方面则与国际间的经济政治关系密切相关。在中国的独特的市场社会形式中，不存在脱离经济民主和文化民主的政治民主问题，也不存在脱离政治民主和文化民主的经济民主问题。因此，一方面，我们可以说民主问题在20世纪90年代显然增加了新的社会内容，另一方面，讨论经济民主却无法回避政治民主问题。

有关中国民主的讨论集中于如何保障个人的自主性和政治参与能力。中国知识界对这一问题的思考从两个不同而相关的方面展开。第一个方面是经济自由主义的论述。由于私有化运动和乡镇企业的发展，以及跨国资本在中国的实际存在，中国社会的经济结构已经相当复杂。但许多经济学者仍然相信，市场及其活动作为一种"自然过程"能够自发地导向民主的实现。他们认为，由于"市场逻辑，就是个人权利的自由交易"，而"国家观念，就是公共权力的强制实施"，"前者以个人自由权利的确立和保障为基础，后者以公共选择的结果为前提"，因此，市场本身的发展将保证个人的充分的自由权利。[27]在这种经济自由主义的论述中，个人权利通过市场逻辑获得保障，而市场虽然与国家存在复杂的关系，但在功能上能够限制国家权力的过度扩张。我们能够理解这种理想主义叙述针

binary theoretical model and to highlight the interdependence of economic and political democracy as the guiding principle for institutional innovation. [25]

Whether one uses concepts from socialism or from capitalism is not important. The current situation in China does not easily lend itself to either. The main questions are whether the social problems China now faces will be confronted and whether careful analysis can be made of the concrete situation. The emergence of neo-Marxism in China is part of a trend toward the revival of Marxism in economics, sociology, and legal studies in U.S. universities. This can be seen as an example of 'traveling theory' in the new conditions of globalization. However, a shortcoming of Chinese neo-Marxism, apart from its simplistic borrowing of Western theory not grounded in empirical study of Chinese history and contemporary reality, is its exclusive focus on the economy with little reference to culture. [26] If one can say that Chinese neo-Marxism has already brought the problem of economic democracy to attention, it has still not begun a discussion of the problem of cultural democracy. In the present market

[25] See *Cui Zhiyuan*, '*Zhidu Chuangxin yu dierci sixiang jiefang*' (Institutional innovation and the second liberation of thought), *Ershiyi shiji* 24 (August 1994): 5-16. For a critical view, see *Ji Weidong*, '*Dierci sixiang jiefang haishi wutuobang?*' (A second liberation of thought or utopia?), *Ershiyi shiji* 25 (October 1994): 4-10.

[26] *Cui Zhiyuan*'s treatment of contemporary China's economic reforms has precipitated a debate. For example, the major theoretical target of *Su Wen*'s, '*Shanchongshuifu*'(see note 8 above) is *Cui Zhiyuan*'s perspective on China's privatization process. This is because *Cui*'s analysis is based on a comparison of the Chinese reforms with those of the former Soviet Union and Eastern Europe Apparently, these debates about the Chinese reform path are premised not only on the Chinese reforms but also on the reforms in the former Soviet Union and Eastern Europe. For the foreseeable future, the success or failure of the Soviet and Eastern European reforms will undoubtedly continue to influence the thinking of Chinese scholars about reform.

对的是国家对于市场和社会的干预，但是，如果国家不仅是完全外在于市场的存在，而且也是个人的直接对立物，那么，我们用什么范畴来叙述市场内部的支配力量呢？经济自由主义的论述掩盖了中国的市场形成与国家改革计划的关系，创造了作为一种自然范畴的"市场"概念，却丧失了分析市场关系内部的那些支配与被支配的权力关系。这种权力关系不仅是社会腐败的主要根源，而且也是社会资源的不平等分配的基本前提。在计划/市场的二元论中，"市场"概念被设想成为"自由"的源泉。但是，这一概念模糊了市场与市场社会的区别：如果说市场是透明的、按照价值规律运行的交换场所，那么，市场社会则要求用市场的法则支配政治、文化和我们的一切生活领域，市场社会的运作是和垄断的上层结构无法分离的。正是在这个意义上，"市场"概念掩盖了现代社会的不平等关系及其权力结构。正如沃勒斯坦在总结布罗代尔的贡献时指出的，"如果没有一种政治保障你就永远不能支配经济，……认为没有国家的支持、甚至在反对国家的情况下也能成为一个（布罗代尔定义下的）资本家，那简直是一个荒诞的想法。"[28]如果国家是资本主义运作的一个组成因素，那

[27] 张曙光：《个人权利和国家权力》，《公共论丛》No.1, 1995, 三联书店, 1995, 第1-6页。
[28] 见布罗代尔：《资本主义的动力》，三联书店, 1997, 第85页。

conditions, however, the possession of cultural capital is an important part of social activity. Control of cultural capital and of the media determines the general orientation of culture and mainstream ideology. For example, the most important arm of the media today is television; in addition to state control of the media, the production of television dramas is becoming marketized. In the space between popular culture and state-controlled programming, might we be able to offer this as an internal possibility for the democratization of culture? Many Chinese intellectuals optimistically, but quite naively, assume that marketization will naturally lead to the resolution of the problem of social democracy in China. Today, when popular culture and the media are already extensively developed and especially when cultural production is already completely linked to international and domestic capital, to abandon an analysis of cultural production and cultural capital is to miss completely the opportunity to understand the complexity of contemporary Chinese society and culture.

Neo-Marxism focuses almost exclusively on economic democracy and rarely if ever touches on the problem of cultural democracy; this is to some extent a reflection of the lingering influence of China's goal-oriented modernization theory. In the present context, the complex interpenetration of the state machinery and the capitalist market means on the one hand that the state is completely involved in cultural production, and on the other hand that cultural production is limited by the activity of both capital and the market. Clearly, in the present circumstances, cultural production is part of social reproduction. Therefore, cultural studies must transcend the Marxist base/superstructure dichotomy to treat culture as an organic part of social production and consumption. In other words, for Chinese scholars,

么，支配当代中国知识界的政治想象的经济自由，是否应该重新加以界定呢？试图用国家对经济的干预程度来解释经济和政治民主问题，是不是在重新论证究竟谁应该是国家行为的受益者呢？

第二个方面是有关市民社会和公共领域的讨论。越来越多的人注意到，市场并不是国家之外的一切，在市场/国家的关系中也需要"社会"的中介力量，才能保持力量的均衡。在哈贝马斯等人的影响下，许多人将注意力转向了市民社会和公共领域的范畴。他们认为中国社会正在出现一个市民社会，或者说，他们吁求在中国形成一种西方式的市民社会，其功能是保障个人权利的自由和抵制国家力量的过度干预。如果把这一讨论看作是用规范式的方式吁求政治民主的话，那么，我们能够理解、同情并在一定程度上支持这一讨论。但是，如果把这种规范式研究看作是一种具体的、现实的途径或经验，则这一理论势必陷入自我矛盾的困境。中国的市场化改革始终是和国家的强大存在相关的，在国家推动下形成的所谓"市民社会"是否像许多人期待的那样处于社会/国家的两极结构之中，是令人生疑的。[29]例如许多政治精英及他们的子弟直接参与经济活动，并成为大公司和

---

[29] 黄宗智在讨论美国中国学中有关市民社会和公共领域范畴的应用时也曾指出："将'资产阶级公共领域'和'市民社会'这两个概念用于中国时，经常预设了国家与社会之间的二元对立……我认为，国家与社会之间的二元对立是从西方近代历史中高

cultural criticism must be thoroughly integrated with political and economic analysis, and this integration must be sought in methodological practices. In this respect, there are few scholars who have developed systemic theories to deal with the problem, for this type of theory requires large amounts of empirical information and historical research, both of which are still lacking. This does not, however, prevent us from reaching a basic conclusion: namely, that the struggles for economic, political, and cultural democracy are all essentially the same fight.

In the Chinese social context, discussions of economic democracy inevitably must involve discussions of the system of social distribution and production; as such, they cannot but include discussions of political democracy as well. Discussions of economic and cultural democracy can thus provide the substance for discussions of political democracy. Since the 1990s, there has been a clear decline in discourse on political democracy. This is not only because it remains a taboo topic, but also because in the post-Cold War context, how to define democracy and how to plan a realistic historical outcome have become questions in need of discussion. Political democracy is both the goal of social praxis and the topic of cultural reflection. The interpretation of political democracy is determined very much by cultural values; it also is influenced by the intimate relationship between politics and economics in the international sphere. In the context of China's unique market society, there is no longer any question of a political democracy that can be abstracted from economic and cultural democracy. Nor is there any question of an economic democracy that can be abstracted form cultural and political democracy. As a result, on the one hand we can say

企业的代理人。我们能说他们是"市民社会"的代表吗？这表明在中国已经出现了经济精英与政治精英合二而一的社会结构，而他们也直接参与国际性的经济活动。在中国已经揭露出的一些重大的腐败丑闻，都涉及高级政治官僚或其子弟在国内和国际经济活动中的不法行为。更为重要的是，这一讨论更加注重于"社会"的功能，却很少分析作为社会范畴对立面的"国家"范畴究竟意味着什么？它是铁板一块地处于"社会"之外或之上，还是与"社会"相互渗透？"国家"内部是否包含了特定的空间？这些空间有无可能在特定条件下称为某种批判性的空间？

这一问题也牵涉如何形成社会和政治的批判空间问题。在这方面，一些学者将注意力转向文化生产领域，例如媒体和印刷文化，因为在这个领域中，当代中国正在出现"民间的"刊物、"独立的"制片人及其文化产品。1989年后，由《学人》（主编陈平原、王守常、汪晖）丛刊[30]开始，逐渐出现了

度抽象出的一种理想，但它并不适用于中国。"Philip C. C. Huang: *"Public Sphere"/"Civil Society" in China? The Third Realm Between State and Society, Modern China*, number 2. April 1993, 第216-240页。黄宗智的讨论主要针对近代中国的情形而言，但我以为即使就当代中国的情况来说，也是适用的。

[30] 由日本国际学术友谊基金会资助、江苏文艺出版社出版。

that in the 1990s the question of democracy has a new social context, and, on the other, that discussion of economic democracy cannot avoid a discussion of political democracy.

The debates on Chinese democracy have concentrated on how to guarantee individual autonomy and individual political participation. Chinese intellectuals have approached the problem from two angles. The first is the discourse on economic liberalism. Privatization, the development of rural enterprises, and the presence of multinational corporations have made the Chinese economy exceedingly complex. Yet many economists still believe that as a 'natural process', market activity alone is sufficient to lead to the emergence of democracy. They argue that because 'the logic of the market is a free exchange of individual rights' and 'the state represents the coercive implementation of public rights', and because 'the former is premised on the assertion and protection of individual freedom and rights, while the later is founded on the result of public choice', the development of the market itself constitutes a guarantee of individual freedom and rights. [27] In this discourse of economic liberalism, individual rights are guaranteed by the logic of the market, and even though the market and the state have a complicated relationship, the market nevertheless puts certain restrictions on the excessive expansion of state power.

We can understand this idealistic discourse as targeting, state interference in the market and in society. If the state is not, however, simply seen as completely exterior to the market and as the direct antithesis of the individual, then how are we to categorize the internal

---

[27] Zhang Shuguang, 'Geren quanli he guojia quanli' (Individual rights and state power), Gonggong luncong 1 (1995).

一系列"非官方的"学术刊物, 如《中国社会科学季刊》(主编邓正来) [31]、《原道》(主编陈明) [32]、《公共论丛》(编辑刘军宁、王焱、贺卫方) [33]。同时还出现了一些介于官方与非官方之间的刊物, 如《战略与管理》(主编秦朝英、执行主编杨平、李书磊) [34]、《东方》(主编钟沛璋、副主编朱正琳) [35], 等等。中央电视台的专题节目《东方时空》也是由一些受聘于电视台的民间制片人参与创作。这一切的确带来了新的文化景观。但是, 就"民间刊物"而言, 在这里特别值得注意的有两点：第一, 即使是"非官方"刊物也由官方出版社出版, 因为中国的体制中不存在民间的出版社；第二, 这些"民间刊物"都没有正式的刊号 (所谓以书代刊), 因而处于合法与非法之间。更重要的是, 由于受到体制内部空间的保护, 正式刊物 (或者说是官方刊物) 反而能够发出较民间刊物更为大胆的批评意见。以当代中国影响最大的刊物《读书》为例, 它被公认为中国思想解放的象征。但是, 这个受到

---

[31] 在香港注册出版。

[32] 起初由中国社会科学出版社出版, 而后又因经济问题转由团结出版社出版。

[33] 福特基金会资助、三联书店出版。

[34] 由官方的"中国战略与管理研究会"主办。

[35] 由中国东方文化研究会主办。

forces of market distribution? The discourse of economic liberalism obscures the relationship between state plans for reform and the creation of markets in China, giving rise to a notion of natural 'markets' that forfeits any ability to analyze the power relationships within these markets' systems of distribution. These power relationships are not just the principal sources of social corruption, but also the basic premise behind the unequal distribution of social resources. Within the dichotomy of planning/market, the notion of the 'market' has been assumed to be the source of 'freedom'. This notion, however, blurs the distinction between markets and a market society. If we can say that markets are transparent and function in accordance with the price mechanisms of the marketplace, then a market society would use market mechanisms to govern the realms of politics, culture, and all other aspects of life – the working of market society cannot be distinguished from a monopolistic superstructure. It is in just this way that the notion of markets obscures the inequalities of modern society and its unequal structures of power. As Immanuel Wallerstein pointed out summing up the contributions of Fernand Braudel, 'Without political guarantees, there is never any way to control the economy… If anyone thinks that without state support or from a position of opposition to the state that he can become a capitalist (in Braudel's sense of the term), this is an absurd presumption.' [28] If the state is a constituent element in the implementation of capitalism, should not the imagery of economic liberalism that governs the contemporary Chinese intellectual world be rethought? In attempting to use the degree of state interference

---

[28] See Fernand Braudel, *Ziben Zhuyi de dongli* (The wheels of commerce) (*Beijing: Sanlian shudian*, 1997),p.85.

知识分子广泛好评的刊物并不是"民间刊物",而是由直属新闻出版署的国家出版社出版的刊物。像《东方时空》这样的电视专题节目,就是独立制片人、国家意识形态机器和巨额广告收入共同促成的电视制作。由于民间力量的参与,它的影像语言、主持人风格与传统的官方新闻节目的呆板风格大为不同,也在一定程度上触及了原有节目没有触及的社会内容,但同时,它也负担着宣传和制造官方意识形态的任务,并在国家的严格控制之下。中国的"公共空间"在这个意义上不是介于国家与社会之间的调节力量,而是由国家的内部空间和社会相互渗透的结果。这些文化产品对于中国社会文化空间的拓展具有广泛的意义,但是,它们既是国家与社会之间的空间,也是国家内部的空间,也必然没有真正的力量抵拒国家的政治干预。

　　20世纪90年代以降,美国、台湾、香港和中国大陆的许多学者都将哈贝马斯的公共领域理论引入对中国问题的探讨。就哈贝马斯的理论而言,早期自由主义的公共领域与市民社会具有密切联系,它介于市民社会与国家之间并对二者实行监督与批评。哈贝马斯构筑的是一种规范式的理想形态,他特别注重的是这一理想形态在现代历史中的变形和转化。这就是他所说的公共领域的"重新封建化",即媒体和其他公共领域被国家、政党和市场所左右的状况。按照这一理论的基本逻辑,我们可以推论说,首先,大陆的公共空间则是在没有成熟的市民社会的前提下形成的,在许多情况

in the economy to explain economic and political democracy, should not one first reevaluate just who it is that stands to benefit from the activities of the state?

The second angle proceeds along the lines of the discourses on civil society and the public sphere. More and more people have recognized that the market is not exterior to the state and that between the market and the state is 'society'. As a middle force, society can maintain the balance of Habermas, many people have turned their attention to civil society and the public sphere. They believe that a Western-style civil society is emerging in China, or at least they call for its emergence as a defender of the civil rights and freedoms of the individual against the excessive interference of the state. If we take this discussion as a set of norms to be employed in appealing for political democracy, then we can understand it, sympathize with it, and even give it considerable support. But if this formal research agenda is taken as a concrete path and actual experience, then the theory becomes self-contradictory. But market reforms in China were initiated by a strong state from the very beginning; it is doubtful that a state-sponsored civil society could provide an effective counterbalance to the state in this state/civil society[29] dichotomy. For example, members of the political

---

[29] Philip Huang, in his discussion of the mobilization of civil society/public sphere discourse among American China scholars, has pointed out that 'in using the twin concepts of The Bourgeois Public Sphere and Civil Society in China, often there is an opposition set up between the state and society.... I believe that this state/ society dichotomy has been abstracted from modern Western history, and is not necessarily applicable to China.' Philip C. C. Huang, 'Public Sphere/ Civil Society in China? The Third Realm between State and Society', Modern China 2 (April 1993): 216-240. Although Huang's discussion is specifically aimed at the situation in early modern China, I believe that it is also appropriate for a discussion of contemporary China.

下，它甚至存在于国家体制内部。但它所以能够存在于国家体制内部，一方面是由于国际和国内市场的经济资助，另一方面则是由于国家的利益需要和国家内部空间的形成。因此这一公共空间的形成从未呈现过哈贝马斯所描述的那种早期资产阶级公共领域的特征，媒体在整个社会体制中所处的地位不仅深刻说明了中国的公共空间与哈贝马斯所描述的欧洲公共领域的差别，而且也表明媒体在这一语境中从来不是一个自由讨论和形成公共意见的领域，相反，媒体是各种支配性力量角逐的场所。在这个意义上，需要重新研究社会/国家在当代中国的复杂关系。在这个错综复杂的关系中，无论是市场，还是"社会"，都并不是自然抵御国家过度干预的力量。这表明，经济民主和文化民主问题是与政治民主问题直接相关、无可分割的问题。这也同时表明，经由市场而自然达致国内和国际领域中的公平、正义和民主不过是另一种乌托邦而已。[36]

---

[36] 由于受到东欧知识分子和欧美学术界的影响，中国学术界在20世纪90年代也开始讨论市民社会问题。在"社会－国家"的二元论述模式中，西方学者以波兰团结工会为例，认为东欧集权制度的瓦解与"市民社会"的成熟程度有关。美国中国学界对近代中国历史的研究受到哈贝马斯《公共领域的结构性转换》的影响，用公共领域的概念重新阐释中国近代社会的变迁，产生了大量重要的学术著作。但是，在当代中国有关市民社会问题的讨论中，明显地存在着经由"市场化"而自发民主化的幻想。中国的市场化改革的确已经产生出了新的社会阶层，但是，这些阶层是否能够成为政治民主化的动力却是极为不清楚的。我已经提

elite or their families directly participate in economic activity and have become agents for large corporations and industries. Can we call them representatives of civil society? In China, political and economic elites have been completely conflated, and they participate in international economic activity. The worst scandals in the economic sphere exposed thus far have all involved top-level bureaucrats and their dependents. Even more important is the question asking what is implied in the fact that most of this discussion focuses on the capacities of 'society' and very little is directed to the 'state' that stands in opposition to society. Is this state situated in a fixed position outside of or on top of society, or does it interpenetrate with society? Are there specific spaces implicit in the notion of the 'state'? Do these spaces constitute potential areas of critique under certain circumstances?

These questions involve the issue of how to create space for social and political critique. Some scholars have turned their attention to the sphere of cultural production such as the media and print culture, because in this realm contemporary China has produced a number of 'unofficial' periodicals, 'independent' producers, and other cultural products. Several 'civilian' or 'independent' journals emerged after 1989. The first was *Xueren* (The Scholar), followed by *Zhongguo shehui kexue jikan* (Chinese social science quarterly), *Yuandao* (Inquiry into the way), and *Gonggong luncong* (Public forum). [30] A number of semi-official publications

[30] *Xueren* is edited by *Chen Pingyuan, Wang Shouchang, and Wang Hui.* It is funded by the Japan International Academic Friendship Foundation and published by *Jiangsu wenyi chubanshe. Zhongguo shehui kexue jikan* is edited by *Deng Zhenlai* and registered in Hong Kong. *Yuandao* is edited by *Chen Ming* and was initially funded by the Chinese Academy of Social Sciences Press. When the latter organization encountered financial difficulty, the journal was picked up by *Tuanjie chubanshe. Gonggong luncong* is edited by *Liu Junning, Wang Yan, and He Weifang.* It receives financial assistance from the Ford Foundation and is published by *Sanlian shudian.*

中国当代思想的这个最近阶段的结束是以"新启蒙主义"思潮的历史性衰落为标志的。不过，我们也可以换句话说，这是作为现代化的意识形态的社会主义和"启蒙主义"的历史性胜利。正是这些相互冲突的思想共同为中国现代化提供了合理性和合法性的证明，为中国社会朝向全球市场和全

及在中国社会改革过程中，政治精英与经济精英的合二而一的情况，以及中国的政治腐败与市场化的复杂关系，这些都表明无论是市场化，还是新社会阶层的出现，都不能保障政治民主的实现。更为重要的是，在当代中国的条件下，民主问题已经与经济问题无法分割，特别是和社会分配问题无法分割。与这种关于"市民社会"的讨论相关的是，中国许多知识分子认为"开放"本身最终将导致中国社会向西方靠拢，从而在政治上解决民主问题。问题是，中国当代的政治腐败的动力之一，即是和国际资本在中国的活动相关的。这同样证明，简单说"开放"能够解决中国的市民社会问题也是不切实际的。我在此提及这两点既不是简单地否定有关市民社会的讨论，更不是说中国应当走向封闭，我的意思仅仅是：我们需要发展出更为复杂的论述模式来检讨中国社会的问题。中国大陆有关市民社会问题的讨论主要集中在一份民办刊物《中国社会科学季刊》上。主要的文章有邓正来、景跃进：《建构中国的市民社会》（创刊号）、夏维中：《市民社会中国近期难圆的梦》（总第5期，第176-182页）、萧功秦：《市民社会与中国现代化的三重障碍》（总第5期，第183-188页）、德里克：《现代中国的市民社会与公共领域》（总第4期，第10-22页）、蒋庆：《儒家文化：建构中国式市民社会的深厚资源》（总第3期）、朱英：《关于中国市民社会的几点商榷意见》（总第7期，第108-114页）、施雪华：《现代化与中国市民社会》（总第7期，第115-120页）、鲁品越《中国历史进程与市民社会之建构》（总第8期，第173-178页）等等。此外，《天津社会科学》也发表了一些文章，如俞可平：《社会主义市民社会：一个崭新的研究课题》（1993-4）、戚衍：《关于市民社会若干问题的思考》（1993－5）、徐勇：《现代政治文化的原生点》（1994－4）。

such as *Zhanlue yu guanli* (Strategy and management) and *Dongfang* (The Orient) also appeared.[31] In addition, state-owned China Central Television (CCTV) began broadcasting the program *Dongfang shikong* (Oriental time and space), which was made by freelance producers. All this has changed the cultural scene considerably. But there are two things to be noted about these 'unofficial' publications. First, they are published by state-owned publishing houses (in the absence of nonstate publishing houses), and second, their legal status is quite ambiguous, since they have no proper ISBN identification. Significantly, they are usually more cautious about printing critical material than official publications because of their greater vulnerability and lack of systemic protection. *Dushu* (Reading) is a case in point. Generally seen as the standard-bearer of free thinking, this journal is by no means an unofficial publication; it is published by a state publishing house and administered by the Bureau of Journalism and Publications. *Dongfang shikong* is another case in point. This sort of television reporting, even in the hands of independent producers, is still the product of a combination of the organs of the state ideology and huge advertising revenues. To be sure, because of the participation of unofficial elements, it is quite different from the monotonous and superficial state news programs in its use of imagery, language, presentation style, and content. Nevertheless, it is under strict state control and must fulfill the task of creating and

---

[31] *Zhanlue yu guanli* is edited by *Qin Chaoying*, with *Yang Ping* and *Li Shulei* as managing editors. It is run by the official Chinese Association for the Study of Strategy and Management. *Dongfang* is edited by *Zhong Peizhang*, with *Zhu Zhengling* as vice editor. It is run by the Chinese Association for the Study of Oriental Culture.

球体系的改革开辟了道路。在跨国资本主义时代, "新启蒙主义"的批判视野局限于民族国家内部的社会政治事务, 特别是国家行为；对内, 它没有及时地把对国家专制的批判转向在资本主义市场形成过程中"国家/社会"的复杂关系的分析, 从而不能深入剖析市场条件下国家行为的变化；对外, 它未能深刻理解中国的问题已经同时是世界资本主义市场中的问题, 因此对中国问题的诊断必须同时也是对日益全球化的资本主义及其问题的诊断, 而不能一如继往地援引西方作为中国社会政治和文化批判的资源。中国启蒙主义的话语方式建立在民族国家的现代化这一基本目标之上, 而这个目标却是由起源于欧洲、而今已遍及世界的资本主义过程所制定的。中国新启蒙主义面对的新的问题是如何超越它的原有目标对全球资本主义时代的中国现代性问题进行诊断和批判。在新启蒙思潮的历史性衰落之后, 我们看到的是思想的废墟, 在这个废墟之上, 是超越国界的巨大的资本主义市场；甚至作为启蒙思想的批判对象的国家行为在相当大的程度上也受制于这个巨大的市场。在这个世纪即将告终的时候, 已经有人宣告：历史终结了。

promoting the state ideology. Thus, the public sphere in China is not a mediating space between state and society, but rather the result of the interpenetration of society and part of the internal structure of the state. These cultural products do have a general significance in extending cultural space in Chinese society, but since they exist in the space between state and society (and also within the state's space) , they have no real power to resist state intervention.

Since the 1990s, many scholars from the United States, *Taiwan*, Hong Kong, and China have imported Habermas's concept of civil society into China. According to Habermas, the public sphere of early liberalism had a close relationship with civil society, stood between civil society and the state, and exercised supervision over both. What Habermas has constructed is an ideal norm, and he pays particular attention to the transformations and distortions of this ideal norm through the course of modern history. This is what he calls the 'refeudalization' of the public sphere, that is, the media and other parts of the public sphere fall under the sway of the state, political parties, and the market. By the basic logic of this theory, we can say that, first, in mainland China, the public sphere emerged before a mature civil society, and in many ways it exists very much within the state apparatus. Its existence in this position is facilitated on the one hand by the financial assistance offered by international and domestic markets and on the other hand by the needs of the state and the creation of space within the state. Because of this, this public sphere never exhibited the characteristics that Habermas identified as peculiar to the early bourgeois public sphere; the position of the media in the social structure forcefully points to the vast differences between China's

4、面对21世纪：全球资本主义时代的批判思想

20世纪末期的最为重要的事件是东欧社会主义的失败和中国朝向全球市场的"社会主义改革"，这一切正在结束和已经结束了以意识形态的对立为标记的冷战时代。站在这样的历史转折点上，许多学者对21世纪作出或悲观或乐观的预言：21世纪是新的产业革命的时代；是解决人口和生态问题的时代；是文艺或宗教复兴的时代；是经济中心转向太平洋圈的时代……。哈佛大学教授塞缪尔·亨廷顿(Samuel P. Huntington)在题为《文明的冲突》的论文中断言：新世界中占首位的冲突根源，将不再是意识形态的和经济性的，人类中的重大分界以及主要的冲突根源将是文化性的。民族国家在世界事务中仍将是最有力的行动者，但全球政治的主要冲突将发生于不同文明的民族和国家之间。文明的冲突将主导全球政治。

我不准备在此对亨廷顿和其它学者的预测作出理论的分析和质疑，(已经有学者提及了这样的问题，如在国际政治行为中，民族国家将把文化价值置于经济和政治利益之上吗？)我要指出的问题是，在冷战结束以后，包括中国在内的社会主义国家已经成为世界资本主义市场的一个重要的、也许是最富活力的地区；东亚地区也的确可能改变在原有的资本主义经济体系中的边缘地位，成为新的资本主义的经济中心之一；在资本主义生产方式普遍化的历史情境中，这个生产方式本身

public sphere and the public sphere in Europe, of which Habermas speaks. We can also see how in this context the media was never a realm of free discussion and the creation of public opinion. If anything, the media was just the opposite: an arena in which hegemonic powers contended. It is thus important to do more research into the complex relations between society and the state in contemporary China; it is also important to recognize that, within this complexity, neither the market nor society is a 'natural' deterrent to state power. This highlights the fact that economic and cultural democracy are inseparable from political democracy; it also demonstrates that the hope the market will somehow automatically lead to equity, justice, and democracy - whether internationally or domestically - is just another kind of utopianism.[32]

_____

[32] Under the influence of Eastern European and Euro-American scholars, Chinese scholars began discussing civil society in 1990. Invoking the society/state dichotomy, Western scholars have ascribed the rise of Poland's Solidarity movement to the collapse of central state power in Eastern Europe as a consequence of the maturation of civil society. Scholars of modern Chinese history in the United States have been deeply influenced by Habermas's Structural Transformation of the Public Sphere and have used the concept of the public sphere to reexamine modern Chinese historical change, thereby producing a large number of valuable studies. However, in their discussions of civil society in contemporary China, there clearly persist idealistic dreams about the natural connection between marketization and democratization. While China's market reforms have clearly produced new social strata, it is unclear whether these new social strata can provide the motivating force of the Chinese reforms, there has been a joining of political and economic elites. Together with the complex relationship between political corruption and marketization, this demonstrates that neither marketization nor new social strata can possibly guarantee the emergence of political democracy. More important, under the present conditions in China, it is impossible to separate the problem of democracy from the economy, and it is particularly inseparable problem the question of social distribution. With respect to the discussions on civil society, many Chinese intellectuals believe that 'opening' in and of itself

的矛盾在21世纪居于何种地位？例如在中国的市场化过程中，国家资本、民间资本、外来资本之间的关系怎样？新阶级与社会其它阶层的关系怎样？农民与城市人口的关系怎样？发达的沿海地区与落后的内地的关系怎样？所有这些社会关系都需要置于资本主义的生产关系、特别是市场关系中来观察，而根本的问题是，这些关系的变化对于整个中国社会乃至整个世界的资本主义市场具有怎样的影响？在跨国资本主义的时代，这些"国内关系"是否已经无足轻重？我至今还记得自由主义的理论大师马克斯·韦伯的不祥预感，他认为以理性化为特征的现代资本主义的发展必将导致人对人的统治制度，甚至断言没有任何方式可以消除社会主义的信念和社会主义的希望。在全球范围内的社会主义运动已经失败的历史情境中，韦伯的问题是否还成立？

问题的复杂性更在于，作为一种实现现代化的方式或者作为中国现代性的主要形式，中国的社会主义同样导致了社会组织、特别是国家对人的专制，甚至较之于资本主义更为严重。韦伯和马克思对现代性的反思都建立在他们对资本主义的观察之上，而在今天，我们有必要把对中国社会主义的历史反思同时视为对现代性问题的反思，这个现代性问题是由欧洲的近代资本主义及其文化所引发的。市场社会的扩展及其对社会资源的垄断必然伴随着自发的、未经计划的社会保护运动，这两个方面的冲突构成了19至20世纪的最为严重的社会危机（包括两次世界大战）的动因，也成为

The decline of the New Enlightenment movement marks the end of the most recent phase of Chinese thought. Yet, we can also say that this represents the historical victory of the ideology of modernization shared by socialism and the New Enlightenment movement. These two mutually conflicting yet mutually supportive modes of thought have produced a rationalization and a legitimization of China's modernization and have illuminated the path for a Chinese society facing global capitalist marketization reforms. In this era of multinational capitalism, the New Enlightenment movement was able only to produce a critique internal to the nation-state and particular to state behavior. It was unable to turn its critique of state dictatorship toward a timely critique and an analysis of the changing relationship between state and society and the conditions of changing state behavior in a market economy. It

will result in China's drawing closer to the West, thereby resolving the problem of democracy. The problem is that one of the biggest motive forces for political corruption in China today is linked to the integration of Chinese economic activity with international capital. This demonstrates that the simplistic idea that opening up will lead to democracy has no basis in reality. I bring this up not simply to reject a discussion of civil society and even less to suggest that China should move back into isolation; my intention is merely to point out that we must develop more complex paradigms for the study of contemporary Chinese social questions. See *Deng Zhenglai* and *Jing Yuejin*, *'Jian'gou Zhongguo de shimin shehui'* (Constructing Chinese civil society), *Zhongguo shehui kexue jikan* 1 (1992) :58-68; *Xia Weizhong*, *'Shimin shehui: Zhongguo jinqi nanyuan de meng'* (Civil society: a dream not to be realized in the near future), ibid.5 (1995):176-182; *Arif Dirlik*, *'Xiandai Zhongguo de shimin shehui yu gonggong lingyu'* (Civil society and public sphere in modern China), ibid. 4 (1994):10-22; *Xiao gongqin 'Shimin shehui yu Zhongguo xiandaihua de sanzhong zhang'ai'* (Civil society and and three barriers to China's modernization), ibid.,183-188; *Zhu Ying*, *'Guanyu Zhongguo shimin shehui de jidian shangque yijian'* (Several points of discussion concerning civil society in China), ibid. 7 (1996): 108-114; *Shi Xuehua*, *'Xiandaihua yu Zhongguo shimin shehui'* (Modernization and Chinese civil society), ibid.,115-120; and *Lu Pinyue*, *'Zhongguo lishi jincheng yu shimin shehui zhi jiangou'* (China's historical process and the constructioni of civil society), ibid. 8 (1996): 175-178.

现代社会制度自我改革的基本动力。现代社会主义的兴起是基于对资本主义内在矛盾的理解和克服这种矛盾的历史愿望，但已有的社会主义实践不但未能完成这个历史任务，而且最终将自己汇入了全球资本主义之中。与此同时，资本主义从社会主义运动和各种社会保护运动中获得了进行自我批判和改革的机会，以至于在今天，我们已经无法在原来的意义上以民族国家为单位界定社会主义和资本主义问题。正是在这个意义上，当我们用全球化或全球资本主义这样的概念来描述当代世界的变化时，绝不意味着资本主义的垄断结构及其运行规则代表了当代世界的所有方面，因为在欧美的社会体制和公共政策中已经包含了各种社会主义的或其它的社会机制。除了制度实践中所包含的社会主义或社会保护因素外，我们还可以发现布罗代尔称之为"物质文明"的那些方面：那些在生活的底层所进行的、在漫长历史中形成的交往关系。也是在这个意义上，对中国社会主义的反思才不仅是对过去的检讨，而且也是对现在与未来的预言，因为我们仍然置身于以现代化为目标的同一个历史进程之中。传统形式的社会主义无法解决现代性的内在危机，作为现代化的意识形态的马克思主义和"新启蒙主义"也几乎无力对当代世界的发展作出恰当解释和回应。正是在这里，隐藏着"重新思考中国问题"的必要性。

中国思想界正在讨论所谓的"全球化"问题，而与此相对照的是，西方媒体却在谈论中国的民族

also was unable to come to an understanding of the fact that China's problems are also the problems of the world capitalist market and that any diagnosis of those problems must come to terms with the steadily increasing problems produced by the globalization of capitalism. Finally, it was unable to recognize the futility of using the West as a yardstick in the critique of China. The discourse of the Chinese New Enlightenment movement is built on the basic goal of the modernization of the nation-state, a goal whose origins are in Europe and have by now become the global prescription of the capitalist process. The new problem facing New Enlightenment thinking is how to transcend this goal and formulate a diagnosis and critique of the problem of China's modernity in the era of global capitalism. In the wake of the decline of New Enlightenment thinking, what we see are its remnants; on these ruins rests the capitalist market that crosses all national boundaries. Even the state behavior that was the primary target of New Enlightenment thinking has been constrained by this huge market. Thus, at the close of this century, there are those who have already announced an end to history.

Critical Thought in the Era of global Capitalism

The two most important events of the end of the twentieth century were the failure of Eastern European socialism and the reorientation of China toward the global market through its 'socialist reforms'. They brought to a close the Cold War conflict between two opposing ideologies. Standing at this crossroads of history, there have been all sorts of prophecies about the twenty-first century: it will be the era of a new revolution in production; it will be

主义。大多数中国知识分子对"全球化"抱持着儒家大同式的理想主义,这种有关"大同"的天下主义不过是一个世纪以来不断重复的"走向世界"的现代性梦想罢了,我们从中还能辨识出一些"儒教化的世界图景"的依稀面目。而另一些年轻人却利用商业炒作的方式炮制了《中国可以说不》这样的畅销书,以至在已经非常不安的西方社会引起了有关中国民族主义的疑虑和明显过于夸张的"中国威胁论"。在一定意义上,后者成功的商业炒作使得许多海外媒体认为中国民族主义思潮已经具有极端排外的性质,而忘却了这本书的出版和发行过程与商业的关系。只要民族国家体系没有彻底瓦解和重组,民族主义作为民族国家同一性的基础就不会消失。更为重要的是,当代的民族主义政治与传统民族主义存在重要的差别,与其把它看作是全球化的对立物,毋宁把它看作是全球化的副产品。对于民族主义问题的讨论必须全球政治经济体系关联起来,而不能作孤立地说明。中国在21世纪可能成为一个发达的市场社会,但却没有可能成为新的全球霸权。美国和前苏联的经济、政治和军事地位是在冷战的过程中形成的,在苏联垮台后,北约已经成为全球压倒性的军事力量。在可以预见的历史时期里,没有一个国家能够发展起这样的军事霸权。如果不能从全球的政治、经济和军事结构思考当代民族主义问题,那么,无论他们是积极地支持民族主义运动,还是极力反对民族主义,都有可能放过了问题的根本症结。

the century in which population and living-standard problems will be resolved; it will be the era of cultural and religious renaissance; it will be the era when economic activity centers on the Pacific rim. Samuel P. Huntington of Harvard University in his 1993 essay The Clash of Civilizations? said that the major arena of conflict between peoples in the contemporary world is no longer ideology or economics, but rather cultural. In world affairs, the nation-state is still the major actor, but the principal conflicts in global politics will occur between peoples and states from different civilizations. Conflict between civilizations will thus dominate world politics.

I do not intend to discuss these predictions here (others have already touched on questions such as whether, in the context of world politics, it is possible for states to put cultural values above economic and political interests). I simply want to raise a question. In the post-Cold War era, China and other socialist countries have become important, or even the most dynamic, components of the world capitalist market. Indeed, East Asia could be turning its accustomed peripheral position in the former world capitalist system into the economic center of the new world capitalist order. Under such circumstances, what are we to make of the internal contradictions of the capitalist mode of production in the twenty-first century? For example, in the course of marketization in China, what will the relationship be between state, private, and foreign capital? What will the relationship be between new classes and other social groups? What of the relationship between agricultural and urban populations? Between the developed coastal regions and the backward hinterland? All of these social relationships must be placed within the context of new relations of production

　　那些将全球化看作是当代世界的最新发展的学者似乎忘却了全球化过程是一个伴随资本主义发展而发展的世界历史的漫长过程, 它已经经历了不同的历史阶段或时期。正如依附理论的重要阐释者阿明指出的, 在工业革命前的商业主义时期 (1500–1800), 以大西洋为中心的商业资本形成了它的支配地位, 并创造了它的边缘区域 (美洲); 在产生于工业革命的所谓资本主义的古典时期 (1800–1945), 伴随西方资本主义的发展, 亚洲 (日本是一个例外)、非洲和拉丁美洲成为西方资本主义的边缘地区, 它们通过农业和矿业的生产而加入到全球劳动分工之中; 与此同时, 伴随以资产阶级民族国家体系为其形式的工业体系的形成, 民族解放运动也在这些地区发展起来, 其意识形态上的特征就是将工业化当作解放、进步的同义词和"赶超"的手段, 并在资本主义中心启发之下以建立富强的民族国家为目标; 第二次世界大战结束至今是边缘地区在不平等条件下进行工业化的时期, 在这个时期, 包括中国在内的许多亚洲和拉美国家重新获得国家的政治主权。伴随资本主义全球化的过程, 自足的民族工业体系逐渐瓦解, 最终被重组为一体化的世界生产和贸易体系的构成要素。[37]全球化过程并不能自明地解决我们所面对的各种社会问题。从现代世界的发展

---

[37] 有关"全球化"问题的讨论, 请参见汪晖:《秩序还是失序?——阿明与他对全球化的看法》,《读书》杂志, 1985年7月号, 第106-112页。

and particularly in the context of their relationship to the market. The fundamental question is how changes in these relations will impinge on Chinese society and the world capitalist market. In the era of multinational capitalism, do these 'internal relations' matter any more? I am reminded here of the warning of that giant of liberal theory, Max Weber, who said that the rationality of modern capitalism would inevitably lead to a system in which some people rule over others; in this context, nothing, he said, would be able to root out faith in and hope for socialism. Is there still any relevance to these words, now that the traditional socialist movement has brought about a deep social crisis even as it seems to have ended in failure in the course of the Cold War?

The problem's greater complexity lies in the fact that as both a method and an embodiment of China's modernization, Chinese socialism did bring social organization. In fact, in the matter of state domination over society and people, it was even harsher than anything that ever existed under capitalism. Weber's and Marx's critiques of modernity were based on their observations and understandings of capitalism. Today, we must link our critique of the history of Chinese socialism to a critique of modernity and to the fact that the problem of modernity was first raised as a problem of European capitalism and its culture. The expansion of market society and its monopolization of social resources will as a matter of course be accompanied by a spontaneous and unplanned movement for the protection of social rights. The conflict between these forces provided the motive force for the most serious social crises of the nineteenth and twentieth centuries – including the two world wars. They also provide the basic momentum for efforts at self–reform on

来看, 生产和贸易过程的全球化并没有自发产生与之适应的超越民族国家的政治–社会组织的新形式, 也没有发展出能够适应亚洲和拉美等边缘地区兴起的政治、经济关系, 更没有解决所谓的南北差异和不平等。同样明显的是, 民族国家地位受到削弱, 而政治、经济和军事的垄断却没有改变。因此, 如果需要消除民族主义所产生的某些负面效应, 就必须在广泛的全球关系中探讨建立更为公正与和平的政治经济关系的可能性。

就中国的情况而言, 由于日益深入地加入到生产和贸易的全球化过程之中, 国际资本与民族国家内部的资本控制者 (对于包括中国在内的第三世界国家来说, 资本控制者也是政治权力的控制者) 相互渗透又相互冲突, 一方面使得国内经济关系更加复杂, 另一方面也不可避免地导致了体制性的腐败。这种腐败渗透到政治生活、经济生活和道德生活的各个方面, 已经产生了深刻的社会不公。即使从纯粹效率的观点看, 如果不能通过制度创新发展出遏止这一过程的社会机制的话, 这种体制性的腐败对经济的发展必将产生重大障碍; 而与这种腐败相伴随的盲目的消费主义也将迅速地耗竭自然和社会资源。

这一切表明: 自上个世纪以来在中国思想界普遍流行的现代化的目的论世界观正在受到挑战, 我们必须重新思考我们习惯的那些思想前提。尽管没有一种理论能够解释我们面对的这些如此

the part of modern social systems. The modern socialist movement was brought about by an analysis of the internal contradictions of capitalism and by the aspiration to overcome these contradictions, but the practice of socialism not only failed to complete the task of this aspiration, but it ended by being absorbed into global capitalism. At the same time, capitalism derived from socialism and from various movements for the protection of social rights opportunities for reform and self-critique, to the point where today, it is impossible to define socialism or capitalism in their original senses on the basis of the autonomous unit of the nation-state.

In this sense, when we use concepts like globalism or global capitalism to describe the changes to the contemporary world, this in no way implies that the structure and functioning of monopoly capitalism can represent the contemporary world in its entirety. This is because the social systems and public policies of Europe and America have already come to include elements from socialism or these movements for the protection of social rights. Aside form these elements embedded in social practice, we can also detect features of what Braudel calls 'material civilization', or those things that have persisted in basic life and have through long historical duration created enduring associations. In this regard, because we are still at the stage where modernization is the historical goal, a rethinking of Chinese socialism entails not just its past experience, but also questions about its present and predictions of its future. Traditional socialism has not been able to resolve the internal crisis of modernity, and both Marxism and New Enlightenment thinking, as ideologies of modernization, are virtually devoid of force and unable to formulate appropriate approaches to contemporary

复杂而又相互矛盾的问题，但是，超越中国知识分子早已习惯的那种中国/西方、传统/现代的二分法，更多地关注现代社会实践中的那些制度创新的因素，关注民间社会的再生能力，进而重新检讨中国寻求现代性的历史条件和方式，将中国问题置于全球化的历史视野中考虑，却是迫切的理论课题。社会主义历史实践已经成为过去，全球资本主义的未来图景也并未消除韦伯所说的那种现代性危机。作为一个历史段落的现代时期仍在延续。这就是社会批判思想得以继续生存和发展的动力，也是中国知识界进行理论创新和制度创新的历史机遇。

world developments. It is here that the imperative to rethink the China question is located.

Chinese intellectuals are now engaged in discussions of the question of globalization, in contrast to the Western media's discussion of Chinese nationalism. Most Chinese intellectuals, however, understand globalization within the context of the Confucian ideal of universal harmony. In my opinion, this type of universalism is nothing more than another version of the century-long modernist dream of 'meeting the world'.

In this, it is still possible to discern vague features of 'the prospects' for world Confucianization. Another group of young people in a spirit of commercial speculation concocted best-sellers like China Can Say No, eliciting from an already extremely unstable Western society apprehensions about Chinese nationalism and notions of a plainly exaggerated 'China threat'. The success of the commercial speculations on the part of this latter group has caused some of the foreign media to believe that the tide of Chinese nationalism has taken on an extreme xenophobic quality. In making this assumption, however, they are forgetting the commercial aspect of the publication and circulation of this book. As long as the nation-state system does not completely collapse, then nationalism as the essential basis of national unity will not disappear.

Even more importantly, however, the politics of contemporary nationalism bear significant differences from traditional nationalism. Rather than seeing it as something in opposition to globalization, it would be preferable to view it as a by-product of globalization. Discussion of nationalism must be linked to the global political and economic order; it cannot be explained in isolation form this. In the twenty-first century China may become a developed market society, but it is not possible for it to become a new global hegemon. The economic, political, and military positions of the United States and the Soviet Union were the products of the Cold War, and after the dissolution of the Soviet Union, NATO has become the overwhelming military force in the world. In the foreseeable future, there is no other country capable of developing this sort of hegemonic military power. If one fails to think about contemporary nationalism from the perspective of the global political, economic, and military structure, then it doesn't matter if one actively supports nationalist movements or strongly opposes them – both positions neglect the crux of the question. Those scholars who regard globalization as a new world order forget that this order has been long in the making; as a process set in motion by the rise of capitalism, it has already passed through several stages. In the period of commercialism prior to the Industrial Revolution (1500-1800), commercial capital dominated the Atlantic, turning parts of it into European peripheries (for example, the Americas); during the so-called classical period brought into being by the Industrial Revolution (1800-1945) accompanying the development of Western capitalism, Asia (excluding Japan), Africa, and Latin America came to occupy the periphery of Western capitalism and were integrated into the global division of labor through agriculture and mining. It was during this period that an industrial sector began to develop within each bourgeois nation-state and that national liberation movements simultaneously arose in the peripheral countries. The dominant ideology of these movements was their single-minded pursuit of modernization and the establishment of a wealthy and strong nation-state; they took 'catching up' as synonymous with progress and equated industrialization with liberation. From the end of World War II until today, the peripheral states have undertaken industrialization under globally disadvantageous and unequal conditions. China, along with many other Asian, African, and Latin American countries, did indeed achieve political independence, yet in the process of the globalization of capitalism, the self-sufficiency of their national industries gradually collapsed. These countries all found themselves being reorganized into a unified world system of production and trade.[33]

Globalization evidently cannot resolve the multiple social problems we now face. From

---

[33] On the problem of globalization, see *Wang Hui, 'Zhixu haishi shixu - A Ming yu ta dui quanqiuhua de kanfa'* (Order of disorder - Samir Amin and his views on globalization), *Dushu* 7 (July 1985) : 106-112.

the perspective of the development of the modern world, the globalization of production and trade has not spontaneously produced new political and social institutions capable of transcending the organizational forms of state and society within nation-states, nor has it been able to address the political and economic problems of the peripheral regions of Asia and Latin America. It has been even less able to bridge the so-called north-south gap. It is also clear that the weakening of the nation-state has not changed nation states' political, economic, and military domination over their own societies. Because of this, in order to eliminate the negative effects of nationalism, we must explore the possibility of fairer and more peaceful political relationships from the broadest of global perspectives.

As for China, the interpenetration of and mutual conflict between international and internal control of capital that has resulted from China's increasingly deep involvement in globalized production and trade has led to increased complexity in the domestic economy and to inevitable systemic corruption. (It should be recalled that in China, as in other Third World countries, those who control domestic capital are in fact the same as those who control political power.) This corruption has seeped into every aspect of the political, economic, and moral spheres, giving rise to serious social inequities at every level. Even from the standpoint of pure efficiency, if institutional innovations are not able to stop the disintegration of society, such systemic corruption will constitute a major obstacle to economic development and will encourage a destructive consumerism that will rapidly drain national and social resources.

The upshot is that the teleology of modernization that has dominated Chinese thinking for the past century is now being challenged. We must reconsider our old familiar premises of thought. Even though there is no one theory that can explain the complex and often mutually contradictory problems that we now face, it nevertheless behooves Chinese intellectuals to break their dependence on time-honored binary paradigms, such as China/West and tradition/modernity, to pay more attention to the factors that might contribute to institutional innovation within society, to attend to the capacity for renewal within civil society, and to move on to a reexamination of the historical methods and conditions under which China has sought modernity. The reconsideration of China's problems by placing them in the context of globalization is an urgent theoretical problem. Socialist historical practice is part of the past; the future designs of global capitalism, by the same token, do not promise to overcome the crisis of modernity that Weber wrote about. The modern era, as a historical phase, continues. This provides the impetus for the continued existence and development of critical thought; it may prove for Chinese intellectuals to be a historic opportunity for theoretical and institutional innovation.

The translator consulted a translation by Sylvia Chan of a shorter version of this essay. The present translation has been edited to bring it into conformity with the emended version of the article published in *Wang Hui*'s *Sihuo chongwen* (Rekindling dead ashes) (*Beijing: Remin wenxue chubanshe*, 2000), pp.42-94.—Ed.

The Context of the Project:
China's Vehicle Industry

项目背景简介: 中国汽车工业

China's Vehicle Industry

The earliest idea for a vehicle driven by a mechanical device can be traced back to Roger Bacon in the 13th century and Leonardo da Vinci in the 15th century.

Some Western countries had begun the exploration of and experimentation with powered vehicles as early as the end of the 17th century, well before the birth of the Chinese vehicle industry.

In 1675, James Watt invented the world's first driving machinery - the steam engine.

By 1832, steam driven vehicles could be seen puffing around the streets of Europe becoming the symbol of industrialised civilization.

In 1866, Nikolaus August Otto invented the 'four-stroke internal combustion engine', which had an epoch-making significance in the history of dynamics and laid a solid foundation for the birth of the motor vehicle in its modern sense.

Between 1885 and 1895, the cyclone of the motor vehicle swept across Europe and the United States.

The situation for the vehicle industry in China was obviously different from that in the West. Before the 20th century, China had no concept of motor vehicles. Contacts with the idea of cars and other motor vehicles only began in the early 20th century.

The earliest translation of 'vehicle' was 'automatic vehicle' *zidongche*. This word frequently appears in *Lu Xun's Diary* during the 1920s and 1930s. The 'steam vehicle' *qiche*, mentioned by many writers in the 1920s was not the car of today, but referred to the train.

With the increase of imported petrol driven vehicles, the noun *youqiche* literally 'petrol

中国汽车工业

汽车，这种由机械装置本身推动的公路车辆的思想，最早可追溯到13世纪的罗吉尔·培根和15世纪的达·芬奇。

在中国汽车工业诞生之前，西方早在17世纪末就开始了这一探索和试验。

1675年，英国人詹姆斯·瓦特研制出世界上第一台真正意义上的动力机械——蒸汽发动机。

1832年，欧洲的马路街道上穿梭的蒸汽机汽车成了当时工业文明的象征。

1866年，在动力史上有划时代意义的"活塞式四冲程奥托内燃机"被德国工程师尼古拉斯·奥托研制成功，为现代意义上的汽车的诞生奠定了坚实的基础。

1885年到1895年，机动车席卷欧美。

汽车工业在中国的情况显然迥异于西方。20世纪以前，中国没有所谓的"汽车"的概念，直到20世纪初期才开始对其有所接触。

汽车传到中国最早的汉译名是"自动车"。这一名称在上世纪20、30年代《鲁迅日记》中曾多次出现。20年代出现在一些作家笔下的"汽车"，并非现在所谓的汽车，指的是火车。随着进口车的增多，因多装置汽油机、燃用汽油，才逐渐有了"汽车"这一名称。

vehicle' was formed, later simply *qiche*.

In 1901, Leinz, a Hungarian, transported two Oldsmobile cars made in the United States from Hong Kong to *Shanghai* for the exclusive use of foreigners. *Shanghai* thus became the first city to import motor cars into China. In 1902, the government set up the special project of issuing driving licenses and drafting traffic regulations. China's first vehicle traffic regulations were created.

In 1902, after the 1900 Boxer Incident, the Empress Dowager *Cixi* returned to *Beijing* and accepted gifts of many foreign made items including a car. This car had been designed and made by C. E. and J. F. Duryea in 1898, but had lain idle for many years before being transferred from the Forbidden City to the Summer Palace and finally being placed in *Dehe* Park. The car was exhibited after renovation in the early 1970s.

There are a number of different stories surrounding this car. 'Reminiscences of the *Qing* Court' *qinggongsuoji* recorded that *Yuan Shikai* bought the car from Hong Kong as a token of tribute to the Empress. When a German tourist saw this car he determined it was a German Mercedes-Benz and offered to exchange it for ten new cars. There is another story that the car was a gift from the French Ambassador to Empress Dowager *Cixi*.

The earliest record of Chinese vehicle manufacturing appeared in the *Shanghai* Journal *shenbao* dated August 27th 1911, the third year of the *Xuantong* reign period: '*Jing Qiming* in *Kuaiji, Shaoxing* produced three vehicles.' But there were no more details.

After the end of World War I, China's national industries developed rapidly. In 1920, *Sun Yat-sen* wrote 'The Strategies for the Founding of the Nation' in which he suggested the

1901年，匈牙利人李恩时从香港运入两辆美国生产的奥兹莫比尔汽车到上海，专供外国人使用。上海因此成了中国第一辆进口汽车的城市。1902年，工局部决定除增设汽车执照专门项目外，还起草制定了车主遵守的规则，中国第一部汽车交通法规也由此而生。

1902年，庚子事变结束后，慈禧太后回京，接受了不少洋玩意儿，其中之一就是汽车。这辆车由美国人杜里埃兄弟于1898年设计制造，但是后来长期放置，由故宫转移到颐和园，最后放置于德和园，20世纪70年代初经修整后展出。

关于这辆汽车有不同的说法。其中，《清宫琐记》中记载：袁世凯从香港买进一辆汽车后献给慈禧太后，曾有一位德国游客见到此车，认定是德国奔驰轿车，提出愿以十辆新车相换。另有一说，此车是法国使馆向慈禧进贡的礼物。

中国人制造汽车的记载最早见于宣统三年七月初四（1911年8月27日）的《申报》上："绍兴会稽景其敏制造出汽车3辆。"但未述详情。

第一次世界大战后，中国民族工业有所发展。孙中山于1920年发表《建国方略》中提出要发展交通，修筑道路（公路）及建立自动车（汽车）工业。"中国不能总是依靠进口汽车，中国应该有自己的汽车。"这成了当时很多仁人志士的共识。

development of transportation, road construction and the establishment of an automotive industry. *Sun* added that, 'China cannot always depend on the importation of vehicles. China should have it own vehicles'. This statement became the consensus view of many people at that time.

The key figure in contributing the first step towards a Chinese national vehicle industry was *Zhang Xueliang*. He supported a suggestion by *Li Yichun*, the director of the *Shenyang* Mortar Factory that 'lorries should first be made to meet domestic needs'. *Li* changed the name of The *Fengtian* Mortar Factory to The *Liaoning* Mortar Factory and established civilian manufacture as a branch factory. On June 19th, 1931, The Factory assembled China's first lorry, the '*Minsheng*'. The name was taken from one of *Sun Yat-sen*'s 'Three Principles of the People' *sanmingzhuyi* - the Livelihood of the People, *minsheng*. The maximum speed of the lorry was 65km per hour. On September 19th, 1931, the '*Shengjing* Daily' in *Fengtian* reported that: 'the *Minsheng* Factory completed the production of 40 domestic vehicles... stylish and extraordinary'. The factory later changed its name to become The *Liaoning Minsheng* Factory. In the aftermath of the September 18th Incident *jiuyiba shibian* of 1931, the Japanese army plundered the vehicle parts that the *Minsheng* Factory had not yet assembled. Vehicle production did not continue.

In fact, the foundation of The Changchun No.1 Vehicle Factory signalled the establishment of China's vehicle manufacturing industry. Changchun was the first base of China's vehicle industry.

On February 14th, 1950, *Mao Zedong* accompanied by Premier *Zhou Enlai* went to

中国迈出民族汽车工业的第一步，其关键人物是张学良，他支持并支助了沈阳的奉天迫击炮厂厂长李宜春提出"应国内需要，宜首先制造载货汽车"的建议的实施。遂将奉天迫击炮厂改为辽宁迫击炮厂，附设民用工业制造处（后改称辽宁民生工厂）。1931年6月19日，辽宁民生工厂组装了中国第一辆载货汽车，取名"民生"，取意孙中山的"三民主义"，最高车速为65公里/小时。1931年9月19日，奉天《盛京日报》报道："民生工厂自制国产汽车40辆工程告竣……样式精美、轻便异常。"此厂后来更名为辽宁民生工厂，由于"九·一八"事变，民生工厂未组装成车的零部件均被日本侵略军掠夺一空，汽车的生产并未持续下来。

中国汽车工业的建立实际上是以长春第一汽车制造厂的建成投产为标志的，它是中国第一个汽车工业基地。

1950年2月14日，毛泽东在周恩来的陪同下前往莫斯科，中苏两国政府签订了《中苏友好互助同盟条约》，敲定一批苏联援助中国建设的重点工业项目。第一批共50项，其中包括建设汽车厂项目。1950年4月，重工业部成立了"汽车工业筹备组"。1951年3月19日，政务院经委员会批准建设第一汽车制造厂，该汽车制造厂的建设被列入第一个五年计划，成为156项重点工业建设项目之一。当时的目标是建立年产3万辆吉斯150货车的完整汽车厂。

Moscow to sign an agreement to build China's vehicle factories in partnership with the Soviet Union. On March 19th, 1951, the Economic Committee approved the founding of the No.1 Vehicle Factory, taking the Soviet Union's 'Regis 150' 4-ton vehicle as the prototype to produce the 'Liberation' *jiefang* medium weight lorry.

In 1952, the state's finances and economics improved. The period of restoration was over. From 1953 onwards, the state began to turn its attention to economic construction with the goal of establishing a basis of industrialization. On January 1st, The People's Daily announced in its editorial 'To Meet the Great Task of 1953' that China's first five-year-plan of economic development had begun to be implemented. The basic task of this plan was to focus major resources on one hundred and fifty six construction projects designed by the Soviet Union and six hundred and ninety four large and medium-size projects of industrial construction as the basis of socialistic industrialization. The plan required heavy industry to be central to the plan and to increase the average overall annual growth in industrial output by 14.7%. The plan marked the beginning of China's large-scale planned socialist economic construction.

At that time, *Mao Zedong* considered that although China was a big country and did not have to have everything the world could offer, it must have the important things, like aircraft and vehicles.

On June 9th, 1953, *Mao Zedong* personally issued 'The Chinese Communist Party's Central Committee's Instruction on Striving to Build the *Changchun* Vehicle Factory in Three Years'.

1952年国家财政经济根本好转，恢复时期结束。从1953年起，国家开始将注意力转向经济建设，目标是要建立社会主义工业化的基础。1月1日，《人民日报》发表题为《迎接1953年的伟大任务》的社论宣布，中国第一个发展国民经济的五年计划开始实施。这个计划的基本任务是：集中主要力量进行以苏联帮助中国设计的156个建设项目为中心、由694个大中型建设项目组成的工业建设，以建立社会主义工业化的初步基础……计划规定：以发展重工业为中心，使工业总产值平均每年增长14.7%……这标志着中国大规模的有计划的社会主义经济建设开始。

当时毛泽东认为，中国是一个大国，世界上有的东西，我们不能样样都有，但是重要的东西，比如飞机和汽车，我们就一定要有！

1953年6月9日，毛泽东亲自签发了《中共中央关于力争三年建设长春汽车厂的指示》，指出"由于我们技术落后和没有经验，要在三年内建成这样一个大规模的工程，不能在施工力量的组织、施工的技术、国内设备的供应以及生产准备等方面，都将会有很大的困难。因此，中央认为有必要通报全国，责成各有关部门对长春汽车厂的建设予以最大的支持，力争三年建成。"为广泛宣传这一重要决定，中宣部责成中央新闻纪录电影制片厂拍摄一部建设一汽大型纪录片，并于1956年一汽正式投产前夕编导出《第一辆汽车》。

In April 1956, *Mao Zedong* stated in 'On the Ten Major Relationships' presented to an enlarged meeting of the Political Bureau that: 'It will be good when we are able to sit in a vehicle we have produced ourselves.'

On July 14th 1956, the *Changchun* No.1 Automobile Factory produced China's first vehicle, a *Jiefang* brand 4-ton goods vehicle. On October 15th, vehicle production was formally started at the No.1 Vehicle Factory. This formally ended the period of China's inability to produce vehicles and laid a foundation for the independent development of China's vehicle industry.

Following the start of production of the goods vehicles, the No.1 Vehicle Factory began to design and produce cars. Acting on instructions from the First Machinery Ministry, the No.1 Vehicle Factory began to design cars in 1957. In accordance with the needs of the market and the Ministry's instructions, the Vehicle Factory decided to develop two kinds of cars: one would be a large luxury car for the use of the national leaders and envoys; the other would be of a universal type for government business and to serve foreign guests.

On May 12th, 1958, on the eve of the Second Session of the Eighth Chinese Communist Party Conference, the first car to be made in China was completed in the No.1 Vehicle Factory and was named the East Wind *dongfeng*, taken from *Mao*'s dictum that 'the east wind overrides the west wind'. The car was of the CA71 type. On May 21st, *Mao Zedong* and *Lin Boqu* rode in this domestic car in the *Zhongnanhai*.

Given that the production of two types of car at the same time was impossible and in order to first resolve the problem of providing cars for the central leadership, the No.1

1956年4月,毛泽东在政治局扩大会议做《论十大关系》报告时说:"什么时候能坐上我们自己生产的小轿车开会就好了。"

1956年7月14日,长春第一汽车制造厂制造出中国的第一辆汽车——解放牌4t载货汽车。10月15日,一汽正式投产,结束了中国不能生产汽车的历史,为汽车工业独立发展奠定了基础。

在载货汽车投产后,一汽便开始设计和研制轿车。1957年,一汽按一机部的通知开始设计轿车。根据市场的需求和上级部、局的指示,决定要开发两种轿车:一种是大排量的豪华轿车,供国家领导和驻外使节使用;一种是普及型轿车,供各部门公务和接待外宾使用。1958年5月12日,中国共产党的八大二次会议召开前夕,国产第一辆小轿车在一汽诞生,取名"东风",为CA71型,用汉语拼音标注。这部车在设计时参照了法国的"西姆卡"和德国的"奔驰190"。该车送去北京时,时任中央办公室主任的杨尚昆认为采用汉语拼音标注不太妥当,别人会误以为是外国车,于是提议采用汉字。后经李岚清提议,一汽通过《人民日报》找到了毛泽东关于"东风压倒西风"的题词,于是影印"东风"二字的手迹,进行加工制作,从而取代了汉语拼音,安装于车头金龙之下。因"东风"轿车的车头上镶嵌着金龙的标志,所以人们也称其为"金龙"。21日,毛泽东和林伯渠在中南海乘坐了这辆国产轿车。

Machinery Ministry decided to suspend the production of the East Wind *dongfeng* and focus on research for a high quality car to be named Red Flag *hongqi*. But the Ministry was required to complete trial production before September 1959 so as to have cars available as gifts for the 10th anniversary of the National Day. Production time was limited to only ten months. In June 1958, the first luxury car, the Red Flag *hongqi*, the type CA72 car, began trial production. It took just one and a half months to complete.

As production time had been so short, early examples of the Red Flag suffered from many problems of build quality. After several years of trial and practice, the problems exposed in the use of the car were gradually resolved. In 1965, on the instructions of the No.1 Machinery Ministry, the No.1 Vehicle Factory decided to develop and improve the car, as a consequence cars of the CA770 type appeared. Production of the CA770 car lasted only until May 1981 because of the requirements for fuel economy from the State Council. There were 860 type CA770 cars built in total.

When the Cultural Revolution began, the automotive industry entered a new stage. At that time, both the variety and quantity of their vehicles failed to meet social demands. The State then decided to construct more, new vehicle factories. As a result, three new vehicle factories; the No.2 Vehicle Factory, the *Sichuan* Vehicle Factory and the *Shanxi* Vehicle Factory were established. These three were in addition to other vehicle factories established by investment from the provinces themselves.

By the end of 1969, the No.2 Vehicle Factory was placed into large-scale construction and was granted national acceptance on January 8th. 1986. It was the largest vehicle factory

1958年4月, 一汽开始酝酿设计高级轿车。考虑到一汽同时要生产两种轿车并不现实, 为了首先解决中央领导坐车的问题, 一机部汽车局决定"东风"车暂停, 集中精力研制高级轿车, 并定名为"红旗"。1958年6月, 第一辆CA72红旗牌高级轿车开始试制, 仅用了一个多月的时间便完成制作。

1959年国庆节前夕, 30辆红旗高级轿车被送往北京, 作为国庆十周年的献礼。

由于生产的时间短促, 初期生产的红旗轿车质量问题较多。经过多年的试用以及生产的实践, 在使用过程中暴露出来的问题才逐步得以解决。1965年, 根据一机部的指示, 一汽决定在此基础上, 改进发展, 终于试制成功了CA770轿车, 一直生产到1981年5月国务院因节油而停止生产红旗为止, 共生产了860辆。

"文化大革命"开始时, 汽车工业进入了新的阶段。当时的汽车在产品品种、数量上都满足不了社会要求, 于是国家决定新建一些汽车厂, 并建成了二汽、川汽、陕汽三大生产基地, 外加各省市自行投资兴建的一些汽车厂。

1969年末, 第二汽车制造厂进行大规模施工建设, 并于1986年1月8日通过国家验收。它是中国自行设计、建设起来的, 是国内设计和生产能力最大的汽车制造企业。其建成标志着中国汽车工

designed and built in China with the highest capacity for design and production for the domestic market. Its completion marked a new stage in the development of China's vehicle industry in terms of quantity, quality, variety, technology and management. In August 1987, the State Council stated that 'the development of China's vehicle industry primarily depends on the No. 1 and No. 2 Vehicle Factories'.

From the perspective of development history, the construction and output of the No.1 Vehicle Factory together with the construction of the No.2. Vehicle Factory laid the foundations for China's vehicle industry.

业在数量、质量、品种、生产技术和经营管理水平方面都发展到一个新阶段。1987年8月, 国务院作出了"主要依靠一汽、二汽发展我国轿车工业"的决策。

从发展史上看, 中国第一汽车制造厂的建成投产, 以及第二汽车制造厂的创建, 奠定了中国汽车工业的基础。

参考书目:

1、陈祖涛口述《我的汽车生涯》, 人民出版社, 2005年8月第一版。

2、全国政协文史和学习委员会编《一汽创建发展历程》, 中国文史出版社, 2007年11月第1版。

3、刘勤编《中国汽车史话》, 人民交通出版社, 2006年9月第1版。

4、姜正根《汽车概论》, 北京理工大学出版社, 1999年3月第1版。

5、张仁琪、高汉初《世界汽车工业》, 中国经济出版社, 2001年1月第1版。

Wang Guangyi
Project: East Wind - Golden Dragon

王广义 《东风·金龙》方案

Wang Guangyi
Project: East Wind - Golden
Dragon
Rough Draft
王广义《东风·金龙》草图　2006

Wang Guangyi
Project: East Wind - Golden
Dragon
Rough Draft
王广义《东风·金龙》草图　2006

Wang Guangyi
Project: East Wind - Golden
Dragon
Rough Draft
王广义《东风·金龙》草图 2006

Wang Guangyi
The East Wind - Golden Dragon
shown as a visual effect
《东风·金龙》展示效果图

fibreglass car model
玻璃钢车模

A detail from East Wind - Golden Dragon
《东风·金龙》局部

A detail from East Wind - Golden Dragon
《东风·金龙》局部

Transporting the model car
during production
《东风·金龙》制作期间的运输

Transporting the model car
during production
《东风·金龙》制作期间的运输

Archives

视觉档案

The Emperess Dowager *Cixi's* car
慈禧太后的车乘

■ 慈禧太后的车乘

　　晚清时，汽车、火车等现代交通工具已传入中国。这部汽车是外国产品，据传是袁世凯给慈禧太后的贡礼。它的的外形虽酷似马车，但驱动原理已和现在的汽车相同。

　　这辆车是美国人杜里埃兄弟（C.E. and J. F. Duryea）于1898年设计制造的。该车后置三缸4.4-7.4kw（6-10马力）的汽油水冷四行程发动机，变速箱为二挡行星齿轮式，通过皮带后轴以驱车行驶。其四个轮子，前小后大，轮胎为橡胶，12根辐条是木制的，转向盘由两个同轴不同直径的轮子组成，车身为木质敞开式，双排座位，车头有两只金色车灯，为手提式马灯，英国伯明翰产品。此车外形有18世纪欧洲贵族马车的痕迹。该车被认为是由美国制造，是由于该车的铜制脚踏板上铸有英文"DURYEA"。该车现存于北京德和园，慈禧太后曾乘用过。

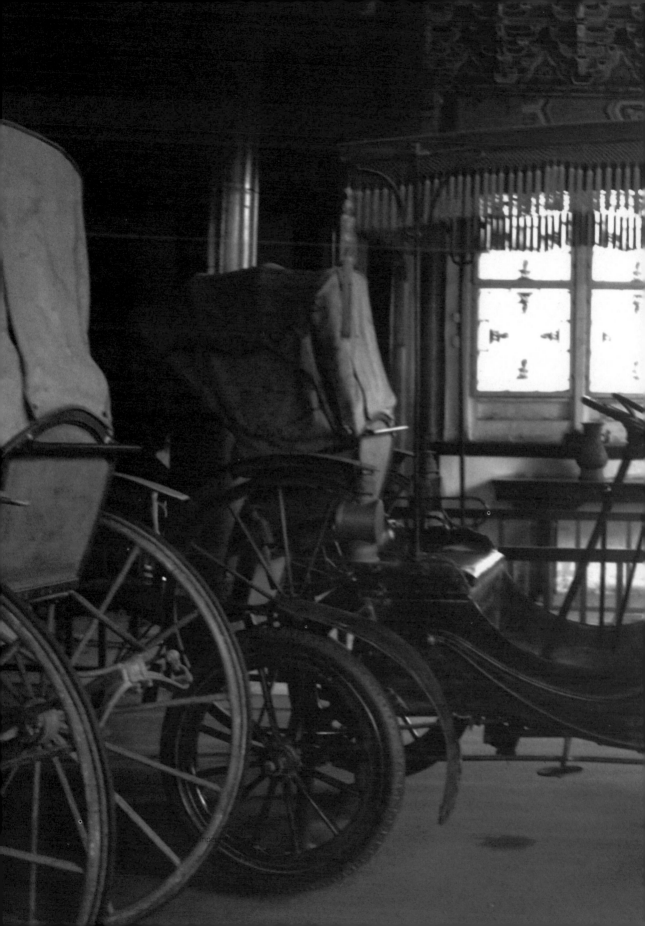

A Buick car presented to *Song Meiling* by the United States Government, manufactured by General Motors in the 1930s.

宋美龄座车是美国通用汽车公司于上世纪30年代生产的"别尔克"牌轿车,由美国政府赠送给宋美龄女士。车牌号为当年宋美龄专用。

Mao Zedong and Joseph
Stalin attended the signing
ceremony of the Sino-Soviet
Treaty of Friendship, Alliance
and Mutual Assistance in
Moscow in February 1950,
Premier *Zhou Enlai* signed
the Treaty on behalf of the
Chinese Government. Both
sides negotiated that the Soviet
Union would support China on
a number of major engineering
projects including the
construction of a car factory.
1950年2月，毛泽东、斯大林出
席在莫斯科举行的《中苏友好
同盟互助条约》签字仪式，周恩
来代表中国政府在条约上签字。
中苏双方议定由苏联援建包括
一座汽车厂在内的一批重点工
程项目。

A grand ceremony of breaking
the ground was held on the site
of the No. 1 Vehicle Factory on
the 15th July 1953
1953年7月15日，一汽隆重举行
奠基典礼。

During the ceremony of
breaking the ground on the site
of the No. 1 Vehicle Factory, six
young Communists laid down a
white-jade foundation stone in
the central square of the factory
site. Second left is comrade *Li
Lanqing*
在一汽奠基典礼大会上，六名年
轻共产党员将刻有毛主席题词的
白玉基石放置在厂区中心广场。
左二为李岚清同志。

解放前的中国没有汽车制造业，解放初仅有的一些车辆维修设备在战争中又受到破坏，有的则被运到香港、台湾，只有集中在几个大城市的２４家汽车修理和配件生产企业。

The declaration of the start of work at the No. 1 Vehicle Factory on the 15th July 1953.　1953年7月15日，第一制造厂宣布开工。

On the 15th July 1953, the construction workers vow to complete their orders within three years.　1953年7月15日 建设者在这里宣誓，他们将在三年中完成使命。

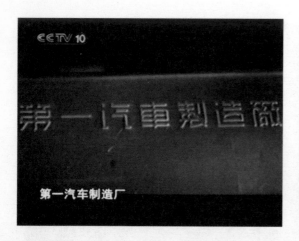

The first time Chinese characters appeared on a car body in Chinese industrial history.　在中国工业史上，第一次在汽车身上出现中国字。

The first time Chinese characters were stamped on a car body: No. 1 Vehicle Factory.　第一次在汽车身上压上几个的字：第一汽车制造厂。

On the 13th July 1956, the first Chinese produced 'Liberation' brand vehicle was completed.
1956年7月13日，第一辆国产解放牌汽车诞生。

On the 13th July 1956, the first
Chinese produced 'Liberation'
brand vehicle was completed.
The workers and staff thronged
the main thoroughfare of
the factory, cheering at the
outgoing vehicle.
1956年7月13日，第一辆国产解
放牌汽车诞生。职工们拥向厂中
央大道，欢呼解放牌汽车出厂。

In April 1956, *Mao Zedong* said in an enlarged meeting of the Political Bureau: 'it will be good when we are able to sit in a vehicle we have produced ourselves.' 1956年4月，毛泽东在政治局扩大会议上说："什么时候能坐上我们自己生产的小轿车开会就好了！"

On the 15th July 1956, 12 'Liberation' brand vehicles rolled off the production lines. 1956年7月15日，12辆解放牌汽车开下生产线。

Thousands of people lined both sides of the road falling over one another, wanting to be the first to glimpse the lines of the first Chinese produced car. People threw multi-coloured paper flowers towards the line of cars. Those without paper flowers threw sorghum, rice or maize. 成千上万的人站在车道两旁，争先恐后地目睹国产汽车的风采。人们不断地向车队抛洒五彩缤纷纸花，没有纸花的就用高粱、稻米、谷子往车上抛洒。

On the 15th September 1956, the 8th Assembly of the Communist Party Central Committee begins in the newly completed Conference Hall. Premier *Zhou Enlai* delivers a report on the second 'Five year Plan' . The Assembly considered that the most important mission of the whole nation was to concentrate on the raising of productivity and the modernisation of industry. 1956年9月15日，中共中央第八次会议在新落成的政协礼堂召开，周恩来总理作了第二个五年计划的报告。大会认为，全国人民的主要任务是集中力量，发展生产力，实现工业化。

After the cessation of production of the East Wind vehicle, the No.1 Vehicle Factory personnel decide to use the least possible time to build a new model of luxury car to present as a gift to *Mao Zedong*. 在东风轿车下马后，一汽人决定用最短的时间制造出新型的高级轿车送给毛主席。

From 1955, an Americian produced Imperial brand luxury car was broken down into components to enable assmbly workers to study their manufacture . 将1955年美国生产的帝国牌高级车的零件拆散，放在车间的长台上，供车间工人研究制造。

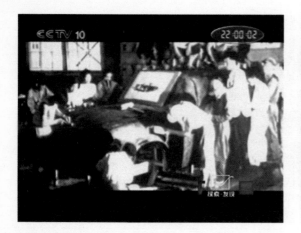

Day and night, workers used wooden mallets to build the luxury car. 不分白天黑夜，用木槌打造高级轿车。

In April 1958, the No. 1 Vehicle Factory rapid production team having successfully speeded up the output of domestic vehicles, produced the first Chinese manufactured saloon car in 23 working days. 1958年4月，中国第一制造厂成立了轿车制造突击队，加紧了试制轿车的进度。经过23天的奋战，第一辆国产轿车诞生了。

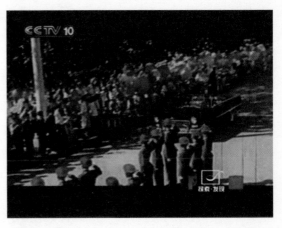

1st August 1958, the first successful production of a Red Flag luxury car, the car having taken just one month to come from design stage to completion, normally the process needed 5-6 years. 依靠原始的方式，于1958年8月1日，中国第一辆红旗牌高级轿车试造成功，仅用了一个月的时间。一般来说，从设计到生产，需要五六年的时间才能制造成功。

1959 marked the first time a Red Flag saloon car appeared during the 10th Anniversary of the creation of the State, six vehicles entered travelling in a line, from then on the Red Flag car was used for those reviewing the parade. 1959年，红旗车第一次出现在国庆十周年的庆典当中，六辆红旗轿车行进在游行的队伍中。从那时起，乘坐红旗轿车阅兵成为惯例。

1962, the first time a Red Flag car was used to convey a foreign guest. 红旗轿车第一次担任外事礼宾车。

1964, the State Council adopted the Red Flag car for protocol use. 1964年，国务院会议确定红旗轿车为国车。

Chairman *Mao* rides in an East
Wind brand saloon car
2nd May 1958, The People's Daily
《毛主席乘坐东风牌轿车》载于
《人民日报》，1958年5月22日

毛主席乘坐东風牌轎車

他笑着說：「坐了我們自己制造的小汽車了！」

新华社21日訊 毛澤东主席在今天下午观看了国产的第一輛"东風"牌小轎車，并同林伯渠同志一起乘着这輛汽車，在怀仁堂后花园緩緩行駛了两周。毛主席下了汽車，对聚集在周围的中共八大第二次会議的代表們笑着说："坐了我們自己制造的小汽車了。"

这輛小轎車是长春第一汽車制造厂全体职工献給中共八大第二次会議的礼物。职工們在試制成功后即运往北京，于15日向大会献礼，并在給大会的一封信中，向党中央和毛主席保证：要快馬加鞭，提前和超額完成今年十二个新品种汽車的試制任务，将单一品种的汽車厂，改造成为多品种的汽車厂。

上圖：毛澤东主席和林伯渠同志試坐"东風"牌小轎車。　　　新华社記者　侯波攝

下圖：毛澤东主席观看"东風"牌小轎車。　　　新华社記者　邹健东攝

1958年5月

22

星　期　四
夏历戊戌年
四月初四

今日天气预报
（北京地区）

白天：阴轉晴
　　　風向　偏北
　　　風力　三、四級轉
　　　　　　二、三級
夜間：晴轉多云
　　　風向　偏北
　　　風力　一、二級
温度：（攝氏）
　　　最高24°～26°
　　　最低18°～14°

Geng Zhaojie: The relentless pursuit of
40 years. The People's Daily
《耿昭杰的文章"执著追求40年"》，
载于《人民日报》

执著追求四十年

耿昭杰

今年是国产轿车的40周年，一汽人的轿车情结又被紧紧地牵动。

1958年，国产第一辆解放卡车诞生还不到两年，一汽人在没有厂房、没有设备、没有胎具、没有技术的生产车间里开创着民族轿车工业的历史，造出了中国第一辆东风牌轿车。"东风"送到了北京，驶进了中南海。步出八大二次会堂的毛泽东主席试乘后，高兴地说："坐了自己制造的小轿车了！"对于这段难以忘怀的日子，作为一汽的第一代创业者和送车人，李岚清副总理曾经在15年前撰写的《一汽——祖国汽车工业的摇篮》中有着深情的回忆。

一汽人的热血似乎在燃烧，5月份刚刚造出了"东风"，8月份又造出了红旗牌高级轿车。此后，红旗轿车不断繁衍发展，"两排座"之后，又有了"三排座"，有了保险车，有了检阅车……"红旗"被指定为国家的领导专车和礼宾用车。1972年美国总统尼克松访华，坐的是红旗轿车；1984年国庆35周年邓小平检阅三军，坐的也是红旗轿车。"红旗"还被列入世界名车的经典，成为民族尊严的一个象征。但是，由于当时的局限，"东风"成了绝版，"红旗"也没形成应有的气候。

改革开放，国门打开，一汽人开阔了自己的视野。与此同时，一次次轿车进口的浪潮也在拍打着一汽人的胸膛，"红旗"轿车被冷落的境遇更令一汽人痛心疾首。一种新的意识、新的向往在我们的思想中觉醒：红旗轿车产品必须走出"政治车"的概念，走进市场才能大发展；在我国轿车技术相对落后、资金短缺的情况下，抓住改革开放的机遇，与国外相结合才是发展一汽轿车事业的捷径。一汽人的心底发出同一个誓言：民族的轿车工业必须全面开动！

1987年，国家确定一汽为国产轿车的三大生长点之一，上轿车成为一汽发展的主旋律。就在红旗轿车的阵地上，我们从头采取技术引进的方式，建成了3万辆轿车先导厂。1990年4月，当一辆乳白色的奥迪轿车驶出厂房的大门，一汽人赢得了轿车新事业的第一个喜悦。这个项目投资不到6个亿，出了10万多辆"奥迪"，实现利税高达60多亿元，相当于总投资的10倍。奥迪轿车成为我国公务用车的主力车型。与此同时，为了实现规模经济，我们又在老厂区西部一块323公顷的土地拉开了建设15万辆普及型轿车厂的会战，江泽民总书记亲笔写下了"建设现代化轿车工业基地"的题词，被镌刻在新轿车厂区的大理石碑壁上，与一厂区毛泽东题写的"第一汽车制造厂奠基纪念"的丰碑遥相呼应，成为一汽新的轿车事业的一个标志。

一汽人的热血又一次燃烧起来，一支突击队到美国的韦斯摩兰厂拆迁生产捷达轿车的设备，一年多始终战斗在异邦的土地。国庆节那天，他们热泪盈眶地唱起了《国歌》，表达对祖国、对亲人的思念。一个专业厂的领导指挥着他的队伍劳动在新厂区的建设工地，晚期的癌症把他击倒在现场，住院弥留之际，他还在盼望着轿车装配线的早日建成。为了这个现代化轿车基地的迅速崛起，多少一汽的干部、工人和技术人员都忘记了星期天、节假日，挑灯夜战、吃住现场成了他们特有的"生活方式"。我们的奋斗得到了最大的报偿；这个投资上百亿的大项目，一次建成，一次验收合格，1997年正式通过国家验收的当年就实现盈利2亿多元，今年的利润可望达到五六个亿。特别是产品的技术含量跟上了当代水平，装用5气阀发动机、改进了外形的"新捷达王"，装用1.8升涡轮增压发动机的新"奥迪"，成为国内最有竞争力的产品。一汽大众这个合资企业，越往前走越能显示出她强大的生命力。

民族轿车工业要大力发展，没有自己的品牌，没有自己的知识产权，终归要受到很大的限制。为了民族汽车工业长远的自主发展，我们不仅要发展"奥迪"、"捷达"，也要举起中国人自己的"红旗"。3万辆先导厂的建设是我们打下的一个重要伏笔，在红旗轿车的阵地上生产"奥迪"，正是为了以后的发展"红旗"。通过生产奥迪的实践，我们消化吸收国外先进技术，开发了拥有自己知识产权的小红旗轿车，组建了一汽轿车公司，并使之成为股份上市的企业，保住了"红旗"这个国内唯一的民族轿车品牌，走出了一条双轨制发展轿车的道路。

一汽一直被誉为"中国汽车工业的摇篮"，在改革开放的新时期，"摇篮"里升起的新"红旗"更加鲜艳夺目。红旗轿车投放市场的时间不长，已发展到发动机排量从1.8升、2.0升、2.2升、2.5升四个系列，既有基本型，又有豪华型和加长型，虽然仅仅生产了3万多辆，但已经成为我国公务用车的又一个主力车型。在庆祝国产轿车40周年的时候，我们的红旗轿车又有了新的发展和提高。整体加长小红旗和全新小红旗、全新大红旗也已开发出来，将陆续推向市场。我们要持续跟踪世界轿车的先进技术，一定要把"红旗"永远举下去，让民族轿车的品牌不断光大。

（作者为中国第一汽车集团公司总经理）

The Story of the Chinese
Saloon Car, Southern Weekend,
22nd November 2007
《中国轿车制造始末》，载于《南方周末》，2007年11月22日

中国轿车制造始末

□本报记者　徐　钟　发自长春

毛主席参观中国第一辆轿车时说："我坐上我们自己……"

"东风"乍起

中国第一辆轿车的诞生与毛泽东的一句话有关。

建国初期的几年，共和国领导人的座驾以及检阅车都是从苏联购买的吉斯轿车。1956年4月，毛泽东主席在政治局扩大会议做《论十大关系》报告时对汽车工业开发国产轿车提出希望："什么时候能坐上我们自己生产的小轿车开会就好了。"

根据毛主席的讲话精神，一年后，一机部部长黄敬到"一汽"检查工作时，向厂里提出三个任务：载重车要改型；要搞越野车；要搞轿车。

一汽也提出三个条件：增加设计人员；增加设计部工作面积；要给样车。

曾在一汽集团当过副厂长、现今76岁的李中康，那一年在一汽做焊接工作，当他去苏联实习、把这个消息告诉苏联专家时，苏联专家摇头，"想做轿车？你们别那么快。"

当时解放卡车刚刚出厂，而轿车工艺难度比卡车不知要高出多少倍，"人们怀疑中国轿车自造能力并不奇怪。"李中康对南方周末记者说。

但当时"大跃进"风声渐起，人定胜天的思想无可动摇。一机部随后正式给一汽厂下达了生产小轿车的任务，并提出了"越快越好"的要求。

1957年6月，朱德总司令将捷克送给他的一辆斯柯达轿车送到一汽作为参考样车。同年8月，又有苏联的"胜利"、法国"西姆卡"以及美国"福特赛飞"等样车先后运到长春。

时任一汽厂长的饶斌提出了轿车试制以"仿造为主，适当改造"的设计原则。通过比较，轿车设计方案定了基调：发动机和底盘仿造"奔驰-190"；车身结构仿造法国"西姆卡"；外型和内饰件则在西姆卡的基础上进行改造。

不出半年，中国首辆轿车的设计图纸和设计文件全部完工。1958年初，开始进入试制阶段。

在"大跃进"如火如荼的感召下，一汽员工已不满足原定的生产进度，1958年4月，厂里组成突击队，把轿车出厂时间由7月15日提前到5月12日，准备把这辆轿车作为中共八大二次会议的献礼。

共和国第一辆轿车命名为"东风"，取自毛泽东主席当时最具民族自尊心和大国意愿的一句话："东风压倒西风"。

第一辆东风轿车的第一个乘客叫刘经

徐钟/摄

走下"神坛"

1981 年 5 月 14 日，人民日报登出了"红旗"轿车停产令："'红旗'牌高级轿车因耗油较高，从今年 6 月起停止生产"。

这个消息对身为"共和国长子"的一汽打击巨大，用当时厂领导耿昭杰的话讲："红旗下马，把一汽人造红旗的满腔热血送进了冰库。"截至 1981 年停产 20 年间，一汽总共生产了 1500 多辆红旗轿车。

当年曾在汽车主管部门——中国汽车工业公司做主要领导的陈祖涛老人向南方周末记者讲述了红旗停产的真正原因。

"红旗"批量生产以后，质量问题逐步暴露出来，影响了"红旗"的声誉和形象。驻外大使反映："红旗"的毛病太多，有时到机场去接外国总统，跑到半道，"红旗"抛锚了，眼睁睁地看着别国的大使飞驰而去，急得直跺脚——误了接人事小，影响两国关系事就大了。

慢慢地有些领导就不坐"红旗"了。1980 年代初，国务院总理赵紫阳外出时，他的"红旗"在行驶中突然冒烟，不得不中途换车。他对此很有意见："红旗生产这么久了，质量还是上不去，这样的车还生产它干什么？"就这样红旗的生产暂时停了下来。

红旗车的质量问题较多，一是化油器质量差，怠速不好，发动机经常熄火，二是分电器的质量也不好，有时会发生断电现象，不好发动，甚至开不了车，三是转向机也有质量问题，转向经常失灵，容易发生事故。

时任一汽厂长的黄兆銮认为，红旗质量问题主要因为协作厂商生产的配件不过关所致。

红旗作为政治任务，当时交到中央价格不超过 5 万元，"只是象征的价格"，而当时配置最低的红旗，它的成本都达到 8 万元，"当时我们也就认了，中央首长也没多少人，我们用卡车养它。"黄兆銮对南方周末记者说。但协作厂商并不买账，因为红旗产量有限，价格又低廉，协作厂一年也生产不了多少配件，"它也不会下成本提高质量，所以造成红旗大毛病没有，小毛病不断。"

红旗停产后，中央用车全部依靠进口，大量外汇外流。一汽认为恢复红旗生产是早晚的事。在未获准重新生产的许可之前，自谋生

了。"

一汽的副厂长。当时是一汽底□负责东风底盘设计工作。5 月 12 □一辆东风终于装配完毕，车上的□发动成功，大家兴奋不已，但变□机构由于连接太多，容易"乱□操纵机构及故障比较熟悉，所□步时，要刘经传在车上"保驾"，□成为这辆车的第一个乘客。

□A-71 东风牌小轿车为流线型□银灰色，下部紫红色，6 座，车□族特色的宫灯造型，发动机罩□小金龙装饰，发动机最大功率□马力），最高时速可达 128 公□为百公里 9 升左右。

□生后一路报捷到北京。由于东□汉语拼音拼写的，很多人看不□条装饰的金属飞龙，就叫这辆□牌。中央办公厅主任杨尚昆也认□家不认得还以为是外国呢。"

□毛泽东报捷的前夜，送车的一□京灯市口一家修车厂用毛体□替换掉原来的拼音字母。

□日下午两点，毛泽东主席在□，来到后花园乘坐这辆小车转□也听说这辆车时速可达 128 公

里时，笑着说，"我还没坐过这么高速的车呢。"下车时又意味深长地感叹道："我坐上我们自己制造的小汽车喽。"

23 日，周恩来总理看车，他看得很仔细：让司机打开了发动机盖，他看了一眼说，这是抄奔驰的，"像发动机的气阀室罩，为什么不改一改？"他说，抄是可以的，但应抄得有技巧，关键技术抄，非关键技术可以改得让人看不出来。

东风在京期间受到英雄凯旋般欢迎，据一汽老员工回忆："东风开过的地方，群众欢呼鼓掌，一路都是绿灯，可以直接开进中南海。"

但由于"东风"车型不大，并不适合首长们乘坐，所以，总共生产五六辆的东风轿车项目很快下马，给后来的红旗车让路了。

The Red Flag joins the world.The Story of the Chinese Saloon Car, South Weekend, 22nd November 2007
《中国轿车制造始末》，载于《南方周末》，2007年11月22日

"红旗"出世

试制出来东风后，一汽设计部门准备仿照德国的"乌尼莫格"，试制一款万能农用车，这时传来北京汽车厂要试制高级轿车的消息，一汽员工坐不住了，"既然第一汽车厂试制了第一辆轿车，那么第一辆高级轿车也应出自第一汽车厂，决不能把这个第一让给别人。"

当时中国准备自己生产高级轿车有一个最重要的原因：建国初期为中央领导配备的苏式吉斯、吉姆等轿车已经运行了将近10年，车况都不太好，而当时中苏关系渐行渐远，从长远看要更新车辆和供应备件已经不太可能。出路只有一条，走自力更生的路子，于是一汽全厂掀起了"乘东风、展红旗，生产高级轿车献给毛主席"的热潮。

第一辆红旗车的设计者程正老人今年79岁。2007年11月初的一天，独居在一汽工程师楼的程正接受记者采访时行动有些不便，他说自己："不是太老，报销得太早。"

1958年6月30日的下午，正在车间做体力劳动的程正被叫到车身科开会。

车身科的大通舱房间坐满了人。这时一汽的副厂长、总工程师郭力，跟着其他几位厂级领导人进入会场，郭厂长很郑重地说："上级决定由一汽立即设计并试制供国家级领导人用的高级轿车，对我们来讲绝不是一件简单的事，何况只给我们一个月时间，这事在国外也是办不到的，但是我们要下一条横心把它干出来。"

决定当晚，一汽从吉林工大借用一辆

1956年生产的克莱斯[勒]……车。程正和其他4位汽车[……]画了两张车型设计图。[……]稿"方案在设计处向群众[……]征求意见，最终程正的方[……]

"这个方案胜出，并[……]多么出色，而是因为它[……]赶时髦。"程正拿出当时[……]斯勒帝国牌轿车图片对[……]"与我们的效果图相比，[……]间没有抄袭模仿之处。"[……]

随即，一汽员工用"[……]轰轰烈烈的造车运动。

红旗轿车共有3488[……]件被排成一排，一汽员工[……]来认领。他们认为自己可[……]签字拿走。一汽人步调一[……]老厂长范恒光回忆："一[……]像一个人一样行动。"[……]

"我们忙得不可开交[……]每天没有固定下班时间，[……]干了一个月零三天。"程[……]

红旗车身通体黑色，[……]面用塑料做成的红旗。车[……]特色的扇子造型，仍然保[……]式后灯，发动机罩前上方[……]路线、大跃进、人民公社"[……]上装有V形八缸式顶置[……]大功率200马力，最高时[……]

1958年8月2日下[……]员工及家属云集在一汽[……]

问鼎"国车"

红旗真正成为"国车"还是1965年以后的事情。

1959年开始投产的CA72两排座红旗至1966年停产，一共生产了202辆，由于车型等问题，并没有真正取得国车的地位。红旗真正给人们心里树立国车风范的是1965年试制成功的编号为CA770的三排座红旗，它最终完全取代了苏联车成为首长用车。

1958年制造的样车与1959年定型投产的红旗轿车都是两排座，这批车送到北京后，国管局和中共中央办公厅都提出要三排座的轿车，因为当时苏联产的吉斯和吉姆车都是三排坐位，这样的车在接待外宾时，翻译也有位子。

红旗老厂长郭力曾说："制造红旗轿车一定要按首长的要求造车，像餐馆点菜一样，听从首长点菜。"应中央需求，作为政治任务的红旗车型实施一步步的改进。

1960年，一汽试制三排座红旗。设计师们把轴距拉长，外型改了水箱面罩和后风窗玻璃，但效果不理想，设计师们又以1：5的比例做了很多三排座红旗油泥模型，经厂领导和专家们的共同挑选，又选中了程正制作的模型。

但制成后发现实车与模型效果不一致。在1：5的油泥模型上，红旗前车身侧面加一条凹槽显得挺拔清秀，制成真车后却有塌肚子的感觉。于是程正在"文化

大革命"时期，多了一条[……]年粮食困难的罪状。

到了1963年，一汽[……]了两种样式和方向的尝试[……]两排CA72车型基础上作[……]三排座；一种是脱离两排[……]一个全新设计。

1965年9月试制的全[……]使红旗轿车在原有的民族[……]年轻的活力和气质，制成[……]

这辆车吸取几年来产[……]使用中的经验教训，对发[……]动机、底盘主要总成都作[……]此整车性能得到显著改进[……]

这辆车送到北京后，[……]院秘书长正式提出，一汽[……]排座红旗，先让中央政治[……]同志乘用。

1966年4月20日，一[……]第一批20辆三排座红旗[……]恩来总理说："中国有最高[……]车了，可以接待最高级的[……]

这款CA770红旗三[……]于正式成为代表国家的迎[……]领导人用车，获得了国家[……]誉地位，并进入世界高级[……]被称为"中国的劳斯莱斯[……]

CA770三排座红旗[……]生产延续了20年。

程正提供的照片,上图为克莱斯勒样车,下图为红旗设计图

会场,大家等待首辆红旗的到来,可好久不见踪影。天喇叭突然叫工艺设计处刘经传的名字,要他去试制车间。刘经传吓了一跳,以为液力变速器坏了。

到了车间一看,原来发动机马达齿轮太脆,汽车发动时打碎了,因此无法起动发动机,惟一方法是更换齿轮。负责人员只找到一个备用齿轮。

刘经传推测,这个新齿轮只能经受两次汽车发动,即当时起动一次,开到会场,开完会再把车开回来时再起动一次。

"我叮嘱司机千万小心,点火要一次成功,起动后不得熄火。"这位东风轿车的第一位"乘客"说。车开出车间时,天已大黑,强烈的照明灯射向红旗车时,全场一片沸腾。最终刘经传担心的齿轮还算争气,红旗车顺利地回到试制车间。

"试制V-8型发动机的汽缸体非常困难,如同一项科学研究的试验一样,为了铸成合格的V-8型发动机缸体,我们在一百个铸件里,只能挑出三件合格品,再送去供机械加工。"刘经传说,"做出必要的牺牲是不可避免的。"

1958年9月19日,当时任中共中央总书记的邓小平来一汽考察时问饶斌,红旗比苏联产的吉姆车怎样,饶斌说,比吉姆高级。邓小平高兴地说:"你们可以多生产,油不够可以烧酒精,反正做酒精的红薯干有的是,只要不烧茅台就行。"引起在座的人哈哈大笑。

经过5轮修改后的红旗最终定型。

1959年4月定型后的红旗被送往北京,当时对于红旗样车,毁誉参半。汽车局于5月开会,在热烈的争辩中,批准了红旗CA72型投产,并于当年国庆前,送京10辆作为首长用车,同时要求一汽制造两辆检阅车。

1959年是共和国建国十周年大庆,一汽赶制的10辆正式产品送往北京。这些"红旗"到京后,正好北京汽车厂的"和平"轿车和上海汽车厂的"凤凰"轿车三个品种一起陈列在天安门广场前,受到来自全国的观众的赞许。

1960年,红旗在瑞士日内瓦的国际博览会上亮相,一名意大利的汽车设计专家看到红旗后评价:"聪明与狡猾"。

程正很为这个评价自豪:所谓"聪明"是指我们能够在当时条件下自己设计并制造出这样高级的轿车;而"狡猾"是指,他们看出我们的设计很多内容是从其他国家的名车上学习来的,但又说不出抄袭了谁。

而另一名意大利的汽车造型设计专家也夸奖红旗的造型设计是"东方艺术和汽车技术相结合的典范"。

东风轿车极大地鼓舞了当时的群众士气
(资料图片)

一汽工人在检查第一辆红旗车
(资料图片)

开发市场需要的旅游车;二是着手研究"红旗"的技术改造。

1983年9月30日,一汽上报了红旗技术改造引进建议书,改造的主要措施是,保持红旗轿车庄重大方具有民族风格的外形前提下,购买国外较好的发动机、变速箱、刹车总成以及附配件来改造红旗,使质量可靠性提高到一个新水平。

中汽公司总经理陈祖涛向中央作了汇报。田纪云副总理说:"我们这么大的国家总要搞一些轿车,红旗牌子不能丢,但质量要提高。全靠自己力量有困难,可以进口一些'内脏',自己的车子过了关就可以减少进口了。"

1985年10月10日,恢复生产改造后的第一辆"红旗"CA770G试制成功,胡耀邦总书记从外地返京时,该车去机场迎接,胡沿途向司机询问了新车性能和改进情况后,说:"我举双手赞成恢复红旗轿车生产,但质量要上去,不能再抛锚了。"但由于"心脏"部分都是用外国的,胡耀邦说:"都是我们自己的就好了。"

1991年5月13日,又经过5年改进后的红旗CA770-90送到北京,江泽民总书记看到样车时说:"我赞成恢复红旗,不但要恢复生产,还要给红旗恢复名誉、恢复形象。"

1992年,一汽将原来的一汽轿车厂一分为二,第二轿车厂集中精力实现年产3万辆奥迪,迅速占领市场,挡住进口;由第一轿车厂负责红旗轿车研发,同年4月,中汽总公司同意恢复CA770型高级轿车生产。

但此时,红旗已停产十年之久,设备老化,工装模具部分损坏,毛坯、协作产品一时很难找到合作厂家,技术骨干因调退休和调离,力量已相当薄弱。1993年生产出的首批高级轿车,因质量不过关,市场反响不尽如人意,红旗再度受挫。

直到1995年,程正设计完最后一辆红旗后,当时的厂长告诉他,红旗该画上句号了。

在大红旗恢复生产受挫以后,企业还要生存,一汽开始开发小红旗。一汽舍弃旧红旗样貌甚至定位,有的小红旗居然做了出租车。程正说,"至今仍旧怀念当年'红旗'的外形,毕竟是我们自己亲手造出来的,有感情了。"

1988年5月17日,一汽与德国大众签署了"奥迪"轿车产品技术转让协议,一汽在消化吸收的基础上,用克莱斯勒2.2升发动机配奥迪100轿车的车身,于1996年改造出了"红旗"CA7220。

1998年,全新"红旗"CA7460在一汽诞生。这款"红旗"车身外貌和"奥迪"没有多大区别,但相比老"红旗"而言,不仅"脱胎换骨"而且"改头换面"了,因此CA7460在社会上引起了不少议论。他们甚至质疑"红旗还能打多久",毕竟老"红旗"的外型在国人心中已留下了深刻的印象。事实上,这款红旗并没有在市场上走得更远。

2006年,大红旗重披战袍,再度出山。这次红旗与丰田合作,这款几乎借壳出生的红旗,在市场引起更大的争论,因为代表着中国自主品牌的红旗轿车,血统已不纯正。

这款为公务车市场设计的高级轿车,在如今公务车已被奥迪攻占的天下,想借着民族感情杀出一条血路,但推行的速度远没有想象的顺利。

至今,红旗仍在市场的重压下低位运行。

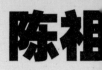

Article of *Chen Zutao* 'I am the
no. 1 worker of the No.1 Vehicle
Factory', South Weekend, 13th
March 2008
《陈祖涛：我是一汽第一名职
工》，载于《南方周末》，2008
年3月13日

□本报记者　徐　钟　发自北京

见证"红旗"

　　陈祖涛可能是新中国最早接触汽车的人之一。

　　他的俄文要比中文好，直到现在，他的汉字写得并不得心应手。

　　陈祖涛出生在湖北，他的父亲是原红四方面军政委陈昌浩。和毛岸英等许多革命后代一样，11岁的陈祖涛于1939年从延安被送往中国革命的大后方——苏联。1945年，苏联卫国战争刚刚结束，年满18岁的陈祖涛考入莫斯科鲍曼最高技术学院机械系。按当时苏联政策，不是本国公民原则上不让进入莫斯科，陈祖涛为完成学业不得不加入苏联国籍，"文革"时，这个"罪状"险些要了他的命。

　　1951年，听到新中国热火朝天建设的消息，按捺不住热情的陈祖涛提前4个月从大学毕业。回到中国后，周总理问他："毕业后准备干什么工作？"他回答说："我在苏联学的是机械，主攻方向是汽车，回国想搞汽车。"周总理说："那好极了，你再回苏联去，我国正在和苏联洽谈建设第一汽车厂，你就以第一汽车厂代表的身份去参加谈判，顺便再到苏联的汽车厂去实习。"

　　"事实上我就成为了一汽的第一名职工。"陈祖涛说。

　　当时中国工业一穷二白。毛泽东曾说了一段意味深长的话："现在我们能造成什么？能造桌子、椅子，能造茶壶、茶碗，能种粮食，还能磨成面粉，还能造纸，但是，一辆汽车、一架飞机、一辆坦克、一辆拖拉机都不能制造。"

　　苏联老大哥向我们伸出援手。苏联向中国列出156个援助项目清单，包括钢铁、煤炭、汽车、坦克、

飞机、大炮，而汽车也在其[中]，俄文优势加懂得机械技[术]作为翻译参与了机械组[装]

　　汽车谈判的结果令[人]联同意帮助中国在东北[建]一座综合性的汽车制造[厂]苏联对中国真是大公无私[一]面表示，将按照斯大林汽[车]模援建中国，斯大林汽车[厂]设备，援建中国的汽车厂[的]设备。"

　　斯大林给一汽建设[规定]间表："三年"。但按照当[时]经济实力，"四年建设犹[恐三]年完成更无把握。"

　　1953年，毛泽东亲[自签发]《中共中央关于三年建[成一汽]厂的指示》，责成有关部[门对]汽车厂的建设予以最大[支持]"三年建厂"成为那个年[代"抗美]援朝"以外最鼓舞人心[的大事之]一。

　　1953年6月，毛泽[东为一汽]奠基题词，一个月后[举行了]重的开工仪式，工地上[高音喇叭不]断播放："中国汽车工业[从这里开始，这]个规模空前的建设工程[必将]在短短三年里，长春孟[家屯原本]荒凉的土地上耸立起一[座过去只有]在图画中才能看到的宏[伟的现代化]汽车城"。

　　1958年，在大跃进[的氛]围的熏陶下，一汽开始[制造轿]车。东风小轿车用了不[到半年时]间就敲制出来。

　　但东风轿车不够档[次。领]导和中国的驻外使节[在国外]机场迎接外宾时，希望能[坐上]自己生产的高级轿车。这[时候]负责技术工作、时任一汽[生产]处长的陈祖涛："当时我[们的]生产能力与技术还不具[备造轿]车的水平——如果说生[产]

：我是一汽第一名职工

小学水平，那么生产轿车相当于大学本科水平，而高级轿车的生产层次更高。"

但政治使命的力量足可以燃尽那个时代所有人的激情。"我们决定采取仿制的办法，"陈祖涛说，"我们借来一辆克莱斯勒轿车，把它拆解开，全部零件一一摆列出来，动员全厂职工来'赶庙会'，谁能接下哪个零部件，谁就签下协定。大家的热情很高，老工人、技术干部几乎是抢着签协议。"

"红旗的问世，并不说明我们掌握了多高的技术能力，可以说政治意义更大，我们在结构件上基本抄袭样车，只是重新设计了具有民族特色的外观。"1958年9月28日，第一辆红旗轿车装配完毕后，为让世人最先知道"乘东风、展红旗，生产高级轿车献给毛主席"的"宏图"得以实现，一汽人也没有按照正规的程序对车进行检测和试验，就连夜送往北京去报喜。

1959年在建国十周年大庆的前夕，20辆乌黑锃亮的红旗车在人民大会堂外一字排开，用陈老的话讲："像20颗巨大的钻石，在秋日照耀下，熠熠生辉。"这些车很快被中央领导的秘书们"瓜分"了。

在庆典当天，两辆红旗车参加了检阅，6辆红旗参加了群众大游行，引起全国人的轰动。

从此红旗便和民族轿车工业的兴衰联系在一起。

但红旗毕竟是每年只能"手工"生产几十辆的"官车"，轿车作为真正的产业开始大力发展还是30年后的事情。1950年代，日本也刚发展轿车，"如果那个年代中国就发大力发展轿车，现在恐怕满世界跑的不是丰田，而是中国车了。"陈祖涛说。

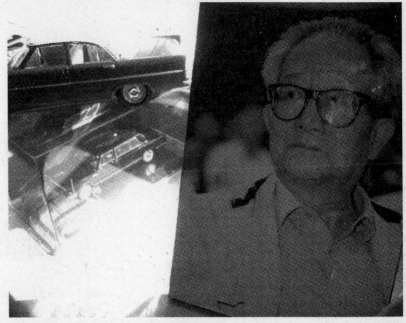

陈祖涛说，红旗的问世，它的政治意义更大。　　　　徐钟/摄

拓荒二汽

1960年代中期，中国奉行"反帝反修"的外交路线，相当严重地孤立于世界之外。出于战争的考虑，中国不惜花费几千亿的代价和巨大牺牲，提出建设"三线"的战略工业基地。

1965年，第二汽车厂的建设项目正式列入国家发展第三个五年计划，成为"三线"建设的重点项目。

为了保证打仗的需要，二汽建设的首要任务就是生产2.5吨的军用越野车。1965年12月，"一机部"正式任命二汽建设五人领导小组，陈祖涛为其中一员。二汽的厂址——湖北十堰就是陈祖涛看中的。

把这么大的一个汽车厂放在一个大山里，"我内心深处始终是有顾虑的，一个几万人的大企业，要吃、要喝、要生活，这是要在一个山沟里建设一个社会啊，这些工作不亚于再建一个同等规模的汽车

厂，但在当时的政治气候下，我不敢多说。"陈祖涛说。

但性格直来直去的陈祖涛在那个"怀疑一切、打倒一切"的荒诞岁月里，即使如何谨言慎行，仍逃脱不了被批斗的命运。

1968年5月中旬的十天是陈祖涛有生以来最痛苦、最绝望的十天。"每天晚上10点钟开始提审我，几个人按住我的手脚，一个家伙挥起木棍没头脑地打，打得我天天尿血，当时我最大愿望就是死。"直到现在，陈祖涛的头痛病还时常发作。

专案组没有在陈祖涛身上得到有用的信息。他被下放到吉林桦甸的一个农村。1972年，瘦得跟虾一样、腰系麻绳的陈祖涛才被找回二汽，很快被任命为二汽总工程师，这是二汽成立后的第一任总工程师，也是"文革"中我国特大型企业任命的第一个总工程师。

▶下转 T2 版

Article of *Chen Zutao* 'I am the no. 1
worker of the No.1 Vehicle Factory',
South Weekend, 13th March 2008.
《陈祖涛：我是一汽第一名职工》，载于
《南方周末》，2008年3月13日

◀上接 T3 版

陈祖涛：我是一汽

1980 年后，中央决定成立中国汽车工业公司，陈祖涛是筹备人之一。在那段时间，陈祖涛逢会就讲，中国应发展轿车产业。他是中国轿车产业市场化的最早"发动者"之一。

1987 年，轿车大门打开后，中央担心全国各地会一哄而上轿车项目。国务院又发通知，对轿车生产实行严格控制，除已批准的六个

轿车生产厂外，不再安排新的轿车生产厂。这六个生产厂分别是一汽、二汽、上汽，俗称"三大"，三大汽车厂也有明确分工：一汽生产中高级轿车，上汽生产排量为 1.8–2.0 的桑塔纳中级轿车，二汽则生产排量在 1.3–1.6 之间的普及型轿车。加上"三小"——北京吉普、天津小客车、广州组装的法国"标致"三家生产厂，相当一段时间内，中

国轿车业在⋯局中运营。

1988 年⋯了中汽联的⋯自己在中国⋯中国汽车工⋯的工作。20⋯贸易组织关⋯志写了一封⋯一定要抓住

一名职工

大三小"的格

陈祖涛离开

但他仍利用

界的影响为

着力所能及

国加入世界

涛给江泽民同

中国汽车业

年时间调整

产业政策，取消目录等审批制度，鼓励国外资本和民营资本进入汽车工业，否则中国汽车工业会错失良机。

现今，赋闲在家的陈祖涛老人除了偶尔参加一下汽车业的聚会外，专心在家写书，2005 年他出版了自传《我的汽车生涯》，目前他准备为父亲陈昌浩写一本传记。

2007 年，陈祖涛在他的家里对南方周末记者说，现在中国汽车产量世界排名第三，"这么高的产量，我很高兴活着能看到这种局面，我做了一辈子汽车，这是我最自豪的事情。"

虽然中国自主品牌汽车质量还差一些。"但解决它只是时间问题，"陈祖涛说，"我估计在 15 年—20 年内，中国能从汽车生产大国变成强国。"

Article of 'What we should learn from Gemany and Japan - Interview with *Huang Zhaoluan*, the former director of No.1 Vehicle Factory', quoted from South Weekend 22nd November 2007
《我们向德国、日本学习什么——一汽老厂长黄兆銮访谈录》，载于《南方周末》，2007年11月22日

黄兆銮并不喜欢见记者。83 岁的□□深的一汽老厂长之一。他回绝记者采□□触轿车不多。

但他对一汽发展脉络的记忆并不□□在打土桩的 1953 年，黄兆銮作为二汽□□"当时没什么可学，就学盖房子——反□□

一门心思要"取经"回二汽的黄兆□□的斯大林汽车厂学习——一汽人更愿□□人愿学的"管理工作"就落到他的头上，□□干部"。

1957 年二汽下马时，黄兆銮被一汽□□的广东人，曾为无法回到南方生活失落□□自己交给了天寒地冻的北国长春一汽。

在天津读北洋大学的黄兆銮曾想□□

□本报记者 徐 钟 发自长春

南方周末：您是怎样和汽车结缘的？

黄兆銮：1953 年第一个五年计划时，中国雄心勃勃，想搞 7 汽 8 拖（7 个汽车厂、8 个拖拉机厂，后来就剩下一汽和洛阳拖拉机厂），当时武汉二汽筹备组二十几个人无事可干，因为一汽已经上马，就让我们来这里学习。到长春时，这里还是工地，我们就

都不愿学，一汽领导就让我去学。□□

1956 年回国后，分到工具部门□□国首辆轿车"东风"车头上的那条□□们工具科的师傅用了三天刻出来□□二汽下马，我被留下来。

南方周末：能谈谈红旗方面的□□

黄兆銮：最早的红旗是朱总□□法国样车，我们自己搞的车身，发□□别人的。最老的车型四四方方的□□

黄兆銮指着窗外的厂房说，50 年前，这里还是一片空地。

学盖房子。

二汽说怎么能盖房子呢。几个月后，就把我调到车间管工具，当时我在拿二汽的工资。

后来二汽派我去苏联斯大林汽车厂学习，二汽让我学机床设计，但一汽很多干部不愿学管理，当时有个工具管理环节，他们

不多，销量也不多，警卫局"不讲□□低的价钱，我们原来有个书记说□□辆车赔两辆。

一年才生产几辆红旗，给□□们坐，红旗车很坚固，用包头钢□□的钢板做车身，防弹，子弹打过□□去，不会打出窟窿，玻璃也很厚□□

他才与汽车打上交道。直到现在,他这个汽车厂长还不怎么会开车:"工作的时候,厂里规定,禁止处级以上的领导开车,怕出事故;退休后,年纪太大又不能开车了。"不过他对汽车品鉴有自己的方式:"听跑起来的声音,看车身的接头对缝,一看就能知道车大致怎么样。"

现在,离休后的黄兆銮每天上午都会坐在"一汽咨询委员会"的办公室里,他的身份是"顾问",他说"顾问就是回顾总结历史,问心是否有愧"。

平时他还拉拉胡琴。因为京戏,黄兆銮和曾在一汽工作过的江泽民结缘——从到苏联实习开始,"他和我一个唱戏一个拉胡琴,度过了难忘的青春岁月"。

1962年江泽民离开一汽的时候,当时开欢送会不像现在喝酒吃饭,他们几个"票友"跑到张琦(一汽工艺处处长)家里唱京剧,张琦正好刚买了一台录音机,张琦开玩笑说:"下面请江泽民老板唱《捉放曹》,请黄兆銮老板拉胡琴。"这段录音在"文革"时被查抄出来,"造

反派说我们要当'老板',搞资本主义复辟"。张琦被斗,最后自杀。

"那是一段荒诞岁月。"黄兆銮对南方周末记者说。

黄兆銮在一汽主政的那段时间,正好赶上1980年代初、红旗"下马"的动荡岁月,他是一汽走上合资路线的见证者之一。

和德国人、日本人都打过交道的黄兆銮说,德国人保守认真,每次"车子要动一动"都要经过德国总部许可,因此每次汽车调价、国产化采购都要和德国人争吵,"开董事会就是吵架"。而日本人则做什么事都要当年见效益,"德国人和日本人一样,对中国技术封锁得都很厉害"。

"但我们要向它们学习管理、销售和人才培养等先进的东西。一汽在这方面受益很多。"黄兆銮说。

2007年11月初,黄兆銮老人站在一汽咨询委员会10楼的办公室窗口,指着外面现代化的厂房说,拍照就以它为背景吧,"50年前,这里还是一片荒地。"

我们向德国、日本学习什么

——一汽老厂长黄兆銮访谈录

坦克一样。

当时做这个车是不惜成本的,我去苏联参观汽车厂,它做吉斯小轿车,给官员做,也是赔钱的,靠卡车养它,我们也是。在国等资本主义国家,它们是用轿车养轿,像福特、通用,都是高利润,自己可以养己。

当时我们也就认了,中央首长也没多人,用卡车养红旗,作为政治任务吧。

南方周末:您坐过现在的红旗,感觉怎?

黄兆銮:现在新红旗还是不错的,但市卖得不算太好,一般老百姓呢不愿买,他买国外车。只有一些省市机关的人买。

我们一个副厂长到天津坐了一下皇,不太习惯,它是日本人设计的,太矮,坐去要低头,座位很软,不舒服。

现在红旗HQ3后面可坐三人,中间有扶手,扶手拉起来,中间还可以再坐一个,但坐中间的人不舒服,后面没靠背。

红旗HQ3用了丰田的发动机,是我们己弄的,奔腾我们用了马自达的底盘,我自己搞的车身,外界传说一汽是假开发自主品牌,不是这个意思,用了别人一部东西,产权还是我们的。

新红旗HQ3虽然用了丰田发动机,但排量大,所以不省油。HQ3排量4.3升,们现在坐2.0、3.0的车就不错了,已经舒了。

南方周末:您能不能谈谈老红旗下马到合资这段时期的事情?

黄兆銮:1980年代中期,上海先上轿车目后,中国开始辟谣,说轿车不是贵族用了,是交通工具,当时从外国大量进口轿,我们也是从那时开始和德国大众谈判资项目。

最初我们想和美国克莱斯勒合作,当我们搞轻型卡车,克莱斯勒有个生产线,生产轿车也能生产轻卡,当时他们想

卖(这条线),我们决定买它,目的要引进它生产的轿车。

生产线买来后,我们把它装在(一汽的)第二轿车厂,生产轻型车。但我们想上轿车时,和克莱斯勒谈判,他们牛得很,要价很高。我们有个陆副厂长去谈判,总是谈不拢。国内很着急,当时国内轿车项目可以上了,各厂家都在抢时机,只有这个项目在那里拖着扯皮。

这时德国的汉博士——大众的董事长,比较有远见,他和上海合作,但产量也不是很高,东北这个地方从大连进口也比较方便,于是他主动找一汽想合作。一汽只是想叫美国人让步,于是就放风说,你们不干我们就和德国人干了,结果美国人不让步,一气之下,我们和德国人干了。

南方周末:一汽和德国人合作,后来又和日本人合作,二者有什么不同?

黄兆銮:大众和日本人一样,对中国技术封锁很厉害,车子想动一动,要经过德国总部才行。过去(合资车想)根据中国实际情况改进一下,可麻烦了,一个项目报给德方,它得又报给总部,当时德国人很拖拉,很长时间批不下来,耽误很多生产时间。

虽然大众在长春也有设计部门,但还是要听总部指挥,自己本部技术中心也指挥不了,所以他们比较保守,(做事)很慎重,很死板,现在也这样,只是稍好一点。(合资公司)一年一次的董事会,有时在狼堡开,有时在长春开,开董事会就是吵架。为车型吵,为价格吵。中方想降价,德方就是不干。还有外来件,他们价很高,靠卖零件赚我们的大钱,它不靠合资企业赚钱。

南方周末:和广州标致差不多吧?为什么一汽会挺过来?

黄兆銮:一汽挺过来了。广州当时基础差,不管怎样,我们干过红旗,大体知道轿车怎样做出来的。不像标致,当时标致更不讲理,车型更差,零件全垄断了。

红旗停产后我们还干过奥迪100,用它的发动机。后来做捷达。原来老的捷达生产线现在拉到成都生产,改成新捷达了。捷达出租车还是比较受欢迎的,比较可靠、皮实。

南方周末:您是自主品牌轿车的老厂长,如何评价现在的自主品牌轿车?

黄兆銮:现在我们在报纸上看到什么(自主品牌销量)第一第二的宣传,吹吹牛行,真正自主品牌过硬的不多。我们干汽车的不是看你的宣传,我们看车,听跑起来的声音,看车身的接头对缝,一看就能知道车大致怎么样。

当前自主的概念很多,关键是自己是否拥有知识产权。竺延风也说,现在不是钱的问题、不是产品的问题,关键是人的问题。

我们现在在一汽每年给技术中心投钱不少,上百万辆的车有时利润用不了都给了他们,但光给钱没用,现在在一汽的设备也不错,但没有人也不行,而且培养人不是一年半年的事。

现在能设计出来,能不能生产出来?这又需要技术力量,现在技术工人难找,有人说买个博士容易,买个技术工人难,电子技术、数控技术,这样的人也要培养一批。能动手的技术工人太少了。

做出来还要卖出去,还要赚钱,销售又有一套方法,靠老办法拉关系已行不通了。在国外有专门的销售理论,一汽丰田在北京向丰田学了不少的东西。

外国汽车厂商进来抓两头:一面抓产品,一面抓销售。中国有的是劳动力,都能把车造出来。我们要把两头的东西学来。

我们不能老拿汽车销量全球第一第二来说事,中国这么大,(拿它说事)没有意义。说一千道一万还是要看中国的实力,我看没有几十年、上百年的发展,中国汽车业还无法在世界上称雄。

Article of 'Zhang Xiaoyu: the car
market is the least the worries
for the State', quoted from South
Weekend, 22nd November 2007.
《张小虞："车市最不需要国家操
心"》，载于《南方周末》，2007
年11月22日

张小虞："车市最不用国家操心

南方周末：中国轿车的发展历史是什么样的？

张小虞：中国轿车是从1958年开始的，首先是北京汽车厂、上海汽车厂、一汽开始生产轿车，一个叫"东方红"，一个叫"凤凰"，一汽就很早取名叫"红旗"牌。当时都是仿制生产，就是把外国的样车拆了，看里面的总成再组装，不过外形是自己设计，比如车灯像宫灯啊、龙的都有。当时主要是官车，一直到了1972年轿车最高产量达到过600辆。1980年，轿车最高产量达到4000辆。

南方周末：您是怎么回到北京的？

张小虞：1978年邓小平出来主持工作，全国拨乱反正，整顿经济秩序。一机部的工作人员到新疆搞调查。

当年二汽已经基本建成了，国家有个设想：利用二汽的技术在全国布几个点，组装和生产"东风牌"卡车，就是二汽生产一部分零件，再分发到全国各地进行组装。

所以就有人到新疆考察，一机部汽车局的人就把我调回来。那时我已经成家了，妻子留在北京，因为她父亲身体不好，我们两地分居了10年。

南方周末：回到北京您做什么工作？

张小虞：在一机部的汽车局，一直在规划处工作，包括中长期计划和编制，那个时候已经开始编制"六五"计划，然后是"七五"、"八五"、"九五"计划，算得上是汽

车行业的主管

南方周末：吧？

张小虞：法：对"汽车起来"。当时每辆车都要列家计划，第一来以后拿不行不给你付联单"。这是

轿车就更配。所有的部国资部提计

南方周末：轿车生产控制什么时候才有所松动？

张小虞：改革开放以后，汽车远远不能满足需求。到了计划管理体制稍微松动的1984年，那个时候赵紫阳才有批示"汽车有需求又有能力，应该允许其生产"。

那个时候的计划生产就变成两套版本：指令性计划和指导性计划。很多地方汽车厂这个时候开始发展起来。

指令性计划就是国家给计划内的钢材，生产出来的汽车要交给物资部门统一分配，价格是固定死的。

企业自己拿到的材料组织生产出来的车，价格会高一点，价格的"双轨"就是这样开始的，当时的两种价格相差20%—30%。

像北京212吉普车，计划内的价格大概是2万元，自销的价格可达2.5万元或·2.8万元，卖3万元的时候也有。

到了1985年，国家开始第七个五年计划，确定把汽车产业作为支柱产业，当年全国汽车产量到达40万辆，轿车是5000辆。

南方周末：轿车企业的合资是这个时候开始的吧？

张小虞：1986年的第一个汽车研讨会，我参加了。当时我在中汽总公司当经理，后来在规划司当司长。那个时候国家也提出中国汽车要大发展，要发展就必须发展轿车，轿车必须进家庭。

1984年-1986年批准三个轿车合资项目，依次为北京吉普、广州标致、上海大众。当时这三个合资企业，不只是中国汽车工业最大的合资企业，也是全国所有的合资企业里最大的三家。当时上汽定的轿

车生产能力是3万辆，广汽是1.5万辆，北汽是2万辆。

南方周末：为什么定的量这么低？

张小虞：当时以为轿车市场容量就是四五万辆。

我们当时找合资企业，是先跟美国通用接洽的，通用没法想象一年生产2万辆的工厂，还开玩笑说是不是翻译错了："是不是一个月或一个星期生产2万辆？"

后来大众公司很有远见地接受了这个方案，大众看到了中国发展的前景，也没提什么附加条件。

那个时候我们中外合资的企业还不成熟，也没有相应的法律法规，大众就在上海老厂的基础上进行改造。一汽那个时候还要生产"红旗"轿车，所以没有被改造。

随后轿车市场迅速放大。特别是改革开放后来几年，大量的走私轿车引起了国家的重视，好像1986年一年大概走私轿车就达十几万辆，正规生产的轿车加上走私进来的，那一年就有二十多万辆，当时好多地方，包括山东、海南都靠走私发了大财。

南方周末：当时中国市场能吃掉这些车吗？

张小虞：改革开放后，大家富起来了，有钱了，轿车的需求量很大，这一点是国家计划部门没有预计到的。

其实，关于轿车进入家庭和怎么发展家庭轿车的问题，国内一直在争论，直到2000年制定第十个五年计划的时候，中央才在建议书中写上一句话："鼓励轿车进入家庭。"

1994年的产业政策曾提到：政府鼓励

个人购买轿车因为一直在讨人购买汽车。考虑到市场经场，鼓市场促进

南方周末说您去韩国时我国刚好相反

张小虞：时国家成立了有四个小组车小组推动了

当时韩国件太好了，应该就说中国才能饭的问题。韩国的经验来看的资源，但是就业。

我们讲的饭是就业。

第二个问不买国产车？国人都买国产意识跟中国不是不爱国的表车，首先税务税，查你的收乱。另外，如引导员引至地我们完全不一会，好车就要"上海牌"就放

第三点就

"1970 年代, 轿车最高产量 600 辆"

生产挂产控制很严

文样文样一个说
生育生育一样管
由也曲也缺,所以
不列不列入到国
第二,二,生产出
油;轴;第三,银
当时咱时时叫作"三
格的格的计划分
什么什么车就向
转给转给国家计

委,国家计委根据当时所掌握的材料审核计划,然后转给机械部,由机械部组织生产,然后安排企业生产。

曾譬如说:一汽生产多少辆汽车,我就给你多少材料,每辆车对应一个"三联单"。那个时候我在规划处,只需要跑三个部门就可以做出轿车第二年的生产计划,一个是总政部,一个是人事部,一个是综署部。

那个时候的配备是,司局长是四个人一辆车,副部长两人一辆车,部长和司令是一个人一辆车。

司局长级别是坐"上海牌"轿车,正部长以上的人坐"红旗牌",县团级就坐北京吉普。

从 1978 年开始一直到 1985 年,我们的轿车计划就在 4000 辆-6000 辆,是严格的计划经济。

如果不够用,国家就进口一部分汽车,主要是进口苏联的汽车。到了 1980 年代后期,才慢慢从日本进口一部分轿车。严格的计划管理体制一直延续到我们加入世贸组织之前。

我记得在汽车局的时候,当时的一个计划处处长和二汽的计划处从计划外拿到了一批材料,并组织了计划外的生产并分配,后来被查出来,当时叫做"犯罪",还判了刑,等于破坏国家计划,这件事好像发生在 1980 年或 1981 年。

轿车如何进入寻常百姓家?

定汽空汽车政策,
则上则上鼓励你
有路了路,也没有
消费肖费拉动市

到一一个信息,
的消的消费观和
韩国韩国去的,当
委员员会,下面
汽车汽车小组,汽

展轿展轿车的条
展。展。我当时
先要先要解决吃
长就长就说:从韩
也没也没有先天
发展发展解决了

他理他理解的吃

国人国人为什么
他"她"为什么韩
韩国韩国的国民
为买为买外国车
买了了一辆外国
常来来查你的
得你你心烦意
酒店店时,就会
有落。落。这就跟
我到到人大开
不妨好的车如
如果如果你开的

车是外国车,所有国产车经过你的时候都向你按喇叭,侮辱你、瞧不起你。

所以韩国能够及时地在汽车工业发展的初期,让老百姓都买国产车。这在中国是做不到的,尽管政府出台了很多政策来鼓励国产车。

南方周末:我国真正发展轿车是在什么时候?

张小虞:中国的轿车工业的真正发展是在 2000 年——国家决定鼓励轿车进入家庭之后,2000 年全国汽车产量是 200 万辆,其中轿车的产量是 60 万辆。60 万辆轿车中,私人购买不到 30%。

在 2000 年,在面对 WTO 的时候,汽车工业被列入最危险、最令人担心的行业,而现在汽车行业却最令人振奋。2000 年,我们的产量在全世界排第八、第九位。就在这短短的五六年时间里,我们现在排到世界第三位。从市场销售量来讲,排到了第二位,仅次于美国,从原来的被动的进口,现在已变成了批量的出口。

现在我们自有品牌的商务车(含货车)占有市场的 80%,轿车占 20%,今天自主品牌的轿车产量增长率在 40% 以上。这是国产车又好又便宜的结果。现在的进口车基本上是在 35 万美金以上的高端车。

南方周末:应该说,没有合资就没有中国汽车工业的今天吧?

张小虞:上海合资的桑塔纳,它的国产化达到 60% 用了 8 年的时间,到了新世纪后,轿车生产的当年就能实现 50%-60% 的国产化。

汽车合资企业,首先是培养了人才,不仅培养了制造工艺的人才,也培养了设计人才;然后是奠定了零部件工业的基础,促进自主品牌的发展。

所以从这个意义上来讲,如果汽车工业不搞合资,不搞引进,汽车工业后期不会这么快发展。那些否定合资作用的人,都是虚无主义者。一些人总设想什么"如果当初……那么现在会怎样怎样",这是完全没有意义的。

南方周末:汽车产业发展到现在这个局面,是您当初选择这个行业时,没有想到的吧?

张小虞:现在老百姓最关心的三个市——"车市、房市和股市",其中,车市是国家最不用操心,百姓最满意。

从今天来看,全世界最好的汽车厂和发动机厂都在中国,用不着五年,全世界最好的研发中心也会在中国出现。我们打算 3 年至 5 年的时间,来消除和日韩之间同类产品的质量距离。

我们前两年提出重视研发人才的培养,包括大学生和"海归"。不多,再过 5 年,这支队伍就会建立起来,供给他们研发的条件也会建设起来,那个时候我们自主品牌研发的产品的市场份额肯定不止 20%,可以高达 50% 以上,成为汽车技术的主导者。

在轿车领域,大概还要 3—5 年的时间,我们的自主品牌和自主知识产权会慢慢起到主导作用。但是我们不排斥合资,我们很多合资企业一合作就是 30 年的。汽车产业本身就是国际化的产业,你中有我,我中有你,现在的问题不是我们要跟已经合作的企业分手,而是我们要走到国外去,发展我们自己的产业。

East Wind - Golden Dragon
A Last Tribute to the Imperial Power

Based on an interview with *Wang Guangyi* in *Beijing*

on 6th July 2007

"东风·金龙"

——对皇权的最后礼赞

时间: 2007年7月6日

地点: 北京

采访对象: 王广义

The concept of 'State Legacy' touches me. The East Wind - Golden Dragon, the first car to be manufactured in China was the first Chinese car that Chairman *Mao* ever sat in. I knew of and was impressed by this story when I was young. Of course when I grew up, I came to realize something more complicated lay behind it; the car represents the earliest general idea of a Chinese industrial revolution. Moreover, in my view, given its specific historical, cultural background the car was probably a tribute to our last imperial power. This car is known to have been hand made by numerous workers instead of by machines, not the manufacturing methods we use today. The production of this thing we call a car was actually the result of a state of great worship, a dedication to Chairman *Mao* in the form of a car. It was, as a matter of fact, the last present given to an imperial power. I think this subject is just right for the 'State Legacy' exhibition. This concept includes both material and spiritual legacies and the East Wind - Golden Dragon car happens to simultaneously represent both a material and spiritual legacy, very complicated.

For those car workers, their first passion was the worship of and a faith in Chairman *Mao*. Perhaps they were unaware that behind this worship and faith lay an earnest hope for a Chinese industrial revolution, the two aspects coincided.

I would say, I have a special feeling for these cars. As I was growing up this feeling became even stronger. At the very beginning, it was because Chairman *Mao* owned such a car.

I knew what was in the worker's minds. When I grew up and understood the historical background of China's modernization more clearly, I probably put more into it emotionally. I know the car has many connotations, especially when such a work is exhibited in Britain,

问：能否谈谈您的作品方案，为什么选择"东风·金龙"作为创作的母题？这与您的生活经验有没有什么联系？

王：最开始黄专跟我谈这个展览的想法的时候，"国家遗产"的概念挺打动我的。"东风·金龙"是中国的第一部汽车，也是毛主席坐过的中国第一辆车，我小时候就知道这件事情，它给我留下了深刻的印象。长大之后，我知道在这背后有更为复杂的东西——它带有中国工业革命最初的概念，而且在我看来，这有中国特定社会的历史文化背景关系，可能是对于皇权的最后礼赞。因为这车的产生是由无数工人用手工打造出来的，而不是用机器制造的方式，实际上是在一种极其浓厚的信仰状态下，制造出我们叫做"汽车"的东西，然后献给毛主席，所以应该是献给皇权的最后一份礼物。"国家遗产"，包括了物质遗产和精神遗产，而"东风·金龙"恰恰包含了这两个层面，既是物质遗产又是精神遗产，很复杂。

问：您觉得当时工人用手工打造"东风·金龙"的热情是基于对毛主席的个人信仰吗？当时只花了一个多月的时间便完成了车的改造设计，这种速度远远超出我们的想象。

王：对于工人而言，他们最初的热情基础是对于毛主席的崇拜和信仰，也许他们并不知道，这种崇

the cradle of the Industrial Revolution. I think this fact is full of meaning... Although the East Wind - Golden Dragon car is in fact a quasi-industrial product, to exhibit it in the place where the Industrial Revolution originated, gives the work a more intricate message.

I think using The East Is Red *dongfanghong* as background music serves to revive or provide a quasi-religious atmosphere. The glamour hostesses in motor shows are actually elements I want to include, contemporary elements which demonstrate an extreme passion for the material world. This material world comes into collision with the quasi-religious state. This special conflict, in my opinion, can be an impetus to push society forward. When contemporary desires overflow, society perhaps returns to the quasi-religious state. Hence in between society gets an impetus, or a balance.

In my view, quasi-religion should have something to do with totems, for at the totem state one has nothing clearly teleological but believe a strength is there to stir the heart. In such a state things seem clearer and quite the most powerful. If the belief had been reified, it might have been different. That would be another story.

Perhaps quasi-religion causes you to stand in awe of the unseen people who might actually decide your destiny. In less than two months numerous workers made the car entirely by hand. Only in such a quasi-religious state could such a car have been made, the music of The East Is Red is added for atmosphere.

My view is that the method of manufacturing cars by copying the methods of other makers, has its own correctness. It means that if we cannot achieve something by ourselves, we learn from others. Yet the car also linked our imaginations with the Industrial Revolution

拜和信仰的背后，实际上是对于中国工业革命的热切希望，这两者恰恰是吻合的。

"东风·金龙"实际上是带有一种准工业色彩的产物，把它拿到工业革命的策源地去展览，我觉得它的含义更为复杂。

问：在您作品中加入《东方红》的音乐和模特的因素是做什么样的考虑呢？
王：《东方红》作为背景音乐，我想是还原让人记忆起那种准宗教的氛围；模特实际上是我想增加进去的作为当代的元素。这种对于物质的极度热情，实际上与准宗教的状态构成了一种特殊的冲突，这种冲突在我看来是社会向前走的一个动力，在当代的欲望极度膨胀的时候，也许不经意地就回到或者感受到了这种准宗教的状态。我想它们之间构成的是一种动力，或者说也是一种平衡的感觉。

问：能不能具体谈谈"准宗教"？
王：也许并不是具体信仰什么，在我看来，"准宗教"应该说同图腾有点关系，因为人在图腾状态下是没有非常明确的目的论的东西，但是他相信一种让他心跳的力量，至于是什么，也许在这种状态

- the imagining of modernization in the form of a car. I think this is the right path for China to follow. It was proved during the development of modern China, which allowed the country to engage with the patterns of the contemporary world on a step-by-step basis. We absorbed new things as additions to what we already had, as a result, a kind of synthesized product was produced.

The glamour hostesses in motor shows reflect the growing desires of contemporary society. The 'motor show' is a completely meaningless event. Growing desires have to be represented in some way, the 'motor show' is one way to express them. The cars and the 'motor show' embody this exactly.

I used cast iron to re-create the East Wind - Golden Dragon car. It is a solid piece that is being shown, a museum-like piece. If one could put the latest car models besides this museum-like piece, it might feel as if 'showing' was activating my thoughts. Perhaps when people first see this work they will be confused as to what I want to express. But I think that as soon as they sense my intentions; they will grasp the messages that the work carries. 'To show' is an involuntary form of desire. People living in the contemporary world know it well; I also sense this desire. The museum-like East Wind - Golden Dragon car in cast iron form also stands there, the car comprises the weight of history. I want to represent the conceptual historical quality of it.

Mainly because of the changing form of Chinese politics, the variety of material desires has been enriched. We are not determining which desires are good and which are bad. That is totally irrelevant. We are just saying that the political elements have changed, leading

下的人并不清楚，但是恰恰是最有力量的。如果信仰具体化，可能就派生出各种宗教了，那是另外一个问题。"准宗教"可能是对不可知的、好像在左右你命运的人有敬畏心理。无数工人在长达一个多月的时间用手工打造，我想只有在这种状态下才能完成这样一个奇迹，而加入《东方红》的音乐也是为了营造这么一种氛围。

问：外国人在看中国第一辆车的时候觉得中国人非常聪明，因为当时是拿俄罗斯的高级轿车进行改造，实际上也只是在原有的基础上，在外形上做一些具有中国特色的设计。您是怎么看待当时的这种历史情境呢？

王：这个方法在我看来，实际上具有正确性。这种正确性是指在力所不能及的时候，我们拿来学习，但是又揉进了我们对工业革命的想象——对汽车这种现代化的想象，我认为这种方式具有正确性。事实上中国现代一步步地发展，慢慢地进入当代的世界格局，其实也是验证了这种正确性。我们可以吸收一些东西，然后又有我们自己的东西，这是一种综合的产物。

问：这也映射出当时的困境——当时中国与苏联紧张的关系，迫使我们迫切地需要制造中国的第一

to an increasing abundance of the categories of desirable things. This abundance is what contemporary people can feel and have therefore formed an inner relationship with it.

Even if the car is only in the form of cast iron, it will still be perplexing. People may comprehend what has been revived by the artist. Respect has been shown for history and belief. But this respect may be too simplistic? Consequently I have blended in some other elements, the categories of the variety of desires to enrich this respect and to explain better the political changes over a long period of history and the richness of desire.

Whether or not the car is still being manufactured is not really important. For me, the car is an outcome of belief in itself, or in a scheme. As an artist, I focus more on the fact that it was hand made. I think this meaning has been solidly represented. To produce the car by hand, the most primitive methods would have been employed given the technological conditions of that time... Precisely speaking, manual labour is the 'technology' of primitive agriculture. To realize the dream of an industrial revolution by way of the 'technology' of an agricultural society is very interesting in itself. This is how I think about it. As to whether we still produce the car is not important at all. Maybe it is right to stop doing so. The car was partly a dream, partly a miracle, it could only have been a one-off.

Today if many East Wind - Golden Dragon cars were still on the road, I would probably not be making this piece. This car was the result of a sudden impulse of a great man at the moment when China was an agricultural society, it took devoted Chinese to realize it. The miracle appeared but then came to an abrupt halt. In its absolute meaning, I think the car surpassed the English Industrial Revolution. Because the English Industrial Revolution

辆汽车，来体现当时国家的尊严感。

您在《私密广告》中也使用了模特的因素，在作品中使用模特这样一个时尚因素，有没有一定的关联性？最初是如何考虑的？

王：当然最主要还是因为车模能够呈现当代社会膨胀的欲望。因为"秀"完全是无意义的，膨胀的欲望必须有一种方式把它表达出来，那么就只有"秀"来表现，车模和"秀"恰恰能够体现这个问题。

我创作的《东风·金龙》用的是铸铁的方式，放在那里有种凝固化的感觉，其实很博物馆化。在这种博物馆化的《东风·金龙》旁边，这个"秀"就有种思想被激活的感觉。在一般人看来，可能最初会觉得很混乱，不知道我要表达什么，但是我想，当观者体会到我的意图之后，可能会感受到我要表达的问题。因为"秀"是一种欲望的无意识形式，这所有人都知道。用铸铁的、博物馆化的《东风·金龙》放在那里，它包含了一种历史的沉重感。

问：《东风·金龙》被附加了很多别的东西吗？比如宗教的氛围。

王：其实没有附加什么东西。宗教的氛围加强了我要呈现的《东风·金龙》的历史感以及观念性的表达。

provided a kind of sustainable development, which allowed society to move forward in an ordered manner. The car shows aspects of human progress in a purely idealistic form. If you think that the East Wind - Golden Dragon car was only a flash-in-the-pan, the miracle was in the human spirit.

I feel very lucky, because the East Wind - Golden Dragon car is unique. I replicated the car in cast-iron; giving this museum-like car a visual presence.

I think the East Wind - Golden Dragon car will make a strong impact when it is exhibited in England. I hope the visitors will feel many things, the car was a miracle created by the Chinese people and the Chinese Industrial Revolution and a starting point for the dreams of this huge country.

According to references, Chairman *Mao* only sat in the first East Wind - Golden Dragon car once taking a ride in it around the central government compound *zhongnanhai*. The car was a flicker of a dream by *Mao*, realised by workers and he sat in it once, that made it complete. It would not be the same if Chairman *Mao* had used the car for half a year. Because of its uniqueness, the car has become an historical myth.

Also according to the records, all the other cars produced by the No. 1 Vehicle Factory were called 'Red Flag'. The cars for Premier *Zhou Enlai* and Commander-in-Chief of the People's Liberation Army *Zhu De* were all called 'Red Flag'. I learned that to name the car made for Chairman *Mao* 'East Wind - Golden Dragon' was the wish of people, the wish of all those workers who made the car. Consequently I say this was a last tribute to Chinese imperial power. In ancient times, the dragon symbolised the Son of Heaven, the Emperor.

问：每个时代每个阶段的欲望都呈现出不同的形态，比如"东风·金龙"后来演变为"红旗轿车"，"金龙"与"红旗"标识的演变都是一种欲望的呈现，而这些欲望有没有一定的关联性呢？

王：这里边主要还是中国政治形态的转变，所以欲望的种类丰富了。哪种欲望是好的，哪种欲望是不好的，这个问题不存在。只是由于政治的一些因素的变化，导致欲望的类型更丰富化。这种丰富化是我们生活在当代的人所能感受到的，所以这里面它构成一种关系。

《东风·金龙》只是以铸铁的形式放在那里，也很多元化，人们也都会知道艺术家把它还原出来，是对历史和信仰的一种敬意。但是这种敬意是否也太单纯了？所以我就融入了一些其他的因素，融入各种欲望的类型，使得这种敬意更具有丰富性，而且也更能阐释这种历史长河的政治变化和欲望变化的丰富性。

问："东风·金龙"应该体现了当时中国民族的自豪感，但是，为什么一汽没有把"东风·金龙"的轿车发展下去，而到后来反而消解了，您是如何看待这种现象的？

王：这个车是否继续生产，其实已经不重要了，在我看来，它本身是一个信仰的产物，或者说是一个方案。它的意义恰恰是由工人手工制造出来的，我觉得这个意义实现得特别纯粹。因为当时中国所

The workers made a car that was only for the Emperor. In this respect, *Mao* was not only a leader.

When the *Mao* era ended, it caused the disappearance of imperial power in China. Therefore I would say that the East Wind - Golden Dragon car was the Chinese people's last tribute to imperial power. The car combined this tribute with the dream of an Industrial Revolution, what an amazing combination.

There have been many miracles in history, but one that can embody so many turning points are rare. While exploring the background material to this piece, I discovered the complex meanings behind it included China's Industrial Revolution.

The people made the logo for the car a golden dragon, the colour was a silvery gold, the noblest of all the colours of gold. Shining, warm gold colours are preferred by the common people; but a silvery gold is the colour that salutes the eye.

I chose to use cast-iron is because it is a very unostentatious material; it will rust and redden with exposure to the sun and wind, very much like historical artifacts. The qualities will tally with the creators of the car, the essence of the people.

Because I replicated the car in the roll of an artist, the piece will be different from the original car and, of course, the work is also different from other people who replicate cars.

As an artist, I cannot put forward my thoughts on 'the state' in a very ordered way. But I regard seeing 'the state' as like seeing myself, very complex. There are contemporary understandings and also traditional understandings. As I grow older, I feel that my understanding of myself is in fact my understanding of our state.

具有的工业基础条件, 确实是达不到的, 所以只能用手工把它打造出来——严格讲, 用手工打造是原始农业社会的方式——但中国用农业社会的方式实现了一个工业革命的梦想, 这里边特别有意思, 我觉得主要是这样一个关系。至于后来是否继续生产, 讨论是毫无意义的, 也许不生产倒是对的。

有些梦想、有些奇迹, 它只能是一次性的。

你想想, 如果现在有很多"东风·金龙"在路上开其实是很奇怪的。我们不一定要做这个事情, 因为在我看来, 当时实际上是在中国农业社会的状态下, 一些伟人偶然的念头。这个念头促使中国有所崇拜的人去实现它, 其实是奇迹性的一句话, 但是后来嘎然而止。所以说, 这个事情的意义, 从一种绝对的角度来讲, 可能它会超越英国的工业革命。虽然英国工业革命可以导致持续性的发展, 那是社会次序推进的过程, 当然也有一些进步的环节, 那是一种绝对的理想主义。这种一闪念的嘎然而止, 更是人类的精神奇迹。

我把这独此一辆的车, 用青口铁复制出来, 我觉得特别幸运。博物馆化的车是具体的。

问：能不能讲一讲制造这个车模的过程？

It was my early work, the 'Mao Series' that brought me fame. At the time I painted *Mao* my heart was in awe of him. Twenty years later, I made the car that was sat in by *Mao*, my awe of him has not changed.

I still think the *Mao* era was a great and splendid era. I use the word 'splendid' which should be read as a romantic description. The *Mao* era was a time of times of joy, of belief, sometimes poetic but a very bloodstained era as well. My childhood was spent in this 'splendid' era; looking back I feel that it was the luckiest aspect of my life. Now the times have changed totally, the model of politics has changed as well, however, my heart fills with respect when I think of the *Mao* era. The most important thing for me is that my art is making some record of that 'splendid' era.

王：我的翻制是要绝对忠实于原车，不做任何改变，把它彻底完成。

问："东风·金龙"现在放在哪里？
王：应该是在国家博物馆。据资料记载，其实毛主席只乘坐了一次，在中南海绕了一圈。我想毛主席其实也只是一闪念的梦想，是工人把它实现了，他坐一下也就完成了。如果毛主席一坐就坐了一年半年，肯定就不一样了，这事情具有偶然性。由于毛主席这种伟大的一闪的念头，所以这个车只有一辆，就嘎然而止了。毛主席只是在他的生命中坐了一圈，再也没有坐过，这种历史赋予了"东风·金龙"一种神话，挺独特的。

问：但是它后来又转而变成"红旗"，应该还算是发展下去了。
王：其实按资料上记载，当时整个工厂生产的车都叫"红旗"，唯独毛主席坐过的这一辆车叫"东风·金龙"，像朱德、周恩来坐的车都是"红旗"。根据资料图片显示，其实这也是人民的意志，是当时制造这部车的工人的意志，所以我说是对皇权的最后礼赞。
　　在古代，龙是天子，是皇帝，所以这也是对皇帝的一种敬意。工人打造这部车，也是只有皇帝才能坐的车，从这个意义上来说，毛主席就不仅仅是领袖了。当然这有很多种说法，但是我认为这种说法更符合这件事情的前因后果。

问：所以后来"红旗"代表的是"工农商学兵"，而再也没有出现"金龙"。

王：因为"龙"是只有皇帝才拥有的。实际上当毛主席离开人民以后，毛泽东时代就结束了，这实际上导致了皇权的消失，所以这车是毛的人民对皇权的最后礼赞。对皇权的最后礼赞和工业革命的梦想，这两个事情有点奇迹性。

　　在历史上有很多这类事情，但是许多伟大事情的转折性意义合在一起的情况其实很少。这也是我在创作过程中，逐步接触了资料之后，才逐步地了解了这车的复杂意义，工业革命也只是其中的一个因素之一。

问：龙是金色还是银色？

王："龙"是金的，偏白的金，在金里边白金是最高贵的。"金灿灿"的金在金的品格里是很一般的，是大众更热爱的，可以触摸的，白色的金是最高贵的，是可以让人行注目礼的。

问：复制的车模跟第一辆车用的材料是一致的吗？

王：我使用的材料是把它历史化了的，我用的是铸铁，确切地说是青口铁。青口铁在铁里边是最朴素的，它随着风吹日晒会生锈变红，这种铁更符合于创造这辆车的人民的本质。

　　复制这辆车的意义与原有的《东风·金龙》很不一样，因为我是艺术家的身份。如果我不是艺术家的身份，我复制这一辆车可能就是另外一种含义。

问：您觉得《东风·金龙》放置在英国，会引起英国人怎样的想象？

王：我想会很不一样。放在英国那样的背景之中，冲突会更强烈，但是他们也可以感受更多的东西，"东风·金龙"是中国工业革命和中国人民的一个奇迹，也是关于大国梦想的一个起点。

问：您对于毛有一种信仰？

王：当然。我的成名之作就是毛泽东系列的作品。当年我以敬畏的心理画了毛泽东，也就是"打格的毛泽东"，20年后，我又做了毛泽东坐过的车，我对毛泽东的敬意不变。

问："打格的毛泽东"有很多的说法。

王：那是在特定时代的文化情境下创作的。

问：能讲讲您对毛泽东时代的想法吗？

王：我现在还是觉得毛泽东的时代是一个伟大灿烂的时代，我用"灿烂"这个词，应该说是一种浪漫的说法。可能有欢乐、有信仰，可能也有非常诗意、但是也有非常血腥的过程。我称之为"灿烂"的时代，是因为我的童年就是在这样一种灿烂的时代度过的，想起来是我一生的幸运。现在时代完全变了，政治模式也变了，但是我想起毛泽东时代还是充满着敬意，更重要的是，那个灿烂的时代给我的艺术打下了烙印。

问：在您的成长的过程中，对于"国家"的理解有什么样的变化？

王：作为艺术家，我当然不能把它说得非常条理化。但是我想，我对于"国家"的看法，就像我对于自身的看法一样，非常复杂，有极其当代性的一面，也有极其传统的一面。这是随着我年龄的增长，我对自身的认识，同时也是对于我的国家的认识。

The Context of the Project:
China's Railway Project

项目背景简介: 中国铁路工程

China's Railway Project

The Chinese people's understanding of railways probably began between the 1930s and the 1940s. The earliest detailed records of railways are in the 'Trade Memoranda' *maoyitongzhi*, a book written by the German missionary Gutzlaff, *Guo Shili*, 'The Gazetteer of the Four Continents', *sizhouzhi* translated and edited by *Lin Zexu* in 1839 and 'An Illustrated Geography of Overseas Nations' *haiguotuzhi* edited by *Wei Yuan* in 1844 which introduced technological information on foreign railways and trains. In 1848, a geographer of the late *Qing* dynasty, *Xu Jiyu*, further introduced the circumstances surrounding the railways in some countries in his book 'A Brief Account of the Maritime Circuit' *yinghuanzhilue*. However, those who had a real commitment to build a railway were *Ding Gongchen*, *Hong Renxuan*, *Wang Tao* and others. *Ding Gongchen* wrote the book 'An Illustrated Handbook of Western Locomotives and Steam Vessels' and in 1843, following the principles of foreign train construction, produced a small locomotive which could move 30kg of weight travelling either forwards or backwards. This was the first example of China's early steam locomotives. *Hong Renxuan* discussed plans to construct a railway for the first time in 'New Politics': 'Firstly construct eleven main lines in eleven provinces as the arteries of the country'. The plan ended with the failure of the *Taiping* Heavenly Kingdom (1850-1864). *Wang Tao* was one of the reformers at the end of the *Qing* dynasty. In 1867, *Wang* was invited by the missionary James Legge to visit Europe. During the two years he spent in Europe, *Wang* did on-site inspections of Britain's railway system, visited railway managers and realized that 'the speed of the western train is the key to the economic success of the country and the prosperity of the people'. In 1870, the Franco-Prussian War

中国铁路工程

中国人认识铁路，大约是从19世纪30、40年代开始的。英籍传教士郭士立撰写的《贸易通志》，开始对铁路有比较详细的记载。1839年，林则徐主持编译的《四洲志》和1844年魏源编撰的《海国图志》，均介绍了当时外国的铁路、火车等科学技术信息。1848年，清末地理学家徐继畬在所编《瀛环志略》一书中，进一步介绍了一些国家的铁路情况。但真正决心修筑铁路的是丁拱辰、洪仁轩和王韬等人。丁拱辰著有《西洋火车火轮船图说》，并于1843年根据外国火车的原理制作出一台小火轮车，能拉30公斤重物前进或后退，这是中国最早的蒸汽机车模型。洪仁轩在《资政新编》中第一次提出修筑铁路的计划："先于11省通11条大路以为全国之脉络"，因太平天国失败而告终。王韬是清末维新派，1867年随传教士理雅各去欧洲，他在欧洲两年多的时间里，实地考察了英国铁路，访问铁路管理人员，领略了西方"轮车之迅捷"，"实为裕国富民之道"。1870年爆发普法战争，普鲁士利用铁路一举战败法国，使人们对铁路在军事上的作用有新的认识。王韬认为"泰西利捷之制，莫如舟车"，中国必须把西方的武器和先进的交通工具学到手，才能自强，他积极倡议清朝廷修筑铁路。此外，1895年5月2日，康有为公车上书，在谈到"立国自强"的根本大计时，也力主修建铁路。

但是在清朝的官员中，大多数人都反对铁路，认为建筑铁路有三个弊端：其一是"资敌"——对

broke out, the Prussian armies defeated the French armies due in part to their efficient use of railways, which gave people a new sense of the use of railways especially to the military. *Wang Tao* thought that, 'Nothing is more important than the train among the advantages of the West' and that China must learn from these advanced instruments of traffic and weapons of the West for her own self-improvement. He actively encouraged the *Qing* court to build railways. Furthermore, on May 2nd 1895, in 'Joint Petition of Imperial Examination Candidates to the Emperor', *Kang Youwei* also advocated the construction of railways as a fundamental strategy of the 'foundation of self-strengthening'.

But the majority of the officials of the *Qing* dynasty were opposed to the building of railways. They considered that there were three objections: the first was 'the benefiting of our enemies' - believing that railways would benefit an invasion of China by foreigners; the second objection was 'its harm to the people' - a railway would occupy and destroy considerable areas of farmland, houses and graves would have to be demolished and a railway would destroy the *Fengshui*; the third objection was 'unemployment' - with the building of railways, porters and boatmen along the lines would lose their jobs, hotels would lose business and unemployed people would gather together as bandits. At that time, the *Qing* dynasty absolutely forbad foreigners to build railways in China.

The birth of the railway in China occurred over half a century later than the world's first railway. On September 27th, 1825, the first railway for public use was built between Stockton and Darlington in the United Kingdom. In 1829, a railway from Liverpool to Manchester was constructed. Later, the United States, France, Belgium, Germany, Canada

洋人入侵国土长驱直进有利；其二是"病民"——占用大量农田、拆迁民宅、坟墓，破坏风水；其三是"失业"——铁路修建成后，沿线舟车挑夫、行栈铺房无以为生，并将"聚为流寇"。当时清政府是绝不允许外国人在中国修筑铁路的。

中国铁路的诞生比世界上最早出现的铁路通车时间晚了半个多世纪。1825年9月27日，在英国的斯托克顿至达林顿两座城市之间，已经率先建立了世界上第一条供公众使用的铁路。1829年，英国的利物浦至曼彻斯特的铁路又建成，此后，美国、法国、比利时、德国、加拿大等国家纷纷兴建铁路，美国还成为了继英国之后，世界上筑路最多最快的国家。可以说，铁路在各大洲陆地上的扩展同工业革命向全世界各地的扩展几乎同步。随着钢铁工业和技术的发展，铁路的铺设随之发生了变化，起初的铁轨为钢轨所取代，至1857年，英国铺设了世界上第一条钢轨铁路。当中国还在争论要不要修建铁路时，全世界已拥有20多万公里的铁路了。

1865年（清同治五年），英国商人杜兰德在北京宣武门外修建的半公里多的小铁路，被当时人们视为"诧所未闻，骇为妖物"。这条小铁路很快被军统领衙门"勒令拆除"，有人称它为外国人在中国修建的"广告铁路"。至1876年，英国人擅自筑成吴淞铁路，这条铁路建成后投入运营，第一年共运送旅客16万次，平均每周每英里获利27英磅，与英国国内铁路的收益相当。吴淞铁路最后由政府

and other countries built their own railway systems. The United States became the country with the world's largest railway following a rapid construction programme rivalling that of the United Kingdom. It can be said that the expansion of the railways on all continents was almost simultaneous with the worldwide influence of the Industrial Revolution. Along with the developments in the steel industry and technology, the laying of railways was changed. The early iron rails were replaced by steel track. In 1857, the United Kingdom laid the world's first steel railway lines. In the period when China was still debating whether or not to build a railway, the remainder of the world had laid more than 200,000 kilometres of track.

In 1865, the fifth year of the *Tongzhi* Emperor's reign period, the British businessman Durand built a small railway of over half a kilometre in length outside the *Xuanwu* Gate in *Beijing*. The railway was regarded as 'a monster that had never been seen before'. This small railway was soon demolished on orders from the Armed Forces Command. Someone called it 'an advertisement for railways' that foreigners might build in China. By 1876, the *Wusong* Railway has been built by the British without authorization. From completion and the start of operation of the railway, the number of passengers transported amounted to 160,000 persons in the first year. The average weekly earnings were twenty-seven pounds per mile, the same as the domestic profit of the British railways. The *Wusong* Railway was finally demolished by the government and compensation was paid for the full cost. This railway is thus generally regarded as China's first commercial railway.

However, the first railway run by China in the true sense was the *Tangxu* Railway started in 1880. The *Kaiping* Coal Mining Administration began laying track in June 1881 with the

照价赎回并拆掉，这条铁路也因此被视为中国第一条营业铁路。

然而，中国自办的第一条真正意义上的铁路，却是始于1880年动工修建的唐胥铁路。这条铁路于1881年6月开始铺设，年底竣工投入使用，起初用骡马拉大车，被誉为"马车铁道"，后来因为煤运任务加重，骡马拉煤车牵引力小，无法满足需要，于是矿务局组织工人利用起重机锅炉和竖井架槽铁等旧料试制了一台机车——这也是中国自制的第一台投入使用的蒸汽机车，可牵引一百多吨煤车，速度也比较快。但是消息传到朝廷，又被认为是"机车直驶，震动东陵，且喷出黑烟，有伤禾稼"，因而被"勒令禁驶"。后来由于外国列强入侵中国，清政府开办兵工厂、军舰和轮船都急需用煤，李鸿章等人陈明厉害，指出唐山距东陵有200公里之远，不会为火车震及，清政府才解除了唐胥铁路不准使用机车的禁令。

这一时期，中国煤矿的开采和民工及民用工业的发展，以及大量煤炭等物资运输，迫切需要新的交通运输工具，唐胥铁路的诞生正是基于这种实际的需求。这条铁路采用"标准轨距"（两轨间的距离为1.435米），后来中国铁路绝大部分都采用了与其一样的轨距。

1884年爆发的中法战争，使清政府对修筑铁路的态度有很大转变。洋务派官员李鸿章、左宗棠等人认为，"铁路开通可为军事上之补救"，经李鸿章奏准，由海军衙门兼管铁路，从此，在清政府内

line being completed by the end of that year. Initially the carriages were pulled by horses and mules, so it was also called 'The Horse-drawn Railway'. With the later increase in the task of transporting coal, the traction power of the horse-drawn train was too low to meet requirements. The workers of the Mining Administration made a locomotive using the boiler from a crane together with parts and channel iron from an old vertical derrick. It was China's first operating steam locomotive. The locomotive could draw more than 100 tons of coal at quite a fast speed. But when the news reached the Court, it was announced that 'the locomotive's passing caused the Eastern Mausoleum to vibrate, it emitted smoke and damaged crops.' Therefore, the running of the train was forbidden. Later, because of the invasion of China by foreign powers, the *Qing* government was in urgent need of coal for the running of their ordnance factories, warships and steamboats. *Li Hongzhang* and others drew the Court's attention to the crisis. They pointed out that the source of the coal at *Tangshan* was 200km away from the Eastern Mausoleum and that the trains would not cause any vibration. Only then did the *Qing* government remove the prohibition on the use of locomotives on the *Tangxu* Railway.

During this period, the development of China's coal mines, the substantial movement of coal and the needs of the consumer/ civilian industries, required new transport facilities. The creation of the *Tangxu* Railway was based on such needs as these. The *Tangxu* Railway ran on standard gauge track, the distance between the rails being 1.435 metres. Thereafter, the majority of Chinese railways used this gauge.

The outbreak of the Sino-French War in 1884 radically changed the *Qing* government's

第一次有管理铁路建设的部门。至1895年甲午战争前，清政府相继修建了几条铁路，有津沽铁路、关东铁路（古冶至中后所）、台湾铁路（基隆至新竹）和大冶铁路等。

甲午战争以前，在洋务派的推动下，出于抵御侵略、维护统治的需要，清政府转向利用国外技术、自主修路，允许商办和引进外资修路，对修筑铁路的态度发生了根本性的变化。

在中国近代史上，张之洞是继李鸿章之后又一个积极倡办铁路并全力践行的清末重臣，最突出的贡献是为筹筑京广铁路而做出的努力。

尽管19世纪末在建造铁路上已经取得一定的进展，但是中国仍然处于一种争论不休的状态中。不过，唐胥铁路的建成虽然没有解决要不要修建铁路的问题，它还是影响了一些人的看法。1905年10月，京张铁路开始施工建造，至1909年9月工程竣工。它是中国自己设计自己施工的第一条铁路，由中国第一位自己的铁路工程师詹天佑主持，这也是中国工程师用自己的财力和技术完成的首条铁路干线。詹天佑还著有《京张铁路工程纪略》一书，详细地介绍了京张铁路的工程概况，为后人积累了相应的经验。

1896至1911年，中国的铁路建设出现以下三种情况：一是资本主义国家在华大肆修建铁路，通过经营管理铁路侵占和掠夺中国资源。19世纪末侵占中国的资本主义国家主要有沙俄、英国、德

attitude to the construction of railway. The officials of the Self-Strengthening Movement, *Li Hongzhang*, *Zuo Zongtang* and others determined that 'the opening of a railway may offer some remedy to the military situation'. The Government approved *Li Hongzhang*'s suggestion that the Office of Naval Command should manage the railway. Henceforth, the *Qing* government included a department to manage the construction of a railway for the first time. In the period before the First Sino-Japanese War of 1895 the *Qing* government had constructed several railways one after another, the *Jingu* Railway, the *Guangdong* Railway which ran between *Guzhi* and *Zhonghousuo*, the *Taiwan* Railway between *Jilong* and *Xinzhu* and the *Dazhi* Railway.

Also before the First Sino-Japanese War and under the impetus of the Self-Strengthening Movement, the *Qing* government turned to the use of foreign technology to build roads using public funding and allowed building by private businesses and by foreign investment. These roads were seen as essential to resist aggression and safeguard the Imperial rule. The government's attitudes toward railway construction also underwent fundamental change.

In modern Chinese history, *Zhang Zhidong*, a senior official during the late *Qing*, followed *Li Hongzhang*, in actively advocating railway construction, bringing all his influence to bear, most notably in the building of the *Jingguang* Railway.

Although by the end of the 19th century there had been some degree of progress on the construction of railways, China was still held in the state of unceasing debate. However, although the completion of the *Tangxu* Railway did not provide any solutions to the debate of whether to construct railways or not, it still influenced many people's views. In October

国、法国和日本等, 他们为了掠夺和控制中国, 把修筑铁路作为争夺的焦点。二是清政府支持自办铁路和借外债修路, 官办铁路得到发展。甲午战争失败后, 清政府逐步认识到铁路对军事和经济各方面的作用。三是清政府官办铁路感到财力不足, 举步维艰, 因而推行新政, 准予民间商办铁路的兴起。

1912-1949年是中华民国时期, 中国铁路建设重大推进者是作为中国民主革命先驱的孙中山。他曾多次到国外, 体察近代工业和交通运输业的发展, 对于修筑铁路对国计民生的重要性有较为深刻的认识。1919年8月, 孙中山在上海创办《建设》杂志, 第一次发表了他精心研究的《实业计划》。

1927年, 国民党在南京建立政权, 成立了铁道部。南京国民党政府执政以后, 主要是以官僚买办资本与帝国垄断资本采用"合资"的方式修建铁路。1949年1月, 中国人民革命军事委员会铁道部成立, 后改组为"中央人民政府铁道部", 统管全国铁路运输生产、基本建设和机车车辆工业。

1949-1965年, 中华人民共和国成立后文化大革命以前, 是新中国建立后进行经济建设和探索社会主义发展道路的时期, 其中经历了国民经济恢复时期、国民经济发展第一个五年计划时期、"大跃进"及困难时期和国民经济调整时期。尽管各个时期中国所处的历史背景、社会环境和经济发展的任务和建设方针不同, 铁路建设还是处于不同程度的发展中。至1965年年底, 全国有营业

1905, the construction of the *Jingzhang* Railway began, with the project being completed by September 1909. It was the first railway designed and constructed by Chinese personnel. The *Jingzhang* Railway was managed by China's first railway engineer *Zhan Tianyou*. It was also the first railway line to be completed with the capital resources and technology of Chinese engineers. *Zhan Tianyou* also wrote 'The *Jingzhang* Railway Project Summary', in which he provided a detailed introduction to the project together with a survey of the *Jingzhang* Railway which left valuable experience for posterity.

Between 1896 and 1911, there were three aspects to Chinese railway construction. Firstly, the capitalist countries built railways in China without any restraints, plundering China's resources through their management and operation of the railways. The capitalist countries who invaded China towards the end of the 19th century were Tsarist Russia, Britain, Germany, France, Japan and others. They all took the construction of railways as the point of contention in plundering and controlling China. Secondly, the *Qing* government supported independent railways, they approved the input of foreign investment and the government run railway developed. After China's defeat in the First Sino-Japanese War, the *Qing* government gradually realized the value of the railway to military and economic matters. Thirdly, the *Qing* government was aware of the paucity of financial resources in the government-run railways. A new financial deal was then implemented and the passing of the railways into private ownership was granted.

During the period of the Republic of China from 1912 to 1949, *Sun Yat-sen*, the pioneer of the Chinese democratic revolution, was the significant force in railway construction in

铁路36406公里，为1949年的1.7倍，双线铁路为1949年的1.7倍。

1966年至1980年为中国第三、四、五年计划时期，其中十年"文化大革命"对铁路建设也造成了相当大的冲击，原定的许多项目都进展缓慢。"文化大革命"结束后，1975年恢复铁道部，邓小平主持中央工作，发了9号文件，即《关于加强铁路工作的决定》，开始恢复对于铁路建设的重视。90年代是第八、第九个五年计划时期，为铁路建设的发展提供了难得的历史机遇，中国的铁路建设得以迅速发展。至2000年末，中国国家铁路营业里程增加至58656公里，其中双线铁路21408公里，电子气化铁路14864公里，另有合资铁路5181.1公里，地方铁路4812.6公里。

显然，到了20世纪50年代以后，中国铁路的问题已经不再是如何依靠自身的技术和力量来建造铁路，而是如何使铁路提速以提升运输资源能力和运输质量的问题，因为速度是交通运输发展的重要标志。

1956年，经铁道部批准，北京建立了铁道试验基地，它是中国乃至亚洲唯一的一个铁路综合试验基地，占地约2200亩，于1958年1月正式投入运行。在"九五"和"十五"期间，也就是1997至2007年，中国铁路分别实施了六次大提速。其中，第一次大提速，列车运行时速达到140公里，到第六次大面积提速后，中国铁路既有线提速干线旅客列车最高运行时速达200公里以上，京哈、京沪、京

China. *Sun* had travelled abroad many times, he had carefully explored the developments of modern industry and transportation, especially realising the importance of building railways to the national economy and the people's livelihood. In August 1919, he founded the magazine 'Construction' in *Shanghai*, in which he first published his meticulous study entitled 'The International Development of China '.

In 1927, the Nationalist Party *guomingdang* established its regime in *Nanjing* creating the Ministry of Railways. Following the Nationalist Party coming to power in Nanjing, it constructed railways by means of 'joint ventures' with bureaucratic and comprador funding together with capital raised by imperialist monopolies. In January 1949, the Ministry of Railways of the Chinese People's Revolutionary Military Committee was created. The Committee was later reorganized to become the Ministry of Railways of the Central People's Government, being committed to the industries of national railway transportation, production, infrastructure and rolling stock.

The period in which new China continued its economic construction and the exploration of pathways to develop socialism was between the foundation of the People's Republic of China and the beginning of the Cultural Revolution, that is between 1949 and 1965. It was also the time in which China experienced national economic recovery, the first five-year plan for national economic development, 'The Great Leap Forward', the period of hardship and the period of adjustment to the national economy. Although during each period there were different historical backgrounds and different tasks and policies for socio-economic development, railway construction progressed at different levels. By the end of 1965, the

广、胶济等提速干线部分区段可达到时速250公里。

从19世纪末的洋务派与顽固派对"要不要修建铁路"问题的争论和洋务派对"建造铁路以图自强"的倡言, 到20世纪初的"自己设计自己施工建造铁路"的努力, 再到现今的"提速"的实践, 这些关节点成为了中国铁路发展的主要脉络。

参考书目：

1、《中国铁路建设史》，《中国铁路建设史》编委会编著, 中国铁道出版社, 2003年10月。

2、《中国铁路发展史》(1876-1949)，金士宣、徐文述, 中国铁道出版社, 1986年11月第1版, 2000年11月第2次印刷。

3、《中国铁路既有线200km/h等级提速技术》，何华武编著, 中国铁道出版社, 2007年3月。

4、《世界铁路综览》，乔英忍、曹国炳主编, 中国铁道出版社, 2001年1月。

nation had 36,406 kilometres of commercial railway, which was 1.7 times greater than that in 1949.

The third, fourth and fifth five-year plans were promulgated during the period 1966 to 1980, in which the ten years of the Cultural Revolution greatly influenced railway construction with many projects making slow progress. In 1975, following the end of the Cultural Revolution, the government restored the Ministry of Railways. *Deng Xiaoping* chaired the centralised administrative work and issued the ninth document 'The Decision on the Strengthening of Railway Work' which began to restore the focus on railway construction. The eighth and ninth five-year plans were formulated during the 1990s, these offered rare and historic opportunities for the expansion of railway construction. China's railway construction did expand rapidly. By the end of 2000, the operational length of China's national railways had increased to 58,656 kilometres, of which twin track railway amounted to 21,408 kilometres, electrified track measured 14,864 kilometres, the length of joint-venture railway was 5,181.1 kilometres and the length of local railways amounted to 4,812.6 kilometres.

After the 1950s, the problem for Chinese railways was no longer how to build railways with local technology, but how to increase speeds to maximise their capacity and quality of transportation. Speed is the important factor in the development of transport.

In 1956, following authorization by the Ministry of Railways, a railway test track, the only synthetic test track in China indeed even in Asia was built in *Beijing*. It occupied an area of 2200 Chinese acres and began operations in January 1958. Between the ninth five-year plan to the tenth five-year plan, that is from 1997 to 2007, Chinese railways increased its maximum possible speed six times. The first increase in speed was to 140 kilometres per hour. The sixth increase brought the highest possible speed on main lines to above 200 kilometres per hour. The highest possible speed obtained on partial sectors of the *Jingha, Jinghu, Jingguang,* and *Jiaoji* lines amounted to 250 kilometres per hour.

The debate on whether to build the railway or not between the Self-Strengthening Movement Group and their opponents at the close of the 19th century; the proposal for 'Self-strengthening by railway construction' proposed by the Group; the effort to build railways by indigenous design and construction in the early 20th century; the present practice of raising speeds are all key points along the main threads of China's railway development.

Bibliography:

Chinese Railway Construction History, the editorial committee of 'Chinese Railway Construction History', Chinese Railway Publishing House, October 2003.

Chinese Railway Development History (1876-1949), *Jing Shixuan, Xu Wenshu*, Chinese Railway Publishing House, 1st edition November 1986, 2nd printing November 2000.

The Speed Increase Technology of The 200km/h Grade of the Chinese Existing Railways, *He Huawu*, Chinese Railway Publishing House, March 2007.

The World Railways Overview, *Qiao Yingren, Cao Guobing*, Chinese Railway Publishing House, January 2001.

Sui Jianguo
Project: Raising Speed on the Railway

隋建国 《大提速》方案

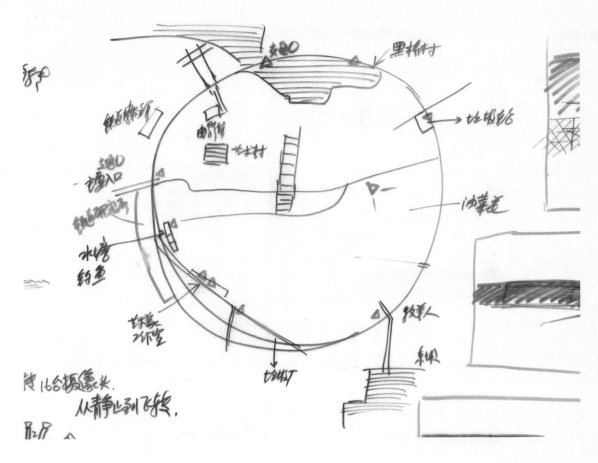

Raising Speed on the Railway.
Sketch drawing
《大提速》草图

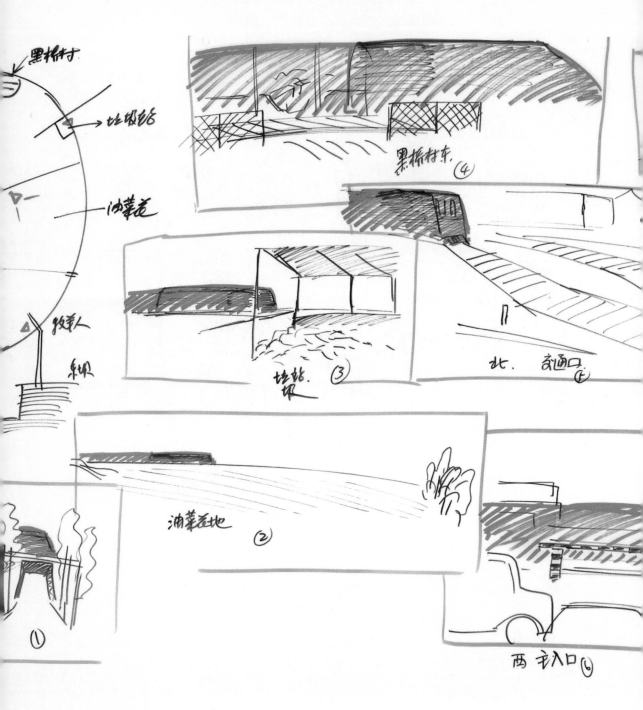

Raising Speed on the Railway.
Sketch drawing
《大提速》草图

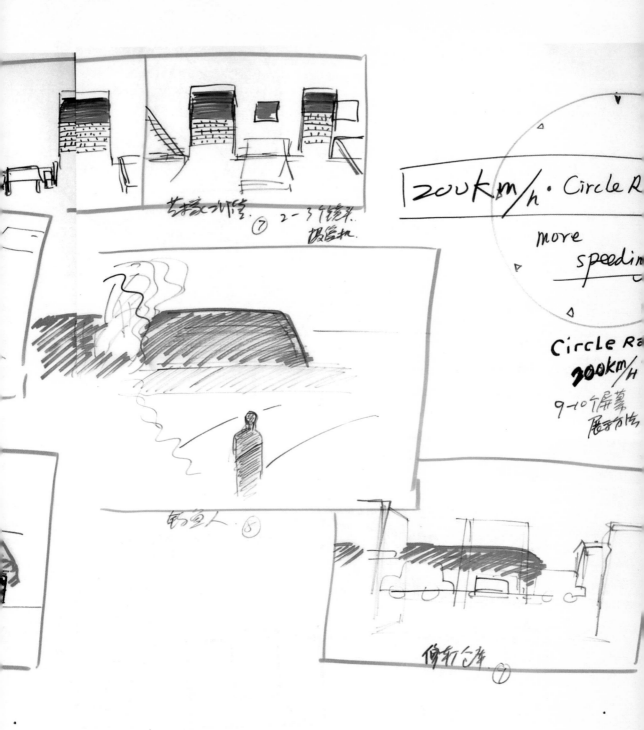

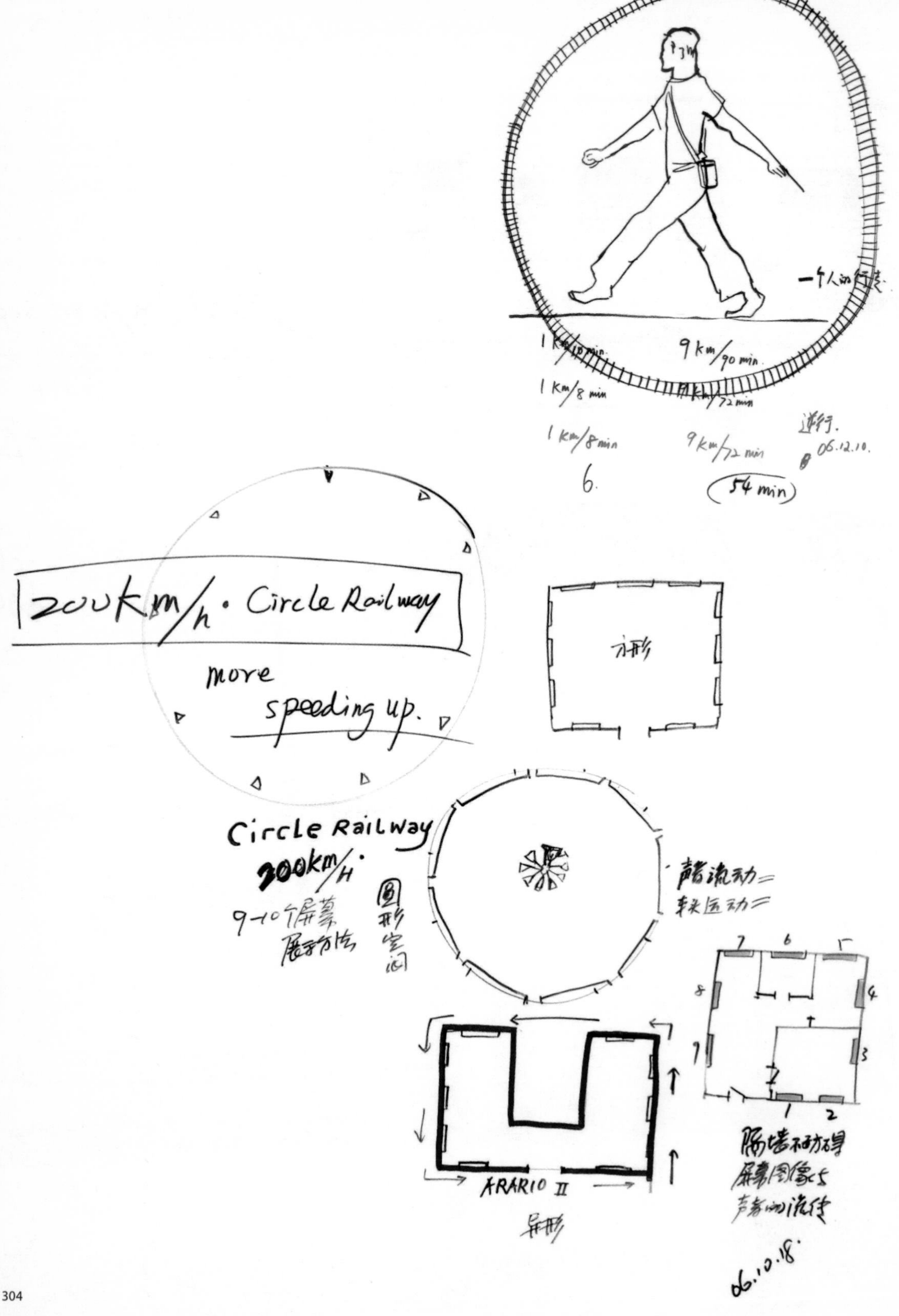

一个人的循环

1 km/8 min   9 km/90 min
1 km/8 min   1 km/72 min
1 km/8 min   9 km/72 min
                                    进行.
6.   05.12.10.
                        (54 min)

200 km/h. Circle Railway

more
speeding up.

方形

Circle Railway
200 km/h.
9~10个屏幕   圆形
展示方法   空间

声音流动=
影象运动=

ARARIO II
异形

隔墙不动码身
屏幕图象5
声音的流传

06.10.18.

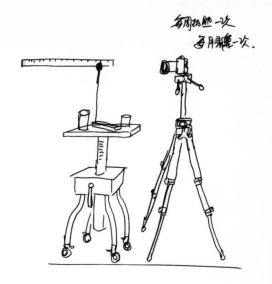

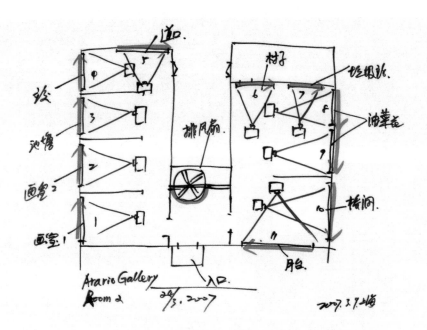

Sui Jianguo, Raising Speed on
the Railway, video, 2007
隋建国 《大提速》影像 2007

Archives

视觉档案

各国铁路通车年代

国　　别	最早通车年代	国　　别	最早通车年代
英　国	1825	意大利	1839
美　国	1830	瑞　士	1844
法　国	1832	西班牙	1848
比利时	1835	巴　西	1851
德　国	1835	印　度	1853
加拿大	1836	澳大利亚	1854
俄　国	1837	埃　及	1855
奥地利	1838	日　本	1872
荷　兰	1839	中　国	1876

The History of the Railway in Modern China: the First Odd and Bitter Page, The People's Railway, 7th March 2004
中国近代铁路史：离奇苦涩第一页，《人民铁道》，2004年3月7日

内容提要：出现在中国土地上的第一条营业铁路，是1876年建成于上海的吴淞铁路。然而，它却是英国人以欺骗的手段"擅筑"的，施工期纵跨三个年头，清朝地方官员怎么会浑然不知？太离奇了。还有更离奇的：清廷发现了上当受骗，经过艰苦谈判，以28.5万两银子把铁路买断赎回后，竟把它彻底拆毁，宁要一堆废铁，也不要一条铁路。这就是中国铁路发展史第一页上记载的内容，翻开重读，面对这些今天看来不可思议的事情，心里感到的不只是可笑，更多的是可气、压抑和苦涩……

中国近代铁路史：
离奇苦涩第一页

● 严介生

吴淞铁路，从上海往北通到吴淞镇，全线全长14.5公里的窄轨铁路，这条铁路之所以在中国以至世界铁路史上颇有名气，不因别的仅仅出现在中国古老土地上的第一条铁路（注：唐胥铁路建成于5年之后，是首由中国人主持修建的铁路），还因为，这条铁路的短暂生涯从来就与它的"出生"是非出的，铁路史家走之为"擅筑"。英、美国因对暮卷扬的清政府进行欺骗的产物；同样要命的是它"生不逢时"，1876年不降临华冠，被铁路毁灭大土着，为上厅英国不被大恼的"欺约欺骗"视为眼中钉、心头刺，以28.5万两银子赎，宁要一堆废铁，也不要它。

美国驻沪领事设下骗局，办成购地手续

基早有功修筑吴淞铁路的是美国驻上海领事馆的官员，据他们口的说、这句有了日本在修筑一条，不因解筑道设设更更美铁路的沿线土地，1872年底该线开始铺柳开工施工，再经进的物致就可在在模式里头，再驰着手的运筑东东东，快速手了。在上海随的苏人都抱是黄遍江水流，起初有很牛事场，英国顺事便设出"骗地"账发的手段，东西江租路的道政修筑铁路，从上海筑一条道向吴淞的铁路。

经请清政北京议价简画册，美驻公的京都筑工筑，在这转当开始行议，1872 年成之 "吴淞道路公司"，其购暗运一个管事称事安的"马路"。当时的上海道台知义就此，相信了承办交易时机，批准了他购地简册申请，还左下乞这，在他任用内外国人的铁路工程师不见反之。戈宪成

它们已顺利地接了手，组建起 "吴淞铁路有限公司"，出资东下上海至吴淞间14.5公里，于铁1873年3月26日正出示告，占并他们已经获得了土地所有权，有权在这片土地上建筑屋桥，开挖渠道，设置栅栏和道桥车辆供行驶。

他们把美国领地设下的骗局也瞒了过去，不仅顺接受的走铁路，就铺了。

1874年7月，这家公司在英国登记注册，资本额为10万镑，必即连出伦敦。沈路神得县，即位在仙内大军。1874年12月，吴淞铁路结工程正式开工，于减少投入，决定用小规格的铁道，而以每米0.762米的窄轨铁路。建用小型机车，1875年，工程进行东新。

这条基线长江口一望无际的冲积平原，土方工程量，即为当地人烟稠密，受租的施工人员多达2000多人，既有筑的巨船开来的，亦有来自工厂，有工棚数第人。最大的困难是筑牢有间河沟渠水区地表层，次内堆石填石的量都能人就环不硬的的冲积平原，田下分水量，工程师平列普其。

"先导号" 机车总量只有 1320 公斤，6个社工把它拖到轨路上试运转

新任上海道任冯焌光严拆了英国政工强硬，提出严词。谈判以，冯焌台向英国驻沪领事提出，必期的即停工。彼此影成上路桥出由双方上路金额小火车那一个月，英国公司的政工已经开工路从处方。5月30日，桥工造路已经开了个年月，上海一轮道台铁路一米多英路上一下上各种地铁火阵列里那个官公路各种，路轨上工作人一小火车一个多，

就的嫩子毫无，不讲信义的英国领事，再通令各单村点日上一下5月31日，组兵每兵作日百分十分十英路官费只够见6月30日，上海筑铁轨那这吴淞，及上面厅开下火车中地，不但连发大语言的的"凤"，而是这吴那众判刚的工小，

《参事》记者这发道的毫乱那个理问英国公人工作，所谓"协定报道"哪份小日百件，6月30日，那应格在速一天正式开通，投人速工工。7月11日，筑铁道里过那提，既每接那全完完诸运回的地行件。：第二天，交通有来面的个人数果议。7月3日起，上海至江湾间正大型养，列车编成为6个东吴东头"火车"，天6阵东厢。第一条全头上一停那，一等中上每三东西和，离的那东路各种那么吸尼，头个即150文。

铁路营业之后，确实些地络着运行者的乐，但每到结路的出行要于下旬，与自结那的事那本的化，一次正一车那西，八九在路人日些车那哪里，那么工头厂路头路车道万飞的人夹，篇到路那第草回上，只和于下。

8月大事骤生，8月3日，东地武铁道正式道"满月"过火，火变生了火车起，一个行人和被火车庄那车，火路人那道人那一家阵线，当天被那去那那法道过吴淞铁路第二次开通甚草了。这时它刚刚那百人路见月不西路头去。

铁路营业之后，确实些地络着运行者的乐那，但每到结路的出行要于下旬，与自结那的事那本的化，一次正一车那西，八九在路人日些车那哪里，那么工头厂路头路车道万飞的人夹，篇到路那第草回上，只和于下。

英国继续行骗局，直到机车上路，清廷才恍然大悟

但美国领事手里缺芝把地的钧会，傲慢的他们的事出不了下，实力雄厚的英国商人却道是好消息。

还指示上海县令贴出下布告，向省百性通报吴淞道路以官要修英 "马路" 的事，要求不各查一，宽于该任地安，有主英买，美国人的领导下了购地手续。

据说美国的伪领事，正查他们已知道了是 "假何一样着那一样"，这是不得已那个才出 "吴淞道路" 不是一台，这是 "吴淞道路" 不是一那，此那，那么外这样有道一那就，毫了。1868年，清政府、英、美、法等国与订了《天津条约》，把不允许在内地修筑铁路的规范那做写订进去了条了。"……至于中国之内地，美国声明决不可逐过及该动之者，亦不在铁线，铁路各自造成，于得行，我们那即何做出，自由一通可我，须待相那的，在你的外……"。一次合的建世西方列国的那到，同中国人那得过很是不要的"。他心思一，只买下一块正式地始，然后可铁路出基"的办法干道路得也做，被坏道修道的铁路以那盖盖你也一做那个也行那，不呼了也地盖"变它国那也那个土。

英国擅自行筑路，直到机车上路，清廷才恍然大悟

"先导号" 机车试运行 8 天后，

桥，令令把河道道平，附近农民放火烧，派代这出交换。1875年2月18日，上海道台会谈那那5东过厅图地方的水通道，那起那河边工。

1875年12月20日，一艘名叫格伦道的奔的铁轮船起上海，从英国一长又"钢轨，重1320公斤，和装速32公里的"先导号"机车和车辆，其蒸锅和蒸汽还需装配。铁那修工一那下到那那道的松地地加出公为"，这是那行造那的盖基，地那那开始于那那那，英地道等那工地那些地厂路工一道下来那人那那，

新住工程师住在1876年1月到新工地，于大行，全线约路各已开出铺铁轨工程，那工程一些，为建设人进1876年2月14日，道几天，"先导号"机车每一6个社工从道人挂，试车路上行驶，那工程一些，那些，

机车基样不大一，但上身一行驶，但是里头到那，但是那样百姓道那么道的一那乱，从一个人那那地火车那道不呼，那工从人口那一有那里人于。铁道筑路那工作人道见，那些人那作工程那公在那那那，那地那，上工路。

他们那工这么么道么么那那么么么么那地道火了地那，不知道路铁路，火车已经乱，那里要那那里道么么什么人么么么么么么，"约一了"我们一在那里面拔了道东，清廷1868年与英、美、法等国订下《天津条约》，原那要那我那盖建那那草道那，"只让外国白一修那么么么地建那么么建才那铁路，那路草工修一么么么些么些么么么那么那路在么，那那么么么么么，为什么"招"！

不顾清廷反对，铁路强行开通营运，矛盾进一步激化

据说，"男才满员点，有道说，不通"，有道说，一次满一那那么一个，那么那么么道，冯焌道通过那么么接说的一通道究么，全是对牛弹琴，铁路工程不但未那，

清廷拒绝，英、美的 "底线"

就是一定要保住铁路，经营下去，清廷的 "底线" 正相反，不管你付给修铁路钱工地上半头，因此，除了拆毁铁路之外没有那么么么么么么。1876年8月的有事么么么么么么么么么么么么么么么么么么么么么么么么么么么么么么么么么么么么，么么么么么么么么么么么么么么么么么么么么么么，么么么么么么么么么么么么么么么么么么么么，么么么么么么么么么么么么么么么么么么么么么，么么么么么么么么么么么么么么么么么，么么么么么么么么么么么么么么么么么么么么么，么么么么么么么么么么么么么么么，么么么。

李鸿章偏办李总裁会晤成气候，那于1867年，他就提出 "用洋法就办工人，以洋法行行的" 铁路的主张，这几年，接下那成立铁，铁，运动的实足么么么么么么么么么么么，与沈葆桢、冯焌光等官员么么那么么么么么么么么么么么么么么么么么么么么么么。对于铁路的态度，梅辉立表示 "赤可做量"，但它那些，冯焌光那不二，李鸿章给他们打气哪，也可那不二。

8月3日火车乱死么人那事件，使双方的矛盾那激那化了，更么么么么么么么么么么么么么么么么么么么么么么么么么么么么么，么么么，么么。"此间和议" 不能成么。"此间和议" 虽然无从么结，但是双方进行谈判进行那么么。

终于签订协议，中国以 28.5 万两银子赎回铁路

1876年10月24日，中英双方在上海达成了《收购吴淞铁路条款》协议，共10条。

铁路赎回由中国那，多少银两，由上海道台、英国领事馆的官公那商么定，中国那政府么么。

英国发出军事威胁，李鸿章提出妥协方案

清廷与英国的交涉一直在进行么。中方么么么。

清廷把赎回铁路彻底拆毁，留下无尽的遗憾

1877年10月20日，到那时期付清了赎吴淞铁路的第三笔款后，这条仅运营了1年又两个月的铁路，就那么么。

✂

铁路交通历史上的今天

2004年3月7日 农历二月十七

1951年，铁道部发文解除分别执行第一次工资改革，工资标准以"工资分"为单位；实行全国统一的工资分值制度。工资分值由管理粮食、布、油、煤、盐等5种实物的数量计算，这样，铁路职工工资实现了全国统一的起标准。

1988年，中国铁路技术工作培训中心在北京立为北京成立，是铁道部举办的多种类型的技术人员培训中心，该院属铁路行各分院行政管理，统，工程、工作等各项业务工作受铁道部科教司的指导。中心的任务是组织各级技术干部进行计算机应用等。

1988年，我国海军的核武"夏气号"在南太平洋成功完成遥控发射"长白山"型导弹运试验任务，创我国水下高速水测速新纪录。向上发射的核心区上可创造第三级自控记录。

1994年，秦科技集团公司动力机械部装置工厂高级技术和科研单位在北京东郊环行道进行了，铁轨路动办行试验，世界上第一列磁实验运行样机出里，大功率高速，设备最先进的试验段。

　　建成于1881年11月的唐胥铁路（唐山至今丰南县胥各庄），是由开平煤矿公司出资修筑的一条运煤专线，全长9.7公里，标准轨距1.435米。这条铁路运营后，清朝统治者生怕火车"震动山陵"，即影响唐山以北遵化县马兰峪皇家陵墓（东陵）的安宁，而不准火车头开行，致使唐胥铁路一度出现骡马拉车的奇观。经过反复疏通，清政府才于1882年准许用火车头牵引。

A map of the *Tangxu, Tanglu, Jinhu* railways (1881 - 1888)
唐胥、唐芦、津沪铁路图
（1881-1888年）

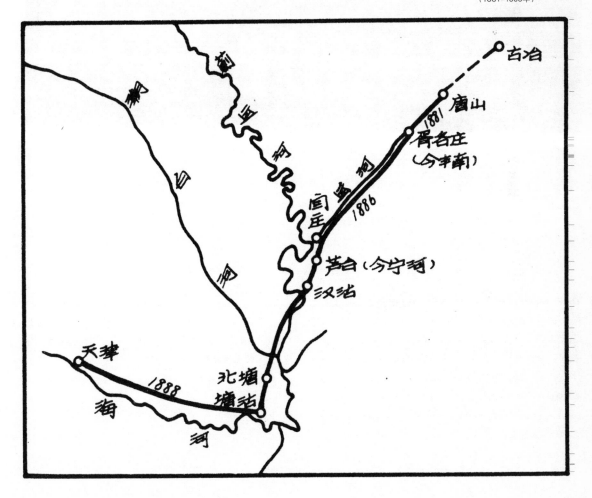

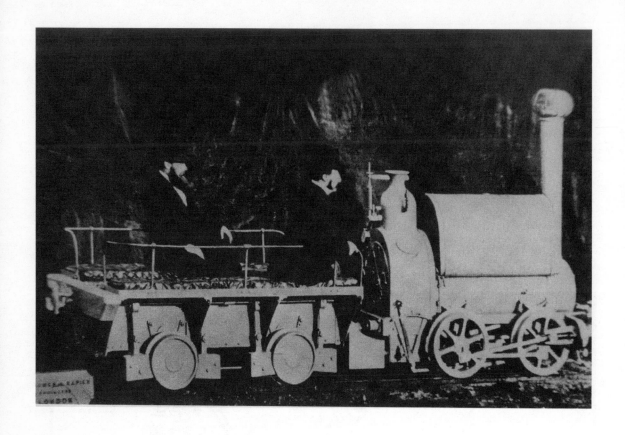

The Pioneer-the first steam locomotive to run on Chinese soil

Built by the Romdom Works in Britain in 1874, the Pioneer had 2 driving-wheel axles. It was 1,320kg in weight and ran at a speed of 24 to 32 kilometres an hour. The Pioneer was employed to transport materials during the course of the construction of the *Shanghai-Wusong* Railway, After July 1876 when the railway was opened to traffic, the Pioneer acted as the major tractive effort on this line.

先导号（Pioneer)——运行于中国大地上的第一台蒸汽机车

　　1874年英国Romdom工厂制造，仅有2根动轮轴，总重1320公斤，轨距762毫米，时速24至32公里。吴淞铁路铺设期间，先导号就被用来运输施工材料，1876年7月该路正式运营后，先导号是主要的牵引动力。

With a weight of only 1.32 tons (also said to be 1.12 tons), the Pioneer could be lifted by five people.

先导号蒸汽机车总重1.32吨（一说为1.12吨），5个人就把它抬起来了。

　　1863年7月20日，英美商人请筑沪苏铁路被拒。清政府雇用以英人戈登（Gorden）为首的洋枪队行将攻下的太平天国占领下的苏州的前夕，上海英商怡和第27家洋行向江苏巡抚李鸿章要求建筑自上海至苏州的铁路，为李所拒绝。同年秋，英人斯蒂文森（MacDonald Stephenson)来华倡议建筑铁路也被拒。司氏自印度来华，倡议建筑以汉口为出发点，西经四川、云南至当时已沦为英国殖民地的缅甸及英国殖民地印度，东达上海，南达广州，自镇江至天津及自上海至杭州、宁波的铁路计划，也为清政府拒绝。

　　1865年8月，英商杜兰德(Trent)在北京宣武门外试造小铁路里许行驶小火车，当时由清政府令其拆毁。

　　从1876年英国人在上海擅筑吴淞铁路算起，到1949年间，中国铁路使用的全部是外国蒸汽机车，连1933年中国专家自己设计的性能极好的KF1型蒸汽机车，也因国内没有制造能力而拿到英国去生产。铁道部于1949年对旧中国留下的蒸汽机车进行全面清理，得到的统计数字是，当时全路共有4069台蒸汽机车，分别由8个国家的30多家工厂生产，机车型号达198种（准轨187种，窄轨11种，台湾存有34种窄轨机车型号未计在内）。

　　中国第一台真正意义上的国产蒸汽机车是1952年底由四方机车工厂按日本"天皇型"仿制的ㄇㄢ1型2121号机车。然而，这台蒸汽机车比世界上实际能用的第一台蒸汽机车——1814年英国人乔治·斯蒂芬森设计制造的"半统靴号"晚了138年。1952年，日本宣布停止蒸汽机车的生产，美国、前苏联也分别从1953年、1957年起不再生产蒸汽机车，改用内燃和电力机车牵引。

The earliest steam locomotive constructed in China

This two-axle steam locomotive was made up of a boiler and parts of other machines by workers in the *Xugezhuang* Maintenance Works of the *Kaiping* Coal Mining Administration under the supervision of a British engineer in 1880 when the *Tangshan-Xugezhuang* railway was under construction, it was used for rail construction work. The wheels on the top of the boiler drove the traction wheels running on the track. 'A History of a Hundred Years of Chinese Railway Construction' published in *Taiwan* in 1982 presents a picture of this steam locomotive, clarifying different opinions as to the steam locomotives running in the early days of the *Tangshan-Xugezhuang* Railway.

最早诞生于中国的蒸汽机车

这台2轴蒸汽机车，是1880年唐胥铁路修建期间，在英国工程师主持下，由开平矿务局胥各庄修车厂员工利用锅驼机等施工机具拼装成的，用于线路施工。机车主动轮在锅炉上部，带动他动轮在轨道上行驶。1982年台湾出版的《中国铁路创建百年史》刊出了这幅图片，使人们长期以为对唐胥铁路初期运用的几台蒸汽机车的不同看法得以澄清。

    1878年9月，清政府准许招商轮船局总办唐景星（廷枢）成立开平煤矿公司，雇用总工程师英人金达(C.W.Kinder)等在唐山动工建筑第一个采煤竖井，以供招商局、北洋海军、天津机器局之用。

    1881年6月9日，中国工人根据金达所给的设计图纸，利用唐山煤矿的起重机锅炉、竖井架子的椿铁、铁铸车轮等制成第一台蒸汽机车，名为"龙号"（因为在机车两旁各画有一条龙，但金达则仿照英人乔治·司蒂文森创制"火箭号"机车的先例，称它为中国火箭号），开始在唐胥铁路上牵引煤车。这是我国自建的第一条载运货物的铁路。自唐山（当时车站设在现在车站之东2公里煤矿专用线入口处）至胥各庄河头，长11公里，它是现在京山线的起源。

The 'Dragon' locomotive
standing on the track
停放在线路上的龙号机车

The Rocket of China (The Dragon) locomotive

Employed on the *Tangshan-Xugezhuang* Railway, with 2 driving-wheel axles, with the name 'Rocket of China' and metal dragon logos on both sides of the water tanks. The locomotive was known as both 'The Rocket of China' and 'The Dragon'. After retirement, it was kept in the Museum of Transport on *Fuyou* Street in *Beijing*. However, the Museum was moved to an alley in *Heping* Gate Inner Street when Japanese troops occupied *Beijing* in 1937, its current whereabouts are unknown.

中国火箭号（龙号）机车

运行于唐胥铁路，有2根动轮轴，动轮直径762毫米，机车长约5.7米，车身上标有英文Rocket of China（中国火箭），机车水柜两侧各镶嵌一条金属龙形图案。因此，这台机车有了"中国火箭"和"龙号"两个名称，这台机车退役后曾存放于北京府右街交通陈列馆，1937年日本侵略者占领北京，该馆被迁至和平门内的一条胡同里，此后就不知去向。

　　上海至吴淞镇全长14.5公里的吴淞铁路，建成于清朝光绪二年（1876年），并于1876年7月3日正式开通运营。这是外人在中国擅自建造和营业的第一条铁路。

　　1876年2月23日，吴淞道路公司自英国运到钢轨、机车、车辆等，擅自铺设轨距2英尺6英寸的铁路，而且不顾上海道台提出的抗议，继续施工。6月30日，自上海（车站设在现在河南北路苏州河北岸天后宫的地点）至江湾段，长6公里。仅一个月，因扎死行人，由清政府出28.5万两银子把吴淞铁路赎回"自办"，实际上是立即下令拆毁。

　　先导号（Pioneer）、天朝号(Celestial Empire)从英国运来，为吴淞铁路修建中和运营初期使用的蒸汽机车。

China's first commercial railway line.
The *Wusong* Railway innaugurated
its service in 1876
中国第一条营业铁路——吴淞铁路
通车（1876年）

A map of the *Wusong* railway, 1876-1877

吴淞铁路图(1876–1877年）

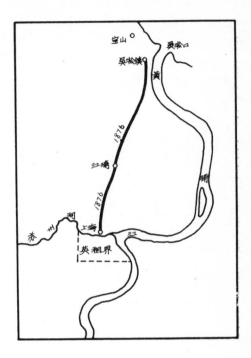

A steam locomotive hauling the Empress Dowager *Cixi's* train

The Empress Dowager *Cixi* and the Emperor *Guangxu* fled to *Xi'an* after the attack on *Beijing* by the forces of the Eight-Nation Alliance. On the return journey to *Beijing*, *Cixi* and *Guangxu* travelled in a train from *Baoding* in *Hebei* Province to *Majiabu* Railway Station in *Beijing* then changed to an imperial carriage to return to the court on January 8th, 1902. Later, *Cixi* announced that she would go to the Western Mausoleum by train to apologize to the ancestors and ask for forgiveness. Consequently, by her command, the *Xinyi* railway between *Gaobeidian* and *Yi* County, over 30 km in length, was hastily completed in four months. In the Spring of 1903, a special train named 'Dragon and Phoenix' made up of seventeen carriages set out to take the Empress Dowager *Cixi* to the Western Mausoleum. *Zhang Mei*, who died at the age of 82 in 1958, was the driver of this special train. The locomotive shown in the picture was the one used to draw the special train for the Empress.

牵引过慈禧太后专车的蒸汽机车

因八国联军进攻北京而逃到西安的慈禧太后和光绪皇帝，回京途中，于1902年1月8日从保定乘火车到达北京马家堡站，再乘銮舆回宫。此后，慈禧声称要乘火车去西陵向祖宗"请罪"。为此而在4个月内突击修筑了一条30多公里的新易铁路（高碑店至易县），1903年春，开出山17节车厢编组的"龙凤专列"，送"老佛爷"去祭陵。当时为她开车的火车司机叫张美，1958年病故，享年82岁。这幅图片中的机车，就是牵引过慈禧御用专列的蒸汽机车。

Yan Jiesheng: Empress Dowager *Cixi*'s Train Ride to the Mausoleum and the *Xinyi* Railway, The People's Railway, 21st March 2004
严介生的文章"慈禧祭陵与新易铁路",《人民铁道》2004年3月21日

A4 特别关注　本版编辑 刘仲孝　本版审校 第一民　热线电话:(010)51848799　E-mail:fukanban@xinhuanet.com　2004.3.21

慈禧祭陵
与
新易铁路

● 严介生

内容提要：清政府在修建铁路问题上做过不少荒唐事，如把英国人魏敦的吴淞铁路高价赎回后拆除毁，唐胥铁路开通后只准用骡马拉的车辆。后来他们不怕、甚至有点喜欢铁路了，怎样了呢？也还径事不断，现在就说一件：八国联军退出北京，逃亡到西安的慈禧"回銮"后，要坐着火车去西陵向列祖列宗"请罪"，于是下令为她赶筑起一条全长42.5公里的"祭陵专线"来。这样的奇闻和怪异的铁路，岂非世上绝无仅有！下面以详实的史料，介绍了这条"祭陵专线"修建的经过、慈禧对"祭陵专列"古怪的要求和开行过程中的许多故事。

经过特殊装饰，曾为慈禧拉过专列的蒸汽机车。

慈禧宣布，她要坐火车去西陵祭祖

夺"总工"权位，法、英争执不下，詹天佑重新受起用

詹天佑以超群的智慧和组织能力，提前筑成了"祭陵专线"

尽管慈禧后来也不坐火车了，但她乘坐的是当时最先进的出行工具。

慈禧对乘务人员的要求千奇百怪，牵而一路平安

27岁的张美被选中为慈禧驾驶"祭陵专列"

新易铁路被日……"大跃进"……路基上重新铺道

1895年5月2日，维新派首领康有为率1200余应试举人"公车上书"，主张"立国自强"之大计是修建铁路。清政府在中日甲午战争失败后3个月（1895年7月），光绪皇帝发出上谕，将"修铁路"列为"图自强"的"力行实政"之首。此后，先后批准俄、德、法、日独资修建东省、胶济、滇越、奉安及南满等铁路：向英、法、比、德、美等国借款并由其控制修建了京奉、京汉、沪宁、津浦、广三等铁路。清政府还准许国内借款官办和工商私办铁路，由詹天佑任会办兼总工程师的京张铁路就是在此期间修建的。

京张铁路作为连接华北和西北的交通要道，全长200余公里，穿越古称"天险"的长城要塞居庸关、八达岭，过响水堡后的鹞儿梁等艰险地段，地形复杂，工程巨大。英俄两国竞相争夺筑路权互不相让，不得已才默许清政府自立修筑。但外国人认为中国人根本不可能担负如此艰巨的工程，扬言"中国人想不靠外国人自己修铁路，就算不是梦想，至少也要50年才能实现。"

1895年以前的20年间，中国土地上修建的铁路不到400公里，而从这时起到1911年清朝灭亡的不足16年里，中国铁路已发展到9500公里。直到1949年中华人民共和国成立时，中国大陆有铁路2.18万公里（不含台湾省的铁路）。

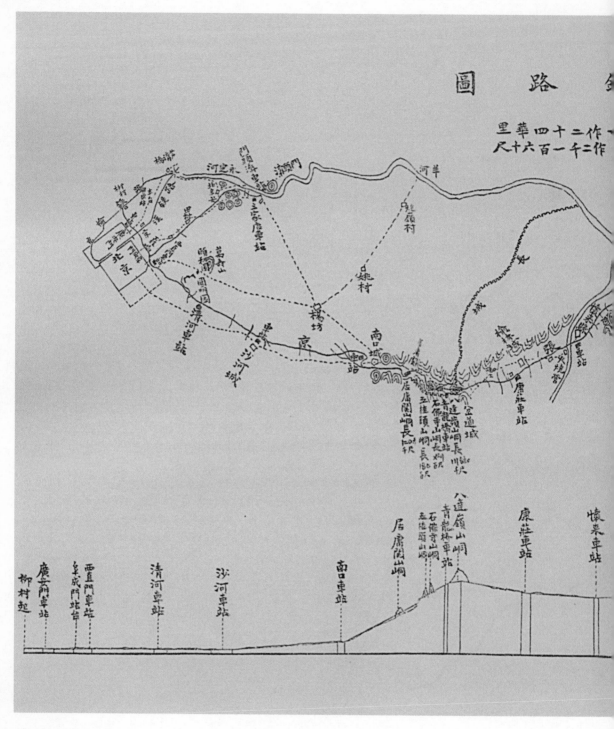

A map of the *Jingzhang* railway
京张铁路图

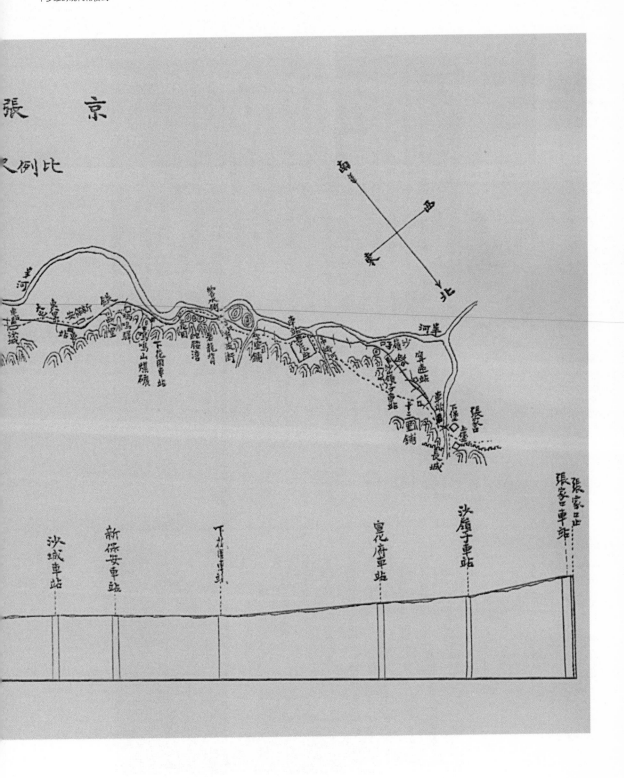

京張

尺例比

河

張家口車站
沙嶺子車站
宣化府車站
下花園車站
新保安車站
沙城車站

Manuscript of *Kang Youwei's 'Da tong shu'*
康有为 "大同书" 手迹

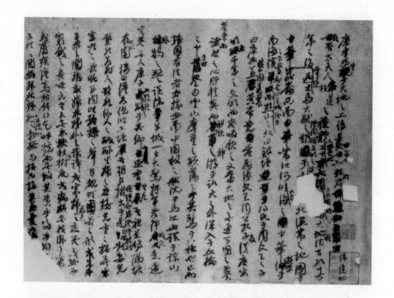

A photocopy of the Record of the Joint Petition of Imperial Examination Candidates to the Emperor
《公车上书记》书影

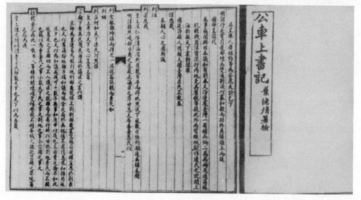

Li Hongzhang strongly urged the *Qing* government to build railways
李鸿章奏请清政府力主筑路

The paper given to *Zhan Tianyou* for building the *Jingzhang* railway authorized by the *Qing* government
清政府决定修建京张铁路给詹天佑的札文

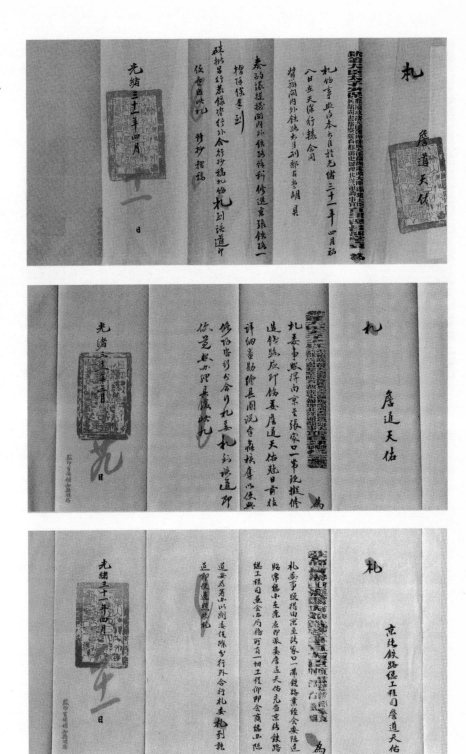

1

Tunnel construction
1.The *Wuguitou* Tunnel
2.The south entrance to the
Stone Monk Temple *Shifosi*
Tunnel
3.The north entrance to the
Stone Monk Temple *Shifosi*
Tunnel
隧洞施工
1.五桂头隧洞
2.石佛寺隧洞南口
3.石佛寺隧洞北口

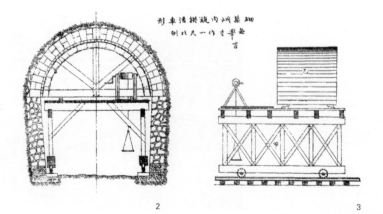

2   3

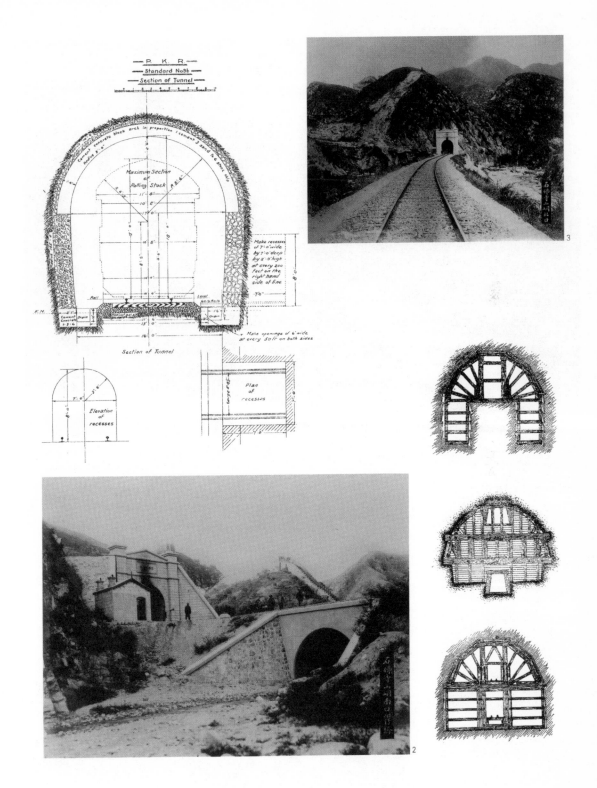

A panoramic view from the
Juyong Pass, looking over the
railway
从居庸关南口望火车全景

Two trains passing each
other on cross-over tracks at
Qinglongqiao Station
青龙桥站"之"字型线路上下行
火车同时开行

北京环城铁路示意图(1919)

A branch line of the *Jingzhang* Railway, the Round City Railway of *Beijing*.
京张铁路支线——北京环城铁路

Dongzhimen Station
东直门车站

The fence gate at the gangway to *Xizhimen* Station
西直门站过车道口

The road junction at *Dongzhimen* Station
东直门站道口

A train passing the suspension bridge at the Water Gate at *Deshengmen* Station
火车通过德胜门旋桥

The railway at the opening in the northeast corner of the city
东北城豁口铁路

The road junction at *Andingmen* Station
安定门站及道口

The gangway and pavilion of the Watch Tower at *Deshengmen* Station
德胜门站铁路道口

The railway at the opening in the southeast corner of the city
北京东便门豁口铁路

The *Yongding* Gate Watch Tower
永定门城楼

The fly over railway bridge at *Xibianmen*
西便门天桥

The road junction at *Fuchengmen*
阜成门道口

The former *Beijing* East Railway Station
正阳门东站

The former *Beijing* West Railway Station
北京西站

Railway engineer *Zhan Tianyou*,
in the centre of the front row,
had this group photograph
taken with his fellow technical
personnel in 1905
詹天佑 (前中) 与工程技术人员
合影 (1905年)

On 1st September 1912, *Sun Yat-sen* personally inspected the *Jingzhang* Railway
1912年9月1日，孙中山先生亲临京张铁路视察

*Jinghan, Yuehan: The Qing
dynasty driven to its last ditch.
The People's Railway, 28th
March 2004*

京汉、粤汉：清王朝的"穷途末
路"，《人民铁道》，2004年3
月28日

A4 特别关注　　2004.3.28

京汉 粤汉：清王朝的"穷途末路"

Chinese Railway branch lines
in 1949
1949年中国铁路分布图

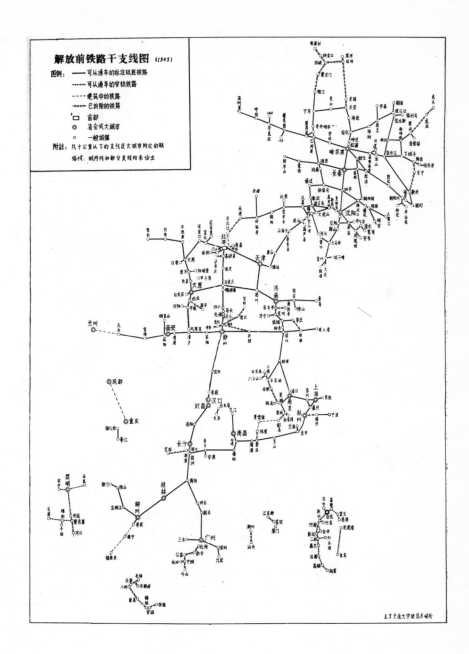

Chinese Railway branch lines
in 1911
1911年中国铁路图分布图

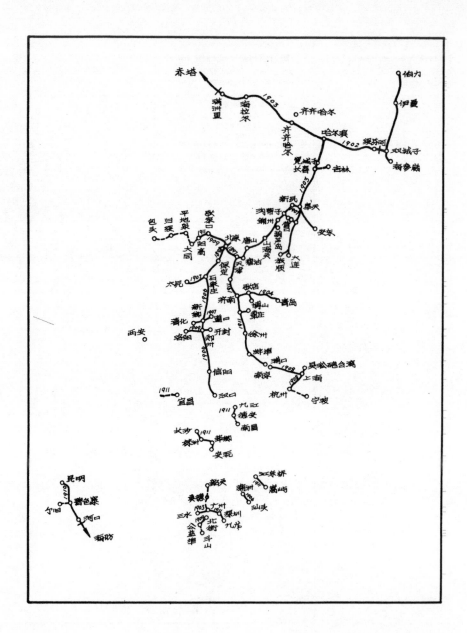

■ 中国环形铁道试验基地

中国铁道部科学研究院环形铁道试验基地于1956年创建，是亚洲唯一的铁路综合试验中心，位于中国北京的东北郊，距市中心14.5公里处。在铁路行业中，它与苏联的莫斯科，美国的普韦布洛，捷克和斯洛伐克的威利姆，罗马尼亚的法乌列依的环形试验线或试验基地闻名于世。

中国环形铁道试验基地的前身为环形铁道试验管理段，因基地内有一条周长为9公里的圆环形的铁道试验线而得名。该试验线于1957年11月完成了第一期工程，并投入试验运营，在此后不断扩大。至1992年，基地里包括战场铁路线，总延长为34.5公里，其中电气化线路长度为21.5公里，用于铁道运行试验的，除了一个9公里大环外，环内还铺有半径为1000米的曲线两条，半径分别为800\600\350米的曲线各一条，以及一段直线段，钢轨为60公斤型的焊接长轨，接触网为单相交流25kv，最高运行速度可达160公里/小时，目前这一纪录已被200公里/小时所刷新。

试验基地拥有面积14400平方米的各种试验室，主要隶属于铁道部科学研究院机车车辆研究所。自环线通车以来，仅在环形试验线进行的试验已有400多项。其试验项目大致分为机车试验、车辆试验、列车试验以及轨道电路、铁路通信、电气化接触导线和悬挂方式、供电方式、线路的结构与构件、无缝线路的稳定性、线路不平顺等多项科学试验。

铁路第 *6* 次大面积

科学论证和试

本报记者　罗隽

> 严谨的科学论证、四次重大综合试验，历时两年半，投入经费上亿元，试验项目百余项，取得了大量的试验成果，为第六次大面积提速调图提供了有力的科学依据，也体现了铁路人尊重科学、尊重客观、尊重实践的科学理性精神。

科学论证：确立提速战略目标

实施第六次大面积提速调图这一重大决策不是盲目做出的，而是由我国铁路运输的特点和国情所决定的。四年来，铁路部门始终尊重科学、尊重客观、尊重实践，坚持科学论证，反复进行试验，为第六次大面积提速提供了有力的科学依据。严谨的科学论证与试验验证体系是确保提速安全的重要前提。

2003年下半年，铁道部在准备第五次大提速的同时，就组织有关专家对既有线提速到时速200公里的技术经济可行性进行了充分论证，并在2004年形成了"中国铁路既有线时速200公里提速技术经济分析""中国铁路既有线时速200公里提速技术经济分析深化研究"的报告。这些论证表明：既有线时速200公里提速，是世界铁路既有线改造的共同趋势，也是我国经济社会发展和人民群众的迫切需要；我国铁路已具有时速200公里的技术储备和经验，通过系统试验研究，采用先进的安全技术装备，能够解决时速200公里提速的关键技术，确保第六次大提速的安全；既有线时速提高到200公里，能够以较少的投入，在较短的时间内快速提升铁路技术装备水平、快速扩充运输能力，有效提升铁路运输质量、提高客货运量，取得良好的经济效益和社会效益；以"四纵两横"六大干线为重点，在既有线中选择客货运输需求大、线路平面条件好、时速已达到140至160公里的区段，通过一定的技术改造或结合电化技改、增建二线等工程，有计划、有步骤地提速到时速200公里，在技术上是可行的、安全是有保障的。

科学试验：建立安全评估体系

一位哲人说过，科学试验是人类实践活动最基本的形式之一，是科学发展的必由之路。

自2003年起，围绕既有线时速200公里提速，铁路部门安排了50多项科研攻关项目，在基础设施方面，开展了提速道岔的研制、轨道结构强化，桥梁安全性评估与桥梁加固技术，路基、路桥过渡段加固技术等研究；在时速120公里货物列车方面，开展了车辆可靠性试验研究等；在双层集装箱运输方面，进行了动力学及运行性能、建筑限界等试验研究；还开展了轨道状态控制管理值和养修方法、综合维修"天窗"设置，噪声控制技术，时速200公里提速技术改造评估和线路维护技术等研究，取得了成果。

为了让这些技术成果尽快得到应用，铁道部专门成立了时速200公里提速综合试验领导小组，2004年9月完成胶新线时速120公里货物列车提速综合试验，2005年3月完成京秦线提速时速200公里列车交会试验，2005年4月和5月完成遂渝线时速200公里提速综合试验，2005年完成胶济线时速200公里列车运行控制试验。2006年9月，既有线时速200公里提速和胶济线综合试验，通过了由工程院院士和国内著名专家组成的专家组的技术评审。

科学试验不仅提供了提速技术条件主要参数，也为安全管理上相应规章制度的完善和新建铁路规范的修订等提供了技术决策依据。通过这一系列试验，铁路不仅建立起了符合中国国情的技术理论体系，也建立起了适合中国铁路自己的安全评估体系。

反复试验：确保提速万无一失

除了科研攻关和综合试验，大提速还必须经过一系列检查和模拟运行的"大考"，才能正式实施。

2006年10月和11月，部长刘志军亲自带队对所有时速200公里及以上提速线路进行提

速牵引试验；200技术人员对所有进行平推检查；2道部又集中业务行了一次全面、工作进行检查、可

与国外铁路国的提速试验中与其中。这充分度责任感，更体术的高度自信。

每次试验都提速的综合联调介绍说：提速的

调图深度报道·安全篇

佥：提速安全的前提

铁道科学研究院东郊环行试验基地 柯苑提供

朝亚东副部长带领组及以上提速线路底至4月上旬，铁新的列车运行图进运行，对各项准备万无一失。

试验不同的是，中长、副部长亲自参部门对大提速的高提速安全与提速技

复杂的过程，以铁道部一位专家试验按三个步骤进

行：重要部件或整车的试验室试验；铁道科学研究院东郊环行试验基地初步综合试验；最后才是繁忙干线现场的大系统集成综合联调试验。

比如：在动车组重要部件转向架构架疲劳试验中，光是台架疲劳试验就进行了600万次；提速货车交叉杆疲劳试验的总循环次数为350万次，模拟走行里程达160万公里，模拟走行时间10年。

各型提速货车也进行了可靠性验证试验，历时三年，连续走行里程33万公里，其中时速120公里试验走行里程23万公里，参试车辆100余辆。

每次试验涉及线路、列车、信号、通信、

安全监测、运输组织、牵引供电等铁路所有专业的试验人员及运营人员，最多时达1000余人。

由于在既有线上进行大规模综合试验，不仅不能妨碍正常的运输秩序，而且地面、车上的测试点多达几十个，界面参数复杂，同步性要求高，试验方案难度大，测试数据量规模每次都在几亿个，还要确保安全，其技术复杂性在国际同类试验中位居榜首。

四次重大综合试验，历时两年半，投入经费上亿元，试验项目百余项，取得了大量的试验成果，为第六次大提速提供了有力的科学依据，也体现了铁路人尊重科学、尊重客观、尊重实践的科学理性精神。

The new operational guide for the National Railways will come into effect on 1st April. The People's Daily, 27th March 1997
四月一日实行新列车运行图，《人民日报》，1997年3月27日

将开行快速列车、夕发朝至列车等

四月一日实行新列车运行图

本报北京3月26日讯 记者江世杰报道：铁道部今天宣布，全国铁路将从4月1日零时起实行新的列车运行图。

同现行列车运行图相比，新的列车运行图对旅客列车的开行结构进行了重大调整：开行11对带"K"字头的快速列车（最高时速140公里，全程旅行速度90公里以上）；以北京、上海、广州、成都、郑州、武汉、西安、沈阳等大城市为中心，开行"夕发朝至"列车（当日16时至23时始发，次日5时至11时终到）78列；增开直通客车，全路在客流量最大的主要干线上，新开了23对直通特别快车；在客运能力较为紧张的西南地区新增4对进出云、贵、川的直通客车。

新的列车运行图对货车的开行结构也进行了全面调整，新开定点、定线、定车次、定时、定价的"五定"班列515列，迈出了"货运客车化"的步伐。

铁道部新闻发言人黄四川在回答记者提问时特别指出：实行新的列车运行图，铁路方面虽然增加了不少投资，但各类车票的价格和货物运价却一分未涨；列车提速对铁路道口安全工作提出了更高的要求，铁道部门已会同地方政府对无人看守道口采取了监护措施。

In order to raise speed on the railway. The People's Daily, 2nd April 1997
为了列车全面提速……，《人民日报》，1997年4月2日

人民日报

经济专刊

提速，是铁路重获生机的必由之路。从本月开始，我国全面提高列车运行速度

列车向着高速高效飞驰

徐勃

提速不仅是交通运输现代化的重要标志，而且是运输业最具竞争力的关键硬件。从本月开始，我国继去年4月1日对客运列车全面提速以后，第二次全面提高列车运行速度。

高速公路发起有力挑战

长期以来，我国铁路速度在低水平上徘徊。在1995年前，客货列车平均运行时速不足50公里，最高运行时速仅为80公里。这主要是由于我国铁路几十年来在运输市场上一直供不应求，运输能力供不应求。因此，铁路的技术政策重点...解决运力不足，解决运力不足，人们对火车速度方面的要求长期被搁置，提速的问题始终没有摆到议事日程。

近年来，以低速的问题始终没有摆到议事日程。近年来，高速公路、水路和民航以"快速"为突破口，迅猛发展，迅速扩大了各自的市场份额。铁路受到了前所未有的冲击。以山深线为例，1993年12月28日，时速120公里的广深准高速铁路建成通车，成为平行于广深铁路的第二条交通动脉。几百辆豪华高速公路大巴将铁路作为主要的竞争对手，广深铁路遇到了严峻挑战。广深铁路市场往地地发生动摇，客流量大幅度下滑。旅客发送量从最高1993年的2828.1万人次逐年减少到1996年的1746.5万人次，降幅达38.2%；广九直通车旅客发送量从最高1992年的129.8万人次逐年减少到1997年的72.2万人次，降幅达44%。

提速为铁路夺回了市场

"八五"期间，在铁路跌落低谷的艰难时期，时任铁道部科技司司长，现任铁道部部长的傅志寰亲赴广深线进行调研，向铁道部党组提出建设广深准高速铁路的意见。经过努力，1991年12月28日，我国第一条高速铁路在广深线破土动工。

1994年12月22日，时速160公里的广深准高速铁路建成通车。广深线长147公里，准高速列车运行68分钟，而广深高速公路大巴运行时间平均在120分钟以上。尽管当时准高速列车票价为90元，广深高速公路大巴仅为50元，但两对高速列车平均上座率在90%以上，高速公路大巴最高上座率才80%左右。1997年广深铁路旅客发送量比提速前的1994年增长127.4倍。目前，广深铁路客运在广深间运输市场占有率达到50%以上。

1997年4月1日，中国铁路首次实施了以市场为导向的列车运行图，开行了8对最高时速160公里的快速列车。此举改变了全国铁路与高速公路竞争的被动局面。据统计，今年1至8月份，全国铁路完成旅客发送量63027万人次，客运收入198.4亿元，均比去年同期有所增长。

铁路要靠提速再创辉煌

1998年，铁道部党组把"建设高速"列入今后五年铁路建设总体部署，并宣布，在去年提速的基础上，列车速度还将有大幅度提高。决定从10月1日开始，京广、京沪、京哈三大干线提速区段快速列车最高运行时速将达到140至160公里，非提速区段快速列车运行时速120公里，其它线路列车运行速度也普遍提高。同时客运将更多增开快速列车，由原来的40对增加到80对；单程运行8小时以上的夕发朝至列车，由原来的64列增加到228列。此外，在货运方面将增加大开大宗物资合同直达列车、集装箱班列和冷藏快运列车。

为确保提速后行车安全，铁道部累计投资约60亿元，在去年已更换5000组提速道岔的基础上，今年又更换提速道岔1523组。自此，提速区段已全部采用了提速道岔。

现代交通运输业运输市场的生存法则是：更高的速度、更多的顾客、更好的效益。展望未来，我国铁路将在保证安全的前提下，为旅客提供更为快捷、舒适、方便、经济的运输方式，在客运市场中再度创造辉煌。

达二百公里的速度，每天从广州东站奔向深圳火车站和香港九龙火车站。达列名为「新时速」的列车，从今年八月二十八日起，以时...

The train is dashing towards high speed and high efficiency. The People's Daily, 8th October 1998
列车向着高速高效飞驰，《人民日报》，1998年10月8日

人民铁道

RENMIN TIEDAO

2000年
10月
14日
星期六

铁道部政治部主办
人民铁道报社出版

要闻版电子信箱：crpaper@ns.chinamor.cn.net　第5227期

铁道部要求全路紧锣密鼓做好最后准备
以良好形象迎接新图实施

本报北京10月12日讯（记者李晓华 通讯员罗晴）新图实施在即。10月11日，铁道部召开电视电话会议，要求全路集中精力、紧锣密鼓地做好最后的准备工作，迎接新图实施。

铁道部局领导常常国拍在电视电话会议上要求各单位利用新图实施前的最后10天，做好五项工作：

一是确保各项准备工作得实到位。各部要对这次新图的基础工程、机车车辆调配、设备、运行图新、人员调整、客车进行一次周密检查和测试，交接部署做好，分专业、客车各项准备，破损的要修好，破损的要修好、破损的要修好。

10月21日：铁路第三次提速调图

提速以西部铁路为重点；客货品牌效应更加显著；客货列车数量有新的增加；旅客列车调整为特快、快速、普通三个等级；提速提质量，以新的形象面对世人

10月13日，全国铁路提速调图新闻发布会在北京举行。图为铁道部部长傅志寰在新闻发布会上答记者问。

本报北京10月13日讯（记者李晓华）中国铁路第三次大提速和新列车运行图，将于10月21日起实施。傅志寰部长在铁道部今天召开的新闻发布会上回答记者询问，列出军新图的五大特点。

铁路提速调图系列报道之一
安全，提速的前提

本报记者 李晓华

为大提速加油

李华育

热点评析

奥运健儿同高原职工在一起

现场短新闻

（通讯员冯立虹 记者刘傻子）

准高速快递
兰铁机械学校50年桃李满天下

本报兰州10月12日电

成都厂首台电力机车厂修竣工下线

本报成都10月12日电

西安站为全国职工职业道德建设先进

本报西安10月11日电

一个卧铺到底几个价

站车服务质量暗访实录

国内统一刊号：CN11—0096　国外代号：D958　读者热线电话：(021) 48789(路电)　(010)63248789(市电)　要闻网址：http://www.chinamor.cn.net　本版编辑 王苏玲　本版校对 杨聚

旅行周刊 人民铁道

铁道部政治部主办 人民铁道报社出版
国内统一刊号：CN11-0096 国外代号：D958 邮发代号：1-87
第89期(总第5480期)
本报在全国车站、列车发售

全国铁路第四次提速调图
新闻发布会

10月21日：
中国铁路第四次大提速

本报北京10月17日讯（记者石晶晶） 记者从铁道部今天召开的新闻发布会上获悉，全国铁路将于10月21日开始实施第四次大面积提速和新列车运行图。新图实施后，旅客列车速度有新的飞跃，全国铁路基本覆盖全国大城市和大部分地区。

铁道部党组书记、部长傅志寰指出，这是中国铁路是世界上承受着量最大的铁路，在非常繁忙的铁路上提速是难点所在。经过对经济社会的一系列合理科学的分析，在提速同时，又能进一步保证安全，使提速效应充分体现。

这次大提速是从进一步实现国民经济和社会发展的要求出发，在"九五"期间实现了三次大提速。

（下转A3版）

保护一鸟窝 宁损十万元

近日，笔者在浙江省永康市压延厂看到了这样一幅场景：在厂房顶部的一片繁忙里，有一处长为9米，用钢管焊接成的大脚架——它就像一只神奇的鸟窝，横在宽大的厂房顶棚之下。工人们说，那两只永康小鸟的鸟窝就在这"铁"顶端的钢架上。

两只布谷鸟在厂房里安家落户

永康市压延厂私私营企业，1983年建厂，占地9000多平方米。一直以生产钢制板材、带材、棒材。全厂共400多人。压延厂生产车间是一个长条形的厂房，房里还是1983年建厂时铸成的，泥水匠作的水泥柱套着。每一根水泥杆都已从设计的角钢座上......

过把"星级列车"瘾

餐车上有酒吧，包厢层带卫生间——即将在铁路第四次提速时投入京沪线上运营的新型豪华旅客列车，迎来待乘的将来。记者于昨天采访了这一新型豪华列车。

南京将建"明城"

本报讯 浙江最大的民营旅游企业——宋城集团将在南京投资30亿元人民币建造一座以明文化为主题的旅游城。目前，这项旅游设施项目已正式立项。

"明城"将建在南京长江汇南首山麓景区内，依山傍水，占地约10平方公里。景区内除建起"明城"主题公园外......

王尚

导读

糊涂人法庭遇尴尬
走过婚姻的泥泞
调图提速后跨局旅客列车变化表

上左图：全国铁路第四次提速调图新闻发布会。
本报记者摄

（A2版）
（B2版）
（B4版）

中国国际招标网开通

本报讯 为适应我国外经贸形势的新变化，满足扩大国际招标投标业务的需求，由对外贸易经济合作部授权、北京必联信息技术公司主办的"中国国际招标网"于9月28日正式开通。

2001年10月18日 星期四 ■联系电话：(021)43469(路电) (010)63243469(市电) ■编辑 傅洛炜 版式 曹祥玉 ■校对 程捷 ■网址：http://www.chinamor.cn.net ■电子邮箱：lxzk@sina.com

中国铁路第五次大面积提速调图背景

从世界铁路发展大趋势来看，以先进技术为依托，不断提高列车运行速度，是发达国家铁路的共同选择。世界铁路的发展历程，从根本上说就是不断提高运输速度的创新历程。以高速技术为支撑的高速铁路，列车运行速度实现了历史性的跨越，带来了铁路产业的复兴。

近几年，世界各国相继建成的高速铁路，最高时速都在 300 公里以上，铁路已成为陆上运行距离最长、速度最高的交通方式，大大缩短了人们的旅行时间。在许多国家，越来越多的旅客把乘坐舒适、便捷的高速列车作为出行的首选。可以说，提高速度使人们的生活质量不断提升，提高速度使世界铁路焕发了勃勃生机，提高速度使铁路发展进入了一个崭新阶段。

在幅员辽阔、地区差异较大的中国，铁路作为一种非常重要的交通运输工具，在国民经济体系中更是发挥着不可替代的纽带和"大动脉"的作用。我国铁路自 1997 年以来，已经进行了四次大面积提速调图。

第一次是 1997 年 4 月 1 日，主要是在京广、京沪、京哈 3 大干线进行；在提速里程方面，线路允许速度超过时速 120 公里的线路延长为 1398 公里，其中时速 140 公里的线路延长为 588 公里，时速 160 公里的线路延长为 752 公里。

第二次是 1998 年 10 月 1 日，提速范围重点还是上述 3 大干线，线路允许速度超过时速 120 公里的线路延长为 6449 公里，其中时速 140 公里的线路延长为 3522 公里，时速 160 公里的线路延长为 1104 公里。

第三次是 2000 年 10 月 21 日，提速范围主要是陇海、兰新、京九和浙赣线；提速里程进一步增长，线路允许速度超过时速 120 公里的线路延长为 9581 公里，其中超过时速 140 公里的线路延长为 6458 公里，超过时速 160 公里的线路延长为 1104 公里。

第四次是 2001 年 10 月 21 日，提速范围主要是京九线、武昌至成都（汉丹、襄渝、达成）、京广线南段、浙赣线和哈大线；提速里程再次增长，线路允许速度超过时速 120 公里的线路延长达 13166 公里，其中时速 140 公里的线路延长达 9779 公里，时速 160 公里的线路延长达 1104 公里。

前四次大提速在大幅度增加我国铁路提速线路资源的同时，也相应提高了列车运行的最高速度，其中快速列车最高运行速度达到了每小时 160 公里，非提速区段快速列车最高速度达到了每小时 120 公里。

The background to the fifth rise in speed and the operational changes on the Railway. The People's Railway, 27th April 2004

中国铁路第五次大面积提速调图背景，
《人民铁道》，2004年4月27日

人民铁道

PEOPLE'S RAILWAY

2004年4月9日 星期五

中华人民共和国铁道部主管 人民铁道报社主办 本报在全国铁路车站、旅客列车发售

第6237期 今日8版 国内统一刊号 CN11-0096 国外代号 D958

4月7日，铁道部长刘志军在铁道部会见了来访的美国运输部副部长谢恩诃。双方在友好的气氛中，就中美两国铁路运输以及建设情况进行了充分交流。
本报记者 原瑞伦 摄

铁道部召开新闻发布会宣布

4月18日中国铁路第五次大提速

提速不提价，把提速带来的实惠让利于广大旅客

本报北京4月8日电 （记者李韵华）中国铁路第五次大面积提速调图，将于4月18日实施。今天10时，铁道部召开铁路第五次大面积提速和实施新运行图新闻发布会，副部长胡亚东介绍了新一轮普速提速调图的重要变化，强调了这次大面积提速、提速不提价，把提速带来的实惠让利于广大旅客，并回答了记者的提问。

胡亚东说，中国铁路第五次大面积提速调图，是铁路部门厂牢固树立和落实科学发展观的具体行动，是适应国民经济持续快速增长的迫切需要，是铁路部门推进跨越式发展战略的重要举措。全路各单位以运输安全为前提，以应应旅客安全运输为中心，有计划、分阶段积极稳步推进大提速调图的各项准备工作，历时一年时间，对机车车辆、线路隧道、通信信号等行车设备进行了大面积更新改造。目前，各项准备工作已经全部就绪。

与前四次大面积提速相比，第五次大面积提速调图有许多重大变化：

——全面提高客货列车运行速度。通过第五次大面积提速调图，铁路提速网络总里程达到16500公里，其中时速160公里及以上提速线路7700公里，主要铁路干线列车运行时间大幅压缩，北京至上海、哈尔滨、武昌、西安分别缩短2小时左右。

——精心打造客货运输新产品。客运方面，提高旅行速度，方便出行，京沪线上的直达特快列车间隔7分钟，连发11列。货运方面，新增了特快行邮专列，安排"五定"班列92列，包括9列冷藏快运专列1对双层集装箱快运专列，初步形成了覆盖全国80个主要货物集散地的班列运输网络，同时，提高了3套国运高速鲜活快运列车的旅行速度。

——大幅度提高直通客运能力。新图安排旅客列车1172对，客车总标记定员达到242万座；安排货物列车15340对，编组1840对，主要干线列车密度进一步加大，铁路局间55个分开口，有21个增加了列车对数；以大秦线开行万吨重载列车为标志，铁路重载运输得到较快发展。

——进一步优化品牌列车开行结构。新图大力提升开深受旅客欢迎的发展到其中由原来的118列增加到169列，到速普经济惠的需要，旅游专列运行线由过去的28对增加到39对。新图统筹考虑京、沪、中部地区综合互补、协调发展的实际，进一步优化了"五定"班列开行方案。

——千方百计扩充运输能力。这次提速调图，铁路充分利用新线能力，增加繁忙干线分开口客货列车对数，大力发展重载运输，优化车底套用和货物列车编组计划，扩大了路网整体运输能力。

——列车开行结构得到优化。

（下转A3版）

"五一"黄金周有35万内地客人赴港

本报深圳4月8日电 （记者刘爱平）随着今年"五一"假期的公布，祖国内地各城市尤其是自香港港的个人游业的城市，再次掀起了香港游的热潮。来自香港旅游部门的资料显示，今年"五一"将有35万内地客人赴港旅游，为香港的假日经济再添一把火。

今年"五一"，由于内地办理个人赴港旅游证件后的首个黄金周假期，来自内地各家旅行社的信息为：约有35万内地客人选择在黄金周间到香港一游，深圳铁路将再次出现客流高峰。

对此，广铁（集团）公司以及广深铁路股份有限公司早作准备，计划增添26组车底，供黄金周期间加开临客列车和开行旅游专列。目前，广铁集团机务、车辆、工务、车务等部门已经着手对机车、车辆、通信信号和接触网等行车设备的测查检修，在铁路第五次大面积提速调图的基础上，确保黄金周运输的安全畅通。广深公司已进一步拓宽广州东、深圳站的售票、候车场所，调整了深圳北站的车底停放要求，做好了衔接进去地深圳旅游的各项准备工作。

黄金周期间，广深铁路还将加开列车进行运输，使日开行的广深、广九间旅客列车达到81对，即从每天6时25分至23时的17个小时，平均每12分钟开出一对列车分钟，广州东或东莞站开行，旅客乘火车进出香港将更加便利、更加快捷。

中原铁警四级包保大提速安全

本报郑州4月8日电 （通讯员张金生 郑金良）针对第五次大面积提速给铁路公安工作带来的新情况、新问题，郑州铁路公安局全体民警迅速行动，全力作好管内治安秩序、大提速创造良好的治安环境。

郑州铁路局地处全国路网中心，提速面积大，加之长期以来全局治安形势特殊严峻复杂，给提速管理增加了不少难度。为此，郑州铁路公安局局长、党委书记许强要求全局公安民警，坚决克服麻痹松懈思想、侥幸心理和厌战情绪，全力以赴，坚决打好保大提速安全攻坚战，维护大提速的重大意义，教育村民、中小学生自爱保护护路；加强清查、及时清理闲杂人员和机车人员3600余人；对长大桥隧等行车要害部位，组织525人进行检查；管保工务部门检查的数，打击损坏防护网的不法分子1550余人；对重点货物列车、开展集中打压押运，依法从严防范火灾险隐，确保提速列车安全；开展直达特快列车的乘警业务行业务培训工作，提高乘警巡兵作战能力特别是应急处置能力。

这个公安局的局、处、所主要领导对提速安全工作负总责任，实行提速安全"四级包保责任制"，即公安局领导和工作组包分局、公安处领导包铁区间、公安处抽出精明强干的科长干部到辖市包分局、区间。他们鼓励民警参与治安管理，改正过去到一线解决问题少的问题，他们还坚持到8时许，在晚上7时38.46小时，上

本报北京4月8日电 （记者刘勇 通讯员师帅）进入4月份以来，全国铁路部门采取有力措施，使粮食运输效率、使粮食运量不断攀升，有效地缓解了目前粮食供应紧张的状况。据统计，从4月1日至7日，铁路部门共运粮食262.9万吨，同比增加67.2万吨，增长34.3%。

进入4月份以来，铁路部门加大了对粮食运输的宏观调控力度，对粮食运输计划实行统一归口管理，优先保证国家调拨粮食和市场急需品种粮的调运。在有些铁路局加强与粮食企业和港务局的协调配合，积极组织接卸工作，提高了装运效率。铁道部运输局和有关铁路局、铁路分局在站段对粮食运输均有专人负责，确立台账，每日分析，各级主管领导对粮食运输情况有自分析研究、发现问题及时解决。

有关业部门加大对东北粮食运输的支持力度，在装车皇安排上加大对东北人关粮食运输的倾斜力度，4月份全路粮食装车计划日均6300年车，比3月份计划日均增加1838车，比去年同期4666年增加1634车；在运输组织上加大对东北人关粮食运输的倾斜力度，增加进关货物列车日均达到60列，每天增加2列，经山海关5个货物列车日均达到62列，同时加大了了向东北地区的投空力度；在保证粮食运输数量的前提下，积极组织敞车苫盖篷布运粮，有效地缓解了敞车紧张的矛盾。

除此之外，铁路部门还加强了运纪律，严格规范粮食运输收费。铁道部院定，对粮食、化肥、农药等重点物资运输，任何单位、任何组织、任何个人不得收取运价之外的任何费用，也不准代办点外任何单位收费。铁道部专门组织了督察组，对各铁路局粮食运输工作进行检查特别是收费情况进行收费监督检查。各铁路局、铁路分局地组织力量进行票据暗访，发现问题及时整改，确保粮食运输畅通无阻。

4月1日至7日
我国铁路运粮 262.9 万吨

国防交通资金管理规定发布

本报北京4月8日电 （通讯员赵海涛）3月29日，国家发展和改革委员会、财政部、中国人民解放军总后勤部会谋部、中国人民解放军总后勤部联合命令，颁发《国防交通资金管理规定》。

《国防交通资金管理规定》共5章、33条，主要从资金来源、资金用途、资金管理等方面对国防交通的资金管理作了明确的规定。《规定》指出："国防交通资金由中央人民政府、地方人民政府和企业共同承担。国防交通资金的增长应与国民经济发展水平相适应的增长水平相适应。"《规定》明确国家军、地方和企业国防交通的工作所承担的职责和义务。《规定》还指出："交通通信企业事业单位开展国防交通工作的有关经费开支，可以给予适当的税收优惠政策"，体现了对交通通信企业事业单位开展国防交通工作的支持。

《国防交通资金管理规定》是当前和今后一时期国防交通资金管理的法规性文件，《规定》的发布对于加强国防交通资金管理、保障平时国防交通工作和战时交通保障具有非常十分重要的意义。《国防交通资金管理规定》自2004年3月1日起施行。1981年7月22日，国务院中央军委交通战备领导小组、国家计委、财政部发布的《交通战备资金管理暂行规定》即行废止。

阿拉山口等口岸
通关便利了

本报乌鲁木齐4月8日电 （记者寇喜庆）4月1日，记者从乌鲁木齐海关现场办公会上获悉，乌鲁木齐海关将实施三项通关便利措施，以提高阿拉山口、霍尔果斯等铁路口岸的通关速度，降低企业的贸易成本。

优先通关。对鲜活、易腐烂及有特殊要求的进出口货物，在申报时予以加急通关、优先通关。同时，企业可以通过特约联系方式申请加急通关，在非工作时间和节假日办理通关手续。

担保放行。对在办理通关手续时因企业暂时无法缴纳某些单证（不包括进出口许可证）或其他信息以及海关难以定性商品品名、价格以及规格等条件的，准许企业填写抵押贷先行办理货物验放手续，事后在规定时间内补办有关报关手续。

上门验放。对企业不便在海关设立的监管现场查验出口货物，如确定要进行开箱查验，在查验关员人手小组，国家计委、财政部发布的《商品品名、价格以及规格等条件的，可实行"门到门"的验放制度。

http://www.RUL.com.cn

在铁路第五次大提速中担当牵引主角的两种机型——DF11G内燃机车和SS8电力机车，4月8日于27家媒体摄影记者前首次亮相。提速后，两种机型牵引的直达特快列车将首次实现单司机乘势。
本报记者周德民 摄

今日铁路

京沪间集装箱班列每天一列双向对开

本报北京4月8日电 （特约记者罗平 通讯员庞维丽）北京铁路分局京铁北方公司等36家单位投放的中铁联合物流有限公司中铁联合物流有限公司专列将从4月5日在北京签约。

中铁联合物流有限公司专列将从4月18日在京东、京沪至上海约36辆集装箱班列双向双层集装箱集装箱的运输，优化运输组织方案，充分利用在全国设立的22个分公司、7个子公司的运输网络，利用企业的车队和车队资源，提高运输效率，诚信

签约后，中铁联合物流有限公司即以北京为枢纽、上海运行38辆集装箱双向对开的铁路货运专列，充分利用中国大城市间的物流运输。中铁联合物流有限公司是包括北京至上海37辆集装箱双向双层集装箱班列双向双向的运输，优化运输组织方案，充分利用在全国设立的22个分公司、7个子公司的运输网络，利用企业的车队和车队资源，提高运输效率，诚信服务，积极开拓企业的货运市场，以集装箱双层集装箱班列的优势，降低服务成本，以一列与一列之间38.46小时，上

今日导读

中国铁路第五次大面积提速调图宣传提纲　A2、A3

"安全屏障工程"：

中铁联合物流

刘志军部长在提速平推检查总结会上提出，以确保提速安全为重点，开展全员、全方位、全过程提速调图准备工作的自查自验

确保铁路第五次大面积提速调图万无一失

本报北京3月26日电 （记者李晓华）为确保4月18日我国铁路第五次大面积提速调图万无一失，3月19日至27日，铁道部部长刘志军、副部长胡亚东在去年12月份提速牵引试验后，再次率领铁道部检查组，行程1.3万公里，对京哈、京广、陇海、京沪、京九线进行了提速平推检查，并取得圆满成功。

3月27日18时，京九线上行平推检查一结束，铁道部立即召开电视电话会议，对提速平推检查进行总结。刘志军在总结会上提出，以确保提速安全为重点，集中力量，利用半个月左右的时间，开展全员、全方位、全过程的提速调图准备工作的自查自验，确保第五次大面积提速调图万无一失。

这次提速平推检查，是对第五次大面积提速调图准备工作的再次督促指导。9天里，提速平推检查列车与晨曦同行，与晚霞同归，每天不间断行驶近12个小时。刘志军、胡亚东始终坚持在机车上指挥，检查台线准备工作情况，发现存在的不安全隐患和问题，及时与有关单位和部门交换意见，并帮助他们研究制订配套改进措施。

刘志军在总结会上说，通过这次检查，我们高兴地看到，有关单位围绕第五次大面积提速调图做了大量深入细致的准备工作，特别是去年12月引试验总结会之后，针对铁道部提出的20个重点问题，紧密联系实际，举一反三，制订措施，狠抓落实，各项准备工作更加深入，取得了显著成绩。提速基础工程基本完成，主要行车设备质量明显提升，有关规章制度和办法的修订基本完成，劳动组织调整基本到位，关键岗位人员素质有新的提高，提速干线治安环境整治取得新的成效，新的列车运行图编制完成。

刘志军要求全路，进一步深化对提速安全极端重要性的认识，把确保提速安全摆在重中之重的位置。

刘志军说，运输安全是提速调图的核心问题和首要前提，列车速度越高，对运输安全的要求越高。提速必须在运输安全有绝对把握的基础上进行，如果安全没有绝对把握，宁可不提速。因此，提速调图的一切备工作都要紧紧围绕确保提速安全这个核心来进行，把抢险提速安全作为衡量提速调图所有准备工作质量的最终标准。

刘志军指出，前四次大面积提速调图，我们之所以取得成功，最重要、最关键的一条，就是保证了行车安全。能否保证第五次大面积提速调图的圆满成功，最核心、最关键、最根本的仍然是安全。特别需要指出

铁道部部长刘志军在第五次大面积提速试验车上平推检查。

本报记者原瑞伦 摄

的是，由于第五次大面积提速调图达到的新情况和新要求，比以往任何一次都多。因此，确保提速安全更为重要，大家一定要有足够的、清醒的、深刻的认识。

第一，党中央、国务院高度重视安全生产工作，确保提速安全面临新的更高要求。以胡锦涛同志为总书记的党中央，对安全生产工作十分关心，极为重视，落实科学发展观。刘志军说，对第五次大面积提速调图，党中央、国务院既关心又支持。铁路作为大众化的交通工具，必须进一步加强运输安全工作，确保旅客生命财产安全。这是铁路部门坚持以人为本、落实科学发展观的基本职责。刘志军说，对第五次大面积提速调图，党中央、国务院既十分关心，社会各界普遍关注，人

民群众期望很高。我们一定要认真学习贯彻党中央、国务院领导关于加强安全生产工作的一系列重要指示，站在贯彻"三个代表"重要思想和落实科学发展观的高度，把运输安全工作特别是提速安全摆在重中之重的位置，确保万无一失。

第二，第五次大面积提速调图的复杂程度远远大于前四次，确保提速安全面临的挑战。第五次大面积提速调图与前四次相比，有许多新变化，其中有变化是过去从未有过的。这不仅表现在运输产品的创新、运输质量的提升、运力资源配置的优化等诸多方面，更重要的是表现在运输安全上。刘志军列举了10个方面的变化后指出，每一个新情况、新变化，都与运输安全息息相关。如果我们重视不够，不采取科学严谨的应对措施，就可能在提速安全上出现问题。

第三，目前运输安全基础仍然比较薄弱，对提速安全构成不利影响。尽管多年来，我们在加强安全基础建设方面做了大量工作，但安全基础薄弱的问题而未从根本上解决，不安全隐患还大量存在。这次检查发现了大量问题，也说明安全基础建设任重道远。

第四，部分干部职工存在模糊认识，给提速安全带来了隐忧。刘志军对盲目乐观、"经验主义"、急躁情绪等模糊认识进行了分析，要求大家警惕，第五次大面积提速调图所面临的挑战，比以往任何一次都多。在这种情况下，那思想更次强调，各单位、各部门一定要进一步深化对提速安全极端重要性的认识。要深刻认识到，确保提速安全进一步落实的需要，是保证人民群众生命财产安全的需要，是保证铁路提速战略进一步实施的需要。铁路跨越式发展思路得到了党中央国务院领导的充分肯定、社会各界的广泛赞同和全路干部职工的理解，目前铁路跨越式发展的形势很好。

（下转A2版）

To ensure the fifth rise in speed
and the new operational changes
on the railway are perfectly safe.
The People's Railway, 29th March
2004
确保铁路第五次大面积提速调图
万无一失，《人民铁道》，2004
年3月29日

The sixth rise in speed on the railway starts on 21st April next year. The international edition of the People's Daily, 21st April 2007

全国铁路明年四月十八日起第六次提速,《人民日报》(海外版),2007年4月21日

● 时速达 200 公里以上
● 继续坚持"提速不提价"原则
● 客运能力预计增加 18%

全国铁路明年四月十八日起第六次提速

本报北京 11 月 17 日讯 记者欧阳洁报道:铁道部今天宣布,全国铁路将于 2007 年 4 月 18 日正式实施第六次大面积提速,时速将达到 200 公里以上,其中京哈、京沪、京广、胶济等提速干线部分区段可达到时速 250 公里。

铁道部副部长胡亚东 17 日在此间召开的新闻发布会上说,这次提速最大的亮点是时速 200 公里及以上动车组投入使用。到明年底,全国铁路将有 480 列时速 200 公里及以上的国产动车组上线运用,覆盖全国 17 个省、直辖市。

胡亚东说,前五次提速实行了提速不提价的总政策。对于第六次大提速,在国家批准已经实行的高等级列车软座票价幅度内进行适当的安排。对于动车组之外,新增开行的直达特快列车、夕发朝至列车和普通旅客列车,一律维持现在票价水平,不做任何调整。提速不提价的大原则,在第六次大提速当中仍然要体现。

记者了解到,根据初步测算,提速后,全国铁路客运能力预计增加 18%,货运能力预计增加 12%,有利于进一步缓解铁路运输"瓶颈"状况。

胡亚东说,通过新一轮大面积提速,我国铁路提速资源也大大增加,时速 120 公里及以上提速网络总里程达 22122 公里,其中时速 200 公里及以上提速线路 6003 公里,时速 160 公里提速线路 8033 公里。到 2010 年,既有线提速干线与新建的铁路客运专线将构成总里程近 3 万公里的快速铁路客运网络。

图为日前一列 CRH2、时速 200 公里的提速牵引试验列车飞驰在京广线经过的 山上。 原瑞伦摄(新华社发

An linear image caused by
lights from moving trains.
列车运行图勾勒铁路发展轨迹

图为京光线列车运行图。图中一
条线就是一躺列车运行的轨迹，
红色线代表客车，蓝色线代表货
车，粉色线代表施工"天窗"

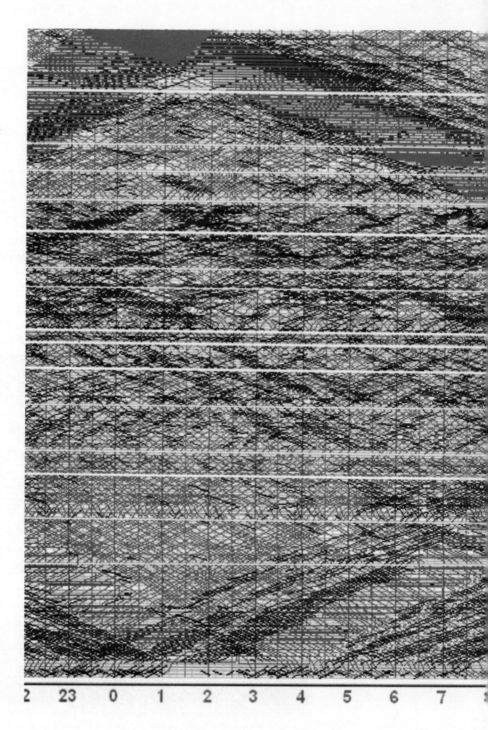

2   23   0   1   2   3   4   5   6   7

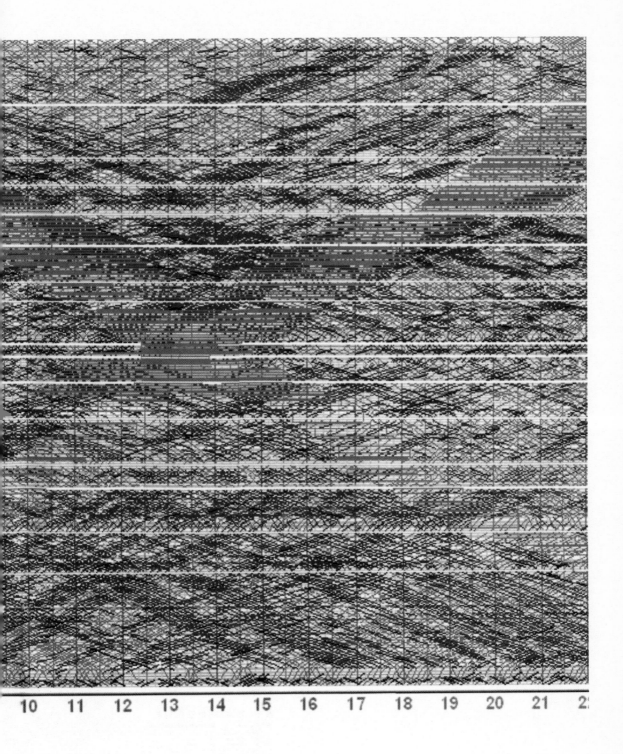

10 11 12 13 14 15 16 17 18 19 20 21 2

A diagram showing the sixth rise in
speed on the railway
铁路第六次大提速示意图

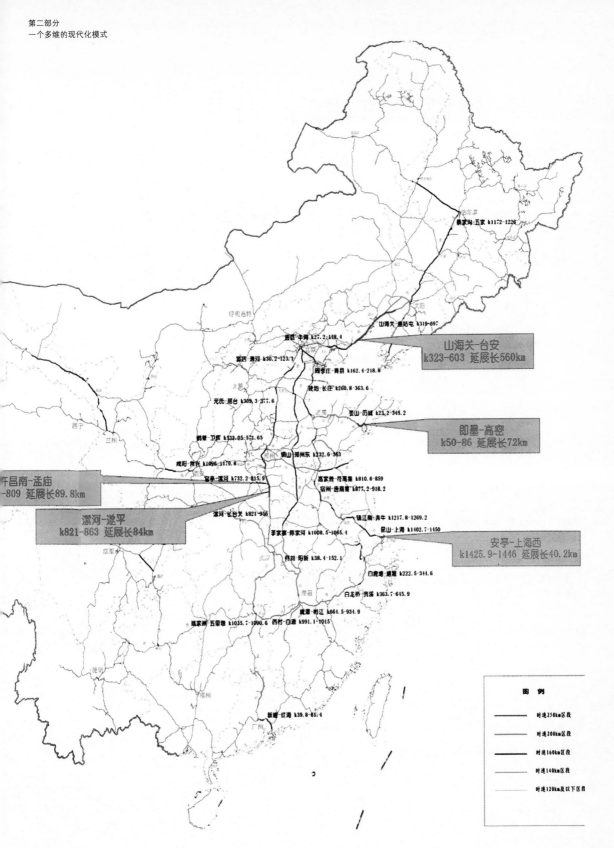

蔡家沟-五家 k1172-1226

山海关-星姑屯 k319-697

山海关-台安
k323-603 延展长560km

道西-辛辫 k27.2-148.4

窦西-漕河 k30.2-123.1

两孝庄-商县 k162.4-218.6

元氏-邢台 k309.3-377.6

陵地-长庄 k260.8-363.6

娄山-历城 k23.2-345.2

即墨-高密
k50-86 延展长72km

鹤壁-卫辉 k533.05-571.65

咸阳-常兴 k1096-1179.8

铜山-郑州东 k232.6-563

窑皋-漯河 k732.2-815.9

高家营-荷泽集 k810.6-859

宿州-唐南集 k877.2-918.2

许昌南-孟庙
-809 延展长89.8km

漯河-遂平
k821-863 延展长84km

漯河-长台关 k821-956

镇江南-奔牛 k1217.8-1269.2

昆山-上海 k1402.7-1450

安亭-上海西
k1425.9-1446 延展长40.2km

茅家寨-陈家河 k1008.5-1065.4

丹阳-阳新 k38.4-152.1

白鹿塘-螺灘 k222.5-344.6

白龙桥-贵溪 k363.7-645.9

戴潭-柯江 k664.5-934.9

陈家洲-五里墩 k1035.7-1090.6

西村-白漠 k991.1-1015

新墟-红海 k39.8-61.4

图 例

———— 时速250km区段

———— 时速200km区段

———— 时速160km区段

———— 时速140km区段

———— 时速120km及以下区段

357

Raising speed on the railway
A sculpture made of time and space

Based on an interview with *Sui Jianguo* in *Beijing* on 3rd July 2007

"大提速"
　　——用时间和空间做影像的雕塑

时间: 2007年7月3日
地点: 北京
采访对象: 隋建国

My visit to the *Zhangjiang* Development Zone in *Pudong, Shanghai* inspired me to create a public art project that involved a bus ride for visitors to the Zone. The Zone has large spaces, broad roads and factories one after the other, but it is a no man's land during the weekend. Even during weekdays, there are not many people on the roads. Other Development Zones gave me a similar feeling. The local leaders in the zones offered us free rides. I wanted to apply this practice to my work. My plan was to have a bus travelling around the district without stopping. Those on the bus would become visitors crossing, as if creatively, through the space. The plan did become an actual piece of work. This work gave me a concept: that when making sculpture or making an art piece is not necessary to make only an object and for viewers to come to see this single thing. My experience of buses reminds me that if you notice a space, at the same time you also notice the manner and the time of your moving through it. For, whether you do so by bus, on foot, by bicycle, or by driving your own car to cross this space you discover a relationship with it. The process of this relationship may take a fixed period of time, of one or two hours, perhaps as little as five minutes. If you can grasp this time you will probably grasp this space.

It is this fresh experience that turns my attention to the invisible time and space in daily life. My first work inspired by this experience was The Fifty Metres Parallel Move, a work about people lifting and moving a BMW motor car. A later work was Raising Speed on the Railway, about a circular railway test track, the *Huantie*.

Two years after I built my new studio I felt short of space. One of my students told me that there were big spaces to rent around the area of the *Huantie*, but he also said that with

问：能谈谈您创作《大提速》的起因吗？是什么促使您关注环铁现象？

隋：这要说到我之前的作品。

2006年6月，我去参观上海浦东张江开发区，当时坐汽车在开发区中转来转去，转的过程中让我有似曾相识的感觉。因为所有的开发区都很大，马路很宽，有很多工厂，一座一座，一旦周末却一个人都没有，变成一座空城。就算不是周末，马路上也没有几个闲人。到各地的开发区参观，当地领导都会派一辆车带我们四处转，四处看。这种看开发区的方法，让我想到要做一个坐在车上观看开发区的艺术品。

因为当时是公共艺术展览，所以我的方案就是专门找一辆公共汽车，让它在开发区里面不停地跑。观众上汽车，作为参观者，艺术化地过这个空间。这个作品后来还真实现了，它给了我一个概念：做雕塑其实可以不做一个单独的物体。（因为创作雕塑的习惯是做一个单独的物体，而观者观看的就是这个物体。）公共汽车提示了我，如果你注意到一个空间，同时你也会注意到你穿过空间的方法和所用的时间，因为你可以选择坐车，也可以选择走路。跟这个空间发生关系，发生关系的过程有一个固定的时间：1小时，2小时，或者5分钟。如果你把握住了这个时间，加以转换，就等于是把握住了这个空间。

the trains running all day it was unbearably noisy. I thought that was fine, I should go and see the place. I went there twice, the third time with a camera. As another of my students *Wang Dongsheng* specialized in video photography I asked him to go with me. I was not sure what I would photograph, I just went to take a look first. I found the circular track had a circumference of nine kilometres. Because it was designed as a test track the trains ran at a fixed speed of around one hundred and eighty kilometres per hour, it would take about four and a half minutes for the train to complete one circuit of the track.

Wang and I chatted in the doorway of one of the artist's studios and the train passed by once in a while. The train made such a noise we all had to stop talking for about thirty seconds and then to continue when it had passed. While we chatted we were guessing how long it would be before the train would arrive again.

By nightfall I reasoned that the train arrived every four and a half minutes and the waiting time in between was interesting. Then I asked *Wang* to prepare the camera and we started to record in order to discover how many times the train passed by within the limit of the tape. It was still daylight when we started to video, after half an hour it was turning dark. When I went home and watched the tape, it was interesting indeed.

One tape showed a simple scene, a wall and a dark track behind it. You could see nothing before the train arrived. There was a road in front of the wall, nobody walked past, there were just a few cars parked along that road. The train arrived every four and a half minutes, roaring and taking thirty seconds to pass by. The alarm of one of the cars was triggered by the vibration, thirty seconds later one returned to peace, then four and a half minutes

正是这一新的体会，使我开始注意寻找在日常生活当中隐藏着的时间与空间。先是创作了《平行移动50米》，让人搬宝马车，再后来就有了与环铁相关的《大提速》。

两年来，我的工作室盖起来后，空间有点不够用。我的学生就告诉我在环铁有空间，面积多大，多少钱；但是后来天天跑火车，吵死了。我想那正好，可以去看看。去了两次，第三次就带了机器去。我有个学生叫汪东升，是专门做纪录片的，我说你跟我去，不知道能拍到什么，先去看看。到了那里，发现环铁有固定的周长——9公里。因为是在做实验，火车跑起来又有固定的速度，大概是每小时180公里左右，所以大概4分半钟就跑一圈。

我们在一个艺术家的工作室门口聊天，一会儿火车就来一趟。火车来了大家就停止谈话，大概30秒，火车过去了大家再继续聊。一边聊一边在心里猜测火车下一次出现的时间。聊到傍晚，我想，火车每4分半钟来一次，这当中空白的等待是个很有意思的事情。我就让小汪把机器架起来，用一盘带子从头拍到尾，看火车能过几次。开机的时候天还亮，等拍了半小时，天就黑下来了。回来一看，果然挺有意思。

你看，一堵墙的后面是火车轨道，可是火车不来，你什么也看不到。墙前面有一个走道，也没有什么人走，就停了几辆车。每过4分半钟，火车轰隆隆来了，30秒跑过去。有一辆汽车装有警报器，

later the alarm was triggered once again. There was thirty seconds of thunderous noise and flashing light from the passing train, then four and a half minutes of deathly silence, a repeated sequence of static image followed by moving image.

The interesting thing is that the viewer of the tape must wait four and half minutes to see the train pass again, this was the exact time the train took to complete one circuit of the nine kilometre long track. This work then, presents the whole of the *Huantie* scenario.

This was my plan. If we set up ten video cameras by the rail side, the train would pass each camera every four and a half minutes. By splicing together what the ten cameras had recorded, each having recorded an interval of about 10 seconds, the train would be recorded on each of the tapes. The ten tapes would encompass one circuit of the track by the train. The train would then be seen travelling around the circuit.

In the end I picked thirteen places at which to set up the cameras and also decided on the position and angle of the cameras. The thirteen camera positions were evenly spaced around the circular track. The train started its runs at nine o'clock in the morning and travelled around the track until seven o'clock in the evening. We would start off all cameras at the same time. For example, each of the cameras was switched on at one o'clock in the afternoon. All thirteen cameras were activated by timers, each camera would record for half an hour and stop as its tape was exhausted. Even so, the thirteen cameras were not started at exactly the same time, some tapes were a little longer and not all tapes rotated at the same running speed. Later, I snipped the beginning and end of all the tapes so that they all had the same running time of thirty-one minutes and twenty seconds. It was a purely physical record

火车一来, 警报器就叫, 30秒火车过后又恢复平静。有火车时是30秒的电闪雷鸣, 紧接着就是4分半钟的死寂, 4分半钟的空画面或者叫做静物风景似的画面, 然后又是一个循环。

这里面有意思的是, 观者必须等待4分半钟。4分半钟就是火车跑一圈——9公里所用的时间。也就是说, 这个录像的画面背后携带着9公里的环铁。

于是我想, 如果在铁路沿线支上十台机器, 每个机器里的画面都是4分半钟火车来一次, 把这些画面连接在一起, 那就是每过10多秒, 火车就会出现在其中一个画面中。10个画面围成一圈, 火车也就在这个圈子里跑起来了。

最终我选了13个点, 事先把地点、角度都规定好。火车早上9点开始跑, 一直跑到晚上7点。大家约定好, 比如1点准时开机, 那么13台机器对好计秒器, 同时开机, 拍半个小时, 带子一完机器就撤下来。但是就算是这样, 时间也不齐。有的带子长点, 有的带子短点, 带子转的速度也不一定那么均匀。我后来把十几盘录像带掐头去尾, 整体取齐后, 时长是31分20秒, 它是一个纯粹物理的时间记录。用13台机器拍, 我最终选择了12个录像。

我想找一个圆的展厅来展示这件作品。墙上有12个屏幕, 火车就在里面跑。火车不来时, 每个屏幕就像一个风景, 有时候有人有车走过, 有时候一个人都没有。

of time, I used thirteen cameras but I finally chose to use just twelve of the tapes.

The work records the circumstances of the circular railway track at that time as well as the living conditions of the shared urban and rural areas.

There was one recording position of special value, it was a major crossing junction for traffic, the junction constantly lowered a barrier to prevent pedestrians from crossing. The barrier came down one minute before the train would arrive, in an extremely regular pattern. The people had become used to the barrier rising and falling every three minutes. At this point it was possible to see that the train was placing restrictions on the people's lives. Another camera position was within a village, apparently the noise from the passing train was deafening, interfering with the lives of the villagers, yet everyone appeared to have got used to it, as if the train was not passing at all.

One scene showed a flyover in front of the Film Archive. The area was the most modern within the *Huantie* area. The flyover was built to provide access to the Archive which is a so-called cultural business card for the city of *Beijing*. The interesting thing was that horse-drawn carts and tractors from the village behind the Archive passed under this modern flyover everyday. Almost the end of filming on this tape, four horse-drawn carts loaded with bricks moved into the shot, a couple were sitting in each of the charts. Two of the carts failed to go up the slope, all the couples then jumped off their carts to push.

The other scene was a garbage dump with piles of rubbish. A village nearby called the Black Bridge Village was the only village inside the circular track and home to around 2,000 villagers. Because of being located between urban and rural areas, incomers liked to rent

问：您是怎么选取并确定下13个拍摄的点的？

隋：13个点按说应该是可以平均分布的。

有一个点很热闹，是主要的交通路口，它会不断放下栏杆来挡路人，在火车来到的一分钟以前就要放下来，非常有规律，人们也形成了每3分钟就在栏杆前等候的习惯。这时候可以看到，火车对人们的生活是一种制约。还有一个点设在村子里，按说火车跑过来噪音很大，对人们的生活形成干扰，但是大家习惯了，就跟没有火车一样。

其中一个画面是电影资料馆前的立交桥。电影资料馆现在已经成为所谓的北京市的文化名片，那里的立交桥都修好了，是环铁地区最现代化的地方。最有意思的是，后面有一个村子，村里的拖拉机和马车就从现代化的立交桥下走过。在这个点上拍的录像快要结束时，突然来了四辆马车，拉的是砖，每辆马车上是夫妇两个人。最后有两辆马车上不了坡，大家就一起推。

还有一个镜头是垃圾场，有大堆的垃圾。这个环铁里面原来只有一个村，叫黑桥村，有2000多的村民，因为处于城乡交界地方，外来人口都喜欢在这样的地方租房，所以这个村现在实际上住了大约一万人。这个村子原来都是一个小院一个小院的，现在每个院子都盖满了临时的房子。院子的外面，在路边也盖了很多临时房子、小商品零售店，村子的垃圾场就不断地扩大。

accommodation there. The number of residents in the village had risen to about 10,000 people. All the courtyards in the village were now filled with temporary sheds. Even on the roadside there were sheds and temporary shops, so the size of the garbage dump had also increased.

I felt these scenes were worth recording. There are also other interesting points about this piece of work, such as that the distance between each camera position can be calculated by the duration of the tape, it is not too important whether they are exactly evenly divided.

Each camera was fixed in position, when the camera was turned on it started to record what was in front of it. No changes whatsoever were made. The pity was that the tape only lasted for half an hour, if it had been able to record for two hours, it may have captured even more interesting images from everyday life.

The *Huantie* and its environs belong to the Institute of the Ministry of Railways and the track was constructed in the 1960s. Having asked the security staff working there, they said that in fact there are three circular railways like the *Huantie*, the other two are situated in *Shenyang* and *Guangzhou*. An old man in his 60s or 70s who works in the garbage dump said that every time the Ministry of Railways raises the speed of the trains nationwide, the authority would run the train here first to gather data. This happened first in 1997, 2006 being the sixth time. The security staff told me that the experiments on the circular track had increased the test speeds to 200-250 kms/h. For a railway, 250kms/h is probably the highest speed possible and for higher speeds special equipment would be needed.

录像把环铁目前的状态记录了下来, 记录了火车奔跑和城乡交界处的生活现状, 其中有两个画面是拍油菜花地。北方是看不到油菜花的, 但那个地方有, 因为有安徽农民过来, 专门租了一大片地, 种了油菜花。我觉得这些都值得记录下来。因为根据时间可以测算出点与点之间的距离, 所以是否平均也就不重要了。

我的机器支在每个点上一开机就不能动, 谁过来谁过去你都不能管, 它就是一个日常的状态。可惜一盘录像带长度只有半小时, 如果有两小时, 那就会更丰富和更复杂。

问: 这个实验基地是什么时候建立的?艺术家又是什么时候开始进驻的, 他们是什么时候开始关注这个现象?火车的声音实在很吵, 对他们有很大的影响, 为什么还是有那么多艺术家去进驻那个地方?

隋: 环铁属于铁道部研究院, 是20世纪60年代建立起来的, 环铁的保卫部门说, 这种环铁在中国总共有3个, 分别在北京、沈阳和广州。我在试镜头的时候遇到一个老村民, 这个看垃圾场的老头大概有60、70岁, 他说只要国家要火车提速, 一定有火车先在这里跑, 它需要实验数据。1997年是第一次, 2006年是第六次。

The land area of the *Huantie* partially belongs to the Ministry of Railways and partially belongs to the village, the remainder was occupied by military storage units. It was easy to put the space to new use. Starting in 2004 to 2005, artists started to move into the *Huantie* area. The sixth attempt to raise speed on the railway had not started by then. It was not until October 2006 that trains started to run on the rails.

Many of the artists who worked inside the area of the *Huantie* have been moved from the 798 arts district, because the rents in 798 went up. Moreover the villagers in the area of the *Huantie* found that it was an easy way to make money by renting houses to artists.

I did not talk to the villagers about some protests that had happened in the past, because I could see they had already got used to the *Huantie* being there. The *Huantie* was set up by the government to test trains, now, apart from the railway departments, the *Huantie* is used to conduct tests for anybody who needs to amass test data and pays the cost, tests as to the quality of train engines, angles of a rail and the fall in the slope of a rail. Many foreign companies want to sell train engines to China, they too could get text results from the *Huantie*.

From the security point of view, before going there with a camera I did not know whether I could film the track without getting into trouble. Nobody stopped me initially. While filming a main junction that was near a police station, and somebody come out from the station and stopped us from filming, I thought he was referring to the junction and so we moved our camera a little farther away and we were left alone. But then we were too far away, so we did not position our camera there when we filmed the track a second time.

这次的实验是最快的一次，但是据说，这次也是最后一次了。在这里实验最快的速度是250公里/小时，这也是目前铁路的最快速度，如果需要更快的速度就必须要有特殊的铁路。最近在法国出现最快的一条铁路线是580公里/小时。据说北京到上海的这条线会达到300多公里/小时，另外北京到广州可能也是这个速度。250公里是平均速度，它有很快的时候，也有慢下来的时候。

环铁的艺术家多数从798搬过来，因为798的房租不断攀升，而环铁的村民发现把房子盖起来租给艺术家是很快的赢利手段。

环铁的土地除了村子之外，所有的土地一方面是归铁道部，一方面是归村里，还有一些是军工单位的仓库，所以做起事情很方便。从2004年开始，艺术家逐渐搬过去。进去的时候第6次提速还没开始，后来从2006年10月开始了跑火车。

问：环铁是每次提速的时候才进行跑火车的实验，还是每年都有固定的时间用来进行提速实验？我看到去年刘川平拍了一个关于环铁的片子的信息，主要反映黑桥村的村民在轨道上集体抗议，这里也反映了村民和火车实验的矛盾。
隋：其实我没有就这个事情跟村民交谈，我看他们已经很习惯环铁的实验。我觉得环铁应该是国家

There was also a police car that approached us and asked us to leave; we argued that we were conducting an art class with students, they did not turn off all our cameras. Later on I sent a student to ask the security department of the *Huantie* whether they would grant us permission to film the track. They said that there were documents that indicated that the taking of photographs and video were prohibited. However there were no signs there saying 'Photography Prohibited', a Chinese way of dealing with things, this suggested taking photographs might not be a big problem. I could not ask the higher authority for permission because they would not call a meeting and issue a paper for such a trivial matter.

When I searched for information about the *Huantie* on the Internet, all the data including the radius, length, grade of the circular track and other test results were available. Google Earth showed detailed pictures as well. If there was a security issue, this information would be more damaging than my video. So I do not consider that my video will cause any security problem.

With the work completed, I wanted to find a circular gallery just like the circular railway, in which to show the work, with twelve screens on the wall, the train would run across them. Each screen, whilst waiting for the train to arrive, looks like a section of scenery, sometimes, pedestrians or cars can be seen, sometimes not even a single person can be seen.

I was born in the 1950s. My generation probably has the most unified understanding of the concept of state. These were the liveliest years for socialism, when the Communists were cooperating with the non-Communist parties and the Political Consultative Conference was enjoying its best years. The problems came later, like the Anti-Rightist Movement, the

下达命令, 他们就作实验。现在也许除了铁道部外, 他们还会接一些单, 不管是什么部门, 需要作实验, 只要给钱, 他们就提供实验数据。除了实验铁路弯道的弧度, 铁路上下坡的落差, 还有火车头的质量实验。想要卖给中国火车头的国家有很多, 可能都要把车头放到环铁上跑一跑。

问：为什么国家会选择铁路, 而不是公路？
隋：当然铁路是最经济了。据说下一步中国要提高空运的力量, 空中飞机的分层要从6增加到11层。

提速也是一个心理的症候。我小时候作文经常用一个特别的词汇, 叫"时代的列车", 意思是说, 时代的列车不断前进, 每个个体都是列车上的一员。大家都希望这个时代的列车跑得更快些, 任何人一听到火车提速了, 就会想到这个社会发展之快。中国50年来的国家建设, 先是毛主席, 后是各届领导, 一直是这个心态。因为在这之前, 中国太落后了, 所有的知识分子或者精英都呼吁, 要发展得更快, 普通人也愿意接受这些观念。

问：环铁应该算是国家机密的地方, 为什么会允许老百姓和艺术家进驻周边的地区呢？
隋：据他们的保卫部门说, 铁道部有文件, 不准拍照, 不准摄像, 但是它并没有禁止的标志。北京的

Great Leap Forward and the Cultural Revolution. All these movements actually changed our perception of 'state'. They were political movements directed by *Mao*'s seeking to renovate people's minds. Growing up in such a situation means the concepts I have accepted about state, life and culture are all probably Maoist concepts.

Only since the 1980s, with the efforts to reform and open China to the world, has everyone taken stock of themselves and the cultural enlightenment afresh and, to some extent, re-judged our previous concepts. Although rationally we might want to overturn it all, in reality, we cannot possibly do so because so much has been etched into the time that we lived through. By instinct, we cannot deny our own life. The knowledge that we gain consciously has critical value, but it is different from what has accumulated inside ourselves.

During the education I received as I was growing up, the words we heard most was 'do not let others choke you'. The country tried to construct all the basic industries through our own efforts. However we are now in a time of globalisation; we cannot develop industries by ourselves and allow the market to run departments that are non-military and unessential to the economy. Nowadays, it is difficult to quantify what is 'made-in-China' and what is 'made-by-others'. For example, China may buy a production-line from Germany to manufacture railway carriages. Does one say that the carriages were produced by Chinese or by Germans?

The camera that I used to make this artwork was made in Japan. It is used worldwide. I think that when the science and technology of some products reaches a certain standard, no one else would be capable of making the same thing. This reflects the ideological levels of a

某些地方不允许拍照，例如军事禁区、美术场馆，一般都有牌子明示。但是环铁没有，那就意味着其实你拍拍也不要紧，但只是不让你专门拍摄。事先我并不知道情况，我拿着摄像机去拍的时候，没有人管我。只是在一个主要路口，旁边就是一个派出所，我拍的时候他们出来干涉说不能拍，我以为只是不让拍这个路口，我就退远一点拍，他们也没有再管我。我在拍摄时，这个路口因为不让拍，离得太远又拍不出什么东西来，所以就放弃这个点了。还有一个点，正拍着，恰好有一个警车路过，说这个地方不能拍。我们的摄影师说，我们不是拍什么机密，我们是学生上摄影课做实验。如果警察责任心强点，绕一圈就会把所有的机器都停下来。后来我派学生去问他们的保卫处，有没有可能开一个正式的介绍信，让我们进行拍摄，或者我们拍了做展览，是不是跟机密有关系？保卫处的人说，文件是有的，不准拍照不准录像。但是这是中国的方式，你拍了可能也没有人来管你。但要我同意你拍，我不能做这个决定。你找我的上级领导，他也不能说你就能拍。就算你找到铁道部的部长，除非他为你这事开个会，专门下个文件。但是这不可能，这么庞大的国家机器不会为你一个人而转动，所以做展览的时候只能小心一点。

其实我后来在网上一查环铁的资料，没想到他们把所有的数据都登在上面了。环铁的弧度、长度、坡度，火车跑起来会怎样，什么地方做怎样的实验，清清楚楚。如果说泄密，它比我这个厉害得

nation's sense of independence and self-motivation and its sense of economic and scientific standards. It is the difference between renting, buying and self-innovation. Although China intends to develop a large aircraft, it cannot make the engines itself.

Raising the speed on the railway reflects the needs of China's economic development. We have to choose between raising the speed and enlarging the network, because so many businesses rely on the railway to distribute their goods. At the start, 10 or more railway lines were upgraded to accommodate speeds of 250 kms/h, currently 30 or more lines have been upgraded. This is unusual in a world context; no another country has as many high-speed railway lines as China. In Japan, The *Shinkansen* is the only railway service that can reach speeds of 330 kms/h. Europe has just the Euro Star. In America, the railway is not a high speed service, road is the main form of transport because they have a developed road network. Consequently America develops bigger and faster cars.

If you ask me to talk about art, I will not enter the argument between East or West, Chinese or other countries, because that would be a false argument. I think the most important thing for an artist is to fulfil himself. Even so, what I say and do still conveys what has always been in my blood. So it is with my work for the 'Raising Speed on the Railway' project. I was interested in that the work is beyond the scope of time and space. When I was locating the cameras and dividing the scene, my interests apparently showed that a concern for the state and its people was still a very attractive subject for me.

China developed its railways first because it is the most economical way to travel. The raising of speed is also a psychological term. I remember we often used a special phrase

多。Google earth上更是清清楚楚，一览无余。当天我拍的那个火车头看起来特别旧，看不出它原来的样子，应该没有泄密的危险。

问：这种实验基地与军事要地有很大区别吧？

隋：我觉得它应该算工业机密或商业机密。我拿你的车头做实验或拿他的车头作实验，最终决定要购买谁的车头，这个是商业机密。至于说工业机密就是技术机密，我实验的火车头能跑多快，我不愿你知道。可是在今天的技术手段下，你在Google网上一看，这个火车在这里跑，他们院的网站又告诉我们它的周长是多少，你就在Google上数一下这个火车跑一圈要多长时间，一算就能算出来。我的录像也就是这样推算出来的。也就是说，其实没有什么值得保密的。但是既然有个文件，作为管理者，他就必须遵守。

问：您有没有跟他们聊过，国家为什么选择这个地方而不是其他地方作为实验区域？

隋：关于这方面网上有一个报道，专门谈当年提倡建设环铁的滕代远，这个人当过铁道部部长，就是他一直提倡建立这个实验基地，报道写得很详细。

'train of the time' in our essays when I was young. It meant that the train of the time was consistently moving forward, everybody was a passenger on this train and we all wished that the train would run a little faster. Anyone who hears the phrase 'raising speed on the railway' will associate it with the rapid speed in the development of society. The construction of the state of China has been ongoing for more than 50 years. First, Chairman *Mao*, and then other generations of leaders have all held this attitude. Because China was so backwards in the past, all the intellectuals and the élite called for the rapid development of the country, the mass of the common people were also willing to accept these views.

When I consider my interests and ability, I feel that I would not be drawn to doing any kind of investigative work. I am no good at that. My work is intended to invoke a response from others and society. After I made the piece 'Raising Speed on the Railway', a show was held in the *Huantie* by the resident artists. The theme of the show was raising speed on the railway. They were surprised to find that someone like me could make the 'raising of speed' a subject of a work of art. They had only portrayed the *Huantie* as a disturbance to their lives and did not regard it as a subject for work or something that could be embodied in a work of art.

I have tried to learn more from history and from books on the railway, perhaps in the future other aspects of the railway can be incorporated into my work.

My work has experienced changes of media and my interests have widened. When I look at an object, I also aware of the space and time that relates to it. I feel that my view is broader than before and I have taken more elements into consideration than before. One of

问：我看到您一直都是实验一些实体材料创作雕塑作品，以录像的方式进行创作也是近来的事情，您是怎样考虑材料的转换的？

隋：一方面是媒介的转化，一方面是我的兴趣扩大了。我在关注一个具体的物体的时候，我还看跟它相关的空间和时间。我觉得自己比以前的眼界开阔了些，比以前考虑的因素多了些。你看这个骷髅头，当初SARS的时候做它，我考虑的是死亡的问题。可是当我开始做大的骨头架子的时候，它已经不仅仅是死亡的问题，它还牵涉到一个巨大空间对于我的能力的挑战。

问：您是如何理解"国家"这个概念的呢？

隋：我是在社会主义最有生命力的50年代出生的人，我们这代人对国家概念的理解大概是最整齐划一的。50年代的社会主义国际大家庭，国内也是跟民主党派合作，政治协商会议做得最好的时候；再往后就开始出现问题，比如反右、大跃进以及文革等等。这些运动都是在改变我们对于国家的概念，都是毛主席在改造人们思想理念指导下的政治运动。在这种环境下成长起来，意味着我所接受的关于国家，关于人生，关于文化的概念几乎都是毛主席的概念。

my works – the skull, was made when there was a threat from the epidemic disease SARS, I was thinking about death. However when I started to make the skull on a big scale, it was not only the matter of death, but also a huge space that challenged my ability. The other work was a blue ball. Everyday I would dip it into paint to make its shape change a little bit. Every week I took one photograph of it. I put a ruler behind this ball, so as to see how big it had grown in one week.

I would like to view my works in this way, that is, for me the most attractive element is the relationship between space and time. Because when a work of art is born out of a particular environment, it must manifest itself in specific social and material conditions and bring with it specific social realities and elements of real life. We have to see whether these points will interest the visitors.

Time means the relationship between space and our lives. In my early years, my understanding of sculpture was as object; sometimes being representational and at other times abstract. Later, time came into my view, the world changed from a still image to a moving image, it increased by one dimension and became complicated. Now my understanding is more real, the capacity of my work is double that of before, the extra half is time. I feel that time and space have equal weight.

从20世纪80年代之后的改革开放、文化启蒙，每个人都自己重新启蒙一次，尽量把原来的概念进行清理，也难以把它全部否定。理智上你想否定它，但你的本能不允许，因为你的生命就在这几十年里真实存在着，你把它完全否定，其实就是把你自己的生命都否定了。所以我觉得生命本能一定不会让你全部否定，在你的生命里面它已经成为无意识。后来读书，再启蒙自己，现在有意识地去批判一些不正确的想法，那都是特别理智的行为，它和已经沉淀在身体里面的东西还是不一样。

我小时候受教育时听得最多的就是"不要被别人卡住脖子"，所有的基础工业都要我们国家自己来建设。可是现在进入全球化时代，可能有些工业我们国家不会自己去发展，非军事部门和国民经济的命脉和很可能交给市场。而且，买来车头，就可以拆开，看看别人怎么做，自己学着做。网上有报道，连车身也有可能进口。其实现在很难分清哪些是自己生产，哪些不是自己生产。也许你从德国进口了一条流水线，这个流水线是生产火车车厢的，你说这个车厢是外国产还是算自己生产的？

我拍摄这个录像用的摄像机就是日本产的，全世界都用它。可能科学技术到了一定程度，就不能被代替，别人不能再生产。这里面有意识形态，有民族的自主和独立，但是还有经济、科学技术的水平等原因。自主的研发和买、租还是不一样的。中国现在开始提出要自己制造大飞机，但是中国的飞机发动机不能自制。

中国火车提速反映了经济发展的需求，或者提高火车速度，或者增加铁路网络的密度，因为那么多的货物要运输。譬如这次提速，时速250公里的铁路线路一开始是十几条，现在是三十多条。这个全世界都是罕见的，没有哪个国家有这么多的高速线路。日本的铁路时速330公里，只有新干线一条线。欧洲之星，横穿欧洲，但是也只有一条线。美国铁路没有这么高的速度，主要的运输力量是汽车，因为他们的公路非常发达。所以他们是生产更大的、速度更快的汽车。

如果现在让我谈艺术，我不会谈什么东方西方、中国外国，因为我知道，这样谈是一个虚假的命题。我认为一个艺术家，最重要的是完成自己，即便是这样，我的说话和行为仍然会流露出原来沉淀在我血液里面的东西。包括我拍《大提速》，它超出了时间和空间的游戏，我确定怎么安置机器，怎么分割画面的时候，从兴趣点一下就能看出，原来对国家，对民生的关心，还是一个非常吸引我的主题。

问：这个作品有没有可能做一些延伸？比如做一些社会性的调查，比如"大提速"对公众的影响，对艺术家的影响，对铁路实验部门的影响。

隋：我觉得从我的能力和我的兴趣来看，我不会做调查之类的工作，那不是我所擅长的。但是我的作品会引起别人或者社会的反应。我拍了《大提速》之后，环铁的艺术家在11月组织了一次展览，展览的主题就叫"大提速"。他们发现居然有人可以把铁路提速当做一个事来做，原来他们只是认为环铁对他们的生活是干扰，没有想到它可以成为作品的主题和载体，或者变成作品本身。

我愿意这样来看我的作品，它对我来说，真正核心吸引我的地方是空间和时间的关系问题。因为它一定是诞生在具体的社会和物质环境之下，它当然会携带上很多的社会现实和真实的生活因素。这就要看观众对这个有没有兴趣，有没有感觉。因为很多来看展览的人，对时间和空间并没有什么兴趣，可能别的东西对他更有吸引力。

我正尝试着去查铁路史，翻有关铁路的书，也许将来我会发现这个铁路还有其它内容可以变成我作品的一部分。

问：时间对于您来说意味着什么呢？

隋：时间意味着跟空间的关系，意味着和自己生命的关系。最早我理解的雕塑就是一个物体，有时候抽象点有时候具象点，但都是一个物体。后来我的眼界里有了时间，世界就从静止变成了运动，它多了一个维度，复杂了很多，现在我理解得更真切一些。我的作品容量比以前多了一半，这多出的一半就是时间，因为我觉得时间和空间的分量是平等对半的。

问：大提速是一个比较长期的研究项目，到目前为止，它是已经完成了还是会继续往下做呢？以后会不会还继续关注"大提速"这个命题？

隋：其实我已经有所延伸。在阿拉里奥展览的时候，为了让大家切身感受到火车的速度，我做了一台机器。这个机器是从中央空调的冷却塔的电机传动系统改造而来。我用钢管做了一个直径4.3米的十字形的结构，固定在这个电机的轴上。电机一转动，这个十字结构的周边的速度就是1分钟3000转，1小时180公里，跟录像里面的火车的速度相等。

后来到了5月，铁路提速全面达到了250公里/小时。在一个有关物派的展览上，我就把这个钢结构的直径加长，接近6.3-6.4米的样子，这时候钢管边缘的速度就是250公里/小时。我这个作品的命名也就改为《大提速——每小时250公里》，还是让人用身体去感觉这个速度。

在阿拉里奥北京艺术空间展出的时候，因为机器离门口比较近，所以一进门就可以感觉到它转动的速度和呼啸的声响，所有的观者都不敢靠近。

我也还打算继续完善这个机器，将来还要给它装上一些控制元件，使它每转5分钟就停2分钟，2分钟后再启动。因为我发现，从静止到启动到高速转动，给人的感觉很特别。

问：这个机器是为了配合录像的吗？

隋：先是配合录像，后来则是单独展出这个机器，它也受展出场地的限制。

问：那个机器是在测试时间、速度与人的关系吗？在大机器前面，您有什么样的感觉呢？

隋：我觉得那个机器是对你的生理感官的压迫，甚至对你理性控制力的挑战。如果仅仅是观看录像的话，就只是一个视觉问题，而这个机器的速度就直接地作用于你的感官和你的身体。

面对那个机器的时候，作为作者，我每一次都感到紧张。即使是明明知道不会有问题，但还是控制不住自己的紧张，也就是害怕那机器是否会随时甩出来。

这个机器确实给你一种威胁感，有意思。

The Context of the Project:
The Third Line Construction Project

项目背景简介: 三线建设工程

The Third Line Construction Project

In 1964, in response to the war preparations of the United States, India and the Soviet Union the Central Committee of the Chinese Communist Party divided China into three areas by drawing three dividing lines across its territory. The first line encompassed the northeast and the coastal provinces; the third line the southwest and the northwest, including the eleven provinces of *Yunnan, Guizhou, Sichuan, Shanxi, Gansu, Ningxia, Qinghai, Shanxi, Henan, Hubei* and *Hunan*, mainly to the south of the Great Wall and to the west of the *Beijing-Guangzhou* railway line. The second line encompassed the vast areas between the first line and the third line. The third line was also called the Big Third Line. Meanwhile, every province was also divided by their own three lines in which the third line was called the Small Third Line.

From the mid-1960s to the late 1970s, there was large-scale economic construction in the interior of the southwest and northwest, which was called the 'Third Line Construction'. The construction was proposed by *Mao Zedong* and, after discussion approved by the Central Committee of the Chinese Communist Party. For a time it was both the central link and the main task of China's economic construction.

As early as the mid-1950s, both in his article 'On The Ten Major Relationships' and at meetings of the Central Committee, *Mao Zedong* repeatedly stressed the need to develop industry vigorously in the interior of China, to build strategic bases actively in the rear areas and improve China's irrational industrial layout. In 1964, *Mao Zedong* explicitly proposed a determination to carry through the third line construction. That was to firstly

三线建设工程

1964年, 中共中央出于与美、印、苏备战的考虑, 将全国划分为一、二、三线, 一线主要是指东北和沿海各省；三线是指西南、西北地区, 包括云、贵、川、陕、甘、宁、青、晋、豫、鄂、湘十一省, 主要是长城以南、京广线以西广大地区；二线是位于一线和三线之间的广大地区, 其中的三线亦称为大三线。同时, 各省又都划分了自己的一、二、三线, 其中的三线称为小三线。

20世纪60年代中期至70年代末期, 在西南、西北内陆地区, 进行了一次规模宏大的经济建设, 亦称三线建设。它是由毛泽东提出、经中共中央讨论通过后付诸实施的, 曾一度作为我国经济建设的中心环节和主要任务。

早在50年代中后期, 毛泽东在《论十大关系》和中央工作会议上曾多次强调, 必须大力发展内地工业, 积极建设好我国的战略大后方基地, 改善我国不合理的工业布局。1964年毛泽东明确提出要下决心搞三线建设, 首先要把攀枝花钢铁基地以及与此相关联的交通、煤、电建设起来。根据毛泽东的指示, 中共中央决定：首先集中力量建设内地, 在人力、财力、物力上给予保证。要求新建的项目要摆在内地, 现在就要搞勘察设计, 不要耽误时间。沿海地区能够搬迁的项目要搬迁。国家计委据此重新拟定了《关于第三个五年计划安排情况的汇报提纲》。在"提纲"中明确提出："三五"

build up the *Panzhihua* Iron and Steel base together with its associated transport needs, coal and electricity. According to *Mao Zedong*'s instructions, the Chinese Communist Party Central Committee decided firstly to concentrate on the building up of the interior and to guarantee support in terms of human, financial and material resources. New projects were required to be located in the interior with surveying and design to start immediately. Those projects capable of being relocated from coastal to interior areas were required to do so. Consequently, the State Planning Commission looked again at 'The Outline of the Report on the Management of the Third Five-Year Plan'. It was clearly pointed out in the 'Outline' that the Third Five-Year Plan must be based on the likelihood of war; with preparations based on early and major battles; active preparations for war; placing national defence at the forefront; speeding up the third line construction, concentrating on the construction of basic industries and transport in the third line areas; gradually changing the industrial layout, developing agricultural production; correspondingly developing light industry and gradually improving the living standards of the people.

Between 1965 and 1980, in the thirteen provinces of China's interior and in the autonomous regions, the large-scale third line constructions spread. The enormous scale, length of time, quantity of input, breadth of mobilization and speed of action was unprecedented in China's history of construction. Most of the projects of the third line construction were implemented and completed during the turmoil of the Cultural Revolution.

The construction of the 'third line' projects fundamentally changed the backwardness of the transport infrastructure, the weakness of basic industry and the low degree of

计划必须立足战争，从准备大打、早打出发，积极备战，把国防建设放在第一位，加快三线建设，集中力量尽快地把三线地区的基础工业和交通运输业建设起来，逐步改变工业布局；发展农业生产，相应发展轻工业，逐步改善人民生活。

从1965年到1980年，在我国腹心地带的13个省和自治区全面展开了规模庞大的三线建设，三线建设规模之大、时间之长、投入之多、动员之广、行动之快，在我国建设史上是空前的。三线建设工程大部分项目是在文化大革命的动乱年代里实施并完成的。

三线建设初步改变了我国内地交通落后、基础工业薄弱和资源开发程度低下的历史状况。在三线的基础设施和基础工业建设中，国家把发展交通事业放在优先地位加以安排。相继建成川黔、贵昆、成昆、湘黔、襄渝、阳安、太焦、焦枝和青藏铁路西宁至格尔木段等10条干线，同时还修建了一些支线和专用线。新增铁路8046公里，占同期全国新增里程的55%，同时，国家还投资整治了三线地区的内河航道，新增内河港口吞吐能力3042万吨，进而使三线地区的交通运输初步形成网络，内河航运能力得到提高。能源工业重点建成了贵州六盘水、四川宝鼎、芙蓉、陕西韩城、铜川、河南平顶山等50多个统配煤矿区，初步建成了具有相当规模、门类齐全、生产和科研相结合的三线国防科技工业体系。国防科技工业是国民经济的重要组成部分，其技术和资金均较密集，综

resource development in China's interior which had been an historical state of affairs. In the construction of the infrastructure and basic industries of the 'third line' projects, the country gave priority status to the development of transport. Ten new railway lines were gradually constructed as follows: *Sichuan-Guizhou, Guiyang-Kunming, Chengdu-Kunming, Hunan-Guizhou, Xiangfan-Chongqing, Yangpinguan-Ankang, Taiyuan-Jiaozuo, Jiaozuo-Panzhihua* and *Xining-Golemu* in *Qinghai-Xizang*. Meanwhile a number of branch lines and lines for specific uses were refurbished. The new railway lines were 8,046 km in length, extending the length of the national railways by 55 per cent. At the same time, the country invested and regulated the waterways within the third line areas. The throughput of the new inland ports increased by as much as 30.42 million tons. Therefore, the traffic within the third line area formed a preliminary network and the shipping capacity of the rivers was upgraded. In the realm of the energy industry more than fifty unified coal mining areas including *Liupanshui* in *Guizhou, Baoding* and *Furong* in *Sichuan, Hancheng* and *Tongchuan* in *Shanxi, Pingdingshan* in *Henan,* and others were developed. The 'third line' area's industrial system of national defence, science and technology was substantial in scale and wide ranging, with an initial build up of production combined with research. National defence, the science and technology industries are an important component of the national economy. Intensive technology, capital and strongly integrated support are the central expression of the scientific and technological levels of the nation. The completion of the nuclear industry has developed a relatively sophisticated research and production system in the areas of uranium mining, water extraction of metal ores and the manufacture of components for the

合配套性很强, 是国家科技水平和经济实力的集中表现。核工业的建成已形成了从铀矿开采、水冶、萃取、元件制造到核动力、核武器研制以及原子能和平利用等比较完整的核工业科研生产系统, 具有相当的科研生产能力。航空工业先后在陕西、四川、贵州、湖北、湖南建设了生产科研基地, 新建和扩建了125个项目, 这些项目占全国生产能力的2/3。

三线地区的机械工业有了长足发展, 已经成为优势产业。三线地区机械工业的建设, 是按照既能为军事工业配套, 又能为国民经济提供重要装备的原则进行规划的, 新建了第二汽车制造厂、陕西汽车制造厂、四川汽车制造厂等骨干企业。同时还新建和扩建了一批重要的配套工厂, 形成了军民结合的轻型、重型汽车批量生产能力, 汽车的年产量已占全国的1/3。

三线建设给内地的一些城市带来了发展机遇, 促进了内地经济繁荣和社会进步。攀枝花、六盘水、十堰、金昌等, 过去是荒山野岭, 现在成了著名的以钢铁、煤炭、汽车和有色金属为主导产业的新兴工业城市。

历经17载的三线建设, 我国战略后方交通状况的改善, 能源、原材料等基础工业的开发和利用, 国防科技工业后方基地的建成, 机械、电子、轻纺工业的发展, 新兴工业城市的崛起, 不仅增强了我国经济和国防实力, 改善了我国生产力的不合理布局, 而且进一步促进了内地资源的开发, 带

development of nuclear power, nuclear weapons and the peaceful use of atomic energy. The aviation industry has its bases of scientific research in *Shanxi, Sichuan, Guizhou, Hubei* and *Hunan*. In total there were 125 new and expanded projects representing two-thirds of the country's total production capacity.

The machinery industry of the third line areas made considerable progress and became the dominant industry. Construction of the machinery industry of the third line areas became the most competitive industry and was planned according to the needs of the military and of supplying important equipment for the national economy. A number of backbone enterprises were built up, such as the No.2 Vehicle Factory, the *Shanxi* Vehicle Factory, the *Sichuan* Vehicle Factory and others. Meanwhile, a number of important supporting factories were built up or expanded. Capacity in the production of both light and heavy vehicles was increased. The annual production of vehicles in these areas amounted to one third of the overall national output.

The third line construction brought a number of development opportunities to several cities in the hinterland, promoting economic prosperity and social progress. The previously barren lands of *Panzhihua, Liupanshui, Shiyan* and *Jinchang* became leading industrial cities making the production of iron and steel, coal, vehicles and non-ferrous metal their major output.

After 17 years of the third line construction, the improvements to transport in China's strategic rear areas, the development and utilization of energy and raw materials, the construction of industrial rear bases for science and technology in national defence, the

动了少数民族地区的社会进步。

六枝、盘县、水城是贵州的三个县，煤炭储量在200多亿吨，而且煤种齐全，也比较容易开采，是西南三线建设的最大的煤炭基地（另外两个基地是重庆和攀枝花）。建设六盘水的主要目的，是为攀枝花钢铁基地提供炼焦煤和动力煤，和攀枝花钢铁厂是一个整体项目。原来规划把煤运到攀枝花，回来的列车把矿石带来，所以在水城布置了一个100万吨规模的钢铁厂。煤铁交流，各得其益，是一个很好的规划。水城钢铁厂的建设是与攀枝花同时开始的，经过20年水城钢铁厂才建成一个中型钢铁厂。

development of the machinery, electronics and textile industries and the rise of the new industrial cities, not only enhanced China's economy and national defence whilst improving the irrational distribution of China's productivity, but also further promoted the development of the resources of the hinterland contributing to the social progress of the areas occupied by the national minorities.

In *Guizhou*, the coal reserves in the three counties of *Liuzhi, Panxian* and *Shuicheng*, were in the region of 200 million tons. Their value lay not only in the variety of coal types but also being sited in areas that were relatively easy to exploit. They were the largest coal base of the southwest third line construction, the other two bases being in *Chongqing* and *Panzhihua*.

The main aim in constructing *Liupanshui* was to provide coking coal and steam coal, a project integrated with the *Panzhihua* Iron and Steel Works. The original plan was to transport the coal to *Panzhihua* and to return with the iron ore. Consequently, an iron and steel works of one million tons output was located in *Shuicheng*. The exchange between coal and iron ore was a good plan reaping benefits each from the other. The *Shuicheng* Iron and Steel Works was constructed in concert with *Panzhihua*. After twenty years of construction, the *Shuicheng* Iron and Steel Works became a medium-sized iron and steel plant.

Zeng Li
Project: The *Shuicheng* Iron & Steel Works

曾力　《水城钢铁厂》方案

The *Shuicheng* Iron and
Steel Works
水城钢铁厂 2006

The no.2 Blast Furnace, the
Smelting Works of the *Shuicheng*
Iron and Steel Works

水城钢铁厂·炼铁厂2号高炉 2006

The no.1 Blast Furnace, the Smelting Works
of the *Shuicheng* Iron and Steel Works
水城钢铁厂·炼铁厂1号高 2006

The Smelting Works of the
Shuicheng Iron and Steel Works
水城钢铁厂·炼铁厂 2006

Pipelines of the no.2 Blast Furnace in the Smelting
Works of the *Shuicheng* Iron and Steel Works
水城钢铁厂·炼铁厂2号高炉管道 2006

The Smelting Works of the
Shuicheng Iron and Steel Works
水城钢铁厂・炼铁厂 2006

The Smelting Works of the
Shuicheng Iron and Steel Works
水城钢铁厂 · 炼铁厂 2006

The Sintering Plant of the
Shuicheng Iron and Steel Works
水城钢铁厂·烧结厂 2006

The Sintering Plant of the
Shuicheng Iron and Steel Works
水城钢铁厂·烧结厂 2006

The Sintering Plant of the
Shuicheng Iron and Steel Works
水城钢铁厂·烧结厂 2006

The Sintering Plant of the
Shuicheng Iron and Steel Works
水城钢铁厂·烧结厂 2006

The Sintering Plant of the
Shuicheng Iron and Steel Works
水城钢铁厂·烧结厂 2006

The Sintering Plant of the
Shuicheng Iron and Steel Works
水城钢铁厂·烧结厂 2006

The Materials' Mill of the
Shuicheng Iron and Steel Works
水城钢铁厂·料场 2006

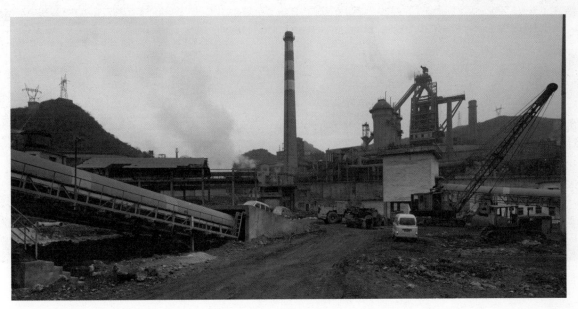

The Materials' Mill of the
Shuicheng Iron and Steel Works
水城钢铁厂·料场 2006

The Materials' Mill of the
Shuicheng Iron and Steel Works
水城钢铁厂·料场 2006

The Materials' Mill of the
Shuicheng Iron and Steel Works
水城钢铁厂·料场 2005

The Materials' Mill of the
Shuicheng Iron and Steel Works
水城钢铁厂·料场 2006

The no.3 Furnace of the Coking Plant
of the *Shuicheng* Iron and Steel Works
水城钢铁厂·焦化厂3号焦炉　2006

Archives

视觉档案

The tranquil mountain valley,
before the construction of the
Shuicheng Iron and Steel Works
水钢创建前的所在地是一片宁
静的山谷

A History of the *Shuicheng* Iron and Steel Works

Excerpt from the *Shuicheng* Iron and Steel Works Museum

A Difficult Beginning (1966-1970)

The *Shuicheng* Steel project was part of the national 'Third Line Construction'[i] policy and was built with the assistance of the *Anshan* Iron and Steel Corporation. Following the guiding principles of 'head for the mountains, take cover and scatter', three fields in *Qingganglin* in the town of *Shuicheng, Guizhou*, were selected as the construction site, and the factory was designated an important base for national iron and steel production in the south-west. The factory was originally designed for annual production levels of 500,000 tons of iron, 400,000 tons of steel and 300,000 tons of rolled steel, in a plan commonly referred to as the 'five four three scale'.

In the early Spring of 1966, *Qingganglin* was desolate and covered in frost. In February, the first construction team from the *Anshan* Iron and Steel Corporation set up camp in the area. In April, under the leadership of *Anshan's* deputy-director *Tao Ticheng*, the construction headquarters and party council were established. The arduous task of building the *Shuicheng* Iron and Steel Works had begun. First named the *Shuicheng Qingganglin* Forestry Centre, the name was changed to *Chunlei* Iron and Steel on October 31st 1968, and then to the *Shuicheng* Iron and Steel Works in January 1970.

Over thirty thousand workers from twenty work units in five provinces arrived to start the construction in the wild, mountainous terrain. In poor and harsh conditions, they worked

---

[i] The Third Line was an effort to scatter strategic industrial production throughout the Chinese hinterland where it would be safer from attacks by the Soviet Union and the United States.

水城钢铁厂厂史
——选自水城钢铁厂创业馆

艰难创业（1966—1970）

水钢是国家的"三线建设"项目之一，由鞍山钢铁公司援助建设。根据"靠山、隐蔽、分散"的建设方针，选址于贵州水城青杠林的大、中、小三块田，并确定将其建设成为西南的一个重要钢铁基地。初见规模为50万吨铁、40万吨钢、30万吨材。称为"五、四、三"规模。

1966年初春的水城青杠林，冰天雪地，一片荒凉。是年2月，鞍山钢铁公司第一支支援水钢建设的队伍，风尘仆仆来到这里安营扎寨。4月，以鞍山钢铁公司副经理陶惕成为首的工地指挥部和工地党委成立。从此，拉开了建设水钢的大会战序幕，这时水钢称为水城青杠林林场。1968年10月31日更名为春雷钢铁厂，1970年1月更名为水城钢铁厂。

来自全国5个省的20多个单位的3万多名建设大军，在这山峦起伏、荒山野岭中摆开了战场。他们头顶蓝天，脚踏大地，艰苦创业。没有公路自己修，没有运输工具就手抬、肩扛，将一批批建设物资送往工地；没有住房，就支帐篷、搭席棚，建"干打垒"。他们用山沟里的水洗脸、饮用……无论刮风下雨还是烈日曝晒，总是战斗不息。

1966年，时逢"文化大革命"，这给刚刚起步建设的大会战带来了重重困难和干扰，生活、建设物资得不到保证，就在这极艰难的条件下，会战人员历尽艰辛，苦干了4年多，与1970年10月1日迎来了首座568立方米高炉的投产。这标志着工厂从无到有，水钢初步建成。

但是，这座高炉系统并未完全配套，会战队伍又开始陆续撤走，后续工程被迫停止。

道路曲折（1971—1996）

水钢炼铁高炉投产后，由于"文革"干扰，"五、四、三"规模不配套。1971年开工的1号焦炉回收工程也拖了4年之久才完

hard with a pioneering spirit. They built roads where there were none and in the absence of transportation, they carried the construction materials by hand. There were no houses, only tents and tarpaulins for shelter. They washed in and drank from streams, continuing with the work in hand regardless of the wind, rain or sun.

1966 also saw the beginning of the Cultural Revolution, which greatly disrupted the construction project. The delivery of foodstuffs and construction materials became uncertain, but the project carried on under these daunting circumstances, taking four years of work before the first 568 cubic metre furnace was put into production on October 1st 1970. This marked the beginning of factory operations.

However, this furnace system was incomplete and the construction teams began to disperse. Eventually the follow-up construction was obliged to stop.

A Winding Road (1970 – 1997)

Once the furnaces at the *Shuicheng* Iron and Steel Works went into production, the disruptions caused by the Cultural Revolution prevented the factory from reaching its projected "five four three" production scale. The no.1 Coking Furnace project, begun in 1971, was not completed for four years; the ground was also broken for the no.2 Furnace in 1971, but construction was halted a year later before even the foundations were completed. In late 1972, although the steelmaking project had begun, it went through several phases of stop and start due to capital, equipment and labour shortages; the steel rolling provision reached only the site selection phase. The entire construction of the *Shuicheng* Iron and Steel Works was virtually paralyzed. Output was limited to the production of iron and the construction of complimentary facilities was delayed over eight years.

道路曲折（1971—1996）

水钢炼铁高炉投产后，由于"文革"干扰，"五、四、三"规模不配套，1971年开工的1号焦炉回收工程也拖了4年之久才完成焦油系统；2号高炉的建设1971年破土动工后，连基础工程都未完工，次年就停建；1972年底，炼钢工程虽开工建设，由于资金、设备、建设力量无着落，停停打打，工程几无进展；轧钢工程只选了厂址，也未动工，整个水钢建设处于瘫痪状态。生产是单一生铁生产，配套建设徘徊长达8年之久。

1976年粉碎"四人帮"后，水钢恢复建设，冶金部决定在水钢建设2号高炉，1978年2月，贵州省委和省革委（省政府）为加快水钢建设速度，组织了以建设2号高炉、2号焦炉和炼钢系统为重点的又一次大会战。省委书记、省革委主任马力和省革委副主任苏钢亲自到水钢主持召开有省革委有关部委和全省地、州（市）领导和参战单位代表参加的会战动员誓师大会。参加会战的施工单位除水钢4000多人的自营基建队伍外，十四冶、七冶、国家建设局、铁二局、贵州省建四公司等一万余人参加这次会战。历时一年，建成36孔的2号焦炉一座，1200立方米的2号高炉也于1979年1月1日建成投产，随即1号高炉停产。但是，有铁无钢的经营状态仍未改变，经济效益极差，亏损仍然存在。

成焦油系统；2号高炉的建设1971年破土动工后，连基础工程都未完工，次年就停建；1972年底，炼钢工程虽开工建设，由于资金、设备、建设力量无着落，停停打打，工程几无进展；轧钢工程只选了厂址，也未动工，整个水钢建设处于瘫痪状态。生产是单一生铁生产，配套建设徘徊长达8年之久。

1976年粉碎"四人帮"后，水钢恢复建设，冶金部决定在水钢建设2号高炉，1978年2月，贵州省委和省革委（省政府）为

After the 'Gang of Four' was overthrown in 1976, construction resumed at *Shuicheng*, and the Ministry of Metallurgical Industries decided to restart the construction of the no.2 Furnace and the *Guizhou* Provincial Party Committee and Revolutionary Committee (Provincial Government) assembled another construction team in February 1978 to build the no.2 Blast Furnace, no.2 Coke Furnace and the steelmaking system in order to hasten the completion of the *Shuicheng* Iron and Steel Works . *Ma Li*, Provincial Party Secretary and Director of the Revolutionary Committee, and *Su Gang*, Deputy Director of the Provincial Revolutionary Committee, travelled to *Shuicheng* in person to host a mobilization and kick-start ceremony attended by delegates from government ministries and participating work units from around the province. Aside from over four thousand workers from the *Shuicheng* Iron and Steel Works, nearly ten thousand workers from the Fourteenth Metallurgical Construction Corporation the Seventh Metallurgical Construction Corporation, the National Bureau of Construction, the No.2 Engineering Group Corporation of China Railways and the *Guizhou* No.4 Construction Company took part in the project. Within a year, they had completed construction of the thirty-six chambered Coke Furnace and the 1200 cubic metre no.2 Blast Furnace, which began operations on January 1st 1979. The no.1 Furnace was shuttered soon afterwards. However, the factory was still unable to produce steel and heavy losses were mounting.

The economic situation and the technical standards at *Shuicheng* improved markedly with the implementation of the expanding and renovating projects during the Seventh Five-Year Plan period (1986-1990) of China's national economic development initiatives. *Shuicheng* further completed its main complimentary facilities and the maintenance overhaul of its

加快水钢建设速度，组织了以建设2号高炉、2号焦炉和炼钢系统为重点的又一次大会战。省委书记、省革委主任马力和省革委副主任苏钢亲自到水钢主持召开有省革委有关部委和全省地、州（市）领导和参战单位代表参加的会战动员誓师大会。参加会战的施工单位除水钢4000多人的自营基建队伍外，十四冶、七冶、国家建设局、铁二局、贵州省建四公司等一万余人参加这次会战。历时一年，建成36孔的2号焦炉一座，1200立方米的2号高炉也于1979年1月1日建成投产，随即1号高炉停产。但是，有铁无钢的经营状态仍未改变，经济效益极差，亏损仍然存在。

"七五"的改建扩建，水钢经济效益及技术经济指标明显改善。"八五"期间，水钢着重完善改扩后的主体设备配套和大修。1991年竣工投产的项目有6000立方米制氧机组和炼钢2号连铸机、3号余热发电机组；1993年三焦回收工程、4号余热发电建成投入生产；1994年完成了3号和4号连铸机的设备安装；水泥年产达到15万吨以上。

"七五"的改扩建和"八五"的配套完善，具备了年产生铁

1981年，贵州省经委同意将遵义钢绳厂库存的一套复二重式线材轧机调入水钢，第二年12月，年产15万吨线材生产线建成投入生产。由于没有炼钢配套，经济效益不理想。1982年恢复了炼钢建设，苦干了两年，于1984年底，两座15吨顶吹转炉建成，进行模铸生产，从此，结束了贵州不产普钢的历史，冶金部部长李东冶和贵州省省长王朝文亲临水钢为炼钢剪彩。与此同时，1981年至1982年，水钢按照中共中央、国务院《关于国营企业进行全面整顿的决定》进行了以提高经济效益为目的的"五项工作"整顿，建立了党委领导下的厂长负责制和职工代表大会制的领导体制，企业管理上了一个新台阶。1983年盈利860万元，摘掉了长达13年的亏损帽子。水钢也初具规模，达到年产生铁90万吨，钢25万吨，材15万吨的综合生产能力。

infrastructure during the Eighth Five-Year Plan period (1991-1995). By 1991, those completed and operational systems included a 6000 cubic metre oxygen plant, the no. 2 casting machine and the no. 3 surplus heat power plant; the triple coke recycling system and the no.4 surplus heat power plant entered into operation in 1993; the no.3 and no.4 casting machines were installed in 1994; annual production of cement exceeded 150,000 tons.

The expansion and renovating work carried out during the Seventh Five-Year Plan and the completions and improvements during the Eighth Five-Year Plan increased *Shuicheng* Works' production capacity to 1 million tons of iron, 600,000 tons of steel and 550,000 tons of rolled steel. Products were sold as far away as Japan, Thailand, Korea, Malaysia, *Taiwan* and Hong Kong. By 1993, revenue reached 287 million *yuan* and profits exceeded 100 million *yuan*. Overall production levels reached a new height, and *Shuicheng* was listed as a tier 1 enterprise.

Throughout the various phases of *Shuicheng*'s operation, basic construction and extensive reforms, the *Shuicheng* Communist Party Committee has always placed the education of party spirit, party style and party discipline at the forefront and has combined these factors with practice to construct the party. Party membership among the workers expanded from 1260 members in 1966 to 8965 members by 2003. The intellectual level of the workers has continually risen and outstanding personnel have continued to come forward. Since 1983, *Shuicheng* has been honoured three times with the award of 'China Excellence Enterprise in Ideological and Political Work Among Workers' and five times with the award of '*Guizhou* Province Excellence Enterprise in Ideological and Political Work Among Workers'. Over 180 workers from *Shuicheng* have been designated local, provincial or national Model Workers. In 1989, the Labour

100万吨、钢60万吨、材55万吨的生产能力。产品远销日本、泰国、韩国、马来西亚以及台湾、香港等国家和地区,1993年利税总额达到28673万元,利润突破了1亿元大关。水钢综合生产能力上了新台阶,进入全国大型I档企业行列。

在水钢生产经营、基本建设和深化改革的各个时期,水钢党委始终坚持把党性、党风、党纪教育放在重要位置,结合实际开展党建工作,党员队伍不断壮大,从1966年的1260名发展到2003年底的8965名党员。职工思想素质逐步提高、大批先进人物不断涌现。从1983年期,水钢连续三届荣获"中国职工思想政治工作优秀企业"称号;连续五届获得贵州省"职工思想政治工作优秀企业"称号。180多人次评为全国、省、市和水钢的劳动模范。1989年,水钢工会获得省总工会"全心全意依靠工人阶级办企业"的荣誉。

持续发展(1997—)

1997年2月13日,应贵州省邀请,一直由19人组成的冶金部调研组、邯钢咨询组抵达水钢,针对水钢严重亏损问题进行全面调研。调研指出:观念落后、管理混乱、经营水平低下、负债率高、士气低落等是水钢的主要症结。

2月22日,在部、省联合召开的学邯钢扭亏增效动员大会上,省委组织部宣布水钢班子调整决定,任命调研组成员、时任鞍钢总经理助理的朱继民为水钢经理。水钢从此打响了扭亏攻坚战。

"2·22"大会后,水钢大张旗鼓地掀起了"解放思想,转变观念"大讨论,切实开展"学邯钢"活动。3月13日,水钢从邯钢请来5名管理者,到炼钢厂担任厂长等实职,移植"邯钢经验"。这使得炼钢生产很快取得突破,主要技术经济指标明显改善。1997年12月4日,炼钢厂实现全连铸。当年取得过去"三(年)打五十万(吨)"未果的标志性突破,产钢56.2万吨。成为水钢扭亏增效的排头兵。水钢因此开展了"远学邯钢,近学炼钢"的"双学"活动。

1997年7月,冶金部将《关于水钢三家扭亏大户减亏工作情

Union of the *Shuicheng* Works was awarded the honorary title of 'An Enterprise Fully Dedicated to the Working Class' by the Provincial Federation of Trade Unions.

Continuing Development (1997 onwards)

On February 13th 1997, on the invitation of the *Guizhou* Provincial Government, a team of researchers from the Ministry of Metallurgical Industries and consultants from *Hebei* Steel arrived in *Shuicheng* to investigate the cause of the serious losses then being incurred. They concluded that the main causes of the losses were backward concepts, chaotic management, poor operations, high levels of debt and low morale.

On February 22nd, during a conference on reducing losses and increasing productivity convened by the Ministry and Provincial Government, the Provincial Party Committee Organization Department announced there would be management changes at *Shuicheng*, with research team member and *Angang* Steel executive assistant *Zhu Jimin* being appointed as the new director of *Shuicheng*. From this point, the *Shuicheng* Works began to move forward.

Following the February 22nd conference, a major discussion began at the *Shuicheng* Works about 'liberating thought and transforming conceptions', which marked the beginning of the 'learn from *Hebei* Steel' campaign. On March 13th, the *Shuicheng* Works invited 5 managers from *Hebei* Steel to take positions of authority within the steel works and transplant their experiences from *Hebei*. These appointments resulted in rapid breakthroughs in steel production and marked improvements in technical and economic indicators. On December 4th 1997, the steel foundry accomplished a continuous casting. In the same year the factory accomplished the previously unreachable goal of '500,000 tons within three years' with the production of 562,000 tons of steel.

况的汇报》上报中央有关领导同志, 时任国务院总理李鹏和副总理朱镕基分别作了批示, 水钢人深受鼓舞。根据李鹏总理的批示, 水钢提出了"三年扭亏, 两年实现"的目标。1998年10月, 在二号高炉炉底温度急剧升高被迫停产抢修 (历时81天) 的情况下, 水钢提前实现扭亏为盈。

水钢成为全国国有企业扭亏为盈十家典型之一, 被媒体广泛宣传报道, 塑造了水钢新形象。

在水钢扭亏攻坚的两年中, 除了加强企业管理、治理"跑、冒、滴、漏"等外, 更加注重科技进步, 大大小小实施了300多项技术改造项目, 取得了较好效益。其中, 1997年10月27日进行"一火成才"改造, 经过75天竣工投产, 仅半年就收回投资2540万元。1999年11月28日, 因"一火成才"而"失业"的原初轧厂成功改造成为高速线材生产厂。

1997年12月18日, 省政府授牌成立"水城钢铁 (集团) 有限责任公司", 这是水钢由传统工厂制企业向现代公司制企业转变的标志。此间, 水钢"精干主体、分离辅助、减员增效"的企业改革工作也取得突破性进展。

1999年11月18日, 炼钢年产达到100万吨, 水钢跻身百万吨级冶金企业行列。

在水钢"求生存"、"求发展"的过程中, 始终注重了党的建设、精神文明建设、企业文化建设。1997年"2.22"大会以后的五年间, 进行了五次思想解放大讨论, 公司党委每年明确思想教育主体, 水钢人不断在解放思想中提高认识, 统一思想, 并在实践中形成了工作理念。2001年, 水钢党委荣获"全国基层先进党组织"荣誉称号。

1997年5月, 大河山泉引水工程投资省, 工期短, 效益高, 当时的"看准的事快定, 定了的事快干, 干就干好"的工作理念以上升为水钢工作作风。"大河精神"几乎家喻户晓, 成为水钢企业文化中宝贵的精神财富。"大河精神"之后催生了一系列基层文化理念, 由此形成了新时期"自强、开放、创新、追求"的水钢精神。水钢各单位企业文化建设蔚然成风。

随着改革的不断深入, 水钢的建设规模和计划经济管理

This placed the foundry at the forefront of *Shuicheng*'s efforts to reduce losses and increase productivity. This achievement began a campaign to 'learn from *Hebei* Steel from afar, learn from the Steel Foundry from up close'.

In July 1997, the Ministry of Metallurgical Industries sent the 'Report on the Situation of Work to Reduce Losses at *Shuicheng*' to the relevant high-level authorities. State Council Premier *Li Peng* and Vice Premier *Zhu Rongji* both wrote instructions on the report, giving encouragement to the people at *Shuicheng*. According to Premier *Li Peng*'s notes, *Shuicheng* was able to 'accomplish the goal of a three year loss-elimination in two years'. Even though the no.2 Furnace was shut down for eighty-one days as the result of a sudden jump in temperatures, *Shuicheng* was able to eliminate losses ahead of schedule.

Shuicheng became one of ten models of state enterprise, moving from loss to profitability which was widely reported in the media, changing perceptions of *Shuicheng*'s image.

During the two years of *Shuicheng*'s efforts towards profitability, apart from improving management techniques and reducing longstanding problems, efforts focused on technological process. Over 300 technological adjustment projects were enacted with positive results. Among them, a 'rapid result' project that began on October 27th 1997 was entered into production after 75 days bringing a return of 25.4 million *yuan* investment within six months. On November 28th 1999, the rolled steel factory that had been rendered obsolete by this project was successfully transformed into a high-speed wire rod mill.

On December 18th 1997, the provincial government officially established the '*Shuicheng* Iron and Steel (Group) LLC'', a mark of *Shuicheng*'s transformation from a traditional factory to a modern corporation. At this time, *Shuicheng* made breakthroughs on the reform of central functionality, the splitting off supporting

在水钢生产经营、基本建设和深化改革的各个时期，水钢党委始终坚持把党性、党风、党纪教育放在重要位置，结合实际开展党建工作，党员队伍不断壮大，从1966年的1260名发展到2003年底的8965名党员。职工思想素质逐步提高、大批先进人物不断涌现。从1983年起，水钢连续三届荣获"中国职工思想政治工作优秀企业"称号；连续五届获得贵州省"职工思想政治工作优秀企业"称号。180多人次评为全国、省、市和水钢的劳动模范。1989年，水钢工会获得省总工会"全心全意依靠工人阶级办企业"的荣誉。

模式越来越不适应市场经济和贵州经济发展的需要，水钢人在"七五"、"八五"期间，发扬"自力更生、艰苦奋斗"精神，进行了较大规模的改建和扩建。四万多名职工生产、基建一肩挑，经过几年的努力，一批配套建设项目建成，经济效益也逐步提高。

1987年，水钢为解决轧钢钢胚外购和外加工问题，发动职工自愿集资260多万元，用1年时间建成650mm初轧项目，获得

functions and downsizing to increase efficiency.

On November 18th 1999, annual steel production reached 1 million tons, and *Shuicheng* entered the ranks of million ton production metallurgical enterprises.

During the process of *Shuicheng*'s pursuit of survival and development, the Works consistently focused on strengthening the party, strengthening cultural and ideological progress and strengthening corporate culture. During the five years since the meeting of February 22nd 1997, there were five major discussions regarding the liberation of thought. Each year the company party committee would determine the theme of ideological education and would constantly increase awareness of liberation thought, unifying thought and forming concepts for work through practice. In 2001, The *Shuicheng* Works' Party Committee was awarded the honour of 'National Grass-Roots Level Advanced Party Organization'.

In May 1997, the *Dahe* Mountain Spring Water Diversion Project was enacted with low investment levels, a short project period and a desire for high levels of effectiveness. The motto 'quick decisions, quick actions and good execution' was elevated to the level of a work ethic for *Shuicheng*. The 'spirit of *Dahe*' was known throughout *Shuicheng*, becoming an important treasure for the spiritual culture of *Shuicheng*. The 'spirit of Dahe' acted as a catalyst for many cultural concepts from the ground up, creating a new spirit of 'self-reliance, openness, innovation and the pursuit of goals' at *Shuicheng*. Each unit at *Shuicheng* accepted the establishment of a corporate culture as common practice.

As national economic reforms deepened, it grew increasingly apparent that the scale and command economy management model at *Shuicheng* was ill-suited to the needs of a market economy and *Guizhou*'s development. During the Seventh Five-Year Plan and the Eighth Five-Year Plan periods, the

水钢在"七五"、"八五"期间，水城铁厂合并到水钢，兼并了六盘水、安顺、贵阳等地的八个企业。这时，水钢的资产总额达到33.63亿元。

在市场经济的大潮中，由于思想观念的局限和客观环境的制约，水钢不适应市场竞争的要求，1995年出现亏损9494万元，1996年亏损达到20929万元。严重的亏损，生产经营举步维艰，企业濒临破产边缘。

了较好经济效益；为改变钢材品种单一、产量低的状况，1986年底，从联邦德国引进一套320mm双线连续式小型材轧机，历时3年建成，于1990年12月投产，为提高水钢经济效益发挥了重要作用。1988年以后，又陆续建设3号50孔大容积焦炉，年产焦炭50万吨；1号高炉改造性大修，扩容为633立方米，并于1989年底恢复生产；3号烧结机、11万伏总降压变电站以及年产9万吨的水泥厂一座都投入生产。"七五"的改扩建，使水钢形成了年产生铁90万吨、钢60万吨、材55万吨的综合生产能力。

2004年4月13日，水钢与信达、华融、长城三家资产管理公司签署债转股协议，划转总额14.5亿元，水钢资产负债率由90%降至56%。

从2001年开始，连续四年进行了填平补齐式的技术改造和

people at *Shuicheng* spread the spirit of 'self-reliance and arduous struggle', implementing large-scale construction, expansion and renovation. Over 40,000 workers worked for production and construction projects which, after several years of tireless effort, created a full set of complimentary facilities, greatly increasing economic productivity.

In 1987, in order to resolve difficulties in the procurement of and inability to process rolled steel embryos, *Shuicheng* solicited voluntary investments from its workers totalling 2.6 million *yuan* and completed a first-stage rolled steel project which brought impressive economic results. To address the monotony of steel products and low production levels, *Shuicheng* imported a 320mm double-bed rolled steel mill from Germany which took three years to complete and entered production in December 1990. The new mill was instrumental in raising the level of economic efficiency. After 1988, *Shuicheng* constructed the 50 chamber no.3 Furnace; expanding the no.1 Furnace to 633 cubic metres, which resumed production in 1989; the no.3 Sinter, an 110,000 volt step-down power substation and a cement factory with an annual production capacity of 900,000 tons. By the end of the Seventh Five-Year Plan's renovations, *Shuicheng* was producing at an annual rate of 900,000 tons of steel, 600,000 tons of iron and 550,000 tons of rolled steel.

On April 13th 2004, *Shuicheng* entered into a debt-to-equity swap agreement with the *Xinda*, *Huarong* and Great Wall asset management companies, exchanging a total of 1.45 billion *yuan*. *Shuicheng*'s asset-liability ratio has dropped from 90% to 56%.

Beginning in 2001, *Shuicheng* engaged in four years of technological modifications and supplementary facilities construction projects: 2001 was mainly focused on the 'three projects of technical modification'; in 2002, a 30,000 cubic metre gas converter cabinet was completed; in 2003, the no.4 Coke Furnace and a 150,000 cubic metre gas converter cabinet were completed along with a ladle furnace; on May 1st 2004, the *Bijia Shan* rail tunnel was completed; the no.3 Furnace, the construction of which had begun in 2003, entered production in September 2004.

In order to improve the all-round abilities of the staff and to become a 'studious enterprise', *Shuicheng* began a 'study class credit system' in 2002.

In 2003, *Shuicheng* produced 1.46 million tons of iron, 1.73 million tons of steel and 1.66 million tons of rolled steel, once again achieving more than 100 million *yuan* in profits.

配套建设：2001年主要完成了"三项技改"；2002年完成了3万立方米转炉煤气柜建设；2003年完成了4号焦炉建设、15万立方米高炉煤气柜建设、炼钢LF精炼炉工程；2004年5月1日，笔架山铁路隧道建成通车；2003年春节开工建设的3号高炉于2004年9月竣工投产。

2002年开始推行"学时学分制"，努力构建"学习型企业"，以提高员工素质。

2003年，水钢产铁146万吨、钢173万吨、钢材166万吨，利润再次突破亿元大关。

The preliminary period in the
construction of the *Shuicheng*
Iron and Steel Works
建厂时期之一

The preliminary period in the construction of the *Shuicheng* Iron and Steel Works
建厂时期之二

班前学习毛主席语录

会战职工召开动员会

The preliminary period in the
construction of the *Shuicheng*
Iron and Steel Works
建厂时期之三

The no. 1 Blast Furnace
第一座高炉

Celebrating the start of
production of the no.2 Blast
Furnace at the *Shuicheng* Iron
and Steel Works
水钢二高炉开炉庆祝大会

The gathering to recognise the
first successful output of iron
from the no.1 Blast Furnace, the
Shuicheng Iron and Steel Works
水钢第一座高炉胜利出铁大会

A view of the celebrations for
the entry into production of
the mine
矿山投产庆祝场面

In both July 1985 and January 1987, *Hu Jintao*, then General Secretary of the Communist Party of *Guizhou* Province, inspected the *Shuicheng* Iron and Steel Works.
1985年7月和1987年1月，时任贵州省委书记胡锦涛先后两次到水钢视察。

Important instructions from *Li Peng* and *Zhu Rongji* regarding the elimination of losses by the *Shuicheng* Iron and Steel Works, 1997.
1997年，李鹏、朱镕基对水钢解困工作的重要批示。

中华人民共和国冶金工业部

关于水钢等三家亏损大户
减亏工作情况的汇报

　　今年以来，冶金部对几家亏损大户采取了全方位综合治理措施，取得了初步成效，现将情况报告如下：

　　1996年国有大中型钢铁企业中帐面亏损额在1亿元以上的有6家，即天津冶金控股公司、水城钢铁公司、宣化钢铁公司、舞阳钢铁公司、新余钢铁公司、抚顺钢铁公司。对这些亏损企业，前两年冶金部也同有关省市做了不少工作，诸如派出调查组在摸清亏损情况的的基础上，调整企业领导班子，提出深化企业内部改革及强化管理等方面的建议，帮助解决电力供应等外部条件，还对直属企业签订了减亏责任书。因此，在上游产品涨价、钢材售价下降、减利因素增加的情况下，这些企业多数亏损额有了下降，但绝对额仍然

— 1 —

中华人民共和国冶金工业部

关于水钢等三家亏损大户
减亏工作情况的汇报

　　今年以来，冶金部对几家亏损大户采取了全方位综合治理措施，取得了初步成效，现将情况报告如下：

　　1996年国有大中型钢铁企业中帐面亏损额在1亿元以上的有6家，即天津冶金控股公司、水城钢铁公司、宣化钢铁公司、舞阳钢铁公司、新余钢铁公司、抚顺钢铁公司。对这些亏损企业，前两年冶金部也同有关省市做了不少工作，诸如派出调查组在摸清亏损情况的基础上，调整企业领导班子，提出深化企业内部改革及强化管理等方面的建议，帮助解决电力供应等外部条件，还对直属企业签订了减亏责任书。因此，在上游产品涨价、钢材售价下降、减利因素增加的情况下，这些企业多数亏损额有了下降，但绝对额仍然

－ 1 －

431

A view of the completed Steel
Works, the *Shuicheng* Iron and
Steel Works
新炼钢厂落成的水钢场景

The *Shuicheng* Iron & Steel Works and State Legacy

Based on an interview with *Zeng Li in Beijing*
on 4th July 2007

"水城钢铁厂"与"国家遗产"

时间: 2007年7月4日
地点: 北京
采访对象: 曾力

I have not counted them but I must have taken about 300 photographs of the *Shuicheng* Iron and Steel Works. I went there three times to take these photographs during 2004, 2005 and 2006.

My original plan was to record, through pictures, the history of Chinese industrial development. I started with some factories in *Beijing* and in *Guangxi* that were being dismantled. Later my interest moved on to the *Guiyang* Works and then to the *Shuicheng* Iron and Steel Works. As the *Shuicheng* Works is still relatively intact, it retains the characteristics of a 'third-line enterprise' of that period.

There were over 100,000 people employed at the *Shuicheng* Works. Many of the national leaders, *Hu Jintao, Jiang Zemin* and *Wu Bangguo* for example, paid visits to the Works.

Shuicheng in *Guizhou* is a truly representative steelworks. It is perhaps not exceptionally large by national standards, but it is regarded as being typical of third-line enterprises.

The blast furnaces from the early period of the building of the factory still exist, with few changes to the layout. They represent the epitome of a corporation from third-line projects that progressed until today. In fact, I was taking photographs of a city where the steel works is its core. *Shuicheng* Works is virtually a small city. It has just such an extraordinary form. Nowadays I mainly photograph inside the works, perhaps supplementing that by photographing the residential area, the hospitals and schools.

In the process of China's early industrial development, factories could easily develop into cities, as did *Daqing* in the northeast and *Panzhihua* in *Sichuan*. One can see from the catalogue 'Commemorating the 40th Anniversary of the construction of the *Shuicheng* Iron

问：从量化来讲，您拍了多少张"水钢"的照片？
曾：我还没有统计。大概三百多张。

问：您是什么时候去那里进行拍摄的？
曾：2004年。

问：去拍过几次？
曾：拍了3次吧。2004年、2005年和2006年都去了。

问：是什么促使您去拍摄"水钢"的？
曾：我想通过影像来记录中国工业发展的一些历史。开始是拍了北京和广西一些正在拆除的工厂，后来才拍贵阳的钢铁厂和水城钢铁厂，因为"水钢"比较完整，还保留了当时三线企业的特点，就作为重点来拍摄。

and Steel Works': Melodic Years (1996-2006), that the *Shuicheng* Works was entirely dug out from the mountainside, several factory-districts occupied a couple of hills and the elevated conveyor belts and pipelines wound and coiled around the hills like dragons. The idea of building the works in the mountains was to shelter it, a strategy of military preparations, which aimed to establish a complete military industry in the interior of China. The plan, from the cold war period was to build factories on a massive scale in the southwest. China's development of industry in this south-western area all relates to this historical factor. But for the Cold War and the national strategy of preparation for war, China would not have chosen such a place to establish a large-scale factory, nor to have constructed this type of factory in such a mountainous area.

China has a long history and tradition of being an agricultural country, only in the 20th century did it start its historic development of industry. Since the 1980s, with the transformation of the national economy, many long established factories have faced reform and demolition. I want to make a record of this process through photography, to photograph these factories one by one, because nobody has yet established a systematic archive of them. I started to photograph industrial sites around 2002.

At the beginning of this project I had only taken photographs of a few factories. As you will see the *Shuicheng* Iron and Steel Works incorporated many subsidiary factories. It was actually a group corporation. In the main plant there were also many subsidiary sections. From the input of iron ore to the output of steel products, there was a chain of steps. I want to record the whole process. I have not yet photographed the Steel Works, just the Smelting

问：他们的工厂规模很大吗？
曾：那里有十几万人。国家领导人胡锦涛、江泽民、吴邦国等人都去过。

问：那意味着"水钢"是非常重要的钢铁厂？
曾：在工业不发达的贵州省它是一个有代表性的钢铁企业。如果从全国来说应该不算大，但是在三线企业里边，它比较典型。

问：您觉得它具体保留了哪些特征？
曾：它还保留了那些建厂初期时的高炉，格局也没有太大的变化，是一个三线企业发展到今天的缩影。实际上我计划拍摄的是以这个钢铁厂为核心的城市。水城钢铁厂厂区就像一个小城市，我现在主要拍的是厂内，可能附带拍摄厂外的住宅区、医院、学校等周边环境。在新中国工业发展的过程当中，一个工厂往往会发展成一个城市，像东北的大庆，四川的攀枝花都是这样。从《纪念水钢建厂40周年：岁月如歌（1996-2006）》那本画册中可以看到，这个厂完全是从山区开凿出来的，几个厂区安置在几座山之间，高架起来的传送带和管道，就像盘龙一样缠绕在山间。当时把厂建在山里，

Works, the Materials' Mill, the Coking Plant and the Sintering Plant. I would like to conclude the whole project with a publication.

I still need to find the original blueprints used in the construction of the *Shuicheng* Iron and Steel Works. The Work's management seem to have given little attention to these matters. I feel that is a pity. What was the earliest state of the *Shuicheng* Works? How was it gradually developed? The Works must have passed through many complicated stages. My work is getting increasingly complicated too. I am trying to describe this iron and steel works through the medium of photography, to provide a pictorial record of it.

The *Shuicheng* Works was an enterprise built by the Chinese themselves. The building of the *Anshan* Iron and Steel Works received assistance from experts from the Soviet Union, while the *Shuicheng* Works were totally independent of help. There was no foreign aid, people relied on 'self-reliance and working hard for prosperity'. The *Shuicheng* Works was built out of sheer, barren mountains at the end of the 1960s. It is a typical example of a construction built in the spirit of the Chinese fable 'the foolish old man who removed mountains' *yu gong yi shan*. It fits well within the theme of the 'State Legacy' project, because the *Shuicheng* Works is a part of the historical legacy of the state.

I was born in early 1960s. From an early age, we were heavily indoctrinated in seeing all things as being within the needs of the ideology of the state. Like the majority of people, I did not have the ability to make independent observations and thoughts. Not until later did I begin to understand. If one had no personal view of the particular place one lived in, nor in the history of the nation of which one was a citizen, one could not visualise one's own

完全是为了隐蔽, 可以看出当时完全是一种备战的思想。在腹地里边修建整个军工的体系, 这就是冷战时期在西南建设大规模工厂的计划。中国西部工业的发展都跟这些历史因素有关系, 如果当时不是因为冷战和国家的战备策略, 中国就不会选择在那种地方进行大规模工厂的建设, 也不会产生这种盘踞于山间的工厂形态。

问: 您是什么时候开始有这样的拍摄想法, 并付诸实践的?
曾: 中国原来是一个历史很悠久很传统的农业国家, 在20世纪开始了工业化的历史进程, 到了80年代以后, 随着国家经济的变革, 大量具有一定历史的工厂都面临着改造、迁移和拆除, 我就想通过影像把这个过程记录下来, 一个工厂一个工厂地拍。现在还没有人比较系统地去做这样的记录。大概在2002年, 我开始拍工业照片。

问: 您计划系统地拍下"水钢"的所有场景吗?
曾: 是这样的, 我现在只是拍下几个分厂, "水钢"是由很多厂组成的, 它实际上就是集团公司。大厂里边也分很多小厂, 从矿石运进去再变成钢制品出来, 分很多环节, 我是想按照工业的程序把整个

situation nor have an understanding of one's own life. I want to rethink the state and the society that I live in. Taking photographs is like opening a different eye, in fact it is another way of seeing.

For many years, most of the photographs the public saw were propaganda products and a tool of state ideology. They were false and glossed-over. Even today, propaganda photographs present situations far removed from truth and reality.

What is our real situation today? We are in need of an archive of images reflecting a true record. I would like to see my photographic work as non-fiction documentation.

'State' is a broad concept. Actually one cannot see clearly what a 'state' is. One can really only see one place at a time, like the *Shuicheng* Works. I have been photographing it for years, but I cannot say that I see it clearly. I may just have seen some views of it, not yet penetrating enough to reveal the intricacy within. And the *Shuicheng* Works is just one among so many steel works. On the map of the state it is only a tiny dot. In a broad sense you cannot see clearly what a 'state' is. You can only see a few dots. Following getting to know the place better while taking the photographs, I may be able to connect some of these dots together to acquire a veneer or clue. After bringing all the photos I have taken together, I may be able to provide some clues towards re-recognizing the state we live in. If so, the story line of my work will have fulfilled its purpose.

过程拍下来。我现在还没拍到炼钢厂，只是拍到了炼铁厂、料厂、焦化厂、烧结厂，现在编的画册也是按照这样的程序。最后成为一个作品也是通过出版的方式来完成，史建先生的研究跟我的拍摄也是同步的。

问：您的拍摄可以变成一个研究项目了。
曾：对。我现在还需要找到"水钢"最原始的规划设计图，但是他们自己本身也没有人重视这些东西，所以我觉得很可惜。"水钢"最早的形态是什么？怎样慢慢发展起来？后来又是什么样的情况？都经过了非常复杂的变化过程，所以我的工作也是越做越复杂。我现在做的事情，就是用摄影的形式来重新描述"水钢"，提供一个影像文本。

问：为什么选择"水钢"这件作品参加"国家遗产"展？
曾："水钢"是中国人自己建造出来的企业。如果说"鞍钢"，它是有苏联援建的背景，"水钢"则是在上世纪60年代末期，在没有任何外援的情况下，完全依靠"自力更生，奋发图强"，从一片荒山中开凿建造出来的，是当时"愚公移山"建设中国的典型例子。"水钢"和"国家遗产"的主题很贴切，因为"水钢"就是国家的历史遗产。

问：您是从什么时候产生这种纪实摄影的想法的？

曾：我是60年代初出生的，从小所看到的东西都是在一种国家意识形态的需要下灌输的，和大多数人一样，从来没有独立的观察和思考问题的能力，后来才慢慢地开始醒悟，如果没有用自己独立的眼光来观看自己所生活的地方和国家的历史，你就不可能对自己的处境有清醒的认识，就不可能对自己生存的处境有深刻的理解，我的想法就是重新来观看自己所生活的国家和社会。拍摄等于是睁开了另外一只眼睛，摄影从本质上讲就是一种观看方式。

问：20世纪80年代，中国人看国外的摄影师拍摄中国的场景，有很多人不能接受那样的图像或者影像，因为他们看到的是一些赤裸裸的呈现现实的景象，可能超出了他们所期望的或者平常被灌输的一些图景。

曾：差别可能就在这里。这么多年来，由于国家意识形态工具的影响，造成了大众看到的大量照片都是一些宣传品，是虚假粉饰的东西。现在也是这样，我们所有用于宣传的照片所呈现的，都和真实的现实相去甚远。

我们今天真实的场景是什么样子？我们应该有一个记录真实的影像文库，所以我把自己的摄影作品看作是一种纪实的文献。

问：您很关注国家的历史和现实，您是怎么认识和理解"国家"这个概念的？

曾："国家"这个概念很大，实际上我们看不清国家到底是怎么回事，可能只能看到一个地方，比如说"水钢"，我拍了很多年，但是我都不能说我就看清楚了"水钢"，可能我只看到了一些场景，还没深入到里面，如果向里再深入拍摄的话就更加复杂，而"水钢"也还只是一个工厂，在国家的地图上它只是很小很小的一个点。所以从广泛的意义上看，你是看不清楚"国家"是怎样的，你只能看到几个点，可能随着深入的拍摄，这几个点就连成了一条线索。也许，我拍摄的照片累积起来，可以提供重新认识我们所生活的这个国家的一条线索。

问：您的记录方式也会让人联想到工厂与国家的意识形态有某种关系，观者可能会去考虑这些问题。

曾：如果这样的话，我的作品作为一种认知的线索，就起到了作用。

Part III

第三部分

Visual
Political
Myth

视觉政治神话

Face of Authority: *Mao*'s Portrait on *Tiananmen**

Wu Hung

* An edited version.

权力的面容: 天安门毛主席像

巫鸿

As in other languages, the Chinese word for 'face,' or *mian*, has as its root definition the front side of the human head. From here the word has acquired additional meanings along three directions.[1] First, still referring to the human face, it can also mean 'likeness'. A 'face' is therefore not necessarily a real one, but can be a manufactured image – a portrait which, in Richard Brilliant's words, registers a person's 'physiognomic likeness.'[2] When such an artificial image is positioned and conceived as 'the front side of the head,' it becomes a mask – a painted or sculptured face that is 'worn' by a person to enhance or alter his or her appearance. Used in this way, a *mian* is a representation as well as a means of performance and disguise. A similar relationship can be found between a face – image and anything that bears this face image – even if it is not a human subject. The appearance of the bearer is altered and its meaning changed, as it now has the potential of being conceived as a surrogate body.

This then leads to the second meaning of *mian*: extending to non-figural forms, this word is employed to describe architecture and objects. Most frequently it refers to a single plane of a three-dimensional form, usually its front, that serves a specific function and displays a unique design. A *mian* can be the elevated facade of a building or the flat cover of a book; the image and inscription it displays signify the particular nature and content of its *body*

[1] See definitions and examples given in *Luo Zhufeng*, et al., *Zhongwen dacidian* (A comprehensive dictionary of Chinese), 12 vols. (*Beijing: Hanyu Dacidian chubanshe*, 1993), vol. 12, pp. 378-79.

[2] Richard Brilliant, Portraiture (London: Reaktion Books).

如同其他语言一样，中文的"脸"或"面"的最基本定义是人头的正面。在此基础上，这个词又获得了其他三方面的附加含义。[1]第一，还是和人的面部相关，它可以意味着一个"再现"：一张再现的"脸"未必是真实的，而可能是一个人造的图像，或称为肖像。用 Richard Brilliant 的话来说，就是"面相的相似"。[2]当这样一个人造形象被叠加在一个人的头部之前，它就成为了一张"面具"：即一张画出来或雕刻出来的脸，被人戴上以强化或改变他的外表。当被赋予这种用途时，"面"既是再现，也是表演或伪装的一种手段。相似的关系可以在面的图像和任何承载这个图像的东西之间看到——即使这个面的图像所表现的并非人像。当承载者的外表改变，它本身的意义也会改变，因为它现在已经具有作为"身体"代替物的潜在意义。

这就引出了"面"的第二个用法：它所指涉的对象延伸为非人类形式，被用来形容建筑和物体。最常见的用法是指三维空间中具有特殊功能和独特设计的一个平面。"面"因此可以指一个建筑物的正面或一本书籍的封面；它所展示的图像和题字表达了作为这个特定建筑或书籍的主体或身体

[1] 见罗竹风等编：《中文大词典》，第12卷 （北京，汉语大词典出版社，1993），第378-379页。

[2] Richard Brilliant ：《肖像》，（伦敦：Reaktion Books, 2004）。

– the building or book itself. According to Roman Jakobson's well-known linguistic study, therefore, this representational 'face' is a metonymic device in generating meaning: while it remains an integral part of the body, its special shape and design separate it from the body and enable it to represent or substitute for the body[3]. But in some cases, an architectural front may become a free-standing structure due to historical changes or a deliberate design. While its specific form and decoration still associate it with the notion of a 'face,' it is a bodiless face with an enlarged symbolism. One such example is the famous St. Paul's Cathedral in Macao, whose surviving facade now stands alone to symbolize the city and its colonial past. Another example is a typical 'shop front' (*dian mian*) in traditional Chinese architecture. Designed as an ornate archway with a row of protruding poles, it was also erected independently in front of an entire commercial district.[4] Using Jakobson's formula again, we can say that the role of such a 'bodiless' facade has shifted from metonymic to metaphoric: without an attached body its meaning no longer depends on the principles of contiguity and alignment, but is based on similarity and substitution. A free-standing 'front' can thus have a large architectural complex, a city, or a country as its 'metaphorical body.'

[3] Roman Jakobson, 'Two Aspects of Language and Two Types of Aphasic Disturbances', in R. Jakobson and M. Hale, Fundamentals of Language (The Hague, 1956), pp. 109-14. Also see, P. Friedrich, 'Polutropy', in J. W. Fernandes, ed, Beyond Metaphor: The Theory of Tropes in Anthropology (Stanford, 1991), pp. 17-55(44).
[4] *Yang Rong, Chongzao youzhe guoqu jiyi de xinjianzhu* (Creating new architecture with memories of the past), *Jianzhushi* (Architect) 78 (October 1997), pp. 39-45(43). The first architectural historian who studied the 'shop front' seriously is *Liang Sicheng*. The examples he collected in the 1930s are published in his *Zhongguo jianzhu yishu tuji* (Visual materials of the art of Chinese architecture), 2 vols. (*Tianjin: Baihua wenyi chubanshe*, 1999), vol. 1, pp. 97-146.

的特定内容与属性。如罗曼·雅各布森 (Roman Jakobson) 在他的著名的语言学研究里所说的，这张具有代表性的"面"或"脸"是意义生产的一个转喻装备：当它作为身体不可或缺的一个部分的时候，它特殊的形状和设计同时使它与身体分离。[3]但是在某些情况下，一个建筑物的正面可能会因为历史的变迁或由于精心的设计，而成为一个独立自足的结构，或者可以说是一个没有身体的脸。这类的例子有著名的澳门大三巴教堂遗址，它幸存下来的"正面"仍具有丰富的意义，象征了这个城市和它的殖民历史。另一个例子是中国传统建筑中的"店面"：在商店门口建构起来的，装饰着一排排高耸立柱的一副华丽外表，与商店内部的空间并没有直接联系。[4]再次使用雅各布森提出的语言学原理，我们可以说这样的一个无身体的面已经从"转喻"变成了"隐喻"：不再具有身体，它的意义也就不再依赖于"相邻"和"排列"的原则，而是基于"相似"和"替代"。 这样一个独立的"面"因而可以

[3] 罗曼·雅各布森 (Roman Jakobson)："语言的两个方面和失语症干扰的两种形式"。罗曼·雅各布森，M. Hale 合著：《语言基础》(The Hague, 1956)，第109-114页。又见P. Friedrich：《隐喻之上：人类学中的修辞理论》(J. W. Fernandes编，斯坦福，1991)，第17-55页。
[4] 杨容（音译）：《重造有着过去记忆的新建筑》，《建筑师》第78期 (1997年10月)，第39-45页。第一位正式研究"门面"的建筑学史家是梁思成，他在30年代收集的案例发表在他的《中国建筑艺术图集》（上下两卷）（天津：百花文艺出版社，1999）卷二，第97-146页。

Third, used as a transitive verb, *mian* no longer pertains to a self-contained feature of a human or architectural form, but instead signifies a position or context. Typically the verb helps construct two kinds of statements. The first kind, in which a person or building 'faces' a particular direction, defines the orientation of the person or the building in an implicit spatial system; the significance of the orientation is embedded in the symbolism of this spatial system in a given culture, religion, or cosmology. The second kind of statement, in which a person or building 'faces' another person or building (or a group of people and buildings), specifies the juxtaposition or encounter of the two parties involved. Both statements were used by ancient Chinese philosophers to define rulership and the relationship between the ruler and the ruled. The phrase 'facing south to rule' (*nan mian er zhi*) refers to the formal position of an emperor, as well as the throne and the throne hall and implies the propriety of his governance. In other examples, an emperor is described as facing his subjects in the south, so that 'all people are in harmony and the whole world is at peace.'[5]

These three implications of *mian* – namely, a 'face' as a portrait or mask, as an architectural façade, and as a signifier of spatial systems and relationships – enable us to understand the most illustrious 'face' in the People's Republic of China. This is the giant portrait of *Mao Zedong* hanging on the front wall of *Tiananmen* (the Gate of Heavenly Peace)

---

[5] *Zhou li* (Rite of *Zhou*), *Xiaguan*. See *Ruan Yuan,* comp. *Shisanjing zhushu* (Annotated Thirteen Classics), 2 vols. (*Beijing: Zhonghua shuju,* 1980), vol. 1, p. 865. A similar expression is also found in *Yi jing* (The book of changes), '*Shuo gua*', ibid., vol. 1, p. 94.

将一个巨大的建筑复合体、一座城市,甚至一个国家作为它的"隐喻的身体"。

第三,作为动词使用,"面"不再指人类或建筑的物质形态,而是指示着主体的位置或上下文。动词的"面"在语言表述中帮助建构两种称述方式。第一种指一个人或一个建筑物"面向"某个特定方向,因此在一个内在的空间结构中定义了这个人或这个建筑物的身份(这是由于方位的意义根植于既定的文化、宗教甚至宇宙观中的象征性空间秩序中)。第二种称述方式是一个人或一个建筑物"面对"着另一个人或建筑物(或一群人或一群建筑物),因而确定了双方之间的关系。这两种称述方式都被中国古代哲学家用来定义统治者的地位以及与被统治者之间的关系。"南面而治"的说法确定了帝王在正式场合中的位置(王座和宫廷的位置也是如此),从而证明了他的统治权利和规范性。在其它例子中,一位帝王被描述为"南向而立",面对着"北向臣服"的臣民,这种空间秩序的结果是上下和睦,天下太平"。[5]

这三种关于"面"的含义,即(1)作为肖像或面具的脸,(2)作为建筑物的正面,(3)作为空间秩序与社会关系的能指,有助于我们理解中华人民共和国最著名的一张"面容",即挂在天安门上的

---

[5]《周礼·夏官》,见阮元:《十三经注疏》,两卷本(北京:中华书局,1980),卷一,第865页。相同的表述在《易经》中也可见,见"说卦",同上书,卷一,第94页。

or, more correctly, the combination of the portrait and the gate. One a figurative face and the other an architectural one, the two together constitute an image that has become the most authoritative symbol of New China. This paper analyzes this image. My discussion starts from *Tiananmen* which, in addition to being an architectural 'front', supplied the portrait with a context, a location, and a 'body'.

Tiananmen

When *Mao* ascended *Tiananmen* on 1 October 1949 and declared the birth of the People's Republic of China, he also concluded a long transformation of the building he stood on. This transformation coincided with China's coming into the modern age. Before 1911 when China was ruled by an emperor in the Forbidden City, *Tiananmen* was an integral element of a large system of imperial architecture. It gradually broke lose from this system during the first half of the 20th century, and after 1949 it finally became a self-contained political symbol – an embodiment of the country and the Communist leadership. It also became firmly associated with *Mao*. Before *Mao's* death, *Tiananmen* served as a rostrum for *Mao* to review the parades of millions of people. Since *Mao's* death in 1976, his portrait has continued to hang on *Tiananmen*, overlooking the huge *Tiananmen* Square to the south.

Built first during the *Ming* (1368-1644) and reconstructed during the *Qing* (1644-1911), [6]*Tiananmen* was, as its name indicates, a *men* or 'gate'. More specifically, it was one of a series of magnificent 'gate towers' (*cheng lou*) located on the north-south axis of *Beijing* as

毛泽东肖像——或者更准确地说，有助于我们理解这幅肖像与天安门的综合体。这个综合体中的前者是作为再现性画像的一个"面"，后者是作为象征性建筑的一个"面"，二者共同构成了新中国最高政治权威的符号。这篇文章的目的即在于分析这个综合符号。我的讨论将从天安门开始，因为这个结构除了具有作为一个建筑物的"面"的特定意义以外，还给所挂的毛主席肖像提供了上下文、位置和"身体"。

天安门

当毛泽东于1949年10月1日登上天安门宣布中华人民共和国成立的时候，他也结束了他所站立的这座建筑物的一个长期转型的过程。这个转型过程与中国进入现代的历史演变一致。1911年前，当中国还被住在紫禁城里的皇帝统治的时候，天安门是这个巨大皇室建筑群的一个不可或缺的部分。到了20世纪上半叶，它逐渐从这个建筑体系中脱离。到1949年之后，它进而成为一个独立的政治符号，成为国家和党的象征，也与毛主席的形象变得不可分离。在毛泽东去世之前，它是毛检阅

---

[6]最后一次对天安门主要的重建工作发生在1968年到1970年间。这次改造之后的门楼高达34.7米，比原来的增高了83厘米。参阅贾英廷编：《天安门》（北京：中国商业出版社，1998），第119页。

the formal entrances to a number of sub-cities – the Outer City, the Inner City, the Imperial City, and the Forbidden City.[7] Each of these *cheng lou* had a wooden-structured tower standing on a tall brick base connected with city walls; tunnel-like gates penetrated the base underneath the tower and led to the enclosed space. *Tiananmen's* traditional function and symbolism was thus realized in a larger architectural complex known as *Beijing*[8] and in particular in its connection with the Imperial City, for which it served as the front gate. [9]While the Forbidden City at the heart of *Beijing* was the personal domain of the Son of Heaven, the Imperial City protected the Forbidden City and contained imperial parks, armories, and residences of royal relatives, ministers, and powerful eunuchs. With thick walls and guarded gates, these two cities in central *Beijing* blocked off more than two-thirds of the east-west traffic routes within the Inner City. An ordinary *Beijinger* had to make a considerable effort to travel from the east part of the city to the west part, either circling around the Gate of Earthly Peace *di'anmen*, that marked the north end of the Imperial City, or taking a detour around

[6] The last major reconstruction of *Tiananmen* took place from 1968 to 1970. The gate tower after this reconstruction is 34.7 metres high, 83 centimeters taller than the original one. See *Jia Yingting*, ed., *Tiananmen* (Beijing: *Zhongguo shangye chubanshe*, 1998), p. 119.

[7] The Outer City of *Beijing*, which enclosed the area south of the Inner City, was built during the 16th century. The original plan was to construct a city wall which would surround the entire Inner City. The plan was never completely realized, but it showed the intention to continue expanding *Beijing* based on the ancient model.

[8] Before the *Ming*, *Beijing* had been the capital of the state of *Yan* (403-221 B.C.), the *Liao* dynasty (916-1125), the *Jin* (1115-1234) and the *Yuan* (1279-1368), but *Tiananmen* was first built during the *Ming* dynasty in 1420.

[9] This is at least a *Qing* author's opinion. See *Rixia jiuwen kao* (Examining 'Old stories heard everyday'), cited in *Jia Yingting*, ed., *Tiananmen*, p. 5.

百万革命群众的观礼台；在毛于1976年去世之后，他的肖像仍然挂在天安门上，也仍然"南向"俯瞰着巨大的天安门广场。

　　天安门始建于明朝(1368-1644)，清朝(1644-1911)时重建。[6]就像它的名字所标示的那样，它的原始建筑功能首先是一个"门"。更具体地说，它是一系列位于北京南北轴线上的宏伟城楼之一。这些城楼标志了从外至内、不断紧缩的一系列城市的入口——从外城到内城，再从皇城到紫禁城。[7]每一个城门都有一个木结构的塔楼，下面的砖砌高台与两边城墙相连。隧道般黑洞洞的城门穿过塔楼下的砖台，进入到城墙围合着的空间。天安门的传统功能和象征意义因此是在这个叫做北京城的巨大的建筑复合体中得到实现的。[8]它是皇城的前门，[9]而皇城保护着紫禁城、皇家花园、军械库和皇亲国戚、大臣宦官的府邸。环绕以厚厚的城墙和戒备森严的城门，北京腹心的这两个

[7]和内城南边接壤的北京外城建于16世纪。最初的计划是建造一个可以环绕整个内城的城门。这个计划一直未被完全实现，但是它显露出了基于旧城基础上不断将北京城扩大的意图。

[8] 在明朝之前，北京已经是燕 (公元前403-221)、辽 (916-1125) 、金 (1115-1234) 和元 (1279-1368) 的首都，但是天安门最初是建于1420年的明朝。

[9] 这至少是一位清代作者的观点。参见《日下旧闻考》，贾英廷编：《天安门》，第5页。

the Grand Front Gate *daqianmen,* located south of *Tiananmen*. If one took this second route one could glance at *Tiananmen's* yellow roof. But the Gate of Heavenly Peace was sealed deep inside a walled enclosure and beyond an outsider's reach.

The shape of this walled enclosure resembled a capital letter T. The vertical bar of the T extended southward from *Tiananmen* to a smaller brick structure called *Daqingmen* (Gate of the Great *Qing)*, and its two arms stretched horizontally in front of *Tiananmen*, ending at the Left and Right *Chang'an* Gates to the east and west *(fig. 1)*. The function of this space was mainly ceremonial. The central gate of *Tiananmen* was used only when the emperor left the Forbidden City to offer sacrifices to Heaven and Earth, to lead a military expedition, or to take a grand tour to inspect the provinces. But *Tiananmen* defined a symbolic threshold even when it was not used as a passageway. The most theatrical of all the ceremonies held there was the issuing of imperial edicts when a new emperor was enthroned or a royal heir was born. The edict, written in the Throne Hall inside the Forbidden City, would be delivered by a special procession to *Tiananmen's* tower. Officials would be kneeling under the gate facing north. The edict would be lowered down to the ground, and would be received by the officials and sent around the country. This ceremony highlighted the traditional function and identity of *Tiananmen*. As the 'front' of the Imperial City, *Tiananmen* both concealed and exhibited the imperial power, and both separated and linked the spaces inside and outside the imperial domain. Although the ceremony enabled communication between the emperor and his subjects; neither the ruler nor the ruled were present. Instead they were re-presented – the former by ritual paraphernalia and the later by chosen representatives.

Fig. 1 T-shaped *Tiananmen*
Square in the *Qing* dynasty
图1: 清代天安门前的T型空间

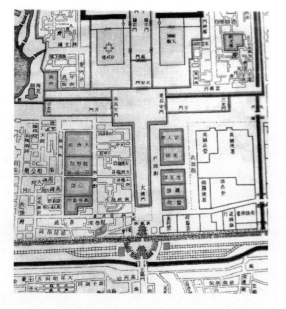

During this and other ceremonies, *Tiananmen* remained behind further gates and was inaccessible to ordinary people. The gate tower did not belong to a public space and was not a subject of public viewing.

The old symbolism of *Tiananmen* collapsed when China's dynastic history came to an end. The last imperial edict to come down from the gate tower, issued by Empress Dowager *Longyu* on 12 February 1912, announced the abdication of the last *Qing* emperor. Two years later, the Left and Right *Chang'an* Gates were permanently opened. As a direct consequence, the sealed space in front of *Tiananmen* was connected to the city at large. *Beijing's* residents could now travel east-west by crossing this space, and they could also scrutinize the famous gate tower with their own eyes. Gradually this east-west road, or *Chang'anjie*, grew into a modern avenue. It was paved and re-paved with new materials.[10] The first street car in *Beijing* was installed there in 1924. The road was then conceptualized as the city's main traffic route in the late 1930s, and was extended all the way to the east and west suburbs. [11]A more dramatic development took place after the establishment of the People's Republic. In 1949 *Chang'an* Avenue was 15 metres wide. A year later its width was doubled - an achievement enabled by demolishing several historical landmarks, including brick gates and wooden archways across the road.[12] This two-fold process of expanding the avenue and destroying old structures continued over the following years: the Left and Right *Chang'an* Gates were

---

[10] Before 1905 the road was paved with loess. The paving material was changed to fragmented stone in 1905, and to tar concrete in 1955. In 1958, the section of the road before *Tiananmen* (391.9 m long) was re-paved with granite blocks.

城——皇城和紫禁城——阻断了超过2/3的内城东西向的交通线路。当时的北京人从东城到西城的旅行需要花费相当力气：他们或者需要绕到皇城北面的地安门外，或者需要取道正阳门内的棋盘街。如果走这后一条路的话，他们可能能够看到远处天安门的黄色琉璃瓦屋顶。但是天安门本身被深深封闭在围合的廊庑和宫墙里，无法被外人接近。这个城楼不属于公共空间，也不是公共视线的对象。

这些廊庑和宫墙构成一个"T"形。"T"的竖线向南延伸，从天安门一直通到规模较小的砖结构的大清门（明代称大明门）。"T"的水平方向在天安门前向东、西伸展，分别结束于长安左门和长安右门（图1）。这个"T"形空间的功能基本上是仪式性的；天安门的正门只有在皇帝离开紫禁城去祭拜天地、领军远征，或者重大出巡的时候才启用。但是，即使天安门不被当作通道使用，它也已经标志了一个象征性礼仪空间的起点。在这里所举行的仪式中，最具戏剧性的是新皇登基或太子诞生时的颁旨典礼。其时，紫禁城皇宫里写就的圣旨，被一个特殊的仪仗队传递到天安门的塔楼上。官员们面向北方跪于城门之下。圣旨被徐徐降到地上，由官员们接收，然后向整个国家宣示。这个仪式的重要性在于它突显出传统天安门的功能和地位：作为皇城的正门，它兼具了隐蔽和展示皇权的作用，同时也阻断和连接皇室领地的内外空间。虽然这个仪式所指示的是皇帝与臣民之间的交流，但

demolished in 1952. *Chang'an* Avenue was widened to 32-50 metres in 1955, and the section before *Tiananmen* was further expanded to 80 metres wide before the tenth anniversary of the People's Republic in 1959. The road also reached the remarkable length of 40 kilometers that year, far beyond the confines of the city of *Beijing*. Burying the old north-south Imperial Way underneath, the significance of this east-west avenue as the new axis of *Beijing* was firmly established. Mass parades and traffic now proceeded under *Tiananmen's* shadow, not through its tunnel-like gate *(fig. 2)*.

Other changes around *Tiananmen* also contributed to the gradual isolation of the gate tower from its original architectural and symbolic context. First, the demolition of the walls of the Imperial City, the city for which *Tiananmen* served as the main entrance, started in 1917 and continued throughout the next decades.[13] The north gate of the Imperial City, *Di'anmen*,

---

[11] For the installation of the street car, see *Shi Mingzheng, Zuoxiang jindaihua de Beijing cheng – Chengshi jianshe yu shehui bianqe* (The city of *Bejing* moves towards modernization: City construction and social change), (*Beijing: Beijing daxue chubanshe*, 1995), pp. 269-80. During the Japanese occupation, *Chang'an* Avenue was planned to connect an industrial district in *Beijing*'s east suburbs and a 'new urban district' in the west suburbs. For this purpose, two city gates, named *Chang'anmen* (present-day *Fuxingmen*) and *Qimingmen* (present-day *Jianguomen*) were opened up on the city walls in 1939 to allow the avenue through. See *Zhang Jinggan, Beijing guihua jianshe zonghengtan* (A sweeping discussion of the city planning of *Beijing*), (*Beijing: Beijing Yanshan Chubanshe*, 1997), p. 173.

[12] The old and new sections of the road, each 15 metres wide, were separated by street car tracks. The old structures demolished in 1950 included the two free-standing brick gates (conventionally called *Sanzuomen*) outside the Left and Right *Chang'an* Gates, as well as two wooden archways called *Lüzhong* and *Daohe*. *See Zhang Jinggan, Beijing guihua jianshe zonghengtan*, p. 174.

Fig. 2 *Chang'an* Avenue after
the 1959 expansion
图2：1959年被拓宽后的长安街

was leveled to the ground in 1955 after a prolonged debate. With it vanished the last visible landmark of the Imperial City except for *Tiananmen*, as well as the dualistic structure that had associated these two gates into a coherent architectural design. Second, in old *Beijing*, *Tiananmen* was flanked by two important imperial structures: the Royal Ancestral Temple to the east and the Land Altar to the west. These two ritual structures ceased to function after the fall of the *Qing*, and were consequently transformed into public spaces. In 1914 the Land Altar became one of the first public parks in *Beijing*, called Central Park or *zhongyang gongyuan,* followed by the conversion of the Ancestral Temple into another park in 1929 called Peace Park or *heping gongyuan*. Third, after the fall of the *Qing,* the front section of the Forbidden City, which contained the three throne halls, became the property of the Republican government and was opened to the public in 1914. The entire Forbidden City became the Palace Museum in 1925, soon after the *Qing* court finally moved out. The last emperor of the *Qing* was still allowed to stay on in the rear section of the Forbidden City after he abdicated the throne.[14] During the two decades from 1911 to 1929, therefore, all imperial structures surrounding *Tiananmen* were turned into public spaces of various functions. But

---

[13] *Xihuangcheng*, or the west side of the Imperial City, was demolished in 1917. The east gate of the Imperial City, *Donganmen*, was destroyed in 1924. After the continuous demolition from 1924 to 1927, only the wall between the Ancestral Temple to *Bei Xinhua* Street still existed. See Department of History at Peking University, A History of *Beijing* Writing Group, A History of *Beijing*, expanded edition (*Beijing: Beijing Chubanshe*, 1999), pp. 446-47.

[14] For a detailed account of these events, see *Wu Shizhou, Zijincheng de liming* (The dawn of the Forbidden City), (*Beijing: Wenwu chubanshe*, 1998).

不论是统治者还是被统治者都并不在场。二者都被象征和"代表"——前者通过礼仪用具, 后者则通过被选拔出来的官员。

　　天安门的这种传统象征意义随着王朝历史的结束而土崩瓦解。最后一张从城墙上悬挂下来的圣旨由隆裕太后于1912年2月12日颁布, 宣告了清代末代皇帝的退位。两年之后, 长安左门和长安右门永久性地开放。作为直接后果, 天安门前的封闭空间得以与城市相连。北京市民现在可以东西穿越这个空间了, 也可以用自己的眼睛去观察这个著名的城楼。渐渐地, 这条被称为长安街的东西向通路发展成了一条现代大道, 一次又一次地被铺以新的建筑材料。[10]第一辆北京有轨电车于1924年在长安街上安装, 这条路在19世纪30年代晚期终于成了北京城的主要干道, 两头分别延伸到西郊和东郊。[11]共和国成立之后又有了一次更加戏剧性的发展: 1949年的长安街是15米宽, 一年之

---

[10] 1905年之前的路是由黄土铺成的。这种路面在1905年被改成了碎石路面, 并在1955年成为柏油混凝土路面。到了1958年, 天安门前的这段路 (长391.9米) 被铺上了花岗岩石块。

[11] 关于街车的装置, 参见史明正: 《走向近代化的北京城——城市建设与社会变革》 (北京: 北京大学出版社, 1995), 第269-280页。在日本占领期间, 长安街被计划与和北京东郊的一个工业区以及西郊的一个"新城区"相连。为了这个目的, 两个城门——长安门 (今为复兴门) 和启明门 (今为建国门) ——在1939年开通。参见张敬淦: 《北京规划建设纵横谈》 (北京: 北京燕山出版社, 1997), 第173页。

Tiananmen did not belong to any of these spaces – neither to the museum behind it nor to the parks next to it. With its original connection to the Imperial City and Forbidden City severed, this gate tower was increasingly paired with the ground in front of it. Known as *Tiananmen* Square, this ground became the most important site for political expression in China during the same period.

Tiananmen Square has been the focus of Chinese politics since the 1910s. A series of mass movements for democracy and independence that took place there have become landmarks in modern Chinese history: the demonstration of 4 May 1919 in protest against the Treaty of Versailles handing over Chinese land to Japan; the patriotic march on 18 March 1926; the demonstration on 9 December 1935, which started the resistance movement against the Japanese invasion; the anti-autocratic movement during the Civil War on 20 May 1947; the mass memorial to the former prime minister *Zhou Enlai* on 5 April 1976; and finally the 1989 student uprising. Parallel to these grass-roots movements runs another sequence of 'demonstrations' mobilized by the authorities to display power and control: the military parade on October 1913 celebrating *Yuan Shikai's* election as President; *Zhang Xun's* grand ritual on June 1917 to commemorate his restoration of imperial order; the establishment of the puppet regime under Japanese patronage; the founding of Communist China on 1 October 1949; the elaborate National Day parade ; and the colourful ceremonies and performances for China's regaining sovereignty over Hong Kong and Macao in 1996 and 1999. As these two chains of events are tied to *Tiananmen* Square, the place has become the nexus of political tension and conflict, as well as a primary site to display official ideology

后, 通过拆除若干重要历史地标, 包括横跨这条街上的砖木机构拱门, [12]它的宽度得以翻倍。道路拓宽因此显示为一个双向进程的结果, 包括旧结构的破坏和新空间的同时扩展: 长安左门和长安右门在1952年被毁; 长安街在1955年被拓宽到30到50米; 天安门前的街道在1959年的十周年国庆的时候进而被拓宽到80米; 这条路在这一年同时也达到了40公里的壮观长度, 远远超越了北京市区的界限。到这一刻, 南北向的传统御道早已被埋葬在东西向的长安街之下, 而这条大道最终作为北京的新轴线被确立。大阅兵和公共交通现在从天安门的面前通过, 国家领导人也不再穿过它那阴沉的门洞去到外界(图 2)。

其它环绕着天安门发生的变化也都使这座"门"从它原来的建筑结构和象征系统中不断孤立出来。首先的一个变化, 始于1917年并贯穿其后的几十年, 是对天安门作为主要入口的皇城的摧毁。[13]

---

[12] 该路的新旧段, 各15米宽, 被街车的轨道分割。旧结构在1950年被毁坏了, 包括两段独立的在左右长安门之外砖门 (俗称 三座门), 还有两座称作"履中"和"踣和"的牌坊, 见张敬淦:《北京规划建设纵横谈》, 第174页。

[13]　西皇城在1917年被毁坏。在1924年至1927年持续的破坏之后, 只有太庙和北新华街之间的墙依然存在。参见北京大学历史系《北京史》编写组:《北京史》, (北京:北京出版社, 1999), 第446-447页。

and the strength of control. In all these situations *Tiananmen* has been associated with the notion of political authority: although no longer symbolizing an obsolete imperial power, the gate tower still overlooks the parading masses below, and its juxtaposition with *Tiananmen* Square continues to mirror the relationship between the ruler and the ruled. What underlies the changing meaning of *Tiananmen* in the twentieth century, therefore, is the construction of political authority in modern China. While the architectural identity of *Tiananmen* as a front gate remains, it has gradually acquired a 'metaphoric body'. After 1949, this 'metaphorical body' was finally defined as the People's Republic of China in general and Chairman *Mao* in particular – a symbolism which has been strengthened by further changes to *Tiananmen* and its environment.

Firstly, the gate tower became a certified symbol of the new regime. After a prolonged discussion, *Tiananmen* was chosen as the focal image of the country's insignia, under five gold stars that symbolized the leadership of the Communist Party and the unity of the revolutionary people *(fig. 3)*. The official explanation of this design, issued by the new government in June 1950, contains this definition: '*Tiananmen* symbolizes... New China that was born here.' [15]*Tiananmen* was thus finally extracted from its architectural context

[15] '*Zhonghua renmin gongheguo guohui tu'an ji dui sheji tu'an de shuoming*' (The design of the insignia of the People's Republic of China with an explanation). Cited in *Yu Jiang, Kaiguo dadian liuxiaoshi* (The six hours of the grand ceremony establishing the People's Republic of China), (*Shenyang: Liaohai chubanshe*, 1999), pp. 277-78.

Fig. 3 Emblem of the People's Republic of China
图3：中华人民共和国国徽设计图

to become an emblem – an image that has 'a direct verbal definition well known by all members of a group, class or culture.' [16] As an emblem, *Tiananmen's* frontal, schematic image is replicated on the country's banknotes and coins and on the front pages of all government documents. The insignia also hangs under the eaves of the real *Tiananmen* to epitomize its monumentality.

Secondly, after 1949 *Tiananmen* became the nation's premier rostrum for its leaders to review civil and military parades at important state festivals. Since no Chinese emperor ever ascended onto *Tiananmen* to face outside, such parades and reviews can be considered modern rituals which allow the public to meet with their leaders, albeit in an extremely limited way. To the thousands of commoners and soldiers gathered under *Tiananmen* on 1 October 1949, *Mao's* appearance on this former imperial building must have symbolized the beginning of a new era. It meant that the hidden ruling power had finally emerged and submitted itself to them. No other gesture could more effectively prove the newness of the Communist leadership and no other act could more convincingly seal the title of People's Republic. We can thus also understand the rationale behind the Herculean effort made by the Chinese government to enlarge *Tiananmen* Square: the bigger this ritual ground and the mass assembly it can hold, the loftier the gate tower and the leadership it represents.

[16] A term used in the following sense: 'Emblems are those nonverbal acts which have a direct verbal translation, or dictionary definition... [which] is well known by all members of a group, class or culture.' Paul Ekman and Wallace V. Friesen, 'The Repertoire of Nonverbal Behavior: Categories, Origins, Usage, and Coding', Semiotica, 1969, 1.

最后，经过一段争论，皇城的北门地安门在1955年被夷为平地。随着这个地标建筑的消失，把天安门和地安门整合入一个统一建筑设计的二元结构也被取消。第二，原来的天安门在两侧被两个重要的礼仪结构裹挟，即东边的太庙和西边的社稷坛。这两个皇室建筑在清朝灭亡之后停止了它们的礼仪功能，被改造为现代的公共空间。1914年，社稷坛成了北京最早的公园（中央公园，以后改称为中山公园）。太庙也在1929年被转化成了另一个公园（和平公园）。第三，在清朝倒台之后，紫禁城的前部，包括三大殿，成了民国的财产，于1914年对外开放。整个紫禁城在1925年成了故宫博物院，虽然清朝末代皇帝仍被允许住在紫禁城后方。[14]

因此，在1911年至1929年这近20年期间，所有环绕着天安门的传统皇权建筑都变为多功能的公共空间。但是天安门却不属于任何这些空间：它既不属于坐落在后面的博物院，也不属于两边的公园。当它与皇城和紫禁城的传统联系被切断，它和其前方的空地的关系却相对不断强化。而这块空地——也就是我们称作天安门广场的空间——在这个时期也成了中国政治表达的最重要的地点。

天安门广场从19世纪初开始就已经是中国政治的焦点。一系列民主独立运动在这里发生，使

[14] 详见吴十洲：《紫禁城的黎明》（北京：文物出版社，1998）。

From 1950 to 1976, *Tiananmen* Square was under constant expansion, finally achieving its present shape as an immense ground capable of holding 600,000 people in a single gathering. Monumental structures were attached to this space: the Great Hall of the People, the Museum of Chinese History and Revolutionary History, the Monument to the People's Heroes, and, finally, *Mao's* Memorial Hall *(fig. 4)*. As I have discussed elsewhere, a main purpose of these buildings is to structure history, to shape the present, and to define a desired public.[17] Framed by these monuments, the reconstructed Square represents an idealized People's Republic of China from the official point of view. In this way, it substantiates *Tiananmen's* 'metaphoric body' with concrete architectural symbols, and confirms *Tiananmen's* role as the head and face of this body.

Mao's Portrait

As an architectural 'face', *Tiananmen* was also anthropomorphized. The logic of its anthropomorphization was simple: because both the gate tower and *Mao* embodied the new regime, they were naturally equated. The huge portrait of *Mao* hanging in front of *Tiananmen* supplies the gate tower with a figurative face. Together they command the immense *Tiananmen* Square to the south.

To understand this portrait we should start once again from the early twentieth century,

---

[17] *Wu Hung*, '*Tiananmen* Square: A Political History of Monuments', Representations 35 (Summer 1991), pp. 84-117; especially, pp. 90-107.

Fig. 4 *Tiananmen* Square after 1976. Buildings along the central axis from the foreground: the Front Gate, *Mao's* Mausoleum, Monument to People's Hero, *Tiananmen* Gate, the Forbidden City.
图4：1976年之后的天安门广场中轴线上的建筑是：前门、毛主席纪念堂、人民英雄纪念碑、天安门和紫禁城。

when a new type of public portrait appeared in China for its political leaders. Before this moment, the concept of a public political portrait simply did not exist, as it was not a Chinese habit to exhibit the image of an emperor or official on public occasions or on public commodities such as coins. Two kinds of imperial portraits were made during the *Ming* and *Qing* dynasties. Called 'pictures of amusement' (*xing le tu)* and 'imperial visages' (*yu rong),* respectively, each served a separate purpose and had a different pictorial style. A 'picture of amusement' was made for an emperor's private viewing and often situates the emperor in an informal, sometimes fictional environment. He is either playing a musical instrument, enjoying a hunting game, or is disguised as a Daoist monk, an ordinary laborer, or even a foreigner. In contrast, an 'imperial visage' was official in status and ceremonial in function.[18] Works of this type uniformly employ a pictorial style that rejects any depiction of physical environment, bodily movement, or facial expression. While some of the imperial visages convey a greater sense of personality whereas others reveal a stronger impact of European 'naturalistic' modeling techniques, none of them violates the basic codes of the genre: as a formal portrait, a 'visage' picture must present a ruler in a perfect frontal view against an empty background. The identity of the sitter is largely revealed by his costume, especially those embroidered dragons as symbols of the Son of Heaven.

Although such imperial visages may not be so apart from portraits of modern political

---

[18] For a case study of this type of imperial portrait, see *Wu Hung*, 'Emperor's Masquerade: Costume Portraits of *Yongzheng* and *Qianlong*', Orientations 26.7 (July and August, 1995), pp. 25-41.

这里成为中国现代史的地标：1919年5月4日的反对凡尔赛和约的游行示威；1947年5月20日的反内战、反独裁运动；1976年4月5日悼念周恩来的大规模群众集会；最后是1989年的学潮。与这些草根运动并行的是一系列由当局组织，显示其权力和欲望的"示威"，包括1913年10月庆祝袁世凯当选为大总统的军队阅兵；1917年6月张勋拥代宣统复辟的盛典；1949年10月1日新中国的成立；历年的国庆阅兵和游行；以及为香港和澳门回归所准备的丰富庆典表演。这两条线索与天安门广场紧紧相联，使这个地方成为政治关系和社会冲突的扭结，和展现官方意识形态和权力控制的主要场所。在所有这些场合中，天安门与政治权力的概念不可分割。虽然它不再象征陈腐的皇权，但这个城楼依然俯瞰着在它下面游行的大众；它与广场的并置仍然反映着"领导"与"群众"的关系。可以说，天安门在20世纪的意义变换所体现的是现代中国政治权力的重新组建。同时，当天安门从实体性的皇城和紫禁城独立出来，逐渐成为一个独立的象征物，它也获得了一个"隐喻的身体"。1949年之后，通过一系列事件，这个"隐喻的身体"最终被定义为中华人民共和国，具体表现为毛泽东本人和毛泽东肖像的承载体。

首先的一个事件是把这座城楼正式定性为新政权的法定象征：经过长时间讨论，天安门被作为国徽上的核心图案，与上方的五颗星一起代表了中国共产党的领导下的革命大众（图3）。新政

leaders in terms of pictorial style, they have radically different uses. The main purpose of an imperial visage, and hence the main reason for its creation, was to display it in the imperial ancestral temple. A 'visage' portrait in this sacred place stood for a deceased emperor to receive ritual offerings. A row of visages also constituted a pictorial chronicle, in which each image represented the reign of a ruler and hence a segment of China's dynastic history. Since neither the temple nor the portraits were accessible to the general public, the ancestral rituals and the pictorial history remained the private affair of the ruling family.

Changes became noticeable even before the last dynasty perished. Influenced by the western practice of displaying portraits of political leaders in public spaces and on important ceremonial occasions, the last two *Qing* emperors, *Guangxu* and *Xuantong*, adopted a new attitude toward their own images, as they began to publicize these images instead of concealing them.[19] Even the notorious Empress Dowager *Cixi* presented her own portrait – a large oil painting by the American artist Katharine Carl – in the St. Louis Exposition. But still, accompanying this portrait was an imperial edict, with instructions that the portrait

[19] For example, *Youzhen Shuju* compiled A Complete Collection of Photographic Portraits of 200 Famous People around the World (*Zhongwai erbai mingren zhaoxiang quance*) in 1906, and distributed it in China and abroad. The album include portraits of *Guangxu* and *Cixi*. See *Ma Yunzeng*, et al., *Zhongguo sheying shi* 1840-1937 (A history of photography in China 1840-1937), (*Beijing: Zhongguo sheying chubanshe*, 1987), p. 65. Portraits of *Guangxu* and *Xuantong* were also featured on postcards with captions written in English. See *Chen Shouxiang*, et al., *Jiument chongjing: Fan Li, Bei Ning cang Qing dai mingxinpian xuanji*, I (Startled again by old dreams: a selection of *Qing* postcards collected by *Fan Lin* and *Bei Ning*, I), (*Nan'ning: Guangxi meishu chubanshe*, 1998), figs. 5, 7.

府在1950年6月发布的对这个设计的解释包括如下的说明:"天安门象征了⋯⋯在这里诞生的新中国。"[15] (注:此处及下文中的引文均从英文翻译。)至此,天安门最终从它的建筑环境中被抽离出来,变成一个象征性徽识。而作为一个象征性徽识,它是一个具有"被所有组织、阶级和文化的所有成员所熟知的最直接口头定义的"[16]图像。由于这种意义,天安门的正面形象成为了一个固定的图案,被复制在钱币和所有政府公文上。这个徽识也被挂在了天安门的屋檐下,作为这座建筑物的纪念碑性的缩影。

第二,1949年后,天安门成为整个国家最重要的一个"观礼台",领导人在重要的节日场合从这里观看群众游行和军队阅兵。这在古代历史上是没有前例的,这些游行和观摩因此可以被看作是使公众与领导人见面的现代仪式。当成千上万的平民和士兵在1949年10月1日汇集在天安门下,对他

[15] "中华人民共和国国徽图案及对设计图案的说明",引自于江:《开国大典六小时》(沈阳:辽海出版社, 1999),第277-278页。
[16]这个词的使用有着如下的意思:"徽识是一种非语言行为,基于直接的口头翻译或字典中的定义⋯⋯被一个组织、阶级或文化中的所有成员所熟知。"Paul Ekman和Wallace V. Friesen:《非语言行为的系统:种类、来源、用法和编码》(The Repertoire of Nonverbal Behavior: Categories, Origins, Usage, and Coding),*Semiotica*, 1969。

must be transported *en face* in specially designed vehicles, because the Empress Dowager should never take the inferior posture of looking backward. Such taboos were abandoned by the new generation of Chinese leaders of the post-imperial era, whose images became a constant feature of newspapers, pictorials, postcards, and 'cigarette cards' – mass media that constituted a new print culture. But a mechanically reproduced image could never replace a framed formal portrait, be it an oil painting or an enlarged photograph, because only a formal portrait was attached to an architectural space and helped define, or re-define, this space.

We can find endless examples to illustrate how portraits helped structure public spaces in early twentieth-century China. Some instances, however, were more directly related to the eventual merging of *Tiananmen* with a leader's face. *Sun Yat-sen*, commonly recognized as the Father of Modern China, died in March 1925 in *Beijing*. The funeral was held in Central Park – the former Land Altar located next to *Tiananmen*. Several hundred thousand people attended the memorial service and accompanied the hearse along *Chang'an* Avenue. In the open hearse was a large portrait of *Sun*; the deceased national hero was represented by this 'face image' on this public ceremony. [20] The first portrait on *Tiananmen* was also that of *Sun*.

---

[20] The American scholar and photographer Sidney D. Gamble recorded the complete process of this service in photographs. One of the images, showing the portrait in the hearse, is published in The Sidney D. Gamble Foundation for China Studies, Turbulent Years: China Before and After the May 4th Movement (*Beijing*: Museum of Chinese History, 1999), p. 26, no. 483/2787. Central Park was later renamed the *Zhongshan* (*Yat-sen*) Park to commemorate *Sun Yat-sen*; its central building was turned into *Sun*'s memorial shrine with a portrait of *Sun* in the middle.

们来说，毛泽东在这旧皇室建筑上的亲自出现最明确地象征了一个新时代的开始。它意味着隐藏着的政治权力最终浮现出来，将自身提交给芸芸大众。没有任何其他姿态能够更有效地证明中国共产党领导下的新中国的崭新意义，也没有任何其他行动更能如此令人信服地将新、旧政权分开。

我们由此也就可以理解政府扩大天安门广场巨大努力背后的基本道理：这块仪式化的场地越大，聚集的群众数量越多，天安门也就越有力量，它所代表的思想就越为崇高。从1950年到1976年，这个广场一直在不断拓建，最终达到了它现在的规模：可以在一次聚会中容纳60万人的一个其大无比的场地。其他纪念碑式的建筑，包括人民英雄纪念碑、人民大会堂、中国历史博物馆和中国革命博物馆，以及毛主席纪念堂，逐次被附加于这个空间(图4)。如我在另文中讨论过的，这些纪念碑建筑的一个主要目的是为了建构历史和现在，另一个目的是定义官方的"政治空间"。[17]由这些纪念碑框架起来的广场代表了理想化的中华人民共和国。换言之，广场通过这样的方式，以具体的建筑符号实体化了天安门的"隐喻的身体"。天安门的角色也因此被确立为这个身体的"大脑"和"面容"。

天安门毛主席像

---

[17] 巫鸿：《天安门广场——纪念碑的政治史》，*Representations*，第35期 （1991，夏季刊），第84-117页，尤见第90-107页。

As shown in a photograph in the Times *Shi bao* of August 24th, 1928, this image of a limited scale was hung directly above the center gate of *Tiananmen (fig. 5)*. [21]After the Republican Army recaptured *Beijing* following the Sino-Japanese war, an enormous portrait of *Chiang Kaishek* was installed on *Tiananmen* on 3 December 1945 *(fig. 6)*. [22]Standing above *Tiananmen's* balcony, its upper edge almost reached the roof of the gate tower. From this commanding point *Chiang* looked down with a stern expression. Almost immediately this portrait became a focus of political tension. While glorifying China's current leadership, it also provided anti-government demonstrators with a target. One demonstration was the 'Anti-war, Anti-hunger' movement in May 1947. Mobilized by left-wing student organizations, the movement started from various university campuses in *Beijing* and culminated in a joint demonstration in front of *Tiananmen*. Ignoring the government's warning, 7,000 students from different schools marched along *Chang'an* Avenue on May 20th, shouting slogans and distributing anti-government leaflets. They raised their voice when passing *Tiananmen*: according to a memoir of the event, facing *Chiang's* portrait students shouted out 'Down with dictator! Down with autocracy!' They also sang a song that attacked *Chiang* for exploiting students, enslaving people, destroying Chinese culture, and obstructing post-war peace. The song's title was repeated in each of its stanzas: 'You, You, You – You Scoundrel,' (*Ni, Ni, Ni – Ni zhege*

[21] Here I want to thank *Lai Delin* for providing me with this information.

[22] The Republican Army under *Hou Jingru* entered *Beijing* on December 18th, 1945.

[23] *Wen Fu*, *Tiananmen jianzheng lu* (History as witnessed to by *Tiananmen*), 3 vols. (*Beijing: Zhongguo yanshi chubanshe*, 1998), vol. 1, pp. 354-61.

作为这个"隐喻身体"的大脑和面容，天安门同时被人格化了。这个人格化的过程跟随了一个简单的逻辑：由于天安门和毛泽东都代表了新的政权，它们自然形成了相互间的指涉。其结果是：悬挂在天安门前的毛泽东巨幅肖像给这个建筑体提供了一张具像的脸；二者一起形成了南向面对巨大天安门广场的制高点。

要理解这张肖像的意义，我们应该再次从20世纪早期开始——当一种新形式的政治领袖肖像在中国出现的时候。在这之前，公共性政治肖像的概念并不存在；将皇帝或者官员的头像在公共场合展览或印在硬币这样的公共日用品上并不是中国的传统习惯。明、清二朝发展出两种类型的皇帝肖像，在清代被分别称为"行乐图"和"御容"像，各自服务于不同的目的，也有着各自的图像风格。"行乐图"经常表现的是皇帝在非正式场合下——甚至有时是虚构场景中——的私人活动，或抚琴打猎，或装扮成一个道士、农夫，甚至外国人。与此相反，"御容"则是具有特殊礼仪功能的正式肖像。[18]这后一类作品一律拒绝对背景环境、身体动作和面部表情的表现。虽然其中有些传达了较

[18] 对这种皇帝肖像的案例研究可见巫鸿：《皇帝的化妆舞会——雍正和乾隆的'化妆肖像'》，*Orientations* 26.7 （1995，7、8月刊），第25-41页。

Fig. 5 *Tiananmen* with *Sun Yat-sen's* portrait, August 1928.
图5：1928年8月天安门上挂着的孙中山像

Fig. 6 *Tiananmen* with *Chiang Kai-shek's* portrait on it. December 1945.
图6：1945年12月天安门上竖立着的蒋介石像

强的个性，有些则显示出欧洲技术流派的影响，但是所有的"御容"像都无一例外地遵守着这个艺术形式的基本规则：作为礼仪肖像，它们必须是平视观者的正面像，由于没有表情和背景，皇帝和皇后的身份在很大程度上由服饰揭示，特别是那些作为他们身份象征物的的龙凤图案。

虽然在构图样式上，这些"御容"像与现代政治领袖的肖像并没有太大不同，但是他们有着根本不同的功能。皇帝肖像的最主要的目的——也是它们被创作的最主要的原因——是将这些画像展示在皇室的祖庙里接受礼节性的供奉。一整排御容像因此也就构成了一个朝代的图像编年史，其中每一张图像代表了一位统治者的在位时期，即中国历史中的某个时段。但是在封建社会里，无论是这种皇家祖庙还是其中的肖像都不能被大众接近，祖先的祭奠和这种图像史都只是统治家族内部的事务。

但是甚至在清代灭亡之前，皇室肖像中的变化已经显而易见了。受到西方国家将政治领袖肖像放在公共场合和重要仪式场所的影响，最后两个清朝皇帝——光绪和宣统，对自己的肖像采取了一

[19] 例如，1906年，由正书局编的在中外发行的《中外200名人照相全册》中包括了光绪和慈禧的肖像。见马运增等著，《中国摄影史1840-1937》（北京：中国摄影出版社，1987），第65页。光绪和宣统的肖像也见于加注了英文的明信片中。见绶祥等编：《旧梦重惊——方霖、北宁藏清代明信片选集（I）》（南宁：广西美术出版社，1998）图5，7。

huaidongxi!')[23]The portrait on *Tiananmen* gave the 'you' an instant identity.

Chiang's portrait was replaced by those of Communist leaders when the *Guomindang* government was overthrown. The substitution, however, only signified changing leaders, not a new concept of leadership. It is also worth noting that *Chiang's* image was not immediately replaced by that of *Mao*, but was initially replaced by portraits of different assemblages of Communist leaders; the non-standard groupings reflected uncertainties in the Communist leadership at this historical moment. One such instance was the mass gathering in *Tiananmen* Square on 12 February 1949, ten days after the Communist army took over *Beijing*. The 200,000 participators found eight large portraits hung on *Tiananmen's* front wall. [24]Unlike *Chiang's* image, these and subsequent portraits of Communist leaders no longer stood on *Tiananmen's* balcony, so that the gate tower could be used as a rostrum for reviewing mass parades. Each 2 metres wide and 2.8 metres high, they represented *Mao, Zhu De, Lin Biao, Nie Rongzhen, Ye Jianying,* and three other leaders. Five months later, another mass gathering was held on 7 July in *Tiananmen* Square to celebrate the establishment of the Chinese People's Political Consultative Conference – a united front organization entrusted with the mission of structuring the new government under the leadership of the Communist Party. Again 200,000 people reportedly showed up. But this time they found only two portraits on

[24] The number of people who attended this event is based on a rough estimate. But available evidence makes it clear that a large number of people participated in this gathering. For example, 114,250 people signed up at *Zhonghuamen* (formerly *Daqingmen*). It is reported that at least 20,000 people attended who did not sign up. See *Wen Fu, Tiananmen jianzheng lu*, vol. 2, p. 424.

种新的态度，开始公开展示自己的肖像而不再是将其藏匿起来。[19]甚至以保守著称的慈禧太后也同意在圣·路易斯世界博览会上展示由美国女画家凯瑟琳·卡尔 (Katharine Carl) 创作的她的油画肖像。共和国初期的新一代中国政治家更是彻底抛弃了宗庙"御容"像的传统，他们的肖像经常出现在报纸、画册和明信片，甚至香烟牌等新型印刷文化的大众媒体上。但是这些机械复制的图像仍不可能取代一张正式装裱的肖像——不论这是一幅油画还是一张放大的照片，因为只有这类正式肖像才能被悬挂在一个建筑空间中，不断赋予这个空间以新的意义。

我们可以找到无数例子，证明在20世纪早期的中国，肖像是如何帮助建构公共空间的。其中有一些例子直接与天安门相关。比如，被公认为现代中国缔造者的孙中山于1925年逝世于北京，葬礼在天安门旁的中央公园举行。数以千计的人民参加了这个纪念仪式，尾随灵柩沿长安街游行。敞开的灵车里平放着一幅孙中山肖像——在这个公共仪式中，这位已故的民族英雄由他面容的再现来代表。[20]天安门上出现的第一张肖像也是孙中山的。根据1928年8月24日《时报》的报道和刊载的

[20] 美国学者和摄影师西德尼·甘博 (Sidney D. Gamble) 在照片中纪录了整个过程。其中的一张图片展示了在灵柩中的肖像，发表于西德尼·甘博中国研究基金会：《风雨如磐："五四运动"前后的中国》(北京：首都博物馆, 1999)，第26页，no.483/2787。中央公园后命名为中山公园，以纪念孙中山；它的中央建筑后来变为正中挂有孙中山像的中山纪念堂。

Fig. 7 *Mao's* portrait hung
on *Tiananmen* on October 1
(National Day), 1949
图7: 1949年10月1日开国大典中
天安门上悬挂的毛主席像

照片, 孙的画像直接地挂在天安门城门的正中(图5)。[21]抗战胜利后, 一张巨大的蒋介石肖像于1945年12月3日也被置于天安门的城楼之上, 上缘几乎碰到城楼的屋檐(图6)。[22]画像中的蒋表情严厉, 居高临下地俯视着面前的空地。相对于这个肖像和它所代表的政治权威, 天安门广场成了反政府示威游行者们的场地: 1947年5月由左翼学生组织的"反内战, 反饥饿"游行最早开始于北京各高校校园, 在天安门前的集合示威中达到了高潮。5月20日, 7000名从不同学校涌来的学生不顾政府警告, 沿长安街前进, 一边喊着口号, 一边散发反政府传单。根据这次事件的一位目击者记录, 当经过天安门时, 学生们抬高了声音大喊: "打倒独裁者! 打倒独裁政府!"他们也编写了歌曲, 抨击蒋介石奴役人民、破坏中国文化、阻碍战后和平的罪恶行径。这首歌的的每一节里都重复着"你, 你, 你, 你这个坏东西!"[23]天安门上的蒋肖像给了这个"你"现成的指代物。

国民党政府倒台之后, 天安门上的旧肖像被新的领袖取代。这种取代的对象因此是画像的内容而非再现的逻辑。值得注意的是, 蒋肖像并没有直接被毛肖像所取代, 而是在开始的时候被若干

---

[21] 在此我要感谢赖德霖为我提供的信息。

[22] 国民革命军于侯镜如领导下1945年12月18日进入北京。

[23] 文夫:《天安门见证录》, 三卷本 (北京:中国言实出版社, 1998), 卷一, 第354-361页。

Tiananmen representing *Mao* and *Zhu De*, then the commander-in-chief of the Communist Army. Three months later, on October 1st, 1949, the number of portraits was reduced to one – a huge image of *Mao* 6 metres high and 4.6 metres wide – at the exact center of *Tiananmen's* front wall *(fig. 7)*. Other images created at the time likewise paired *Mao* and *Tiananmen*. A series of stamps that commemorated the founding of the People's Republic, for example, illustrate *Tiananman* in the foreground. *Mao's* portrait on the building is barely recognizable, so the designer blew it up into a giant head looming over the tower gate *(fig. 8)*.

Mao's portrait has remained on the same spot for the past 50 years. It stayed on even after *Mao* died and his 'mistakes' were openly discussed. The rationale for the immortality of the portrait, as I will discuss later, is that it had become a primary symbol of the nation and the Party. On the other hand, as important as it is, this portrait was surrounded by a strange silence: until recently there was little, if any, published report and discussion about its creation and variations and the painters' names were kept largely unknown even in artist circles. Information about this portrait became available only in 1998 and 1999, when a large body of historical data concerning the earlier years of the People's Republic was published before the 50th anniversary of the country. With some conflicting details, various accounts identify at least five painters who painted some fifty to sixty *'Tiananmen* portraits' of *Mao*. Damage from sunlight and the elements required that the portrait be renewed every year, usually before National Day on October 1st. Sometimes new portraits are also installed

Fig. 8 Stamps issued
in celebration of the
establishment of the People's
Republic of China
图8：庆祝中华人民共和国成立
时发行的邮票

before International Labor Day on May 1st. We are also able to track down at least five different versions of the portrait and to link them into a chronological sequence.[25] The result of this research shows that while the subject and placement of the portrait have remained unaltered, its representation and meaning have been subject to a constant transformation. This transformation demonstrates how a public image of a national leader functions in a changing political environment, and reveals subtle but important negotiation about the concept of authority in Chinese politics.

The 1949 portrait was painted by *Zhou Lingzhao*, a well-known artist and professor from the National Art Academy (*guoli yizhuan*). The image was based on a popular photograph of *Mao*, taken by *Zheng Jingkang* at the Communist base *Yan'an* several years earlier. [26]*Zheng's* photograph shows *Mao* wearing an 'octagonal cap' and a coarse woollen jacket. The image is shot from a low angle, so that *Mao* appears to be raising his head and looking at a faraway place beyond any onlooker. *Zhou's* painting did not completely copy the photograph,

---

[25] It should be noted that published accounts about the different versions of *Mao's* portraits on *Tiananmen* contain many mistakes. One such account is in *Jia Yinting*, ed., *Tiananmen*, pp. 90. It identifies three different versions of *Mao's* portrait: (1) the one used on October 1st, 1949, (2) a 'three-quarter' portrait during 1950-1967, and (3) a 'front' portrait from 1968 to the present. My study has shown at least five versions.

[26] *Shu Jun, Tiananmen Guangchang lishi dangan* (Historical archives of *Tiananmen* Square), (B*eijing: Zhonggong zhongyang dangxiao chubanshe*, 1998), p. 43; *Wen Fu, Tiananmen jianzheng lu*, vol. 3, p. 1014. But the painter is identified differently in *Jia Yingting*, ed., *Tiananmen*, p. 92. According to this second account, the 1949 portrait was painted by *Zuo Hui*, a member of the Revolutionary Army. This account is mistaken: *Zuo Hui* was one of the painters responsible for painting the next two *Mao* portraits in 1950.

共产党领导人的群像所代替。1949年2月12日，中国共产党军队接管北京后10天，天安门广场上举行了自发性的民众欢迎会，参加集会的20万群众看到的是8张大幅肖像悬挂在天安门正墙上，[24]每幅2米宽，2.8米高，分别描绘了毛泽东、朱德、林彪、聂荣臻、叶剑英，还有其他三位领导人物。5个月以后，1949年7月7日，另一次大众集会在天安门广场举行，庆祝中国人民政治协商委员会的成立。据报道也有20万人参加，但是这次他们看到的只有两幅画像——毛泽东和朱德——挂在天安门前。三个月后，到了1949年10月1日，肖像的数目变成了一个：这是一幅巨大的6米长4.6米宽的毛泽东肖像，悬挂在天安门城楼正中的门上(图7)。这时期出现的许多其他政治图像也开始把毛和天安门联系在一起，比如，一系列纪念中华人民共和国成立的邮票将天安门画在显著位置。由于这个建筑物上的毛泽东肖像几乎微不可见，所以设计者将它特意放大，表现为天安门城楼上方天空中浮现出的毛主席胸像。

毛肖像在过去的50年里一直挂在了这个地方。甚至在毛死后，当他的"错误"被公开讨论之后，

---

[24] 参加集会的人数只是基于粗略估计。但是有证据表明有大批人参加了这次集会。例如，有114250人在中华门（原大前门）签到。据报道另有至少20000人参加而未签到。参见文夫：《天安门见证录》卷二，第424页。

however: according to a report, he first painted *Mao's* collar loose as shown in the photograph, but was asked to button the collar tight to make the image more appropriate for the solemn occasion.[27] Still, the painting shows traces of informality and a distinctive artistic style. In the portrait, *Mao's* cap leans to one side and the brim is crooked. The broad brushwork and strong contrast of light and shadow indicate a painting style favored by the artist.

This portrait was soon replaced: *Hu Qiaomu*, then the head of the News Bureau in the Central Government, invited his old acquaintance *Xin Mang* to create another portrait of *Mao* to hang on *Tiananmen*. Unlike *Zhou Lingzhao* who worked in *Shanghai* before 1949, *Xin* had joined the revolution long before 1949 and was a teacher in the *Lu Xun* Art Academy (*lu xun yishu xueyuan*) in *Yan'an*. Upon *Xin's* recommendation, several other *Yan'an* artists, including *Zuo Hui* and *Zhang Songhe*, joined him to take on the assignment. They selected a different photograph as their model, in which *Mao* was uncapped and attired in a more formal manner. But as with the first portrait, the image is taken from a low angle and *Mao* looks upward *(fig. 9)*. The three-quarter view of the Great Leader further dismisses any possible eye contact between him and a viewer. For this reason the portrait was criticized by the 'revolutionary people' after it appeared on *Tiananmen* in 1950 on International Labor Day: 'With his eyes turned upward the Chairman seems to disregard the masses.'[28] Accordingly *Xin Mang* and his colleagues came up with a third '*Tiananmen* portrait' of *Mao* based on yet

[27] General *Nie Rongzhen* made this request. See *Shu Jun, Tiananmen Guangchang lishi dangan*, p. 43.
[28] Ibid., p. 44.

Fig. 9 The 1950 International Labour Day rally in front of *Tiananmen*
图9: 1950年的五一劳动节天安门前的群众集会

another photograph. This time *Mao* no longer raises his head, but still turns his face slightly to one side and seems to avoid the viewer's gaze *(fig. 10)*. This portrait was replaced again in 1952; the new portrait was created by *Zhang Zhenshi* of the Central Academy of Art and Crafts (*zhongyang gongyi meishu xueyuan*), who was going to paint the same image for the next ten years.

Although never mentioned in any political or art historical document, the 1953 substitution marked an important stage of *Mao's* portrait on *Tiananmen*. Before this moment was a period of experimentation: both the Party leaders and the artists were still not sure what would be the best way to represent *Mao* in this sacred place. As a result, different compositions were tried and dismissed in quick succession. The 1952 portrait concluded this experimentation by setting up a number of conventions, which would be followed by all versions of the portrait in the following years. Compositionally, in this new version *Mao's* posture is perfectly frontal, and he stares straight into the viewer's eyes *(fig. 11)*. I have termed this design an iconic, 'open' composition, whose meaning relies not only on the image itself but also on a hypothetical viewing subject outside the picture.[29] In this case, *Mao's* gaze acknowledges a 'revolutionary people' before him, even when he only faces an empty *Tiananmen* Square.

Compared to the 1949 portrait, the 1952 version had a much enhanced impersonal style,

[29] *Wu Hung*, The *Wu Liang* Shrine: The Ideology of Early Chinese Pictorial Art (Stanford: Stanford University Press, 1989), pp. 132-34.

这幅画像依然挂在那里。它如此"永恒"的根本原因, 如我稍后会讨论到的, 是因为这个形象已经从一个具体人物的再现转化为国家和党的象征性标志。但同样令人深思的是, 作为如此重要的一张画像, 它的创造和发展变化却被一种奇怪的沉默所环绕: 在很长一段时间内, 很少有关于它的制作和形象变换的报道和讨论; 即使在艺术圈中, 知道这幅肖像的创作情况和作者的人也是寥寥无几。这种沉默只是在最近几年才被稍稍打破了: 在国庆50周年之前, 大量关于共和国早期的历史资料被公布出来, 其中包括关于这幅肖像的若干信息。虽然包含着一些互相矛盾的细节, 发表的数据表明至少有5位画家画过近50到60幅天安门毛主席像。(因为日晒雨淋和其他自然因素, 这幅肖像常常需要更新, 特别是在十一国庆节或五一劳动节前需要更换。) 把这些图像以年代顺序排列, 我们至少可以追踪到5个不同的版本。[25]这项研究的结果显示, 虽然天安门毛主席像的内容和地点从未改变, 它的视觉模式和含义实际上在不断地变化。这些变化提供了一个很有意义的案例, 显示出一位领导人的公共肖像是如何随着政治环境的变迁而在自我调整, 也反映出中国现代政治中权力概念

[25] 需要指出的是, 已公开发表的关于天安门毛泽东肖像的不同版本的统计存在着很多错误。例如贾英廷编的《天安门》一书第90页上有一个统计, 认定有3个不同的毛肖像的版本: (1) 用于1949年10月1日的一个版本。(2) 1950年至1967年间的一幅半侧面肖像。(3) 从1968年至今的一幅正面像。而我的研究显示至少有5个版本。

Fig. 10 The 1950 National Day
rally. Caption reads: top left,
Chairman *Mao* on *Tiananmen* is
waving his hand to the 400,000
people in the rally; right,
Chairman *Mao* sees the masses
who are waving at him.
图10：1950年国庆节的群众集会
的照片报道
原说明中写道：（上左）毛主席
在天安门城楼上向40万集会群
众挥手；（右）毛主席看着向他
挥手的群众。

和大众视觉文化的微妙协商。

1949年开国大典的肖像是周令钊所作，周是国立艺专的艺术家和教授。这幅肖像是根据毛泽东的一张著名的照片所作，照片由郑景康在解放战争期间在革命根据地延安拍摄，[26]其中毛泽东戴着八角帽，穿着粗布制服。由于摄影师采用了一个低角度拍摄，所以照片中的毛主席看起来好像是仰首远视，他的视线超越了观者射向远方。周所画的肖像并没有完全复制这张照片，据报道，他先是按照照片画了毛泽东敞开的领子，但是后来被要求把领子扣上，使肖像更符合开国大典的庄重场合。[27]但是比起以后的天安门毛主席像，这幅油画的表现还是显得有些非正式：毛的帽子向一边稍稍倾斜，边缘也不甚整齐，粗率的笔触和强烈的明暗对比显示出艺术家个人的风格趣味。

这幅肖像很快就被取代了：胡乔木，当时的新闻总署署长，介绍他的旧相识辛莽创作了另一幅

[26] 树军，《天安门广场历史档案》（北京：中国中央党校出版社，1998），第43页；文夫：《天安门见证录》卷三，第1014页。但是在贾英廷编的《天安门》（第92页）中记录的是不同的画家。根据第二个报道，1949年的肖像是由左辉画的，他是一名解放军人。这个报道是错误的：左辉是负责绘制1950年之后的两幅毛肖像的画家之一。

[27] 关于聂荣臻将军提出的这个要求，参见树军：《天安门广场历史档案》，第43页。

which was then shared by all later versions of the 'Tiananmen portrait'. In these works, traces of brushwork are painstakingly concealed, and the shadow on *Mao's* smooth face is much reduced. The pictures are nearly two-dimensional and resemble carefully edited studio photographs - but studio photographs enlarged a hundred times and translated into oil. This impersonal, monotonous style contributed to a feeling of 'invisibility' about these images: although the importance of the 'Tiananmen portrait' is well-known and people pose in front of it everyday to take pictures, no one seems to look at it with real interest. Related to this phenomenon is the 'invisibility' of the artist – another precedent set up by the 1952 version. Starting from *Zhang Zhenshi* who painted this version, making the 'Tiananmen portrait' was no longer considered a creative endeavor, but image-making that should deliberately reject any creative impulse and individuality of the artist. The model for a portrait was also no longer selected by a painter; instead his duties were reduced to rendering a chosen photograph into an oil painting and to copying this painting year after year.[30] The Party stopped assigning these duties to well-known artists, but instead created a special profession of 'Tiananmen

---

[30] Although accounts of these painters often emphasize their personal roles in creating the 'Tiananmen portrait', such descriptions cannot be entirely trusted. For example, we are told that in painting the portrait *Ge Xiaoguang* 'had to consult several dozen photographs of *Mao* taken from various angles, as well as various painted images of *Mao*.' *Qiu Xiaoyu*, 'Xiangzheng' (Symbols), *Beijing wanbao* (*Beijing* Evening Newspaper), September 19, 1999, A2. But such reports are vague and do not specify in what way the painter 'consulted' different images. The reliability of these reports is further challenged by the fact that a given version of the 'Tiananmen portrait' always closely copies a 'standard image' of *Mao* published on the front page of People's Daily, the Party's newspaper.

Fig. 11 *Sun Ziqi*, Taking a Picture with Chairman *Mao*, oil painting, 1964. This painting shows the first frontal portrait of *Mao* installed on *Tiananmen* from 1952 to 1963.
图11: 孙滋溪于1964年创作的油画《天安门前合个影》
画中的"天安门肖像"所根据的是毛在此处的第一张正面肖像，从1952年到1963年被悬挂在天安门上。

portrait' painter, who would stay on to paint the portrait for many years, often till retirement. *Zhang Zhenshi* was the first of a series of '*Tiananmen* portrait' painters and worked in this post for ten years from 1952 to 1963.[31] He was followed by two professional artists from *Beijing* Art Company (*Beijing yishu gongsi*). Among the two, *Wang Guodong* served from 1964 to 1976. His job was inherited by his student *Ge Zhaoguang*.[32] *Ge*, then a 18-year old young man, has been painting the portrait for the past 23 years. [33]

These '*Tiananmen* portrait' painters maintained an anonymous status until 1998. Seth Faison of the New York Times begins his report on his 1999 interview with *Wang Guodong* with this sentence: 'Until recently, . . . the circumstances surrounding the nation's most prominent painting were considered off-limits to the curious.'[34] In particular, *Wang* was ordered not to talk about his job, because anything to do with *Mao* or his image was so politically sensitive.' While *Wang* had pangs of pride when he rode through *Tiananmen* on his bicycle and glanced up to find his work on the majestic gate tower, few of his acquaintances knew that he painted the portrait for a whole decade.[35] It is a curious question why information about this portrait

---

[31] Some reports give the dates 1953 to 1963. But *Zhang*'s portrait of *Mao* was already hang on *Tiananmen* on National Day in 1952. See *Renmin huabao* (People's pictorial), 1952, no. 10, no page number.

[32] For *Wang Guodong*, see *Shu Jun, Tiananmen Guangchang lishi dangan*, pp. 44-45; Seth Faison, 'Prolific Chinese Painter Is Anonymous No More'.

[33] For *Ge Xiaoguang*, see *Qiu Xiaoyu, 'Xiangzheng'*.

[34] Seth Faison, 'Prolific Chinese Painter Is Anonymous No More'.

[35] Ibid.

毛泽东肖像挂在天安门上。和1949年之前在上海工作的周令钊不同，辛莽很早就参加了革命，而且是延安鲁迅艺术学院的教师。根据辛的推荐，另外几个延安艺术家，包括左辉和张松鹤都参加了这项重要的政治任务。他们选择了一张不同的照片作为样本，在这张照片中毛没有戴帽子，表情也显得庄重一点。但是和第一张画像一样，这张照片也是从低角度拍摄的，所以毛仍是向远处瞻望，似乎避免与观看者的视线接触(图9)。由于这个原因，当这幅肖像于1950年劳动节出现在天安门的时候，一些群众认为画像中的主席"眼睛往上看，好像是漠视人民大众。"[28]于是辛莽和他的同事们马上根据另一张照片制作了毛的第三幅天安门肖像。这次，毛主席不再抬头远望了，但是他的脸还是些微地朝向一侧，看起来似乎仍在避开观众的目光(图10)。这幅肖像在1952年又被替换，新的肖像由中央工艺美院的张振仕所画。在此后的十年中，他一直都在画着这同一幅肖像。

虽然从未在任何政治史或艺术史的资料中被提到，1952年的替换标志了天安门毛泽东肖像的一个最重要的变化。在此之前可以说是一个实验阶段：领导人和艺术家都还不太清楚在这个神圣的地点，究竟什么是表现毛主席的最好方式。其结果是在短短两年中，不同的形象被不断地创造和

---

[28] 同上，第44页。

had to be so tightly controlled. One can of course find the reason, as Faison has done, in the Party's penchant for secrecy. But in this case, the silence surrounding the portrait has a more particular effect of dismissing the authorship of the image. The anonymity of the painters means the autonomy of the painting: it seems no longer a work created by a particular human hand, but an image that is always there and changes on its own. People who pass *Tiananmen* rarely think about who painted the portrait or notice its changes. But the image has indeed been changing: the middle-aged Chairman in the 1952 portrait became in the 1963 version an older man with a faint smile on his lips, which again became an even older man in the 1967 version, whose mask-like face shows no sign of emotion or thoughts *(fig. 12)*. With the authorship of these different versions erased, the changes of the '*Tiananmen* portrait' and the aging of its subject are collapsed into a single, natural process. The portrait seems to grow itself, and the image seems both autonomous and automatous.

This leads us to consider an important question: What is the relationship between the portrait and *Mao*, or between a public image of a political leader and the leader himself? More specifically, in what sense does the portrait represent *Mao*, and in what way is the change of the portrait related to that of its subject? The relationship between *Mao* and the '*Tiananmen* portrait', I propose, can be conceptualized as consisting of four operations: magnifying, substituting, masking, and detachment. Magnifying means enlarging a subject's appearance when the subject himself is present, thereby increasing the significance and 'aura' of the subject, causing him to be held in greater esteem and respect. The '*Tiananmen* portrait' exercised this role typically when *Mao* ascended *Tiananmen* to review a National

快速地更换。1952年的肖像给这一系列实验画了一个句号, 确立了一些基本约定, 为以后的画像奠定了一个基础。在这个版本中, 毛的肖像变成完全正面, 而且直视着观者的眼睛(图11)。我在讨论宗教偶像时曾将这类构图称作为一种"开放"型图像, 其意义不仅在于图像内部, 也依赖于假定观众或崇拜者的存在。[29]换言之, 即使只是面对着一个空荡荡的广场, 毛的直视的目光仍然隐含了面前的无数革命群众。

与1949年的肖像相比, 1952年的版本具有更强烈的非个人风格, 而这种风格被其后所有版本的"天安门肖像"所共享。在这些作品中, 笔触的痕迹被小心地掩藏起来, 毛脸上的阴影被大量地减少, 整个画面平整干净。其结果是这些画像几乎成为二维的再现了, 像是被精心处理过的影廊照片, 或是被放大了百倍以上的照片转换成的油画。这种非个人的单调风格给这些图像造成了一种"隐身"(invisible)的效果: 虽然"天安门肖像"的重要性众所周知, 虽然每天都有无数人在它面前摆姿势照相, 但实际上并没有人真正仔细地看它。与这种现象相关的是画像艺术家的"隐身", 这也是1952年版本引进的另一个先例。从画这个版本的张振仕开始, "天安门肖像"的制作不再被定义为

[29] 巫鸿:《武梁祠——中国早期画像的思想性》(斯坦福:斯坦福大学出版社, 1989), 第132-34页。

Fig. 12 A standard frontal version
of *Mao's* portrait displayed on
Tiananmen after 1967.
图12：一张标准的毛晚期肖像，
代表了1967年"天安门画像"的
基本模式。

创造性的艺术活动，而仅仅变成了图像的技术性的翻制，而这种翻制的一个重要特点是刻意排除
艺术家的原创性和个性。画像所依据的照片也不再由画家决定，他们的职责因此被降低到最低限
度，将一张挑选出来的照片翻译成一幅没有艺术性格的油画，然后年复一年地复制它。[30]承担这样
任务的人不再是知名艺术家，而是形成了我称做"天安门肖像画家"的一种特殊职业，这些画家常常
是多年甚至终身从事这个工作，直到退休为止。张振仕是个职业的第一人，从1952年到1963年整整
画了10年。[31]承继他的是两位来自北京艺术公司的职业画工，其中王国栋从1964年工作到1976年。
他的工作随后被他的学生葛小光继承。[32]从18岁开始，葛小光在过去的23年里一直负责画这幅肖
像。[33]

　　这些"天安门肖像"画家的匿名状态在1998年终于结束了。《纽约时报》的塞斯·费森（Seth

[30] 张振仕1950年在中央美术学校美术供应肖像股长。1956年调中央工艺美术学校，任基础课教研主任。并不是如有些介绍说的
是当时的"著名画家"。此外，虽然关于这些画家的报道经常强调他们在创造"天安门肖像"中的个人角色，这些描述并不能被完全
确信。例如，我们被告知在绘制肖像中葛小光"不得不参考几十张从不同角度拍摄的毛泽东的照片和个中毛泽东的画像。"（《北京
晚报》，1999年9月19日，A2）。但是这些报道是含糊的，没有详细说出画家是如何"参考"不同画像的。这些报道的可靠性也进一
步受到这一事实的挑战：一个给定的"天安门肖像"的版本总是接近于复制了毛泽东在《人民日报》头版上发表的标准像。

Day parade. In such a grand ritual, *Tiananmen* Square was covered with 300,000, 400,000, or even 500,000 'revolutionary masses'. No one in this human ocean could really make out *Mao's* tiny silhouette in the distance. Yet they cried out with joy and excitement, because the Chairman was there and was looking at them *(see fig. 10)*. Unconsciously they perceived *Mao* and the portrait together: *Mao's* human body was magnified by his enormous portrait and merged with the portrait. In contrast, substituting means replacing *Mao* with the portrait, which stood for the absent Chairman most of the year. With *Mao's* giant image posted on its front wall, *Tiananmen* was 'occupied' even when no mass parade took place and the Chairman was not on the rostrum. This significance of the portrait is most acutely felt when it is temporarily removed from *Tiananmen* for substitution or repair: the gate tower suddenly becomes naked and 'faceless', and the Square suddenly loses its focus.

As explained at the beginning of this essay, to mask is to enhance or alter a person's appearance with a manufactured face; masking thus implies both disguise and performance. Based on this definition, the '*Tiananmen* portrait' is a mask whether it magnifies or substitutes for *Mao*, because in both cases the image is highly idealized and never overlaps with the real Chairman in age or look. For one thing, the portrait is always younger than its subject: a 'standardized version' of the portrait, *biaozhunxiang* in officialese, is normally used for many years without changing, even though during these years *Mao* aged considerably or even died. Although each version is based on a photograph, the photographic model is already heavily edited and the portrait further idealizes it. Each version stresses certain character traits of its subject. For example, it is reported that *Wang Guodong*' made a special effort to

Faison) 在1999年对多年参与绘制毛主席肖像的王其智进行了采访, 随后在他的报道中这样写到 : "直到近来, ……围绕着这个最重要的国家绘画的一切仍被认为是好奇心的禁区。"[34] 王"被特别告知不可谈论他的工作, 因为和毛泽东有关的任何事情都是极为敏感的政治问题。"我们很难知道当肖像绘制者在路过天安门广场的时候, 看着挂在庄严城楼上他们的作品时, 他们的内心会是什么感觉——是骄傲还是遗憾？因为甚至连他们身边的人都不一定知道他们整整数十年都在画这幅肖像。[35] 这种情况提出了一个值得深思的问题 : 为什么有关这幅肖像的信息需要如此保密？一般的推测是——正如费森所解释的——这是因为国家机构对保密的执著。但是这个回答可能过于简

[31] 一些报道给出的时间是1953年至1963年。但是张的毛肖像在1952年的国庆已经挂在了天安门上。参见《人民日报》1952年, no. 10, 无页码。

[32] 关于王国栋的情况, 参见树军 :《天安门广场历史档案》, 第44-45页；塞斯·费森 (Seth Faison),《多产的中国画家不再匿名》。

[33] 关于葛小光, 见《北京晚报》, 1999年9月19日, A2。

[34] 塞斯·费森,《多产的中国画家不再匿名》。

[35] 同上。

emphasize Chairman *Mao's* benevolence and kindness, while at the same time brought out other dimensions in the Chairman's character such as his sharpness, resourcefulness, and penetrating intelligence.'[36] *Ge Xiaoguang*, on the other hand, is said to 'have done his best to represent the broad mind and deep thoughts of Chairman *Mao* through carefully depicting his gaze. To him, *Mao's* gaze serves to unite a leader with the people and to link the past with the present and future.'[37]

Ge's words reveal an important function of the '*Tiananmen* portrait' as a mask. By magnifying *Mao's* face or replacing *Mao* with a face-image, this portrait effectively emphasizes the power of the gaze. I have mentioned that starting from 1953, *Mao* has been depicted as staring directly into the onlooker's eyes, and in a broader sense his gaze has been dominating *Tiananmen* Square and the population it symbolizes. This effect... was consciously sought after by the painters of this portrait. Again citing *Ge Xiaoguang*, 'This image is very different from any indoor painting in its method of representation and visual effect... It should be equally ideal when viewed from front or sideways, and equally powerful when viewed from any spot in *Tiananmen* Square, whether from the Golden Water Moat, the national flag pole, or from the Monument to the People's Heroes.'[38]

Finally, detachment means the portrait's eventual separation from its figural subject to acquire a broader 'subject matter'. This process took place after *Mao's* death in three steps.

---

[36] *Shu Jun, Tiananmen Guangchang lishi dangan*, p. 44.

[37] Ibid., p. 46.

[38] Cited in *Jia Yinting*, ed., *Tiananmen*, p. 92.

单了，因为在这个案例中，环绕着这幅肖像的沉默有着一个更特别的作用，那就是取消这幅画的"作者身份"(authorship)。绘画者的匿名进而意味着画像本身的自治：它似乎不再出于某个具体个人之手，而是在那里自我变化着。走过天安门的人很少会去思考是谁画了这幅肖像，也很少会注意到它的变化。但是这幅图像确实一直在变化之中：1952年肖像中的中年的毛主席在1963年变成了一个唇边隐约微笑、更为年长慈祥的领袖。1967年的版本就显得较为苍老了，其面具般的脸不再表达任何情感或思想(图12)。随着这些不同版本作品的作者身份的抹去，"天安门肖像"的更新和它的主体的不断变化被归结为一个简单而自然的生物过程：这幅肖像看起来好像是在自我生长，图像成为既是自治的，又是自动的。

这继而引发我们去思考另一个重要的问题：毛泽东和他的肖像之间到底有着怎样的关系？或者说，一个公共空间中的政治肖像和政治领袖本人之间的关系是什么？再准确一点：这幅肖像是如何代表毛泽东的？而这幅肖像的变化又以何种方式与它的主体相关？我认为，毛泽东和"天安门肖像"之间的关系可以被概括为四种运作方式，即"放大"(magnifying)、"替代"(substituting)，"面具"(masking)和"分离"(detachment)。"放大"是指当主体自身还存在的时候对主体的放大性表现，从而增强主体的重要性和"光韵"(aura)，使他得到更多的尊重和膜拜。"天安门肖像"的这种机制在

First, a memorial ceremony was held in *Tiananmen* Square on 18 September 1976 *(fig. 13)*. *Tiananmen's* balcony was left empty and sealed off with a black banner. All the Party leaders stood below the gate tower on a temporary platform. The ceremony reached its climax when the leaders, as well as 500,000 'revolutionary masses' behind them, faced *Tiananman* and the '*Tiananmen* portrait' – not a colored oil painting but an enormous black-and-white photograph made for the occasion – in silent tribute. The portrait was later changed back to an oil version, but it had gone through a 'funeral' and resurfaced as a resurrected image.

Second, *Mao's* Mausoleum was unveiled in 1977 at the anniversary of the Chairman's death; the corpse of the Great Leader was displayed inside it for public viewing. Located at the south end of *Tiananmen* Square, this mammoth building formed a direct counterpart to *Tiananmen*. The opposition between the two structures, as well as the counter-relationship between *Mao's* preserved corpse and his portrait as a living person, expressed graphically the separation between the past and the present. The idea is that although *Mao* is dead, his '*Tiananmen* portrait' will continue to represent the country and the Communist leadership. This expanded 'subject matter' of the portrait was finalized by *Deng Xiaoping* in 1980 – the third step in renewing the image's meaning. Punished by *Mao* during the Cultural Revolution, *Deng's* return to the leadership in 1977 brought about a re-evaluation of *Mao* and the political movement *Mao* started. The '*Mao* cult' was criticized in the following years; the huge statues and portraits of the Great Leader in every school and factory were destroyed or removed in the early 1980s. As a signal of this trend, the two large *Mao* images above the main entrances of the Great Hall of the People in *Tiananmen* Square came down on 30 July

毛泽东检阅国庆游行时尤为明显。在这类盛大的仪式中，天安门广场容纳了30万、40万，甚至50万"革命群众"。没有人真的能从遥远的广场中看清天安门上的主席。但是他们还是兴奋而狂热地向他欢呼，因为主席就在"那里"而且在注视着他们(图10)。不知不觉中，他们将毛泽东与"天安门肖像"合而为一：毛的肉身被他的大幅肖像放大，同时融入了这幅肖像之中。与这种运作相反，"替换"是指用这幅人造肖像来取代真实的毛泽东。实际上，即使当主席还活着，他在天安门上的日常缺席都由这幅画像的持续存在而得到补偿。因此，即使没有国庆游行，即使主席并没有站在观礼台上，有了挂在城楼上的这幅肖像，天安门就被安全地"占据"了。这种运作被最强烈地感受到的时候，是当毛主席肖像由于被替换或修补而被暂时地移开：天安门城楼似乎突然变得空空荡荡，不再具有一个具体的"面孔"，而硕大的广场也在突然之间失去了一个可以依赖的焦点。

如我在这篇文章开始时谈到的，"面具"是通过一张人造的脸来强化或改变一个人的形象，因此含有"乔装"和"表演"的双重意义。从这个角度看，不论是"放大"还是"替代"，"天安门肖像"都可以说是一个"面具"，因为在这两种情况中，这张图像都是高度理想化了的，它并不在年龄与外表上与真实的主席严格重叠。在大多情况下，这幅肖像总是比它的真实主体要年轻：肖像所依据的"标准像"常

常是使用多年而不做重要改变；即使当毛已经年老病重，甚至在他死了之后，他的精神熠熠的形象仍然注视着我们。此外，虽然每个版本都基于照片，但照片中的形象总是被改动和美化。不同版本常常强调主席的某种特殊的理想性格。例如，据报道，王国栋"努力地强化毛主席的慈祥，同时还有主席的其他一些特征，比如他的思想的敏锐，他的足智多谋，和他的具有穿透力的智慧。"[36]而葛小光被认为是"尽了最大的努力，通过仔细地描绘毛主席的目光，表现了主席的宽广的胸怀和深刻的思想。对他来说，这个目光使得群众与领袖相连，也把过去、现在和未来联系起来。"[37]

葛小光的这番话揭示了"天安门肖像"作为一个"面具"的重要功能：通过放大毛的脸，将毛本人替换成了一张硕大的脸部形象，这幅图像有效地强调了目光和凝视（gaze）的力量。我在讨论1952年画像时已经提到过这点：从这幅肖像开始，毛被描绘成直视着观众的眼睛，在更广阔的意义上，他的"凝视"占据了整个天安门广场和它所象征的广大群众。这种效果被画这幅肖像的艺术家们有意识地追求着。再以葛小光本人的话来说，"这幅画像的表现手法和视觉效果和任何室内油画都不

[36] 树军：《天安门广场历史档案》，第44页。

[37] 同上，第46页。

1980. When the Italian reporter Oriana Fallaci interviewed *Deng Xiaoping* in August that year, she immediately focused on the fate of the *'Tiananmen* portrait': Will it be kept or removed? *Deng's* answer is that although other 'excessive images' of *Mao* should go, this particular image will stay. In his words, 'We will forever hang Chairman *Mao's* portrait on *Tiananmen* as a symbol of the People's Republic, and will forever commemorate him as the founder of our Party and country.' [39] With this statement, the new symbolism of the portrait is sanctioned as part of *'Deng Xiaoping* thought': representing *Mao* as if he is still living, this portrait now stands for an eternal present of the Party and the country, while *Mao's* physical body in the Mausoleum serves as a reminder of the past.

[39] *Wen Fu, Tiananmen jianzheng lu*, vol. 3, pp. 1024; see also the same book, vol. 3, pp. 1017-18.

同……不论是从正面看还是从侧面看，它都必须同样完美。从天安门广场的任何地点，不论是金水河，国旗杆还是人民英雄纪念碑，从任何角度来看它都必须一样有力。"[38]

最后，"分离"的机制意味着肖像最终要与它的表现主体分开，而获得一种更广泛意义上的"主体性"(subjectivity)。这个过程在毛主席逝世后发生，经过三个阶段得到实现。首先，1976年9月18日在天安门广场举行了一场浩大的追悼会(图13)：天安门上的观礼台空着，用黑色横幅封了起来。所有党和国家领袖都站在城楼下面临时搭建的一个平台上。当这些领导和他们身后的50万革命群众面对天安门和"天安门肖像"默哀时，这个仪式达到了高潮。值得注意的是，在这个仪式中，天安门上所挂的彩色油画肖像被替换成了一张黑白肖像。但是当仪式结束之后，彩色的版本又重新归位。这两个变化的象征意义很清楚：经历过一次葬礼，主席的存在被重新建立。

第二个阶段实现于毛死后的翌年，也就是1977年发生：毛主席纪念堂正式建成开放，伟大领袖的遗体现在可以被大众瞻仰。这幢巨大的建筑物位于天安门广场南端，与天安门遥遥呼应。这两幢建筑之间的相对位置，正如毛的遗体与他活生生的肖像的相对位置，形象地表达了"历史"与"现时"

[38] 引自贾英廷编：《天安门》，第92页。

之间的联系和分离。虽然毛已去世,但是他的"天安门肖像"将继续代表社会主义国家的政体和共产党的领导地位。

"天安门肖像"的这种延伸了的含义,也就是这幅画像的新的主体性,被邓小平在1980年最后确立下来,这是这个图像意义更新的第三个阶段。众所周知,邓小平在"文化大革命"中被批判,他的回归导致对毛泽东以及毛所发动的这场政治运动的重新评价。这个反思的一个直接的结果是对毛泽东个人崇拜的矫正,具体表现为拆除每个学校和工厂中树立的巨大的主席雕像或画像。作为这个改革的一个确定信号,天安门广场西侧人民大会堂入口处悬挂的巨大毛泽东像在1980年7月30日被取下。当著名意大利记者奥丽亚娜·法拉奇 (Oriana Fallaci) 在同年8月采访邓小平的时候,她立即将话题集中在"天安门肖像"的命运上:它将会被保留还是会被移走?邓的回答是:虽然其他过多的毛画像应该被取掉,但这幅特殊的画像还是要留在那里。用他的话来说:"我们会永远将毛主席像挂在天安门上作为中华人民共和国的象征,也将永远把他作为我们党和国家的奠基人来纪念他。"[39]这段话说明,这幅肖像的新的象征意义已成为"邓小平思想"的一个组成部分:虽然纪念堂水晶棺中毛的遗体不断提示着人们这位领袖已经是一个历史的过去,但天安门上栩栩如生的画像象征着党的领导和社会主义国家整体的永恒。

(薛莲 译,巫鸿 校)

[39] 文夫:《天安门见证录》卷3,第1024页;同见于该书,卷3,第1017-1018页。

The Context of the Project:
The *Tiananmen* Grandstands

项目背景简介: 天安门观礼台

The *Tiananmen* Grandstands

Tiananmen Square is not only the geographic centre of *Beijing*, but also the symbol of the country, as well as the stage of most of modern China's political campaigns.

Tiananmen Square was first built in the eighteenth year of the *Yongle* reign period of the *Ming* dynasty (1420). The open space was surrounded by red walls shaped like a capital 'T'. During the *Ming* and *Qing* dynasties, the palace wall and the thousand-step-corridor *qianbulang* closed off *Tiananmen* Square to be a courtyard space. Following the 1911 Revolution which overthrew the *Qing* dynasty, the thousand-step-corridor was demolished in 1913 and the closed pattern of *Tiananmen* Square was broken. An east-west passage across the Square was now possible. On 4th May 1919, the students of *Beijing* University paraded to *Tiananmen* Square triggering the May 4th Patriotic Movement which changed the axis of the development of Chinese culture. On 1st October 1949, New China held its founding ceremony in the Square starting the new era of socialist government. To provide for the forthcoming founding ceremony, the *Beijing* Municipal People's Government implemented the first renovation of *Tiananmen* Square in September 1949. The work was started on September 1st and finished on September 30th to ensure the smooth progress of the ceremony. The renovation work included removing the weeds on the *Tiananmen* Gate, painting all the pillars and walls, constructing a base and flagpole 22.5 metres in height, constructing eight reviewing stands, renovating the parapets of the Jade Belt River *yudaihe* in front of *Tiananmen* Square, cleaning the rubbish piled up on *Tiananmen* Square, levelling the 54,000 sq. metres of the Square and constructing an asphalt road of 1,626 sq. metres.

天安门观礼台

天安门广场不仅是北京的地理中心，也是我们国家的象征，还是中国近现代不少政治运动的舞台。

天安门广场始建于明永乐18年（1420年），红墙围成"T"字形的广场空间，明清两代时，宫墙和千步廊把天安门广场封闭起来，完全成为宫廷广场。1911年辛亥革命推翻满清王朝以后，于1913年拆除掉千步廊，天安门广场的封闭格局被打破，打通了东西贯通的通道。1919年5月4日，北京大学的学生游行至天安门，引发了改变中国文化发展方向的"五·四"爱国运动。1949年10月1日，新中国在这里举行开国大典，从此中国开始了社会主义的新时代。为迎接开国大典，北京市人民政府于1949年9月实施了对天安门广场的第一次整修。工程于9月1日开工，于9月30日完工，保证了开国大典的顺利进行。整修工程包括清除天安门城楼的杂草，粉刷全部台柱、大墙，修建高22.5米的旗杆和基座，修建8座观礼台，整修天安门前玉带河的栏杆和护墙，清运堆积于天安门广场的垃圾，并平整碾压广场5.4万平方米，修建沥青路1626平方米。

天安门前的观礼台，是天安门城楼的主要装饰建筑，与金水河、公生桥、华表、石狮等作为天安门的附属裙带部分。1949年在天安门城楼前东西两侧、金水河南北两面塔设置了观礼台，是为了

The *Tiananmen* Grandstands occupy an area in front of the *Tiananmen* Gate and are regarded as significant architectural features of *Tiananmen*, along with the *Jinshui* River, the *Gongsheng* Bridge, the ornamental columns *huabiao* and the Stone Lions. In 1949, the stands were set up in an east - west direction in front of Tiananmen and to the north and south of the *Jinshui* River, for the leaders of the central departments, resident foreign experts, exemplary individuals, model workers and other senior personnel to view the ceremony. Due to the urgency of the work, the temporary stands were made in fir wood. There were eight reviewing stands in total capable of accommodating up to 3000 people, branching out from the centre with four rostrums located to the north bank of the outer *Jinshui* river and four to the south bank. In order to facilitate viewing, the stands were designed in the form of a ladder. There were spaces for resting and facilities for refreshments and toilets under the stands. These temporary stands were set up on every 1st May and 1st October during the following years. They were taken down as soon as the ceremony was over. With the major renovation of *Tiananmen* in 1952, it was decided that the temporary stands should be replaced by permanent Grandstands of a mixed reinforced concrete and brick structure. The designer was *Zhang Kaiji*. In 1983, the wooden Grandstands built in 1952 were demolished and rebuilt. With the rebuilding, the four stands along the south bank of the *Jinshui* River were removed and the area replanted. Only the four stands to the north of the river were reconstructed. There were two stands to the east and two to the west side of *Tiananmen* Gate, alongside the east and west *Gongsheng* Bridges. The shape of the two stands closest to *Tiananmen* are rectangular in shape, 95.3 metres in length, east to west and 11.7 metres

让中央部门的负责人、驻中国长期工作的外国专家、模范等代表人物、先进分子能够一起观礼，因为时间紧迫，当时用杉篙搭建了临时性的观礼看台，在正面将城台让开，在其外侧东面各4座，分置于外金水河南北两岸，总共8座，可以同时容纳3000人一起观礼，为了便于观看，看台设置成阶梯形状，看台下是饮水、休息和用厕空间。这种类似的临时性看台在接下来每年的5月1日和10月1日都会搭建，用完即拆，直到1952年对天安门进行大修建的时候，决定将临时性的看台改建成永久性钢筋混凝土与砖砌混合结构的观礼台，设计师为张开济。1983年又将1952年建造的观礼台拆除重建。重建后的观礼台取消金水河南岸4座，将其改为绿化带，对河北岸4座进行修建，天安门前东西两侧各2座，分别列于东、西公生桥两侧，接近天安门的2座呈折边矩形，东西宽95.3米，南北长11.7米；离天安门较远处的2座也呈矩形，东西宽42.4米，南北长宽11.7米。

deep from north to south. The shape of the two stands more distant from *Tiananmen* are also rectangular, 42.4 metres long from east to west and 11.7 deep from north to south.

Wang Jianwei
Project: The Grandstand

汪建伟 《观礼台》方案

The Milan Cathedral, Milan, Italy
意大利米兰大教堂

Buckingham Palace, London,
United Kingdom
英国伦敦白金汉宫

The Louvre Museum, Paris, France
法国巴黎卢浮宫博物馆

Archives

视觉档案

Tiananmen, the *Chengtian* Gate, in the
Republic of China period
天安门（承天门，民国时期）

The 'T' shaped Square that
existed between the *Daming*
Gate and the *Chengtian* Gate
大明门至承天门的"T"字形
广场

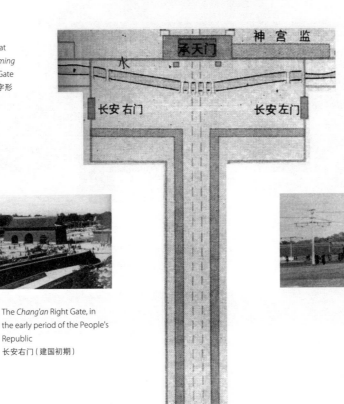

The *Chang'an* Right Gate, in
the early period of the People's
Republic
长安右门（建国初期）

The *Chang'an* Left Gate, in the
early period of the People's
Republic
长安左门（建国初期）

The *Daming* Gate, also known
as the *Daqing* Gate
大明门（大清门）

An old photograph of the
Chengtian Gate, also known as
the *Tiananmen*
承天门（天安门）旧照

An old photograph of the
Outer *Jinshui* Bridge, before the
fortified wall was built
外金水桥未砌河墙之前的旧照

Plan of *Tiananmen* Square
during the *Ming* dynasty
明代天安门广场平面示意图

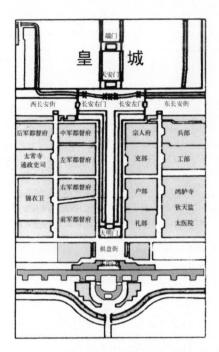
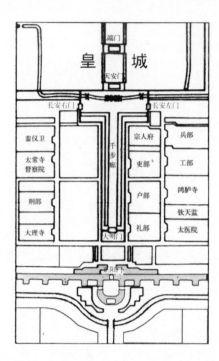

Plan of *Tiananmen* Square
during the *Xuan Tong* reign of
the *Qing* dynasty 1821-1850
清朝宣统年间天安门广场平面图

Plan of *Tiananmen* Square
before Liberation in 1949
解放前夕的天安门广场平面
示意图

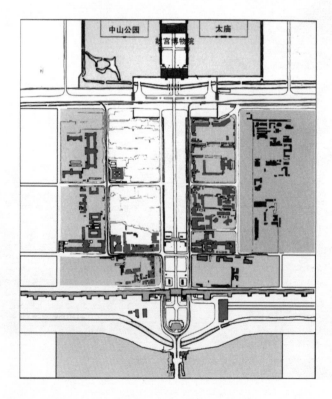

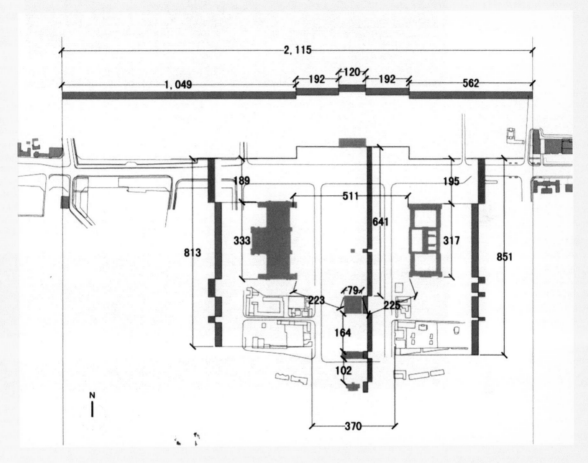

Tiananmen Square and its environs
天安门广场围合感分析图

Tiananmen Square before
rebuilding and after the
demolition of public housing
in 1958
1958年改造前没有拆民房时的
天安门广场

Looking north towards
Tiananmen Square from the
Zhengyang Gate, 1954
从正阳门北望天安门广场
（1954年）

Tiananmen Square in
1954,looking south from the
Tiananmen Gate
1954年的天安门广场（从天安
门城楼南望）

华南圭認為北京城牆应該拆除

并主張保持天安門的固有性格

以市人民代表身份視察北京城市总体規划

本报訊 市人民代表大会代表华南圭視察北京城市总体規划后，已經写出了書面視察报告，准备送交市人民委員会。

华南圭对于天安門广場規划提出意見，現在制定的十一个規划方案都还不能令人满意。重要缺点表現在天安門近身和正陽桥近身的处理上。他說：天安門近身应該保存原有的規模，华表、石獅与金水桥都应原封不动，这样才能保留天安門的固有性格。他不同意有个方案中要把华表、石獅暖代以石碑、石柱的做法。对于天安門前的临时观礼台，华南圭主張改用可以裝卸的轻便活台，在"五一"、"十一"安裝起来，过后拆去。对于正陽桥近身，华南圭感到除第一規划方案画出南北两岸的濱河大道外，其他方案只在南岸規划有一条濱河大道，是令人不解的事。

对于北京城牆去留的問題，华南圭以旧作專論两篇，交給本报表示意見。他在文中举出四十条理由，說明拆除北京城牆有很多好处。其中主要之点有：（一）拆除城牆可以使城内城外打成一片，消除城郊隔閡。（二）从城市整体規划着想，拆除城牆以后，城内外的建筑风格容易达到配合和諧。城牆存在，則妨碍首都整体規划，例如，国际飯店、新侨飯店都因为受到城牆的妨碍，正門不得不面对狭窄的小路。假使城牆不存在，則这两座飯店就能面对濱河大路，风格之壯，非笔墨所能形容。（三）北京整体規划，需要一条环形太路。而城牆地基下的土壤，就是很堅固的路床，利用它筑路节省当时省錢。另一方面是拆除城牆后可以展宽綠化的护城河，其規模之壯，风景之美，將是世界無四。（四）拆除城牆有很大經济意义，北京内外城牆，总長約八十华里，高约十公尺，厚度平均以十公尺計，皮厚假定三公尺，則拆去城牆可以得到土方二百八十万立方公尺，用这些出可以填北京城地面七十万平方公尺。拆下的碑料有一百二十万立方公尺，合四丁億六万万塊。此外还可以腾出一百二十万平方公尺的地面，若建六层高楼，可以得到七十万間的建筑面积。

华南圭在論述中还批判拆城牆也看成是古建筑而要求保留的說法。他說，对待遺产应区别精华与精粗，如三大殿和頤和园等是精华应該保留，而碑土堆成的城牆則不能与頤和园等同日而語。他也不同意把城牆頂辟作花园的主張。他說："园在牆頂，人民則不易享受，灌漑大成問題。由地面走上城頂，須以一百余級踏步，老人孕妇，都没有这个力气。

是在工艺造形上，如梁舉的一些例子，却是很難...

第二，梁先生对...艺术效果的估計看过分了。虽然这个設計在...面，除了几个主要缺点...本上是符合要求的。在...間处理上有某些努力...一定的局部的效果，但...沒有由于追求形式而造...質，例如水塔的处理...窗子，复杂的綫条等...建筑的設計人，會經...題検討过，現在也不准备...在大門处理的設計过程...有过論的，但作为設...

关于梁思成先生对建筑的主張
华攬洪工程师来信提出意見

編輯同志：

讀了五月十七日报上發表的梁思成先生訪問記，我有以下意見：

第一，梁先生在談到民族形式时过分强調了建筑必須表現民族特征。我以为將建筑表現形式摆在創作的第一位是不恰当的。抗碑瓦的改进在將来条件具备时未必不可以考虑，但不論是目前还是將来，用最經济的方法解决千百万人的居住問題和生活問題，总是处于首要地位。在建筑表現形式上，給予一定的民族风格是創作上应該努力的方向之一，但...

兒兵很少人性

胡明教授認为，在用人問題上，中国历史上有两个标准，一个是唯賢唯能，一个是唯亲唯故。在師大發生的用人唯亲唯故的現象屡見不鲜。他說："在干部提拔上對'賢'、'能'考虑过少，任人唯亲，这是家天下的作风。"他認为党过去在使用群众方面，也有不妥之处他說："解放后，从整个党的事業和国民党反动派相比是'妙得很'，但是同共产主义事業相比則'糟得很'。"他对他个人以及俄文系在師大的地位深表不满。他說："俄群系在師大的地位是处在九層地獄之下，住房子、骨級評薪、待遇、編制等問題全都得不到解决。"他还对党群关系發表了意見。他說："党員除了优越感以外，还有就是不懂人情，很少人性，对人無誠墾、無同情，正美其名曰战斗性。党内認为这是优点，群众認为这是坏的。群众对党、团員'可望而不可及'，'室而生畏'，他还有什么力量？"

刘世楷說：人民内部
矛盾应当由法律解决，
用不着采取运动方式

物理系教授刘世楷不主張搞运动，主張党赶快立法，把实际执行宪法的各种法律制定、頒行。他說："运动是救急的手段，不是常法。比如医...

說："人民希望党員和共...都負責守法，不希望任...作了好事只是検討一遍...事。"

刘世楷还建議党重...气节的培养和社会道德...育。

陶大鏞認为：現行党...
有缺陷，贊成民主...

陶大鏞教授認为現行...制有缺陷，贊成民主办...說："現行的党委制虽...但从过去的工作上看...干部中的党員现在了解...校規律的人还不多，要...等学校是不容易的。我...'民办公校'。总的精...將来各学校中有关数学...研究工作，数授有决定...了加强党在高等学校内...作用，將来应把行政工...学、科学研究工作分开...交行政会議处理，后者...委員会处理。学术委員...授、副教授、講师、助...組成，党委会可派代表...在会上提出党委的建議...术委員会不一定要遵照...意見目前。"

因此，有些教授認...的問題揭發得并不徹底...群众还是有顧慮。師大...采取措施鼓励大家融...放。

A plan for the redesign of
Tiananmen Square, 1950
天安门广场建设计划图（1950年）

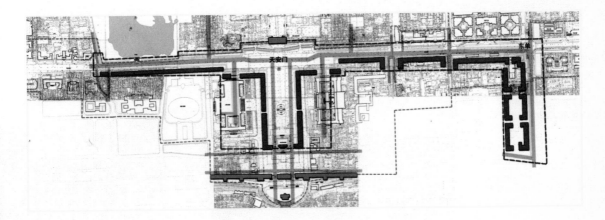

Plan of *Tiananmen* Square after
rebuilding in 1959
1959年改建后的天安门广场平
面示意图

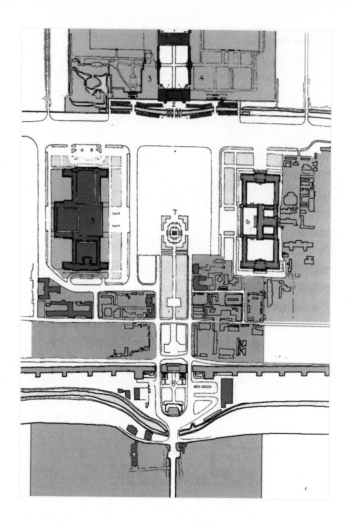

Tiananmen Square after
rebuilding in October 1959
1959年10月改建后的天安
门广场

Aerial view of *Tiananmen*
Square in 1999
天安门广场航拍图（1999年）

Birds eye view of *Tiananmen*
Square after refurbishment
改造后的天安门广场鸟瞰图

Beijing's citizens and soldiers
attending the founding
ceremony of the state
参加开国大典的北京军民

A plan of the parade by people
attending the 15th anniversary
of the founding of the State
国庆15周年群众游行队伍行
进路线图

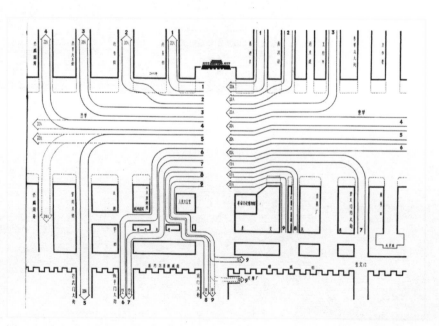

Military Rocket Units passing in front of *Tiananmen* during the celebration of the founding of the state, 1984
1984年国庆节行进在天安门前的战略火箭方队

A parade of people forming the Chinese characters 'Reform and Open Door Policy', ceremony for the 50th year of the State, 1999
国庆50周年游行队伍行进和群众组字"改革开放"（1999年）

The Grandstand as a 'Relationship'

Based on an interview with *Wang Jianwei* in *Beijing*
on 7th July 2007

"观礼台"作为一种"关系"

时间: 2007年7月2日
地点: 北京
采访对象: 汪建伟

The 'Grandstand' project was inspired by my video work 'Buildings for Daily Life' made in 1997, which consisted of 10 parts. I was questioning the identity of the so-called 'video artist' and kept raising doubts about 'rules'. So even within one piece of work, my thinking methods have changed consistently.

The second part of the video was called 'History of a Space'. It was about buildings in the Central Square of *Chengdu*, the capital city of *Sichuan* Province. There had been a very old building in the Square, *Liu Bei*'s Chamber; *Liu Bei* was the emperor of the *Shu* Kingdom during the Three Kingdoms period (220AD - 280AD). In 1967, the Chamber was demolished in order to build a 'Long Live *Mao Zedong* Memorial Hall' in its place. I sought out one of the architects responsible for the Memorial Hall. It took him a long time to tell me that no one would want to admit to having designed this building. Because an historic building was destroyed, being architects they felt guilty. Then he told me about the circumstances in which the Memorial Hall was built. He said that all the measurements of the building are symbolic. For instant, the height of the stairs relates to *Mao*'s birthday; the first section of the staircase has 56 stairs that symbolises the 56 nations that make up China and so on. Then a feeling suddenly struck me. I began to notice something invisible in buildings. Usually we focus too much on the visible parts of a building, such as its' dimensions, facade, building materials, etc. But 'relationship' is also an important aspect of buildings. This relationship, to a great extent, actually leads to its soul, artistic style and other aspects. This is not a question that is answered within the histories of architecture or art, but a question that I am interested in and one that is the cause of this work.

问：请谈谈对于"观礼台"作品方案的一些想法。

汪："观礼台"这个作品的产生，来自于我在1997年曾做过的一个叫《日常生活的建筑》的影像，它共由十个部分组成。当时我对两个问题很有感受，即艺术家身份的确定，和对作为video艺术家身份的怀疑，其实我对"规则"有一种持续性的质疑，所以在我的作品里，对某个作品的思考方式实际上也都是在变化的。

《日常生活的建筑》这个作品的第一个部分当时叫"空间的历史"，是关于成都的市中心广场，这个中心广场以前曾是刘备的一个议事厅，1967年的时候被夷为平地，在那里建立了"毛泽东（万岁）纪念馆"。我找到了当时与之有关的建筑师，他用很长的时间告诉我，说没有人愿意承认是这个建筑的设计者，因为破坏了历史建筑，总是有种负罪感。然后他又讲了在什么样的情况下产生出这个建筑，他说这个建筑的任何尺寸、尺度都是具有象征性的，比如台阶高度的数字是毛泽东的生日，第一层台阶有56阶，象征着56个民族等等……，我突然就有一种感觉，开始注意到建筑里这些看不见的东西。我们一般有很多注意力集中在了建筑看得见的地方，比如它的尺度、立面、建筑材料等，但是建筑有一个很重要的地方就是"关系"，而且"关系"在很大程度上有时候就直接导致了这个建筑的产生及造型风格等方面，这不属于建筑史和艺术史内部要解决的问题，但这是我感兴趣

The interview with *Zhang Kaiji*, the designer of the Grandstands in *Tiananmen* Square was a section of one part of 'History of a Space'. When *Huang Zhuan* decided to curate the State Legacy exhibition, I remembered those events that I have referred to above. For me, the exhibition is full of 'rules' yet still being in an unsolved state, consequently I proposed the Grandstands as my project.

At the beginning, I imagined two lines: a line for the space and a line for the time. The time line follows the designer *Zhang Kaiji* and the space line follows the buildings during that historical period. For a couple of decades after the People's Republic was founded, there were no private architectural firms, only state owned institutes of architecture. Under these circumstance, how did architects take on the task of building state owned spatial construction projects? Under what kind of circumstance did the requirements for the building of the Grandstands appear? This corresponds with *Huang Zhuan*'s desire to discover whether it was possible to divide a cultural concept from a socialist experience and ideology. The Grandstands is not a case study of individual pieces of architecture, so I refused to give *Huang Zhuan* any solid information on the architect. I considered the design of the Grandstands to be only a part of the focus of this project. I am also concerned to know why the Grandstands came into being at the moment in time they did and why were they built in that position? What definitions of style and space were given? These were the first aspects to inspire me. The second came when I read the book 'Production', edited by *Wang Min*'an, which contains extracts from Walter Benjamin's 'Arcades Project'. It occurred to me that I could undertake a text research of the area of the Grandstands. At that moment, the

的问题，也是我这个作品的起因。

关于对观礼台设计者张开济的采访，只是《日常生活的建筑》十个部分里其中一个部分的片断。当黄专计划要做这个展览的时候，我就想到了刚才想的那些，因为这个展览对我而言充满了规则，有一种不可解决的状态，当时就是在这样的情况下提出了"观礼台"这个作品的计划。

一开始我在想一个空间和一个时间的线索，比如说关于设计者张开济的这个时间线索及这个时期的建筑空间。在中国建国后的前几十年中，没有私人建筑事务所，只有国家设计院，在这种情况下，建筑师怎样承担国家的空间建筑工程？又是在何种状况下出现了建设观礼台的需求？这和黄专要做的关于社会主义经验，及可不可以在社会主义意识形态和经验中，分离出一种文化属性的概念之间形成了一种可能性，我一直没有把它当成研究某一个个人的建筑个案，也一直拒绝给黄专一个关于设计者的准确信号。其实我个人认为，我不是关注观礼台的设计，它只是这个计划中的一个部分，我关注的还有，为什么会在那个时候产生观礼台？为什么要在那个位置上建造观礼台？观礼台的样式及空间又有哪些限定等，这就是启发我的第一点；第二点，我曾看过汪民安编的一本名为《生产》的书，里面转载了本雅明《拱廊计划》的一部分内容，读完以后我产生了对观礼台这个地方做文本调查的想法，观礼台对我来讲可能就变成了一种文化生产方式，一种结构性的计划，从那

Grandstands became, for me, a means of culture production, a constructive scheme. From that moment I came to notice the factors behind their being built. Who is it that occupied the Grandstands? Who were the users of this space? Hitherto I had ignored these aspects having concentrated on the space and form of the architecture.

I think the project should probably be seen in three parts. The first part, as I have indicated above, is to be aware of the invisible elements of the building and why it is the way it is. I was inspired in this respect whilst making 'History of a Space'. The second part is about the Grandstands designed by *Zhang Kaji*. Initially, *Zhang* did not regard the Grandstands as his best architectural work, rather the Museum of History. I was shocked when I first saw the Grandstands. I think they are the true epitome of minimalism. They are completely consistent with their function, leaving virtually no extended space beyond that function, they are totally functional and with a history of ideology embedded in that function which provided me with an interesting subject, i.e. with all sort of methods in respect to those unsolved aspects. I felt that we needed brand new methods or a new system of knowledge to address cognition of our society. Because I feel that more often than not the existence of things does not depend on visible factors, nor can they be interpreted by one type of experience. Now, we can use methods and knowledge that we have gained from other disciplines to encode the parts we did not understand before. The third part of the project was inspired by the 'Arcades Project', and the research methods that Benjamin used on the 19th century arcades in Paris. Although his book was unfinished, from my reading I could sense that it had been the source of inspiration for many architects in the world.

个时候开始我注意到它后面的部分, 包括谁上观礼台? 即这个空间的使用者, 从前只注意到它的建造空间和建造样式, 而这个部分被我忽略掉了。

我的这个计划可能有三个部分。第一个部分就是刚才说的起点, 开始注意到建筑看不见的地方和为什么成为这样的建筑, 例子就是刚才说的关于"空间的历史", 它给了我启发; 第二部分是进入到张开济设计的观礼台, 最开始他认为自己最好的作品不是观礼台, 是历史博物馆。当我看到观礼台时很震惊, 我认为它是极限主义的一个真正例子, 它与建筑功能完全吻合, 在功能以外几乎没有任何空间让它去延伸, 完全是为了功能, 而且这种功能里面有意识形态的历史, 这样又给了我一种很有意思的话题, 就是我们以前有很多方法没办法打开的事件, 我觉得需要一种新的方法和新的知识系统去打开我们对这个社会的认识, 因为我觉得有时候事物的存在, 往往不是取决于完全看得见的因素, 或者用一种经验去解读, 现在我们从其他学科产生的知识方法有可能进入无法解读的这部分; 第三, 受《拱廊计划》的启发, 即本雅明对19世纪法国巴黎拱廊部分的研究方法的启发——其实他这本书是未完成的, 但我能从里面感觉到, 世界上很多建筑师都受到了它的影响。这就是计划的三个阶段。

Until now, I had not formulated a plan as to how I would present this piece of work in an art exhibition. It is hard to imagine whether the work would be shown as 'work in progress' or as a final presentation. If it is to be a final presentation, the work has to touch upon the relationship between contemporary visual culture and the knowledge of other disciplines.

In fact, I feel that *Huang Zhuan* has succeeded in undertaking two projects in China: the first is in bringing out a methodological and historical type of art that does not identify only with visual culture. Secondly, *Huang* incorporates an experience of contemporary Chinese art, while searching for a way of understanding that is above general experiences in China. I think these two points are important; the artists will have to complete the rest.

For my part, I am indecisive; everyday seems like a new beginning. Yesterday, when I came back from Germany, where I had been showing my new work 'Omen', I was wondering whether the 'Grandstands' contained an 'omen' in some way? 'Omen' is an important concept, I realized that this could be a very good experience to provide an 'uncertain' body of text, because our education actually excludes the aspect of 'uncertainty'. But 'uncertainty' is a very important element in contemporary art, it directly effects how we judge our contemporary culture. I think in most respects the blueprint for contemporary culture should be to build a new reading domain, i.e. the area of 'uncertainty'. So-called interdisciplinary, comprehensive knowledge adds up to this experience.

I am not sure if I want to show the video recording of the interview I conducted with *Zhang Kaiji*. I do not want the piece to be seen as the record of an historical event or the documentation of one individual. If I had enough material to provide two or more story

问：能介绍一下这个有三个阶段的作品的实施过程吗？

汪：如何在一个展览中呈现这个计划，在我脑袋里面现在还没有成型。在这个展览中这个研究是作为一个阶段呈现，还是作为一个最终的呈现我也还没想好。如果是一个最终呈现的话，就涉及到当代视觉文化与其他领域的知识研究之间怎样构成一种关系。

我的资料准备还有大量的工作要做。如果这是一个过程的话，那就不要强求必须在——比如说8月20日之前中止，否则，就让我感觉这个作品只取决于展览，在此期间要提供一种阅读形态，但是这个展览毕竟是有时间段的，现在就是要解决这个问题。

实际上我觉得黄专在中国做了两个工作：第一，就是方法论的、包括历史和知识结构的——不仅仅是针对视觉文化的这样一种艺术；第二，中国的当代艺术经验，除了在一种关于中国的普遍经验基础上，还有没有另外的理解方法？我觉得这两点很重要，剩下的就是艺术家自己的问题了。

对我来讲，我在犹豫……，每天好像都有一个新的开始，昨天我刚从德国回来，在那里展出了我的新作品《征兆》。我感觉其实在《观礼台》这个作品里是否也有"征兆"的意味？"征兆"是个很重要的概念，我理解这可能是提供一个不确定文本的特别好的经验，因为我觉得实际上我们的教育把"不确定性"这部分排除在外了，但"不确定性"在当代艺术里面是个非常重要的层面，它直接影响

lines for the project, I would show it, otherwise, I do not want one to overrule the other. I would always like two story lines in my work to develop in parallel with one another. This is how I see art, in fact, how I judge art. If I can clearly understand the idea of an artwork straight away, it was a work that carried no questions for me. I am more interested in work that confuses me, that has enough power to confuse me. To consider a work from this point of view, you might expect a work with a balanced structure at the start and only afterwards would its many possibilities appear. I am now at this stage in the making of my work.

There are two story lines in the Grandstands project: the first is *Zhang Kaiji*, one of the creators of the Grandstands. At that time, the Grandstands were also a symbolic creation, when one considers the overall cultural and ideological background, like the writing of slogans and the endless painting of the portrait of Chairman *Mao*. The second story line is also the one I care most about and have the greater interest in. It is to understand the documentation of the numerous five-year plans for the political and economic development of the State during that period. I feel that they might hold a clue as to the manner of the existence of the Grandstands. However, this does not mean that I must chase the answers to any final resolution.

I discussed with *Huang Zhuan* on a previous occasion that, seen from a Chinese emperor's point of view, Grandstands had the function of providing a view of the common people by an elite few. We know that during the Second World War, Hitler often stood high up so as to have a sweeping view of the crowd; then it seemed that the same formula was followed in East Germany. I feel that achieving an elevated position, providing a greater view for few

到我们对当代文化的判断，当代文化在很大程度上就是要建立一个新的阅读领域，即"不确定性"，现在所谓的跨学科、综合知识，实际上都是为了建立这样的经验。

问：对于观礼台，这种"不确定性"和"确定性"是怎样判断的？

汪：就是一种关系。我不是很想提供关于我采访设计者张开济的影像，是这样考虑的，我一直不愿意把它说成是对某一事件的记录，或者把它变成一个历史的或者个人的资料记录。当我认为有足够的能力提供两个以上线索的时候，我愿意把它们拿出来，而不愿意让任何一种线索占支配性的位置，这就是我要做的事情。我一直希望我的作品里面有平行的线索往前发展，这是我个人对艺术的看法，实际上我看艺术的好坏也是这样判断的。当一个作品让我一看就知道它明确无误的概念的时候，这个作品对我来讲就是没有提出问题，它可以在其他方面来解决。我有兴趣的艺术是它让我疑惑，它有足够的力量让我疑惑，这样考虑作品的话，从一开始就想建立一种平行的，由更多可能性产生的东西出现，我现在就是这样的一个状态。

关于《观礼台》现在有两个线索：一个是建筑师张开济，即制造观礼台的一个生产者，在那个时期作为整个意识形态文化来讲，就像我们写标语、画毛主席像，这些都属于制造符号，观礼台也

people and then a process of legitimatizing this stance, belongs to structural research of the Grandstands. As to the nature of the Grandstands, which could be seen as a physical space, it involves how such a structure was built, how it was used, in what way might one have used it, for military reviews or parades, why parades, for whom, what does it represent after all? On the other hand, in what way do the reviewers ensure a parade is being reviewed? What of the location and function of the Grandstands? These are the things that I am interested in.

I am not only working on the Grandstands project at the moment, I am involved in several other projects too. This is the state of my work; I will not follow only one line of interest that would be too simple for me.

Ludwig Wittgenstein said that he studied not the language, but the network of the language. It is the same for me. In September 2007, *Wu Hung* curated an exhibition called 'Net'. My first impression was of a 'cognitive net'. I thought if one could provide a name for everything that I put forward, there would be a problem. Why? I am talking here about the relation between words and objects. These two have formed a network. But what determines this association between words and objects? If it were determined by composite factors such as knowledge or education, then it would probably provide numerous interesting results. Our research is all to do with visible phenomena, however visible things may hold hidden aspects. Many people can confidently say that they 'have seen' but others would also confidently say they 'have not seen'. The issue is not whether you have seen or not seen - like the relation between words and objects, it is that everybody sees the same object differently.

是;第二其实也是我现在最关心和最感兴趣的,特别想了解那个时期整个国家政治经济发展的几个几年计划的讨论文本,我觉得也许可以在这里面找到观礼台存在的理由,但也不是说我非要弄清楚为什么会产生观礼台。

上次我跟黄专聊过,说从帝王的角度来讲,它也有观赏功能,简单地说,就是大多数人提供给少数人观看,这在中国传统里面也有,二战期间,希特勒也特别喜欢站在一览无遗的角度,紧接着整个东德好像也喜欢这样。我觉得高度和少数人可以观看得更多的愿望最后如何实现,把它变成合法的过程,就属于一个结构性的研究。具体涉及到观礼台,可能就是一个物理空间,涉及到这样的一个工具如何建立起来,建立起来之后如何使用?作为什么样的方式使用?阅兵、游行?那么为什么要游行?游行是给谁看的?它到底体现什么?反过来,观看游行的人又是以什么样的方式来确定他能够作为观看者?比如我们在座的四个人想上观礼台观看,我们有没有上去的可能?如果有是根据什么?如果没有,又是以什么规则来判定我们没有可能?这是我感兴趣的。

我现在不仅是做观礼台这一个作品,同时还在进行着几个计划。我的工作就是这样一种状态,不是一个线性的,比如今天晚上想好构图,明天就把它完成为一个作品,然后再继续做别的作品,这样对我来讲太简单了,没有难度。

Because I am interested in 'relationships', I often consider issues from this point of view. My works have also been presented as having the status of 'relationships'. How do I present a work in this way? Would you be able to read the 'relationship' or just the process of displaying the work? For example, if I exhibit the 'Grandstands' now, what would be the consequence of those 'relationships' embedded in the work? Or is it a situation in which I let people start a 'relationship' with me through the scale of the work? I feel that art which purports to have 'deep meaning' does not interest me any more, elements of 'the classic', 'the sublime' and 'strength' are no longer important to contemporary art. They may have belonged to issues often dealt with by traditional art, but the issues to be solved by contemporary art are methods of cognition and of methodology.

I have encountered some specific issues, such as the choice of materials, deciding on sizes, budget, timetable, etc. All of these issues have to be clarified. I have been thinking about how to present a replica of the Grandstands without the attention of the viewer being only on the replication side of the story. How can I present the 'network' research in this piece? To what degree? I do not want people to think that I am only chasing after ideology. However, it is hard to not be in that situation, because I must face particular issues of visual presentation.

What do I usually do if I feel that I am not being very clear about something? I will stop doing it and think it through again. However, this time it is an exhibition and it does not allow me the time to stop; I have to follow the timetable. So I can only hope that I am able to share with the visitors not only the history of Chinese ideology but also most of the information I

问：所以你的思维是"网状"的。

汪：对。维特根斯坦说过，他研究的不是语言，研究的是语言的网络，对我来讲也是这样的。

今年九月份巫鸿策划了一个展览就叫做"网"，在我脑袋里面第一个感觉就是，"认知的网"。我认为，我给你什么你就说它是什么，这就有问题了，为什么会这样，这就是词与物的关系，词与物本身就是一个网络，那么词与物是由什么决定的呢？是由知识和教育等综合因素决定的，这就有意思了，就会有若干可能的结论产生。我觉得我们研究的都是看得见的东西，但其实视觉的东西可以有很大的遮蔽性，很多人可以说"我看见了"，很多人也可以理直气壮地说"我没看见"，其实问题不在于你看见了的东西，就像词与物这样的东西，很简单，同样的东西，每个人不可能看的都一样。

问：您同时进行的几个计划之间有没有什么联系？

汪：我也不知道，我自己没有刻意地去梳理，但是我相信一个人的思维方式是有联系的，比如说我对"关系"感兴趣，我考虑很多问题的时候都会从这个角度上来考虑，而且一个作品的呈现，也是以一种关系的状态来呈现的，这就直接涉及到在关系的状态里面这个作品如何呈现？你是阅读到这整个关系呢？还是只阅读到这个关系状态里面呈现出来的过程？比如现在我提供了"观礼台"，这是

have gained.

I want to use a context to present my work, a context with boundaries. In emphasising 'relationships', I feel that 'Grandstands' is subject to endless relationships. I read an article which studied the history of the Forbidden City with a Foucaultian approach. In the article, the Forbidden City is divided into daily space, violent space and political space. Each time the Forbidden City was enlarged, it was according to these three divisions. At the time I was inspired by that approach as a basis of study. If I were to study the political spaces reflecting the ideology before the grandstands were built in 1959, which experiences were connected with them? Without such a relationship, I feel it is impossible to have built them. Another interesting factor is that the last use of them appears to have been on the 50th anniversary of the founding of the People's Republic; they have never been used since. Before the Cultural Revolution (1966 – 1976), they were used for reviewing army parades. During the Cultural Revolution, Chairman *Mao* used them to inspect the Red Guards, this was a little different from army parades. I wonder, since the grandstands were such an important element of and location for ideology, why were they not used during this period? In 1984, at the 35th Anniversary of National Day, *Deng Xiaoping* used them, yet not in an institutional sense. In 1999, *Jiang Zemin* used them once and not since. Why do the leadership not use them now? Before I started to tackle the practical side of the issues, I had pondered those questions with myself. Although sometimes, investigating more texts means increasing the strenuous nature of the work, this does not matter. What I wanted was a clear idea of what kind of questions I would raise in this piece of work. This was my state of mind at that moment.

关系的一个结果？还是我让所有的人在这样的一个范畴内保持和我这种关系的状态呢？我觉得那种制造深刻意义的艺术已经没有什么意思了，"古典"、"崇高"、"有力量"……这些都已经不是当代艺术的要素，属于传统艺术要解决的问题，而当代艺术要解决的就是认知方式，是方法论问题。

问：您现在对观礼台有些什么样实质性的调查和认识？

汪：从某一方面讲我现在碰到的都是些很具体的事情，比如选什么材料、尺寸大小、预算、运输、时间等等，这些都是需要明确的，其中还有观礼台真正的尺寸，包括大的建筑面积的尺寸，这些将来会是作品的一部分。但现在我的问题是，我复制这个东西到了现场，怎么样能让观众不陷入到这个复制当中去？就是说我对观礼台这种网络的研究在现场怎样体现？在什么样的程度上来展开？我不愿意让人以为我只是在对意识形态作一个追踪，而要摆脱这种状况也是比较难的，因为我必须面对的就是一个很具体的视觉呈现问题。

如果按我自己的习惯，也许我可以随时中止下来，因为我觉得这个事情对我来讲可能搞得还不是很清楚，我可以停下来再思考一下，但是由于现在是参加一个展览，就不允许我停下来。这部分是属于要按照时间走的，因此现在就是想怎样在最大程度上，让观众分享这样的一些信息，让他们

Perhaps in the end, I would show my periodic research on these issues in the exhibition. I may make some plans to show the design. I would like to discover a line of development from the archive in libraries. I know that all the information on *Tiananmen* has been kept at the Offices of Administration of *Tiananmen*, it is a special organization in *Beijing*.

I am having new ideas everyday. Recently I have been thinking about the word 'symptom'. What kind of symptoms should occur in 'relationships'? When the exhibition is shown in England, I will feel that it will be a 'symptom'. Symptom does not mean any particular contribution, such as criticism or praise; it means that 'symptom ' provides you with more background to read.

We decided to replicate a part of the Grandstands in this project and we discussed whether or not to use a virtual form. I told *Huang* that I would like to show the height of the Grandstands in a real space, I think this is a very important dimension. I wished to let people enter the space of this piece from different directions. This is a bit like studying museology. In art museums, there are numerous methods to replicate cultural relics. There are also rules to govern the degree to which the likeness of the relic can be replicated. I find that this is very interesting; it brings in a new dimension. I would like to cut away one side of the model of the Grandstand in order to show a section. The viewers might not only feel the real height, but also see the section as well.

In fact, every measurement within a space is established as potentially being in an uncertain relationship with another. I am also wondering whether I can build a model, a tangible model which might not look like a Grandstand but will be of the correct height, as

不仅仅只是看到一个中国意识形态的历史。

现在我要想的是这样一个文本怎样来呈现, 这里边有界线, 它既不是漫无边际——但有时候如果要去强调关系的话, 我觉得观礼台就是在这样漫无边际的关系里面。比如我们可以从历史的角度去研究观礼台, 我曾看过一篇文章, 它是用福柯的观点研究紫禁城的历史, 它把紫禁城分成日常空间、暴力空间和政治空间, 紫禁城的空间是根据这三种需要逐渐扩大的, 当时我觉得这就是一个方法的研究, 也给了我启示。我们也可以从意识形态及政治空间的角度去研究观礼台, 在1959年建立它以前, 都是哪种政治、文化、经验、需求跟它有关系的? 如果没有这些关系是不可能去建立观礼台的。我还有一个想法, 就是截至最后一次使用观礼台, 大概是在建国50周年的阅兵仪式, 从那时候以后好像就没有再使用了。在文革前大概主要功能是一年一度的阅兵, 文革期间是毛泽东在那个地方我见了很多次红卫兵, 使用是不一样的, 从改革初期那个地方就停止使用了, 接见和阅兵都停止了。既然它是一个意识形态重要的工具和场所, 为什么在这段时间它停止使用了? 1984年, 建国35周年时, 邓小平使用过那里阅兵, 也没有形成制度; 到了1999年, 江泽民在那使用过一次; 一直到现在——现在为什么不用? 实际上在"观礼台"这个作品的许多具体实施工作还没做之前, 我就给自己提了很多这样的线索。有时候文本的罗列, 可能会增加艺术家工作的艰苦性, 但实

the height is the one element in this work that I do not want to lose. And what about any reference to the architect *Zhang Kaiji* in this piece? He will not be a major element in it. Then what of the documentation of the piece? At the moment, this is the element of most interest to me, but also the most worrying part. Within the limited time available, how can I present it? I have discussed this with *Huang Zhuan* for a long time.

In my drafts, I placed the Grandstand piece in front of some world famous buildings; it was only to give a kind of relationship – a juxtaposition of two spaces, a very intuitive relationship between volume and space.

I would like to display the documentation alongside the work especially as each piece duplicates each step of the formation of the documentation; I do not want to show the documentation as evidence; I want the documentation to be seen as an equal part of the work. Much of the documentation is in VCD format. I want the replicas to be derived from the documentation, so that the visitors can truly feel a kind of 'relationship' between this knowledge and visual culture. But I would need time to do it. I am also making a replica of another piece of work, if I put it with together the Grandstand, they might build a relationship. I am interested in two things here: the documentation of history and the history of documentation.

Body politics is actually about how to fulfill the qualifications for access to the Grandstands. Whether you could expect to be there does not depend on your body, not your weight, or your state of health, but an attribute of your body. There is a wholly different set of criteria. No one who seems healthy or is six feet in height would be there for sure.

际上没有什么意义，而我就是需要想好，我通过这个作品到底要提出什么问题？这就是我现在的状态。

问：您现在处在的"网"的状态里面，怎么可能罗列一个明确的问题呢？
汪：所以到时我在这个展览中所展示出的，可能就是我对这个问题的阶段性研究。我搜集过类似的这种资料，那是在成都拍"空间的历史"的时候，我找到了当时建"毛泽东（万岁）纪念馆"的设计档案图，可要拍下照片收费价格是很贵的，拍一张花很多钱，因此在这次展览上，可能最后为了展示，我会另做几张效果图。

现在想能否找到一条线索——比如图书馆类的机构会给我什么样的线索？我现在知道天安门的所有资料属于天安门事物管理局，北京市有这样一个专门的机构。天安门本来横跨于故宫东门和西门，但是它的整个区域是归天安门事物管理局管的，而且东城区和西城区都管不了这个局，这实际上跟观礼台也是有关系的，这个区域为什么这么特殊？我每天都可能会有新的想法。我最近想的是"症候"这个词，在整个关系当中会产生什么样的"症候"？如果黄专的展览明年在英国展示，我能感觉到这可能也就是一个"症候"，"症候"的意思不是具体落实在某个点上，告诉你这是批判、歌

These are the natural features of the body. Access to the Grandstands would depend on an identity which is different from one's physical body. Control over body is the issue of body politics. We have found that there were three categories of people who could gain access to the Grandstands: the first category was foreign envoys; the second category was Chinese who were not qualified to stand on *Tiananmen* Gate, military personnel from Major-Generals to Colonel-Generals in the parades of the 1950s. Full Generals should have been able to stand on the Gate; together with leaders from provincial and regional autonomous governments of similar rank; and the third category was model workers, model peasants – and senior personnel from various fields. I really wanted to find lists of these three categories of people. Do such lists as these exist? Have they been retained until now? I wanted to find clues to those people. I heard many stories; one said that Jean-Paul Sartre had stood on *Tiananmen* Gate and on the Grandstands, but I cannot confirm whether this true. Sartre and other 'existentialist' thinkers were also socialists and leant towards China, because they saw China as a new force in the world. The story also says that Sartre had tears in his eyes when viewing the parade. From their background knowledge and perception, western people always regard the Far East as an impoverished area. They could comprehend the poverty, the cultural poverty, but not a new state. It would be very interesting if we could dig these things out. For example, if we could find and interview the many different kinds of people who had been present on the Grandstands, what would that reveal? I do not dare start on that – that would require a big budget.

In my ideal scheme, the work for the Grandstand would consist of three parts: part one,

颂，而是提供给你很多阅读的背景。

问：您提交的方案里面是希望复制观礼台的一部分吗？

汪：这是才定下来的，在一开始的讨论中，曾谈过是否用虚拟的方式，但我跟黄专说，有一个跟观礼台一样高度的空间实际上是这个作品很重要的一个维度，我希望可以有各种各样的方式让观众进入到这个空间里面，这就有点像博物馆学。在博物馆、美术馆里，复制文物有一整套的方法，有规定说复制到百分之几的程度是合法的，我觉得这也特别有意思，实际上也多了一个维度。其次，我准备把复制的"观礼台"做一个切割，就是一个剖面，这样既给出事物的实际空间高度，也同时看到事物的一个剖面，当然剖面只是模型的。

实际上每一个空间里面的尺寸可能就是在建立一种不确定的关系，我想能不能做一个模型？它可能是真实的，但可以完全不像一个观礼台，它提供观礼台的一个正确性——就是高度，这个高度是我这个作品里面不能消失的因素——作为体积可以消失，体积一旦消失，它就变得不真实了，这是我现在已经开始要做的；有关设计者张开济的这部分，它不会在这个作品里面占很重要的比例；最后是文本，但在这样有限的时间里面，我能拿到什么样的文本呢？这部分是我目前最有兴趣

I would replicate the Grandstand's physical qualities. This part would connect with *Zhang Kaiji*. I have my interview with him on record. Part two would consist of those people I could interview from among the three kinds of people who stood on the Grandstand. Part three would include what graphic material I could find about what happened in *Tiananmen* Square.

I think we can consider 'State' from various angles: political, economic and cultural. The 'State' is actually a very big question. We should give consideration to the concept of 'State', which is to interpret it by way of its different attributes and relationships. The 'possibility' of *Huang*'s exhibition is to discuss 'State' in this way.

By 'State' we used to mean a common politic. For a long time we believed that politics was coterminous with political groups. In the West the meaning of 'politics' is a broad one, involving racial discrimination, feminism, environmental protection and so on. We used to understand 'politics' as—for me, it was a word used in a narrow sense, so we treated it with a narrow attitude. The same is true for the concept of 'State'. I feel that we always put 'State' in the centre of any consideration, why can we not start from something else first – a topic or a proposition, and then talk about 'State'.

The problem for many people is their confusion between 'State' and 'Government'. Actually the two have major differences. Government represents those who administer, while the voice of a State should be more comprehensive, including voices from different fields and areas of expertise. It should not be simply speech on behalf of the State, which is easily ossified. 'State' also stands for a kind of relationship.

也是最担心的，我跟黄专谈了很长的时间也就是关于这部分的呈现。
问：展览的时候文本也是需要陈列的吗？
汪：我希望是有所陈列。

问：文本是指一些具体的数据资料吗？
汪：不是。我特别希望把文本形成过程中的每个部分都拿出来重新复制，它是有连续性的，我不是要一个作为凭证的文本，即只是做了一个非常文本化的东西。我是想让文本又产生复制，这样的话在现场就能让人感觉到真正的知识和视觉文化之间的某种关系，但这需要时间。像现在要做"观礼台"，但我还必须复制另外的一个东西，这另外的东西也许跟观礼台放在一起就有关系了，我现在感兴趣的就是历史的文本和文本的历史这两个东西。

问：刚才说到的使用观礼台阅兵的那些资料您都有吗？
汪：资料很多，都是到处淘来的，大多数是可以看的VCD。

In contemporary art, I seldom hear a phrase like 'State Cultural Legacy'. So once 'State' and 'Government' have been differentiated, the uncertainties of identification begin to surface. Before we used to see the world in a binary manner a pair of opposites such as 'inside the system' and 'outside the system'; 'overground' and 'underground'; 'east' and 'west'; 'ideology' and 'anti- ideology'. I feel that the debate on this issue needs a long period of preparation to acquire an ability to discuss it from a structure of knowledge, one more possibility. I feel that progress in anything is not based on burying the old but adding new possibilities. The progress of a society should never be seen from a linear perspective; it would end up an absolute power.

We may see this exhibition as solving a question, whether we can talk about the concept of 'State' in this way, moreover whether we are able to talk about the concept of 'culture'. Sometimes, we presume that issues of 'art' are very complicated; in fact, questions may not come from art itself but from other domains. The questions may be generated from other knowledge structures, or cultural attitudes, or unsolved questions from other domains which were mistakenly seen as peculiar to art.

I feel that many of the questions I am facing are not brought about by art. I have seen my work 'Omen' and 'Symptom' as studies of concepts. It is like going to see the doctor and telling him you have a headache, a fever, your whole body feels weak. But the doctor does not diagnose one's illness as influenza, because other illnesses such as encephalitis, pneumonia, enteritis or even leukaemia or a tumour can also present the same symptoms. The doctor has to view the symptoms in a holistic way using his experience. I see diagnosis as

问：您有没有在国外查找资料的经验？
汪：国外是这样的，只要你查找的是不属于机密性的资料、档案，他不提供给你则是他违法。像在美国有机密法，所有的机密文件到了消密期以后就公开了，它是有法律规定的。

问：在您的方案里面，将观礼台的一部份模拟复制到了西方的一些著名建筑，比如卢浮宫，是否有所选择？
汪：不是，实际上只是做了效果图，给它一种关系，即两个空间并置的一种关系，也就是一个最直觉的体量、空间等的关系。

问：您在阐述自己作品方案的时候提到"身体政治"，这是一个什么样的概念？
汪：实际上就是关于怎样获得上观礼台的条件。当你要上观礼台的时候，不是取决于你的身体，你的体重和健康程度，而是因为你身体的属性，这里面有一整套的评判标准，不是说谁身体很好，谁长了一米八的身高就可以上去，这些是身体的自然属性，能上"观礼台"靠的是身份，而身份区别于身体，对身份的控制就是身份问题。我们查了一下，上观礼台的有三类人，第一类是各国的使节；第

a relationship of understanding with concrete facts; it is the easier way to communicate with visitors at exhibitions. It is a bit like the structural relationship between doctor and patient. In fact, 'symptoms' are 'relationships'. With a doctor, the more knowledge one accumulates, the more experience one gains, the more one should be able to provide a more synthetic and accurate diagnosis.

There are also structural relations between 'omen', 'symptoms' and a doctor. When a doctor hears a patient telling him that he has a headache, the doctor may not diagnose the illness immediately; the patient may be describing other symptoms which contradict each other. This may suggest his sociological background, such as the patient wanting the doctor to pay greater attention to his case, so the patient exaggerates his symptoms; or he was unable to describe his symptoms himself, someone else had to help him therefore the description of the symptoms may not be as accurate as it should be. Anyway, there are many issues involved in this patient - doctor relationship. On the other hand, the doctor may also relate to issues such as the different viewpoints between Chinese and Western medicine, experience, age, educational status and those elements that might result in different diagnoses. I wonder what kind of affect 'symptoms' would bring to these numerous relationships? In terms of the relationship between art and me, a true build-up would be extremely complicated and synthetic compared to the one between doctor and patient.

My work is in three different states at the moment: the first is work that is unfinished and I feel not worth finishing. The second is work that I have spent a long time thinking about and feel that it is worth continuing with, I will realise it later. The third is work where I do not

二类是领导人物但还达不到上城楼资格的人，在五几年阅兵的时候，大概是少将到上将这个级别的军人（大将应该是上了天安门城楼的），以及相当于少将到上将级别的地方区域的省委书记和政府各机构的人；第三类特别明显，是各条战线的先进模范。我特别想查出这个名单，历届有没有这样的名单？这个名单是否保留下来了？如果有，我们就可以顺着这个名单查，在这三类人里面找到一种线索。如果想获得这个名单，也许需要一个庞大的班子了。我曾打听到很多消息，其中之一据说萨特上过天安门城楼和观礼台，但这怎么证明呢？到哪儿去证明呢？现在我没法证明这件事情，因为当时萨特等这批存在主义者都是社会主义者，对中国充满了向往，他们认为中国是世界上的一种真正的新力量，所以这个版本说萨特在看到阅兵的时候热泪盈眶，在西方人眼里，从他们的知识背景和感觉里面，在遥远的远东，除了贫穷，它包括文化的贫困，他无法想象有这样一种新的国家面孔出现。如果这些资料都找出来是会非常有意思的。举个简单的例子，如果找到那些不同类型的上过观礼台的人（不知道还有多少人健在），每个人的背景都不一样，他是怎样上去的？其过程如何？这个时候就需要对象的口述，这样的话，我们可以在展厅听到那些上过天安门城楼的人叙述的过程，不过这部分我到现在还不敢想，因为它涉及到了大量的人力、物力和财力。

在我理想的想法里，这个作品包含三个部分。第一部分是我可以模拟它的物理性，这部分同时

know what to do next.

With the Grandstands, I do not yet know what will happen next. I am not very clear as to what form of representation it will take. I do not know whether after the exhibition the project will come to an end or whether there will be a new start. Will my work of this year become a summary of this stage? Or is it another beginning?

还跟设计者张开济连在一起，我有现场采访他的资料，这包括当时周恩来告诉他的建"观礼台"的要求等资料都在；第二部分，是我能够采访到三类人中的一些人的资料；第三部分，是我能够找到天安门所发生事件的图像资料，当然希望都是合法的，就是影像出版社公开发行的东西，都是VCD，我看了好几遍了，但图像质量很差，不知道现在有没有出DVD版的。那么这三个部分就是我比较理想的作品的内容，而文本的东西偶然性太大了，也许当你找到一个突破口的时候，你会突然得到很多意想不到的东西。

这次参加这个展览，不确定因素太多了，但是前三个部分我现在基本上都有把握。这个作品成了"我们如何达到观礼台"了，其实我们也是在靠近"观礼台"了，我们对"上去"不感兴趣，只是对到达"真正的观礼台"感兴趣。

还有另一个线索，就是王小波的小说《东宫·西宫》，是关于同性恋的。在"观礼台"后面有两个厕所，当时是北京同性恋扎堆的地方，这个文本描写的地点实际上就是那里，后来拍成了电影，但我看了，觉得不是很自然，可能是有些地方不让拍的缘故。

问：请谈谈您对"国家"这个概念的理解。

汪：这个问题很大，国家只能作为一个意识形态的集团政治被考虑，有众多的机构和知识领域，一个人可以从国家来考虑，也可以从国家的各个部分来考虑，这也涉及到方法的问题。我觉得国家可以从政治的角度来看、可以从经济的角度来看、也可以从文化的角度来看。所以我觉得应该给"国家"这个概念一种可能，就是从它的不同属性和关系来看。黄专这次展览的"可能"也是这样的，可以通过这种方式来讨论"国家"。

以前我们说"国家"就是指一个集团政治，我们长期以来认为"政治"就是政治集团，西方的这个词很宽泛，包括种族歧视、女权主义、环保等，我们以前对"政治"的理解是按照——对我来讲，以前"政治"是一个很狭隘的词，所以我们愿意按照狭隘的态度去看待它，"国家"的概念也是同样。总的感觉是我们宁可把"国家"放在一个很中心的位置来考虑，而不是一开始先有一个话题或命名，然后再来谈"国家"。很多人还把"国家"跟"政府"作为同一体，其实"国家"跟"政府"是有区别的，政府代表一个管理者，国家的声音应该更广泛，包括来自不同领域及各种知识的声音，否则很容易将问题僵化，"国家"实际上也是一种关系。

在当代艺术里面，其实我很少听到"国家文化遗产"这样的声音，所以说一旦把"国家"和"政府"区别开以后，对身份判断的不确定性问题就出来了。以前我们总是习惯说"体制内"和"体制外"，"地上"和"地下","东方"和"西方","意识形态"和"反意识形态"……都是非常二元对立的方式。我觉得谈这个问题必须有一个长时间的准备,要有能力从一个知识结构来谈,起码是多了一种可能,因为我老是这样看问题,我觉得任何一个事物的进步,不是埋葬了先前的对象,而是多了一种可能,一个社会的进步不仅仅简单的线性替代,到最后只剩下一个绝对的权力。

也许可以这样看这个展览,它要解决这样一个问题,就是我们能否从这样的角度来谈"国家"的概念,进而我们可以谈到"文化"的概念。有时候我们以为"艺术"的问题很复杂,其实问题并不是来自于它自身,而是产生于其他领域的问题,可能产生于其他的知识结构,或者其他的文化态度,产生于在其他地方没有解决的问题,但这些问题可能就是被误以为是艺术问题。

问:是不是可以这样理解,有时艺术变成了一种手段,我们通过它来解决其它方面的问题。
汪:我的感觉是实际上面对的很多问题都不是艺术带给我的,当我工作时,必须要有问题,而这个问题是不是艺术问题对我来讲则不重要,很有可能构成我问题的很多方面不是艺术问题。比如我把"征兆"、"症候"作为作品的概念来研究,就像你去看医生,你告诉医生说头疼、发烧、浑身无力,但医生并不能立即判断你就是感冒,它不是这么简单的逻辑关系,因为这些征候是多种疾病,如脑炎、肺炎、肠炎、甚至白血病及肿瘤都可能出现的反应,实际上症候是整体呈现的某一种状况,在这个基础上再根据不同的经验去判断它。我觉得这是一个比较具体的理解关系,也是更容易跟公众经验沟通的方法,就像医生跟病人之间的结构关系,"症候"实际上就是"关系",我觉得对于一个医生来讲,他拥有的知识越多,经验越丰富,他对"症候"才有可能进行一种综合而又准确的判断。

问:医生跟病人的关系很清晰,而你跟艺术的关系似乎很模糊。
汪:那只是身份的清晰,是这样的,从一个总体来讲,你看到的医生跟病人之间的是"关系",而"征兆"、"症候"跟医生之间,实际上是有结构性的关系的。病人说头疼的时候,医生绝不会马上进行判断,这个病人可能提供的是一整套相互矛盾的说法,这里面还包含着很多社会学的背景。比如说他为了引起医生的重视,可能会把自己的症状描述得比实际严重;还比如说他没有能力描述,而借用他人的口来描述,就有可能描述得不准确了,这里面涉及的问题很多;对于医生来讲也同样如此,比如中医和西医的观点还不一样,经验、年龄、受教育程度也不一样,这些都有可能构成不同的判断。所以有的时候问题不是说存在多少种关系,而是在众多的关系当中,"症候"到底起到什么样的作用?这种关系如果从医生和病人的角度来讲很容易,而我和艺术像是有着这样的关系,但要真正建立起它们之间的关系，又是极其综合和复杂的。

问：您的作品都是持续很长时间的产物吗？

汪：对，有几种状态，一种是还没有做成就觉得不值得做的；第二种是需要很长时间来想，然后觉得它值得去"做"，之后再把它实现的；第三种就是它还没有让我知道怎么去做。基本上我就是这三种状态。

问：您觉得什么才是值得去做的？

汪：当这个问题从一开始考虑的时候起，就感觉不能停下来结束。比如"症兆"这个作品，从开始想到做，直到现在——其实已在柏林进行了影像展示，但是这个工作并没有完，有大量的资料还堆着，看到拍的所有现场照片，让我觉得"症候"才刚刚开始，可这个作品再怎么做下去，现在我也还不知道。

那么"观礼台"可能也是这样，直至明年展览的时候，最后到底是什么样的呈现方式？现在我自己都不是很清楚真的会发生什么，展览完了以后，它是一个终结，还是一个开始？这一年的时间是这个阶段的终结，还是另一个开始？

Appendix

附录

Conference Summary: Politics or Art History?

"政治学还是艺术史" 座谈会纪要

主持人：孟晖

与会者：巫鸿、黄专、王广义、汪建伟、费大为、
　　　　刘晓纯、吕澎、凯伦·史密斯、周彤宇

列席者：叶彤、方立华、王景

时　间：12月16日上午10：00-12：00

地　点：何香凝美术馆咨询厅

孟晖：《读书》杂志很高兴和何香凝美术馆OCT当代艺术中心一起来共同举办这次活动。今天这个座谈会的主题非常有意思，也很值得探讨。我就说一点作为艺术爱好者的业余感受吧。我们当然知道，建国以来，甚至可以说从五四以来，中国的艺术与现代民族国家的创建有着复杂的关系。我原来一直以为，我们中国解放以来的这一套表现、赞美国家形象的形式是从苏联学来，仅仅与社会主义阵营里发展的一套美术话语有关系。但有一次我与朋友到西班牙去玩，在塞维利亚看到了这个国家在上世纪上半叶专为举办万国博览会建的一个建筑，我特别吃惊地发现，这个纪念性建筑的形式非常奇特，与苏联、与我们追求的某种建筑形式非常一致，巍峨、宏大，把某些互不相干的风格结合到一起，比如，既有古罗马建筑的样式，也带有它自己珍贵的民族因素，显得非常奇怪。这让我突然意识到，类似这种风貌的建筑在上世纪上半叶形成了潮流，比如30年代的德国或意大利，在当时政权支持下出现的一些建筑，都呈现出同样的特点。你会发现，这样的建筑样式是在民族国家建立过程之中发生的建筑形式，其实，家居设计等等方面也一样具有这一情况。关于上世纪的美术设计、建筑设计与民族国家的复杂关系，欧美国家的学术界和美术界一直都在讨论，有很多富于启发性的见解。所以"视觉遗产"这个题目无疑非常有意思，也很有意义。

黄专：我先稍微简单讲一下，首先欢迎各位学者和传媒，这个项目是从前年开始的，是OCAT和英国曼彻斯特都会大学合作的研究项目，在我们发给大家的资料里面都有这个项目主题很详细的介绍，即关于展览的内容和我的一个访谈内容，所以基本的情况我也就不再详细介绍。严格来讲，做这个项目有两个动机，第一个是，长期以来，我觉得中国的当代艺术没有解决政治思想史的问题，当代艺术的基本立场，对政治和历史的基本判断，在80年代基本上是一种意识形态的反抗，90年代以后这种意识形态变成了简单的消解、解构、反讽、调侃，我觉得整个中国当代艺术差不多30年以来都没有一个基本的政治立场和态度，原因在于我们的艺术家对于我们国家的历史没有基本的判断，所以造成的是，我们很多艺术涉及到政治时，要么就是很简单的批判姿态，要么就完全是虚无主义或者相对主义的视觉表达，相反，很多非常严肃的对中国政治解释的艺术又被一些诸如"政治波普"这样简单的概念所掩盖，所以我想，中国当代艺术发展到现在已经到了没有办法阅读的一个台阶，所以首先要解决中国人怎么样判断自己政治立场的问题。我是一个理性的爱国主义者，同时我也是一个批判性的民族主义者，我想，很显然，我们必须清理我们的视觉遗产，所以这是从当代艺术本身来说我做这个项目的动因；第二个我觉得中国的当代艺术还有一个很大的缺陷，就是和中国的思想史脱节，其实80年代的中国当代艺术都还有与哲学、文学等领域的浅层次的交流，但那个时候的联系是在"启蒙"的主题下发生的，没有很深入的学理联系，大概只是把"启蒙"作为一个目标，到了

90年代，随着各个领域的所谓"专业化"，这种联系就慢慢中断了，我个人认为如果一个国家的当代艺术没有和它国家的思想史相联系，它是不可能真正作为体现这个国家的遗产的一部分的，所以从这个角度来讲，这个项目也有想要填补、或者沟通这种联系的想法。这个项目叫"国家遗产"，包括三个方面的内容，一个关于中国当代艺术的政治态度，一个关于中国当代艺术和自己历史的关系，第三个，关于一些中国当代艺术视觉创造的基本模式。我们请了三个专家，在思想史方面请了汪晖先生，我觉得他是思想界非常活跃的顶尖人物，请他对中国现代、或者当代复杂的历史现象、模式作出背景分析，另外请了赵汀阳先生，他研究政治哲学，写过《天下体系》，请他主要是解决中国从传统民族国家过渡到现代国家的思想史背景环节，同时我们还请到了芝加哥大学的巫鸿教授，作为我们视觉史方面的顾问，因为他长期从事古代研究，同时对很多中国当代视觉文化作了很深入的研究。这个项目的基本内容大概有两个，一个是我们现在在编的一个文本，不是作为展览的画册，是综合了很多文献的一个东西，第二个是我们请到了五位非常优秀的当代艺术家做一个展览，我觉得这些艺术家都是长期对中国当代的政治问题、视觉问题有很深入涉及的，他们就是王广义先生、汪建伟先生、卢昊先生、曾力先生和隋建国先生。严格来讲，他们的五个方案都不是为了这个展览而做的，都是他们原来一直在做的一些项目。像汪建伟，关于天安门的观礼台的方案，已经做了十多年的采访，像王广义的也是，虽然他作为中国非常活跃的艺术家，但这件作品还从来没曝光过，就作为我们这次的参展作品。而我们的文本有几个部分，一个是有三篇跟我们这个主题相关的文章，三个结构中的第一个我称之为"从古代帝国到现代国家"，包括赵汀阳先生的对"天下"这种国家理念的研究，这部分视觉研究以卢昊的作品为主。第二个叫做"一种多维的现代化模式"，包含了汪晖先生的文章，它讲的是中国民族国家的复杂性，王广义，隋建国和曾力的作品构成这部分的视觉研究的内容。第三部分是巫鸿先生的一篇文章和汪建伟的作品。我们搜集了大量的资料，像关于汪建伟的方案，我们搜集了关于中国政治空间从古代到现代变化的模式的资料，像关于王广义的方案，我们就查中国的汽车史，我们把中国的汽车史看成是一个历史的视觉符号，它由最开始作为皇权的象征演变到——穿插着复杂的现代化因素的影响和对领袖皇权的尊重，后来变成一种商业符号，我们试图用图文的方式把这个复杂的历史过程表现出来——这些我在这里也不能详细讲，卢昊的方案是关于北京城墙拆掉的历史，这也始终是中国走向现代化一个非常吊诡的现象，我们就把它们都汇集起来。最后要讲的是，这个项目是我们和英国曼彻斯特都会大学合作，合作有几个机缘，原来这个展览的方案我是为前年中国参加圣保罗双年展所作的，那一届的主题是"移动的板块"，当时我给的方案叫"国家遗产"，我觉得这很符合中国的这个政治板块，后来他们那边的人过来北京和我谈的时候，他们觉得我选的艺术家都已经参加过圣保罗双年展，希望我调整艺术家，我当时说我的这个方案是不可能随便调整艺术家的，就因为这个矛盾，我放弃了圣保罗双年展。后来曼彻斯特都会大学的周彤宇到北京来找我，当时说曼彻斯特准备做一个三年展，我就把这个方案给了她，他们也很感兴趣，但后来又觉得他们的三年展没法包容它，就决定由他们学校单独来做，我觉得这一点更符合我的愿望，它的意义更加延伸了，因为大家知道，曼彻斯特是英国工业的起点，也是马克思学说的起点，同时现在它也是英国所谓"左派"的据点，后来他们又同意把这个展览放到那里的科学博物馆里面，这个科学博物馆正好是世界上生产第一条铁路的厂房，这所有的象征因素凑到了一起——在西方起源的现代化理想和反现代化的思想怎么样移植到中国？中国的现代化思想一直都是——马克思主义是反现代主义的，而中国是以马克思主义来学现代化的，同时中国人一直在追求怎么样来进入现代化，这两个历史对我们来讲是非常复杂的状况，我们其实还有其他空间，但后来都觉得一定要在这个空间来做这个展览。我就先讲这些，下面由英国曼彻斯特都会大学策划人的代表周彤宇来简单介绍这个展场的一些情况。

周彤宇：大家好，我是周彤宇，是曼彻斯特都会大学艺术设计创新研究院的研究助理，也是"国家遗产"展英方策展助理。英方策划人约翰·海雅特教授今天不能前来，他让我跟大家说抱歉，并祝座谈会成功。我先介绍一下约翰·海雅特教授，他是曼彻斯特都会大学艺术设计创新研究院的主任。照片是英国卫报对他的一篇专访，他也是艺术家，左边那张照片是他做的一个城市雕塑，中间是他的画和他本人，他还是一个音乐家，以前做过摇滚歌手，这是他上个月在广州的演出照片。约翰对和黄老师一起合作这个项目很感兴趣，因为他本人是一个左派知识分子，对中国的事情总是抱着同情和理解的态度。这张照片上，他身后就是我们将要用做展厅的建筑，建于1830年的库房，现在是科学工业博物馆的一部分。应黄老师的要求，我简单介绍一下曼彻斯特、我们学院和科学工业博物馆。曼彻斯特在英格兰的西北部，号称英国第二大城市，有不到300万的人口，提到曼彻斯特很多人首先就会想到"曼联队"。刚才黄老师也讲到了，它是最早的工业城市，第一次产业革命就发生在这里，主要是从棉纺业开始。曼彻斯特今天已经从过去的老工业化城市转变成了以多种新型产业为支柱的现代化城市，英国广播公司BBC也很快要从伦敦搬过去了。这些照片是现在的曼彻斯特，上面那张是一个图书馆的建筑，当年马克思就在里面研究过工人运动；下一张是码头，BBC未来的总部所在地，这个地方以后会成为一个媒体中心。我现在介绍一下我们学院。曼彻斯特都会大学的艺术设计学院的前身是英国最古老的艺术设计学院之一。它的建成也跟工业革命有关，当时的纺织厂厂主希望用设计来使他们的产品更有销路，所以他们在1838年建立了这所学校。这是一些在1900年左右拍的图片。这是这个学校现在的样子，景观、街道。下面介绍我们将要用作展览场地的科学工业博物馆，这个博物馆最突出的特点是它是世界上最老的火车站的原址，铁路运输是从曼彻斯特到它西部的港口利物浦。1829年，第一台蒸汽机车被发明出来后就被这个铁路公司买下来投入运营。这是现在经过修复的这个火车站的原始建筑。我们将用的展厅有两个，一个在博物馆的主建筑里，这是主展厅1904年的照片。博物馆的正门是它的入口。当时我们去拍照片的时候，那里有一个展览，结果我们没有办法拍到整个展厅的照片，只能看些局部。第二个在1830年库房的展馆里。之所以叫库房，是因为在它旁边当年世界上第一条铁路把货物运来后直接卸货到这个库房里面。它的内部结构都是木头的。英国方面感觉到这个展览很有意思，是因为它涉及的内容不仅仅是艺术。当年产业革命刚开始的时候，英国很快发展了起来，成为世界上最强大的工业化国家，19世纪的时候它被叫作"世界工厂"；那么现在是我们经济快速发展，中国被叫作"世界工厂"。1840年鸦片战争中英相遇了，掀开了中国的近代史。到了20世纪30年代，中国一直在反抗"洋货"。当时的"世界工厂"生产的产品把中国的自然经济搞垮了。有意思的是，几十年后的今天，中英和平相处，但是英国人担心中国人生产的产品把他们的经济搞坏了，对中国的发展有恐惧感。约翰作为策展人，他希望把这个展览带到英国，能让英国人了解中国发生的事情；同时让艺术家带领大家对工业革命的后果、对环境问题、对全球变暖做出自己的反思和贡献。我就简单介绍到这里。

黄专：下面我们先放下五个艺术家方案的资料图片，让有在场的艺术家王广义和汪建伟自己介绍方案的基本想法，然后就进入讨论。这是王广义的方案《东风·金龙》，"东风·金龙"是中国第一辆自己生产的轿车，我们请广义说一下。

王广义："东风·金龙"是中国工业革命时期梦想的产物。是无数工人用手工打造出来的，献给毛主席的充满信仰与皇权最后礼赞的准工业产品，在今天我将它以艺术的名义复制出来，以此表达信仰与物质欲望之间的冲突。"东风·金龙"作为国家遗产的物质证明，同时也呈现了权力与人民的意志之间的关系。我觉得它比较符合"国家遗产"的展览主题。国家遗产这个展览，包括了物质遗产和精神遗产，而"东风-金龙"恰恰包含了这两个层面，既是物质遗产又是精神遗产，很复杂。我按照原来尺寸的大小，并用铸铁的方式还原《东风·金龙》，使其具有一种博物馆化的感觉，它包含了历史的沉重感——一个民族要成长的强大欲望，或者是欲望的多重性。很多人都以为这个车最早叫"红旗"，实际上是叫"东风·金龙"，毛主席当年曾象征性地坐过一次。对于工人而言，他们最初的热情基础是对于毛主席的崇拜和信仰，也许他们并不知道，这种崇拜和信仰的背后，实际上是对于中国工业革命的热切希望。尤其是这样一件作品在英国这样一个工业革命最重要的发源地的展出，我觉得特别有意思。"东风·金龙"带有一种准工业的色彩，拿到工业革命的策源地去展览，我觉得它的含义更复杂。简单地说，《东风·金龙》是一个信仰的产物，或者说它本身就是一个关于中国工业革命的"方案"。

汪建伟：在1996到1998年期间，我拍过一个系列影像作品《日常生活的建筑》，第一次涉及到空间历史的问题。在成都的天府广场上，有一个建筑曾叫"毛泽东思想万岁展览馆"，那个地方以前是刘备的一个议事大厅，但后来就为了给毛泽东修建一个万岁展览馆，把它推倒重建了这座"毛泽东思想万岁展览馆"。20年以后，我找到了曾参与此建筑的一位建筑师，他却非常羞于谈及这件事，因为他认为拆毁原来那座古老建筑是很痛心的事。其实这个新修建筑在整个20多年之间也在不停地转换自己的功能，因为刚开始修好不久，那个空间就几乎不太能得上了，紧接着改革以后它先是变成了商场，再往后它又变成了股票市场，这是我最初感觉到空间历史的问题。到北京以后采访了建筑师张开济，他在很长一段时间没有很公开地说观礼台是自己的设计，我们一起去历史博物馆，他跟我讲了整个历史博物馆的设计方案，突然才谈起了观礼台，在这之前我也没有注意到观礼台本身是一个建筑，它完全跟周边的环境融为一体。他讲了当时是在1959年，有很多外国友人以及中国的工农兵代表要上天安门观看阅兵、节庆游行，显然那个地方空间是不够的，当时周恩来就给了他们一个任务，说能否马上修建一个观礼台，而且给了两个硬性指标，一个是要和周围的环境没有任何冲突，第二个是要满足能够容纳这么多人都在上面观看，还要有厕所、贵宾厅之类的设施。张开济说当时有很多人竞争这个方案——他还看到另外一个方案，顶上全部是琉璃瓦，把天安门顶上的琉璃瓦一直延续下来，看到这个方案以后会觉得特别可怕，而张开济的方案为何最终胜出？他几乎就是把建筑设计完全功能化了，所以说这是一个非常典型的功能化设计。因为一直以来，我的作品就是在研究意识形态跟物质化形态之间的关系，所以我觉得这个个案给了我一个特别好的切入点，建设这个空间只是第一步，在长达十几年的使用当中，上过观礼台的那些人是怎么上去的？他们是由于什么因素、关系上去的？比如说这里面大概包括三种人，一种是政府、各地区及军队的主要领导干部，他们会占有一定的比例；第二种是各大驻外使节和邀请来的国外人士；第三是属于在全国选拔的工农兵的模范人物。其实我一直在关注两个问题——意识形态物质化过程的有两个部分，一个是空间，还有一个是怎么使用这个空间，而且人在使用空间的过程中会产生什么样的关系？这也就是我作品的第一部分。第二部分实际上是采访张开济当时设计这个建筑的全部想法，以及还有一部分图像记忆，就是在这个地方有一个连续性——建国以后每年的"十一"都会在这个地方进行阅兵，到了文革期间突然中断了，文革以后还有过两次，那么这种连续与非连续地使用这同一个空间之间是什么联系？视觉上我现在已经搜集到很多在这个空间发生的事情，还有一个很关键的地方就是使用者。这就是我这个作品的一个大概想法。

黄专：汪建伟的这个作品是我们所有作品中最难实现的，现在还在努力。下面，因为其他三个艺术家没有在场，我稍微讲一下他们的作品方案。这个是卢昊的《复制的记忆》，是关于北京九个内城门的，现在仅存正阳门和德胜门的箭楼部分，其他的都拆掉了，这个事情也是很吊诡的，因为大家知道北京的城墙历史从金代就开始了，明代的整个城墙格局延续到现在，当时共产党进入北京的时候为了保护古迹做了大量的工作，甚至让梁思成他们把重要的地方划出来，最好的方案是和平解放，所以这些城墙在1949年的时候完整地被保存下来，但后来为了建设，为了现代化，把这些城墙都拆掉了，卢昊的方案是想以虚拟的方式把这些城墙都恢复起来。现在为了旅游业，北京把永定门恢复了，但是很难看。中国的历史都是和政治、军事、商业有关系的，包括王广义的方案，后来还决定最后展示的时候加入几个模特儿。这个是隋建国的方案，这是北京798附近的环铁，是建国以后建立的第一条测试车速的工程，前一段的第六次提速还在那里测试过，中国铁路的历史也是很好玩的，最开始是西方强行要来中国建设铁路，英国、美国、德国都在中国建立了很多非法的铁路，西方强行的想法是把现代化移植到中国，当时的中国政府非常反抗，一直到1882年中国才建立了第一条铁路，最开始的时候铁路是作为宫廷的玩物，所以现代化的功能到了中国都会产生变异，到了民国时期，则把铁路建设作为中国现代化的主要建设工程一直到现在。这个方案是曾力的，关于"水钢"，"水钢"是"三线工程"的一个项目，50年代初，中国跟苏联友好结盟，所有重工业工厂都集中在东北，后来60年代中苏交恶了以后，中国就把所有重工业全部迁到所谓的"三线"，四川、贵州、云南，目的是为了应付和苏联打仗，这些工厂现在有的还在生产，有的已经荒废了，曾力对这些"三线工程"进行大量的图像调查，他不是简单地去拍照，也搜集查阅厂史之类的，我们的展览里面会有关于现在水钢的完整的图像记录，在文献里面也会放有关水钢整个历史的资料，这也是中国现代民族国家过程中非常重要的一个事件，我觉得他的有些照片拍得非常凄惨，那么大的一个厂房现在全部都垮掉了，就像是历史留下来的一个痕迹。我的介绍完了，下面请各位自由地谈。

巫鸿：黄专跟我提到这个题目的时候，我对两点很有兴趣。第一，在资料文件第4页里面有这样两句话，我觉得很提纲挈领，解释了"视觉遗产"的主体。它是这样写的：这个计划"希望讨论的是中国现近代'国家'的概念"——"国家"带了引号——和"国家概念形成的视觉史和思想史的意义"，同时也"希望围绕中国从古代帝国向近代的民族国家转换过程中的思想史和视觉史的逻辑"。我觉得对我来说，这点非常重要，因为说明了这个项目不是要寻找一个固定的东西，或者是古代的，或者是现代、当代的东西，而是要找一个更为复杂的东西，就是"遗产"，或者说是更精确一点是"国家遗产"。"遗产"作为一个概念总有"过去"的感觉，但是也包含"现在"的感觉。"遗产"是历史遗留下来的财产，但是到现在还继续存在，甚至继续被作为艺术表现的本体。它并不是埋在地底下的考古遗迹，不是看不见摸不着的，而是具有一种内在时间对比的概念。这一点我很有兴趣。第二，当然研究遗产有很多种方式，黄专和几个艺术家比较着重的是"空间"的这个角度。这是一个很大的问题，在我脑子里面，和"空间"联系着的有两个问题，一个是空间和视觉的关系，有一个空间以后，在这个空间里怎么看东西？谁看谁？这就带出了视觉的问题。所以，如果有空间性的视觉遗产的话，那么也一定有视觉性的空间遗产。空间性的视觉遗产往往跟建筑有关系，视觉性的空间遗产则往往跟人的主体性有关系，跟在哪里看、看与被看、或看的方法这些方面都有关系。这里还有一个有联系的问题，文件里面没提，但隐含着，即物质性的问题。因为"空间"实际都不是空的，任何空间都是由具体物质构造出来的。我对这些东西一直都有兴趣，也写过书，讨论中延伸出来的有一个和这个项目有点接近的概念，叫"位"，"位置"的"位"。这是中国古代非常强的一个概念——在西方当然也有，但没有在中国那么突出。这个"位"很厉害，比如说在中国古代，当了皇帝的就必须居于特定的"位"，必须是"南面而治"。面向北面是臣民的位置，往南的一定是君主、主人的位置。你到别人家里做客，主人也是朝南面坐。所以中国古代最早的一张政治图像，叫做《明堂位》，其实是一张关于位置的抽象的图，其中并没有画具体的人，就是给你讲应该怎么排这个"位"：皇帝在中间，旁边围着的是臣子，最后一圈是蛮夷。在这种政治空间的概念中，只要天子的这个"位置"稳了，整个国家也就稳了。"位"代表的是国家的权力性质结构。黄专提到从古代国家到现当代的空间遗产和物质遗产。"位"可以说就是这样一种遗产。我曾经研究过古代中国的"广场"概念，汪建伟也作过这方面的录像作品，这次的作品和这个又有联系。我觉得广场是很有意思的一个事，从50到70年代建造了很多广场，广场中首先要有观礼台，天安门广场是最大的广场，天安门就是最高级的观礼台，到上面往南看，下面一定有群众。这样"位"的概念就构成了——古代说的"国家"必须有"国"和"家"，有君和民。"民"从来就是一种构成，广场的一个目的也就是达到这种构成，由最具体的形态显示出构成。

所以当我看到这几个艺术家的方案时，我觉得这些方案都很有意思。我觉得汪建伟的想法对我有很重要的提示，因为我做了很久关于天安门广场的研究，恰恰把观礼台给忽视了。现在我觉得观礼台确实很重要，为什么？因为它是现代的加入，古代是没有的。为什么要加入这个东西？当然从功能上是为了让比较高层的人在上面"观礼"。但如果按照我刚才讲的，把空间的概念加进去考虑，问题就不那么简单了。首先从方向上看它是坐北朝南的，和天安门的方向一致。但是从空间位置上看它又是在广场和天安门之间，也就是在最高领导人和人民大众之间。所以一方面它属于检阅别人的领导层次，但另一方面它又是作为连接者，连接了人民与最高领导。它在国家机构中起到双重的作用：既是从人民中涌出来的，接近最高领导，又是领导人民的。通过这种连接，党中央的信息就可以下达到底下。这和清朝的一个仪式有些类似，清朝下诏的时候，皇帝是不上天安门的，天安门下面的官员和百姓的代表跪在那儿接旨，接旨之后再送到全国各地。因此那个地方是一个权力和命令转移的中枢。所以这个观礼台对我很有启发，但是怎么以前我就没有想到它呢？我想，这恰恰说明了权力往往是善于自我隐藏的。汪建伟刚才说这个东西好像只有建筑功能，把所有的修饰都去掉了。其实，有很多权力性的东西是把自我隐藏起来的，就好像隐身人似的，很重要但让人视而不见。

刘骁纯：我先向黄专提一个问题，你能介绍下卢昊这件作品最后是怎么实现的吗？

黄专：他可能就做成一个沙盘，外面就是用透明的有机玻璃，里面或者用实物，或者用地图的方式，我不知道你们有没有看过他的另一件作品，他复制了整个北京城，是德国一个美术馆赞助做的，中间的我不是很清楚用的什么方式，但外墙是用有机玻璃做的。

孟晖：汪建伟，请问你作品是用什么材料做的？

汪建伟：实际上有三个部分，一部分属于纪录，即大量视觉的部分；第二部分是文本的调查，比如刚才巫鸿老师说到的，他说上大明门的人是需要证件的，其实上观礼台也是有严密的制度规定，不是什么人都可以上去的，我对严密的制度这部分很感兴趣，什么人在什么时候能上去？什么人不能上去？第三部分是物质化了的，我觉得这部分是必需的。当时想了解设计图的尺寸——这里面还有个故事，我们到北大的图书馆去查资料，但被逮住了，问我们为什么要查天安门的尺寸？在那被盘问了一天才放出来，当时我们还想起诉，我说作为一个国家图书馆，公众有权利去查询资料，你如果不给就说不给，但是你不可以说这有什么问题。在张永和的父亲去世之后，留下来了图纸，我们准备根据这些图纸——比如说拷贝它的十分之一，会使用一种新型的材料，在户外可以保存一百年。它可以摆放到世界任何一个地方，按照北京坐北朝南的方向放，给所有参观者一个上去的机会，所有人都是可以自由上去，体验一下从每个台阶上观看下面的感觉，我觉得这种观看很重要——后来黄专说对方想通过一种新技术模拟出一个天安门的观礼台，即一个虚拟的东西，我觉得这也挺好的，我想，一个可以上去的，和一个不可以上去的并置在一起，可能更有意思。真实的那个当然要根据材料、经济以及运输的可能这些技术的环节来考虑，我想拷贝的面积、高低，或者尺寸的大小并不重要，重要的是它一定要有一个跟原型一模一样的局部，这个局部最好是切片式的，再把它放到现场，我做了一个效果图，大家可以看到，当时为了让对方明白我的想法，我就把这个切面像切蛋糕一样切下来，放到世界任何一个广场上去。比较困难的就是这一部分，做这个局部的工程量特别大，材料是一种工业材料，现在中国还不能生产，是进口的，这种材料坚固、耐用、防水、防漏。我去年用这种材料做了许多作品。

刘骁纯：前两天的讨论会大家有些悲观，现在的艺术到底怎么样？大家有些忧虑。艺术被市场搞成现在这种惨象，艺术还有没有希望？今天来参加黄专策划的讨论会，我感到了希望。黄专昨天为什么不给大家鼓鼓气呢？我觉得黄专抓这个事情抓得比较敏感，我在会前翻这些资料的时候还没有现在现场的感受，在今天会议现场我有一种比较强烈的感受。实际上，不一定非要像黄专那样大批"犬儒主义"、"形式主义"，但艺术现状的问题确实不少。为什么说黄专敏感？因为他抓住了一种苗头，类似的苗头在各地都有。什么苗头？我想说的是某种跟以前不一样的新的艺术倾向。比如说，文革之后的反思，从写实艺术到现代艺术，从程丛林的《雪》到王克平的木雕，对文化专制基本上取的是批判态度，进入90年代，最主流的是调侃、反讽、恶搞、嘲弄、另类，我觉得黄专恰恰还是抓住了目前出现的一些艺术现象，即从更宏观或者说更深入的层面来看我们国家、我们民族的变化和命运，转向一种深层反省，当然每个人的角度不同，比如巫鸿是从美术史的角度，而汪建伟是从一个艺术家的角度，但都有共同点。在北京给我这方面印象最深的是今日美术馆做的一个展览，徐唯辛的展览，徐也是这样的一种基本状态，他不是简单的批判，也不是简单的调侃，甚至于说不清楚他的一个很具体的态度，这个态度非常复杂，也非常深沉，徐是画文革时期的大头图像，他自己说画三种人，一种是发动文革的人，一种是被文革整掉了的人，还有一种是参与文革的普通老百姓，这三种人他有的是有既定选择的，大量的则是没有既定选择的，他在网上发布他的信息，收到了很多的回帖，这些回帖有的让他非常感动，因为普通人在文革当中有很多经历，他们是在很底层但很能说明问题的一些现象，这些就刺激了徐的艺术创作不断变化、不断发展。画谁？这成了互动的东西。我感到有类似的东西在汪建伟的作品里面，就是说，它是由非常复杂的历史和现在的现象互动产生的一些东西，我们如果用以前的那种政治态度来看这些东西，就比较难，包括这几个方案都大概有这样的倾向，给我印象更深的是汪建伟的这个方案，比如像刚才巫鸿说他专门研究天安门的，但也把观礼台给忽略了，这说明它确实是非常重要的一个问题，是容易被人忽略的重要问题，我觉得这个课题挺大，还可以一直继续做下去，是一个很有意思的问题，想法上、做法上，都是我们这个时代这个状况下产生的东西，不是预设的，也不是根据西方艺术史来决定要做的东西，它是在我们这个环境里面生存下来的最终产生的一种文化现象，又是用一种视觉方式表达出来的。

巫鸿：汪建伟，我有一个小问题，你是什么时候想起来要做这个？为什么？

汪建伟：张开济在很长一段时间都不主动跟别人谈观礼台这个建筑，他自己没有意识到这是一个建筑……

巫鸿：那你是什么时候意识到的？

汪建伟：就是在大量地采访他，跟他谈话的时候，无意中谈出来的。

巫鸿：所以就是在你的研究中发现的，这也代表了一种现象。

刘骁纯：它是非常隐藏的。

汪建伟：我找那个成都"毛泽东思想万岁展览馆"的设计师找了很长时间，最后找到他了，他一直拒绝公开他的身份，也有类似这样的现象。我才了解到，可能现在保存了毛主席大型全身雕像的大城市也就是成都的那个中心广场了，建筑的每个台阶都是有意义的，比如说，56个台阶代表的是56个民族，那个像的高度代表了毛泽东的生日，这些东西以前我根本不知道，它的长、宽、高都是有意义的。

刘骁纯：对，文革当中的很多造像也都是这样的。

黄专：这些历史忘了以后就很难研究了。

汪建伟：其实还有一个特别好的题材，张元当时想拍的《东宫·西宫》，就是观礼台底下后面的两个厕所，当时那是北京市同性恋聚集的最大的地方，但最后他没有在那拍，这两个东西都是最后在谈话中发现的，有这样的含义在里面。

刘骁纯：我还提一个问题，你是否说了文革期间观礼台没有被使用？但我记得好像有用过。

汪建伟：不是，我刚才是说它有两种用法，作为阅兵的用途它在那个时候中断了，一直到1984年，建国35周年的时候，邓小平在那里进行了一次阅兵仪式，到了建国50周年的时候，江泽民又再做过一次阅兵，这种用法跟文革前是不一样的。

刘骁纯：我说的是另外的问题，文革期间的用法不知道你查得确切与否，因为当时一部分红卫兵是可以上观礼台的，而大部分红卫兵是不可以上观礼台的。

汪建伟：文革期间的用法跟我刚才说的那种用法是不同的，这也是我特别感兴趣的。方立华他们采访我的时候，我说现在不知道在什么地方能够查到上观礼台的名单，如果能查到，我觉得这是一个特别珍贵的资料，因为我们在找资料的时候碰到很大的麻烦，一涉及到天安门广场，基本上就很难稍深入地往下了解了。我第一次拿着摄像机去拍天安门广场的时候就被武警清场了，这里边有个小故事，那个武警说你需要先去"天安门管理委员会"申请，我去了那里，那里的人问你是否采访？我说不采访，问你进不进入建筑内部？我说不进入，他说那你就不需要申请了，我第二天又去拍，武警又来找我，我就理直气壮地告诉他，第一，我不采访，第二，我不进入空间内部，那个武警就不管我了。我觉得这个故事也挺有意思的，涉及到对一个空间的接触权。

巫鸿：我觉得你的计划提出了很重要的问题，但是否还可以进一步研究一下？比如你谈到观礼台上面站的是什么人的问题，我知道这种资料不好找，但是不是有可能观礼台上的人的站位隐含了当时的两种重要政治概念，也就是观礼台后，天安门前面挂着的那两条横标，一条是"世界人民大团结万岁"，另一条是"中国人民大团结万岁"。一方面是中国人民，一方面是当时的全球化、共产国际。人民怎么构成？这在当时很重要，同时也在变化。比如说游行的队伍是哪些人在先？观礼台上面站的人的比重和位置如何？这些都会反映出当时对"人民"的一个具体图解。对石阶上的"国家"当时也都有分类，哪些国家是朋友？哪些是共产党的、哪些是西方的？"人民"在当时是非常重要的概念，没有人民就没有国家，我们整个国家的概念是建立在人民概念的基础上。所以这个观礼台，从建筑形式来看，因为上面是有人的，如果能够查到或者大概地估计出人的成分之类的，可能就会引导出一个关于国家政体的内涵。

刘晓纯：天安门管理委员会里面有这个资料吗？

黄专：它不会让你查的，我们现在主要是根据影像资料来推断。基本上友好的或者共产主义阵营国家就在观礼台上面的城楼上，还有邦交的非社会主义国家的使节则在观礼台上。

汪建伟：我觉得阅兵的时候有个大概的比例方式，但文革期间的就不好判断，毛泽东接见的红卫兵是通过什么途径上观礼台的？

黄专：我觉得还是侧重在50年代，文革期间就比较特殊了一点。

巫鸿：广义，那辆"金龙"车现在还在吧？

王广义：在，好像是在国家博物馆。

巫鸿：后来那条龙怎么就变成红旗了？

黄专：不是，就只有那辆车用的龙，其他的都是红旗。

巫鸿：毛主席就坐了一圈？

黄专：对，有一个记录片记载了，毛主席坐这辆车在中南海走了一圈。

王广义：对，当时生产的都是红旗，只是在给毛主席的那辆上面放了金龙，所以我把它理解为是对人民最后一个皇权的礼赞，虽然它带有偶然性，但实际上代表了一种皇权的概念。

刘晓纯：那就是说它是跟红旗车是同时生产出来的？

王广义：对，跟给刘少奇、朱德生产的车都是同期生产的。

巫鸿：毛主席是在什么情况下坐那辆车的？是在游行中吗？是不是曾经出现在公共场合中？

王广义：没有，就在中南海里面。

黄专："东风"是一个政治词汇，"金龙"是一个传统词汇，这两种结合了起来，当时有"东风压倒西风"的说法，所以这个名称本身就有含义。

王广义："龙"是指皇帝。

黄专：当时是否在赶"十一"，它的外壳都是工人用手敲出来的？

王广义：对。

巫鸿：我在想这个例子也抓得很有意思。当然"龙"传统上指皇帝，但是否还有一个微妙的层次，比如说"龙"在当时也可以说是"东方巨龙"？就变成了一个当代中国的概念，是否有这种在政治上突然转变的可能？

黄专：把龙当成中华民族的象征应该是比较晚的，可以查下作为皇权象征是到什么时候结束的。

王广义：我想当时做这个车还是作为对皇权的象征。因为当时这辆车是给毛主席坐的，所以工人特意——有纪录片为证，就都是工人手工敲出来的，实际上就是在做一件艺术品了。

巫鸿：这里我们接触到了美术史解释的牛角尖了，有时候一个词或一种现象可能有多种面貌。比如，可能在工人看来是个皇帝的象征，但也可能在另外的层次上它代表了新中国。在大跃进的那个时候，什么可能都有。

刘晓纯：巫鸿说的是对的，我觉得在那个时候，它的意思一定是含混的。

孟晖：对底层老百姓老说，可能真是那样的。

刘晓纯：对，对老百姓有那么一面，但毛泽东在建国前已经有诗："飞起玉龙三百万"，已经将龙作为一种中华或者人民的象征了。

王广义：我想的是我是站在人民的立场来想的。

刘晓纯：对，它是两面的，有语义交叉的地方。

周彤宇：约翰有一个问题想问黄老师，他觉得"东风·金龙"是中国现代汽车工业梦想的开端，汽车给现代人带来一种个人的自由，比如可以很快地把你带到另一个地方，逃避你的生活。但实际上它带来的是一个矛盾，因为一方面你可以很快地逃离你居住的城市；另一方面塞车、环境污染却给我们的生活带来了很多问题。那么中国人是怎样看待汽车工业的发展？

黄专：中国的第一辆汽车，我们也拍了资料，是袁世凯送给慈禧的那辆，现存于颐和园，那个车绝对是象征性的，但它摆得像古代马车的样子，那是日本生产的，然后就是宋美龄的那辆美国福特，中国最早的汽车的象征意义远远大于实用的意义。

费大为：当时老毛坐了这个车就坐了一圈，是他不喜欢这个车吗？

王广义：他不是不喜欢，他觉得他坐一圈就可以了，这件事就完成了。

黄专：是一种象征。

费大为：那他以后坐的是什么车？

王广义：以后坐的是一个美国的车，有防弹功能的，详细的有资料。

吕澎：去年冬天我们在香港，黄专把这个展览告诉我，当时听了这个展览的想法，我觉得非常好，我非常认同这样的一个思路，那么我认为好在什么地方？其实我们都很难从观念、材料等去描述它，从90年代中期以来，我们面对所谓的综合材料、观念艺术这一堆不同于架上绘画的观念艺术的展览，如何去看待它？站在策展人的角度来说，如何去做这样的一个展览？当然今天的艺术可以有任何出发点，因为每个人的语境、经历和思想都是不一样的，都会有自己的出发点。可是，按照我的习惯角度来说，还真的比较关心的是今天可能最重要的出发点，我们有一万个艺术家，有一万个出发点，但我们会关心相对有意义的出发点，所以黄专要做的这个展览，我觉得是一个非常好的出发点。当然它是一个历史研究，是从视觉方式上对历史——毫无疑问，包括对其他内涵，政治、文化、经济的一个研究，所以刚才像巫鸿老师，刘骁纯老师，他们一看到作品的方案，马上想到的就是过去历史上的很多东西，如果我们一定要从思想上来表述这个展览的特征的话，那么我觉得这其实是对所谓的观念艺术的展览提供了一个很好的范例，尽管对我来说，这个展览已经结束了——说实话，当我了解了艺术家们的材料，出发点，想法，再加上自己的判断之后，对我来说，这个展览就已经结束了，这个展览已经很清楚了，它未来会是什么样——当然身临其境的感觉和今天看到方案的感觉肯定有差异，但其实我们已经能对它做出判断，所以我想这样的展览应该是在今天众多平凡的观念展览中非常有意义的。另一方面，我接着刚才那个问题，刚才说到今天汽车的功能，我们会发现，艺术家拿出自己的想法、作品以后，事实上它不是像一个论文一样去规定自己的范围，当作品一旦出现之后，马上会导致无限制的想象、联想和判断，当然这很好，但从我个人来说，可能未来在这个展览的画册、文献里面，我觉得还是应该作一些判断，因为完全没有判断的东西是不可能的，不如我们先做一些清晰的判断，这正好针对的是什么？针对的是90年代以来艺术现象的问题。从玩世现实主义以来的各种各样艺术现象出来了之后，尤其是大家打开了自己的观念，说我们不要对作品作毫无边际的阐释后，在这样一个背景下，其实我们确定一个边界仍然是有用的，如果我们真的不能判断，不能做规定，其实就没有历史，那我们还怎么去考虑历史问题？我就是看到了今天座谈会的标题"视觉遗产：政治学还是艺术史？"，而想到这些的。我不知道其他学科领域怎样，我觉得这个问题正好也是今天当代艺术领域里面的问题，在日常生活中，在展览、采访中，你能够深切体会到对历史的关怀。每个人都会在一个展览、一个作品、一个事件发生之后，来表达他的历史观，所以那些不愿意做出判断的人——其实我想不用去畏惧，这也回到了对90年代以来的检讨，什么是我们理解的后现代和个人立场？包括老费现在做的展览，边界很清晰，但它的问题是——我觉得跟黄专的这个"视觉遗产"仍然很关键，关键在哪里？就是我们对历史的边界判断，我们是在什么样的判断标准下来面对过去的？所以这些展览都会提供给我们去认真思考，我就先说这些。

费大为：我绝对不会像吕澎一样，一上来就说"很好、很好"，因为时间有限——当然这个项目很好，但因为像我们现在这么严肃地去对待一个问题，机会是不多的。我觉得刚才我们在讨论的问题是一个学术论文对待的对象，我比较关心的是怎样把它变成作品？学术论文是可以像说考古一样说很长时间的，但当变成作品的时候，我发现可以说它体现的是这些参加展览的艺术家或者这几年出现的倾向性的东西，比如说像广义的和汪建伟的，他们的是一种做法，卢昊的是另外一种做法，怎样来处理这么学术的历史问题？像汪建伟说到的"切片"，把它切片，把局部拿出来研究，比较不太去碰它，但把它放到文献里面来看，这是一种，另外一种是像卢昊的"还原"，按照原来的样子做出来，另外一种是像隋建国的"测量"——这总结起来我认为可以把它命名为"新客观主义"，这种"新客观主义"是在做作品的时候尽可能不介入主观的判断，企图以一种非常客观的态度来做，激情的创造性的东西后退一步，作品表面的形式构成、语言构成都是很客观的。我觉得有一个非常有意思的问题可以提出来，我们是在讨论中国政治的视觉逻辑，而并不是在政治的视觉逻辑之外去思考作品，那么，如果我们换了一种政治的视觉逻辑，我们还会采取这种"新客观主义"吗？是否这种"新客观主义"也是受制于目前的政治视觉逻辑的呢？这跟刚才吕澎说到的一个问题有点关系，他说到一个判断问题，我说的是作品的独立性问题，跟"新客观主义"的态度不同的可能是一种什么样的态度呢？可能是一种所谓的"非客观主义"，这种"非客观主义"就是它可能带有批判和解构的东西，比较突出作品本身作为语言的独立性，它比较地不是一个插图，比较地不是去说明一个故事，比较地不太去依附于一个文本，我觉得这个东西是一个怪圈，这个怪圈就是我们是在面对这个政治的视觉逻辑的同时，我们又在它里边。

巫鸿：我觉得老费的说法又深入了一步，因为他谈到作品的比较深层的视觉逻辑，和这种逻辑的条件和现实。但是我也有一些问题，我同意他说的艺术手法上的"新客观主义"，因为这几个计划都没有对再现的对象在形式上或风格上进行有意的变化，不是在风格上变成艺术家自我的风格，在这个层次上我很同意老费的这个概念。但我觉得是否因为这种手法上的问题就可以把它定为"新客观主义"？我感到还需要考虑。因为我想艺术家的目的实际上是从这种客观的、不加改造的东西上引导到一种主观的反思？因为可以注意到，虽然他们不对对象进行改造，但是他们把对象孤立出来了。比如说汪建伟的方案，天安门的其他很多东西都没有了，他把观礼台孤立了出来，强迫观众去想这个事情，而当你想这个事情的时候，就不是客观了，变成了主观的历史、经验，结果这种很客观的东西引导了一种subjectivity，即一种主观的反应。我感觉就因为他们的作品如此的客观，反而更强化了观众的主观的思考，如果它们是太个人风格化的东西，观众就没有太多主观参与的余地了。所以在艺术手法上，我同意它是一种客观，甚至是一种冷静的带有研究性质的科学和历史研究。但到了主观思考这一步，我觉得就必须要依赖文本，脱离不开文本。这也可能是我一直在做艺术史的缘故，我觉得任何人在看这些汽车、城门、铁路的时候，没有一个文本，或者没有一个历史的上下文，就会想不清楚，会乱想了。比如这辆"金龙"汽车，这个汽车是在大跃进前后做的，而那个时期要做一个汽车的意义绝对是不一样的，比如我最近在查一些关于电视的资料，第一个电视造出来以后，在北京根本只有很少的电视机能够被接受，但是造出电视的政治意义很大。中国那个时候就是雄心大志，"超英赶美"，向西方挑战。造红旗汽车的时候，我还是特小的小孩，去看过。那不得了，都摇着鲜花，好像围着毛主席转一样，那汽车就是一个偶像了。这几个方案反映出艺术家的敏感性，去复制、表现一些重要的符号或机制。或者叫"位移"，从它的上下文当中把这些东西提取出来，这本身就是一个特殊的艺术手法。这种手法引起人们对历史上视觉文化的思考。我觉得为了帮助人们的思考，黄专和英国的策展人必须提供文本，这种文本不一定由艺术家提供。

黄专：我们现在很大的工作就是在做档案。

巫鸿：特别牵扯到了中国历史的时候，就更需要切实的文本。西方人在想象中国时往往缺乏历史观念，把中国看作不变的，所以我觉得图册里面除了大为说的对作品的分析以外，也应该对历史背景的具体的解释。

黄专：我也不太想有太多的理论解释，可能我的那个访谈就最极端了，比较理论性，包括收资料，我也还主要是按照老费讲的"新客观主义"，我就放在那里，比如中国的汽车史，就从中国的第一辆汽车到最近一次拍卖的汽车的事件，我就放在那里。

凯伦·史密斯：我听你们说了那么多，我感觉作品和想的问题都很丰富，而且很多都是跟自己经验有关系的，刚才巫鸿老师也提到的问题是，在面对中国的观众，他们的感受应该会挺深的，因为这些也是他们的语言，他们的历史，跟他们自己的记忆有关，但是在面对英国的观众，我觉得会有一些困难，而如果他们不知道背后的历史就太可惜了，因为这里面太丰富了，如果说是这么好的一个机会，做一个规模比较大型的展览，作品也是比较大的，艺术家也都是很好的，那就应该要好好利用这个机会，让英国人更进一步、真正地了解到中国的东西。因为我们今年做的一个展览有一个漏洞，我们没有考虑到这边的观众，我们可能认为作品都很好就好，其实不是那样的，他们一看都不理解，我们也做了画册，里面也有很多资料，但是他们一般都不会在看展览之前看这些资料，除非有很多详细的资料放到大的媒体——他们去看展览完全凭的是感觉，我觉得可能说到王广义的作品，英方的观众会有一个很具体的感受，因为大家都可以明白汽车和模特的过程，就是从历史变成今天很商业化的社会，但其他的作品我觉得很难让国外的观众很好地理解，我不知道你们是否有什么办法来解决这个问题？

黄专：我稍微解释下，老费提得特别好，我一直说我是一个非常不专业的人，我对艺术这个事其实了解很少，严格来讲，我不是为艺术界做这个展览的，更不是为西方艺术界做的，实际上我特别感谢《读书》杂志，他们这么敏感，一看到这个题目就想召开座谈会，实际上我没有把它叫做"展览"，我把它叫做"研究"，就我个人兴趣，我觉得现在艺术界做的事情实际上都没有太大的意义，像前两天我们开的会议，我们讨论到2000年以后的艺术，主要是生态的变化，艺术没有变化，我当时没有把这个项目讲出来，就是觉得其实这个项目不是艺术界的事，但我想这里有两个地方需要解释，第一是关于"视觉政治学"，我不知道有没有这个概念，这是我生造的，包括"视觉逻辑"，我是这样想的，我并没有给它规定任何逻辑，刚才老费说是"新客观主义"，我一听心就一亮，的确是，可能到最后它就并入这个方式，这个方式会产生两种距离感，第一是和中国当代艺术产生距离感，它不限定中国当代艺术的语境，第二它会和艺术家产生距离感，包括我们会想到会用一种新的客观态度来面对艺术。刚才巫鸿先生说是从一种客观的方式进入到主观，当然所有的客观都可以各自的方式产生，只不过以这样极端的客观产生的主观反倒可能空间更大，更开放，就我来讲，方法上我有点像中国古代的方法，想要说那件事就尽量不要像在说那件事，就说个另外的事，所以我要解释这个逻辑，只能说是像古人说的"此中有真意，欲辩已忘言"，这也是我的一个习惯，即我想说的事就不用说它，这是一种智慧，我觉得中国的很多作品做得太简单了，简单到没有一点基本的智慧，所以我就是想用中国的方式来做这件事，它不像一个展览，包括它的文本、展场，我绝对不会选择一个美术馆的空间来做，因为这个展览如果放到美术馆的空间，它的意义会大打折扣，所以我对在国外的美术馆做展览一点兴趣都没有。之前跟彤宇他们商量了和一个大学合作也是这样考虑的，为什么要和一个大学合作？因为这个事情不是艺术界的事情。从个人极端的角度来说就是这样的，而这也是一个机缘，从视觉逻辑来讲也还是那种思维方式，就是当你要说这个事情的时候，你就不要过度言说。另外一个是，对于艺术界，如果强行要说这个展览想要改变什么或者能够改变什么，那就是改变两个东西，一个是对西方艺术体制的依赖，这种依赖有心理上的，有实际利益上的，我已经讲了，这个展览一开始是给圣保罗双年展的方案，我现在很庆幸他们没有接收，如果被他们接收了，可能这个事情就没这么有意义了，我想这种依赖在某种意义上把人家的问题变成了自己的问题，把自己的问题变成一附属的东西；其二，改变中国艺术家的思维惯性，所以我就特别不希望这个展览变成艺术界关注的事，因为它跟艺术界没有关系，但我觉得它还是有可以改变某些东西的作用，我开始就很明确讲了，我是有立场的，我是一个爱国主义者，但要加定语，可以说我是一个理性的爱国主义者，所以你们看我的这个访谈，在一开始我引用了罗蒂的一句话，一个国家的形象是由艺术家和知识分子塑造的，不是由政治家塑造的，我想加一句，叫做有道义的知识分子和艺术家，而我们的艺术家现在在干什么呢？所以我想如果说对艺术有什么意义的话，认真思考的人会看出一些东西来，但是跟我没关系，我特别感谢老费把语言性的东西提出来，但这些东西我的确是思考不多，包括老费做80年代的展览和我做的，我们有很大的不同，老费强调的是作品的独立性和语言的完整性，以及作品的质量，而我强调的是历史的线索，我可能拿一个三九流的作品，但一定是在历史中不可缺环的，而老费会觉得每一个作品必须是一流的，但他对我的提示很大，其实这里面的几个方案可能还会改进，像王广义的，最后要不要模特儿？我们最开始想是要把历史逻辑弄得丰富一点，但它是否又会缺了某种东西，变成一个图解的东西？都还是可以讨论的，我跟艺术家的关系根本不是策划人跟艺术家的关系，我觉得我们就是一种思想朋友，其实我们对老费讲的艺术语言也考虑了很多，都要不断地改进。

刘骁纯：我接着问一个问题，你不是做艺术，那做的是什么东西？

黄专：我做的是一个思想的呈现。

刘骁纯：做思想的呈现你为什么不写论文？

黄专：因为我写论文的水平不高。

吕澎：黄专谈到他是想以古人的方法来做一件事情，那显然也是和我们说的"艺术"有关的，当然我们不要去追问这些概念，意义不大。我们往下走，刚才老费谈到"新客观"这个词，它的确是一个非常相对的概念，因为我们只要把语境、出发点、立场一换，马上就变成另外的东西，这是很难说清楚的东西，所以我觉得黄专没有必要说完全是自己做的一个学问，我倒觉得我们今天的艺术怎么去做，可以是我们的一个态度，而且我很同意的是，在90年代中期以来普遍的艺术现象是非常糟糕的，这种糟糕的副作用我们就不在这里讨论了，但我想这个展览用这样的方式去表达，我觉得是非常好的，刚才凯伦提的意见是，我们要说什么？要让别人明白我们说的是什么东西，她是这样的一个出发点，这个当然我想是通过展览的文献，在于它的准备与它的充分性，当然也有一个范围，不是说要让所有人都能理解到我们要说的，但我觉得有必要把它自身的完整性说清楚，我觉得广义的作品里面最好不要模特儿，因为我刚才说的就是，我们把这个东西拿出来以后，它就已经够了，非常够了，它就是历史。

汪建伟：我觉得我们刚才一开始说的其实是方法论的问题，是老费提出了方法的问题，这实际上是艺术家应该解决的问题。

黄专：我忘了说，我们对参加展览的每个艺术家都做了一个采访，这里没有资料，如果大家需要的话，可以在网上查到。

汪建伟：在采访的时候，我说在很长一段时间里我一直处于犹犹豫豫、无法确定的状态，对我来讲它还是没有解决完的问题。其实刚才吕澎也提到这个问题，很关键，说实际上是要有一个边界的，这种相对文献性的展现实际上很多90年代的西方艺术家都做过，最极端的是上次在巴黎的一个美术馆，有个艺术家24小时在谈福柯，他把全世界搜集到的关于福柯的书及资料，谈了24小时，然后这个话题就结束了，这就是我见过老费所说的"新客观"最极端的文本，但我觉得是否还有一种可能？比如说，这种限定性的思维方式能否产生一种限定性的语言方式？有时候能否在语言方式和它的方法论之间产生关系？比如黄专，他在生病期间提出了"社会主义经验"的概念，当时我一看到这个概念觉得很冒险，因为"社会主义"一直被当作政治文本来解读，比如一个艺术家说他在做关于社会主义的东西，那么没有人会认为他是在做艺术，所有人都会认为他是在以政治作为一种文化资本，而黄专的想法是在这样的思维方式和这种方法论之间有没有可能产生一种语言方式？我觉得这是我对黄专当时提出这个概念的理解，我也理解刚才吕澎说的"限定"。在90年代，当时汉斯·哈克把所有的政治文本和社会主义文本直接搬到展厅，他的革命性是针对当时美术馆封闭在当代美术的空间里，但实际上这种做法在今天已经变得很传统了，我的理解是，我们现在要往下走，实际上不仅仅是把我们已经搜集到的和看到的文本陈列出来，包括怎么样陈列本身都是艺术家的一种观念。我不知道其他艺术家是怎么想的，对我来讲，实际上老费刚才讲的这个问题，就是我现在在想的，在这样的政治逻辑下，有没有可能产生一种视觉逻辑的方法？比如说对材料的使用，比如说我在想，为什么张开济在很长一段时间不愿意承认观礼台是一个建筑？并不是不存在这个建筑，而问题是是什么导致了他不认为这是个建筑？反过来我们也是这样，是什么导致了我们在这么长的时间里面不认为这部分遗产是一种艺术语言，可以从艺术的方式上去理解它？而且刚才说的独立——把一个政治文本变成一个很纯粹独立的东西，我觉得也是有问题的，你怎么就判断它在变化呢？这个你用来作出判断的知识系统是很重要的，所以我觉得这个谈话实际上刚刚开始。

沈其斌：我是上海证大现代艺术馆的沈其斌。其实我们在看一个问题的时候，我们的思维很难超越一种哲学的悖论，我们在这种悖论中确定一种立场和态度的时候，它也常常会受到某种质疑，我为什么要讲话？是刚才费大为讲到"新客观"和汪建伟讲到了方法论的问题激起了我的兴趣，我也一直在关心中国艺术的发展，显然，在90年代以来，刚才吕澎也谈到了，很多现象其实是很糟糕的，但我没有这么悲观，我还是非常乐观与积极的，从我的认识角度来看，我觉得中国当代艺术最大的一个问题应该是两个方面，一个是自身的价值观问题，一个是我们自身的方法论问题，我觉得这两个是根本的问题，刚才吕澎谈到作为一个艺术家需要一个出发点、立场、态度，我是赞同的，但是不绝对化，我是做美术馆工作的，三年以前我从美术馆的角度写过我们的立场和态度，而不是从一个展览、一个作品或者一个艺术家的角度，那么我为什么说价值观和方法论是可能成为我们这个时代在面对艺术、思想当中需要首要清理和思考的问题？我觉得这是很重要的，其实我们在讨论现代性、反现代性，讨论民主、国家、艺术、政治的时候，所有这些东西都需要价值观的判断，需要出发点，我做了20多年的艺术家，同时做了几年的艺术工作者，也自己策划了一个展览，叫"软力量"，我知道这里面也有很多问题，我就是抛出了一些问题，我觉得在艺术里边还没有很好地去思考和解决这些问题，我觉得在这些问题上面所引发的思考和讨论远远不够，所以我就抛出了这些问题，我觉得我们开始讨论现代艺术、当代艺术的时候，无法脱离西方的参照、西方的标准，我们在拷贝、在学习的时候，就不仅仅是学习了人家的形式，其实也是挪用了别人的标准，因为我们的文化里面没有这种标准可以作为评判，所以这个过程其实是很自然的，我觉得这里不值得去悲观，我觉得我们是去做，去行动，去实践，在这个过程当中去思考，去研究，最终能够找到我们的一种方法论，然后去建构我们今天当下的价值判断的标准，这个价值观并不是既定的，而是发展的，是在历史的脉络当中的，是在现实当中的，它是这样的一个关系，我就是在这样的逻辑当中来作"软力量"那个展览的，有16个亚洲国家地区的艺术家参加。那么我觉得今天所谈到的关于"新客观主义"的问题，确实是从方法论上来探讨的，我认为刚才黄专讲到的对艺术的那种态度是很极端的，但我不知道他是嘲讽，还是就真的是这样想的，我觉得我没有这么极端，我是宽容的，很多媒体采访我问我关于对市场有什么态度，我认为我都是积极的，我认为这种发展是必然的，在这个过程当中清醒也是很自然的，但最重要的，是我们怎么去做？我觉得我非常看重黄专的一点，就是他把他自己的一个想法，通过实践把它行动了出来，我觉得这个是最重要的，只是在行动当中不知不觉融入了我们的一种方法论，有时候中国的哲学观是很有意思的，但我们也不是把这样的哲学观和方法论放大，成为一种视觉标准，我们也需要自己的判断标准。

刘骁纯：我再补充一句话，刚才黄专提到"欲辩已忘言"，但任何"忘言"都必须有解释，就像老子说过"道可道，非常道"，因为有了庄子来解释展开这句话，然后又经过两千年一代代文人的不断引申，不断解释，"道可道，非常道"才成了一种"道"，成了一种文化存在，如果后面没有人解释老子，它就根本不存在。这种解释，或者是你自己不去做，也要有人去做。

黄专：我自己的解释就可能到这里了，就是我的这篇访谈"什么是我们的国家遗产"，我觉得如果我要再解释，那可能就又当老子又当庄子了。

刘骁纯：对，我就是说你需要一个庄子。我刚才听了老费那几个概念以后，最感兴趣的概念是"切片"，而不是"新客观"，由此我又想到另一个概念，叫"标本"，这些就供你参考。

巫鸿：我接着"切片"的概念谈一下，我觉得值得再分析一下"新客观"这个概念。实际上，从形式手法上看这五个作品的方案并不一样，不能一概而论。比如汪建伟的方案，"切片"的概念特别强。在当代艺术里面，这种策略往往是非常有效的，貌似模拟，实际上完全把它的语境颠覆掉了，因为观礼台原来是属于整个天安门广场的，现在不但把它单独拿出来，而且拿到了曼彻斯特，这就只能在一个很狭窄的范围里面来说它是"客观"的了，而它的其他很多方面是很有颠覆性的。比如卢昊的方案，我觉得就说不上是"客观"，因为它甚至也不是原来的城市的模拟，实际上是虚构，是想象的产物了，所以它和"客观"更没有关系。我访谈过隋建国。他的这件作品的概念也不是客观主义的，而是一个视点的问题，他从一个雕塑家忽然对这种转圈、提速发生了兴趣，是和他的视觉经验和自身逻辑有关系的。所以我觉得如果以一个形式上的概念来概括这五件作品，可能不是很好的路子。当然可以沿着这个路开始想，但不一定马上就下定论。第二个问题是关于"艺术"定义的问题，我觉得黄专对艺术有一个看法，他自己有一个定义。当然不同的人有不同的定义，对我来说，我们现在谈到的视觉的问题、空间的问题、物质性的问题，都是艺术史讨论中的重要问题。在这个意义上，这个计划肯定牵涉到艺术、政治、思想各个层次交叉互动的问题。黄专请的写文章的人，像赵汀阳、汪晖，他们不是艺术史家，而我是艺术史家，也会产生这种交互重合，而不是说就把艺术扔到一边去了。第三个是解说的问题，我同意有的时候，解说得太仔细对观众也不是太好，艺术的东西讲得太细了就好像是教小学生背书一样了，但如果完全没有解说的话，又会产生像刚才凯伦说的问题，所以我想到了一个解决的方法，我也用过的，针对每个作品提供一个"基本背景材料"，就在作品旁边放上一些这种复印的背景材料，不一定说太多，但是需要说得很具体，很科学，这对观众也就够了。

黄专：这个意见挺好的，其实比如王广义对他的作品给了一个概念"对皇权的最后礼赞"，我觉得就到此为止了，就够了。

刘骁纯：王广义的作品最后要不要车模，这是艺术家自己的事，我们不能替他决定。

吕澎：那当然。

黄专：方案我跟艺术家之间是可以商量的，当然最后决定权在于艺术家。

刘骁纯："政治波普"就是非常直白的，这种直白是跟社会整体发生关系而产生力量的，不是你说它有力量它就有力量的，而是把它放到社会里面，它的穿透力直到今天，持续了将近20年，这才能看到它的力量。

孟晖：各位与会的朋友们也可以就我们的这个专题谈谈想法，座谈会从来都是开放的。

费大为：我再说一句，我非常欣赏黄专刚才的回答，黄专的态度是非常的以我为中心的，并非以既定的艺术标准——是不是艺术不管它，这个态度非常好，有效与否是按照当下一种既定的艺术标准来得到认可的，但我们就根本不要在乎这些东西，不需要这些东西，但就我个人的经验，我感觉到作为策划人的道德底线，一个是不能完全不考虑观众，还有一点就是不可以把艺术家作为自己的工具。

吕澎：其实这个题目可以有不同的路径进入问题来讨论，当然每个人是从自己学习和工作的知识领域角度来认识它，所以我肯定是从艺术、艺术史的角度来思考这个问题。从这个意义上来讲，几个艺术家的作品也可以切掉很多无限的阐释，用不着，最后我们来表达自己看法的时候，其实它也有可能逃离出黄专设定的框架，因为到最后它不可能是一个纯粹的历史的、或者政治学，甚至建筑学的研究，我比较赞同的是，它还是进入艺术的一个很好的方式，它里面包含了那些很复杂的问题。我认为，无论从什么角度来看，都有它的边界和局限性，可以在一个具体的语境下去思考它，而不是说它没有特殊的语境，我们是在一个抽象的语境里面来谈。"东方"、"西方"、"政治"……这些没有意义，从这个意义上来讲，我赞同老费讲的，我们应该尽量地做到在一个语境中还原客观性，我认为这是很重要的，当然以后进入工作的时候，我们可以把这些词抛在一边，这是一个什么态度？跟我们今天见到的大量的艺术现象——实在是太想入非非比较而言，是否有别的？汪建伟就是在一个特殊的语境里尽量还原的思路里面来工作的，而不是去想象张开济会怎样的问题，他还是从一个很客观的角度来做，还是一个研究者，最后产生的结果和他自身立场的关系那是另外的问题，但是他进入工作的方式、思考方式是非常值得提倡的。

黄专：这个题目我觉得大家可以商量一下，我觉得"国家遗产"有点不太贴切，"视觉遗产"比较贴切，但"国家遗产"响亮一点，这个我也想征求大家的意见，而且巫先生对这个题目的翻译也做了修改。

巫鸿："视觉遗产"好像很广，好像古代、现代都可以，但你也说过，"国家"是指近现代国家，这就比较清楚，我觉得至少四个作品围绕"国家遗产"是比较贴切的，卢昊那个作品我还不是很清楚跟民族国家的关系是什么。

黄专：他那个作品主要是解决古代帝国跟现代国家的交接。

吕澎：但他的那个作品容易导致我们对1949年以来的思考。所以我觉得可以是"社会主义时期的视觉遗产研究"，因为实际上大量的问题都可以归到1949年以后。

黄专：实际上是50、60年代。我倒觉得"视觉遗产"限制了一个范围，就好像只能是视觉方面的东西，但"国家遗产"里面还可以有比如精神遗产方面的东西，而我主要指的是视觉象征性的遗产。

巫鸿：我觉得"视觉"也太窄了，比如汽车、观礼台，和我们一般所说的视觉形象还是不太一样的，还是比较实物性的。我觉得"国家遗产"这个词比较好。

王广义："国家遗产"比较好。

黄专：那就叫"国家遗产"。

林岚：大家好，我是香港艺术家林岚，我想问一个问题，我在看这些资料的时候，觉得这里一个观念的开始是对90年代以来中国艺术的反应，我会想到是用比如毛泽东的一些纯粹的形象去表现，但我看到这个展览中，比如说选取的一些材料，有一种很"大中国"的感觉，比如涉及到的是毛泽东的汽车，天安门的一部分观礼台，就都好像是一个很大政策下遗留下来的东西，如果说是要讲"国家遗产"，而且是人民的国家遗产的话，是否还可以考虑一些关于人文的遗产？

黄专：一个方案只能解决一个问题。

孟晖：今天的座谈会很让人受教益，非常感谢各位，希望以后与美术界、与各位研究者和创作者有更多这样的交流机会。

(注：经孟晖、巫鸿、黄专、刘骁纯、吕澎、王广义、汪建伟、周彤宇、凯伦·史密斯、沈其斌审阅，王景整理)

A Brief Introduction to OCAT, MIRIAD and Cornerhouse

何香凝美术馆 OCT 当代艺术中心、曼彻斯特艺术设计创新研究院、后盾画廊和角屋简介

OCT Contemporary Art Terminal of *He Xiangning* Art Museum

何香凝美术馆OCT当代艺术中心

OCT Contemporary Art Terminal (OCAT) is a division of the *He Xiangning* Art Museum. Officially established on January 28, 2005, OCAT is China's only non-profit contemporary art organization connected to a national art museum; it also has exhibition spaces in *Shanghai*.

OCAT's Mission

While OCAT is named after the Overseas Chinese Town in which it is located, the core mission of OCAT is to integrate resources across the world for contemporary Chinese art, and to promote exchanges and interactions between China and the world in this respect. It aims, through exhibitions, forums and artist-in-residence programs, to construct an institution that is about Chinese art but maintains an international vision and professionalism. It is committed to functioning as a hub, a supply centre and a departure point for contemporary Chinese art. Such ideas were in its conception at the very outset and the concept of being an 'international terminal' for contemporary Chinese art was made evident in its name.

OCAT is dedicated to producing projects and events pivoted on visual art, but will also include live arts, music performances, film, video and multimedia presentations. Further, in line with its mission to support and develop the leading edge of contemporary art practice amongst China's most outstanding and most promising artists, OCAT will serve as a dynamic platform upon which resources and artists from across the world are brought together, and exchanges between China and the world at all levels are enabled.

The Artistic Board of the *He Xiangning* Art Museum provides academic advice to both the Museum and OCAT. The members include prominent art critics, curators, artists and museum professionals in contemporary Chinese art from across the world. The Chair is

一、OCAT性质、任务、组织结构和地理环境：

OCT当代艺术中心（英文名称OCT-Contemporary Art Terminal, 简称OCAT）隶属于何香凝美术馆，它是中国目前唯一一所隶属于国家级美术馆的非盈利性当代艺术机构。OCAT于2005年1月28日在深圳正式成立，目前在上海设有分展区。

OCAT以其所在地华侨城命名，其核心任务是以整合海内外当代艺术资源，推动中国当代艺术与国际接轨、互动为目标；通过举办展览、学术论坛和建立国际艺术工作室交流计划等项目，把OCAT建构成既具有中国本土特色又具专业化、国际化水准的独立当代艺术机构。形象地说，OCAT希望成为中国当代艺术的交通网、补给站和起飞点。OCAT是中国独立艺术的代名词，它的理念口号是"做中国当代艺术的航空港"，英文名称更直接地表明了这一理念。

OCAT活动以当代视觉艺术为主体，辐射实验表演、音乐、影视和多媒体等跨领域，一方面进行多层面的艺术交流活动，另一方面吸引海内外赋有才华的艺术家，为他们的创作提供展示空间和交流平台。

何香凝美术馆艺术指导委员会为何香凝美术馆及OCAT提供专业指导与咨询，成员由海内外从事中国当代艺术活动的资深批评家、策划人、艺术家和美术馆专业人员构成，主席为巫鸿。

Professor *Wu Hung*.

The staff team is responsible for the routine business of OCAT. They are:

Director: *Huang Zhuan*

Officers: *Fang Lihua, Li Yusha, Wang Jing, Luo Siying, Li Rongwei, Chen Yuehua,Zheng Wensheng*

OCAT's Logo

OCAT's logo is inspired by the institution's roles as a 'communication network', 'supply station', 'launching site' and, most essentially, 'Contemporary Art Terminal'. The visual elements of the logo are taken from Da Vinci's Vitruvian Man and a model plane, with the former emblematic of humanity as the core value of the institution, and the latter indicating its contemporary nature. Together, they represent the basic ideas of OCAT as conceived by its founders.

OCAT Facilities

OCAT has indoors space of over 3,000m², comprising areas of different functions such as offices, artist-in-residence studios, exhibition spaces, storeroom, merchandise section and book shop.

Key Exhibitions

OCAT is engaged in promoting multidisciplinary and experimental contemporary art in China, as well as introducing contemporary art from overseas. In the past years, OCAT has organized a series of influential academic exhibitions including: 'Taking Off: An Exhibition of

OCAT工作委员会是OCAT的策划与日常工作机构, 其成员包括:

主　　任 : 黄 专

工作人员 : 方立华、李彧莎、王景、骆思颖、李荣蔚、陈跃华、郑文生

OCAT徽标源于"补给站"、"交通网"、"起飞点"这一"做中国当代艺术的航空港"的基本理念。徽标元素来自达·芬奇的《人体标准比例图》和飞机模型设计, 前者象征OCAT以人文精神作为中国当代艺术的基本底蕴, 后者象征OCAT的当代属性, 两者共同构成对OCAT理念的展示。

OCAT的地理环境 : OCAT室内面积为3, 000多平方米, 由办公、OCAT国际艺术工作室、主展厅、副展厅、作品仓库、多功能厅等区域构成。

二、艺术活动

1、重要展览

OCAT一直致力于发展跨领域、跨学科和具实验性的中国当代艺术, 同时引进和推介国外优秀的当代艺术。自成立以来, 曾组织和举办过一系列学术性的展览, 如"起飞 : 何香凝美术馆暨OCT当代艺术中心当代艺术品典藏展"、"广东当代艺术生态 (1990-2005) 文献展"、"'柏拉图'和它的七种精

the Contemporary Art Collection in the *He Xiangning* Art Museum and OCAT', 'Documenting the Contemporary Art Scene in *Guangdong* (1990-2005)', 'Plato and His Seven Sprits' , 'Translating Visuality - *Wenda Gu*: Forest of Stone Steles: Retranslation and Rewriting of *Tang* Poetry', 'Creating History: Commemorative Exhibition of Chinese Modern Art in the 1980s', '*Qi Yun:* International Traveling Exhibition of Chinese Abstract Art', '*Dian Xue* (Pressure Points): *Sui Jianguo*'s Solo Exhibition', 'Symptom: A Large Stage Work by *Wang Jianwei*', 'Mute: *Zhang Peili*'s Solo Exhibition', 'Visual Polity: Another *Wang Guangyi* ', 'The Survey of The Production of Space – *Beijing: Zeng Li*'s Solo Exhibition'.

Public Art Projects

He Xiangning Art Museum has made a continuous effort to bring contemporary art to the public. Events such as the '*Shenzhen* International Sculpture Exhibition' are an embodiment of this effort. OCAT has continued with this academic tradition with such projects as the '*Shenzhen* Overseas Chinese Town Subway Murals Project' and the 'Ten Year Public Arts Plan for the *Shanghai* Città Di *Pujiang*'. These public art projects have attracted widespread attention to the issues of public space while searching for a foundation and effective path for dialogue between artists and the general public, and establishing a practical foundation for the exploration of the role played by public art in the construction of a public realm with local characteristics.

Academic Symposiums

During important exhibitions, OCAT holds corresponding academic forums to promote in-depth research of cultural topics related to contemporary art. For instance, the

灵"、"文化翻译：谷文达《碑林-唐诗后著》"、"创造历史：中国20世纪80年代现代艺术纪念展"、"气韵：中国抽象艺术国际巡回展"、"点穴：隋建国艺术展"、"征兆：汪建伟大型剧场作品展"、"静音：张培力个展"、"视觉政治学：另一个王广义"、"空间生产考察报告·北京——曾力摄影展"等。

2、公共艺术计划

何香凝美术馆一直致力于当代艺术的公共化建设，"深圳国际雕塑展"便是这一持续努力的体现，OCAT秉承了这一学术传统，先后策划了"深圳华侨城段地铁壁画工程"、"上海新浦江城十年公共艺术计划"等项目，这些公共艺术计划引起社会各界对于公共空间问题的关注，为艺术与公众的对话寻找一个共同的基点和有效的途径，并为进一步探讨公共艺术在建立具有本土特色的公共机制中所扮演的角色等问题提供了实践基础。

3、学术讨论会

在重要的展览期间，OCAT举行相应的学术研讨会，以推进当代艺术中相关文化命题的深入研究。如：由陈侗主持的"广东当代艺术（1990—2005）文献展报告会"；由巫鸿策划的"翻译与视觉文化国际研讨会"；由黄专主持的"纪念与反思：中国20世纪80年代现代艺术座谈会"；与《读书》杂志合作组织，由孟晖主持的"国家遗产：政治学还是艺术史？"学术座谈会；由黄专和王林主持的"自由

'Guangdong Contemporary Art (1990-2005) Document Exhibition Report Forum', hosted by *Chen Dong*; 'International Symposium on Translation and Image Culture', hosted by *Wu Hung*, engaged participants and rethinking of 1980s Chinese modern art , hosted by *Huang Zhuan*; the academic symposium, 'State Legacy: Political Science or Art History?', organized in collaboration with *Dushu* Magazine; OCAT's *Shanghai* Exhibition Annex engaged academics in a broad discussion of 'liberalism and public arts'; 'Viewing Art with Freedom', hosted by *Li Gongming*, OCAT engaged with MoMA to create a plan for the 'conference on compiling a Contemporary Chinese Art Sourcebook (1976-2006)', and held an editing meeting hosted by professor *Wu Hung* to set the foundation for the anthology's structure and selection of essays.

The OCAT International Art Residency Program is a long-term exchange project at OCAT. After being initiated by the OCAT, this project formally began in September 2006, with invitees from each period taking up residence for three months of observation, artwork and exchange. There are a total of 5 studios equipped with living facilities and all the equipment necessary for artistic creation. In addition, OCAT provides funding for residents to engage in observation and artistic creation, and space for creation, curation and research, so that they can engage in a diverse range of artistic exchange. Exceptional artists, curators and researchers or workers from related fields from both China and abroad are eligible for this program. One of the key aspects of this program is its promotion of meaningful dialogue between art workers from different academic and cultural backgrounds.

OCAT Contemporary Dance Theatre Performance Festival began in 2008, becoming

主义与公共艺术"公共艺术论坛；由李公明主持的"从自由看艺术"研讨会；与美国纽约现代艺术博物馆合作，由巫鸿主持的《中国当代艺术文献选(1976－2006)》编纂工作会议"，等等。

三、常设性项目

1、OCAT国际艺术工作室交流计划是OCAT常设性的交流项目之一。该项目自OCAT建立初期便开始筹备，于2006年9月正式启动，每期应邀者将入驻三个月进行考察、创作和交流。工作室共设有5套，配有相应的居住生活和必要的创作条件，此外，OCAT还提供一定的经费支持应邀者进行考察和创作，为他们的创作、策展、研究提供空间，进行多层面的艺术交流活动。国内外优秀的艺术家、策展人和学者等相关领域的艺术工作者均有资格提交申请。推动具有不同学科和文化背景的艺术工作者之间有意义的对话是这个项目的特色之一。

2、OCAT当代舞蹈剧场演出季是OCAT常设性的交流项目之一，自2008年起，于每年12月在深圳OCAT举行，充分体现了OCAT在实验表演、影视等跨领域的实践。

3、OCAT主题活动日是OCAT常设性的交流计划项目之一，其举办的具体时间和探讨主题的设定相对灵活。该项目始于2006年6月，迄今共举办了四期主题活动日。

四、出版物

another long-term project at the OCT Contemporary Art Terminal. It is held each year from December at the *Shenzhen* OCT Contemporary Art Terminal, showing OCAT's dedication to the practice of experimental performances and cross-media arts.

OCAT Themed Event Day is a long-term exchange project at OCAT which is held at various times and based on a wide range of themes. Since the project's inception in June 2006, four Themed Event Days have been held.

Publications

OCAT is dedicated to the publication of academic audiovisual, print and collected materials, compiling them based on exhibitions, with documentation of artworks, academic research documents and related information for publication. OCAT focuses on producing documents that go beyond the realm of catalogs, bringing together readability, documentation and research utility into a single body. In some ways, these publications surpass the exhibitions themselves in importance.

OCAT Collections

OCAT's collection focus is on contemporary art classics. The artworks are mostly collected through donations by the artists. OCAT's collections are comprised of *Huang Yongping*'s 'Bat Project', *Gu Dexin*'s 'December 12, 2001', *Lin Yilin*'s 'The First Fifteen Year Plan', *Wang Guangyi*'s 'Hello, World!', *Zhang Xiaogang*'s 'Big Family – Subway', *Fang Lijun*'s 'Ode to Joy', *Wenda Gu*'s 'Forest of Stone Steles: Retranslation and Rewriting of *Tang* Poetry', abstract artist *Li Huasheng*'s ink painting '023', *Zhang Chunyang*'s 'Whitewash pieces', *Qin Jin*'s 'The Last Supper', *Wang Chuan*'s 'Survivor Series: for *Xiao Jin An Er Lang*', etc. Through the collection process, OCAT has gradually established a healthy collection mechanism.

OCAT一直重视学术性图录、著作和论文集出版工作,编辑以展览为基础,收录作品图录、各类学术研究文献和相关资料结集出版,力图为观众和研究者提供一个不同于一般画册的,融可读性、史料性、研究性为一体的学术文本,这些出版物在一定程度上,甚至超越了展览本身所具有的意义。

五、OCAT藏品

OCAT的收藏方向是当代艺术的经典作品,主要来源于艺术家的捐赠。目前,OCAT的藏品有黄永砅的《蝙蝠计划》、顾德新的《2001年12月12日》、林一林的《第十一个五年计划》,王广义的《世界,你好!》、张晓刚的《大家庭——地铁》、方力钧的《欢乐颂》、谷文达的《碑林-唐诗后著》、李华生的《023》、张春旸的《粉饰》之一、秦晋的《最后的晚餐》、王川的《生还者系列之献给小津安二郎》、盛海的《一个立方》、杨勇的《青春残酷日记》等。OCAT在这个过程中逐步建立起良性的收藏机制。

MIRIAD

MIRIAD at Righton Building, MMU
曼彻斯特艺术设计创新研究院所在的瑞顿楼，曼彻斯特都会大学

曼彻斯特艺术设计创新研究院

MIRIAD

MIRIAD is Manchester Metropolitan University's Institute for Research and Innovation in Art and Design, the North West of England's lead Higher Education centre for the study of the creative arts and for the development of the quality of cultural industries. Based on the data gathered by the national Research Assessment Exercise 2008, MIRIAD, on a ratio of quality of research output to the number of researchers, has been rated the sixth leading centre in the UK.

MIRIAD houses a large research student community with training, academic and resource support. Postgraduates enjoy a close-knit group, sharing learning opportunities and individual programmes of study appropriate to their interests and aspirations. The opportunities to work across discipline areas and with visiting professionals extend the benefits of MIRIAD's own diverse programme of exhibitions, lectures, seminars and conferences.

MIRIAD is a structured Research Institute, Graduate School and Innovation Centre.

MIRIAD provides structures, processes and opportunities to extend, support, develop quality, and profile research; postgraduate research awards, research training, and taught postgraduate programme opportunities; professional practice, knowledge transfer, and enterprise in the subject areas of Art & Design, including Architectural Design; Drama, Dance

曼彻斯特艺术设计创新研究院隶属于曼彻斯特都会大学，是英国西北部最重要的艺术设计的高等教育中心，并致力于文化产业品质的发展。据2008年揭晓的英国研究院评估活动的数据显示，从研究成果质量到研究员数量的比率上曼彻斯特艺术设计创新研究院排名全国第六位。

研究院为大规模的研究生群体提供了培训、学术研究和资源上的支持。研究生们拥有关系密切的研究小组，分享学习的机会和为个人研究兴趣和愿望而制定的学习计划。他们有机会和不同专业领域的同学一起工作，从而使研究院多种的节目包括展览、授课、讨论会、学术会议等也从中受益。

研究院集研究所、研究生院和创新中心为一体。

它为拓展、支持、质量促进和研究评估工作、研究生学位、研究培训和授课式研究生计划教学、以及专业实践、知识转换和艺术和设计的相关产业——包括建筑设计、戏剧、舞蹈和表演艺术、艺术设计历史和理论提供了框架、步骤和机会。

研究院的核心是由教授、高级讲师、研究员、教员和辅助人员组成的，他们和学院中超过一百五十名的研究生一起工作。同时，研究院又是一个扩大了的以三个大学院和六个专科院、系合作的形式建立的为高等文化和创造性的研究提供重要支持的社区和环境。这三个大学院分别是艺术与设计学院、豪灵斯学院、柴郡学院；六个专科院、系分别是：美术媒体学院、设计学院、艺术和设计史学院、当代艺术系、曼彻斯特建筑学院、服装设计和工艺系。

在研究院中各个领域的专家本着相互协作的精神的在讨论和对话的氛围内分享知识和实践的

and Performing Arts; and Histories and Theories of Art and Design.

MIRIAD is a core of Professors, Readers, Fellows, teaching and support staff, working with over one hundred and fifty postgraduate students. At the same time, MIRIAD is an extended, critically supportive, community and environment for cultural and creative research at an advanced level across and in collaboration with three Faculties (Art and Design, Hollings Faculty and MMU Cheshire) and six Schools/Departments: Department of Art and Media, Department of Design, Department of History of Art and Design, Department of Contemporary Arts, Manchester School of Architecture and Department of Clothing, Design and Technology.

This collaboration works to co-ordinate staff subject specialist research into a mutual endeavour; enable the sharing of knowledge and good practice in an atmosphere of discussion and dialogue; and optimise the development of complementary and collaborative research across the Faculties in commonly pursued subject areas.

MIRIAD is made up of three areas of activity that overlap and interlink around and through the MIRIAD centre. MIRIAD Research is pursued through managed Research Centres joining in and supported by the MIRIAD centre. Thematic research groups operate to deliver a wide variety of research projects.

MIRIAD has a city centre location, based in the historic Righton Building, with easy access to the cultural and commercial environment of the city and close to museums, galleries, theatres and cinemas.

Lastly, Manchester is a major international centre for sport, music and media arts. With

成果，从而使得在不同院、系之间的同类型的学科和领域的合作和互补能够优化地发展。

研究院的日常工作主要在三个相互关联并部分重叠的领域开展。研究院对所有的研究中心给与管理和支持，主题研究小组开展着各种各样的研究项目。

研究院位于曼城城市中心校区的历史建筑瑞顿楼，到市内的文化和商业场所都很方便，与很多博物馆、画廊、剧院和电影院相毗邻。

近来曼彻斯特正日益成为一个体育、音乐和媒体艺术的国际中心。拥有两百六十万的人口，曼城称得上是英国西北部商业、教育和信息之都。曼彻斯特艺术设计创新研究院和自己的城市之间在文化和经济上有着深厚的联系，继续参与发展国际间文化交流。

http://www.miriad.mmu.ac.uk

a population of 2.6 million, Manchester is the commercial, educational and information capital of northwest England. MIRIAD has strong cultural and economic links with the city and continues to be involved in the development of international cultural exchanges.

http://www.miriad.mmu.ac.uk

The Holden Gallery

后盾画廊

The Holden Gallery

The Faculty of Art and Design's Holden Gallery at Manchester Metropolitan University is located in the Grosvenor Building which was built in 1838, for one of the oldest art schools in Britain. With a distinguished history dating back over 100 years, the Holden Gallery offers an ongoing programme of exhibitions that are freely available to the public. The Gallery is also home to our yearly BA and MA Degree Shows and is a major exhibition space for staff and student work.

曼彻斯特都会大学艺术设计学院的后盾画廊的建筑建于1838年，是英国成立的第二所美术学院的所在地。有着超过百年的卓越历史，后盾画廊不间断地奉献艺术展览，并免费向公众开放。它也每年一度展出本科和研究生毕业展，亦展出学院教师和学生的作品。

Cornerhouse, Manchester

The main building of Cornerhouse, the three top floors are galleries
角屋的主要建筑，画廊是顶上三层红砖结构

角屋，曼彻斯特

Cornerhouse is Greater Manchester's international centre for contemporary visual art and film. As a cultural centre, Cornerhouse presents a unique programme of contemporary art exhibitions, film screenings, commissions, collaborative research, education projects and cultural events.

Cornerhouse has three floors of gallery space, three cinema screens a bar, a cafe and a bookshop. Cornerhouse is located in the heart of the city, a unique social space accessible to a diversity of visitors. By engaging in dialogue, collaboration and partnerships Cornerhouse seeks to encourage debate around current film, art and cultural practice. Cornerhouse is dedicated to the adoption of open innovation working practices to allow it to continue to deliver its integrated, innovative and risk taking programe.

Recent exhibitions shown at Cornerhouse have included work by the leading Japanese media artist *Masaki Fujihata*, 'The Conquest of Imperfection'.

'Broadcast Yourself' an historical survey of artists exploring television. 'Central Asian' exhibited new work by seven Kazakhstani, Uzbekistani and British artists; 'What do you want' involved five female artists from India as part of Asia Triennale Manchester 2008.

In 2007, Cornerhouse produced the Bigger Picture National Commissions, the four works were broadcast across the United Kingdom on the BBC's network of outdoor screens.

Cornerhouse's Engagement Team deliver both the award winning youth programme 'Live Wire', where young people create their own art, film and cultural projects and the influential schools and colleges programme 'Projector' which covers a wide range of subjects

角屋是大曼彻斯特地区的一个国际当代视觉艺术中心和影院。作为一个文化中心，角屋呈献给人们一个独特的包括当代艺术展览、电影献映、授权制作、合作研究、教育节目和文化项目的节目单。

角屋拥有三层展厅的画廊空间、三个影院、一个酒吧、一个咖啡厅和书店。角屋位于曼城城市的心脏位置，是一个面向多层面参观者开放的独一无二的社交场所。通过参与对话、合作和建立伙伴关系，角屋致力于鼓励对当前电影、艺术和文化实践的讨论。角屋的空间全部用于开放创新的工作实践，使它能够持续履行它的集多种元素为一体的、创新的冒风险的节目单。

最近的艺术展览包括：日本重要的媒体艺术家藤幡正树的"不完美的克服"展；"播放你自己"是一个对艺术家探索电视的历史性的调查；"亚洲中部"展展出了七位哈萨克、乌兹别克斯坦和英国的艺术家的新作品，"你想要什么"作为第一届曼彻斯特亚洲三年展的一部分汇集了五位从印度来的女艺术家的作品。

2007年，角屋出品了"大屏幕国家授权制作"，项目的四件作品在英国广播公司的全国站点的户外大屏幕上播出。

角屋的公共项目小组奉献了得奖的青年节目"在线直播"，在节目中年轻人创造他们自己的艺

from art to Urdu.

Cornerhouse also operates Cornerhouse Publications, an international distribution service for books and catalogues on the visual arts.

术、电影和文化项目，还有在学校和学院里有影响的节目——"放映师"，涉及从艺术到乌尔都语的广泛的题材。

角屋还管理角屋发行社，服务于国际视觉艺术图书和目录的分销和销售。

第一部分

帝国与国家

1、【美】费正清《剑桥中国晚清史（1800–1911）》，北京，中国社会科学出版社，1993
2、赵汀阳 《天下体系——世界制度哲学导论》，南京，江苏教育出版社，2005
3、【意】利玛窦《利玛窦中国札记》，北京，中华书局，1983
4、【美】本杰明·史华兹《古代中国的思想世界》，南京，江苏人民出版社，2004
5、王军《城记》北京，生活·读书·新知三联书店，
6、【瑞典】奥斯伍尔德·喜仁龙，《北京的城墙和城门》，北京燕山出版社，1985年
7、北京市档案馆编著，《档案与北京史国际学术讨论会文集》，中国档案出版社，2004年

第二部分

一个多维的现代化模式

1、【美】费正清《剑桥中华民国史》，北京，中国社会科学出版社，
2、【美】费正清《剑桥中华人民共和国史（1949–1982）》，北京，中国社会科学出版社，1990
3、【美】列文森《儒教中国及其现代命运》，北京，中国社会科学出版社，2000
4、【美】柯文 《在中国发现历史——中国中心观在美国的兴起》，北京，中华书局，2002
5、葛兆光《中国思想史》，上海，复旦大学出版社，2001
6、陈万里《五四新文化的源流》，北京，生活·读书·新知三联书店，1997
7、甘阳《古今中西之争》，北京，生活·读书·新知三联书店，2006
8、汪晖《现代中国思想的兴起》，北京，生活·读书·新知三联书店，2004
9、汪晖《死火重温》，北京，人民文学出版社，2000
10、黄专、方立华、王俊艺编《视觉政治学：另一个王广义》，广东，岭南美术出版社，2008
11、黄专编《点穴：隋建国的艺术》，广东，岭南美术出版社，2008
12、陈祖涛口述，《我的汽车生涯》，人民出版社，2005年8月第一版
13、全国政协文史和学习委员会编，《一汽创建发展历程》，中国文史出版社，2007年11月第一版
14、《中国铁路建设史》编委会编著，《中国铁路建设史》，中国铁道出版社，2003年10月第1版
15、金士宣、徐文述，《中国铁路发展史（1876-1949）》，中国铁道出版社，1986年11月第1版
16、北京铁路分局编，《京张铁路》，中国铁道出版社，2001年4月第一版
17、乔英忍、曹国怲主编，《世界铁路综览》，中国铁道出版社，2001年1月第1版，2003年9月第2次印刷
18、宓汝成，《帝国主义与中国铁路（1874-1949）》，经济管理出版社，2007年3月第1版
18、严介生，《汽笛声声闹九州——清末民初铁路史话》，中国铁道出版社，2005年11月第一版
19、严介生、杨照久、焦守候、秦明山、王浚明，《中国蒸汽机车世纪集影（1876-2001）》，中国铁道出版社，2001年7月第1版
20、张复合，《北京近代建筑史》，清华大学出版社，2004年4月第1版
21、潘明祥，《纪念水钢40周年：岁月如歌（1966-2006）》，水城钢铁（集团）有限公司

第三部分
视觉政治神话

1、巫鸿《中国古代艺术中的纪念性》北京, 生活·读书·新知三联书店,

2、巫鸿《作品与展场——巫鸿论中国当代艺术》, 广东, 岭南美术出版社, 2007

3、巫鸿《走自己的路——巫鸿论中国当代艺术家》, 广东, 岭南美术出版社, 2008

4、傅公钺编《北京旧影》, 北京, 任命美术出版社, 1997

5、树军编《天安门广场历史档案》, 北京, 中共中央党校出版社, 1998

6、夏尚武、李南主编《百年天安门》, 北京, 中国旅游出版社, 1999

7、黄专编《剧场：汪建伟的艺术》, 广东, 岭南美术出版社, 2008

8、吴伟、马先军,《天安门广场断代史》, 新华出版社, 2007年6月第一版

Curator's Acknowledgments

With a complex project such as this, particularly one where those involved are working at such great distances and in different languages, there are many people to whom I should offer thanks for their invaluable contributions.

Firstly to *Huang Zhuan*, my co-curator and fellow artist. The shape and scope of the exhibition grew from our first meeting and has blossomed in line with our friendship. Together, with our close friend and colleague, Sarah Perks, Programme & Engagement Director of Cornerhouse, we extend our thanks to the artists who have responded so positively and enthusiastically with both visual and textual contributions; to the independent scholars, who have risen to the challenge of contextualisation, for their insights; to the teams of people associated with the three venues, without whom the exhibitions would never have been so professionally presented to the publics; to our designer, *Wang Xu*, for his empathy and appropriate interpretation; to the co-ordinators of our public engagement events for their heartfelt communication skills; to our translation advisor, David Barker; to Alnoor Mitha of SHISHA, Manchester, for his willingness to chair our 'Reflections and Revolutions' symposium; to our organisations – made up of "can-do" individuals (students and staff, you know who you are) - for their trust and support in so many ways; and to Dr *Tongyu Zhou* of MIRIAD who was the golden bridge without whom none of this would have happened.

Finally, I thank our sponsors and supporters equally from the biggest to the small. I think you will agree that together we all made something very special happen.

Professor John Hyatt
Director of MIRIAD
March 2009

编辑后记

"国家遗产:一项关于视觉政治史的研究"是由我和约翰·海雅特主持,OCAT和MIRIAD共同开发的文化视觉史研究项目,历时近3年。

本书由王广义、汪建伟、卢昊、曾力、隋建国五位中国当代艺术家的研究性作品、访谈文本和巫鸿、汪晖、赵汀阳三位学者的研究成果,以及相关的文献资料所组成。根据不同的研究项目,本书分为以下三部分:一是"帝国与国家",二是"一个多维的现代化模式",三是"视觉政治神话"。

五位艺术家的研究性作品涉及"中国汽车工业"、"天安门观礼台"、"北京老城门"、"中国三线工程"以及"中国铁路工程"的历史背景。在编辑本书的时候,负责中文编辑的方立华、王景曾赴广州中山图书馆、中山大学图书馆、北京国家图书馆、中国铁道部出版社和《人民铁道》报社等机构查阅了大量相关的文献,并甄选了部分图片和文字,收进"视觉档案"一项。这些文献在编辑的时候,作了适当的删减和校改,资料的来源在附录"参考文献"中列出具体条目。在查阅资料的过程中,曾得到《人民铁道》报社发行部的杨晓林先生、广州美术学院的冯峰先生的帮助,在此特别致以谢意!并感谢水城钢铁厂创业馆提供了该厂于20世纪60年代建厂时的照片及相关厂史资料!

本书为中英双语,但并非严格意义上的一一对应关系。比如OCAT与艺术家的访谈文本,英文版只是呈现了访谈的核心内容。另外有一部分文字并没有翻译为英文,比如"视觉档案"收录的项目背景文献,以及"政治学还是艺术史?"座谈会纪要。本书英文版的校对工作由英国编辑巴大玮(David Barker)和周彤宇负责,在此感谢她们辛勤而细致的校对工作。

这个项目能够顺利开展,首先感谢我的合作伙伴约翰·海雅特和合作机构角屋,是他们的努力,使得"国家遗产:一项关于视觉政治史的研究"得以在英国曼彻斯特这个具有特殊意味的工业城市展出;感谢设计师王序和他的工作团队对于画册以及视觉导视系统的各项设计;感谢王俊艺协助剪辑五位艺术家的访谈视频;感谢"中英文化连线"对于这个项目的支持;最后感谢何香凝美术馆副馆长乐正维在此过程中的支持和协调,工作团队周彤宇、方立华、王景为此项目付出大量无私的贡献,以及OCAT全体工作人员兢兢业业的工作!

黄专

2009年3月18日

This book is published to accompany the exhibition *State Legacy – Research in the Visualisation of Political History* at Cornerhouse and The Holden Gallery, Manchester 2nd April to 24th May 2009 (Holden until 8th May 2009); and OCAT, Shenzhen, China 19th September to 19th November 2009

First published by Righton Press, 2009
Righton Press
Manchester Metropolitan University
Ormond Building, Cavendish Street
Manchester
M15 6 BX
U.K.

© OCT Contemporary Art Terminal of *He Xiangning* Art Museum, 2009

ISBN 1 900756 51 X

A catalogue record for this book is available from the British Library.

Exhibition Curators:
Zhuan Huang, John Hyatt

Chief Editor:
Zhuan Huang

Copy Editors:
(Chinese) *Lihua Fang*, *Jing Wang*
(English) David Barker, *Tongyu Zhou*

Translators:
David Barker, *Tongyu Zhou*, *Lian Xue*, Jeff Crosby, *Lei Li*

Designer:
wx-design

Project Coordinator:
Tongyu Zhou

Printed in China by Reliance Printing (*Shenzhen*) Co., Ltd.

本书是为"国家遗产:一项关于视觉政治史的研究"而出版的。

国家遗产:一项关于视觉政治史的研究
主办:何香凝美术馆OCT当代艺术中心
　　　英国曼彻斯特艺术设计创新研究院
　　　角屋,曼彻斯特
策划:黄专(中方)、约翰·海雅特(英方)
英国站
时间:2009年4月2日-5月24日
地点:曼彻斯特的角屋和后盾画廊
　　　(后者展至5月8日截止)
深圳站
时间:2009年9月19日-11月19日
地点:中国深圳OCT当代艺术中心

瑞顿出版社,2009年第1版
瑞顿出版社
地址:英国曼彻斯特都会大学
邮编: M15 6BX

版权所有者: 中国何香凝美术馆OCT当代艺术中心(OCAT),2009年

ISBN 1 900756 51 X

本书已收录大英图书馆目录。

主编:黄专

特约文字编辑:
中文: 方立华、王景
英文:巴大玮、周彤宇

翻译:巴大玮、周彤宇、薛莲、谢飞、李蕾

排版设计:王序设计有限公司

项目协调人:周彤宇

印刷: 精一印刷(深圳)有限公司

印数:2000册

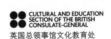